Digital Design
from Zero
to One

T0233897

Jerry D. Daniels
Division of Engineering
Brown University

John Wiley & Sons, Inc.
New York • Chichester • Brisbane • Toronto • Singapore

ACQUISITIONS EDITOR   Steven Elliot
MARKETING MANAGER   Debra Riegert
PRODUCTION MANAGER   Lucille Buonocore
SENIOR PRODUCTION EDITORS   Nancy Prinz, Tracey Kuehn
DESIGNER   Lynn Rogan
MANUFACTURING MANAGER   Dorothy Sinclair
ILLUSTRATION   Ishaya Monokoff

This book was set in Palatino by Publication Services and
printed and bound by Donnelley/Crawfordsville.
The cover was printed by Lehigh Press.

The excerpt from "Little Giddings" in *Four Quartets,* copyright 1943
by T. S. Eliot and renewed 1971 by Esme Valerie Eliot, was reprinted
by permission of Harcourt Brace & Company.

Library of Congress Cataloging-in-Publication Data:

Daniels, Jerry, 1948–
    Digital design from zero to one / by Jerry D. Daniels.
        p.   cm.
    Includes bibliographical references.
    ISBN 0-471-12447-8 (cloth : alk. paper)
    1. Digital integrated circuits—Design and construction—Data
processing.   I. Title.
TK7874.65.D36   1996
621.39'5—dc20   95-50562
                                                        CIP

To my parents
Homer Delmar and Elizabeth Mae Daniels

Digital Design from Zero to One is my one-semester introduction to digital hardware design. The fountainhead of the text is a course at Brown University on digital design that is required of all electrical engineering majors and attended by many students of computer science (CS) and other fields. In transferring my experience from that course to the format of a textbook, I've made a conscious effort to create material understandable to a wide range of students, starting with a primary audience of electrical engineering and CS majors and extending to technicians and even experimental psychologists. On a micro level, the "writing" effort began with attention to graphics: circuit schematics, block diagrams, flowcharts, tables, equations, and so on; the effort continued by integrating clear prose with the graphics. The writing and graphics were tailored to guide the reader through the major themes of digital design with a minimum of digressions. On a macro level, my selection of topics kept in mind the model curricula for introductory digital design courses published by IEEE and ACM. Those curricula, plus the standards of the Accreditation Board for Engineering and Technology Inc. (ABET), emphasize that *design* must be a significant part of hardware education, and so it is in *Digital Design from Zero to One*: from examples to exercises, students are offered a range of design challenges.

Prerequisites   Unlike nearly all other engineering courses, the material in a course on digital circuit design does not depend on knowing calculus. In fact, it's hard to think of much in the way of prerequisites for starting to learn from this book. You don't need to know a programming language or circuit theory, and you don't need to have any specialized knowledge from the lab. Although I normally teach introductory digital design to sophomores and juniors in engineering, I have successfully conveyed the material in this book to motivated high school juniors. Certainly, students majoring in CS should find the topics here accessible. In some ways students with a CS background will have an advantage approaching the material, because they may be generally familiar with base-2 arithmetic, logical operators, register transfers, and other subjects treated here. At any rate, once a student feels comfortable with the material in Chapter 1, the rest of the book is rather self-contained.

Contents   The 11 chapters are grouped into three parts, as summarized below.
   Part One (Chapters 1–4) covers combinational logic. The first chapter, "From Numbers to Switches," introduces the digital idea and outlines advantages of digital over analog processing and transmission of data. Positional and other binary codes for numbers are developed, and methods of converting back and forth between

base-2 and base-10 numerals are presented. I offer conversion algorithms in readable MATLAB scripts instead of pseudocode or PASCAL. After they have learned positional code, students are given methods for adding together pairs of binary numbers. Two's complement code is brought forth as a way to represent negative numbers and accomplish subtraction by *adding* signed numbers. Other important codes for numbers are listed, including bar code and ASCII code.

The last part of Chapter 1 shows how the 0s and 1s of binary can be represented in hardware as the states of on-off and toggle switches. The student sees how switches can be formed into gates for INVERT, OR, AND, XOR, and other logic operators. Design examples for half and full adders bring together the arithmetic topics developed earlier in Chapter 1. At the end of Chapter 1, I foreshadow other topics in the book by outlining the steps involved in modern computer-aided design of digital hardware, from synthesis tools to simulators.

The next three chapters cover the basics of combinational design. Chapter 2 starts with sums of products from truth tables and then motivates and explains Boolean algebra. NAND, NOR, and some XOR circuits are brought forth in examples. At the end of Chapter 2 is a box on fuzzy logic, showing how the same algebraic axioms underlying Boolean algebra can be extended to fuzzy sets. Chapter 3 introduces maps and tabular methods, starting with a segue from Venn diagrams to Karnaugh maps. In the last half of Chapter 3 I vet the Quine-McCluskey algorithms for finding minimum covers of many-input combinational truth tables. At the end of Chapter 3 I outline the widely used heuristic algorithm Espresso, and an evolutionary algorithm from my lab, for finding nearly optimal covers. Chapter 4 starts with SOP encoder/decoder circuits and then opens up the world of programmable logic chips to the student. Read-only memory (ROM) programmable array logic (PAL) and PLAs are presented, as well as combinational aspects of field-programmable gate arrays.

Part Two (Chapters 5–7) is on sequential design, and it takes a student from basic *SR* latches to challenging finite state machine design examples. Chapter 5 starts with the concept of feedback and uses it to develop ring oscillators and latches. *SR* latches are showcased in a switch debouncing example. I bring forth glitches and other timing problems and explain how the master/slave concept offers a solution. Flip-flops—bistable elements with edge-triggered clock inputs—evolve from latches. The importance of *D* flip-flops in modern design is emphasized, and a three-latch *D* flip-flop design is detailed. Chapter 5 ends with an account of maximum clock rate and metastability.

Chapter 6 begins by saying what a sequential circuit is, defining state, and comparing *state* to circuit *output.* Chapter 6 restricts itself to *automatons:* synchronous sequential circuits with only clock for input. A 10-step algorithm, featuring extraction of flip-flop drives from present-state–next-state tables, tells a student how to design any clock-only synchronous sequencer from concept to hardware. Cyclic shift registers are introduced and used in examples such as pseudorandom sequence generators. Hidden units are employed to generate sequences with repeating states. Chapter 6 ends by showing how a counter plus ROM can be used to generate arbitrary sequences.

Chapter 7 extends automatons to synchronous finite state machine (FSM) designs with nonclock inputs. I discuss FSM outputs and distinguish Mealy and Moore circuits. Designs for *synchronizers* are brought forth. The emphasis in Chapter 7 is on states and their transitions. I show that states can be described by state transition tables, by ASM charts, and by coded declarations of an FSM language. I draw on *Finite State Machine Compiler (FSMC)*, written by Don Troxel and his students at MIT over the last 15 years or so; FSMC is available free by anonymous ftp, as explained below. After presenting a six-step algorithm for FSM design, Chapter 7 continues by developing extended counter examples with LOAD, ENABLE, CLEAR, and DIREC controls. At the end of Chapter 7, a counter addressing a ROM morphs into a microprogrammed controller capable of generating arbitrary control sequences.

Part Three (Chapters 8–11) deals with memory, communication, arithmetic hardware, and register transfer logic, all topics that help the student master the combinational and sequential design skills learned in the first two parts of the book. The last four chapters were written so that each could be read independently by a student who had mastered the material of Chapters 1–7.

Memory chips are the single largest market for digital ICs, and an understanding of semiconductor memory is necessary for a hardware engineer. In Chapter 8 both static and dynamic memory (SRAM and DRAM) are considered. I show how latches create SRAM cells and how capacitance on an MOS transistor creates a DRAM cell. DRAM refresh and the internal workings of row-column addressing are explained. I finish Chapter 8 by illustrating designs for and uses of content-addressable memory and first-in–first-out (FIFO) stacks.

Communication is one of the major themes of modern electrical engineering. How digital circuits relate to the world of communication is introduced in Chapter 9. Parallel-to-serial transmission and serial-to-parallel receivers are discussed. RS-232 is explained. I introduce the issues of error correction, encryption, and compression to the student. Good examples of combinational design, particularly with Hamming codes, are developed. At the end of Chapter 9, handshaking is brought forth in the context of sequential synchronous design and an example of considerable detail is worked out.

The last two chapters (10 and 11), on *arithmetic hardware* and *register transfer logic*, extend the student's mastery of combinational and sequential design into the realms of computer architecture. By waiting to the end of the book for arithmetic circuits, I'm able to show off both combinational arithmetic designs and synchronous FSM designs. Multiplication, including Booth's algorithm, is treated in detail. The synchronous multiplier in Chapter 10 motivates the student for the more general discussion of register transfers in Chapter 11. One-register, two-register, and multiregister machines are systematically built up for the student. Design of an ALU and design of a shifter are worked out. Register transfer language algorithms for a multiregister machine illustrate multiplication, taking up again the hardware-specific designs of the arithmetic chapter. The last example of Chapter 11 shows how parallel processing of a sum of products can speed up computation. By the end of *Digital Design from Zero to One*, the student should sense that an understanding of a general-purpose computer is just around the corner and should be well prepared for a subsequent course on computer architecture.

In my opinion, most of the material of the first two parts of this book (Chapters 1–4 and Chapters 5–7) is necessary for an acceptable introduction to digital design. The flow chart below shows chapters of the first and second parts of the book presented sequentially to the student; the chapters of the third part (Chapters 8–11) can be approached individually or in sequence, at the discretion of the instructor.

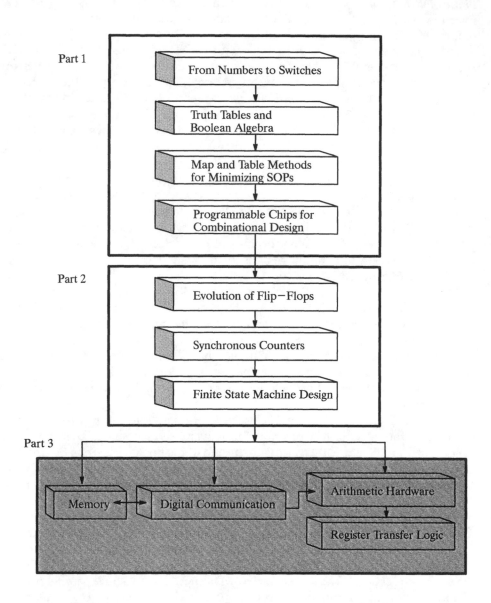

General Features   *Digital Design from Zero to One* is technically up-to-date: boxes highlight such topics as fuzzy logic, evolutionary algorithms, field-programmable gate arrays, and associative memories. Each chapter starts with an overview and ends with a summary. In each chapter general methods of design are balanced by explaining with examples. I have carefully drawn schematics and block diagrams as aids to explanation. A strong effort was made to highlight terms when they first appear and to provide new terms with definitions. Great care has been taken to make the index of over 700 items as thorough and accurate as possible. Likewise the Table of Contents was designed from the beginning as a guide that the student can depend on. There are 534 end-of-chapter exercises, ranging from drill problems to open-ended design questions. All problems have been classroom-tested, and a Solution Manual is available for them.

Pedagogical Materials   The Solution Manual will be available to teachers who adopt the book. At the beginning of the Solution Manual (and at the website discussed below) will be a complete list giving a one-line description of each problem and the location in the text where the problem is relevant. Also available will be a complete list of 600 text figures with their page numbers and captions.

In addition, I have written *Daniels' Digital Design Lab Manual*. The *Lab Manual* is used in the lab component of a digital design course at Brown University and is built around 21 "lab challenges." The lab challenges take the student from seven-segment displays and matrix keyboard decoding to finite state machine design for an elevator controller, design of a successive approximation analog-to-digital converter, and hex multiplication with a 22V10 PAL. A kit of digital ICs plus hardware such as power supplies, logic probes, and keyboards is recommended as the basis of a student's construction of answers to the challenges. The *Lab Manual* offers introductory advice about working on digital hardware, and it has various supplemental sections and case studies to help the student appreciate common practices, from decoupling power supplies to eliminating clock skew. For at least half a dozen of the lab challenges, students are directed to use layout and simulation software that has been loaded on a server for a classroom network at Brown.

Web Sites   I once remarked facetiously to my editor Steven Elliot that the best way to come up with a 600-page book is to write 1200 pages and throw out the worst 600. In fact there are several other "chapters" I have written that don't fit into an introductory 600-page format. These chapters, including graphics, are available at a World Wide Web site at Brown University. The supplemental chapters are

DC Characteristics of Logic Chips

Dynamic Characteristics of Logic Chips

D-A Conversion

A-D Conversion

Asynchronous Sequential Circuit Design

Case Study of the 2910 Sequencer

Microprogramming Case Study with the AMD 2901

Introduction to Digital Signal Processing

Parallel Processing and Neural Networks

sign from Zero to One can be found at the same World Wide Web site. Go to URL `http://www.engin.brown.edu/faculty/daniels` and find the link on my home-page for DDZO.

Software   I recommend that students have access to digital layout and simulation software. Possible packages are LogicWorks from Capilano Computing (PCs and Macs), WorkView from ViewLogic (supported by the Xilinx XACT tools), DigLog (on Sun Workstations), Beige Bag V3.0 (from Ann Arbor, Mich.), and even MacBreadboard for Macintoshes (from Xoeric Software of Hillsborough, N.C.). For state machine design the "Moore" part of PALASM can be used. I should point out that in no way does the value of my book *depend* on use of computer aids to design, nor does it depend on the particulars of the *Lab Manual* I've written.

Downloading Software   I recommend that adopters of the book look at the design tools in OctTools 5.2, from my alma mater, the University of California at Berkeley. OctTools can be obtained by ftp over internet for a fee of $250. Start by requesting information from the Industrial Liaison Program by ftp to `iplsoft.berkeley.edu`. See particularly Espresso and misII for combinational optimization of large truth tables. At Brown we have downloaded these tools to Sun workstations for students to use in digital design courses.

I also recommend that adopters download by ftp a suite of programs from Don Troxel at MIT. Use the anonymous ftp site `sunpal2.mit.edu` and go to directory `pub/digital_tools`. Look at the README files there. I suggest that the Boolean reduction programs `reduce` and `kmap`, plus the finite state machine compiler `fsmc` and the PAL translation program `palasgn`, be brought into your workstation. Chapter 7 discusses the use of `fsmc` in the design of finite state machines.

Acknowledgments   I thank my colleague Bill Patterson, who elaborated to me many of the subtleties of digital design. Don Troxel read over Chapter 7, on finite state ma-chines. Katie Cornog of Avid Technology read through Chapter 9, on communication. I thank Sue Barrett, who read the entire manuscript and corrected many misprints and awkward stylings. Ishaya Monokoff, Illustration Director at John Wiley and Sons, constructively critiqued every one of my 600 interleaf-drawn illustrations and is responsible for a much better-looking book. He deserves thanks, too.

Digital Design from Zero to One was inspected by more than a score of academic reviewers, and I thank them all for their various suggestions, major and minor. I hope some of them see improvement in this edition over what they read in an earlier draft. Over the last two years the reviewers were:

Bruce A. Black
Rose-Hulman Institute of Technology

Martin Dubetz
Washington University

William Freedman
Drexel University

Subra Ganesan
Oakland University

David Harper
University of Texas at Dallas

John K. Komo
Clemson University

Albert McHenry
Arizona State University

Philip Noe
Texas A&M University

John P. Robinson
University of Iowa

Hemant G. Rotithor
Worcester Polytechnic Institute

Majod Sarrafzadeh
Northwestern University

Jill Schoof
University of New Hampshire

Dorothy E. Setliff
University of Pittsburgh

Peter G. von Glahn
Villanova University

Chin-Long Wey
Michigan State University

Finally I thank a generation of Brown students, who discovered that there were no lectures in my course, but only this book to be read and a request to tell me directly what they didn't understand of it. Their questions, and my struggles to provide clear answers, were the fuel and the engine that drove the book from one revision to another and resulted in the edition you have here.

However vigilant and helpful everyone was, I have no doubt that undiscovered errors remain in the text. I am responsible for them and would welcome readers informing me of any significant errors, so at least a second edition can benefit.

BRIEF CONTENTS

CONTENTS

COMBINATIONAL
LOGIC

From Numbers to Switches

....

Welcome to digital circuit design. You are about to begin study of one of the fundamental areas of modern electrical engineering and computer science. Chapter 1 will take you from an abstract look at binary numbers and codes to a concrete account of how such codes are expressed in hardware switches. Along the way in Chapter 1, you will learn how to add numbers in base 2 and then how to build adders out of basic logic gates.

We begin Chapter 1 by considering **digitization.** To understand digitization, first appreciate the human need to **represent** things—pictures, numbers, spoken words—in symbols. To digitize means to force a symbolic representation into discrete categories. An example of numerical digitization is the rounding off of a number with a fractional part into an integer. Another example is the pictures you see on TV. They have been digitized into about 250,000 pixels per 30-ms frame. Even representations that are already discrete can be further condensed, if need be. For example, the letters of the alphabet can be categorized into, say, uppercase and lowercase. The kind of digitization we consider exclusively in digital design is **binary representation,** which relies on base-2 numbers for expression.[1] What advantages result from binary digitization will become clearer as you read on in this chapter.

Digitization is pursued by dividing real numbers into two categories over and over in a way that can represent numbers to an arbitrary degree of accuracy. Decimal digits are in that way replaced by **positionally coded base-2 numbers.** Next in Chapter 1 you find out how to convert between binary numbers and decimal numbers. The **addition** and **subtraction** of base 2-integers and fractions are explained and illustrated. The chapter discusses other nonpositional codes (bar codes, ASCII) and the binary coding of nonnumeric information (letters of the alphabet, for example).

After establishing the importance of base-2 numbers, the chapter shows how binary codes of 0s and 1s are naturally expressed as the on and off states of toggle and complementary **switches.** When switches are combined with power supplies and resistors, they form **gates,** which are the basic building blocks of electronic **logic systems.** The chapter presents the important logic gates AND, OR, exclusive OR, and INVERT. We see how such gates can be combined together to form **adder circuits,** which are fundamental to computer arithmetic.

---

[1]There are two kinds of people in this world: those who divide things into two categories, and all the rest.

3

Chapter 1 concludes with an outline of how digital designs on paper are translated into hardware. It emphasizes modern techniques of computer-aided design, including programs that can compile algebraic descriptions of logic into standard digital gates.

Beyond Chapter 1 *Digital Design from Zero to One* introduces you to one of the most important realms in electrical engineering. By virtue of speed, accuracy, low cost, small size, and little need for power, electronic digital hardware has revolutionized computing, communication, control, and data acquisition. Most complex digital systems involve hardware and software; simpler digital systems may have hardware only. *Digital Design from Zero to One* emphasizes hardware, and it does so in a way that affords you a chance not just to analyze digital systems, but to design them as well. All engineers and computer scientists can profit from a study of digital design. Even if your future work does not involve designing digital hardware, you will still benefit from the understanding you will gain from this text. Programmers will have a better feel for how their code is implemented, and all others will better understand how digitization affects the way their work may be represented and interpreted in a computer.

By the time you finish *Digital Design from Zero to One*, you will know what a truth table is and how to turn any truth table into digital hardware, you will be able to take any sequence (with conditional branching or not) and design a *finite state machine* of flip-flops and combinational logic to generate it, and you will understand details of semiconductor memory, digital communication, computer arithmetic, and register-transfer architecture. Again, welcome to digital circuit design.

1.1 FROM CONTINUOUS TO DISCRETE

1.1.1 Meaning of Digitization

An infinity of numbers lies between any two points on the real number line. Such an infinity of numbers is **continuous-valued.** In this text we will care about only discrete subsets of all possible numbers. How coarse or fine a *discrete-valued function* digitizes numbers is a practical matter only. It will not obscure the first and most fundamental dichotomy in this text: between continuous and discrete numbers (called *analog* and *digital*, respectively, in engineering).

EXAMPLE 1

Digitizing the Real Number Line Confine your attention to the set of all real numbers from 0 to 10.23, a set that can be represented by a line:

0.00   10.23

If we bisect the line, we have two subsets of numbers: those numbers n greater than or equal to 5.12 and those less than 5.12. We can let the **symbol** 0 stand for the subset $\{0 \le n < 5.12\}$ and let the symbol 1 stand for the subset $\{5.12 \le n \le 10.23\}$.

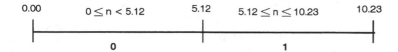

Using 0 and 1 as symbols for the two subsets is our introduction to binary notation. At the centers of the two subsets are the points 2.56 and 7.68. If we bisect again, we have four regions:

If we allow ourselves only the symbols 0 and 1 for marking the four regions, the labeling scheme shown above is reasonable. Let us make one more division of regions:

We extend the 0 and 1 labeling again, as shown. Now we need (at least) trios of 0 and 1 per region to label them unambiguously.

The subdividing and labeling could continue to arbitrary resolution, but we can stop here to make our point. Remove the real number labels and place dots in the middle of each subdivision.

The diagram now emphasizes that only eight numbers are allowed in this digitized representation. We have carried out an **analog-to-digital conversion**: all the real numbers between each pair of consecutive vertical lines have been collapsed to one binary digit, represented by the dot in the middle. For example, all the real numbers between 6.40 and 7.68 are represented by the binary number 101 in our eight-level digitization.

We can further transform our diagram. Remove the continuous number line and the vertical dividers:

●　　　●　　　●　　　●　　　●　　　●　　　●　　　●
000　　001　　010　　011　　100　　101　　110　　111

We now have a coarse digital ruler that lists eight consecutive integers starting with zero in the base-2 number system. (We could just as well present the numbers as a vertical list, and we do so later in Table 1.1 for 16 integers.)

Example 1 was about digitizing. We could have used Greek letters or sports logos to label the discrete regions of the line. The symbols we did use—combinations of 0 and 1—are standard labeling for digitized patterns, be they patterns of numbers, letters, or pictures. The numerals 0 and 1 are the *ciphers* of the base-2 number system and are sometimes referred to as **bits;** *bit* is short for *binary digit*. They will lead us to number codes, which are practical for computing. It is the aim of later sections of Chapter 1 to develop computational codes and to show the use of such codes in binary addition and subtraction. Before we proceed with number coding, we further justify digitization of numbers.

1.1.2   Why Digitize?

If you understand the answer to this question, you will understand why we live in a digital culture, why scientific computations, financial transactions, audio recordings, and (soon) television pictures and phone conversations are handled digitally. It is not enough to say that we live in an information age. We live in an age of binary codes. We store information in binary codes and transform and compute with this information by means of electronic digital circuits designed specifically for binary codes. Digital circuit design is not just one way to solve engineering problems in computation, control, and communications. It is practically the only way, because it has overwhelming advantages over alternatives. For better or worse the digital culture has taken on a life of its own. Not only computer scientists, but all engineers (not only electrical engineers) need to understand something about the workings of digital hardware as the foundation of the digital technology they all work with.

Furthermore, there is a **binary constraint** at work. Digitization can be done in a variety of ways, but we will focus on the binary approach, highlighted by Example 1. So why digitize, and why do it with binary methods? Here are three reasons, each of which foreshadows further discussion in this text.

Digitized Data Are Less Susceptible to Noise Contamination than Analog Data.   This reason for digitizing applies primarily to the acquisition and the transmission of data, in which noise from external sources may be a problem. Any real voltage can be considered a combination of **signal** and **noise.** For example, an unshielded transmission line running near an AM radio may act as an antenna and pick up radiation from the radio's oscillators, adding unwanted oscillations as noise voltage to the transmission line's signals. To the radio's circuits, its oscillators provide signal; to the nearby transmission line, the oscillators are a source of noise.

Return to the binary-labeled dots of Example 1, reproduced in the diagram below. The vertical lines form boundaries between the dots. Suppose the horizontal axis is the amplitude of a signal. Then the zone near each dot bounded by the vertical lines to the left and right is the domain of the analog signal to be converted to the binary label near the dot.

Suppose a signal starts out at the value of the 101 dot. Noise is added. Unless the amount of noise added is greater than the **noise margin** shown, the signal will still be converted to binary value 101. By establishing a noise margin that is greater than any expected noise pulse, you can protect digital recordings, inputs, and transmissions from degradation.

There is a corollary to this noise margin advantage of digitized signals: data can be represented in a computer to an arbitrary degree of accuracy. For example, the irrational number π that is the ratio of the circumference of a circle to its diameter can be crudely marked on a ruler or set as the output of a voltage source, but when it is stored in 32 binary bits in a computer, as

$$11.0010\ 0100\ 0011\ 1111\ 0110\ 1010\ 1000\ 10$$

each of the bits, even the 30th to the right of the decimal point, is absolutely accurate and usable in a way that would be extremely difficult to achieve by strictly analog techniques.

Methods of encoding, transmitting, and receiving digital messages and checking the messages for errors will be the subject of Chapter 9.

Digitized Data Are Economically Processed and Stored in Semiconductor Circuits.   If the noise and accuracy advantages of digital data were achieved only at great expense, digitizing would be reserved for only the most critical missions. In fact, the opposite is true. It is possible to build onto something about the size of your thumbnail millions of semiconductor transistor switches for processing digital data. And the transistors in such an *integrated circuit* can change state millions of times per second, dissipate only microwatts of power, and cost only microdollars per switch. So the economy of digitizing is a fourfold economy of space, time, power, and money.

Binarized Data Can Be Logically Combined and Computed with, Using Theorems of Boolean Algebra.   In 1854, about a century before the advent of electronic computers, George Boole published his mathematical theory of a logical calculus. He set forth a system of axioms and proved various theorems about true-false relationships. If true is represented by 1 and false by 0, Boole's theorems have direct application to the processing of data represented in digital binary. As we will see in Chapter 2, Boole's theorems can help us design forms that minimize the use of hardware. Claude Shannon, a graduate student at MIT in 1938, was the first to realize the usefulness of Boole's work to digital design.

Once converted to digital form, numbers may be added, multiplied, and otherwise used in computations; Boole's theorems can help us design arithmetic circuits to do such calculations. Further, beyond the *combinational* designs addressed by Boolean algebra, there is a substantial theory on *finite state machines* built from bistable circuits called flip-flops. We will introduce finite state machines and methods for the design of counters and sequencers in Chapters 5–7. In sum, there is a body of knowledge for the systematic design of digital circuits, and much of the rest of this text will introduce you to that knowledge. In addition, during the 1990s the art and practice of digital design have advanced to the point that various CAD (computer-aided design) programs are available for the layout, simulation, and optimization of yet more digital hardware. At various points in this text, selected CAD programs will be referenced, and the lab component of your course may give you more hands-on experience with CAD. Chapter 1 concludes with an overview of CAD use in modern digital design.

1.2 THE CONVENIENCE OF TWO STATES

Next we introduce general techniques for creating binary codes. We start with the issue of representation and how the representation of data, or objects, is central to the problem of encoding. After that, we compare the two main categories of things to be encoded: numbers and symbols. In computer jargon the word *symbol* refers to anything that is not a number.

1.2.1 Representation and Encoding

Representation is the art of finding something convenient to stand for something important. In the case of digital circuit design, what is convenient (see Section 1.1.2) is switches in integrated circuit chips. A switch is always in one of only two states: open or closed. Transistor switches can be combined with power supplies and resistors in a way explained later in this chapter to form **gates.** A gate is a small circuit that presents either a high-voltage or a low-voltage output. The high or low output of one gate is a variable that will help represent the important things, namely, digits and letters. One gate's output can be another gate's input, and electronic gates can therefore be cascaded together in logic and arithmetic circuits. (See Fig. 1.1.) The design of such circuits is the theme of this book.

Since 0 and 1 can represent only two condition, we must be prepared to use many bits to encode digits or letters. From combinatorial arithmetic you may recall that N coin flips can result in 2^N different patterns of heads and tails. Thinking of 0 and 1 like tails and heads, you can see that N bits can represent no more than 2^N different

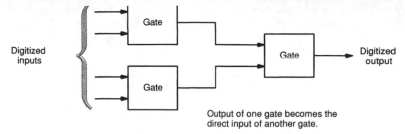

Output of one gate becomes the
direct input of another gate.

Figure 1.1 Gates directly connected.

conditions. For example, $2^8 = 256$, so eight binary bits would be needed to represent the decimal numbers from 0 to 255. How many bits per number would be needed to represent all the three-digit base-10 unsigned integers (that is, the integers from 0 to 999)?

Encoding is the process of turning something important into our convenient representation of 0s and 1s. In what follows, decimal numbers or letters of the alphabet are the important nonbinary elements we wish to encode. At the opposite end of the system may be **decoding,** in which the encoding process is reversed and the decimal number or letter that a particular binary sequence stands for is found. In general, if a set $\mathscr{S}$ has M different elements, the minimum number of bits needed to encode $\mathscr{S}$ is the smallest integer N such that $2^N \geq M$.

EXAMPLE 2

Let us encode the letters of the alphabet. To represent all 26 capital letters by strings of 0s and 1s, we need at least five bits per letter for encoding, since $2^5 = 32 > 26 > 2^4$. Using this minimum number of bits per letter, we can come up with the following positional code:

A	00001
B	00010
C	00011
⋮	⋮
U	10101
V	10110
W	10111
X	11000
Y	11001
Z	11010

Without guidelines, however, there is nothing to stop us from using (say) 26 bits per letter if we like; a 1 in the third place in a field of 25 0s could represent C, for example. The trade-off between compact codes and longer error-detecting codes will be discussed later, in Chapter 9.

How many bits would be needed per letter to represent the alphabet if we distinguish between uppercase and lowercase letters?

Assume that you as a human decoder are given the word "10011 10100 10101 00100 11001 based on the five-bit/letter alphabet code above. Extend the positional code and figure out what the word is. *Hint:* The first three letters of the word are consecutive in the alphabet.

1.2.2 Symbols and Numbers

The letters of the alphabet are **symbols** that imperfectly stand for linguistic sounds. **Numerals** are symbols that stand for numbers. Numbers are abstractions that in turn represent quantity: count, length, duration of time, money. Unlike letters or any other symbols, numbers can be added, subtracted, have their square roots taken, and be otherwise computed with. In algebra, letters can be variables representing unknown numbers, but in the end, when a variable is solved for, a number appears.

Letters at least have an alphabetical ordering—they can be sorted. Many sets of symbols can be neither computed with nor sorted.

EXAMPLE 3

Think of half a dozen nonnumeric, nonalphabetic set of symbols.
Some possible answers:

- Road signs have international icons of gas pumps, cutlery, beds, and so on to inform travelers.
- Flags stand for nations.
- Astrologers use the signs of the zodiac to divide up the annual calendar.
- The icons on the screen of a Macintosh computer are symbols for various kinds of files and directories within the computer.
- A turkey, Santa Claus, the Easter Bunny, and Uncle Sam are symbols for U.S. holidays.
- Baseball coaches use a variety of hand signals to stand for bunt, steal, take a pitch, hit-and-run, and so on. In this case the symbols are *encrypted* so that their broadcast is understood only by a limited audience.
- A general category of nonnumeric, nonalphabetic binary representation is that of images, for example, digitized images for television.

All these sets of symbols could be represented by strings of binary 0s and 1s, should the need arise.

Terminology   **Word** has a specialized meaning in digital design. It refers to a set of bits, usually 2^N bits (N a natural number). If $N = 3$, then $2^3 = 8$ bits are in the digital word and it is called a **byte**. One characteristic of a computer is the word size of its memory, registers, and buses. For example, older Apple Macintoshes have 16-bit words, 386-class and 486-class PCs have 32-bit words, and DEC Alpha computers use 64-bit words. The position of each bit in the digital word matters, each bit plays a specific role in a symbol code. A letter of the alphabet might be represented in the computer by a single digital word. To be expressed in a computer, a word of text may therefore require several digital words, each representing a letter.

Although numerals are legitimate symbols, computer scientists often consider *symbol* to mean a representation of a nonnumerical object; letters in that sense are symbols. *Symbol manipulation*, then, refers to operations on symbols, such as searching, comparing, and sorting. A term for the series of bits representing a symbol is **string**.

Number is a concept independent of its representation; any given number can be zero, an integer (odd or even), fractional, irrational, transcendental, negative, prime, or complex depending on the underlying base system.[2] A **numeral** is an expression that represents a number. In a general sense, three fingers held up, the word *seventeen* written out, and high and low voltages in a computer can all be considered numerals. One meaning of the word **cipher** is a symbol in the first cycle of numerals of a given base system. The digits {0, 1, 2, 3, 4, 5, 6, 7, 8, 9} in that sense are base-10 ciphers. The ciphers of the base-2 number system are 0 and 1.

Section 1.3 considers binary codes for numbers, codes that are suitable for computation. Later in Chapter 1 we take up again the coding of nonnumeric objects.

1.3 ON BASE-2 NUMBERS

Problems disappear as notation improves.

Leon N Cooper

We forge ahead with the binary representation of number, starting with zero and the positive integers. As noted above, we want a code that facilitates computing. We can take a cue from the history of base-10 numbers. The importation from India to Arab lands, at the beginning of the ninth century A.D., of a base-10 set of ciphers that included a mark for zero was an important event in mathematics. Arabic numbers are **positionally coded** groupings of digits. Their gradual displacement of Roman numeral letters in Europe during the Middle Ages made possible more efficient development of arithmetic and algebra.[3] In positional coding each successive cipher position to the left implies multiplication by another power of the base, or **radix**, of the number system.

EXAMPLE 4

The base-10 number 1066 is

$$1 \times 10^3 + 0 \times 10^2 + 6 \times 10^1 + 6 \times 10^0$$

---

[2] "[The notion of plurality] led to the invention of a set of names which in the first instance did not suggest a numerical system, but denoted certain recognized forms of plurality [e.g., many] just as blue, red, green, etc. denote recognized forms of colour. Eventually the conception of the series of natural numbers became sufficiently clear to lead to a systematic terminology, and the science of arithmetic was thus rendered possible." Entry under "number" in *Encyclopedia Britannica*, 13th ed. (1926).

[3] The words *algorithm* and *algebra* are of Arabic origin. The Arabic mathematician al-Khuwārizmi (circa 800 A.D.) wrote a manuscript *ilm al-jebr wa'l-muqābala*, from which the term *algebra* was derived. Al-Khuwārizmi's name itself morphed into *algorithm*.

$$9 \times 10^4 + 6 \times 10^3 + 4 \times 10^2 + 8 \times 10^1 + 5 \times 10^0 + 3 \times 10^{-1} + 0 \times 10^{-2} + 9 \times 10^{-3}$$

The Faraday constant plus 1066 is 97551.309, or

$$9 \times 10^4 + 7 \times 10^3 + 5 \times 10^2 + 5 \times 10^1 + 1 \times 10^0 + 3 \times 10^{-1} + 0 \times 10^{-2} + 9 \times 10^{-3}$$

In each case the *position* of the digit with respect to the decimal point determines the weight of the digit in the number.

In the binary system the ciphers (bits) in positional coding are limited to 0 and 1. The first four nonnegative integers of base 2 in positional code are therefore as follows:

Decimal	Binary
0	00
1	01
2	10
3	11

The radix of the base-2, or binary, number system is 2. In general an integer P in base B can be converted to its decimal equivalent D by the formula

$$D = \sum_{i=0}^{i_{max}} P_i \cdot B^i$$

where i_{max} is the maximum nonzero position of the base B number and P_i is the ith numeral of P.

EXAMPLE 5

The base-8 (octal) number $P = 123{,}567_8$ has $P_0 = 7$, $P_1 = 6$, $P_2 = 5$, $P_3 = 3$, $P_4 = 2$, $P_5 = 1$, and

$$D = 7 \times 8^0 + 6 \times 8^1 + 5 \times 8^2 + 3 \times 8^3 + 2 \times 8^4 + 1 \times 8^5 = 42{,}871_{10}$$

The positions of the numerals in P are indexed starting with 0 and incremented for numerals to the left; therefore, i_{max} in the formula above is $N - 1$, where N is the total number of bits to be converted.

EXAMPLE 6

Convert the base 8 (octal) number 1232_8 to decimal.

Solution

$$D = 2 \times 8^0 + 3 \times 8^1 + 2 \times 8^2 + 1 \times 8^3 = 2 + 24 + 128 + 512 = 666_{10}$$

Table 1.1 Binary, Decimal, Hex, Octal, and BCD
Codes for 16 Integers

	Decimal	Binary	Hexadecimal
	0	0000	0
	1	0001	1
	2	0010	2
	3	0011	3
Octal	4	0100	4
	5	0101	5
	6	0110	6
	7	0111	7
	8	1000	8
	9	1001	9
BCD line	- - -	- - - -	- - -
	10	1010	A
	11	1011	B
	12	1100	C
	13	1101	D
	14	1110	E
	15	1111	F

To extend counting in binary, we need more bits per number. Table 1.1 uses four bits per number to show 0 and the first 15 positive integers in base 2. The table also includes the base-10 and base-16 (hexadecimal) numerals. The six capital letters A through F are the higher ciphers in the base-16 number system. The numerals 0 through 7 indicated by the brace on the left are the eight ciphers of the octal (base 8) number system. The octal ciphers compose the subset {0, 1, 2, 3, 4, 5, 6, 7} of the base 10 ciphers and can be represented by three bits in binary.

EXAMPLE 7

What is the continuation of octal counting up from 8_{10} to 16_{10}?

Answer   10, 11, 12, 13, 14, 15, 16, 17, and 20.

1.3.1 Binary-Coded Decimal

If Table 1.1 stopped at $9_{10} = 1001_2$, it would list the first 10 numbers of the **binary-coded decimal (BCD)** representation. The number 10_{10} in BCD takes five bits: 10000. BCD is not a true positional code. The fifth bit in BCD does not represent 2^4. Computation with BCD is more involved than computation with positional representations. But because the conversion between decimal digits and binary bits is so straightforward in BCD, it is an important representation at the output stages of digital systems that interface to decimal displays.

EXAMPLE 8

What is 903_{10} in BCD?

Solution $903_{10} = 1001\,0000\,0011_2$, where each decimal digit is represented by a group of four bits.

1.3.2 Gray Code

Another important nonpositional binary number code is **Gray code.** From one number to the next, a Gray code changes only one bit. Sixteen four-bit Gray code numbers are shown in Table 1.2.

This Gray code has a reflective quality that is illustrated in Table 1.2 for states 3, 4, 13, and 14. Number pairs that are symmetrically located about a midline (the dotted line) differ by only the first bit, for example, 0011 and 1011 or 0010 and 1010.

In Chapter 3 we will encounter Gray code as a method for labeling Karnaugh maps. Gray code is also useful for encoding multiple inputs that change one at a time, such as input from mechanical encoders. The four-bit Gray code can be shown as linear stripes, as in Fig. 1.2. If the input arrow moves horizontally along the bottom, it encounters only one color change at a time. If the figure is folded in the middle, where the arrow is drawn, the top three stripes are seen to be mirror images and the bottom stripe is reversed contrast, as the reflection quality requires.

1.3.3 Higher Numbers in Positional Code

To list more than 16 integers in a positional code would require a fifth bit in the binary column and a second digit in the hexadecimal (hex) column of Table 1.1. It is

Table 1.2 Reflected Gray Code

	Gray Code	Decimal State
	0000	1
	0001	2
	0011	3
	0010	4
	0110	5
	0111	6
	0101	7
Reflection line	0100	8
	1100	9
	1101	10
	1111	11
	1110	12
	1010	13
	1011	14
	1001	15
	1000	16

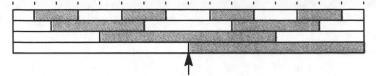

Figure 1.2 Gray code pattern as horizontal stripes.

often convenient to represent binary numbers of many bits in octal (base 8) or hex (base 16) code, because the conversion between binary integers and octal and hex integers is pain-free and because octal and hex codes are more compact. Conversion from binary is a matter of matching binary patterns of three or four bits with octal or hex numerals. The three-bit and four-bit patterns are picked out of Table 1.1. A series of examples will illustrate.

EXAMPLE 9

Convert the 21-bit binary number 1 1100 1000 1100 1110 1100 to octal and hex.

Solution For octal conversion break up the binary pattern into three-bit groups, starting at the right-most bit, and use the integers labeled *octal* in Table 1.1:

$$111\,001\,000\,110\,011\,101\,100_2 = 7106354_8$$

To convert binary to hex, break up the binary pattern into four-bit groups, starting at the right-most bit, and use the hexadecimal column of Table 1.1:

$$1\,1100\,1000\,1100\,1110\,1100 = 1C8CEC_{16}$$

EXAMPLE 10

Convert the 35-bit binary number 10011101010001001011001110011 to hex and octal.

Solution To start with hex, break up the long binary number into four-bit groups, starting from the right:

$$100\,1110\,1010\,0010\,0101\,1001\,1101\,0011_2 = 4EA259D3_{16}$$

For conversion to octal, break up the binary number into three-bit groups:

$$1\,001\,110\,101\,000\,100\,101\,100\,111\,010\,011_2 = 11650454723_8$$

EXAMPLE 11

Convert the base-16 number $94D_{16}$ to binary and octal.

Solution To convert to binary, turn each of the hex ciphers into a four-bit binary code:

$$94D_{16} = 1001\,0100\,1101_2$$

To convert to octal, rearrange the binary form into groups of three and then generate the octal ciphers from Table 1.1:

$$94D_{16} = 100\,101\,001\,101_2 = 4515_8$$

We have now introduced the positional coding of binary bits for representation of 0 and the positive integers. We will extend positional coding to fractions and to negative numbers. In Chapter 10 the floating-point format, which can represent huge and tiny numbers by exponential notation, is illustrated. Our concern now—as 10-fingered humans—is conversion between base 2 and base 10 (decimal).

1.4 CONVERSION TO BASE 10

1.4.1 Conversion to Decimal Using Powers of 2

Our first method of converting to decimal from binary was by use of Table 1.1, which was good for the first 16 integers starting with zero. To find a formula for converting larger binary numbers to decimal, study the powers of 2 in Table 1.1, expressed in decimal and binary:

$$2^0 = 1 = 0001$$

$$2^1 = 2 = 0010$$

$$2^2 = 4 = 0100$$

$$2^3 = 8 = 1000$$

Any other four-bit binary number is a sum of a subset of these powers of 2; for example,

$$3_{10} = 0011 = 0010 + 0001 = 2 + 1$$

and

$$15_{10} = 1111 = 0001 + 0010 + 0100 + 1000 = 1 + 2 + 4 + 8$$

We therefore pick off each 1 in the binary number and count from the right to determine its position. Using a calculator or a table giving powers of 2, we add up the (decimal) powers of 2 associated with the 1 bits in the binary number. Assume that an N-bit binary number is of the form $\{B_{N-1}, B_{N-2}, \ldots, B_1, B_0\}$ where the right-most bit has subscript 0. Table 1.3 gives the first 18 powers of 2. For larger numbers, 2^{10} is abbreviated K; that is, K = 1024.

To convert an N-bit base-2 number with bits B_i (where $i = 0, \ldots, N-1$) to a base-10 number, add up, in decimal, the nonzero bits B_i weighted by coefficients 2^i. The conversion formula is

$$\text{Base-10 number} = \sum_{i=0}^{N-1} B_i \cdot 2^i$$

where B^i is the ith digit of the base-2 number, and B_i is either 0 or 1. For example, in the number 1010, $B_2 = 0$. In words, look up or calculate the power of 2 corresponding to the bit position of each 1 in the binary number.

Table 1.3   Powers of 2 Expressed
in Decimal (K = 1,024)

Bit	Bit Position i	2^i	
B_0	0	$1 = 2^0$	
B_1	1	$2 = 2^1$	
B_2	2	$4 = 2^2$	
B_3	3	$8 = 2^3$	
B_4	4	$16 = 2^4$	
B_5	5	$32 = 2^5$	
B_6	6	$64 = 2^6$	
B_7	7	$128 = 2^7$	
B_8	8	$256 = 2^8$	
B_9	9	$512 = 2^9$	
B_{10}	10	$1,024 = 2^{10}$	1K
B_{11}	11	$2,048 = 2^{11}$	2K
B_{12}	12	$4,096 = 2^{12}$	4K
B_{13}	13	$8,192 = 2^{13}$	8K
B_{14}	14	$16,384 = 2^{14}$	16K
B_{15}	15	$32,768 = 2^{15}$	32K
B_{16}	16	$65,536 = 2^{16}$	64K
B_{17}	17	$131,072 = 2^{17}$	128K

EXAMPLE 12

Convert 110010_2 to decimal.

Solution   Mark off the bit positions, starting with 0. Then for all bit positions i with a 1, add the terms 2^i to find the answer.

Bit position: 5 4 3 2 1 0

Number: 1 1 0 0 1 0 $= 2^5 + 2^4 + 2^1 = 32 + 16 + 2 = 50_{10}$

EXAMPLE 13

Convert the eight-bit number $1100\ 0001_2$ to decimal.

Solution   By use of the formula above and Table 1.3:

$$
\begin{aligned}
1100\,0001 = \quad & 1000\,0000 &= 1 \times 2^7 &= 128 \\
+ & 0100\,0000 &= 1 \times 2^6 &= 64 \\
+ & 0000\,0001 &= 1 \times 2^0 &= 1 \\
\hline
1100\,0001_2 = & & & 193_{10}
\end{aligned}
$$

Expressed in powers of ten, it is $193 = 1 \times 10^2 + 9 \times 10^1 + 3 \times 10^0$.

EXAMPLE 14

Convert the 12-bit number $1001\ 0100\ 1101_2$ to base 10.

Solution   Again, find the 1s and their positions, and add up powers of 2 with the help of Table 1.3.

Note how much less work it is to convert the binary number in question to hex, by use of Table 1.1:

$$1001\ 0100\ 1101 = 94D_{16}$$

1.4.2 Conversion from Octal or Hexadecimal to Decimal

To convert larger base-8 or base-16 numbers to decimal, first convert the base-8 or base-16 number to binary and then follow the formula above. It's also possible to use powers of 8 or powers of 16 to compute the decimal number directly.

EXAMPLE 15

Convert $CAFE_{16}$ to decimal.

Solution 1

$$
\begin{aligned}
CAFE_{16} &= 1100\ 1010\ 1111\ 1110_2 \\
&= 2^{15} + 2^{14} + 2^{11} + 2^9 + 2^7 + 2^6 + 2^5 + 2^4 + 2^3 + 2^2 + 2^1 \\
&= 32{,}768 + 16{,}384 + 2048 + 512 + 128 + 64 + 32 + 16 + 8 + 4 + 2 \\
&= 51{,}966_{10}
\end{aligned}
$$

Solution 2 Using summation of powers of 16 multiplied by the decimal coefficients (a sum of products), we can compute

$$
\begin{aligned}
CAFE_{16} &= C \cdot 16^3 + A \cdot 16^2 + F \cdot 16^1 + E \cdot 16^0 \\
&= 12 \cdot 4096 + 10 \cdot 256 + 15 \cdot 16 + 14 = 51{,}966_{10}
\end{aligned}
$$

The following MATLAB function converts a binary number (expressed as a row of 0s and 1s) to a decimal number.[4] (Actual code is boldface.)

```
function dec = bindec(binin)
% Names the function bindec with input binin and output dec, the
% decimal number answer. binin is stored as a row vector of 1s or 0s.
% The most significant bit of binin is on the left in position 1.
nc = size(binin,2);     % Finds the number of bits in binin.
dec = 0;                % Initializes output dec to zero.
   for index = nc:-1:1  % Starts a loop counting left from nc to 1.
   dec = dec + binin(index)*2^(nc -index); % Creates new value of dec.
                        % dec to right of = sign is previous value of dec.
   end % of ii loop     % End of loop on decrementing index.
```

On the command line type >>bindec([1 1 0 0]) and see 12 returned.

[4]MATLAB is a widely used computational software package from MathWorks, Natick, Mass. MATLAB is written in the C programming language. MATLAB scripts are used in Chapter 1 instead of pseudocode because MATLAB (unlike C or Pascal) is about as easy to understand as pseudocode, and in contrast to pseudocode, if you can find a machine with MATLAB on it, you actually can run these scripts! Text after the % sign is comment, not code.

Let's see how binary numbers can represent positive values less than 1. Computers find it awkward to deal with binary proper fractions of the ratio form

$$\frac{1110}{11000} = \frac{14}{24}$$

but we can turn a binary ratio into a decimal ratio by separately converting the numerator and the denominator, in this case arriving at $\frac{7}{12}$. In Chapter 10, "Arithmetic Hardware," we will discuss a computer algorithm for long division that converts a ratio expression to a decimal-point fraction; for now, assume that you are given a positionally coded binary string to the right of a "binimal point" and you need to convert it to a decimal equivalent.

EXAMPLE 16

Get your bearings by dealing with the base-2 number 0.1.

In the same way that the decimal fraction 0.7 equals 7×10^{-1}, the base-2 fraction 0.1 is 1×2^{-1}, which converts to 0.5 in base 10.

Likewise, 0.01 in base 2 converts to $1 \times 2^{-2} = \frac{1}{4} = 0.25$, and $0.001_2 = \frac{1}{8} = 0.125_{10}$. The number 0.111_2 would convert to the sum

$$0.500 + 0.250 + 0.125 = 0.875_{10}$$

which is the decimal fraction $\frac{7}{8}$.

By induction from the examples above, we see that our formula for converting base-2 integers to base-10 integers can be extended to the case of binimal point fractions by lowering the limit of the power-of-2 summation: Suppose the binary number D has N bits to the right of the binimal point and $M + 1$ bits to the left of the binimal point; its bits are $\{B_M, B_{M-1}, \ldots, B_2, B_1, B_0.B_{-1}, B_{-2}, \ldots, B_{-(N-1)}, B_{-N}\}$. Then the decimal version D of B is given by

$$D_{10} = \sum_{k=-N}^{+M} B_k \cdot 2^k$$

Notice that the first bit to the left of the binimal point is given subscript 0 but the first bit to the right of it is given subscript -1. Care must be taken to make the summation index k match the numbering of the subscripts N and M. In the notation used here, N labels the farthest nonzero bit to the right of the binimal point. The way the formula is written, the index k starts at minus N and increments up to M. The first eight negative powers of 2 are given in Table 1.4.

EXAMPLE 17

Convert the three binimal numbers 101.0101_2, 0.011_2, and 0.100101_2 to decimal.

Solution   In the first number, $N = 4$ and $M = 2$.

Bit position k :	2	1	0		-1	-2	-3	-4	
Number :	1	0	1	.	0	1	0	1_2	$= 2^2 + 2^0 + 2^{-2} + 2^{-4} = 5.3125_{10}$

$$0.011_2 = \tfrac{1}{4} + \tfrac{1}{8} = \tfrac{3}{8} = 0.375_{10}$$
$$0.100101_2 = \tfrac{1}{2} + \tfrac{1}{16} + \tfrac{1}{64} = \tfrac{32}{64} + \tfrac{4}{64} + \tfrac{1}{64} = \tfrac{37}{64} = 0.578125_{10}$$

Table 1.4   Negative Powers of 2

Binary Representation	Decimal Representation
0.1	$2^{-1} = \tfrac{1}{2} = 0.5$
0.01	$2^{-2} = \tfrac{1}{4} = 0.25$
0.001	$2^{-3} = \tfrac{1}{8} = 0.125$
0.0001	$2^{-4} = \tfrac{1}{16} = 0.0625$
0.0000 1	$2^{-5} = \tfrac{1}{32} = 0.03125$
0.0000 01	$2^{-6} = \tfrac{1}{64} = 0.015625$
0.0000 001	$2^{-7} = \tfrac{1}{128} = 0.0078125$
0.0000 0001	$2^{-8} = \tfrac{1}{256} = 0.00390625$

1.5   CONVERTING FROM BASE 10 TO BASE 2

Given a base-10 number, how can we find its base-2 equivalent? Nothing as easy as summation of powers of 2 works. There are two methods for conversion from base 10 to base 2. The first method starts with a list of the powers of 2 and proceeds through **repeated subtraction** of the largest remaining powers until zero remainder is left; the other method is **repeated division** by 2. The subtraction algorithm is first explained and is then shown as MATLAB code.

1.5.1   Repeated Subtraction

The subtraction algorithm starts with a decimal integer DEC. You (or the computer) find the largest power of 2 (2^{EXPO}) less than or equal to DEC. Call the exponent of 2 EXPO. EXPO + 1 is the position of the most significant bit (MSB; in a binary number it is the position of the left-most 1). We increment by 1 because positional code starts with 2^0 in the right-most position.

Next, subtract 2^{EXPO} from DEC. Continue to call the resulting difference DEC:

$$DEC = DEC - 2^{EXPO}$$

Repeat the process of finding the next largest exponent EXPO of 2 such that $2^{EXPO} \le$ DEC.

Whatever the value of the exponent, place another 1 in bit position EXPO+1 of the answer.

If N is the largest integer such that $D_{10} > 2^N$, then MSB $= 1 + N$.

Subtract again: $DEC = DEC - 2^{EXPO}$.

Keep going until the difference is zero.

The algorithm discovers all bit positions where the bit value should be 1 in positional code.

A commented algorithm in MATLAB code is shown below, and then examples illustrating conversion by subtraction follow. In the MATLAB code the top M-function (a MATLAB script that returns a value while computing with local variables) calls the bottom M-function both in the initialization to find the MSB and then in a loop when the algorithm decrements the original number until it equals 0.

The bottom function finds the greatest power of 2 less than or equal to the (positive integer) decimal number it is given.

MATLAB Code for Subtraction Algorithm to Convert
a Positive Base-10 Integer to Base 2

```
function bin = dbsub(dec)   % Names function dbsub to convert
                            % decimal number dec to binary string bin
if (dec <= 0) error('input is not positive'); end
if (dec-floor(dec) ~= 0) error('input is not integer') end
% Algorithm for positive integers only

expo = pwrlt(dec, 32)       % Find the greatest power of 2 <= dec
                            % using function pwrlt below
bin = zeros(1,expo+1);      % Fill bin vector with 0s
bin(expo+1)=1; % Insert a 1 in bin at location expo+1
dec = dec - 2^expo; % Subtraction to initialize while loop

while (dec ~= 0)                 % Eventually dec will decrement to 0
      expo = pwrlt(dec, expo);   % Find the next largest power of 2
      bin(expo+1) = 1;           % Put a 1 in appropriate location of bin
      dec = dec - 2^expo;        % Subtraction in the while loop
end % of while loop

bin = fliplr(bin);              % For display purposes flip bin left to right.

function pwr = pwrlt(dec, max) % Finds greatest power (pwr) of 2 up to 2^max
         % that is less than or equal to positive integer dec
if (dec <= 0) error('input is not positive'); end
if (dec-floor(dec) ~= 0) error('input is not integer') end
flg = 1;

for p = 0:max
      if (2^p > dec) flg = 0; break; end % Stops loop when 2^p > dec
end % of p loop
pwr = p - 1; % Go back to previous power for correct answer

if (flg == 1)
error('input decimal number greater than 2^max'); end
```

```
>> bin = dbsub(100)
```

to see the conversion of 100_{10} to 1 1 0 0 1 0 0 = 64 + 32 + 4.

EXAMPLE 18

Convert 28_{10} to binary by repeated subtraction.

Solution

The largest power of 2 less than or equal to 28 is $16 = 2^4$. The first EXPO is therefore 4, and the most significant bit will be in position $4 + 1 = 5$.

$28 - 16 = 12$. The largest power of 2 less than or equal to 12 is $8 = 2^3$, so store 3 in the list with 4.

$12 - 8 = 4$. The next power of 2 is 4 itself, or 2^2, so store 2 in the list with 4 and 3.

$4 - 4 = 0$. The remainder is 0.

The binary answer has $4 + 1$ bits with 1s in bit positions $4 + 1$, $3 + 1$, and $2 + 1$. Therefore $28_{10} = 1\ 1100_2$.

EXAMPLE 19

Convert 193_{10} to positional binary code by repeated subtraction.

Solution

The largest power of 2 less than or equal to 193 is $128 = 2^7$. The most significant bit of the answer will be in position $7 + 1 = 8$.

$193 - 128 = 65$. The largest power of 2 less than or equal to 65 is $64 = 2^6$; store a 1 in location $6 + 1$ in the answer.

$65 - 64 = 1$. The largest power of 2 less than or equal to 1 is $1 = 2^0$; store a 1 in bit position $0 + 1 = 1$.

Now the subtraction is $1 - 1 = 0$, so we have finished.

The answer is 1100 0001 $= 193_{10}$.

EXAMPLE 20

Convert 5000_{10} to base 2.

Solution

The largest power of 2 less than or equal to 5000 is $4096 = 2^{12}$, so 12 becomes the first value of EXPO, and the most significant bit will be in position $12 + 1 = 13$.

$5000 - 4096 = 904$. The largest power of 2 less than or equal to 904 is $512 = 2^9$; store 9 in the list with 12.

$904 - 512 = 392$. The largest power of 2 less than or equal to 392 is $256 = 2^8$; store 8 in the list.

$136 − 128 = 8$. The largest power of 2 less than or equal to 8 is $8 = 2^3$; store 3 in the list.

$8 − 8 = 0$; we have reached zero and are done with subtracting.

The numbers in our list are 12, 9, 8, 7, and 3. Increment each list item: 13, 10, 9, 8, and 4. These are the bit positions of the 1s: $5000_{10} = 1\ 0011\ 1000\ 1000_2$.

1.5.2 Repeated Division

Instead of conversion from base 10 to base 2 by subtracting powers of 2 from remainders, you can divide by 2 repeatedly and save the remainders (which will be either 0s or 1s). Repeated division works backward from the positional definition of a binary number, as the following examples show.

EXAMPLE 21

To appreciate repeated division as a means of converting from decimal, watch what remainders result from repeated division by 2 of $25_{10} = 1\ 1001 = 2^4 + 2^3 + 1$.

$$\frac{2^4 + 2^3 + 1}{2} = 2^3 + 2^2 \quad \text{remainder of 1}$$

Save the remainder of 1 in a list and divide by 2 the integer part of the quotient minus the remainder:

$$\frac{2^3 + 2^2}{2} = 2^2 + 2^1 \quad \text{no remainder}$$

Note in the list that the remainder is 0; divide the quotient minus the remainder by 2 again:

$$\frac{2^2 + 2^1}{2} = 2^1 + 1 \quad \text{no remainder}$$

Note the remainder is zero again, and divide by 2:

$$\frac{2^1 + 1}{2} = 1 \quad \text{remainder of 1}$$

A final division by 2 of 1 results in a final remainder of 1.

The term 2^4 was divided by 2 five times before the final remainder appeared. Thus the final remainder must represent the fifth bit of the binary answer.

Look at the trail of remainders left: 1 0 0 1 1. Reverse the order. The number 1 1001 results, which is the number we are looking for.

In general terms, repeated division by 2 of a decimal number proceeds as follows. D expressed as a power-of-two expansion is

$$D = \sum_{k=0}^{N-1} B_k \cdot 2^k$$

where the B_k are either 0 or 1. Divide both sides by 2:

$$\frac{D}{2} = \frac{1}{2} \sum_{k=0}^{N-1} B_k \cdot 2^k = \left(\sum_{k=0}^{N-2} B_{k+1} \cdot 2^k \right) + B_0$$

So B_0 is the first remainder, as we saw in the example above. The next division by 2 of the quotient minus the remainder leaves

$$\left(\sum_{k=0}^{N-3} B_{k+2} \cdot 2^k \right) + B_1$$

with B_1, the next bit of the answer, as the remainder. Continue for N divisions. The last remainder will be B_{N-1}.

Below is a MATLAB function DBDIV expressing the division algorithm.

MATLAB Code for Division Algorithm to Convert a Nonnegative Base-10 Integer to Base 2

```
function bin = dbdiv(dec) % Names function dbdiv to convert
      % decimal number dec to binary string bin
dec = abs(dec);    % in case dec is typed in as a negative number
if (dec-floor(dec) ~=0) error('input is not integer'); end
if (dec > 2^32) error('input greater than 2^32'); end

for e = 1:32
      if (2^e > dec) break; end
end % of e loop
% Finds largest power of 2 less than dec

for div = 1:e
      bin(e-div+1) = rem(dec,2); % rem finds remainder after division by 2
      dec = floor(dec/2) % Continue to use dec as the divided down variable
end % of div loop
```

In MATLAB the function FLOOR finds the greatest integer less than or equal to the argument expression.

EXAMPLE 22

Convert decimal 50 to binary by repeated division.

Solution   To follow the division algorithm, begin by dividing 50 by 2 and continue dividing on the quotient minus remainder.

2	50	50 ÷ 2 has a remainder of 0
2	25	↓ 0
2	12	1
2	6	0
2	3	0
2	1	1
2	0	1 $1 \div 2$ has a final remainder of 1

By reading remainders *from the bottom up,* we see the correct answer:

$$50_{10} = 32 + 16 + 2 = 2^5 + 2^4 + 2^1 = 11\,0010_2$$

EXAMPLE 23

Convert 321_{10} to base 2.

Solution

2	321_{10}	Remainder
2	160	↓ 1
2	80	0
2	40	0
2	20	0
2	10	0
2	5	0
2	2	1
2	1	0
2	0	1

The answer is $1\,0100\,0001_2$.

EXAMPLE 24

We convert 168_{10} to base 2 by both division and subtraction.

Division			Subtraction

Division

2	168_{10}	Remainder
		↓
2	84	0
2	42	0
2	21	0
2	10	1
2	5	0
2	2	1
2	1	0
2	0	1

The answer is $1010\ 1000_2$.

Subtraction

Start by finding N such that $2^N < 168$:

$$168 > 128 = 2^7$$

$$
\begin{array}{rll}
168 & & \\
-128 & = 2^7 & \rightarrow \quad 1000\ 0000 \\
\hline
40 & & + \\
-32 & = 2^5 & \rightarrow \quad 0010\ 0000 \\
\hline
8 & & + \\
-8 & = 2^3 & \rightarrow \quad 0000\ 1000 \\
\hline
0 & & \quad\quad\ 1010\ 1000 \\
\end{array}
$$

The answer is $1010\ 1000_2$.

When I tested both DBSUB and DBDIV on my Sparc 5 computer by converting 100,000,000 to a 27-bit binary number, DBSUB required 3 times as much CPU time as DBDIV. Many calculators have built-in decimal-to-binary converters, so in most cases the calculator, not you, needs to remember the repeated division algorithm.

Conversion from decimal to octal or hexadecimal is a two-stage process: first convert the decimal number to binary (by either method), and then group the bits of the answer in 3s or 4s for conversion to octal or hex.

1.5.3 Conversion of Fractions

Let us extend our conversion techniques to the other side of the decimal point. The same methods applied to converting decimal integers to binary form can be applied to fractions. In the case of fractions, however, the process can go on forever, and repeating sequences (such as the decimal fraction $4/13 = 0.307692307692\ldots$) can be generated. The binary fraction conversion process must usually stop at a specified resolution, such as 8 or 16 or 32 (or some other 2^N) bits.

EXAMPLE 25

Convert the decimal fraction 0.4 to 8-bit binary resolution by repeated subtraction. Use the negative powers of 2 from Table 1.4.

Solution

$$
\begin{array}{llll}
0.40 & & & \\
-0.25 & = 2^{-2} & \rightarrow & 0.01 \\
\hline
0.150 & & & + \\
-0.125 & = 2^{-3} & \rightarrow & 0.001 \\
\hline
0.025000 & & & + \\
-0.015625 & = 2^{-6} & \rightarrow & 0.0000\ 01 \\
\hline
0.0093750 & & & + \\
-0.0078125 & = 2^{-7} & \rightarrow & 0.0000\ 001 \\
\hline
0.0015625 & & & \vdots \\
\ \ \vdots & & &
\end{array}
$$

The answer is $0.40_{10} = 0.0110\ 0110\ldots$, a repeating binimal.

Decimal fractions can also be converted with repeated multiplication by 2. Consider the summation form of a binary fraction:

$$ D = \sum_{k=-N}^{-1} B_k \cdot 2^k $$

where all exponents of 2 are negative. If the summation is multiplied by 2, the result R will be such that $0 \le R \le 2$. If multiplication by 2 results in a product greater than or equal to 1, subtract 1 from the result and multiply the residue by 2 again. If the product is greater than or equal to 1, put a 1 in the sequence of bits representing the binary fraction to the right of the binimal point. Put a 0 in the sequence if the product is less than 1. Continue this process until the residue is 0 or the limit of resolution (in bits) is reached.

EXAMPLE 26

Convert $D = 0.25 = 2^{-2}$ to binary.

Solution Multiply D by 2 to find 0.50, a number less than 1. The start of the binimal fraction is therefore 0.0. Now multiply 0.5 by 2 to find 1.00. Since this product is equal to (or greater than) 1, the continuation of the fraction is 0.01. Since the residue is now $1 - 1 = 0$, we have finished.

Program for Conversion Here is a MATLAB M-function that returns a binary fraction array given a decimal fraction (decfrac) and a desired resolution (r). Repeated multiplication by 2 is used.

```
function bin = binfrac(decfrac,r)
% decfrac is between 0 and 1; r is the resolution
if (decfrac >= 1) error('input too large'); end
for ii = 1:r
  decfrac = decfrac*2;
  if (decfrac >= 1)
    decfrac = decfrac - 1;
    bin(ii) = 1;
  else bin(ii) = 0;
  end % of if
end % of ii
```

From the MATLAB command line type

```
>>binfrac(pi-3,16)
```

to see the 16-bit answer,

```
ans = 0  0  1  0  0  1  0  0  0  0  1  1  1  1  1  1
```

Let's work two ways by hand through another fraction conversion.

EXAMPLE 27

Convert 0.34 to binary with a resolution of 8 bits.

Conversion by Repeated Subtraction   Use Table 1.4 to start. Find the largest power of 2 less than 0.34, and subtract it from 0.34. The power of 2 involved will be the bit position of the first 1 to the right of the binimal point. The largest fraction smaller than 0.34 is $0.25 = 2^{-2}$.

$$
\begin{array}{lll}
0.34 & & \\
-0.25 & \rightarrow & 0.01 \quad \text{(binary)} \\
\hline
0.0900 & & \\
-0.0625 & \rightarrow & 0.0001 \\
\hline
0.027500 & & \\
-0.015625 & \rightarrow & 0.0000\ 01 \\
\hline
0.0118750 & & \\
-0.0078125 & \rightarrow & 0.0000\ 001 \\
\hline
0.00406250 & & \\
-0.00390625 & \rightarrow & 0.0000\ 0001 \\
\hline
\end{array}
$$

Add up the binary terms: $0.34_{10} = 0.0101\ 0111$.

Conversion by Repeated Multiplication   Start by multiplying 0.34 by 2 and testing whether the result is greater than 1. If it is, the next bit in the fraction is 1; if it is not, the next bit in the fraction is 0. Continue the process until eight bits have been generated.

$2 \cdot 0.34 = 0.68$; this is less than 1.0, so the fraction starts with $B = 0.0$.

$2 \cdot 0.68 = 1.36 > 1.0$; the residue after subtraction from 1 is 0.36, and now $B = 0.01$.

$2 \cdot 0.36 = 0.72 < 1.0$; now $B = 0.010$.

$2 \cdot 0.72 = 1.44 > 1.0$; the residue after subtraction from 1 is 0.44, and now $B = 0.0101$.

$2 \cdot 0.44 = 0.88 < 1.0$; now $B = 0.0101\,0$.

$2 \cdot 0.88 = 1.76 > 1.0$; the residue after subtraction from 1 is 0.76, and now $B = 0.0101\,01$.

$2 \cdot 0.76 = 1.52 > 1.0$; the residue after subtraction from 1 is 0.52, and now $B = 0.0101\,011$.

$2 \cdot 0.52 = 1.04 > 1.0$; the residue after subtraction from 1 is 0.04, and now $B = 0.0101\,0111$.

The sequence of 1s and 0s generated after eight iterations is $0.34_{10} = 0.0101\,0111$.

Binary numbers with decimal points, as represented here, are *not* in floating-point representation (discussed in Chapter 10). Typically in a computer program noninteger numbers are represented in scientific-exponential format, but here we have worked with fractions as a direct extension of positional coding.

1.6   TRUNCATION VERSUS ROUNDING

If the conversion process for a fraction is simply stopped after an arbitrary number of bits or digits is reached, the number is said to be **truncated**. For example, π truncated four places after the decimal point is 3.1415. If the conversion of π is carried out to one more place it is 3.14159. Because the fifth digit is $9 \geq 5$, a more accurate four-place version of π is 3.1416. Using the next lower place in the decimal fraction to decide the value of the previous digit is called **rounding**. Half of the time it results in a more accurate number than truncation. If the decimal fraction has a 9 in the place to be rounded, the effect can sometimes ripple up through several places. If 1.999963 is rounded to four places the result will be 2.0000.

Note that adding $1.999963 + 0.000050 = 2.000013 \approx 2.0000$. This shows by a computation what the rounded number should be. Since $0.1_2 = 0.5$, a method for rounding a binary fraction at the Nth place is to compute the $(N + 1)$th bit and then add that $(N + 1)$-bit fraction to another binary fraction having N zeros and a 1 in the $(N + 1)$th place. The truncated result is a properly rounded N-bit version of the binary fraction in question.

EXAMPLE 28

Convert the decimal fraction 0.96875 to five binary places, round it to four places, and then convert it back to decimal.

Solution   I used my MATLAB function dbfrac to find that

$$0.96875_{10} = 0.1111\,1000$$

right or 0.0000 1, and add that fraction to the starting fraction:

$$0.1111\ 1000$$
$$+0.0000\ 1000$$
$$1.0000\ 0000$$

This converts back to decimal 1.0. (See Section 1.7 for details on adding binary.)

More refined aspects of rounding are topics of *numerical analysis,* a subject that looks in detail at the use of digital computers in computation. Computation speed often trades off with computation error; rounding can take time, but it can reduce error. In some computation languages, such as MATLAB and Mathematica, the round operation finds the nearest integer. To round a decimal fraction dfrac to two places in MATLAB, multiply and divide it by 10^2:

```
>> dfrac = 0.2975;
>> r2frac = round(100*dfrac)/100
r2frac = 0.30000
```

With the discussion of rounding, we have finished our preliminary look at binary coding of numbers. Next we utilize positional coding to add binary numbers. This look at addition will be preliminary too, confined to addition of nonnegative integers and fractions. After several more chapters of digital design, you will be ready for a more in-depth treatment of binary arithmetic, with topics such as carry look-ahead, multiplication by add-and-shift, division, multiplication of signed numbers, and a consideration of floating-point arithmetic, topics of Chapter 10.

1.7 ADDITION OF NONNEGATIVE BINARY NUMBERS

We first develop methods for adding two bits, and then generalize the method to add multiple-bit numbers. To start with, we deal only with zero and positive integers and fractions.

1.7.1 Half Adders and Full Adders

The rules we know by heart for adding decimal numbers transfer to binary *if the binary code conforms to the positional form of the base-2 numbers system.* In the second grade my kids had to memorize the sums of all pairs of one-digit decimal numbers. It seemed like it took a year before my son could consistently recall that $6 + 7 = 13$. What relief he would have found in binary addition, where the one-bit pairs of addition possibilities are enormously simplified. There are only four cases:

0	0	1	1	A
+0	+1	+0	+1	+ B
0	1	1	10	{carry-out, sum}

The fact that $0 + 1 = 1 + 0 = 1$ implies that binary addition—like addition in any base—is *commutative*. The fourth case, $1 + 1 = 10$, has a two-bit answer, the left bit (C) of which is called **carry-out**. Carry-out is 1 only if both of the inputs A and B are 1. For any number system—binary, decimal, hex, and so on—carry-out from adding any *two* numerals together will be either 0 or 1; thus carry-out for two-number addition in any base is a binary output.

If we add together two N-bit binary numbers,

$$
\begin{aligned}
A_{N-1}&, \ldots, A_1, A_0 \\
+ \ B_{N-1}&, \ldots, B_1, B_0 \\
\hline
C_{OUT}, \ S_{N-1}&, \ldots, S_1, S_0
\end{aligned}
$$

the answer may involve $N + 1$ bits, with the $(N + 1)$th bit a nonzero carry-out bit, here called C_{OUT}. In multi-bit summation any column sum after $A_0 + B_0$ may involve $A_i + B_i + C_i$, where $N > i > 0$ and C_i is the *carry-in* for column i.

Since the adding of two multi-bit numbers may involve three bits (including carry) for each column, let us look at how *three* bits can be totaled. The eight possibilities for three bits to be added are

0	0	0	0	1	1	1	1
+0	+0	+1	+1	+0	+0	+1	+1
+0	+1	+0	+1	+0	+1	+0	+1
00	01	01	10	01	10	10	11

The top row can be thought of as carry-in. The answer is shown in each case as two bits, with the left bit being carry-out again.

EXAMPLE 29

Here is an addition by hand of two binimal numbers with a carry in every column but the first. The equivalent hex addition is on the right.

$$
\begin{array}{cc}
1111\ 111 & 11 \\
1010.1011 & A.B_{16} \\
+\ 1101.0101 & +\ D.5_{16} \\
\hline
11000.0000 & 18.0_{16}
\end{array}
$$

1.7.2 Modular Adding

The four one-bit pairs (which do not involve a carry-in) and their sums and carry-outs can be described by a table and a black box called a **half adder** (see Fig. 1.3).

B	A	SUM	C_{OUT}
0	0	0	0
0	1	1	0
1	0	1	0
1	1	0	1

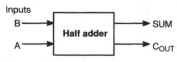

Figure 1.3 Half adder.

Table 1.5   One-Bit Full Adder Table

C_{IN}	B	A	SUM	C_{OUT}	
0	0	0	0	0	
0	0	1	1	0	Half adder table
0	1	0	1	0	
0	1	1	0	1	
1	0	0	1	0	
1	0	1	0	1	
1	1	0	0	1	
1	1	1	1	1	

It will be a goal of digital design (later in Chapter 1) to find an arrangement of switches and logic gates that will convert the inputs A and B to the outputs SUM and C_{OUT}, but for now we leave the half adder as a black box and continue with three-bit adding. The eight one-bit trios and their sums and carry-outs can be described by another table, called the **one-bit full adder** (1BFA) table, given in Table 1.5. The half-adder part of the table is boxed; it represents the output when $C_{IN} = 0$. A 1BFA can be abstracted as another black box, shown in Fig. 1.4. The same schematic symbol will be used frequently for arithmetic operations.

At this point we can foreshadow the development of logic gate designs that is discussed later in Chapter 1 by showing you that the 1BFA can be implemented with two half adders and an OR gate, as shown in Fig. 1.5.

The input-output table of a **two-input OR gate** is shown in Fig. 1.6. An OR gate has a 1 output whenever *any* input is 1. In words, the OR operation says that a 1BFA

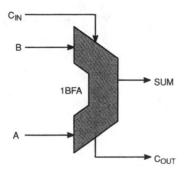

Figure 1.4   One-bit full adder icon.

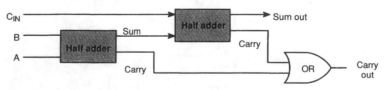

Figure 1.5   One-bit full adder.

B	A	OR
0	0	0
0	1	1
1	0	1
1	1	1

Figure 1.6 Two-input OR gate.

will have a carry-out of 1 if either half-adder carry-out is 1. Later in Chapter 1 OR gates and the half adder itself will be built with switching circuits. For now we continue with our use of the 1BFA black box.

For multi-bit adding, 1BFAs can be chained together, as in the four-bit adder in Fig. 1.7, which adds together $A + B$, expressed bit by bit as

$$\{B_3, B_2, B_1, B_0\} + \{A_3, A_2, A_1, A_0\} = \{C_{OUT}, S_3, S_2, S_1, S_0\}$$

The carry-out of one stage is the carry-in of the next stage to the left. The carry-in of the first stage on the right is set to 0.

The use of two half adders in one 1BFA and the chain method of adding multi-bit numbers draw on a guideline of good digital design, the guideline of **modularity:** when possible, design a system by repeated use of generic subsystems. The 1BFA was designed in units of half adders; the multi-bit adder was designed in terms of 1BFAs.[5] Use of modularity may result in a design that uses more than the minimum amount of hardware of a system built from scratch, but the modular design is likely to be less costly in the long run and easier to troubleshoot in case of problems.

1.7.3 Subtraction and Modularity

In order to subtract $A - B$, we could repeat the efforts we made to perform addition and create tables involving borrow terms and pairs of inputs A and B. However,

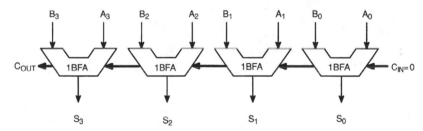

Figure 1.7 Four-bit adder.

[5]Arthur Koestler called self-sufficient components of a hierarchical system *holons*, a term that has not endured. However, Koestler's requirement for holon subsystems, that they can carry out tasks on their own, even when separated from the main system, holds for 1BFAs and half adders. *Holon* might be a good term for the generic subsystems called for in modular design. See Koestler (1978), which includes various engineering examples of holons.

the modularity guideline can be efficiently extended to subtraction. You know that subtraction of one positive number from another can be thought of as adding a positive number and a negative number together. If signed numbers can be represented in binary in such a way that the 1BFA chain could add a positive number and negative number, the same hardware can be used for both adding and subtracting. Two's complement code does the job for representation of binary numbers.

We give here a brief account of 2's complement (2C) code. Basically the user chooses a maximum bit size for the numbers in a system; for the next few problems let that maximum size be four bits. No input or output is allowed to have greater than the maximum number of bits. The left-most bit is the sign bit; a sign bit of 1 signifies a negative number. Now look at the circle of numbers in Fig. 1.8. Marked on the outside, clockwise from the top (0000), are numbers that increase up to $0111 = +7$. Counterclockwise from 0000 are negative numbers that decrease to $1000 = -8$.

A positionally coded number A can be converted to the N-bit 2's complement number A_{2C} by subtraction: $A_{2C} = 2^N - A$. (Similarly a regular decimal number D can be converted to N-digit 10's complement by $10^N - D$.) However, we want a conversion that uses addition: there would be little point in devising a process to replace subtraction by addition if the process required subtracting to get there! It turns out that another way to convert from a positionally coded number N to a negative number $-N$ is to complement (change all 1s to 0s and vice versa) all the bits of N and add 1. Here is what it looks like for a four-bit number: if $+N = \{N_3,N_2,N_1,N_0\}$ then $-N = \{\overline{N_3},\overline{N_2},\overline{N_1},\overline{N_0}\} + 1$, where a bar over a variable means the complement of the variable, and N_s is the sign bit. For example, the complement of 0001 is 1110, and $1110 + 1 = 1111$, the code for -1. If you apply the conversion formula to -1, you get back $+1$. Of course, you do not need to convert to 2C notation if your numbers are already in that format. And for now we just want to add pairs of signed 2C numbers.

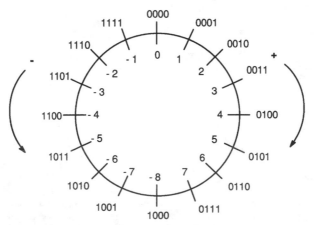

Figure 1.8 Four-bit 2's complement wheel.

EXAMPLE 30

In four-bit 2's complement code add +1 plus −1, 5 plus −2, and 4 plus 4.

Solution

$$
\begin{array}{rl}
+1 = & 0001 \\
-1 = & \underline{1111} \\
     & 10000
\end{array}
$$

Since our word size is limited to four bits, use only the right-most four bits for the answer: $0000 = 0 = 1 - 1$

$$
\begin{array}{rl}
+5 = & 0101 \\
-2 = & \underline{1110} \\
     & 10011
\end{array}
$$

Again, use only the right-most four bits. The answer is $0011 = +3 = 5 - 2$.

$$
\begin{array}{rl}
+4 = & 0100 \\
+4 = & \underline{0100} \\
     & 01000
\end{array}
$$

The right-most four bits say the answer is 1000, which would be +8 in unsigned positional code, but in four-bit 2's complement code the answer is 1000, which is, from the wheel in Fig. 1.8, the number −8. We can see why the answer to $4 + 4$ has turned out wrong: the correct answer is too big for four-bit 2's complement code. The answer has **overflowed** the word size. If we compute $4 + 4$ in five-bit 2's complement code, then $01000 = 8$ will be a valid positive number and overflow will not occur.

Overflow versus Carry-out   There are a couple of different ways to detect 2C overflow. Perhaps the most straightforward way is to compare the sign of the answer with the sign(s) of the two numbers being added. *If the two numbers being added together in 2's complement have the same sign and that sign is different from the sign bit of the answer, then overflow must have occurred.* Overflow cannot occur if the two numbers to be added have different signs, because in fact a subtraction will occur.

Both overflow and carry-out are **status bits** in an arithmetic process; the sign bit is also a status bit. Overflow, unlike carry-out, cannot be used directly in a continuation of modular adding; it only announces that an error has occurred. The fifth bit in the calculations of the previous example is the carry-out of the fourth 1BFA, but it too has no use as input to another 2's complement adder. The fifth bit can be used to detect overflow, as an end-of-chapter exercise shows.

The important points to emphasize about 2's complement code are as follows: 2's complement allows subtraction to be done with the same modules as addition, but the designer must choose a maximum word size for the calculations to take place in.

microprocessors use $2^5 = 32$ bits per word (an exception is the PDP 12 computer, now obsolete, from Digital Equipment Corp.).

1.7.4 Adding Binary Fractions

We conclude our introduction to binary arithmetic with a look at adding fractions. Adding pairs of unsigned binimal fractions by hand follows the same carry-out rules as adding unsigned integers.

EXAMPLE 31

Add 0.5 and 1.75 in binary.

Solution

$$
\begin{array}{r}
1 \\
0.10 \\
1.11 \\
\hline
10.01 \quad = \quad 2.25_{10}
\end{array}
$$

Two's complement code has a fixed word length. Therefore subtraction or addition of fractions by 2's complement addition requires that the decimal point location be set to the same position in both words (numbers) to be added.

If the number N to be subtracted is not given directly in 2C, it must be converted to a negative N through the formula

$$-N = \text{complement}(N) + 1$$

or in the case of word size 4,

$$-N = \{\overline{N_s}, \overline{N_2}, \overline{N_1}, \overline{N_0}\} + 1$$

Note that we add the 1 as the right-most bit, ignoring the decimal point.

EXAMPLE 32

Subtract 0.5 from 2.75 in binary by using 2's complement addition; show that the answer is correct to two decimal places.

Solution   First let us size the larger number: 2.75_{10} equals 10.11 which is four bits. We need a fifth sign bit for 2C, so five bits are required to represent 2.75_{10}. In five-bit 2C, $2.75_{10} = 0\ 10.11$.

Next we need to convert 0.5 to a negative number. Represent 0.5 as a positionally coded binimal fraction, filling out five bits: $0.5_{10} = 0\ 00.10$. Complement the representation: $\text{complement}(0.5_{10}) = 1\ 11.01$. Add 1 bit at the right (ignoring the decimal point):

$$1\ 1101 + 1 = 1\ 1110$$

so -0.5 in 2C is 1 11.10, with the decimal point back in.

$$
\begin{array}{ll}
111 & \\
010.11 & 2.75_{10} \\
\underline{111.10} & \underline{-0.50_{10}} \\
1010.01 & 2.25_{10}
\end{array}
$$

The result has six bits, but we use only the right-most five bits, since we restricted our word size to five bits in setting up the problem. The answer is $010.01 = 2.25$. The sign is positive.

Like the minus sign, the decimal point is another symbol that is not 0 or 1. In our look at fractions we have not worried about how to place or represent the decimal point; we have been able to line up decimal points on paper. In a computer, keeping track of decimal point position is an important task; floating-point representation normally handles decimal fraction numbers by means of a binary version of scientific (exponential) notation. Floating point is developed in Chapter 10.

1.8 CODES AND ENCODING

We started this chapter with a focus on binary codes (representations) for numbers. A good code is one that allows for straightforward addition and subtraction. We covered four codes:

Positional binary

Gray code

Binary-coded decimal (BCD)

Two's complement for signed numbers

(Chapter 10 covers another binary number protocol, floating-point representation.) After explaining number codes, we looked at binary addition and subtraction. Now, before delving into how switches can be used in the design of adder circuits, we look briefly at coding in general.

Codes are ubiquitous. From notation for music, to names for colors, to knitting instructions, to the various computer codes we will consider in this text, codes simplify and organize processes, patterns, and plans. Codes and the art of encoding are an important part of computer engineering. In this introductory chapter you will be given some examples of digital codes and some of the virtues of good codes. Further evaluation of codes, particularly error-correcting codes, will be found in Chapter 9, "Digital Communication." See also MacKenzie (1980, Chaps. 13 and 14).

1.8.1 Examples of Codes

Morse Code   Samuel F. B. Morse, inventor of the telegraph, devised (around 1840) what came to be known as Morse code. Morse code is a system of dots and dashes representing the letters of the alphabet and the numerals 0 through 9. As you can

Table 1.6   Morse Code
for Decimal Numerals

0	— — — — —
1	· — — — —
2	· · — — —
3	· · · — —
4	· · · · —
5	· · · · ·
6	— · · · ·
7	— — · · ·
8	— — — · ·
9	— — — — ·

verify by watching old war movies, the dots and dashes of Morse code can be transmitted by semaphore, flashing lights, or taps on pipes. In the nineteenth century Morse code was mainly sent out by a telegraph key operator as short and long pulses over telegraph wire (the first form of electrical communication). A good key operator could transmit as many as 20 words per minute.

In making up his code, Samuel Morse decided that the more frequently used letters would be coded by shorter sets of dots and dashes. E is one dot, and T is one dash, for example. He created a *variable length code*, a topic treated more in Chapter 9. The full set of letters and their Morse codes are given in an end-of-chapter exercise. Here we will discuss Morse code for the numerals 0 through 9. There are five bits per numeral. See Table 1.6.

The Morse code of the 10 decimal numerals is like Gray code: a number representation differs from its neighbors by only one bit. Unlike Gray code, Morse code cannot be reflected; however, numerals 0–4 are the complements of 5–9 in Morse code. By counting the number of dots in a number and determining whether the dots come before or after dashes, it is possible to devise an algorithm for addition of Morse code numbers, but it would be much more awkward than using one-bit full adders for positionally coded numbers.

Bar Codes for Scanners   Packaged items in supermarkets, books,[6] magazines, and other mass-produced consumer products have bar codes of black and white stripes. For groceries the **universal price code** (UPC) is a 10-digit striped code printed on the packaging. UPC is for numbers only, not letters. Figure 1.9 shows a horizontally stretched UPC from a bag of corn chips. Each digit is allocated seven *lanes*. The central five contain the digit's code, and the outside two lanes are either all white or all black. In the middle and on the outside are longer *registration bars*. The two regions separated by the two middle registration bars have complementary codes (for the central five lanes). If we let black represent 1 and white represent 0, then the seven-bit codes for the numerals are as shown in Table 1.7. The column labeled "Left" contains the code in the region to the left of the two middle registration bars, and the column labeled "Right" contains the code in the region to the right. Adjacent

[6]Publishers print their 12-digit ISBNs (International Standard Book Number) for books using bar code. Study the ISBN number and its bar-code representation printed on the back of this text.

Figure 1.9 Bar code from a bag of corn chips.

Table 1.7 Bar Code for Numerals

Number	Left	Right
0	0 00110 1	1 11001 0
1	0 01100 1	1 10011 0
2	0 00100 1	1 10110 0
3	0 11110 1	1 00001 0
4	0 10001 1	1 01110 0
5	0 11000 1	1 00111 0
6	0 10111 1	1 01000 0
7	0 11101 1	1 00010 0
8	0 11011 1	1 00100 0
9	0 00101 1	1 11010 0

1s appear as a single black stripe. Every number therefore has exactly two black stripes from one to four lanes wide. By studying the table, you can match up patterns from the corn chip bag to the proper numbers.

Note how the numeral 3 is represented differently in the two columns. The complementary number codes left and right of the midline facilitate optical scanning and make tampering more difficult. Tight specifications on relative line widths also contribute to the reliability of laser scanning and the difficulty of counterfeiting.

Curiously, bar code and Morse code both use five bits for numerals. Both codes are difficult to compute with and are awkward to convert to positional code.

ASCII Code The American Standard Code for Information Interchange, or ASCII, is a seven-bit code representing 128 characters, including numerals, uppercase and lowercase letters, and various keyboard symbols. It is partly shown in Table 1.8. An eighth bit can be attached to the left (and become B_7 in the notation of Table 1.8). If used, the eighth bit is for **parity check;** that is, B_7 is appended as a 0 or 1 in order to make the total number of 1s in the eight-bit word even or odd.

EXAMPLE 33

What should be the parity check bits for the numerals 0–9 in ASCII code, in order to have even parity?

you need only count the number of 1s in $B_3B_2B_1B_0$. If the number of 1s is 1 or 3, then B_7 should be 1, to make an even number of 1s. The result is as follows:

Numeral	B_7	$B_6B_5B_4$	$B_3B_2B_1B_0$
0	0	011	0000
1	1	011	0001
2	1	011	0010
3	0	011	0011
4	1	011	0100
5	0	011	0101
6	0	011	0110
7	1	011	0111
8	1	011	1000
9	0	011	1001

Note that even parity does not mean that the numeral is necessarily even. In our list the numerals 1, 2, 4, 7, and 8 required parity check bits. Parity check bits in code words are useful in **error detection** circuits. A digital circuit receiving parity-stamped character codes will check for error by testing whether each character has the correct parity. Error detection in receiver circuits used in transmission of binary data is examined in more detail in Chapter 9, where methods of **error correction** of code words are also vetted.

The bits $B_3B_2B_1B_0$ in ASCII are in BCD positional format. In order to add two ASCII-coded numerals, a program need only strip off (*unpack*) all bits but $B_3B_2B_1B_0$.

Table 1.8 ASCII Character Code*

$B_3B_2B_1B_0$	$B_6B_5B_4$							
	000	001	010	011	100	101	110	111
0000			SPACE	0	@	P	`	p
0001			!	1	A	Q	a	q
0010			"	2	B	R	b	r
0011			#	3	C	S	c	s
0100			$	4	D	T	d	t
0101			%	5	E	U	e	u
0110			&	6	F	V	f	v
0111			'	7	G	W	g	w
1000			(	8	H	X	h	x
1001			)	9	I	Y	i	y
1010			*	:	J	Z	j	z
1011			+	;	K	[	k	{
1100			,	<	L	\	l	|
1101			—	=	M	]	m	}
1110			.	>	N	^	n	~
1111			/	?	O	-	o	Delete

*The ASCII code word B is $\{B_7, B_6, B_5, B_4, B_3, B_2, B_1, B_0\}$. Not shown in the first two columns are various transmission control characters, such as carriage return.

ASCII code is embedded in longer code words. Typing a character on a computer keyboard sends to the computer an 11-bit code that contains an ASCII subcode. The receiver circuit then strips off bits used in transmission and exposes the ASCII bits for further decoding.

Genetic Code   All the proteins in a living organism are synthesized by starting with "software" instructions stored in the deoxyribonucleic acid (DNA) of the organism's chromosomes. DNA molecules are firmly bonded phosphate-and-sugar backbones weakly connected by pairs of bases in such a way as to form a double-helix spiral. There are four bases in DNA: adenine, guanine, cytosine, and thymine. Proteins are the final molecular "hardware" and are assembled from 20 different amino-acid building blocks. A typical protein is a sequence of about 500 amino acids. The **genetic code** describes how the 20 different amino acids are encoded by the four nucleotide bases. Because $4^2 = 16$, pairs of bases could code for only 16 different amino acids. The genetic code represents each amino acid with three bases. A **gene,** which is the code sequence for one protein, therefore averages about 500 triplets. Since $4^3 = 64$, which is greater than 20, there is room for repetition in the code. (How many bits per amino acid would be needed to encode the 20 amino acids with a minimum-length *binary* code?)

The genetic code is traditionally listed in the map form shown in Table 1.9, where the nucleic acids of DNA are abbreviated C, A, T, and G, and the amino acids are given beside the triplet codes representing them. The 21st item in the list—the terminator—is the unit that terminates the amino-acid sequence making up the protein. Considerable order exists in the map; for example, all four codes for proline are in the same box and are not randomly scattered around. The same holds for valine, alanine, threonine, and others.

Another type of nucleic acid, RNA, acts as a "compiler" of the DNA code, actually directing the assembly of proteins from amino acids in the ribosomes of the cell. Terminator triplets begin and end a gene, but otherwise protein synthesis depends on exact replication by RNA of the DNA triplet sequence from beginning to end. No error detection or correction is involved. DNA like yours can code for about 50,000 different proteins; there are about 3 billion base pairs in your DNA. Considerable stretches (in fact, over 90%!) of the 3 billion base pairs in human genes contain nonsense codes, whose function, if any, is unknown.

For general discussions of the genetic code, see Stent and Calendar (1978, chap. 16) and Watson et al. (1987, chap. 13).

Neural Codes   Except for some specialized sensory cells, most nerve cells communicate with each other by pulse codes. A typical nerve cell emits 100-mV digital pulses at rates up to 1000 Hz. Because there are so many nerve cells in an animal (about 10^{12} neurons in humans, each neuron being in contact with, on average, 10^3 other neurons) information in the central nervous system probably has meaning more by *which* cells are involved (spatial code) than by *what pattern of pulses* (temporal code) a particular nerve fiber emits. At any rate, compared with the precision of our knowledge about the genetic code, less is known about the code(s) that a nerve cell may use.

Table 1.9 The DNA Genetic Code

First Base	Second Base A		Second Base G		Second Base T		Second Base C		Third Base
A	AAA	phenylalanine	AGA	serine	ATA	tyrosine	ACA	cysteine	A
	AAG		AGG		ATG		ACG		G
	AAT	leucine	AGT		ATT	terminator	ACT	terminator	T
	AAC		AGC		ATC		ACC	tryptophan	C
G	GAA	leucine	GGA	proline	GTA	histidine	GCA	arginine	A
	GAG		GGG		GTG		GCG		G
	GAT		GGT		GTT	glutamine	GCT		T
	GAC		GGC		GTC		GCC		C
T	TAA	isoleucine	TGA	threonine	TTA	asparagine	TCA	serine	A
	TAG		TGG		TTG		TCG		G
	TAT	methionine	TGT		TTT	lysine	TCT	arginine	T
	TAC		TGC		TTC		TCC		C
C	CAA	valine	CGA	alanine	CTA	aspartic acid	CCA	glycine	A
	CAG		CGG		CTG		CCG		G
	CAT		CGT		CTT	glutamic acid	CCT		T
	CAC		CGC		CTC		CCC		C

42

The designer of a digital code should keep in mind that a code must first of all satisfy the need of some user, whether that user be a human, a computer, or even a ribosome. As users we are interested, in Chapter 1, in codes that facilitate addition and subtraction. It is rare that an entirely new code is brought into use. Codes imply standards. All other things being equal, the more widely adopted a code, the better; Chapter 10 goes over some of the many details of the IEEE floating-point code standard, for example.

Given a digital code, two processes can occur: **encoding** and **decoding.** An encoder takes as possible input objects from a set and produces digital code. The numerals 0–9 form a set that can be encoded as Morse code, for example. At the other end, presumably after computation or symbol manipulation, a decoder transforms code back into another object convenient for the user. (See Fig. 1.10.)

The virtues of good encoders are:

- **Speed** All other things being equal, the faster an encoder does its job, the better.
- **Reliability** The encoding process should produce as few errors as possible; the error rate may turn out to increase as the speed of encoding increases.
- **Compression of input** Codes that compress well have many encoder input lines and fewer outputs. The ability of encoders to express data in compact form becomes critical when large amounts of data, such as millions of pixels from television pictures, must be handled. In the binary coding of numerals, we have seen that positional code uses four bits whereas Morse code and bar code use five bits and ASCII code uses eight bits.
- **Compliance** How well an encoder meets all the specifications of the code can be important. For a simple example, an encoder must set a sign bit in 2's complement encoding; a bar code must be complemented for lines printed to the right of the registration midline in order to comply with the rules of UPC.
- **Security** In some cases the role of a code may be to encrypt a message so that only a decoder with a key can make sense of the message. Designing hard-to-crack codes for encryption is a specialized art. In Chapter 9 we will look at basic methods for scrambling and recovering messages with the help of pseudorandom sequence generators.

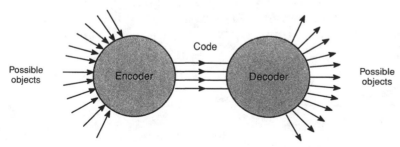

Figure 1.10 Encoding and decoding.

rest of Chapters 1–4 can be considered design of encoders and decoders. We start that design process in Section 1.9 by introducing the basic element of digital hardware: the switch.

1.9 FROM SWITCHES TO GATES

We now "switch" gears and begin consideration of electronic switches as the hardware that underlies much of digital design.

1.9.1 On-Off Switches

Switches and their cousins, the valves, have been around since the dawn of civilization, in such things as water systems and musical horns. A valve regulates flow between two places, and it has varying degrees of openness. A switch, on the other hand, has no in-between positions—its only two states are opened and closed. The handle of a sink faucet is a valve; the lever on a toilet is a switch. Valves (or potentiometers, in electrical terms) will not concern us much in this text. But as you can appreciate from the first part of this chapter, the two states of a switch will be associated with 0 and 1 in binary codes, and digital design will proceed from there. What makes switches so important to digital culture is their fabrication in semiconductor integrated circuits (ICs). Switches in ICs are made of silicon transistors, about which you can read more in *Daniels' Digital Design Lab Manual*. Silicon transistors are successful because they can change state millions of times per second, dissipate only microwatts of power, cost only microdollars per switch, and occupy only microns of space.

Understanding digital hardware starts with the two-position **on-off switch** (see Fig. 1.11). When the switch is open, as shown, RIGHT is disconnected from LEFT. Nothing can flow through the switch. LEFT and RIGHT can be at different pressures, voltages, or levels of illumination. If the switch closes, something can flow through it: water, electrons, photons, etc. Of course, switches for air, water, electrons, and photons will be completely different physical devices, but they all have in common the on-off control of flow from one point to another.

A switch by itself is useless unless employed in a system or circuit that allows flow to be converted to output or control. In digital electronic circuits, the flow of current is switched, and changes in current flow result in voltages shifting from one level

Figure 1.11 An on-off switch.

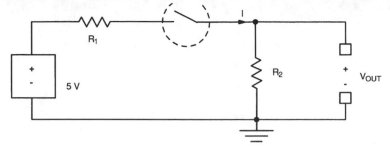

Figure 1.12   Switch in voltage divider.

to another. To continue the discussion, then, we portray the switch in an electric circuit with a battery and resistor. This portrayal will call upon some basic knowledge of basic electricity—voltage, current, and Ohm's law—that you are expected to know.

In Fig. 1.12 one on-off switch is incorporated into a voltage divider circuit. When the switch is closed, the two resistors divide up the 5 V, so that

$$V_{OUT} = \frac{R_2}{R_1 + R_2} \cdot 5\,V$$

The current I flowing through the resistors when the switch is closed is

$$I = \frac{5\,V}{R_1 + R_2}$$

so the expression for V_{OUT} is an application of Ohm's law.

For our purposes we need $R_1 \ll R_2$, so when the switch is closed, $V_{OUT} \approx 5\,V$. If R_1 were the internal resistance of a battery and R_2 were the resistance of a light-bulb filament, the voltage divider circuit could be used to turn the light on when the switch closed. When the switch is open, as shown, $V_{OUT} = 0\,V$. We can associate voltages near 5 V with binary 1 and voltages near 0 with binary 0. If you have any trouble understanding the circuit of Fig. 1.12, imagine that R_1 is zero and see that the switch controls the appearance of 5 V at V_{OUT}.

In the circuit of Fig. 1.12 we allowed a small R_1 to account for the battery's internal resistance. We could also place a small resistor in series with the switch itself; instead, we work in Chapter 1 with **ideal switches,** which have zero internal resistance. Real switches, as transistors or in any other form, always have some finite but small series resistance, which we neglect in this chapter.

1.9.2   What Does the Switching?

For some practical circuits you, the human, control the switching. You can turn on a light by flipping a switch, start your car by turning a key to connect the battery to the starter motor, and turn off the TV by pushing a button on a remote-control unit. At the next level of automation, a sensor or timer can control a switch. A metal

Figure 1.13 The control of a switch.

coil in a thermostat can straighten out in the cold until it makes contact with another conductor and turns on the furnace. Soot from a fire can obscure infrared light detected by a sensor and set off a smoke alarm.

However, the great distinguishing feature of the electronic switches used in digital circuit design—the feature that distinguishes such switches from their manually and sensor-activated cousins—is *the ability of one switch's output voltage to control another switch's open-closed state.* By this means essentially unlimited cascades and interconnections of switches can be built to carry out, in hardware, any digital computation. Transistors are the basis of voltage-controllable electronic switches in integrated circuits.

A switch can therefore be seen to have three pins: LEFT, RIGHT, and CONTROL (see Fig 1.13). CONTROL gates the path between LEFT and RIGHT in the switch.[7] There must be a rule, physical law, or equation saying how the control signal determines whether the switch is open or closed. For example, if CONTROL carries a voltage into the switch, it might be the case that

If CONTROL > 2 volts, the switch is closed.

If CONTROL < 2 volts, the switch is open.

Here 2 V is the **threshold** of the switch control. If a changing control input passes through the threshold voltage, the switch changes from one state to the other. For the switch to stay closed the control input must *remain* above 2 V; some switches have *memory*—they stay closed if the excursion of control above threshold is only momentary. See Exercise 47.

EXAMPLE 34

Draw an input-output curve for the gate in Fig. 1.14 if the threshold for *opening* the switch is 3 V. For avoidance of clutter, the 5-V supply is indicated as a rail at the top of the circuit and its return to ground is not shown explicitly. The internal resistance of the 5-V supply is also not shown in the diagram.

---

[7]Another term, somewhat dated, for a remotely controlled switch is **relay.** *Relay* often refers to electromagnetically operated switches. Relays can be classified as *normally open* or *normally closed,* depending on whether the excitation voltage on the electromagnetic coil closes or opens, respectively, the switch.

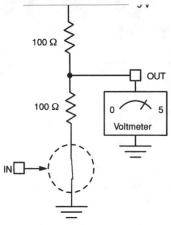

Figure 1.14 Voltage divider.

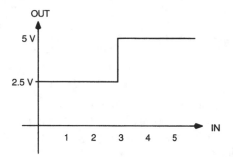

Figure 1.15 Input-output curve for the voltage divider of Fig. 1.14.

Solution   If IN is less than 3 V, the switch is closed, so a current of $(5\ V)/(200\ \Omega) =$ 250 mA flows from 5 V to ground. Output is $100 \times 0.25 = 2.5$ V. If IN > 3 V, the switch opens, so no current flows through either resistor and OUT $= 5$ V. See Fig. 1.15.

Note that whatever is flowing between LEFT and RIGHT of a closed switch or valve does not pass through the control pin. (As you fill a sink, water does not squirt out of the faucet handle!) In electric circuit terms, the CONTROL line has a *high input impedance*, or resistance. At any rate, the output of the switch—or, more likely, the system the switch is embedded in—can become the input to another switch or switches.

Match between Circuit Output and Switch Threshold   We restrict our consideration to two input states: one that keeps the switch closed and one that keeps it open. In order to participate in binary logic, a switch in a circuit must have a reasonable control input threshold—one that is between the two output values the circuit as a whole can obtain. If the low and high outputs of a circuit are designed to be approximately 1 V and 3 V, respectively, a 2-V control threshold is reasonable, but a 4-V threshold is not. See Fig. 1.16.

Terminology   A circuit with one or more electrically controllable switches embedded in it is referred to as a **gate.** Generally *gate* is reserved for a switching circuit just large enough to have a function on its own and versatile enough to be a building block in various larger systems. Where to stop calling switching circuits *gates* and start calling them *systems* is a fuzzy border. AND and OR logic gates go into adder circuits, but adder circuits are not referred to as gates. Further, in this text we will deal with electronic gates based on 5-V switching circuits, but the ideas of logic design can be expressed with optical, fluid, and pneumatic gates as well as with electrical gates.

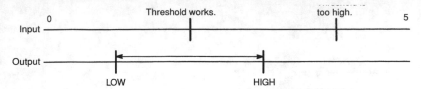

Figure 1.16   Logic thresholds.

For example, oil refineries, where fire hazard is great, sometimes use pneumatic logic control to avoid the danger of sparks from electrical control systems. Finally, the control pin on an MOS transistor is also called a gate. The few times when MOS gate pins instead of logic gates are referred to in this text, the context will make it clear.

1.9.3   An Inverting Gate

With the understanding that the input to one gate can be controlled by another gate's output, let's reexamine our one-switch gate using a switch that has a threshold of 2 V for closure. Assume that IN, shown in Fig. 1.17, has come from another gate's output. Assume further that the input is either approximately 0 V or approximately +5 V. If IN is 0, the switch is open, no current I flows through R, and OUT = +5. If the input is +5 then the switch is closed and OUT = 0.

The following table presents the input-output relationship of the gate:

IN	OUT	Switch
0 V	5 V	open
5 V	0 V	closed

When IN is high, OUT is low; when IN is low, OUT is high. The gate is an **inverter.** The inverter symbol, shown in Fig. 1.17, has only IN and OUT; it omits the power

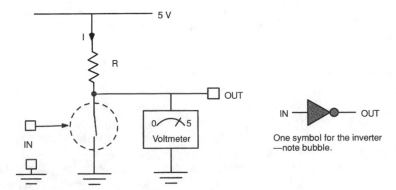

Figure 1.17   Inverter made from a switch.

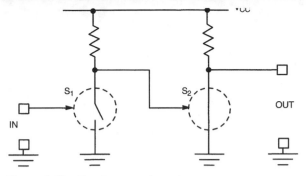

Figure 1.18 Two inverters in series.

supply and ground connections necessary in practice for the gate to work. For an inverter, OUT can be said to equal NOT IN (which can be written $\overline{\text{IN}}$ or IN'), or in other words, OUT is the *complement* of IN.

In Fig 1.18 the output of one switch is controlling the input of a second switch. (The power supply rail is now labeled as V_{CC}. The exact values of reasonable resistors here are unimportant.) This "noninverter" gate is two inverters in cascade, so OUT $\approx$ IN if we continue to restrict IN to values near 0 or V_{CC}. In the case shown in Fig. 1.18, IN is grounded (set to 0 V), switch S_1 is open, and switch S_2 is closed, so voltage at OUT must be ground also. In many digital circuits $V_{CC} \approx 5$ volts.[8] If so, and switch S_2 is open, a reading near 5 V appears at OUT. If switch S_2 is closed, a voltmeter at OUT would read nearly 0.

In some of the circuits in Chapter 1 the value of resistance along the switching pathway has not been calculated or specified. The resistance is there to provide an Ohm's-law voltage drop when current flows and to limit the maximum current flow. Here assume that a reasonable current-limiting resistance is in place, and concentrate your attention on the arrangement of switches in the circuit at hand.

1.9.4 Switches Used for AND and OR Functions

Two switches can do more than noninvert a signal. Place two switches in series, as shown in Fig. 1.19. Assume that a high input closes the switch. Now only if both switches S_1 *and* S_2 are closed is the output voltage zero. Otherwise the output is V_{CC}.

We have our second digital gate. Because the circuit of Fig. 1.19 combines the features of an inverter and the conjunctive AND relationship, it is a two-input

[8]In answer to questions about the mysterious V_{CC}: Subscript letter C stands for the *collector* pin of a transistor. When subscript letters are repeated, as in CC, the reference is to a *power supply*; when the letters are capitalized, the reference is to a *steady* voltage, not time-varying. Therefore V_{CC} stands for a steady power supply voltage on the collector resistor of a transistor. There is no transistor in the figure, but we know that a transistor can function as a switch, so let us leave the label as V_{CC}. The term *power supply* refers to a circuit that, by means of a voltage regulator, maintains a steady output voltage up to a guaranteed level of current demand.

While +5 V has been a standard power supply voltage in logic circuits for decades, there is a movement to convert circuits to 3.3 V; some memory chips already use 3.3 V. Such circuits consume less power and dissipate less heat. See Prince and Salters (1992) for more discussion.

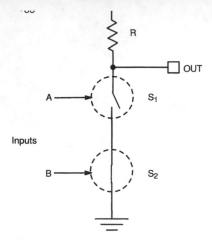

Figure 1.19 NAND gate made from switches.

NOT-AND gate, or NAND gate. In Fig. 1.19, input A is LO (switch open), so the output voltage remains HI. Placing N switches in series between V_{CC} and ground would make an N-input NAND gate. The following table lists all input-output possibilities for a two-input NAND gate:

IN		
B	**A**	**NAND(A, B)**
LO	LO	HI
LO	HI	HI
HI	LO	HI
HI	HI	LO

where LO and HI are shorthand for low and high voltages.

Figure 1.20 shows a standard symbol for a NAND gate, in this case one with three inputs. Note the inverting bubble on the right side of the semicircle. A plain AND gate does not have the inverting bubble on the output. Since any one LO input to a NAND causes the output to be HI, it can be said that a LO input to a NAND or AND gate *disables* the gate, preventing other inputs from affecting output.

A NAND results from switches in series. What about switches in parallel? See Fig. 1.21. In this case, OUT $= 0$ whenever either switch S_1 *or* S_2 is closed; only when both switches are open is OUT isolated from ground and OUT $\approx V_{CC}$. In the circuit

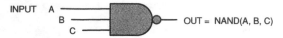

Figure 1.20 NAND gate symbol.

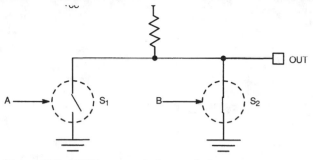

Figure 1.21 NOR gate made from switches.

INPUT A — B — C — [NOR gate symbol] OUT = NOR(A, B, C)

Figure 1.22 Three-input NOR gate symbol.

shown, input *B* is HI so OUT is pulled LO. This relationship between input and output is called NOT-OR, or NOR, and its realization in hardware is a **NOR gate.** The following table lists all input-output possibilities:

IN		
B	A	NOR(A, B)
LO	LO	HI
LO	HI	LO
HI	LO	LO
HI	HI	LO

where LO and HI are again shorthand for low and high voltages. The logic function NOR(*A, B, C,*...) equals HI only when all of *A, B, C,*... = LO at the same time. If *N* switches are in parallel, an *N*-input NOR gate can result.

Fig. 1.22 shows an officially accepted symbol for a NOR gate, in this case with three inputs. Compared with the NAND symbol, the NOR symbol has a curved left-hand input side. The bubble on the right side of the NOR gate means inversion.

1.9.5 An Exclusive OR Gate Designed with Four Switches

EXAMPLE 35

See the circuit in Fig. 1.23. What roles do R_1 and R_{BIG} play? What input-output table results for inputs *A, B*? Assume that switches S_1–S_4 close if their inputs are HI. Switches S_1 and S_2 form an OR combination, and S_3 and S_4 are an AND combination. The output is from the middle of the "totem pole" of the switches. The resistances

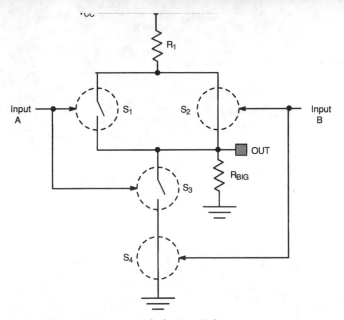

Figure 1.23 XOR gate made from switches.

are such that $R_{BIG} \gg R_1$.[9] The gate has two inputs, A and B, entering from the left and right, respectively.

Solution Resistance R_1 is necessary when both A and B are HI and all the switches are closed at once, in which case OUT becomes LO while R_1 limits the current flow from V_{CC} to ground. R_{BIG} is necessary when both A and B are LO and all the switches are open, in which case OUT has a path to ground and is LO. What if only A or only B is HI? Then the OR gate connects V_{CC} to OUT and the AND gate does not provide a path to ground. OUT goes HI.

The following table summarizes all the input-output relationships of the gate shown in Fig. 1.23.

IN		
B	A	XOR(A, B)
LO	LO	LO
LO	HI	HI
HI	LO	HI
HI	HI	LO

This is the table for an exclusive OR gate, or **XOR gate.** The XOR output is HI when exactly one of the two inputs is HI; it is a digital *comparator*. A symbol of the XOR

[9]Because of R_{BIG} the XOR circuit shown with switches may not be practical. As soon as its output is connected to any low-resistance load, its HI output voltage may drop below a level needed for controlling any other switches the output may be connected to.

INPUT $\begin{matrix} A \\ B \end{matrix}$ ⊃ OUT = XOR (A, B)

Figure 1.24 XOR gate symbol.

gate is shown in Fig. 1.24. Note the two curved input bars on the left, and no bubble on the output. Unlike NAND and NOR gates, XOR gates have only two inputs. (See Exercise 53 on creating a multi-XOR circuit that checks the parity of code words.)

A note on notation:

A AND B can be written $A \cdot B$.

A NAND B can be written $\overline{A \cdot B}$.

A OR B can be written $A + B$.

A NOR B can be written $\overline{A + B}$.

A XOR B can be written $A \oplus B$.

A XNOR B can be written $\overline{A \oplus B}$.

At the end of Chapter 1 we will work through the design of a one-bit full adder using AND, OR, and XOR gates. But first the on-off switch is developed into a more complex and useful form.

1.10 TOGGLE SWITCHES AND MULTIPLEXERS

In its off (open) position the on-off switch pole is not connected to anything. If the switch pole is forced to choose one of two inputs, depending on whether CONTROL is above or below threshold, a more versatile switch, the **toggle switch,** is created. (See Fig. 1.25.) OUT is always connected to one of two inputs; there is no condition of disconnection, such as the on-off switch has during its OPEN state.[10] In switch

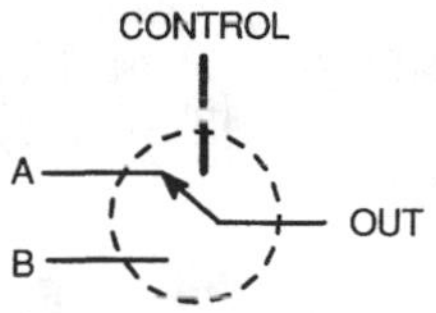

CONTROL

A — OUT

B —

Figure 1.25 Toggle switch.

[10]Later in the text—when timing becomes a concern—it will be of importance in a toggle switch that as the pole (or wiper) rotates from one input to the other it spends a small amount of time in a third state in which neither A nor B is connected to it. For now we ignore this transient state and deal only with the steady state.

An open connection on a high-impedance logic gate input can become a source of noise; use of toggle switches on inputs minimizes the chance of noise pickup, compared with hanging inputs from on-off switches.

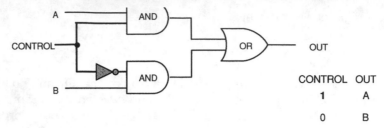

Figure 1.26 Design for a multiplexer.

catalogs a toggle switch is a *single-pole, double-throw* (SPDT) switch, and the on-off switch is *single-pole, single-throw* (SPST). The convention in this book will be that the arrowhead is the moving part of the switch, even though it points against the flow of information in the circuit of Fig. 1.25.

Toggle, a mechanical term, brings to mind a manually operated switch, but in digital design we have more interest in an electronic toggle gate, whose output can control the switching of another toggle. For now let us establish the convention that when the CONTROL input is HI, the top rail (*A* in Fig. 1.25) is selected for connection to OUT.

Yes, a toggle switch can mimic an on-off switch if one of its inputs is left unconnected, but let us explore what a fully connected toggle switch may be useful for. First note that *one* toggle switch is equivalent to the circuit of Fig. 1.26. In this circuit CONTROL *enables* one of two AND gates. The table at the bottom right in the figure shows the value of OUT for the two possibilities of CONTROL input. A direct replacement of the AND, OR, and inverter gates in Fig. 1.26 would require seven on-off switches!

EXAMPLE 36

Consider a room with two entrances and one light bulb in the middle of the ceiling. The light bulb goes on only when one side of the bulb is connected to the hot wire and the other to the neutral wire. At each entrance is an SPDT toggle switch. Design a circuit so that either toggle switch can be used to turn the light on or off. That is, the state the light is in—on or off—will change when either toggle is flipped. Use only the switches shown; no extra logic gates are allowed.

Solution   A diagram of the room is shown to the left in Fig. 1.27. Something must be connected to each side of the bulb. Since we have two toggle switches, try connecting the output of each toggle to the two sides of the bulb. If the hot and neutral conductors are connected to the inputs of each toggle, this electrician's problem is solved! See the diagram on the right in Fig. 1.27.

This switching arrangement for turning off and on room lights should remind you of exclusive-OR logic: only when the two toggle outputs are different does the light bulb go on.

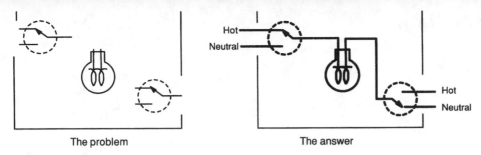

The problem   The answer

Figure 1.27   Two switches controlling one light.

Let us hook up three toggle switches in a two-level circuit. We label the CONTROL inputs SELECT 1 and SELECT 2. (See Fig. 1.28.) SELECT 1 controls both of the switches on the left. The four DATA inputs at the extreme left may come from other switch outputs or be tied directly to V_{CC} or ground. The DATA inputs can become OUT according to the following table:

SELECT 2	SELECT 1	OUT
LO	LO	DATA-D
LO	HI	DATA-C
HI	LO	DATA-B
HI	HI	DATA-A

Such a circuit is called a **multiplexer,** in this case a $4 \rightarrow 1$ (four-to-one) multiplexer. The basic toggle switch is a $2 \rightarrow 1$ multiplexer. An end-of-chapter problem shows how to turn a toggle switch around to create a demultiplexer.

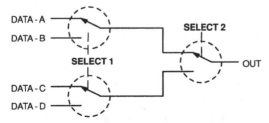

Figure 1.28   Four-to-one multiplexer.

EXAMPLE 37

Make a multiplexer imitate a two-input AND gate.

Solution　The truth table for a two-input AND gate is as follows:

IN		
B	A	AND (B,A)
LO	LO	LO
LO	HI	LO
HI	LO	LO
HI	HI	HI

The $4 \rightarrow 1$ multiplexer can meet the requirements if its DATA inputs are connected to ground and +5 V as indicated in Fig. 1.29. Only when *B* and *A* are both HI will the HI data input be selected.

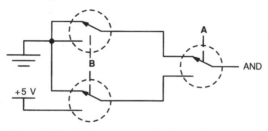 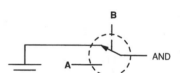

Figure 1.29　Four-to-one multiplexer for Example 37.

Figure 1.30　Two-to-one multiplexer for Example 37.

A $2 \rightarrow 1$ multiplexer (one toggle) can also do the job! See Fig. 1.30. When *B* is LO, ground is selected and the first two lines of the AND table are taken care of. When *B* is HI, output will be HI only when *A* is also HI, meeting the AND requirement. Note that the toggle-switch implementation of an AND gate requires no resistors, as the on-off switch AND does.

1.11　COMPLEMENTARY ON-OFF SWITCH PAIRS

The problem with an on-off switch output floating during its open state led to the evolution of toggle switches. It is possible to overcome the floating output and other limitations of the simple on-off switch by packaging two on-off switches in the totem-pole configuration shown on the left in Fig. 1.31. The two switches in series are controlled by the two inputs on the left; an output is between the two switches. On the right in Fig. 1.31 is shown a more compact icon for the totem-pole switch;

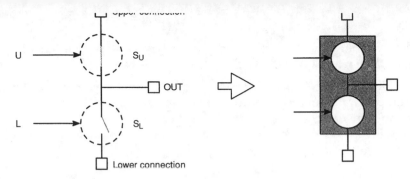

U → S_U

OUT

L → S_L

Lower connection

Figure 1.31 On-off switches in totem-pole arrangement. Assume that each switch closes when its contact input is HI.

that symbol will be used in various gate designs in this chapter. A *complementary switch* is created if the two on-off switches in the totem pole have opposite threshold characteristics.

First we make a complementary **inverter,** shown in Fig. 1.32. The input to the inverter splits. The bottom path goes straight to the lower on-off-switch input, and the top path passes through an inverter on the way to the upper on-off-switch input. When IN is HI, the lower switch is closed and the upper switch is open, connecting the output to LO. If you trace through the effect of IN being LO, you will find that OUT is HI.

Yes, the circuit functions as an inverter, but it already has an inverter built in! What's the advantage? One advantage is that OUT is connected by switches directly to V_{CC} or ground in its two states: the circuit can therefore boost weak input signals and do away with the need for a collector resistor. Another advantage is that MOS transistor switches can be fabricated that close because of either HI or LO inputs (CMOS switch pairs: the one on the top normally closed, and the one on the bottom normally open), eliminating the need for a separate inverter on the upper input.

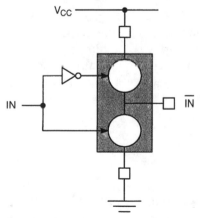

V_{CC}

IN

$\overline{IN}$

Figure 1.32 Complementary inverter.

EXAMPLE 38

It is possible to concatenate complementary switches to implement other logic functions. Let us design an XOR gate with complementary switches.

Solution   Shown in Fig. 1.33 are four complementary switches organized for an XOR gate. The output of the circuit as a whole is now between two levels of complementary switches. Input inverters are represented as bubbles to avoid clutter in the diagram. Connections are shown with black dots. Think of the switches with inverters on their inputs as normally closed.

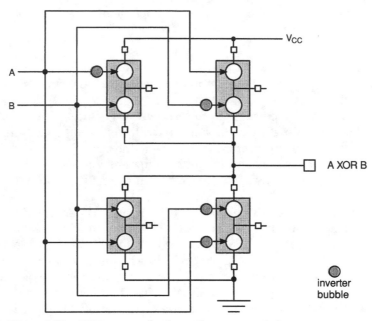

Figure 1.33   XOR gate made of complementary switches.

The bottom complementary switch on the left connects to ground only when both *A* and *B* are HI, and the bottom complementary switch on the right connects to ground only when both *A* and *B* are LO. The top two complementary switches close when either *A* (right) or *B* (left), but not both, are HI. The output is HI when *A* or *B* but not both are HI. Note that the circuit is constructed to avoid resistors between V_{CC} and the switches; no combination of inputs can create a short circuit from V_{CC} to ground.

1.11.1   A Third State

Some situations naturally present two states: a flipped coin lands either heads or tails; an electron has a spin of either $+\frac{1}{2}$ or $-\frac{1}{2}$; a human is either male or female. Other situations can present a third state: win, lose, or draw; left, right, or middle;

past, present, or future. Complementary switches are important because they idealize a major semiconductor fabrication technology used for logic chips: the **complementary metal-oxide-semiconductor** (CMOS) chip, which easily allows for a third output state: disconnection, or the high-impedance (Hi-Z) state. Imagine the basic totem-pole switch with both top and bottom on-off switches open. Then the output is disconnected from both HI and LO. We call a switch with ON, OFF, and Hi-Z states a *three-state switch*.

To be able to disconnect an output from a circuit is useful in memory systems. Chapter 8 will show how many memory chip outputs can be bused together, with only one output at a time enabled (addressed); all other outputs on the common bus wire are in the Hi-Z state.

1.12 SWITCHING CIRCUIT FOR ADDERS

In developing methods for binary addition, we constructed tables for half and full adders. We look again at those input-output tables to help us design an adder circuit.

EXAMPLE 39

What switching circuits will realize a half adder and a full adder?

Solution   Remember from our look at binary addition that a half adder (Fig. 1.34) is described by the following table:

Input			
B	A	SUM	C_{OUT}
0	0	0	0
0	1	1	0
1	0	1	0
1	1	0	1

Figure 1.34   Half adder symbol.

Inspection of the half adder's outputs reveals that carry-out is A AND B and SUM is A XOR B. Therefore, a design for the half adder is as in Fig. 1.35.

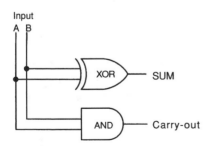

Figure 1.35   Half adder.

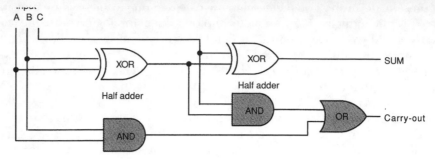

Figure 1.36   One-bit full adder with logic gates.

The XOR and AND symbols in Fig. 1.35 could be replaced by the circuit diagrams for switch-level gates. The gates could be *realized*[11] with on-off, toggle, or complementary switches. To deal with the switches needed in a half-adder design would mean going down a level in the hierarchy, referring to the level of detail at which the problem is considered. The next level *up* would involve combining two half adders into a one-bit full adder. And above that level, 1BFAs can be combined into multibit adders. A modular design philosophy allows the engineer to go from one level of the hierarchy to another without becoming lost in detail.

Earlier in the chapter (Fig. 1.5) we saw that a 1BFA can be realized with two half adders and an OR gate. At the gate level the 1BFA looks like the circuit in Fig. 1.36, in which the second half adder takes carry-in and the first sum as its inputs, and the final carry-out OR is shown at the bottom right.

In the next three chapters you will learn systematic methods for turning logic problem specifications into hardware realizations. You will see other 1BFA designs, including one in which the number of gates between input and carry-out is two, not three as above. In a gate in a real logic circuit, a small gate delay occurs between a change in input and the corresponding change in output. It can be important to minimize circuit delay or to minimize the number of gates involved; both issues will be taken up in Chapter 2.

1.13   COMPUTER-AIDED PROTOTYPING OF DIGITAL CIRCUITS

The final part of this introductory chapter will outline for you what is required to go from a hardware design on paper (such as the adder in Fig. 1.36) to an actual digital circuit. As usual, there are two paths to consider: the "traditional" method, still useful for smaller digital circuits, and the more recent rapid prototyping method, essential for large-scale digital circuits. The traditional method relies on medium-scale

---

[11]In digital circuit design the verb *to realize* often means to turn a problem's solution into hardware; of course, in this text realizations will be hardware on paper.

wire-wrap technology. The 7400-series TTL (transistor-transistor logic) chips and their logic offspring are the mainstay of the traditional method. TTL chips were first introduced by Texas Instruments around 1968. A TTL catalog can describe hundreds of different ICs, from NAND gates to adders and eight-bit counters and registers, which the designer can call on. The design process consists almost entirely in the mixing and matching of ICs by the engineer. Once a design is worked out on paper, the engineer will build and test a prototype. The traditional method can be extended to large-scale projects by breaking up the large project into modules and having each module (which may end up as a separate circuit card in the final system) worked out by a different designer. Changes in the design goals may require an extensive reworking of the chips and their interconnections in a module.

The **CAD method** has arisen in response to pressures for more rapid design of large-scale digital systems, such as automobile engine controllers, which may have to be redesigned for every new model. Other pressures for CAD come from the hardware side, where larger and larger chips, with programmable features, have become available to designers. One large chip can replace many smaller ones and reduce manufacturing cost by eliminating the need for wiring between small chips. For purposes of simplification, the CAD process can be divided into the four phases shown in Fig. 1.37.

- The CAD process may begin with the use of a **high-level design language** (such as Verilog, VHDL, or ABEL). With the high-level design language the designer can describe the problem in terms of equations, tables, or state diagrams.

- A computer **synthesis tool** will translate (compile) the high-level description to a level closer to the intended hardware. A limited library of gates, registers, etc. may be called up by the compiler and interconnected.

- After synthesizing a hardware description in terms of gates and their interconnections, the engineer can test his or her design with a **simulator**. The simulator is a computationally intensive program that will try as realistically as possible to find timing and load problems. Errors in understanding the original design goal may crop up at the simulation level. In any case problems will be caught before hardware resources are committed.

- Once a design has passed the simulator test, the engineer is ready to realize it in hardware. Here again computer methods come into play. Intended hardware products, such as read-only memory, programmable logic arrays (PALs), and field programmable gate arrays (FPGAs), are large logic chips with sometimes tens of thousands of programmable switches (see Chapter 4). For FPGAs a

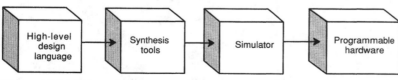

Figure 1.37 CAD method.

place-and-route program will attempt to fit the logic gates from the simulation into the general-purpose modules that reside on an unprogrammed chip. Often the routing (wiring) resources in an FPGA are used up before all the logic modules can be utilized. PALs are less flexible but more regular arrays of AND gates, OR gates, and flip-flops. We will look carefully at PALs in Chapter 7.

At the level of chips, the contrast between the traditional approach and the CAD approach is stark. TTL-type chips are fixed-function units in 14- to 28-pin dual-in-line packages. FPGAs are programmable units with 60 to 160 pins on all four sides of the chip. An FPGA may cost $10 compared with $0.50 for a typical TTL chip, but the FPGA may contain enough logic for 50 of the TTL chips. And once programmed, an FPGA takes care of much wiring internally, eliminating the need for extensive wire-wrapping or circuit-board printing to connect the smaller-scale TTL chips.

The two methods—the traditional and CAD—exist side by side for many design efforts. If you open up your personal computer, you're likely to see circuit boards with one large (50- to 150-pin) chip surrounded by several smaller chips. The internal connections of the large chip have been determined largely by computer methods, and the digital interface represented by the "glue logic" surrounding the large chip may have been done by hand.

In a lab course based on this material, you would probably start out using the traditional approach to get a hands-on feel for logic design on a small scale. By the end of the lab course you would be trying out more automated methods of digital design, perhaps not to produce a big design that would challenge the capability of an FPGA, but to see the advantages of working nearly all the way through to hardware with versatile computer tools. But before any lab design effort can start, you must know what you are doing, and that is what the rest of this book is about!

1.14 SUMMARY

- Digital systems have a number of advantages over analog: signal fidelity is preserved in the face of noise, numbers can be represented to arbitrary degrees of accuracy, and semiconductor technology allows for cost-effective digital processing and memory.

- Binary representation is a convenient way of encoding numbers and symbols. A **bit** is a numeral of the base-2 number system. The two bits of base-2 are 0 and 1 and are complements of each other. Several bits (4, 8, 16, and so on) grouped together are called **words.**

- The **positional code** for a N-bit base-2 unsigned number leads to the conversion formula

$$\text{Base-10 number} = \sum_{i=0}^{N-1} B_i \cdot 2^i$$

where B_i is the ith digit of the base-2 number.

- Repeated subtraction of powers of 2 or repeated division by 2 can convert a decimal number to a positionally coded base-2 number.

- There are other codes for numbers. **Gray code** changes one bit at a time; binary-coded decimal **(BCD)** uses four bits for each of the 10 decimal digits; **2's complement** coding represents negative numbers.

- **Fractions** can be handled by extending the conversion formulas developed for integers. Repeating or irrational fractions need to be truncated or rounded off.

- Addition of positionally coded binary numbers produces a sum and a carry-out. Two bits can be summed by a **half adder;** two bits and a carry-in can be summed with a **one-bit full adder.**

- The method for converting a positionally coded number A to 2's complement is given by the equation $A_{2C} = \overline{A} + 1$. The left-most bit of a 2C number is the sign bit; a sign bit of 1 stands for a negative number. The user must specify the word size of a 2C number so that the meaning of the sign bit is clear.

- Subtraction by 2's complement is done by adding a positive and negative number.

- Since 2C numbers have a specified number of bits per word, the sum of two positive or two negative numbers may result in **overflow.**

- Other digital codes are Morse code, bar code, ASCII code, error-detecting codes, and genetic code.

- Good encoders have the following virtues: speed, reliability, ease of processing, and security.

- A **transistor switch** is distinguished from its mechanical counterparts by its ability to be controlled by the output of another switch.

- The three types of switches—**on-off, toggle,** and **complementary**—can be placed into **gates,** which carry out logic functions such as INVERT, AND, OR, XOR, and multiplexing.

- Circuits for half and full adders can be constructed out of AND, OR, and XOR gates.

- Computer aided design (CAD) software and programmable gate array hardware are methods for the rapid prototyping of digital designs.

Exercises

1. What would be the size of the subdivisions of a scale from 0 V to 10.0 V if four binary bits could be used to describe each subdivision?

2. **(a)** According to "Hooked on Phonics" there are 44 distinct phonetic sounds in English. How many bits minimum would it take to represent the 44 sounds?

   (b) How many bits would it take to represent only the vowel letters in English? The long and short vowel sounds?

   (c) There are about 3000 common kanji characters in written Japanese. How many bits minimum would it take to represent the set of kanji characters?

binary code uses as few 0s and 1s per symbol as possible. When I was in Boy Scouts, we all learned the Morse code for letters and numbers. Morse code is an *efficient* binary code, using fewer dots and dashes for more frequently sent letters, such as E and T. The international Morse code for letters, sorted by binary, is given in Table P1.1. (Á, É, and Ñ require five bits and so are not included in the table.) To transmit a series of letters, the sender pauses briefly after each letter.

Table P1.1   International Morse Code

E	·	D	− · ·	P	· − − ·
T	−	K	− · −	J	· − − −
I	· ·	G	− − ·	B	− · · ·
A	· −	O	− − −	X	− · · −
N	− ·	H	· · · ·	C	− · − ·
M	− −	V	· · · −	Y	− · − −
S	· · ·	F	· · − ·	Z	− − · ·
U	· · −	Ü	· · − −	Q	− − · −
R	· − ·	L	· − · ·	Ö	− − − ·
W	· − −	Ä	· − · −		

(a) Morse code is an awkward binary encoding of the letters, since a given letter may be represented by anywhere from one to four "bits." Can you think of a way to transmit Morse code reliably so that an automatic digital system receiving a sequence of bits in time will have no problem telling when one letter ends and another begins?

(b) Suppose the probability of sending a vowel is 0.16 and the probability of sending a consonant is 0.01. What is the average length in bits of letter transmission? (Count − and · each as a bit, 1 or 0, say).

(c) Look at the alphabet layout of a typewriter (QWERTY) keyboard. How well does Morse code predict the positioning of letters on a keyboard (assuming that more frequent keys are easier to reach)?

4. Shown below is a diagram of a four-column, five-bead abacus. The number 3510 is represented. How would the number 9726 be expressed with the beads?

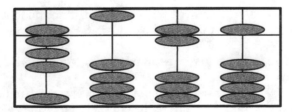

Figure P1.1   Abacus.

5. **Roman numerals**

(a) What do the letters (ciphers) I, V, X, L, C, D, and M represent in the Roman numeral system?

(b) How can you know whether to add or subtract a Roman numeral letter in the sequence it may appear? Explain what to do with XIX.

(c) Convert 1001 0001 to Roman numerals.

6. (a) Notwithstanding the Roman numerals shown on the clockface below, on what number system are clocks based?

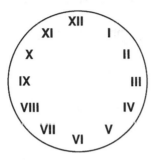

Figure P1.2

(b) How many bits minimum would it take to express the time of day to the nearest second?

(c) The widespread use of digital clocks has produced a generation unsure of what *clockwise* and *counterclockwise* mean. Can you think of a reason why the hands of analog clocks rotate in the clockwise direction? (*Hint:* Think of sundials. Does it matter whether the sundial is in the northern or southern hemisphere?)

7. Too bad we did not evolve with 12 fingers. Computation in base 12 has advantages over base 10. In base 12 the numbers 2, 3, 4, and 6 can divide 12 with no remainder; in base 10 only 2 and 5 can divide 10. The list below shows the conversion from base 2 to base 12:

Binary Number	Base-12 Cipher
0000	0
0001	1
0010	2
0011	3
0100	4
0101	5
0110	6
0111	7
1000	8
1001	9
1010	A
1011	B

Convert the following two binary numbers to base 12: 11 0011 and 10 1001.

8. Coins represent one of the oldest ways of counting. Consider a set M of American currency, $M = \{1¢, 5¢, 10¢, 25¢, 50¢, \$1, \$2, \$5, \$10, \$20\}$, including the modern substitute for coins, paper money. The members of set M are the ciphers of the currency system. Let a dollar be 1.00 unit of currency.

(a) Any finite currency amount can be represented by combinations of elements from the currency set M. Consider currency amounts C between $0.00 and $40. Let the set μ be the minimum number of currency pieces needed to add up to C. For example, μ for $16.27 is $\{2 \times 1¢, 25¢, \$1, \$5, \$10\}$. For what value(s) of C is the size of μ greatest? Is there a value of C for which all elements from M are needed for its μ?

(b) There are few 50¢ pieces and few $2 bills in circulation. Can you suggest a reason why?

9. Convert the following base-8 positive integers to decimal:

(a) 116_8

(b) 7701_8

(c) $55{,}523_8$

(d) $444{,}000_8$

10. What are the following decimal integers in BCD?

(a) 9_{10}

(b) 71_{10}

(c) 503_{10}

11. Shown below is an arrangement of 16 squares with binary labeling for each of the rows and columns. The bits are DCBA. Show on the diagram where the sequence of numbers of the Gray code is. The sequence is started and finished for you.

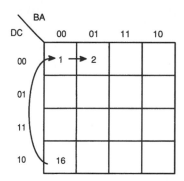

12. The linear form of the four-bit Gray code is copied below, where the least significant bit is the top stripe.

(b) Draw out the horizontal stripe version of the four-bit positional code and show where the code changes by more than one bit at a time.

13. Consider two lists of five-bit binary numbers, each list starting with 00000. List P continues with positional coding, while list G continues with reflected Gray code.

(a) Find a formula to convert P_i to G_i, where P_i and G_i are i items down in the lists.

(b) Find a formula to convert G_i to P_i.

14. Convert the following base-2 numbers to octal and to hexadecimal:

(a) 01 1101

(b) 1000 1011

(c) 1 0011 0101

(d) 1101 1110 1001 0001

(e) 10 1001.001

15. Convert the following base-16 numbers to binary and to octal:

(a) CAB_{16}

(b) $F00D_{16}$

(c) $FEED_{16}$

(d) $DEAD_{16}$

(e) $CAFE_{16}$

16. **(a)** Is hexadecimal A an odd number or an even number?

(b) What is a quick test to decide whether a binary number is even?

(c) Will your test work for Gray code?

17. Convert the following base-2 integers to decimal:

(a) 1 1111

(b) 100 1010

(c) 1 1011 0011

(d) 101 0011 0101

18. Convert the following base-16 numbers to decimal:

(a) BAC_{16}

(b) $D00F_{16}$

(c) 11000_{16}

(d) $9A8B_{16}$

19. What is the decimal equivalent of the binary fraction $1\,100/10\,000$?

20. Convert the following base-2 numbers to decimal:

(a) 10 1001.101

(b) 111.1101

(c) 1 1011.1010 1

(d) 1001.1100 11

21. Why, in the repeated subtraction algorithm for converting base 10 to base 2, do we increment each power of 2 used in the process before inserting 1s in those positions in the binary answer $N_2 = N_{10}$?

22. Convert the following decimal integers to base 2 using repeated subtraction.

(a) 40

(b) 99

(c) 216

(d) 1001

For further information see Schimmel (1993).

23. Convert the following decimal integers to base 2 using repeated division:

(a) 52

(b) 84

(c) 153

(d) 10,000

24. Convert the following decimal integers to hex:

(a) 40

(b) 99

(c) 216

(d) 1001

‡**25.** If you have access to a computer and know a programming language such as C, PASCAL, or even MATLAB or BASIC, write a program to convert decimal numbers to binary. Use repeated division for the algorithm. Make it able to convert numbers up to $131,071_{10}$ and resolve fractions down to 0.002. How many bits above and below the binimal point does that represent?

Here's the shell of a MATLAB function for the job:

```
function [binu, binl] = dbconv(dec)
% dec is a decimal number and
%binu.binl are the bits above.below binimal point
next = floor(dec); % Finds the integer part of dec
frac = dec - next; % The fractional part of dec
binl = binfrac(frac, 9);
% Uses previous function for fractional part conversion
for e = 1:17
if (2^e > next) break; end
% Stops when largest power of 2 less than next is found
end % of e
for div = 1:e
...
...
end % of div
```

To finish, all you need is to figure out the two lines represented by ellipses in the last loop. Not built in to this function is a test for numbers greater than $131,072_{10}$.

Test your function with the conversion of 131,071.002 to

$$1\ 1111\ 1111\ 1111\ 1111.0000\ 0000\ 1$$

26. Convert the following decimal numbers to hex:

(a) 40.3

(b) 91.43

(d) 2001.0625

27. An imaginary frog hops half the distance to its goal with each jump. Its first jump is 32 cm. How far will it have gone after eight jumps? Express your answer in base 2 and in base 10.

28. **(a)** What is π to 12 places after the binimal point in binary?
    (b) What is π truncated to 12 binary places, and what is it after rounding?

‡29. Two 1s added together are 10, three 1s are 11, and four 1s are 100. What formula predicts how many bits will be in the sum of N 1s? For $N = 2, 3, 4, 5$ the answer is $2, 2, 3, 3$.

30. Add by hand the following pairs of binary numbers:

    (a) $110 + 010$
    (b) $1110 + 1001$
    (c) $11\,0011.01 + 111.1$
    (d) $0.1101\,1 + 0.1110$

31. We saw in adding groups of bits that there are four combinations of pairs of bits and eight combinations of trios of bits. What if two-bit numbers are to be added together? Since four bits are involved, there are 2^4 possible combinations of two-bit pairs. But by taking account of commutativity, and not counting the cases of adding zero ($B + 0 = B$), we can see that there are six cases left. What are they? How many result in a carry-out of 1?

32. By writing out the cases for each CARRY of the two half adders involved, show that the OR gate in the one-bit full adder diagram correctly captures the requirements for carry-out. Write your answer out in the form of input-output tables for the final carry-out.

33. **Unary counting** Let $1 = 1, 2 = 11, 3 = 111, 4 = 1111$, and so on, and let 0 represent a space between numbers. Then 2 and 3 transmitted serially would look like 110111.

    Unary coding could be acceptable for small integers, and it is a code that could be handled by a binary switching system, but it is one that rapidly becomes inefficient for even modestly large numbers. It is not clear how to represent negative integers, either.

    (a) What is a rule for adding unary numbers?
    (b) What is a rule for subtracting a smaller unary number from a larger one?
    (c) In what way do Roman numerals represent a unary counting scheme?

34. Add with four-bit 2's complement the following pairs of numbers:

    (a) $1 + 2$
    (b) $4 - 1$
    (c) $7 - 8$
    (d) $-3 - 5$

35. If A is a binary number, let $2C(A)$ be the 2's complement of A. Prove that $2C(2C(A)) = A$.

36. Show that overflow occurs in 2's complement addition when the carry-out of the left-most column is the complement of the carry-out of the column next to the left-most. See the four-bit overflow example below:

$$
\begin{array}{r}
0\,1 \\
+4 = \quad 0100 \\
+4 = \quad \underline{0100} \\
\hline
01000
\end{array}
$$

37. The following subtractions are given in decimal notation. Perform the subtractions in 2's complement, and show your answer truncated to two positions to the right of the decimal point and in a word size appropriate for each problem.
   (a) $1.5 - 0.75$
   (b) $3.625 - 1.875$
   (c) $2.0 - 2.375$
   (d) $-3 - 4.5$

38. Study Table 1.6 showing Morse code for the 10 decimal numerals.
   (a) What is an algorithm for converting Morse code to positional code? The positional code will have four bits, not five.
   (b) Devise a method for adding together two Morse-coded numbers.

39. Study the bar code for numerals shown in Table 1.7.
   (a) Can you see a method for converting the central five bits of bar code to positional code?
   (b) Other than converting bar code to positional code, can you see a method for adding two bar-coded numerals together?
   (c) Look at several UPCs on grocery store boxes. Use a millimeter ruler and find how similar in width are the thinnest black stripes on the different boxes.

40. How many different characters can be formed with a seven-bit code? How many different keys are on the nearest computer keyboard you can find? Count characters formed by SHIFT, ALT, CNTRL, OPTION, and so on, if possible.

41. The way uppercase letters are produced on a computer keyboard is unchanged from the way they were produced on the typewriter keyboard of 100 years ago: hold the shift key down while the letter key is struck. What would it take to transfer the shift operation to a foot-pedal? Look at the bit patterns of uppercase and lowercase letters in the ASCII code and see how they differ. What would a shift pedal input to the computer have to do to take over the role of the SHIFT key on the keyboard? That is, which ASCII bit would the shift key have to control? Would this idea for shifting letters of the alphabet work also for other shifted characters on a keyboard?

42. By stripping off all but the right-most four-bits, an ASCII-coded number between 0 and 9 can be made ready for computation. See Table 1.8. What can be done if hex is transmitted by ASCII? Say how the uppercase letters A–F coded in ASCII could be converted to the six largest hex numerals. Refer to Table 1.1 for the hex code, if necessary.

‡**43.** Before it was cracked by biochemical experimentation in the 1960s, some molecular biologists thought that the nucleic acid-to-amino-acid genetic code

might be an overlapping code, which would include data compression and error detection. In one version of an overlapping code, the last base of one triplet is the first base of the next. For example, if the base sequence were G C A C U U A G A, the triplets would be

$$GCA$$
$$ACU$$
$$UUA$$
$$AGA$$

and four amino acids would be coded in the space that three would need in a nonoverlapping code. The overlapping code could be a comma-free code without the need for special symbols between triplets. In an overlapping comma-free code, only a subset of the $4^3 = 64$ possible triplets can be used without confusion. For example, if GCA codes for an amino acid, then CAG and AGC would not be allowed (or else GCAGC could not be unambiguously interpreted). See Crick, Griffith, and Orgel (1957).

Your question: What is the maximum number of the 64 triplets that could be used in a one-base-overlap code before confusion would set in?

44. In what ways is a switch different from a valve? By valve we mean a three-terminal device, one terminal of which is a *rotational knob* whose position determines the rate at which input (electrons, water, and so on) flows through the main channel of the valve to become output.

45. Imagine a spring attached to the lever of a switch. How is control of the switch affected by the spring? That is, if input is the force applied to the switch, how does the presence of the spring affect the input needed to make the spring change state? Compare the spring-loaded switch to one without a spring.

Is there a spring in the wall switch that controls your room light?

46. Suppose $R_1 = 10\ \Omega$ and $R_1 = 90\ \Omega$ in Fig. P1.3.

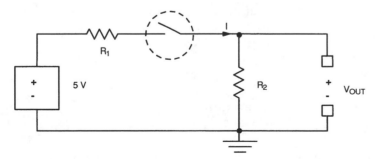

Figure P1.3

(a) What will be V_{OUT} with the switch closed? With the switch open?

(b) Suppose V_{OUT} is required to be 4 V when the switch is closed and that R_1 be fixed at 10 Ω. What should R_2 be?

47. Imagine the control input threshold to a switch *depends on the state of the switch.* If the switch is closed, the threshold to open is 3 V, and if the switch is open, the threshold to close is 2 V. Suppose the switch in question is in the circuit in Fig. P1.4.

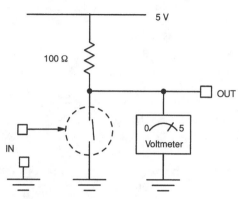

Figure P1.4

(a) Draw a graph of control input versus output for such a switch over the input range from 0 to 5 V. What you will draw is a **hysteresis** curve.

(b) Speculate on what good hysteresis may be in processing sensory input signals. Think about what state the switch is in with IN between 2 V and 3 V.

48. Using a 5-V power supply, resistor(s), and a *one* ON-OFF switch, design a noninverting gate for one input. The input can be any voltage from 0 V to 5 V. Specify what makes the switch open or close. What good is a noninverting gate? Think of it as a digitizer, a circuit that converts a many-valued input to a two-value output.

49. **(a)** Write out tables of all input-output possibilities for a three-input NAND gate and a three-input OR gate.

(b) Draw an arrangement of switches (plus any needed resistors and power supply) that results in a three-input OR gate. Specify the threshold on your switches.

50. **(a)** Describe with *logic functions* (NOT, OR, AND, and so on) what OUT does with inputs A, B, and C in the switching circuit in Fig. P1.5. Write down the input-output table. Assume that a switch S is closed when its control input is HI.

(b) What is the *voltage* output for the switch settings shown?

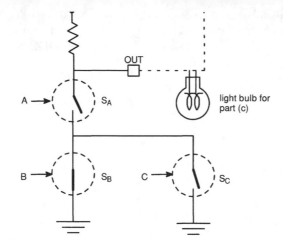

Figure P1.5

(c) Now suppose output of the circuit is HI when a light bulb comes on. The bulb is shown by dotted connections in the figure above. The bulb will light when there is a voltage *difference* across it, that is, when the OUT pin is at a low voltage. Write down the input-output table for the light bulb circuit and compare it with that of the circuit in which the voltage of OUT is considered the output.

51. (a) Design an exclusive NOR (XNOR) gate with five SPST switches, any resistors you need, and a + 5 V power supply. The input-output table of an XNOR gate is as follows:

IN		
A	*B*	**XNOR**
LO	LO	HI
LO	HI	LO
HI	LO	LO
HI	HI	HI

Assume that the two inputs to the gate come from wires connected to either HI or LO.

(b) Design the XNOR gate using only four switches of any type.

52. Design an XOR gate using (a) only two-input NOR gates and (b) only two-input NAND gates. (You can test your design on layout and simulation software such as LogicWorks. See *Daniels' Digital Design Lab Manual*.)

53. The generalization of a two-input XOR gate is a parity-checking circuit. Draw out a circuit of four XOR gates that receive input from eight bits of a code word.

Let the output of the four XOR gates project to two more XOR gates, and let the outputs of the two XOR gates go to one final output XOR. Show that such a circuit responds with a HI output if there is an ODD number of 1s in the eight bits of input. See Fig. P1.6.

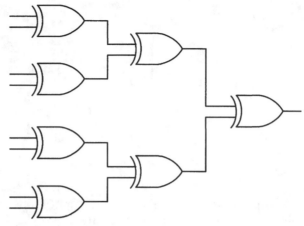

Figure P1.6

54. Show how to replace one toggle switch with a combination of on-off switches. Try to use no more than five on-off switches.

55. How many switches does it take to change a light bulb? Consider a room with three entrances and one light bulb in the middle of the ceiling. At each entrance is an SPDT toggle switch. For the light bulb to light, one side must be connected to the hot conductor, and the other to neutral. We want each toggle to switch the light off or on. Whatever state the light is in—on or off—a flip of any one of the three toggles will change the state of the light bulb.

(a) What is wrong with the design of Fig. P1.7 for meeting the requirements?

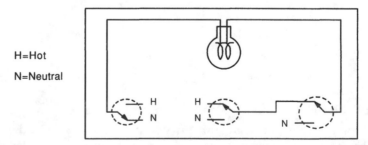

H=Hot

N=Neutral

Figure P1.7

(b) Can you think of a way, using only toggle switches (perhaps more than three), to meet the switching requirements for a three-door room?

(c) What if you are allowed to use only one four-point cross switch? The two positions of a four-point cross switch are shown below:

Position 1   Position 2

You can make a four-point cross switch out of two SPDT switches. Show how. Start by making a cross switch with four toggles.

(d) Using two four-point cross switches and two toggle switches, show how a four-door room can have controls at each door to toggle the light in the middle from any door.

56. What is the relationship between INPUT and OUTPUT in the following circuit? Assume that a HI value on the control of the toggle pulls the wiper up and that HI on an on-off switch closes it.

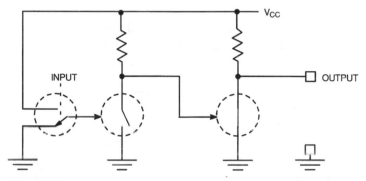

Figure P1.8

57. Show how to select the inputs of a two-to-one multiplexer so that it becomes a two-input OR gate.

58. What is OUT for each of the four possible combinations of SELECT 1 and SELECT 2 in the following circuit? This arrangement of toggles is a three-to-one multiplexer (for inputs V_{CC}, DATA-X and GND).

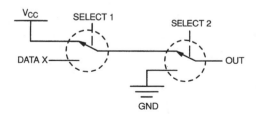

Figure P1.9

59. Under what conditions of C, B, and A does the following circuit have an output of 1? Suppose a switch is pulled up if its control input is HI.

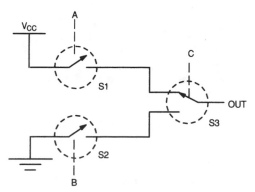

Figure P1.10

60. An SPDT switch can be turned around so that it has one input and two outputs. With the addition of a power supply and a couple of resistors, arrange the wiring around the toggle shown so that OUT_1 is always the complement of OUT_2.

In general, a circuit that directs an input to one of several outputs is a **demultiplexer.**

61. Suppose switches are needed to select which of 16 radio stations will be played on a radio. What is the minimum number of toggle switches that will do the job? Do not worry for now that the 16 "data inputs" to the switches may not be digitized.

62. Study how the XOR gate was fashioned from four complementary switches in Section 1.11. Try the same template of switches, shown in Fig. P1.11, and design (a) a two-input NAND gate and (b) a two-input NOR gate. Use inverters on switch inputs where necessary. On your diagram use solid dots to show connections of crossing wires.

63. Show how to realize a half adder with (a) on-off switches, (b) toggle switches, and (c) complementary switches. The design in the text for the XOR gate with switches is half the job.

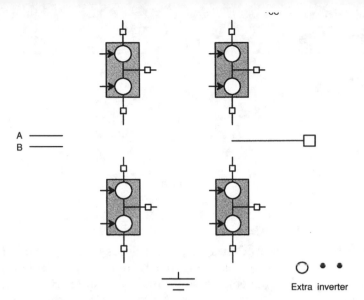

A ————
B ————

Extra inverter

Figure P1.11

64. Assuming that you have at hand several one-bit full adder chips, what else would you need to construct a circuit that changes the sign of a four-bit 2's complement number? Draw out a design for the sign-changing circuit.

65. Show how to realize a one-bit full adder with (a) on-off switches, (b) toggle switches, and (c) complementary switches.

References

CRICK, F., J. GRIFFITH, AND L. ORGEL. 1957. Codes without commas. *Proceedings of the National Academy of Sciences* 43: 416–421.

HAYES, J. P. 1993. *Digital logic design.* Reading, Mass.: Addison-Wesley. Chap. 2.

KATZ, R. 1994. *Contemporary digital design.* Reading, Mass.: Addison-Wesley. App. A.

KOESTLER, A. 1978. *Janus: A summing up.* New York: Random House.

MacKENZIE, C. E. 1980. *Coded character sets: History and development.* Reading, Mass.: Addison-Wesley.

PRINCE, B., AND R. SALTERS. 1992. ICs going on a 3-V diet. *IEEE Spectrum,* May, 22 ff.

SCHIMMEL, A. 1993. *The mystery of numbers.* New York: Oxford University Press.

STENT, G., AND R. CALENDAR. 1978. *Molecular genetics.* 2d ed. San Francisco: W.H. Freeman.

WAKERLY, J. F. 1994. *Digital design principles and practices.* 2nd ed. Englewood Cliffs, N. J.: Prentice Hall. Chap. 1.

WATSON, J., ET AL. 1987. *Molecular biology of the gene.* 4th ed. Menlo Park, Calif.: Benjamin-Cummings.

Truth Tables and Boolean Algebra

The binary restriction brought forth in Chapter 1 limits each *input* of a logic circuit to one of two values, 0 or 1. By the same token, circuit *outputs* are also restricted to the values 0 and 1. The challenge of **combinational digital circuit design** is the following: *Given a binary input-output relationship, design logic circuit hardware that will implement the relationship.* Furthermore, *try to optimize the design* by minimizing the number of gates, the number of connections per gate, or the delay from input to output.

In Chapter 1 the first dichotomy we considered was between analog and digital representation. Here in Chapter 2 we encounter a second dichotomy, that between two kinds of outputs in digital circuits: outputs that depend on a history of inputs, and outputs that depend only on present input.[1] Input-output relationships that involve input histories can be described by *state diagrams* and will be the subject of *sequential circuit design* in Chapters 5–7. Outputs that depend on present input only can be described by an input-output table and are the subject of Chapters 2–4.

There are two important ideas in Chapter 2. The first is that once you express a present-input logic problem in table form, you can find a guaranteed (but probably nonoptimal) hardware solution by ANDing together each input combination associated with one (true) output and then ORing together all the local AND outputs, as shown in Fig. 2.1.

The second important idea in this chapter is that the output of an **OR-of-AND circuit** can be described by an equation in **Boolean algebra;** by applying various theorems of Boolean algebra, you (or a computer) can reduce the number of AND combinations required, in an effort to minimize gate count.

In establishing small truth tables we are led to **hardware primitives:** common logic relationships that occur repeatedly in digital design. In describing Boolean algebra we are led to a **duality principle,** which shows a correspondence between two different forms of Boolean theorems. Later in the chapter we show that NAND

---

[1] As a rough analogy, the flame on a gas burner depends only on the setting of the control knob at the present time, whereas the temperature of an electric burner depends on the amount of current sent through the coil in its recent past. In this and the next two chapters we restrict our concern to circuits like gas burners, whose outputs depend only on their present inputs.

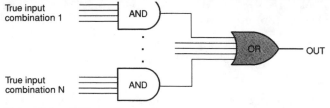

Figure 2.1 AND-to-OR circuit.

gates alone, or NOR gates alone, are capable of realizing any combinational design. At the end of the chapter timing problems of real combinational circuits are discussed, and ways to defeat *timing hazards* are presented.

2.1 COMBINATIONS OF BINARY INPUTS

The subject of present-tense design is called *combinational logic*. Why "combina tional"? We will be exhausting the number of different *input combinations*, where each individual input can be in one of two states.[2] As you may recall from probability, for N coins flipped there are a total of 2^N different combinations of heads and tails. The combinations are position-specific, that is, the combination HHT is different from the combination THH. For N inputs to a combinational logic circuit there are 2^N different input combinations, expressed as 0s and 1s.

The positional code you learned in Chapter 1 provides a good way to list all input combinations. Use a positional code with as many bits as there are separate inputs, and list the positional numbers down the page. By this means the list of input combinations is necessarily complete and the order makes it more readable. For N inputs there will be 2^N lines. Each separate binary input labels a column of the resulting list. The start and end of a 256-line, eight-input table are shown in the following table.

IN_7	IN_6	IN_5	IN_4	IN_3	IN_2	IN_1	IN_0
0	0	0	0	0	0	0	0
0	0	0	0	0	0	0	1
0	0	0	0	0	0	1	0
0	0	0	0	0	0	1	1
			⋮				
1	1	1	1	1	1	0	0
1	1	1	1	1	1	0	1
1	1	1	1	1	1	1	0
1	1	1	1	1	1	1	1

[2]Finding the combinations and permutations of set members is combinatorial arithmetic, and before 1980 or so combinational circuits were frequently called combinatorial. Over time, *combinational* has gained preference, at least in academic usage. Commercial data sheets are another matter. Even in 1995 Xilinx Corporation called part of its field-programmable gate array chip logic block a "combinatorial function generator."

2.2 TRUTH TABLES

A **truth table** defines an input-output relationship of a binary system by listing all input combinations and their corresponding output(s). Normally each input combination is a separate row in the table. The input rows are listed with the positional coding you saw in Chapter 1. The inputs may not actually represent binary numbers in a particular problem, but truth table rows will have the orderly appearance of a series of binary numbers in increments of 1 from 0 to $2^N - 1$, where N is the number of distinct inputs to the system. A combinational circuit may have more than one output. Listed to the right of each line of the input table is the resulting output(s). For M outputs, the total number of columns of a truth table is $N + M$. The entries of a truth table are nearly always 0s and 1s.[3]

When a truth table for a combinational circuit is realized (physically built), each input to the hardware comes on a separate wire and has its own label and meaning. Permuting wires may be a desperate troubleshooting strategy for a malfunctioning system, but it will not concern us in logic system design. We are interested in combinations—not permutations—of the inputs.

2.2.1 Four Examples of Truth Tables

EXAMPLE 1

A truth table needs to be written for the following specifications: If any two consecutive switches out of four on-off switches in a row are on, light 1 is on; if exactly two out of the four switches are on, light 2 is on. Assume positive logic; that is, when a switch is on, it produces a logical 1.

Answer There are four inputs and two outputs, so the number of columns is $4 + 2 = 6$. Let the inputs be $DCBA$ and the outputs be OUT_1 and OUT_2. Since the switches are independent of each other, there are $2^4 = 16$ rows in the truth table:

---

[3]Why put 1s and 0s in the truth table? Why not T and F? Fewer pen strokes is one reason. Another is that 1s and 0s are more suitable for arithmetic than other symbols. In positive logic the "truth" in truth tables can also be called T, ON, +, HIGH, HI, active, or 5 V.

In logic chips voltage levels are related to logic values. Suffice it to say that for positive logic, FALSE = LO = 0 is associated with voltages less than about 1 V (0.8 V for TTL), while 1 = TRUE = HI is associated with voltages greater than about 2 V. Between 1 and 2 V is a zone of indeterminate logic.

In negative logic a low voltage represents a TRUE output, so TRUE = LO = 1; this convention is the opposite of the one in positive logic and can therefore cause confusion. In some cases negative logic can make for more efficient use of hardware. Negative logic will be considered later when we use NOR gates in truth table implementation. In either case, logic conventions are *choices*, whereas voltage levels are *facts*.

D	C	B	A	OUT$_1$	OUT$_2$
0	0	0	0	0	0
0	0	0	1	0	0
0	0	1	0	0	0
0	0	1	1	1	1
0	1	0	0	0	0
0	1	0	1	0	1
0	1	1	0	1	1
0	1	1	1	1	0
1	0	0	0	0	0
1	0	0	1	0	1
1	0	1	0	0	1
1	0	1	1	1	0
1	1	0	0	1	1
1	1	0	1	1	0
1	1	1	0	1	0
1	1	1	1	1	0

In this problem, input order matters for output: it matters that sensor C is next to D and B but not next to A. Note that the truth table clears up possible ambiguity in the specification. For example, does A wrap around to D? (That is, are A and D to be considered consecutive switches?) No: 1001 has output OUT$_1$ = 0. If two consecutive switches are ON, a third is OFF, and the fourth ON, is OUT$_2$ on? No. See the boxed combinations above. Sometimes writing out a truth table is the best way to clarify what is meant in a problem statement.

EXAMPLE 2

Restricted Input Combinations   A truth table input combination can be impossible if there are constraints in the mechanism that generates input. Suppose inputs are sent from level-detectors in a fluid tank. The detectors are labeled A–D in Fig. 2.2. It's impossible for detector D to be active without all three other detectors being active. Likewise C can be active only when B and A are too. So only the five input

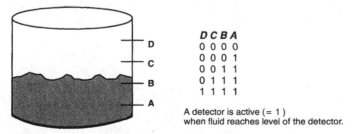

D C B A
0 0 0 0
0 0 0 1
0 0 1 1
0 1 1 1
1 1 1 1

A detector is active (= 1)
when fluid reaches level of the detector.

Figure 2.2   Level-sensor logic possibilities.

combinations listed in the figure are possible. What are the outputs associated with the 11 impossible inputs? Since the designer doesn't care what the outputs are for impossible inputs, he or she can just put an X in the output column for those rows. **Don't care** outputs occur frequently in design. An X in the output column is standard notation for don't-care outputs.

Suppose we want a logic circuit to respond only when the fluid level is between detectors C and B. Then the only line of the truth table with a 1 output would be $DCBA = 0011$. See the table below.

D	C	B	A	OUT
0	0	0	0	0
0	0	0	1	0
0	0	1	0	X
0	0	1	1	1
0	1	0	0	X
0	1	0	1	X
0	1	1	0	X
0	1	1	1	0
1	0	0	0	X
1	0	0	1	X
1	0	1	0	X
1	0	1	1	X
1	1	0	0	X
1	1	0	1	X
1	1	1	0	X
1	1	1	1	0

Two points need to be made about don't-care outputs here: First, after a circuit is built to realize a truth table, an actual definite output, HI or LO, will be produced if a don't-care input combination is somehow reached. If an "impossible" input combination is encountered, one or more of the detectors or logic gates may be malfunctioning. The designer may want to keep that precaution in mind when determining what the don't-care output will be.

Don't-care X's can sometimes be placed on the *input* side of a truth table when several related inputs result in the same output.

EXAMPLE 3

Four input lines from a truth table are shown in the following table. All result in an output of 1. Inspection shows that inputs X and Y do not matter; only when $W = 0$ and $Z = 1$ does OUT equal 1. Therefore the four lines could be condensed to the one shown below the arrow, in which X's are placed in the columns of X and Y in the four lines above the arrow.

Input				
W	X	Y	Z	OUT
0	0	0	1	1
0	0	1	1	1
0	1	0	1	1
0	1	1	1	1
	↓			
0	X	X	1	1

EXAMPLE 4

Seven-Segment Decoder   Here's a multiple-output, pattern-determined system. Consider the truth table of a seven-segment display driver. As you can tell by inspection of a digital watch, the two minutes digits are each represented graphically by an arrangement of seven segments. The labels for the segments (outputs) are shown in Fig. 2.3. Four inputs are shown in Table 2.1. They are the four bits of the BCD code, which you saw in Chapter 1. The four inputs can represent 16 numbers, the first seven of which are listed along with their outputs. The seven-segment driver outputs are shown as 1s where we want a segment to be displayed.[4] One don't-care X has been placed in the row for the numeral 6 because *we* don't care whether segment *a* is lit or not when the numeral 6 is formed. Other don't-cares are shown for binary numbers greater than 9_{10}. Our truth table has the display go blank (outputs *a* through *g* are all 0) for input 1111.

The complete truth table for BCD-to-seven-segment conversion can be found in the data sheets for a display driver chip such as the 7448. The 7448 is a 16-pin TTL chip designed to drive light-emitting diode (LED) segments. Eleven pins on the 7448 accommodate the inputs and outputs listed in Table 2.1, two pins are for power and ground, and three pins are for testing the chip. The 7448 actually has no don't cares

Figure 2.3   Labels for seven segments.

[4]Whether *on* means a lit or darkened segment is another matter. In a back-lit liquid crystal display, the active segments are dark, whereas with LEDs the segments would be lit. We're assuming here that whatever is active for a segment—lit or darkened with respect to background—is driven by a 1 in the output table.

Table 2.1   Truth Table for a Seven-Segment Display Driver

Numeral to Be Displayed	Inputs				Outputs						
	D	C	B	A	a	b	c	d	e	f	g
0	0	0	0	0	1	1	1	1	1	1	0
1	0	0	0	1	0	1	1	0	0	0	0
2	0	0	1	0	1	1	0	1	1	0	1
3	0	0	1	1	1	1	1	1	0	0	1
4	0	1	0	0	0	1	1	0	0	1	1
5	0	1	0	1	1	0	1	1	0	1	1
6	0	1	1	0	X	0	1	1	1	1	1
7	0	1	1	1				⋮			
8	1	0	0	0							
9	1	0	0	1							
	1	0	1	0	X	X	X	X	X	X	X
	1	0	1	1	X	X	X	X	X	X	X
	1	1	0	0							
	1	1	0	1				⋮			
	1	1	1	0							
Blank	1	1	1	1	0	0	0	0	0	0	0

in its table; the higher-order hex numbers appear as truncated versions of numbers 8 or less (a 10 appears as the d, e, g segments of 2 since $2 = 10 - 8$).

2.2.2   Two Examples of Combinational Design

Before using truth tables in a systematic design method, you will learn the motivation for the idea and review material from Chapter 1 through two examples.

EXAMPLE 5

Detecting Two Adjacent Buttons Pressed   Suppose you are given three SPST switches arranged left to right as shown in Fig. 2.4. If a switch is closed, its associated output signal (C, B, or A) is connected to ground and becomes LO (voltage $= 0$). If a switch is open, no current flows through its associated resistor, and the signal (C, B, or A) is HI (about V_{CC}; assume that any load resistance is high). In the particular situation illustrated, CBA = LO-HI-HI (or in binary where HI = true, 011). Design a logic circuit that will produce a HI output if exactly two in a row of the three keys are open (logical 1) at the same time. OUT should not be HI if all three switches are on at once.

Answer   The diagram in Fig. 2.5 introduces the design cloud symbol: the cloud suggests that the input/output relationship is known but a way to express the relationship in hardware has not yet been figured out.

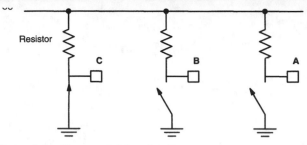

Figure 2.4 Three-switching circuit.

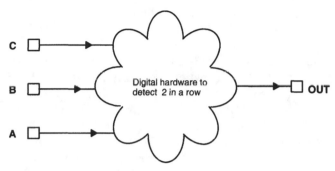

Figure 2.5 Design cloud for detector.

The three input signals A, B, and C provide a total of $2^3 = 8$ input combinations. The input combinations for which we want logical 1 output are C and B only or B and A only. That is, if $C = 1$ and $B = 1$ at the same time or if $B = 1$ and $A = 1$ at the same time, then OUT $= 1$; otherwise, OUT $= 0$. The six cases to result in OUT $= 0$ include the case $C = 1$, $B = 1$, $A = 1$, which is three in a row. The truth table is as follows:

Inputs			
C	B	A	OUT
0	0	0	0
1	0	0	0
0	1	0	0
1	1	0	1
0	0	1	0
1	0	1	0
0	1	1	1
1	1	1	0

In some cases, such as this one, the wording of a problem can lead directly to a solution in hardware. Key words to look for are terms such as *and, or, not,* and *unless*.

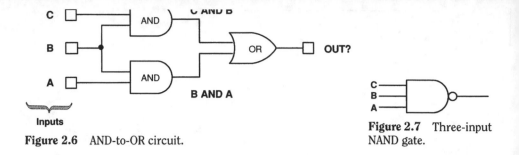

Figure 2.6 AND-to-OR circuit.

Figure 2.7 Three-input NAND gate.

A logic gate solution to the problem can be *started* by using AND and OR gates and substituting the gates for key words in the problem statement. See Fig. 2.6. OUT in Fig. 2.6 is *C* AND *B* OR *B* AND *A*. The detections of *C* and *B* and *B* and *A* occur in parallel.

Unfortunately, this attempt at design fails to stop OUT = 1 when $CBA = 111$. Some way is needed to inhibit the output when too many (three) inputs are active at once. You can detect when all three inputs are HI with a three-input AND gate. If that three-input AND gate can inhibit the final output, the specifications will be met. What should you use for the final output gate? To inhibit or disable an OR gate, use a HI input; to disable an AND gate, use a LO input. Choose an AND gate for the final output gate. Recall from Chapter 1 that the NAND gate provides a built-in inverter. See Fig. 2.7. Only when all three inputs are HI will the NAND output be LO, so you can use this three-input NAND gate to disable an output AND gate.

The original design attempt plus the overload shutdown are now combined in Fig. 2.8, in which the overload part is shaded. The third AND gate is disabled by the NAND at the bottom when $CBA = 111$, forcing the final AND to LO. This circuit works; the design cloud is removed. The circuit of Fig. 2.8 realizes the required input-output relationship.

The trial-and-error approach succeeded here because the problem was small. We will return to this example, with a better solution, both for gate count and delay, after our first systematic design method has been explained. See Exercise 8 for two more attempts to solve the two-in-a-row problem.

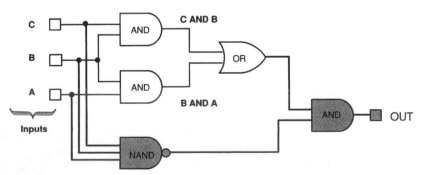

Figure 2.8 Three-level design with disable path.

EXAMPLE 6

A digital logic circuit receives input from five valve position sensors in a system of pipes. Each sensor sends either an OPEN or CLOSED signal. How many different combinations of valve positions are there? The circuit output must respond with HI if an odd number of valves are open. What logic circuit can handle the job?

Answer With five independent inputs, there are $2^5 = 32$ possible combinations of valve positions, including the combinations of all valves open or all closed. All the possible combinations of valve openings $V_1V_2V_3V_4V_5$ are listed in Table 2.2 along with an indication as to whether an odd number of valves are open. The list is in two columns. In the column on the left, valve V_5 is always closed; in the column on the right, V_5 is always open. Note that the two columns have complementary "odd" markings.

Recall from Chapter 1 that detecting an odd number of active inputs is a parity-checking problem. There you learned that XOR gates chained together can test for odd parity. Figure 2.9 shows a way to connect five inputs to four XOR gates. The

Table 2.2 Truth Table for System of Five Valves

V_5	V_4	V_3	V_2	V_1		V_5	V_4	V_3	V_2	V_1	
C	C	C	C	C		O	C	C	C	C	odd
C	C	C	C	O	odd	O	C	C	C	O	
C	C	C	O	C	odd	O	C	C	O	C	
C	C	C	O	O		O	C	C	O	O	odd
C	C	O	C	C	odd	O	C	O	C	C	
C	C	O	C	O		O	C	O	C	O	odd
C	C	O	O	C		O	C	O	O	C	odd
C	C	O	O	O	odd	O	C	O	O	O	
C	O	C	C	C	odd	O	O	C	C	C	
C	O	C	C	O		O	O	C	C	O	odd
C	O	C	O	C		O	O	C	O	C	odd
C	O	C	O	O	odd	O	O	C	O	O	
C	O	O	C	C		O	O	O	C	C	odd
C	O	O	C	O	odd	O	O	O	C	O	
C	O	O	O	C	odd	O	O	O	O	C	
C	O	O	O	O		O	O	O	O	O	odd

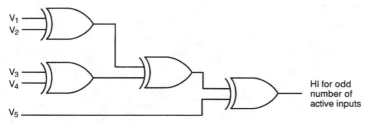

Figure 2.9 XOR cascade for parity check.

2.2.3 Sizes of Truth Tables

The smallest truth table, two lines, can define an inverter. On the other hand, truth tables can be large. Consider a truth table required to list all the multiplication products of two eight-bit binary numbers. The number of eight-bit binary numbers is $2^8 = 256$. Because each row of the multiplication table will have a different pair of eight-bit numbers (16 columns of input), the number of rows will be

$$256 \times 256 = 2^{8+8} = 2^{16} = 65,536$$

which means over 65,000 rows in the multiplication table!

The product of two eight-bit numbers can contain as many as 16 bits, so the *output* part of each row must also have 16 columns. How many bits does it take to contain the whole multiplication table?

$$32 \text{ columns} \times 65,536 \text{ rows} = 2^{21} \approx 2 \text{ million bits}$$

Amazingly, there are single-memory chips with capacity of 2 million bits or more. While none have 16 bits of output per chip, 8 bits of output is not uncommon. Memory chips and their use in realizing large truth tables will be discussed with more detail in Chapters 4 and 8.

Summary   A truth table is an exhaustive listing of all combinations of inputs for a binary system and their associated outputs. Each row of a truth table holds a different input combination. A truth table for N inputs will have 2^N rows. Inputs and outputs in a truth table can be 0, 1, or a don't-care state, represented in the table by X. A truth table is a systematic way to state a problem or define a relationship. A truth table by itself is not a solution to the problem. We now turn to methods for solving, in hardware, problems posed by truth tables.

2.3   HARDWARE PRIMITIVES

The quickest way to turn a truth table relationship into a hardware system is to find an already-built piece of hardware that solves your problem. It could be that a general-purpose circuit chip with many inputs and outputs, such as a memory chip, could realize almost any truth table problem you can think of but would do so at too high a cost ($10 versus 50¢). Later, in Chapter 4, we will consider the use of programmable logic array chips to solve many truth table problems by systematic use of AND-to-OR circuits. For now we focus on coming up with an economical amount of hardware to solve modest-sized problems. As Chapter 2 proceeds, we will look for *minimal* hardware configurations.

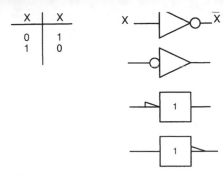

X	X
0	1
1	0

Figure 2.10   Inverter symbols.

With that said, we start with **hardware primitives:** small gates available off-the-shelf[5] that a designer can immediately apply to truth tables; the correspondence between small truth tables and such gates is obvious. A primitive is a commonly useful logic gate that can realize a truth table of one or two inputs.

Our first hardware primitive is the one-input inverter. An inverter turns a 0 into a 1 or a 1 into a 0. If X is a logical variable, let $\overline{X}$ be its inverted, or opposite, value, or **complement.** See Fig. 2.10. The schematic convention is that the whole inverter symbol (top right) is normally used when only one of several inputs to a gate must be complemented. The bubble will be used on a gate input (second from the top) in multi-function chips such as general-purpose arithmetic units, where the question of what is being complemented is decided inside the unit.

Table 2.3 lists the outputs of all 16 possible two-input, single-output combinational circuits. Twelve of the 16 have been labeled. The notation is as follows: + means OR, · means AND, ⊕ means exclusive OR, and a bar over an expression means inversion, or complement. The four output combinations in the unlabeled columns are cases of logical *implication;* they will not concern us as hardware primitives.

In Fig. 2.11 the schematic symbols (for two inputs) of four of the 12 labeled primitives of Table 2.3 are illustrated. Listed in Table 2.4 are the truth tables of the four primitives. Recall that in Chapter 1 these four primitives were built up from switches. Above each primitive name in Table 2.4 is the 74LSXX number of the TTL chip that contains the primitive. For example, a 74LS00 chip has four two-input NAND gates.

Exclusive OR, or XOR, is true only when B and A are different. NANDs and NORs can legitimately have an arbitrary number of inputs; to qualify as primitives, they are restricted here to two inputs. Since NAND and NOR gates combine an inverter

---

[5]Commercial logic gate families are covered in various manufacturers' data books, especially those of Texas Instruments. Some of the hardware primitives in this chapter will be labeled with 7400-series TTL numbers. The 7400 series has a 30-year history of use by logic design engineers, and many of its individual chips have very high status in digital logic. Plain 7400 chips are obsolete; for low propagation delay and low power consumption, 74LS and 74ALS are good choices.

Table 2.3 Logic Functions of Two Inputs

Inputs								Outputs					
B	A	Pass 0	$\overline{A+B}$	$\overline{B}$	$\overline{A}$	$A \oplus B$	$\overline{A \cdot B}$	$A \cdot B$	$\overline{A \oplus B}$	Pass A	Pass B	$A+B$	Pass 1
0	0	0	1	1	1	0	1	0	1	0	0	0	1
0	1	0	0	1	0	1	1	0	0	1	0	1	1
1	0	0	0	0	1	1	1	0	0	0	1	1	1
1	1	0	0	0	0	0	0	1	1	1	1	1	1

~~Table 2.1~~   ~~Truth Tables of the Four Primitives in~~
Fig. 2.11

Inputs		74LS00	74LS02	74LS86	74LS04
B	A	NAND	NOR	EXOR	INVERT A
0	0	1	1	0	1
0	1	1	0	1	0
1	0	1	0	1	1
1	1	0	0	0	0

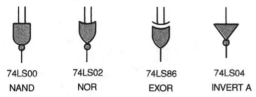

74LS00	74LS02	74LS86	74LS04
NAND	NOR	EXOR	INVERT A

Figure 2.11 Logic function primitives.

with another logical operation, they are versatile as building blocks. We will see later in Chapter 2 that any combinational logic function can be realized by using NANDs only or NORs only.

If a two-input truth table problem looks like any of these standard gate responses, your design is done. Just plug in the correct chip and hook up the inputs. In other cases a combination of two gates may solve your problem. For the larger problems that we are about to consider, more and more hardware primitives may be combined into your design.

We still do not have a systematic method for solving a truth table problem in terms of hardware primitives. That will come in Section 2.4. For now let us merely list various primitives and note that where a problem statement uses words such as *and, or, not,* and *compare,* the primitives may provide a direct solution.

EXAMPLE 7

Suppose when $C = 0$ the output of system S should be $A \cdot B$, and when $C = 1$ the output should be $A + B$. What connection of primitives can realize system S in hardware?

Answer   You may want to write out the truth table for inputs CBA and OUT_2, but the problem statement has enough relationship words to enable us to come up with the circuit of Fig. 2.12. $A \cdot B$ passes through enabled gate AND_2 if $C = 0$; $A + B$ passes through gate AND_3 if $C = 1$. Only one of the outputs of AND_2 and AND_3 can be asserted at any time; whichever is selected passes to OUT_2. The part of the circuit on the right was seen in Chapter 1. It's a **multiplexer**.

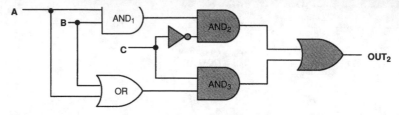

Figure 2.12   AND and OR feeding into multiplexer.

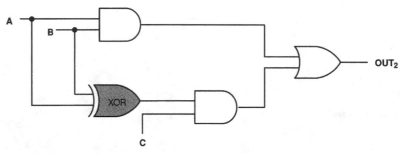

Figure 2.13   Alternative design for Example 7.

As an illustration that the same input-output relationship can be expressed with hardware primitives in more ways than one, another circuit for system S is shown in Fig. 2.13.

The truth table for system S turns out to be the truth table for carry-out in a 1-bit full adder, an arithmetic operation you saw in Chapter 1.

2.4   A METHOD FOR SOLVING ANY TRUTH TABLE

Given a truth table with no obvious solution in hardware, here is a general-purpose hammer guaranteed to crack the nut.

1. Start with a one-output truth table or restrict your attention to one column of output of a multiple-output truth table.

2. Look down the output column for the first 1. *(Find the truth in the truth table!)*

3. Now look across the table at the input values responsible for the true output. The inputs will be some combination of 0s and 1s. AND together all the input terms of that row, *making sure to complement any input term listed with a 0*. The resulting AND expression will realize one line of the truth table.

EXAMPLE 8

If the first line of a six-input truth table with a 1 output reads

F	E	D	C	B	A	OUT
0	1	1	1	0	0	1

then, when the AND combination $\overline{F} \cdot E \cdot D \cdot C \cdot \overline{B} \cdot \overline{A}$ is true, OUT will be 1.

Note the dots between the variables in the expression. Because it has algebraic similarities to multiplication, the ANDing of two or more binary variables is often called a **product,** or product term. The ANDing of one combination of all inputs of a truth table is known as a **minterm.** There are 2^N possible minterms of N inputs. The expression of six inputs or their complements ANDed together above is one of 64 possible minterms of the six-input table.[6]

To continue the recipe,

4. Repeat the ANDing process of step 3 for each row of the truth table with a 1 output, in the process generating more minterm products.

5. OR all the minterms generated. The output of the OR gate is a correct implementation of the truth table.

EXAMPLE 8 (CONTINUED)

To continue Example 8, imagine that only three other lines of the six-input truth table result in true outputs. We list them all together and write out their minterms:

F	E	D	C	B	A	OUT	
0	1	1	1	0	0	1	$\overline{F}\cdot E\cdot D\cdot C\cdot \overline{B}\cdot \overline{A}$
0	0	1	1	1	0	1	$\overline{F}\cdot \overline{E}\cdot D\cdot C\cdot B\cdot \overline{A}$
0	0	0	1	1	1	1	$\overline{F}\cdot \overline{E}\cdot \overline{D}\cdot C\cdot B\cdot A$
1	1	1	0	0	0	1	$F\cdot E\cdot D\cdot \overline{C}\cdot \overline{B}\cdot \overline{A}$
Any other line						0	

Then

$$\text{OUT}_{\text{total}} = \overline{F}\cdot E\cdot D\cdot C\cdot \overline{B}\cdot \overline{A} + \overline{F}\cdot \overline{E}\cdot D\cdot C\cdot B\cdot \overline{A} + \overline{F}\cdot \overline{E}\cdot \overline{D}\cdot C\cdot B\cdot A + F\cdot E\cdot D\cdot \overline{C}\cdot \overline{B}\cdot \overline{A}$$

[6]It is important to understand the word *minterm* exactly. In this text a minterm represents a conjunction (AND) of *all* truth table inputs or their complements for a line of the truth table in which output is true. Therefore a particular truth table has only as many minterms as it has 1s in its output column. A name for the *set* of minterms is the *on-set*.

We continue to use the notation + meaning OR and · meaning AND. The context will prevent confusion when we need to use + for addition. In some digital logic chip data sheets you will see the word PLUS written out where addition is to take place in order to prevent confusion with OR.

OUT_{total} responds to all combinations of exactly three in a row out of six. The system is drawn out as hardware in Fig. 2.14, where the six inputs are repeated for clarity and inverters on inputs are shown as separate gates. The AND gates have six inputs, and the OR gate has four inputs, a little large perhaps for bona fide primitives. The systematic solution does have a look of regularity. As drawn in the figure, inputs A–F are repeated for each of the AND gates; in fact, not shown further to the left there is just one input A that fans out the four A lines shown in the figure. Not counting the input inverters on some paths, the maximum delay from input to output is two gates' worth.

An AND-to-OR circuit such as the one for Example 8 is known as a **sum of products** (SOP, or in Greek letters, Σ of Π) circuit. Multiplication and addition of real numbers are not taking place here, but as we will see later, there are enough similarities between arithmetic and logic that "sum of products" is valid jargon. An SOP design like the one above, which takes each minterm associated with a 1 output, without further reduction, is a **canonical SOP.** A canonical SOP might not have a *minimum gate count,* but it is definitely a correct solution. And in all but degenerate cases an SOP design, whether canonical or reduced, has minimum delay (two gates' worth) from input to output (assuming inputs and their complements are available to the AND gates).

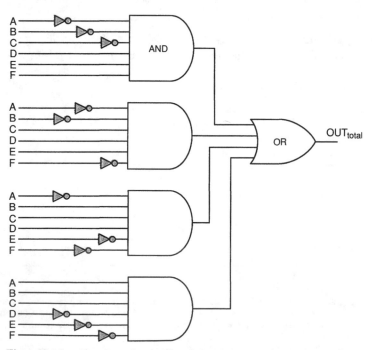

Figure 2.14   Circuit to detect three in a row.

A truth table input IN_i can be considered an argument of the function OUT: OUT $= f(IN_1, IN_2, \dots IN_N)$. When the value of a variable is known (as 0 or 1), it is said to be a **literal**. Each variable IN_i has two literals associated with it, IN_i and $\overline{IN_i}$. The canonical expression

$$\overline{F} \cdot E \cdot D \cdot C \cdot \overline{B} \cdot \overline{A} + \overline{F} \cdot \overline{E} \cdot D \cdot C \cdot B \cdot \overline{A} + \overline{F} \cdot \overline{E} \cdot \overline{D} \cdot C \cdot B \cdot A + F \cdot E \cdot D \cdot \overline{C} \cdot \overline{B} \cdot \overline{A}$$

has 24 literals. Counting literals is a way to see how many input connections will be required in a circuit.

EXAMPLE 9

We return to the problem of detecting two in a row that was treated in Example 5. Here is the truth table:

Inputs			
A	B	C	Output
0	0	0	0
0	0	1	0
0	1	0	0
0	1	1	1
1	0	0	0
1	0	1	0
1	1	0	1
1	1	1	0

Matching the two 1s in the output list with AND combinations of the associated inputs (2 minterms) and ORing those two AND outputs together, we come up with the design shown in Fig. 2.15, which actually has one fewer gate than the trial-and-error result of Example 5, Fig. 2.8. The input condition $CBA = 111$ continues to generate OUT $= 0$ because the AND gates on the left are selective for only the two conditions required in the problem statement.[7]

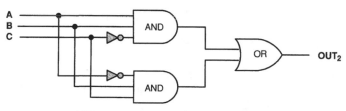

Figure 2.15 AND-to-OR circuit with inverted inputs.

[7] For a brief amount of time, equal to one gate's worth of propagation delay, the input condition $CBA = 111$ will produce a false 1 output of 1 because of the extra delay of the two inverters. Delay in combinational circuits is covered in the last part of this chapter.

EXAMPLE 10

We looked at the one-bit full adder (1BFA) in Chapter 1. Let us return to it here to apply the SOP method. The truth table is repeated in the following.

Inputs			Outputs	
$CARRY_{IN}$	B	A	SUM	$CARRY_{OUT}$
0	0	0	0	0
0	0	1	①	0
0	1	0	1	0
0	1	1	0	1
1	0	0	1	0
1	0	1	0	1
1	1	0	0	1
1	1	1	1	1

As required by the five-part SOP method, first find the minterms associated with 1 outputs. Start with the SUM column. The minterm of the first 1 output (circled above) is

$$\text{First minterm of SUM} = \overline{C} \cdot \overline{B} \cdot A$$

where C stands for $CARRY_{IN}$. The other three minterms associated with true outputs for SUM are

$$\overline{C} \cdot B \cdot \overline{A} \qquad C \cdot \overline{B} \cdot \overline{A} \qquad C \cdot B \cdot A$$

To finish the canonical SOP design for SUM, send the outputs of these four minterm AND gates to one four-input OR gate, whose output will be SUM:

$$\text{SUM} = \overline{C} \cdot \overline{B} \cdot A + \overline{C} \cdot B \cdot \overline{A} + C \cdot \overline{B} \cdot \overline{A} + C \cdot B \cdot A$$

By the same SOP process, gather 1s from the $CARRY_{OUT}$ column and find associated minterms:

$$\text{CARRY}_{OUT} = C \cdot B \cdot \overline{A} + C \cdot \overline{B} \cdot A + \overline{C} \cdot B \cdot A + C \cdot B \cdot A$$

Both SUM and $CARRY_{OUT}$ share the minterm $C \cdot B \cdot A$; therefore a small economy in the design can be achieved by sending the $C \cdot B \cdot A$ AND gate output to the two output ORs. A schematic of the SOP design for a 1BFA is shown in Fig. 2.16. Crossing lines are connected only where there are dots. Beyond the input layer there is two gates' worth of delay to either output.

Recall from Chapter 1 that a 1BFA can be made from two half adders and a two-input OR gate—much less hardware than we see in Fig. 2.16! Except for the $C \cdot B \cdot A$ minterm projecting to both SUM and CARRY, the circuit of Fig. 2.16 is a canonical

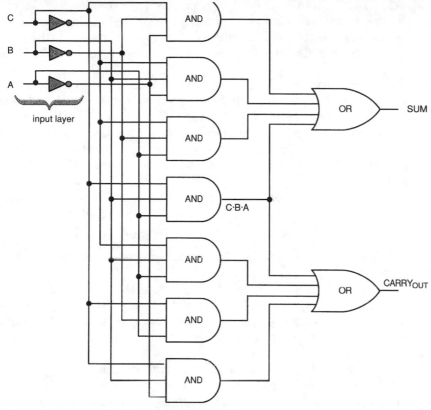

Figure 2.16 One-bit full adder realized as SOP.

realization. Our next concern will be to find ways further to reduce the hardware involved in SOP (or other) realizations. Our first set of methods for reducing gate count will be the use of Boolean algebra.

2.5 BOOLEAN ALGEBRA

Now that we have a systematic way to generate a valid (canonical) solution to any logic problem in the form of a truth table, we need methods to improve the solution by using fewer gates. Those methods are provided by Boolean algebra. Before we discuss theorems of Boolean algebra used to simplify logical expressions, let us review algebra in general in order to appreciate that Boolean algebra offers ideas you have seen before in real-number algebra.

2.5.1 Algebra of Real Numbers

Encyclopedia Britannica defines algebra as "the generalization and extension of arithmetic." As such, algebra is a way of solving equations for *unknowns* that are represented by symbols. In ordinary algebra unknowns turn out to be real numbers; the principal algebraic *operations* among real numbers and unknowns are addition and multiplication. (Subtraction is addition of negative numbers, as we saw with 2's complement code in Chapter 1; division can be construed as multiplication by inverses.)

Variable is another word for *unknown*, and it is often used in the context of computer programs. It is instructive to consider how a variable for a number is treated in a computer. At the level of the program, the variable appears as a word-symbol, such as TEMP, which is set equal to other terms in program statements. However, the location reserved for TEMP in the computer's memory always contains the binary code of a number. The computer always knows the value of TEMP, whether the programmer does or not.[8]

In real-number algebra operations between variables are governed by laws or axioms; for example, a distributive law relates addition and multiplication:

$$A \cdot (B + C) = A \cdot B + A \cdot C \qquad \text{(a real sum of products!)}$$

The laws of algebra are combined to derive theorems handy for solving important equations, such as the quadratic equation.

If the two variables x and y can be separated so that y ends up by itself on one side of an equation, we say that y is a function of x, or $y = f(x)$. When y is a function of x, then x is the *independent variable* (or *input*) and y is the *dependent variable* (or *output*). In a computer program assignment statement, the dependent variable is always separated to the left.

Algebra meets geometry when a relationship between variables is graphed. If, for example, $y = f(x)$ is the function of x given by $y = f(x) = x^2 + 3x + 2$, it has the graph shown in Fig. 2.17. Compare the graph of y versus x to a truth table: the truth table output corresponds to y, and its input corresponds to x. A graph is to real-number algebra what a truth table is to Boolean algebra.

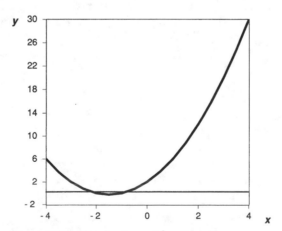

Figure 2.17   Graph of $y = x^2 + 3x + 2$.

[8]In this text we assume that unknowns are numerical variables, which can be involved in computations. The other thing an unknown can be is a symbol, which cannot be involved in computations but can be sorted or otherwise manipulated.

in the algebra of real numbers you learned various methods for reducing expressions to simpler forms. For example, you can factor the numerator and denominator of the polynomial fraction below:

$$\frac{x^4 + 6x^3 - x^2 + 36x + 36}{x^2 + 4x - 12} = (x - 1)(x + 3)$$

We now begin a search for analogous methods to simplify logic expressions.

5.2   Objects in Boolean Algebra

We want to construct a Boolean algebra out of binary objects. Our Boolean algebra will structure relationships between the 0s and 1s we've been using in truth tables. From there we'll prove various theorems to simplify expressions. As with any algebraic system, we need three things: a set of elements to work with, one or more basic operations on pairs of the elements, and rules for combining the operations. Let's start with the elements to work with. In Boolean algebra we restrict our set to just two members, 0 and 1. In Boole's original work of 1854 (reprinted in Boole 1954), his intent was to describe logical discourse formally. The objects of his study were "true" and "false" and their expression in propositions. We use 1 and 0 instead of "true" and "false" and follow George Boole's lead.[9] Note that 0 and 1 in a Boolean algebra do not need to be considered numbers. Our two elements will be operated upon by AND ($A \cdot B$), OR ($A + B$), and INVERT ($\overline{A}$).

5.3   Rules for Operations in Boolean Algebra

The operations of Boolean algebra conform to the following axioms. (The symbol $\in$ means "is an element of.")

$A + B \in \{0, 1\}$	$A \cdot B \in \{1, 0\}$	Closure
$A + (B + C) = (A + B) + C$	$A \cdot (B \cdot C) = (A \cdot B) \cdot C$	Associativity
$A + B = B + A$	$A \cdot B = B \cdot A$	Commutivity
$A \cdot (B + C) = (A \cdot B) + (A \cdot C)$	$A + (B \cdot C) = (A + B) \cdot (A + C)$	Distributivity

The elements 0 and 1 fulfill the identity conditions:

$$0 + A = A \quad \text{and} \quad 0 \cdot A = 0 \qquad 1 \cdot A = A \quad \text{and} \quad 1 + A = 1$$

Finally, there exists a complement of A, shown as $\overline{A}$, such that

$$A + \overline{A} = 1 \qquad\qquad A \cdot \overline{A} = 0$$

The axioms as presented here are known as the *Huntington postulates*, from the work of E. V. Huntington (1904). The axioms are in two columns. If you inspect

---

[9] An algebra with variables that can assume only two values is called a *switching algebra* to distinguish it from other kinds of Boolean algebras that can include more than two elements in their sets of objects. In this text we restrict Boolean algebra to the set $\{0, 1\}$.

the two columns, you'll see that the axioms on the left can be transformed into the axioms on the right by swapping AND and OR symbols and swapping 0s and 1s. This feature, **duality,** will be exploited to reveal various dual forms of Boolean theorems.

Associativity and commutativity should look familiar from high school algebra. Associativity says that the order of single operations—ORing or ANDing—does not matter. Commutativity says that the order of the variables in a sequence of ORs and the order of variables in a sequence of ANDs does not matter.

Closure and the definition of complement guarantee that only 0 and 1 result from operations in Boolean algebra. The definitions of our primary operations—AND, OR, and INVERT—are as we have already seen them in truth tables:

B	A	B + A	B · A	A	INVERT $A = \overline{A}$
0	0	0	0	0	1
0	1	1	0	1	0
1	0	1	0		
1	1	1	1		

As Exercise 28 points out, the definitions of the AND, OR, and INVERT operations are not independent of the Huntington postulates; the tables for the three operations can be derived from the Huntington postulates.

A **Boolean variable** can assume only the values 0 and 1. A **Boolean expression** is any combination of Boolean variables transformed by the Boolean operations AND, OR, or INVERT. In particular, a sum of products is a Boolean expression. We can include other operations in valid Boolean expressions if the other expressions are derived from AND, OR, or INVERT. In particular, $A \oplus B = (A + B) \cdot (\overline{A \cdot B})$, so XOR can be included in Boolean expressions.

2.5.4 Useful Boolean Theorems

Let's start a list of theorems useful for reduction of Boolean expressions. The first is the **involution property,** by which inverting (complementing) a variable twice returns it to its original value:

$$\overline{\overline{X}} = X$$

Now consider Boolean theorems involving one variable X and one constant:

OR	AND
$X + \overline{X} = 1$	$X \cdot \overline{X} = 0$
$X + 1 = 1$	$X \cdot 0 = 0$
$X + 0 = X$	$X \cdot 1 = X$
$X + X = X$	$X \cdot X = X$ (idempotence)

Each of these theorems can be proved by help from the AND, OR, and INVERT truth tables. To list all cases of an expression is to prove by *perfect induction.* There are only two cases for each one-variable theorem. For example, to prove that $X + X = X$, we

right, are the duals of the OR expressions to the left of them. For example, the dual of $X + 1 = 1$ is created by replacing $+$ with $\cdot$ and changing the 1s to 0s to achieve $X \cdot 0 = 0$.

EXAMPLE 11

One-variable theorems are important, but it is tough to think up realistic and difficult Boolean reduction problems with them. Here are three tries.

$$X \cdot 1 + X \cdot 0 = X + 0 = X$$
$$(X + X) \cdot \overline{X} = X \cdot \overline{X} = 0$$
$$\overline{X + 1} = \overline{1} = 0$$

When AND and OR appear in the same expression, AND operations have *priority* and should be carried out first unless parentheses are encountered. In the second expression above, parentheses are used to overrule the normal precedence of AND over OR. Without parentheses, $X + X \cdot \overline{X} = X + 0 = X$, whereas $(X + X) \cdot \overline{X} = X \cdot \overline{X} = 0$.

2.5.5 Distributivity

To handle more that one type of operation in an expression requires *distributivity*. Distributivity takes two forms in Boolean algebra. Let P, Q, and R be Boolean variables. The first form is the familiar sum of products:

$$R \cdot (Q + P) = (R \cdot Q) + (R \cdot P)$$

Its dual, with the $+$ and $\cdot$ signs swapped, is a product of sums version,

$$R + (Q \cdot P) = (R + Q) \cdot (R + P)$$

which is *not* true for real numbers.

Parentheses are required to give unambiguous meaning to the distributive laws; the parentheses are necessary in the first form of the distributive law in order to generate the dual properly. Both versions of the distributive law can be proved with a three-input truth table. Let's write out the truth table for the second (POS) version of the distributive law to see the proof by induction:

Inputs			Outputs					
P	Q	R	$Q \cdot P$	R	$R + (Q \cdot P)$	$R + Q$	$R + P$	$(R + Q) \cdot (R + P)$
0	0	0	0	0	0	0	0	0
1	0	0	0	0	0	0	1	0
0	0	1	0	1	1	1	1	1
1	0	1	0	1	1	1	1	1
0	1	0	0	0	0	1	0	0
1	1	0	1	0	1	1	1	1
0	1	1	0	1	1	1	1	1
1	1	1	1	1	1	1	1	1

both expressions are true whenever R is true or when Q and P are simultaneously true. The distributive laws give us a major resource to use in Boolean expression reduction, especially of SOPs. The distributive laws also help with factoring.

EXAMPLE 12

Let's use the Boolean theorems developed so far to work on the SOP expression for $\text{CARRY}_{\text{OUT}}$ in a one-bit full adder (1BFA). We saw in Example 10 that

$$\text{CARRY}_{\text{OUT}} = \overline{A} \cdot B \cdot C + A \cdot \overline{B} \cdot C + A \cdot B \cdot \overline{C} + A \cdot B \cdot C$$

Since $X + X = X$, we can add two more $A \cdot B \cdot C$ terms to the right-hand side:

$$\overline{A} \cdot B \cdot C + A \cdot \overline{B} \cdot C + A \cdot B \cdot \overline{C} + A \cdot B \cdot C + A \cdot B \cdot C + A \cdot B \cdot C$$

Now apply the commutative law to rearrange terms:

$$A \cdot B \cdot C + \overline{A} \cdot B \cdot C + A \cdot B \cdot C + A \cdot \overline{B} \cdot C + A \cdot B \cdot C + A \cdot B \cdot \overline{C}$$

Apply the SOP distributivity law to make transformations to

$$(A + \overline{A}) \cdot B \cdot C + A \cdot (B + \overline{B}) \cdot C + A \cdot B \cdot (C + \overline{C})$$

Recalling that $X + \overline{X} = 1$, we see that the above form collapses to

$$1 \cdot B \cdot C + A \cdot C \cdot 1 + A \cdot B \cdot 1$$

Recall that $1 \cdot X = X$. The considerably simplified expression is therefore

$$\text{CARRY}_{\text{OUT}} = B \cdot C + A \cdot C + A \cdot B$$

There are only 6 literals in the new expression, compared with 12 in the original. $\text{CARRY}_{\text{OUT}}$ can now be realized with three two-input AND gates instead of four three-input AND gates. It is still an SOP, but now a reduced form; fewer hardware resources are required for realization.

2.5.6 Boolean Theorems Based on Distributivity

Here are more theorems, now combining AND and OR with two variables in the same expression. These can be proved with help from the distributive law:

$X + X \cdot Y = X$	$X \cdot (X + Y) = X$	Absorption
$X + \overline{X} \cdot Y = X + Y$	$X \cdot (\overline{X} + Y) = X \cdot Y$	Adsorption
$X \cdot Y + \overline{X} \cdot Y = Y$	$(X + Y) \cdot (\overline{X} + Y) = Y$	Adjacency

Again, left-right duals are generated by swapping OR and AND symbols. Note where parentheses are required to indicate the ordering of operations. The last theorem—**adjacency**—is of great importance for reducing SOP expressions in computer minimization algorithms. It will be utilized in the second half of Chapter 3.

Again, the various theorems can be proved by perfect induction. As an exercise, let us prove two of the theorems and their duals by application of previous theorems and postulates. First remember that $1 + 1 = 1$, and proceed on the first pair. For the left side,

$$X + X \cdot Y = X \cdot (1 + Y) = X \cdot 1 = X$$

For the dual on the right,

$$X \cdot (X + Y) = X \cdot X + X \cdot Y = X + X \cdot Y = X \cdot (1 + Y) = X \cdot 1 = X$$

To prove the second theorem and its dual, use the distributive laws and apply the relationships $X + \overline{X} = 1$ and $X \cdot \overline{X} = 0$.

$$X + \overline{X} \cdot Y = (X + \overline{X}) \cdot (X + Y) = 1 \cdot (X + Y) = X + Y$$
$$X \cdot (\overline{X} + Y) = X \cdot \overline{X} + X \cdot Y = X \cdot Y$$

The second theorem and its dual will be used to prove one of De Morgan's laws. An end-of-chapter exercise gives you an opportunity to prove the remaining two expressions above.

EXAMPLE 13

In this example a two-variable Boolean theorem is used. Suppose an alarm must sound if a door is open or if the door is closed and the light is on. This specification can be written by the expression ALARM $= D + \overline{D} \cdot L$, where

$$D = \text{door open}$$
$$\overline{D} = \text{door closed}$$
$$L = \text{light on}$$

The direct formula for ALARM uses three gates: OR, AND, and INVERT. Is there a way to use only one? Yes. By the first theorem in the two-operation list above, which states that $X + \overline{X} \cdot Y = X + Y$, we can reduce the expression for ALARM to a simpler formula,

$$\text{ALARM} = D + \overline{D} \cdot L = D + L$$

which uses one gate (an OR gate) instead of three.

2.5.7 Duality and Negative Logic

As was noted when the Huntington postulates were presented, the dual of a theorem or postulate is found by changing all ORs to ANDs, all ANDs to ORs, 0s to 1s, and 1s to 0s. As a result, if the theorems used in the proof of a new theorem are replaced by their duals, a new dual theorem will be proved.

There is a restriction here: Taking the dual of an equation of *separated* variables is not a valid operation. In Examples 12 and 13, terms such as ALARM, SUM, and CARRY$_{OUT}$ were functions of *input* variables. Boolean equations such as ALARM $= D + L$ resulted. Incorrect Boolean expressions will result if duality is applied in circuit design to Boolean equations with separated variables. In the alarm example above, it is *not* true that ALARM = $D \cdot L$.

On the other hand, if *all* variables in a Boolean equation are complemented and all AND and OR operations swapped, the equation remains correct. $\overline{\text{ALARM}} = \overline{D} \cdot \overline{L}$, after applying DeMorgan's Law. Complementing all variables and swapping all AND and OR operations converts the expression of the problem to **negative logic** form. In negative logic, 0 represents TRUE and 1 represents FALSE. Negative logic signals are called **active low** in data books. In either case—positive or negative logic—the voltages in a hardware circuit are *physical facts*, while the TRUE and FALSE they represent are *conventions*.

Signals are asserted. The verb *to assert* in digital design means to make TRUE, regardless of logic convention.[10] "The enable input was asserted to allow memory access" is a typical sentence and means that enable was set HI or LO depending on whether positive or negative logic convention was in effect. Unless otherwise stated, assume that signals in this text are active-high positive logic. An end-of-chapter exercise explores some of the consequences of the negative logic convention.

2.5.8 Parentheses, Tree Structures, and Parallel Processing

Parentheses enforce precedence of operation in an algebraic expression. An algebraic expression can be drawn graphically if the parentheses are replaced by a tree structure. The standard version of the distributive law generates the two examples in Fig. 2.18. These two tree structures are two different hardware solutions for the same problem. The one on the left uses fewer operators. The one on the right has two multiplications taking place in parallel. If the operator blocks have equal computation delays, then both circuits have the same maximum delay from input to output. However, as we will see, the circuit on the left may generate transient glitches if all inputs change simultaneously.

When you are translating a Boolean expression directly into hardware, remember that the operations deepest inside parentheses are done first.

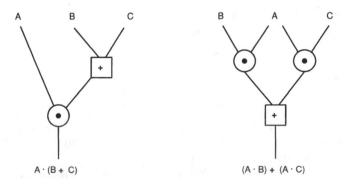

Figure 2.18 Distributive law tree diagrams.

[10]See Fletcher (1980) for 10 pages of discussion at the beginning of his chapter 2 about the correct use of the verb *to assert* in digital design!

EXAMPLE 14

Draw a circuit to realize the following Boolean expression for OUT:

$$\text{OUT} = \overline{E \oplus (F + (G \cdot (H + J)))}$$

Answer   The solution is shown in Fig. 2.19.

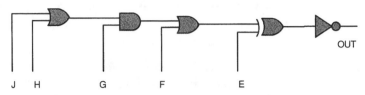

J   H   G   F   E

Figure 2.19   Gates in series to realize the Example 14 output.

Exercises 42 and 43 ask you to turn other circuits back into Boolean expressions.

2.5.9   De Morgan's Laws

We saw in the discussion of two-input primitives that NAND and NOR gates are especially versatile building blocks. The next Boolean theorem and its dual, known as **De Morgan's laws**, offer a way to transform between NAND and NOR operations, provide still more machinery for simplifying Boolean expressions, and help a designer move between positive and negative logic forms.

$$\overline{A + B + C + D + \cdots} = \overline{A} \cdot \overline{B} \cdot \overline{C} \cdot \overline{D} \cdots$$
$$\overline{A \cdot B \cdot C \cdot D \cdots} = \overline{A} + \overline{B} + \overline{C} + \overline{D} + \cdots$$

On the left of the first expression is the NOR operation on an indefinite number of inputs; on the left of the second expression is the NAND operation. The second of De Morgan's laws says that the NAND of many variables is equal to the ORs of all the complements of the variables. The circuits in Fig. 2.20 illustrate the De Morgan transformations for three-input NAND and NOR gates. The gates on the right have

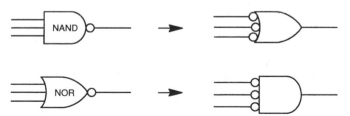

Figure 2.20   De Morgan transformations in hardware.

complement *bubbles* on their inputs because all inputs to the gates are complemented; if not all inputs were complemented, then separate inverter *gates* would be shown.

As an exercise, let's prove, by recourse to previous Boolean theorems, the second of De Morgan's laws for two variables F and G. First, notice that De Morgan's second law is a statement about complements. De Morgan's second law says that $\overline{E} = \overline{F} + \overline{G}$, where expression $E = F \cdot G$ is the uncomplemented version of E. Therefore, if we can demonstrate that the complement of E is $\overline{F} + \overline{G}$, the proof will be finished. What do we know about complements? From Boolean theorems involving only one variable, we know that complements imply that

$$E + \overline{E} = 1 \quad \text{and} \quad E \cdot \overline{E} = 0$$

giving us a way to test whether expression E is the complement of $F \cdot G$.

Let's first test $E \cdot \overline{E} = 0$, the equation on the right above. We know that $E = F \cdot G$ and $\overline{E} = \overline{F} + \overline{G}$; then by the distributive law,

$$E \cdot \overline{E} = (F \cdot G) \cdot (\overline{F} + \overline{G}) = F \cdot G \cdot \overline{F} + F \cdot G \cdot \overline{G}$$

Rearrange terms using commutativity and find

$$E \cdot \overline{E} = F \cdot \overline{F} \cdot G + \overline{G} \cdot G \cdot F$$

Now since $X \cdot \overline{X} = 0$,

$$E \cdot \overline{E} = 0 \cdot G + 0 \cdot F = 0$$

Therefore one test for complement is passed.

Now check whether $E + \overline{E} = 1$. By associativity,

$$E + \overline{E} = (F \cdot G) + (\overline{F} + \overline{G}) = \overline{F} + F \cdot G + \overline{G}$$

Now recall the Boolean theorem of two variables, $X + \overline{X} \cdot Y = X + Y$, and apply it to $\overline{F} + F \cdot G$:

$$\overline{F} + F \cdot G + \overline{G} = \overline{F} + G + \overline{G} = \overline{F} + 1 = 1$$

where $G + \overline{G} = 1$ is used. Therefore both tests for complement are passed, and De Morgan's second law is proved for two variables.

EXAMPLE 15

Here is a verbal illustration of De Morgan's second law: To make Baby Bear B, Papa Bear P and Mama Bear M are required. The complementary way of expressing this is to say that Baby Bear will not result if Papa Bear is not involved or Mama Bear is not involved.

The first statement about Baby Bear is expressed in symbols as $B = P \cdot M$. Complement B and use De Morgan's second law to find that $\overline{B} = \overline{P \cdot M} = \overline{P} + \overline{M}$, the second statement about Baby Bear's conception.

EXAMPLE 16

De Morgan's laws can be used to convert a product of sums to a sum of products, or vice versa. Change the expression $(E + F + G) \cdot (H + J) = \text{OUT}$ to a sum of products.

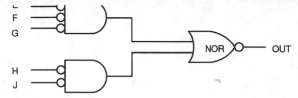

Figure 2.21 Sum-of-products conversion example.

Answer

$$(E + F + G) \cdot (H + J) = \overline{\overline{(E + F + G) \cdot (H + J)}}$$
$$= \overline{\overline{(E + F + G)} + \overline{(H + J)}} = \overline{(\overline{E} \cdot \overline{F} \cdot \overline{G}) + (\overline{H} \cdot \overline{J})}$$

The first move is to complement the whole expression twice. Apply De Morgan's laws until the desired form is reached. (If you apply De Morgan's laws one time too many, you'll end up with the original expression!) Yes, the resulting form looks a little awkward, with all the complements involved, but it is in SOP form. The hardware, in Fig. 2.21, goes in and out of negative logic; that is, the complemented inputs on the left are processed as negative logic by the POS circuit, and then the output bubble on the right returns the result to positive logic form.

2.5.10   Law of Consensus

We have so far seen De Morgan's laws, which can be used with an arbitrary number of variables, and all the useful Boolean theorems of one and two variables. Here is a Boolean theorem of three variables that should be added to our collection:

$$A \cdot B + \overline{A} \cdot C + B \cdot C - A \cdot B + \overline{A} \cdot C$$

It has a dual form:

$$(A + B) \cdot (\overline{A} + C) \cdot (B + C) = (A + B) \cdot (\overline{A} + C)$$

This is the **law of consensus.** Three SOP products are reduced to two if the three variables agree with each other in the way required by the law of consensus.

EXAMPLE 17

Law of Consensus in Action.   Suppose a buzzer is to sound if the key (K) is in the ignition and the door (D) is open or if the key is out of the ignition and the brake (B) is off or if the door is open and the brake is off. At all other times the buzzer must be silent.

Answer   Assume there are digitizing sensors for K, D, and B so that $K, B, D \in \{0, 1\}$; let $+$ mean OR and $\cdot$ mean AND; and let $K = 1$ if the key is in, $D = 1$ if the door is

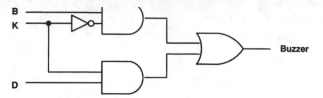

Figure 2.22   Door-unlocking circuit.

open, and $B = 1$ if the brake is off. Then

$$OUT = K \cdot D + \overline{K} \cdot B + D \cdot B$$

is a way to express as a formula the statement of the problem. With this formula we could proceed directly to a hardware SOP realization using an inverter, three two-input AND gates, and one three-input OR gate. But, by the consensus law, we reduce it to

$$OUT = K \cdot D + \overline{K} \cdot B + D \cdot B = K \cdot D + \overline{K} \cdot B$$

saving one AND gate and shrinking the size of the output OR gate from three inputs to two inputs (see Fig. 2.22). Here is the truth table for the buzzer output:

Key In	Door Open	Brake Off	Buzzer On (Output)
0	0	0	0
0	0	1	1
0	1	0	0
0	1	1	1
1	0	0	0
1	0	1	0
1	1	0	1
1	1	1	1

Inspection of the truth table proves (by perfect induction) the consensus law.

2.5.11   Shannon's Expansion Theorem

(This section is optional.) It sometimes helps to factor Boolean expressions. For example, breaking up a large expression by factoring can aid in the generation of a *modular* solution suitable for programmable logic arrays such as we will see in Chapter 4. Here is a pair of theorems that help with factoring. Let $F(X_1, X_2, X_3, \ldots, X_N)$ be *any* Boolean expression of N variables. Then **Shannon's theorem** in the SOP form says that

$$F(X_1, X_2, X_3, \ldots, X_N) = F(1, X_2, X_3, \ldots, X_N) \cdot X_1 + F(0, X_2, X_3, \ldots, X_N) \cdot \overline{X_1}$$

and its dual, formed by swapping ANDs and ORs and swapping 0s and 1s, says that

$$F(X_1, X_2, X_3, \ldots, X_N) = [F(0, X_2, X_3, \ldots, X_N) + X_1] \cdot [F(1, X_2, X_3, \ldots, X_N) + \overline{X_1}]$$

The term X_1 has been factored out; by "factored out" we mean, in Boolean terms, that the literals of X_1 have been isolated as products of another expression. Another way of saying it is that the function F has been expanded in terms of X_1.

EXAMPLE 18

Suppose $F(W, X, Y, Z) = W \oplus X \cdot \overline{Y} + Z$, where precedence requires that

$$F(W, X, Y, Z) = (W \oplus X) \cdot \overline{Y} + Z$$

Factor out X and Y.

Answer   First factor out X using the SOP form of Shannon's theorem.

$$F(W, X, Y, Z) = X \cdot [(W \oplus 1) \cdot \overline{Y} + Z] + \overline{X} \cdot [(W \oplus 0) \cdot \overline{Y} + Z]$$
$$= X \cdot [\overline{W} \cdot \overline{Y} + Z] + \overline{X} \cdot [W \cdot \overline{Y} + Z]$$

where we use the fact that $W \oplus 1 = \overline{W}$ and $W \oplus 0 = W$. Next factor Y out of both parts in the line above:

$$F(W, X, Y, Z) = X \cdot [\overline{W} \cdot \overline{Y} + Z] + \overline{X} \cdot [W \cdot \overline{Y} + Z]$$
$$= X \cdot Y[\overline{W} \cdot \overline{1} + Z] + X \cdot \overline{Y}[\overline{W} \cdot \overline{0} + Z] + \overline{X} \cdot Y[W \cdot \overline{1} + Z] + \overline{X} \cdot \overline{Y}[W \cdot \overline{0} + Z]$$
$$= X \cdot Y[Z] + X \cdot \overline{Y}[\overline{W} + Z] + \overline{X} \cdot Y[Z] + \overline{X} \cdot \overline{Y}[W + Z]$$

By continued application of Shannon's theorem, function F can be eventually expanded into straight SOP form.

The two forms of Shannon's theorem can be proved by induction on X_1. Try the SOP form. First set X_1 to 0, then set X_1 to 1, and see that the left and right sides remain equal:

$$F(0, X_2, X_3, \ldots, X_N) = F(1, X_2, X_3, \ldots, X_N) \cdot 0 + F(0, X_2, X_3, \ldots, X_N) \cdot 1$$
$$= F(0, X_2, X_3, \ldots, X_N)$$

and

$$F(1, X_2, X_3, \ldots, X_N) = F(1, X_2, X_3, \ldots, X_N) \cdot 1 + F(0, X_2, X_3, \ldots, X_N) \cdot 0$$
$$= F(1, X_2, X_3, \ldots, X_N)$$

Since 0 and 1 are the only values X_1 can take on, the proof is complete.

A similar effort would prove the dual of the SOP form. Note that in forming the dual of the SOP form of Shannon's theorem, the function $F(X_1, X_2, X_3, \ldots, X_N)$ remains unchanged.

Shannon's theorem in the SOP form will prove useful in Chapter 4 for expressing functions to be implemented in multiplexer hardware. The two forms of Shannon's theorem, like De Morgan's laws, are Boolean theorems applicable to N variables. Shannon's theorem is not as widely used as De Morgan's laws.

2.6.1   XOR and Boolean Algebra

We climbed out on the Boolean algebra limb of the combinational logic tree to study ways of trimming sums of products. Before we looked at Boolean algebra, we had been on a nearby shoot of the tree exploring two-input hardware primitives. One of the primitives was the exclusive OR operation. Let's return to XOR gates. What does Boolean algebra tell us about them? It says that the following expressions are equivalent:

$$A \oplus B = (A + B) \cdot (\overline{A \cdot B}) = A \cdot \overline{B} + \overline{A} \cdot B$$

(The two expressions on the right are *not* duals of each other.) These equivalences can be useful in hardware reduction.

The XOR operation is commutative and associative and can therefore be the basis of an abelian group.[11] A few one-operation theorems result. For example,

$$A \oplus A = 0$$
$$A \oplus \overline{A} = 1$$

as the polarity control example below shows. Exercise 53 asks you to test whether XOR can support distributivity with AND.

The direct contact of XOR logic with Boolean algebra is mostly limited to the above identities and to application of Shannon's theorem. Since XOR is not a primary operation in Boolean algebra, it is sometimes neglected as a solution to logic problems. The rest of Section 2.6 will give attention to uses of XOR logic.

EXAMPLE 19

Design logic for an alarm that must sound if either the front or the back door is open, but not if both doors are open or both doors are closed.

Answer   One answer is that from the wording of the problem, an OR gate, a NAND gate, and an AND gate can be combined for a design (Fig. 2.23). On the other hand,

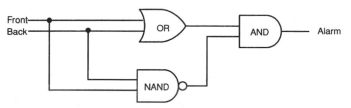

Figure 2.23   Exclusive OR from AND, OR, and NAND gates.

[11]In algebra, a *group* is a set of elements upon which one operation having certain properties is defined. Commutativity does not hold for all groups; those for which commutativity holds are called *abelian groups*. Furthermore, a set upon which *two* operations are defined is an algebraic *ring*. Boolean algebra is a commutative ring algebra.

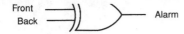

Figure 2.24 Single XOR solution for Example 19.

from the Boolean equivalents above, we have

$$\text{FRONT} \cdot \overline{\text{BACK}} + \overline{\text{FRONT}} \cdot \text{BACK} = \text{FRONT} \oplus \text{BACK}$$

so a single XOR gate can do the job (Fig. 2.24). Considering the finite propagation delay from input to output of real logic chips, the smaller one-gate XOR solution has one gate less delay than the three-gate solution.

Even though the XOR primitive is defined for only two inputs, a generalized XOR operation can be carried out on several variables using a series of XOR gates. A five-input XOR, $A \oplus B \oplus C \oplus D \oplus E$, is realized by the circuit in Fig. 2.25. The output of this circuit is HI only when an odd number of inputs A–E are HI. A practical concern with this particular circuit may be that it has four gates' worth of delay from the A-B input to the final output; nevertheless, the XOR circuit of Fig. 2.25 is a leaner design for the underlying truth table; an SOP realization would have only two gates' delay but would require numerous input inverters, eight five-input AND gates, and one eight-input OR gate. (Can you see a way to reduce the total gate delay in Fig. 2.25 by one?)

A single XOR gate is a **comparator,** responding with a 1 only when the two inputs are not equal (an XNOR gate responds with a 1 when the inputs are equal). The generalized XOR operation, shown in Fig. 2.25 for five inputs, responds only when an odd number of inputs are HI. Inspection of a string of bits to find out whether an odd number of them are 1 is called **odd parity check.** Parity check was introduced in Chapter 1, and we will encounter parity check again in Chapter 9, where it is used as one test on multi-bit binary messages to ascertain whether they have arrived correctly at a receiver from transmission over noisy lines.

Figure 2.25 Five-input XOR circuit.

EXAMPLE 20

Design a circuit that tests eight input bits for odd parity and has no more than three gate delays from input to output.

Answer For interconnections of XORs, it doesn't matter which bits are compared to which other bits, so four comparisons can be made in parallel, as shown in the circuit of Fig. 2.26. The results of the comparisons converge on other XOR gates until only one output remains. In this case $2^3 = 8$, so three levels of XORing are needed. If

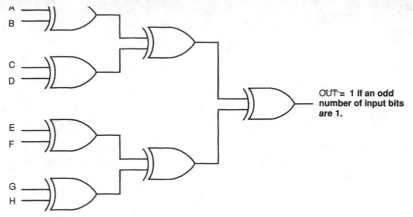

Figure 2.26   XOR convergence.

the eight-bit parity check requirements were met with an SOP circuit, 128 eight-input AND gates would be needed!

Polarity Control   If a digital word passes through a bank of XOR gates, each of which is attached to a common control, the control value determines the polarity of the output, regardless of whether the output passes through as is or is complemented. In the circuit shown in Fig. 2.27, if $PC = 1$, then the four-bit words A and B are related by the equation $B = \overline{A}$. If $PC = 0$, then $B = A$.

2.6.2   Reed-Muller Form of Boolean Expressions

In the **Reed-Muller form** all literals in the Boolean expression are asserted TRUE. No complemented variables or complement operations are allowed. The Reed-Muller

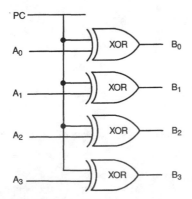

Figure 2.27   Polarity control circuit.

form is normally used with a three-level AND-OR-XOR architecture. Inversions are created by the rule $A \oplus 1 = \overline{A}$. Methods for synthesizing Reed-Muller forms are not as straightforward as sums of products, but since no inverters are needed on inputs, the AND-OR-XOR form has the same total delay from input to output as a sum of products with inverters on the input layer. Like sums of products, Reed-Muller forms can represent any truth table. Reed-Muller forms are important with some programmable array logic (PAL) chips, to be discussed in Chapter 4.

EXAMPLE 21

The 20X8 PAL chip contains the three-level subcircuit shown in Fig. 2.28. There are eight inputs, A–H. What percentage of the $2^8 = 256$ possible truth table lines result in OUT = HI?

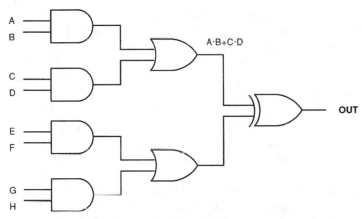

Figure 2.28 PAL subcircuit for Example 21.

Answer The output OUT of the XOR is HI whenever the two OR gate outputs are unequal. For one OR gate output to be LO, both of its AND gate inputs must be LO; for the other OR gate output to be HI, either of its AND gate inputs must be HI.

Consider the truth table for $A \cdot B + C \cdot D$. For how many of its 16 input combinations is *at least* one of the AND gates HI? If you write out the 16-line truth table, you'll see that 7 out of 16 lines result in HI. Conversely, $\frac{9}{16}$ of the lines result in *both* AND gates having LO outputs. Therefore, only

$$\frac{7}{16} \cdot \frac{9}{16} = \frac{63}{256} = 24.6\%$$

of the truth table lines for the circuit of Fig. 2.28 will result in HI. On the other hand, if the output XOR is replaced with an OR gate,

$$1 - \left(\frac{9}{16} \cdot \frac{9}{16}\right) = 68\%$$

of the truth table lines will be HI.

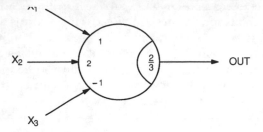

Figure 2.29 Threshold element.

‡2.7   THRESHOLDS

(This section is optional.) Some gate outputs can be classified by threshold. If a gate output changes from 0 to 1 (positive logic convention) after some number θ of inputs are asserted and stays at 1 no matter how many more inputs are asserted, then θ is the **threshold** of the gate. An N-input OR gate has a threshold of 1; an N-input AND gate has a threshold of N. XORs and inverters can't be classified by threshold because increasing the number of active inputs results in the output returning to 0.

An extension of the threshold idea from OR and AND leads to the **majority gate**, which responds when a majority of its inputs are active. For example, the threshold of a majority-of-seven gate would be 4. Exercises 62–64 enable you to develop the concept of majority logic and show you how XNOR gates fit into a commercial majority logic chip.

Threshold, where it is applicable, is a characteristic of output. In its general form a threshold gate can accept weighted analog input, such as we saw in the beginning of Chapter 1. A threshold gate with one analog (real number) input is a one-bit analog-to-digital converter. Fig. 2.29 exhibits a threshold element with three analog inputs. If $X_1 + 2 \cdot X_2 - X_3 > \frac{2}{3}$, then OUT $= 1$; otherwise, OUT $= 0$. See Dertouzos (1965).

2.8   USE OF NAND GATES IN SUM-OF-PRODUCTS DESIGN

We have seen that XORs have a niche for realization of certain truth tables. Now we consider NAND gates. Recall from Section 2.4 that any output column of a truth table can be realized in hardware as a two-level SOP design in which AND gates in parallel feed into an output OR. In its canonical form, an SOP AND gate represents a minterm corresponding to a true output. Here we will see that if all AND gates and the final OR gate of an SOP design are replaced by NAND gates, the output of the circuit remains unchanged.

If we take liberty with the symbols $\sum$ and $\prod$ to say they mean OR and AND respectively, then a canonical sum of products can be expressed by

$$\text{OUT} = \sum m_i$$

where the m_i are the minterms that result in OUT = 1. Now complement each m_i twice, which, by involution, results in no change.

$$\text{OUT} = \sum m_i = \sum \overline{\overline{m_i}}$$

By De Morgan's second law a sum of complements is a complement of products, so we can write the above as

$$\text{OUT} = \sum m_i = \sum \overline{\overline{m_i}} = \overline{\prod \overline{m_i}}$$

The symbol $\overline{m_i}$ represents a NANDing of the minterm literals, and $\overline{\prod}$ is another NAND expression. Therefore the form on the right of the equation above is a two-layer NAND of NANDs. The output NAND is expressed by $\overline{\prod}$. If the starting SOP hasn't been simplified by application of Boolean theorems, the resulting NAND of NANDs will still be canonical. The importance of the NAND of NANDs form is that only one kind of logic gate is needed to realize *any* truth table. In the example that follows, a sum-of-products expression is first reduced by Boolean algebra and then converted to an all-NAND realization.

EXAMPLE 22

Suppose a problem specification results in the following truth table:

C	B	A	OUT
0	0	0	0
0	0	1	0
0	1	0	0
0	1	1	1
1	0	0	0
1	0	1	1
1	1	0	0
1	1	1	1

The minterms of input associated with the three 1s of OUT are

$$\overline{C} \cdot B \cdot A \qquad C \cdot \overline{B} \cdot A \qquad C \cdot B \cdot A$$

so a sum-of-products expression for OUT is

$$\text{OUT} = \overline{C} \cdot B \cdot A + C \cdot \overline{B} \cdot A + C \cdot B \cdot A$$

Since $X + X = X$, we add another $C \cdot B \cdot A$ to the right side of the equation, associate expressions in pairs, and then use various Boolean theorems to reduce it to a simpler form:

$$\begin{aligned}
\text{OUT} &= \overline{C} \cdot B \cdot A + C \cdot \overline{B} \cdot A + C \cdot B \cdot A + C \cdot B \cdot A \\
&= [\overline{C} \cdot B \cdot A + C \cdot B \cdot A] + [C \cdot \overline{B} \cdot A + C \cdot B \cdot A] \\
&= (\overline{C} + C) \cdot B \cdot A + (\overline{B} + B) \cdot C \cdot A \\
&= 1 \cdot B \cdot A + 1 \cdot C \cdot A \\
&= B \cdot A + C \cdot A
\end{aligned}$$

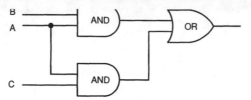

Figure 2.30 AND-to-OR circuit.

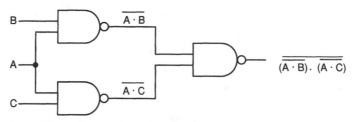

Figure 2.31 AND-to-OR circuit equivalent with NANDs.

This can be drawn out with logic gates as shown in Fig. 2.30. Now replace the ANDs and the OR with NANDs. The resulting circuit appears in Fig. 2.31. Use De Morgan's laws to convert this circuit's output to the sum-of-products form in terms of the minterm inputs:

$$\overline{\overline{(A \cdot B)} \cdot \overline{(A \cdot C)}} = \overline{\overline{(A \cdot B)}} + \overline{\overline{(A \cdot C)}} = (A \cdot B) + (A \cdot C)$$

The NAND circuit could be realized with one 74LS00 quad two-input NAND gate chip.

To repeat the conclusion of this section: *If all the ANDs and the OR in a two-level sum-of-products realization are replaced by NANDs, the resulting output is unchanged.*

2.9 GATHERING ZEROS AND DESIGNING WITH NORs

2.9.1 Product-of-Sums Form

Up to this point we have looked for the truth in truth tables. Now, by changing our focus to the rows where output is 0, we will show how to realize a truth table with a product of sums (POS, or Π of Σ) OR-to-AND circuit. You will see that a POS expression is the negative-logic version of an SOP. Then we will recapitulate the NAND-to-NAND development of an SOP by demonstrating that a two-level NOR-to-NOR circuit is equivalent to the standard POS. The POS form will be convenient for handling truth tables with a few output 0s among many 1s. The starting point of a POS is the understanding that an N-input OR operation on N different inputs has a truth table with a single 0 output.

EXAMPLE 23

Consider the eight-line truth table below, which has seven HI outputs. What is a way to describe the input combination that gives rise to the sole 0 output in row 6?

J	K	L	OUT
0	0	0	1
0	0	1	1
0	1	0	1
0	1	1	1
1	0	0	1
1	0	1	0
1	1	0	1
1	1	1	1

Answer AND($J, \overline{K}, L$) will not work because it would give a 1; NAND($J, \overline{K}, L$), however, will do the job. If we apply De Morgan's law to $\overline{J \cdot \overline{K} \cdot L} = OUT_6$, we find that $\overline{J} + K + \overline{L} = OUT_6$, so another way to produce the 0 in row 6 is to OR together the complements of the inputs of row 6. The only condition in which ($J, \overline{K}, L$) results in LO is the ORing of the complements. A *sum* that includes literals of every truth table variable is a **maxterm**, and it is designated by a capital letter M with a subscript. The subscript indicates the row of the truth table in which the OR of the literals is 0. We have just generated M_6. The minterm m_6 is $J \cdot \overline{K} \cdot L$, and the maxterm M_6 is $\overline{J} + K + \overline{L}$, formed by complementing the variables and changing AND to OR. For N inputs there are 2^N maxterms; each row of the truth table is associated with one minterm and one maxterm. (Assume $JKL = 000$ is row 1.)

What if there are *two* 0s in the truth table, as shown below? We can write the associated maxterms, M_4 and M_6, next to the rows:

J	K	L	OUT	
0	0	0	1	
0	0	1	1	
0	1	0	1	
0	1	1	0	$J + \overline{K} + \overline{L} = M_4$
1	0	0	1	
1	0	1	0	$\overline{J} + K + \overline{L} = M_6$
1	1	0	1	
1	1	1	1	

How do you combine them in an expression that yields the truth table for OUT? You want an operation that results in 0 when either of the two maxterms are encountered. An AND operation results in 0 if any of its arguments is 0. Therefore

$$OUT = (J + \overline{K} + \overline{L}) \cdot (\overline{J} + K + L)$$

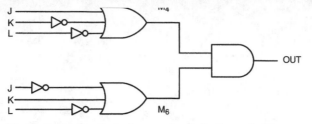

Figure 2.32   Product-of-sums circuit for Example 23.

is the correct POS equation. Whenever any maxterm is 0, the output of a POS circuit is 0. The product-of-sums circuit for the truth table above looks like Fig. 2.32, in which a HI output is TRUE.

If we had used minterms m_4 and m_6 and had formed a sum of products for the output, we would have generated a circuit with truth table output 1s in rows 4 and 6 and 0s elsewhere. We could still recover a correct answer by claiming a negative logic convention.[12]

2.9.2   De Morgan's Laws Applied to a POS Circuit

Collecting maxterms that result in outputs of 0 is called *gathering zeros*. Once the maxterms are collected, they can be expressed as a product for OUT,

$$\text{OUT} = \prod M_i$$

where the M_i are the individual maxterms that result in OUT $= 0$. Now, following for the product of sums the development of the sum of products, we complement each M_i twice, resulting in no change in OUT:

$$\text{OUT} = \prod M_i = \prod \overline{\overline{M_i}}$$

By De Morgan's laws, a product of complements is a complement of sums, so we can write the above equation as

$$\text{OUT} = \prod M_i = \prod \overline{\overline{M_i}} = \overline{\sum \overline{M_i}}$$

The expression on the right is a NOR of NORs. The input NORs are expressed by the $\overline{M_i}$; the output NOR is expressed by the $\overline{\Sigma}$ and is the canonical POS. If the canonical POS can be simplified by application of Boolean theorems (duals), the NOR of NORs will require fewer gates (and perhaps a minimum) to realize the under-

---

[12]It's possible to carry further the point of view that 0s can be the focus of truth table output. In negative logic, variables are asserted LO. As noted earlier, chips described with negative logic conventions use active low inputs and outputs. By complementing all input lines and swapping all ANDs and ORs, a circuit can be converted from positive to negative logic (or vice versa). For example,

$$\overline{A \cdot B + C \cdot D} = \overline{A \cdot B} \cdot \overline{C \cdot D} = (\overline{A} + \overline{B}) \cdot (\overline{C} + \overline{D})$$

Use of NAND and NOR gates in digital design can sometimes lead to simpler negative logic notation. But, like trying to read print in a mirror, designing in terms of negative logic is usually more awkward than with positive logic convention.

lying truth table. The importance of the NOR or NORs is that only one kind of logic gate is needed to realize any truth table. Now you have your choice: NAND or NOR. If there are fewer 0s in the output column, the *canonical* form of the POS will be simpler than the SOP. However, application of Boolean theorems will generally result in SOP and POS realizations of nearly equal complexity, as seen in the next example.

EXAMPLE 24

The truth table below has two 0 outputs. Realize the table with a product of sums and with a sum of products. Draw a circuit having only NORs that implements the truth table with as few gates as possible.

C	B	A	OUT
0	0	0	1
0	0	1	1
0	1	0	1
0	1	1	1
1	0	0	0
1	0	1	1
1	1	0	0
1	1	1	1

The maxterm of row 5 is $M_5 = \overline{C} + B + A$; the maxterm of row 7 is $M_7 = \overline{C} + \overline{B} + A$. Forming the product gives

$$\text{OUT} = (\overline{C} + B + A) \cdot (\overline{C} + \overline{B} + A)$$

which gives OUT as a canonical POS.

To find an SOP form, we could expand the OUT product as nine ANDs, we could eliminate duplicates and gather all the minterms associated with the six 1s, or we could complement OUT and apply De Morgan's laws to the POS maxterm form—

$$\overline{\text{OUT}} = \overline{(\overline{C} + B + A) \cdot (\overline{C} + \overline{B} + A)} = \overline{(\overline{C} + B + A)} + \overline{(\overline{C} + \overline{B} + A)}$$
$$= (C \cdot \overline{B} \cdot \overline{A}) + (C \cdot B \cdot \overline{A})$$

and come up with an SOP for the *complement* of OUT. To find a smaller expression, use a Boolean distributive law on the SOP of $\overline{\text{OUT}}$:

$$\overline{\text{OUT}} = C \cdot \overline{A} \cdot (\overline{B} + B) = C \cdot \overline{A} \cdot 1 = C \cdot \overline{A}$$

It is drawn with only three NORs in Fig. 2.33, where two of the NORs are used as inverters. By De Morgan's laws, again, $\text{OUT} = \overline{C} + A$ for an equally simplified SOP form.

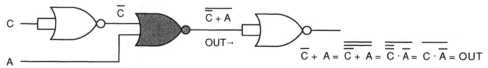

$$\overline{C + A} = \overline{\overline{C} + A} = \overline{\overline{C} \cdot \overline{A}} = \overline{C \cdot \overline{A}} = \text{OUT}$$

Figure 2.33 Sum-of-products circuit using NOR gates only.

Example 24 implies that 0s can be gathered in a truth table and their associated minterms ORed together to produce the complement of OUT,

$$\overline{OUT} = \sum m_i$$

where the m_i are the minterms of 0s in the output.

EXAMPLE 25

Design a one-bit full adder by gathering 0s.

CARRY$_{IN}$	B	A	SUM	CARRY$_{OUT}$
0	0	0	0	0
1	0	0	1	0
0	0	1	1	0
1	0	1	0	1
0	1	0	1	0
1	1	0	0	1
0	1	1	0	1
1	1	1	1	1

Answer Try gathering the four 0s in the SUM column and ORing together the minterms for a $\overline{SUM}$ expression,

$$(\overline{C} \cdot \overline{B} \cdot \overline{A}) + (C \cdot \overline{B} \cdot A) + (C \cdot B \cdot \overline{A}) + (\overline{C} \cdot B \cdot A) = \overline{SUM}$$

an SOP form. If you don't allow yourself access to XOR gates, there's no theorem that can be applied to reduce the $\overline{SUM}$ expression.

Now gather the four 0s in the CARRY$_{OUT}$ column and AND together maxterms. By application of the second form of the distributive law, CARRY$_{OUT}$ can be reduced:

$$CARRY_{OUT} = (\overline{C} + \overline{B} + \overline{A}) \cdot (\overline{C} + B + A) \cdot (C + B + \overline{A}) \cdot (C + \overline{B} + A)$$
$$= (\overline{A} + \overline{B}) \cdot (\overline{A} + \overline{C}) \cdot (\overline{B} + \overline{C})$$

CARRY$_{OUT}$ as a NOR circuit is drawn in Fig. 2.34. SUM's schematic would have four three-input NORs. Curiously enough, because CARRY$_{OUT}$ is a symmetric threshold-of-2 function, if all the NORs were replaced by NANDs, the correct CARRY$_{OUT}$ would still result!

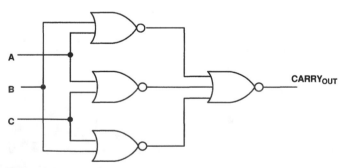

Figure 2.34   Carry-out with NORs.

In Example 22, three three-literal minterms of the canonical SOP were reduced by Boolean theorems to two two-literal terms. These smaller product terms are not minterms; they are called *prime implicants*. An **implicant** is any product term in an SOP expression. A **prime implicant** is a product term that cannot be further reduced (have any more literals removed) without violating the underlying truth table output. In formal logic an implied statement is always true when the implicant statement is true. "There are footprints in the sand" implies "Someone has been here," but there may be other reasons why "Someone has been here" would be true. Likewise, if $P \cdot Q \cdot R = 1$, then always $Q \cdot R = 1$; $Q \cdot R$ is an implicant of $P \cdot Q \cdot R$.

A **prime implicate** is a sum of complements, none of which can be eliminated without altering the meaning of an expression.

EXAMPLE 26

What are the prime implicants and implicates of the carry-out of the 1BFA?

Answer   We saw in Example 12 the reduction

$$CARRY_{OUT} = \overline{A} \cdot B \cdot C + A \cdot \overline{B} \cdot C + A \cdot B \cdot \overline{C} + A \cdot B \cdot C = B \cdot C + A \cdot C + A \cdot B$$

Since none of the implicants $A \cdot B$, $B \cdot C$, and $A \cdot C$ can be reduced further without violating the underlying truth table, they are prime. Furthermore, since none of $A \cdot B$, $B \cdot C$, and $A \cdot C$ can be taken away from the $CARRY_{OUT}$ expression without changing its truth table, each is an **essential prime implicant.** Referring to the terms of formal logic, each product term in an expression is a *sufficient* condition, and all product terms are collectively the *necessary* conditions. The summation of a complete set of essential prime implicants is a minimized SOP expression for a truth table. It will be important, in the graphic and tabular reduction methods we look at in Chapter 3, to find the prime and essential prime implicants of a truth table, but for now let's merely become aware of the terminology.

The prime *implicates* of $CARRY_{OUT}$ are $C + B$, $C + A$, and $B + A$.

.11   OPTIMIZING DIGITAL DESIGNS

At this point you have the sum-of-products method for generating a canonical solution to a truth table problem, and various Boolean theorems to reduce the number of gates involved. Duality gives you the POS option, and XOR gates have a niche in providing efficient solutions to certain classes of problems. But none of what we've done here in Chapter 2 guarantees a realization with a minimum number of gates. Minimizing the number of gates is in general a difficult optimization problem. We've already seen the example of the one-bit full adder: a *reduced* SOP realization requires four three-input AND gates and a four-input OR gate for SUM and three two-input AND gates and one three-input OR gate for $CARRY_{OUT}$, whereas combining two half adders and an OR gate requires only five gates total, none with more than two inputs. The larger SOP design has two gates' worth of propagation from input to output, and the two-half-adder design has three gates' worth of delay on the carry-out path. Chapter 3 will offer the Quine-McCluskey method—two algorithms for guaranteeing a minimal SOP form.

The half-adder design uses fewer gates, and the gates have smaller **fan-in** (number of input pins); on the other hand, the SOP 1BFA design is faster. In general, a designer may have to consider total gate count, total number of literals introduced as inputs, maximum fan-in per gate, and worst-case propagation delay through the circuit as factors to minimize.

Yet other factors, not directly related to circuit performance, may be important too. Chapter 1 discussed modularity as a design principle. How many *different* gates are used may be critical. Larger circuits may need designs that are adaptable, and the speed with which an engineer can revise a design may be a factor. Real-world issues can add to a designer's difficulty, such as power consumption, noise margins, and timing problems. The point is, Chapter 2 has given you a good start on combinational design, but it is worth keeping in mind that a working design from Chapter 2 may not be the best design.

With the knowledge you've learned in Chapter 2, Boolean algebra factoring or expanding of an expression may pay off in a search for an optimal design. Example 14 showed one case in which multi-level design reduced gate count. Here is another.

EXAMPLE 27

The 1s of a six-input truth table have been gathered in an SOP form, and Boolean theorems have produced the expression

$$YUX + YVW + YVX + YUW + Z$$

with 13 literals, which can be reduced no further. Implementation in a sum of products will require four three-input AND gates and one five-input OR gate (17 pins). The total delay is two gates' worth, as it is in every SOP. Is there a way, allowing more delay, to implement with fewer gates?

Answer

$$YUX + YVW + YVX + YUW + Z = Y \cdot (UX + VW + VX + UW) + Z$$
$$= Y \cdot (U \cdot (X + W) + V \cdot (X + W)) + Z$$
$$= Y \cdot (U + V) \cdot (X + W) + Z$$

which is realized in Fig. 2.35 and uses one fewer gate and eight fewer pins, at the expense of a three-gate delay.

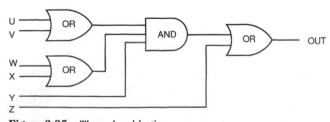

Figure 2.35   Three-level logic.

especially given the SOP architecture as a framework. In the meantime, the final part of this chapter looks at a real-world issue that can be appropriately introduced here: timing.

2.12   OUTPUT TIMING IN COMBINATIONAL CIRCUITS

The truth tables and Boolean equations of this chapter tell us *how* output is modified in response to input changes, but they don't tell us *when*. Under most circumstances, the user of a combinational logic circuit is unaware that a few nanoseconds may elapse between the time new input is presented to a circuit and the later time when output responds. Worrying about submicrosecond delays in a logic circuit may seem like a distraction from the job of designing the Boolean logic implementation correctly in the first place. But, like the flight controller who knows that all the airplanes on the runway will eventually be flying, there are some circumstances in which the logic designer must be aware of delays between the boarding of input and the takeoff of output.

At one level, dealing with delay through combinational gates may mean just waiting at the output for the answer to appear. For example, a combinational circuit may be required to finish a computation 10 ns before the next clock pulse or else data pathways with long delays will cause failure. Applications in which speed is an important factor are one matter, but if there are paths through the logic with *different* amounts of delay, some signals may express themselves at the output before others, resulting in **transient glitches.** A circuit that can produce a timing glitch is said to contain a **hazard.** Like trapeze acrobats who must time their swings so that the flyer is caught safely, sometimes a combinational circuit designer must equalize delays in a circuit to eliminate timing hazards.

Our introduction to issues in combinational circuit timing will consist of three examples. In these examples the term t_{pd} will be used for propagation delay from input change to output change.

EXAMPLE 28

If each XOR gate in the odd-parity circuit in Fig. 2.36 has a propagation delay t_{pd} of 10 ns, what output results when inputs change simultaneously from $PQRS = 0000$ to $PQRS = 1001$?

Answer   Since both input combinations have an even number of 1s, we expect that OUT should remain unchanged (see Fig. 2.36). However, the timing diagram

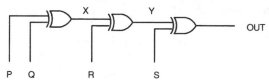

Figure 2.36   Cascade of XOR gates.

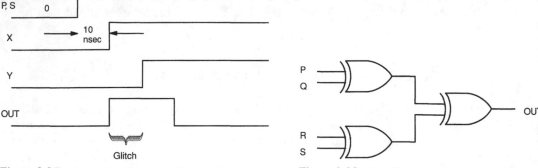

Figure 2.37 Glitch from cascade of XOR gates.   **Figure 2.38** Parallel XORs to eliminate glitch.

in Fig. 2.37 shows that gate output X changes 10 ns after input P does, and Y changes another 10 ns after that. In the meantime, input S has raced ahead to the final gate and has caused OUT to go HI for 20 ns, until the P-pathway catches up and brings OUT back down to the expected LO value. The glitch is a **static-0 hazard** because the circuit was expected to stay at 0 but made a momentary excursion to 1.

Still using only XOR gates, how can the circuit be redesigned to eliminate the glitch? Place two of the XOR gates in parallel, and then have their outputs drive a third XOR as in Fig. 2.38. Now (if the two XORs on the left have exactly the same t_{pd}) the simultaneous change of P and S should result in no glitch. There will be two gates' worth of delay from input to output, whichever input path is considered.

The foregoing example illustrates that an effort to place gates in parallel can sometimes improve circuit timing. The next example shows a use of the Boolean law of consensus in eliminating a timing hazard.

EXAMPLE 29

Consider the SOP circuit in Fig. 2.39. Imagine that each gate, including the inverter, has a 12-ns t_{pd}. Say input is currently $PQR = 111$ and therefore OUT is HI. How does OUT respond when Q makes a sudden change from HI to LO?

Answer   According to the equation for OUT, OUT should remain HI, since $P \cdot \overline{Q}$ is also a prime implicant in the SOP. But because of the delay of the inverter, there will be 12 ns when neither AND gate presents a HI to the OR, and OUT will have a transient LO glitch. See the timing diagram. There is a 24-ns delay between Q's change to LO and X's change to HI because the inverter and the AND gate both contribute to the delay on Q's path.

What can be done to eliminate the glitch and the resulting **static-1 hazard**?

Answer   Run the law of consensus backwards. Let

$$\text{OUT} = P \cdot \overline{Q} + R \cdot Q = P \cdot \overline{Q} + R \cdot Q + R \cdot P$$

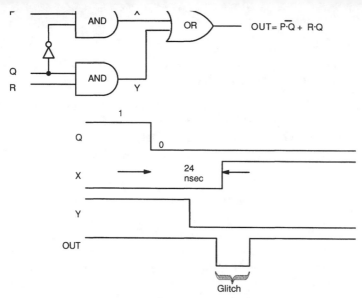

Figure 2.39 Glitch generator.

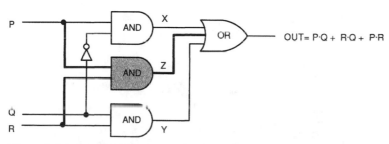

Figure 2.40 Hazard-free circuit, thanks to the law of consensus.

and add back the extra term. Now the circuit looks as shown in Fig. 2.40. When Q goes from HI to LO, OUT does not change at all because the extra term $R \cdot P$ stays HI during the whole time. By adding what seems to be a superfluous gate, a timing hazard is eliminated.

In general, LO-going glitches in SOP circuits can be eliminated by adding extra "cover" as dictated by the law of consensus. The dual of that statement is that HI-going glitches in POS circuits can be eliminated by application of the dual of the POS form of the consensus law.

So far we have seen transient glitches in outputs that we expect to remain unchanged. A glitch can also occur in an output during an interval of change from one state to another. A **dynamic hazard** is a circuit condition that can cause errors during output transitions. The following example of a dynamic hazard basically places a transient glitch generator in parallel with a slow inverter.

EXAMPLE 30

The circuit in Fig. 2.41 consists of a three-input POS part, in which gate delays are 8 ns each, and an inverter for input T, which has a t_{pd} of 32 ns. Describe what happens to OUT when input changes from $TUV = 111$ to $\overline{T}UV = 011$.

Answer   The boxed-in NOR circuit ANDs together two maxterms that are related by the law of consensus. When $TUV = 111$, the boxed NOR output is 0. After the inputs change, the boxed NOR settles again to 0. Before it settles, a positive-going glitch occurs, as seen in the timing diagram in Fig. 2.42. Note that a POS circuit has a positive-going glitch, whereas its dual, the SOP circuit, has a negative-going glitch, whenever a law-of-consensus timing problem occurs. What about OUT? When $TUV = 111$, OUT is 0 because both OR inputs are 0. After the circuit settles, OUT will have switched to 1. During the 32-ns delay of the inverter at the bottom of the circuit, the POS circuit will have sent its glitch through the OR to OUT.

What to do about the dynamic glitch, or *chatter?* In many combinational circuit applications it does not matter that a glitch occurs, because it is just too brief an event; but if, say, OUT is the input to a counter of rising edges, the counter will increment twice, instead of once as we would expect. At any rate, various fixes suggest themselves. A consensus NOR gate with $\overline{V}$ and $\overline{U}$ inputs could be added to

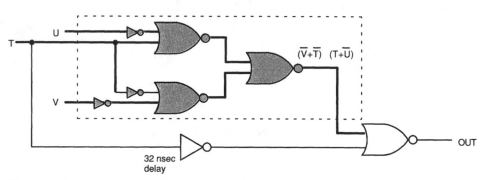

Figure 2.41   Combinational circuit with transient hazard.

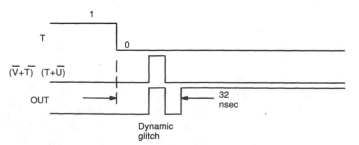

Figure 2.42   Timing diagram for dynamic hazard.

the POS circuit; more delay could be inserted in the POS-to-OR path; a faster inverter could be used to complement T at the bottom. It might be best to arrange that the counter wait until the combinational circuit has settled its output before looking at OUT. In general, elimination of dynamic hazards is more difficult than elimination of static hazards.

Input History and Combinational Circuits   At the beginning of Chapter 2 it was stated that combinational circuits are distinguished by their lack of memory—that the current output of a combinational circuit depends only on present input. Now that we've seen some of the timing glitches that can occur in combinational circuits implemented with gates having nonzero propagation delays, that assertion must be qualified: on a nanosecond time scale it may matter what the recent history of some inputs has been with regard to the present output of a real combinational circuit. Furthermore, although we've seen that different formats, such as SOP and POS, can solve the same truth table with different hardware, it may matter for the sake of timing which circuit is used in practice.

.13   SUMMARY

- **Combinational gates** rely on input only for their output; their outputs have no memory of past inputs. However, real combinational gates have some nanoseconds of input-output propagation delay.

- A **truth table** shows all combinations of input and the resulting output(s) for a problem with input and output digitized to binary levels. A truth table for N inputs has 2^N lines. Positional coding is used to list the input possibilities.

- **Don't-care** (X) is a possible choice on some truth table outputs.

- Primitives such as **AND, OR,** and **XOR** can sometimes directly realize the solutions to small truth tables.

- By picking truth table rows with output equal to 1, you can realize any truth table by a two-level structure of AND gates feeding into one OR gate; this structure is referred to as a **canonical sum of products**. **Minterms** are combinations of input literals ANDed together to account for 1s in truth table output.

- **Boolean algebra** is a commutative ring algebra on the set $\{0, 1\}$. Boolean algebra generates rules for manipulating logical expressions involving OR, AND, and INVERT operations. Through various theorems, Boolean algebra provides a means of reducing logic expressions to simpler forms.

- In Boolean algebra expressions, parentheses enforce precedence of operation, especially in distributive laws. Parentheses can be replaced by a hardware tree structure. The tree structure is the beginning of hardware parallel processing.

- Because of symmetry between AND and OR operations, there is a fundamental **duality** in Boolean algebra. A Boolean expression can be turned into its dual by swapping AND and OR operators and swapping 1s and 0s. Each Boolean theorem has its dual form.

duals of each other:

$$\text{NAND}: \quad \overline{A + B + C + D + \cdots} = \overline{A} \cdot \overline{B} \cdot \overline{C} \cdot \overline{D} \cdots$$
$$\text{NOR}: \quad \overline{A \cdot B \cdot C \cdot D \cdots} = \overline{A} + \overline{B} + \overline{C} + \overline{D} + \cdots$$

The two forms are used to convert between NAND and NOR circuits.

- **Shannon's theorems** for factoring a variable X_1 out of Boolean expression F are as follows:

$$F(X_1, X_2, X_3, \ldots, X_N) = F(1, X_2, X_3, \ldots, X_N) \cdot X_1 + F(0, X_2, X_3, \ldots, X_N) \cdot \overline{X_1}$$

and its dual,

$$F(X_1, X_2, X_3, \ldots, X_N) = [F(0, X_2, X_3, \ldots, X_N) + X_1]$$
$$\cdot [F(1, X_2, X_3, \ldots, X_N) + \overline{X_1}]$$

- **XOR gates** can be viewed as digital comparators. To determine the **parity** of a binary word, pass all the bits of the word through a series of XOR gates.
- N-input AND and OR gates have output **thresholds** of N and 1, respectively. A general form of threshold gate can handle weighted analog inputs.
- If all the AND and OR gates of a two-level AND-to-OR sum of products realization are replaced by NAND gates, the output will be unchanged.
- A **maxterm** is a combination of input literals ORed together that accounts for one 0 in a truth table output. If the truth table rows with output of 0 are gathered, the truth table can be realized by a two-level product-of-sums (POS) structure, which can be implemented entirely with NOR gates, the dual of the NAND SOP circuit.
- Truth tables and Boolean expressions can be realized in different ways that may be optimized for gate count, literal count, fan-in, or propagation delay.
- **Timing hazards** in combinational circuits arise from unequal propagation delays and can cause transient **glitches** in outputs. Adding consensus terms to SOP and POS circuits can eliminate some static hazards.
- Logical operations can use **fuzzy sets** as their inputs. A fuzzy variable has a grade of membership in a fuzzy set. Fuzzy logic is distinguished from probability and may be useful for dealing with qualities that are not easily categorized into distinct compartments.

2.14 FUZZY LOGIC

(This section is optional.) In most of this text variables are restricted to the values 0 and 1; however, in this section we consider the consequences of variables that can take on real values μ, $0 \leq \mu \leq 1$. These new variables cannot be considered logical, except in the limits of 0 and 1; instead, the μ's will form part of a **fuzzy variable**, and the other part is an instance of the variable. We will first investigate the notion of a

fuzzy set, and then the operations that can be performed on fuzzy sets and on fuzzy variables. We will contrast fuzzy variables to random variables, found in probability theory.

Fuzzy logic is designed to deal with common qualities that do not necessarily fit into mutually exclusive categories. For example, although clearly classified as either male or female, a person may not be easily classified as smart or beautiful or even tall or young. Fuzzy logic provides a framework for capturing indistinctness, as opposed to the uncertainty of randomness. Later an example will be given of the use of fuzzy logic to resolve a paradox. By the time you finish this section, you will appreciate that the all-or-none logic of 0s and 1s is a special case of fuzzy logic. (See Fig. 2.43.)

Fuzzy logic controllers show potential for adapting to variable input conditions. In recent years, Japanese companies have made commercial fuzzy logic controllers for washing machines, subways, and other systems. Various Japanese semiconductor makers fabricate fuzzy logic hardware chips.

Let's start with **fuzzy sets**. Compare a fuzzy set to a standard set. A nonfuzzy set or subset has distinct boundaries. For example, given the universe of cars, the set of 1961 Mercurys is a distinct set from the universe. In general, a set S is any collection of things; once the set is defined or enumerated, we can say that things are either in S or not in S. Various operations, such as union, intersection, and complementation, which will be discussed later, can be performed on sets.

A fuzzy set F is a collection of ordered pairs $\{x, \mu(x)\}$ where $\mu(x)$ is the *membership* of x in F; $0 \le \mu(x) \le 1$. The function $\mu(x)$ may be determined arbitrarily or may be computed. For example, we might define the fuzzy set of large real numbers by

$$\mu(x) = \left| \frac{x}{x+1} \right|$$

By this measure the number 7 has 0.875 membership in the set of large real numbers. It is not appropriate to speak of a number being in or not in the fuzzy set of large numbers; rather, a number simply has a membership value more or less close to 0 or 1 for that fuzzy set. One exception here is the number 0; $\mu(x) = 0.0$ suggests that 0 is not in the set of large numbers at all.

Which is the fuzzy variable, x or $\mu(x)$? Both numbers are needed. Like a complex number, the fuzzy variable has two components, the object and its membership value. Together they specify the fuzzy variable.

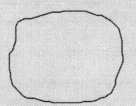

Figure 2.43 A fuzzy circle or a fuzzy square?

Operations on Fuzzy Sets   The **complement** of a fuzzy set F is the set of ordered pairs $\{x, 1 - \mu(x)\}$. For example, given our membership function above for the set of large numbers, the set of not-large, or small, numbers has the membership function

$$\mu(x) = 1 - \left| \frac{x}{x + 1} \right|$$

A number can belong somewhat to both the fuzzy set of large numbers and its complement, the fuzzy set of small numbers. For example, according to the function above, 2.0 has membership 0.67 in the set of large numbers and 0.33 in the set of small numbers.

The **union** of two fuzzy sets F_1 and F_2, $F_1 \cup F_2$, is a set whose membership function is the maximum of $\{\mu_1(x), \mu_2(x)\}$ over all x, where $\mu_1(x)$ is the membership function of F_1 and $\mu_2(x)$ is the membership function of F_2. Consider the union of the large-number and small-number fuzzy sets. The numbers 0.5 and 2.0 both have a membership value 0.67 in the union. Fuzzy set union is a generalization of the OR operation. For example, the OR of the four logical variables $V_i, i = 1, 2, 3, 4$, could be defined as $\max(V_1, V_2, V_3, V_4)$.

The **intersection** of two fuzzy sets F_1 and F_2, $F_1 \cap F_2$, is a set whose membership function is the minimum of $\{\mu_1(x), \mu_2(x)\}$ over all x. Intersection of sets is a generalization of the AND operation. For example, $\text{AND}(1, 1, 1, 0, 1, 1) = \min(1, 1, 1, 0, 1, 1) = 0$.

In general, operations on sets—whether fuzzy or sharply bounded—result in properties such as $A + A = A$ and $A \cdot A = A$ (where A is a set) that have no parallel in the algebra of real numbers. However, Boolean algebra can handle fuzzy logic. See Courant and Robbins (1947, 273ff.).

Fuzzy versus Random Variables   Fuzzy variables are different from logical variables and even from random variables. Although random variables and membership values of fuzzy variables are both restricted to the range [0, 1], they represent different concepts. Here is an example adapted from Kosko (1991). Consider two refrigerators. You are told there is a 50% probability that a peach is inside refrigerator P, and you are told that half a peach is definitely inside refrigerator F. Superficially, it seems that both refrigerators contain the same amount of peach-value, but let us think a little more carefully. What about the half-peach in F? Is it really a peach, or a piece of fruit with 0.5 membership in the set of peaches? F contains a "fuzzy peach." What about P? Once P is opened, either a whole peach or no peach will be seen. Once more knowledge is gained by opening the door of P, the uncertainty disappears. No such disappearance of uncertainty is possible with the fuzzy half-peach; we know for certain what is in F, but we just cannot place it with value 1.0 in the set of peaches.

Fuzzy and random variables can be combined in one expression: For example, in the phrase "a 50% chance of light rain," the "50%" is a probability notion, and the "light rain" is a fuzzy notion.

If we direct our attention from relations between fuzzy sets to the members of one fuzzy set, we can construct a fuzzy algebra. If x and y have membership values μ_x and μ_y, then $\bar{x}$, the complement of x, has membership value $\mu(\bar{x}) = 1 - \mu_x$; similarly:

x OR $y = x + y =$ has membership value $\max(\mu_x, \mu_y)$.

x AND $y = x \cdot y =$ has membership value $\min(\mu_x, \mu_y)$.

Note that these are operations on the members of a set, not operations on sets. Further theorems, similar to the Boolean theorems seen earlier in this chapter, can be proved. Boolean algebra is, in fact, a special case of fuzzy algebra.

EXAMPLE 31

This paradox appears in Kosko (1991). Bertrand Russell reported seeing a barber's sign that said, "I shave those, and only those, who don't shave themselves." Who shaves the barber? If he does not shave himself, he must.

Equate these contradictory statements and solve for the "truth." Let $T(s)$ be the truth that the barber shaves himself; $T(s)$ is a membership function for the set of people who shave themselves. Then

$$T(s) = T(\bar{s}) = 1 - T(s)$$
$$2T(s) = 1$$
$$T(s) = \tfrac{1}{2}$$

Thus the barber must have membership $\tfrac{1}{2}$ in the set of people who shave themselves (and membership $\tfrac{1}{2}$ in the set of people who don't shave themselves).

We see fuzzy logic can be used to resolve glass-half-empty, glass-half-full paradoxes. But true to its name, it is difficult to find a clear example of fuzzy logic *and fuzzy logic alone* being used in the solution of a practical engineering problem. Fuzzy logic applications often involve coordinated use of expert systems, neural networks, or Bayesian estimates. Kosko (1991) describes several fuzzy applications, including a control system for backing up a truck, a filter to separate signal from noise, and an object-recognition system. In each case the fuzzy rules interact with other more conventional engineering approaches to produce results. See Kosko and Isaka (1993), Kandel and Lee (1979), Zimmerman (1985), and Asai and Seguno (1992) for more information. Lotfi Zadeh is considered the father of fuzzy logic; his 1965 paper named and defined fuzzy sets.

Exercises

1. Which of the two circuits in Fig. P2.1 is not a combinational circuit?

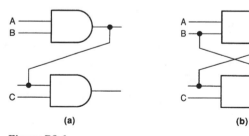

(a)　　　　(b)

Figure P2.1

2. **(a)** Suppose the two digital inputs to a combinational circuit are called A and B. The complement of A is $\overline{A}$. List all the input combinations of A and B in terms of A and B and their complements.

(b) A combinational logic circuit has six independent inputs, $A-F$. How many different combinations of inputs are possible? The order $A-F$ must be preserved, and all six inputs must be considered for each combination.

(c) Eight switches provide input to a logic circuit. Because of mechanical constraints, at least one switch must be on at all times, but not all eight can be on at once. How many valid input combinations are there for the system?

(d) Imagine a combinational circuit with three independent inputs and three outputs. What is the maximum number of different output combinations? How many different output combinations are possible if a particular logic circuit has only two inputs?

3. The Xilinx 3000 series field-programmable gate array (Fig. P2.2) has in each of its configurable logic blocks a "combinatorial function generator" with five direct inputs (a–e) and two "indirect" inputs (di and ec). In its F mode the function generator can be programmed by a user to realize any one five-input combinational function; in its FG mode it can be programmed to realize any two four-input combinational functions, with the outputs being F and G in the diagram of Fig. P2.2.

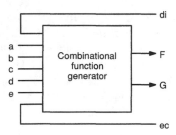

Figure P2.2

(a) Considering that the five inputs for the F mode can be selected from any of the seven total choices, how many different sets of input are possible?

(b) In the FG mode a user is limited to four choices per function but can choose two different functions for the two outputs. Are there more possible input sets in the FG mode than the F mode, or fewer?

4. For the four level-detectors of Example 2, write out a truth table for a system that will report when either detector B or detector C is stuck at 0.

5. A special clock face has 12 detectors, $D_0, D_1, \ldots, D_{11}$, which respond to the hands M and H of the clock (Fig. P2.3). Each detector spans a $30°$ arc and responds with a 1 output when M *or* H is in its range. A clock hand is in one and only one detector arc at a time.

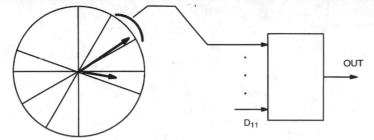

Figure P2.3   One of 12 arcs with detectors.

(a) Out of 2^{12} detector combinations, how many are valid, or possible, as inputs to the logic circuit on the right?

(b) If each detector responds to $M \oplus H$, how many detector combinations give a signal of 1?

(c) If OUT in Fig. P2.3 is true only when one and only one detector output is active, how many truth table lines will have OUT $= 1$?

6. Before a truth table can be filled in properly, the problem needs to be stated clearly. Sometimes that is a matter of finding what the inputs should be.

(a) Consider the following possible inputs: door bolt detector, sound detector, window latch detector, movement detector, temperature detector, dog-bark detector, telephone busy signal detector. Assuming each detector gives a digital output, which of these inputs (or combinations of inputs) may be don't-care for a home burglar alarm system?

(b) Some special cars have breathalyzers, which must generate a low output before the ignition will work. Think of four other factors you might include in a vigilant car ignition guard system.

7. For a seven-segment display, shown in Fig. P2.4, write down the truth table outputs a–g for the digits 7, 8, and 9. Write out lines for the two patterns of the digit 7 shown at the right.

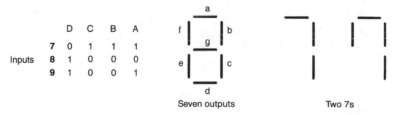

		D	C	B	A
	7	0	1	1	1
Inputs	8	1	0	0	0
	9	1	0	0	1

Seven outputs   Two 7s

Figure P2.4   Seven-segment control for 7, 8, and 9.

8. In Fig. P2.5 are two more tries to detect two in a row (A and B, or B and C). Will either of them work? If a circuit does not work, show what line of the truth table gives an incorrect answer.

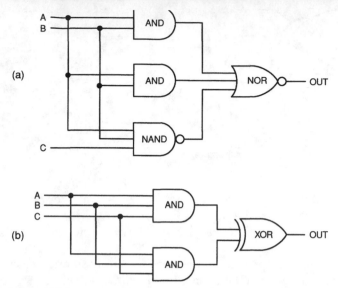

(a)

(b)

Figure P2.5

9. **Voltages versus logic levels** Three light bulbs are input indicators in the circuit of Fig. P2.6. The resistors R are sized to limit current to the bulbs when the switches are closed, and $R \gg$ resistance of bulb. If (say) switch A is closed and its bulb is lit, then voltage at point A is nearly 0. The input switches are manually controlled. Let voltages C, B, and A be inputs to a logic circuit.

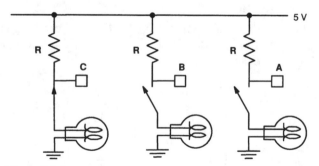

Figure P2.6

Using electronically controlled switches for logic and a *different* bulb as output, design a circuit that responds with the output bulb ON only when bulb B alone or bulbs C and A together are lit. Use on-off or toggle switches and specify control for each switch.

10. **Binary representation of Mastermind** In the game Mastermind the "maker" chooses a pattern of colored plastic pegs and sticks the pegs in holes hidden

from the breaker. The breaker makes a guess about the pattern by placing other colored pegs in a set of holes that the maker can see.

Hidden pattern   Guess

The maker inspects the guess and gives the breaker two pieces of information: the number of the breaker's pegs that are of the right color in the right position, and the number of other pegs that are of a color in the pattern but in the wrong position. The score for the guess in the figure would be (1, 2) for the one yellow peg in hole 4 and the two green and blue pegs in the wrong positions. Let there be eight different colors to choose from and four positions for the pegs to be in (and each position *must* have a peg in the hidden code).

(a) How many bits are needed to represent the eight colors?

(b) If any color can be in any position, how many different hidden patterns are possible?

(c) If the four code pegs must all be different colors, how many different hidden patterns are possible?

(d) If all four code pegs must be different colors, devise a binary code to represent the pattern generated by the maker.

(e) Devise a binary representation for the two-number answer the breaker receives after every guess.

‡(f) Design a combinational logic circuit that will take a pattern from the maker, compare it with the breaker's guess, and produce the two-number answer of information for the breaker.

11. Write out the truth table for a four-bit system that defines even parity; that is, its output is 1 only when an even number of the four inputs are 1 at the same time. (Zero is an even number. Note that parity check does not depend on the order of the inputs, but only on the total number of 1s in the current input pattern.)

12. If whenever P is true, then Q is true, P *implies* Q. Expression Q may be true at other times, too, but P is true only when Q is true. In English, if-then statements signal implication. For example, "If the sun shines through the rain, then a rainbow occurs."

The four implication functions of two inputs are shown below as four columns of OUT.

B	A	OUT			
0	0	0	0	1	1
0	1	1	0	0	1
1	0	0	1	1	0
1	1	0	0	1	1

For each of the output columns, design a logic circuit using the hardware primitives listed in Chapter 2 that will produce that output.

13. Show how the following primitives can be configured as inverters.
   (a) XOR gate
   (b) NAND gate
   (c) NOR gate

14. Assume a vat has, at three different levels, sensors of liquid that have binary output; if liquid is present, the sensor sends out a 1.
   (a) An overflow warning light must come on if all three level-sensors are active. What one logic gate would solve this problem?
   (b) An empty warning light signaling a low level must come on if all three level-sensors are inactive. What one logic gate would solve this problem?

15. The logic expression $A \cdot B \cdot C \cdot D \cdot E$ must be realized using only two-input NAND primitives. Come up with a design using a minimum number of gates. What is the longest delay through your circuit, if we say that each two-input NAND contributes 25 ns of delay?

16. (a) Write out the eight-line truth tables for the circuits in Fig. P2.7, which are composed of logic gate primitives.
   (b) Assuming that all gates have the same propagation delay t_{pd}, which of the four circuits do not have a static timing hazard?

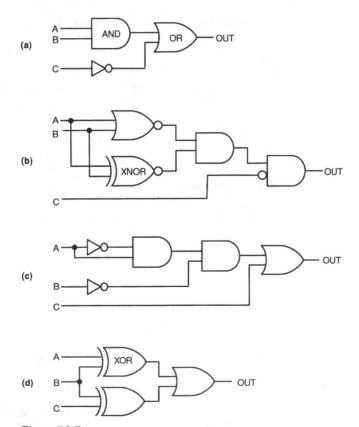

Figure P2.7

17. **(a)** Show how to make a four-input NAND out of two-input NANDs.

   (b) Show how to make a four-input NOR out of two-input NORs.

18. What are the minterms for the following truth table?

R	Q	P	OUT
0	0	0	1
0	0	1	0
0	1	0	0
0	1	1	1
1	0	0	1
1	0	1	0
1	1	0	0
1	1	1	1

   Can you find a Boolean expression for $OUT(R, P, Q)$?

19. Consider the two Boolean expressions of four variables,

$$\overline{(A + B) + \overline{(C + D)}} \qquad (A + C) + (B \cdot D)$$

   (a) For how many of the 2^4 input combinations are these two expressions *both* true?

   (b) For how many combinations are *both* false?

   (c) What are all the minterms associated with the expression on the left above?

20. Which Boolean expression below has more literals? Without further reduction, which expression would require the greatest number of input and output pins to realize with logic primitives?

   (a) $A \cdot \overline{(B + C)} + C \cdot (B + \overline{D}) + \overline{E}$

   (b) $A \cdot \overline{B} + A \cdot \overline{C} + C \cdot B + C \cdot \overline{D} + \overline{F}$

   (c) $A \oplus B \oplus C \oplus D \oplus E \oplus F$

21. A circuit inspects five switches in a row. If the two end switches are the same value (HI or LO) and the three middle switches are all the opposite value to the end switches, then and only then is the circuit output to be HI. Design a sum-of-products implementation for the circuit.

22. Without using XOR gates, design an SOP circuit that will respond with 1 when an odd number of bits of a four-bit word are presented simultaneously as input to the circuit (odd parity check).

23. Find a canonical SOP realization for the three-input truth table below:

C	B	A	OUT
0	0	0	0
0	0	1	0
0	1	0	0
0	1	1	0
1	0	0	1
1	0	1	0
1	1	0	1
1	1	1	0

24. Design canonical SOP solutions for OUT_A and OUT_B as given in the truth table below, where W, X, Y, and Z are the inputs.

W	X	Y	Z	OUT_A	OUT_B
0	0	0	0	0	0
0	0	0	1	0	0
0	0	1	0	0	0
0	0	1	1	1	1
0	1	0	0	0	0
0	1	0	1	0	0
0	1	1	0	0	1
0	1	1	1	1	0
1	0	0	0	1	0
1	0	0	1	0	0
1	0	1	0	0	0
1	0	1	1	0	0
1	1	0	0	0	1
1	1	0	1	0	0
1	1	1	0	0	0
1	1	1	1	0	0

Can you reduce the canonical SOPs to ones with fewer literals in their expressions? Can the two outputs share any hardware?

25. Realize the three five-input truth tables OUT_1, OUT_2, and OUT_3 as sum-of-products AND-to-OR designs. The second half of each table ($E = 1$) is all 0s.

E	D	C	B	A	OUT_1	OUT_2	OUT_3
0	0	0	0	0	1	1	0
0	0	0	0	1	1	0	0
0	0	0	1	0	0	0	0
0	0	0	1	1	0	0	0
0	0	1	0	0	0	0	0
0	0	1	0	1	0	0	0
0	0	1	1	0	1	1	1
0	0	1	1	1	1	0	1
0	1	0	0	0	0	1	1
0	1	0	0	1	0	0	0
0	1	0	1	0	1	1	1
0	1	0	1	1	0	0	1
0	1	1	0	0	0	1	1
0	1	1	0	1	0	0	0
0	1	1	1	0	0	0	0
0	1	1	1	1	0	0	1

26. A safe has a 66-button keyboard. In order to unlock the safe, a teller must *simultaneously* press buttons 6, 27, 33, 48, and 64. If extra buttons are pressed at the same time, the safe will not unlock (pressing all the buttons at once will not work). When a button is pressed, it can send a HI output to a logic circuit.

(a) Design a combinational circuit whose HI output will represent the unlocked safe. Assume you have independent access to each digitized key.

(b) Suppose a thief knows in advance that exactly five buttons must be pressed to unlock the safe, but does not know which ones. How many combinations are there of 66 things taken 5 at a time that the thief may have to try? If the thief has an electronic combination tester that can systematically change five-input combinations every 20 μs (10^{-6} s), what is the greatest possible amount of time he could need to crack the safe?

27. Recall Boolean addition from Chapter 1. Write out a truth table for 2-bit by 2-bit multiplication. How are the Boolean operations AND and OR like the ordinary algebra operations of multiplication and addition?

28. Here is the truth table definition of a two input AND gate:

A	B	A AND B
0	0	0
0	1	0
1	0	0
1	1	1

Each of the lines of the two-input AND truth table can be proved from the definitions of identity and complement in the Huntington postulaton, discussed in Section 2.4, using the · operation for AND. For example, the line $0 \cdot 0 = 0$ comes from the definition of 0. Prove the other three lines of the AND relationship.

29. Simplify these one-variable Boolean expressions:

(a) $X \cdot X + X \cdot 1 + X \cdot 0$

(b) $(X + X + X) \cdot X$

(c) $(X + 1) \cdot (X + 0)$

30. A set, and an operation with closure, but no associativity or commutativity
Imagine a set $\mathcal{S}$ of six arrows pointing orthogonally out of the six sides of a cube—Up, Down, Left, Right, Front, and Back. Now consider pairs of arrows operated on by the right-hand rule. For two orthogonal arrows operated on by the right-hand rule, the resulting arrow is in the direction of a screw turned from the first arrow to the second. The accompanying table shows the arrow that results from the right-hand-rule operation on two arrows A_1 and A_2 that are at right angles to each other, where A_1 is the first arrow and A_2 is the second arrow in the operation. OUT $= A_1 \times A_2$. To keep things simple, we are not allowing operations when $A_1 = A_2$ or when $A_1 = -A_2$. Set $\mathcal{S}$ operated on by the right-hand rule has closure because all the resulting rotations are still members of set $\mathcal{S}$.

	U	D	L	R	F	B
U			B	F	L	R
D			F	B	R	L
L	F	B			D	U
R	B	F			U	D
F	R	L	U	D		
B	L	R	D	U		

First element A_1 in operation

(a) Show (by counterexample) that the set $\mathcal{S}$ of six orthogonal arrows operated on in pairs by the right-hand rule is not associative or commutative.

‡(b) If you allow a seventh element, 0, in the set, what rule can fill in the colored squares, and what results from $A_1 \times 0$ and $0 \times A_2$?

(c) How many bits are needed to represent U, D, L, R, F, B, and 0?

31. What are the duals of the following two theorems?

(a) $X + \overline{X} \cdot Y = X + Y$

(b) $X \cdot Y + \overline{X} \cdot Y + 0 = Y$

32. Show what ambiguities result when the following expression of a distributive law is stripped of its parentheses, even when precedence is enforced.

$$R + Q \cdot P = R + Q \cdot R + P$$

33. Prove the dual adjacency theorems

$$P \cdot Q + \overline{P} \cdot Q = Q \qquad (P + Q) \cdot (\overline{P} + Q) = Q$$

by perfect induction.

34. Use Boolean theorems to help simplify the following expressions:

$$P \cdot Q \cdot R + P$$
$$P \cdot Q \cdot \overline{R \cdot S} + R \cdot S$$
$$P \cdot Q \cdot \overline{R} + P \cdot Q \cdot R$$
$$P \cdot Q + P \cdot Q \cdot R \cdot S + \overline{P \cdot Q}$$

35. Prove the Boolean distributive relationship

$$X + Y \cdot Z = (X + Y) \cdot (X + Z)$$

using the Huntington postulates. (Do not just write out truth tables for both sides.)

36. (a) Prove the Boolean algebra law of consensus:

$$\overline{B} \cdot A + C \cdot B + A \cdot C = \overline{B} \cdot A + C \cdot B$$

(b) By using DeMorgan's Law, distributivity, and definition of zero, prove that

$$(A + B) \cdot (\overline{A \cdot B}) = A \cdot \overline{B} + \overline{A} \cdot B$$

37. Simplify, if possible, the following expressions:
    (a) $A \cdot \overline{B}$
    (b) $A \cdot \overline{B} + A \cdot B$
    (c) $A \cdot \overline{B} + A \cdot B + \overline{A} \cdot B$
    (d) $A \cdot \overline{B} + A \cdot B + \overline{A} \cdot B + \overline{A} \cdot \overline{B}$
    (e) $A \cdot \overline{B} + A \cdot B + \overline{A} \cdot B + \overline{A} \cdot \overline{B} + A \cdot B \cdot C$

38. **Negative logic**   See the NAND circuit of Fig. P2.8.

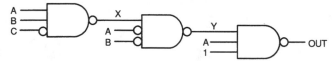

Figure P2.8

    (a) Find a simplified Boolean expression for OUT. You might try finding the intermediate forms X and Y in working toward OUT.
    (b) What is the dual of the expression for OUT? Is it equal to OUT?
    (c) Use De Morgan's law on the middle NAND gate to find an OR gate replacement. Draw out the circuit with an OR gate in the middle. Note that the OR gate replacement allows cancellation of various bubble-pairs in the circuit. All the inputs to the new OR gate are complements of the former NAND input, and the NAND has been replaced by an OR operation. The middle OR gate carries out negative logic, and the circuit as a whole is therefore mixed logic.

39. The following pseudocode was used to compute the expression $A \cdot B + A \cdot C$ of the distributive law, where A, B, and C are real numbers:

    TEMP1 ← A * B
    TEMP2 ← A * C
    ANS ← TEMP1 + TEMP2

    Can you think of code that will find the answer in two steps instead of three?

40. Consider the following Boolean product-of-sums expression:

$$(A + B) \cdot (C + D)$$

    (a) Use the distributive law to find two different hardware realizations of this expression.
    (b) Draw circuits for the hardware. Does one of your realizations have less propagation delay?

41. Figure P2.9 is a block diagram of a combinational circuit, with two identical subcircuits. At time t_1 the inputs are ABC; at time t_2 the inputs are CAB.
    (a) What can be in the combinational subcircuit to ensure that OUT is always the same for both input combinations? (More than one answer is possible.)

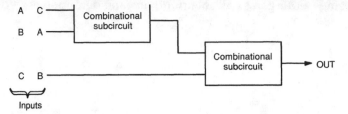

Figure P2.9

(b) What can be in the combinational subcircuit so that for at least some values of *CBA*, OUT for the first input combination is different from OUT for the second combination? *Hint:* Think about associativity.

42. What are reduced Boolean expressions for the outputs of the circuits in Fig. P2.10?

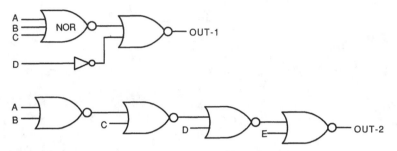

Figure P2.10

43. **(a)** What does the following circuit of NORs do? Write OUT in a simplified expression in terms of *A* and *B*.

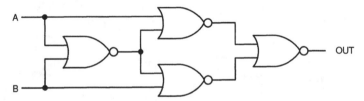

Figure P2.11

(b) What simplified Boolean expression relates OUT to inputs *A* and *B* in the following NAND circuit?

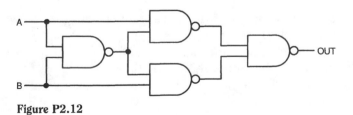

Figure P2.12

44. Prove the first form of De Morgan's law, $\overline{(A + B + C)} = \overline{A} \cdot \overline{B} \cdot \overline{C}$, for three variables A, B, and C. Use the proof in the text, based on the definition of complement, as an aid.

45. Can you find a counterexample to the following assertion, which is similar to duality? "Given any Boolean equation that has only OR, AND, and INVERT operations among variables, swapping all ORs for ANDs and vice versa and complementing all variables (including OUT) results in an equation with the same truth table."

46. Show that the expression

$$(\overline{C} + \overline{B} + \overline{A}) \cdot (\overline{C} + B + A) \cdot (C + B + \overline{A}) \cdot (C + \overline{B} + A)$$

can be simplified to

$$\overline{C \oplus B \oplus A}$$

47. **(a)** Rewrite the Boolean expression $P \cdot Q \cdot R + S \cdot T \cdot U$ in product-of-sum form.
   (b) Rewrite the Boolean expression $P + Q + R \cdot S + T + U$ in sum-of-products form. *Hint:* Use the two forms of De Morgan's law.

48. Can you think of a generalization of the law of consensus to four variables, D, C, B, and A?

49. **(a)** Simplify the following expressions:
       (i) $P \cdot Q + \overline{P} \cdot R + Q \cdot R$
       (ii) $\overline{D} \cdot C \cdot A + C \cdot B \cdot A + D \cdot C \cdot B$
       (iii) $\overline{D} \cdot C \cdot A + C \cdot \overline{B} \cdot A + C \cdot B \cdot A$
       (iv) $\overline{D} \cdot \overline{C} \cdot \overline{B} \cdot \overline{A} + D \cdot \overline{C} \cdot \overline{B} \cdot \overline{A} + D \cdot \overline{C} \cdot B \cdot \overline{A} + \overline{D} \cdot \overline{C} \cdot B \cdot \overline{A}$
   (b) Realize the simplified expressions with only NOR gates.

50. A rectangular surface is inspected by three overlapping photodetectors. Each photodetector signals with a 1 when light strikes it and a 0 when it is in the dark. The three detectors cover the following regions of the rectangle, here shown as three shaded areas.

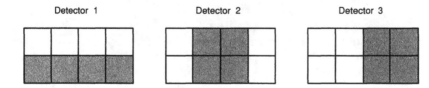

    Detector 1   Detector 2   Detector 3

What logic circuit receives the three detector signals as inputs and gives an output of 1 whenever *any* one of the following colored area is illuminated?

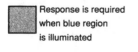

Response is required when blue region is illuminated

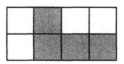

Note that the three detectors cover the rectangle in such a way as to account for the eight lines of a three-input truth table. Design the required circuit in an SOP form with a minimum number of AND and OR gates. *Hint:* The law of consensus may come in handy.

51. **(a)** Apply Shannon's theorem to expand the alarm output ALARM $= D + L$ in terms of D.

   (b) With the help of Shannon's theorem, factor the terms Y and Z out of the following Boolean expression:

$$X \cdot Y + U \cdot Z \oplus Y + W + Z \cdot X$$

52. You saw that XOR is equal to

$$A \oplus B = (A + B) \cdot (\overline{A \cdot B}) = A \cdot \overline{B} + \overline{A} \cdot B$$

If you take the *dual* of the two AND-OR-INVERT expressions on the right, is the result still equal to $A \oplus B$?

53. **(a)** Are the distributive laws of Boolean algebra true if the OR operation is replaced by XOR? If not, show where XOR fails.

   (b) If XOR replaces OR as an operator in Boolean algebra, do closure, associativity, and commutativity still hold?

54. Which is the closest analogy: OR is to exclusive OR as

   (a) Subtraction is to remainder
   (b) Multiplication is to division
   (c) Addition is to the modulo operation
   (d) Circle is to semicircle
   (e) Doughnut is to doughnut hole

55. Consider an AND gate. If any one of its inputs is LO, the output of the AND gate is LO, so we can say that a low input to an AND gate *disables* the AND gate. Similarly, if any one input to an OR gate is HI, the OR gate output must be HI, and we can say that a high input disables an OR gate. Can an XOR gate be disabled?

56. A 74LS51 chip realizes the two functions $\overline{A \cdot B + C \cdot D}$ and $\overline{P \cdot Q \cdot R + S \cdot T \cdot U}$ with AND-OR-INVERT gates in a 14-pin package.

   (a) Turn a 74LS51 into a 2-input OR-gate.
   (b) Make a 74LS51 perform the XOR operation.
   (c) Suppose the output of one AND-OR-INVERT gate of the 74LS51 is fed into one of the inputs of the other AND-OR-INVERT gate. How large a single minterm could such a circuit handle?

57. Suppose the output of a circuit with N inputs $I_0, I_i, \ldots, I_{N-1}$ is true only if I_j *alone* is true for some particular $j, 0 \le j < N$ (a version of implication).

   (a) Design a circuit to realize implication for $j = 2, N = 4$. Can you do it with just XOR gates? What about using a three-out-of-five majority gate in your design?

   (b) Suppose now OUT is required to be true only when I_2 alone is false. Is the *complement* of the answer to (a) the correct hardware? If not, show a design that works.

58. If the 2^n positionally coded binary numbers are applied to the following circuit, what are the four-bit outputs? Write out a truth table. What is special about the output bit pattern of G's?

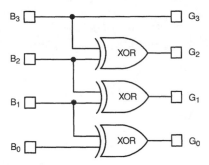

Figure P2.13

59. **(a)** Consider two two-bit binary numbers A_1A_0 and B_1B_0. Write out the truth table that expresses when the two pairs are identical, that is, when $A_1 = B_1$ and $A_0 = B_0$.

(b) Design hardware to realize the equality function. What is the minimum number of 2-input primitives needed to signify equality of the two pairs?

60. N-input NAND and NOR gates have thresholds in terms of negative logic. What are their thresholds?

61. **(a)** Write out the truth table and design a logic circuit to realize a two-out-of-three (2/3) majority circuit. Let the output be 1 if at least two out of three inputs are 1 simultaneously.

(b) Now design the 2/3 majority gate using NAND gates only.

(c) Show how to design a 3/5 majority circuit using 2/3 majority gates.

62. Consider the uses of a three-out-of-five majority gate (call it M5). M5 can be classified as a threshold logic device.

(a) Show how M5 inputs can be routed to configure M5 as a two-input AND gate.

(b) Show how M5 inputs can be routed to configure M5 as a three-input OR gate.

(c) Can M5 be configured as an inverter?

63. A set of four photodetectors looks at a square area ("retina") as shown below.

One instance of "vertical"

Figure P2.14

vvhen light strikes one of the lettered square areas, the detector (A–D) sends out a HI. On the right is shown one of two vertical patterns, in which areas B and D only are lit. Design a circuit that will respond only when a vertical pattern (AC or BD) is on the retina. Use a 3/5 majority gate in your design.

64. A plain majority gate cannot be used as an inverter. In the Motorola 14530 chip the output of a 3/5 majority gate is fed through an XNOR gate, which sees a sixth input. See Fig. P2.15. Show how to configure a 14530 gate as

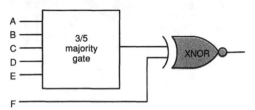

Figure P2.15   One-half of the Motorola 14530.

(a) A circuit that inverts input A
(b) A three-input NOR gate
(c) A three-input NAND gate
(d) What Boolean expression describes the circuit of Fig. P2.16?

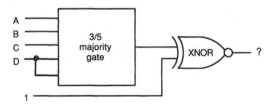

Figure P2.16

(e) There are two such circuits (a 3/5 majority gate with an XNOR) in one 14530 package. Can one 14530 package be used to create a 4/7 majority gate?

‡(f) Using four or fewer 14530 packages, design a circuit that responds when *exactly* two in a row of the inputs A, B, C, D, and E are simultaneously active.

65. Find an SOP realization for the following Reed-Muller four-input circuit (one that contains no inverters):

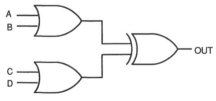

Figure P2.17

C	B	A	OUT
0	0	0	0
0	0	1	0
0	1	0	X
0	1	1	X
1	0	0	1
1	0	1	0
1	1	0	0
1	1	1	1

Design a NAND-only circuit to realize this truth table. What values become assigned to the don't-care lines in your realization?

67. Realize OUT $= A \cdot \overline{B} \cdot C \cdot \overline{D} \cdot E$ using only three-input NAND gates.

68. Suppose a minterm of a six-input truth table is $A \cdot B \cdot \overline{C} \cdot \overline{D} \cdot E \cdot \overline{F}$. Which of the following could be prime implicants of the minterm?

(a) $A \cdot B \cdot E \cdot \overline{F}$

(b) $\overline{A} \cdot B \cdot \overline{C}$

(c) $A \cdot B \cdot E \cdot \overline{F}$

(d) $A \cdot \overline{B} \cdot E \cdot F$

69. How is a prime implicant like a prime number?

70. Which of the conditions below are necessary and which sufficient for the roots of a quadratic equation $f(x) = Ax^2 + Bx + C$ to be real? Which of the conditions are *implied* if the roots of $f(x)$ are real?

(a) $A, B,$ and C are real.

(b) $A, B,$ and C are nonnegative.

(c) $B^2 > 4AC$.

(d) $A, B,$ and C are nonzero.

(e) A is nonzero.

71. What is a POS form for XOR?

72. A minterm is true for only one row of a truth table. The corresponding maxterm is false only for the same row. What maxterms correspond to the following minterms?

(a) $A \cdot \overline{B} \cdot C$

(b) $A \cdot B \cdot \overline{C} \cdot \overline{D}$

(c) $\overline{A} \cdot B \cdot C \cdot \overline{D} \cdot E$

73. A five-input truth table has an output column that is all 1s except for the following rows:

E	F	G	H	J	OUT
0	0	0	1	1	0
0	1	1	1	0	0
1	0	1	1	0	0

Design a POS circuit to implement the truth table. Show an all-NOR realization.

74. The following circuit is built with only two-input NAND gates. The inputs are
$A, B,$ and C.

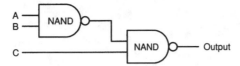

Figure P2.18

(a) Write out the truth table for the circuit.
(b) Redesign the circuit using only two-input NOR gates. Does your design
use a minimum number of NOR gates?
(c) Can this circuit be designed using only XOR gates?
(d) If each NAND gate has 10 ns of propagation delay, under what input
circumstance will OUT show a transient glitch?

75. Write OUT_i as a Boolean function of the four inputs for the two circuits in the
following figure. Note that bubbles on both ends of a connector cancel each
other out.

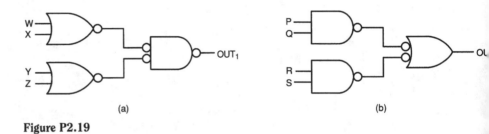

(a)   (b)

Figure P2.19

76. What single Boolean operation does the six-input circuit below carry out?

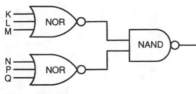

Figure P2.20

77. Consider the following Boolean expressions.

    (i) $(A + B) \cdot (C + \overline{D})$
    (ii) $A \cdot B + A \cdot \overline{D}$
    (iii) $E \oplus F + G \cdot H \cdot (J + K)$
    (iv) $A + 0 + C + (D \cdot 1 \cdot C)$

    (a) Realize the expressions with NAND gates only.
    (b) Realize the expressions with NOR gates only.

78. Redesign the following circuit

    (a) Using fewer two-input NAND gates, with less delay
    (b) Using only NOR gates of any input size

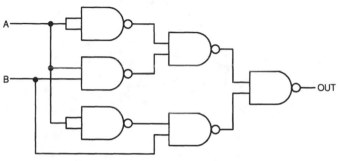

Figure P2.21

79. Make an effort to find the minimum number of gates needed to realize the following Boolean expression, regardless of total delay or gate fan-in:

$$(A \cdot \overline{B} + A \cdot B) \cdot C + (D \cdot E \cdot C) + (A \cdot B)$$

80. **Output timing** A circuit with an XOR is shown below. Assume that each gate in the circuit, including the inverter, has a 12-ns propagation delay t_{pd} from change in input J or K to change in OUT. Under what input circumstances will timing glitches appear at OUT? Could any change in design eliminate the glitch(es) and still realize the same truth table?

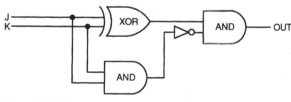

Figure P2.22

81. In asynchronous circuit design the generation of glitches can be a *design goal*, in which case the glitches are called pulses. Given a handful of gates all

with 10-ns propagation delays, can you think of a way to have a combinational circuit generate a 20-ns pulse in response to a rising edge on IN?

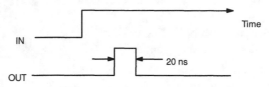

Figure P2.23   Desired output for Exercise 81.

82. Find and eliminate the timing hazard in the following POS circuit.

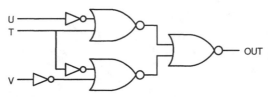

Figure P2.24

‡83. Let TEMP be the temperature of a room, and let there be two numbers θ_H and θ_L such that $\theta_H > \theta_L$. Suppose a temperature controller has three inputs: one input is HI when TEMP $> \theta_H$, another is HI when TEMP $< \theta_L$, and the third input is the on-off output of the temperature controller itself. Design a circuit that will turn on the heater when TEMP falls below θ_L, turn off the heater when TEMP rises above θ_H, and leave the heater either on or off when TEMP is between θ_H and θ_L, depending on what it was before TEMP entered the range between θ_H and θ_L.

Your design will realize **hysteresis** for the temperature controller, preventing the controller from "chattering" around a set point. For this problem you will need one other kind of subcircuit, an *analog comparator*. The analog comparator has two (nondigital) inputs IN_1 and IN_2 and one digital output that is HI when $IN_1 > IN_2$ and LO otherwise.

84. Say an auto-reverse tape deck has four buttons,

   PLAY
   STOP
   FORWARD
   REVERSE

and an internally generated end-of-tape signal. This tape deck is a player only; it does not record. The motor, which receives the output of the controller, has two directions, CW and CCW, and two speeds, NORMAL and FAST. See Fig. P2.25.

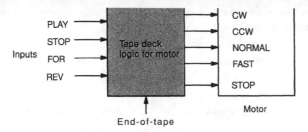

Figure P2.25 Tape controller problem.

Design a combinational circuit with minimal gate count for a tape-deck controller that meets the following specifications. Assume positive logic and that initially all input buttons are inactive, the tape is in the machine, and the tape is not at end-of-tape.

When PLAY is pressed, MOTOR goes CW at NORMAL speed.

When PLAY is active and end-of-tape goes HI, MOTOR reverses to CCW.

When FOR is pressed, MOTOR goes CW at FAST speed until end-of-tape goes HI, and then the motor stops.

When REV is pressed, MOTOR goes CCW at FAST speed until end-of-tape goes HI, and then the motor stops.

If PLAY is asserted during FOR or REV, PLAY has priority and the speed changes to NORMAL.

STOP has priority over the other buttons; when STOP is pressed, the motor stops.

‡85.   *Reverse engineering* is the process of taking apart something, often an integrated circuit, to see how it was put together, often with the intention to reproduce it at a lower cost. The art of reverse engineering an integrated circuit with diamond saws and electron microscopes is a sophisticated one, but in some cases it is worthwhile to desperate competitors. The following is a different approach to reverse engineering, in the form of *reversible logic*.

(a)   Given the output of a logic gate, under what conditions is it possible to know what the input was? Think of a logic circuit example where it is not possible to reconstruct the input, given the output.

Knowing the outputs of a *Fredkin gate* always enables a user to infer what the inputs were (Fredkin and Toffioli 1982). A Fredkin gate has three inputs and three outputs. C_{IN} passes through unchanged to become C_{OUT}. If C_{IN} is LO, then $A_{IN} \rightarrow A_{OUT}$ and $B_{IN} \rightarrow B_{OUT}$. If C_{IN} is HI, then A and B are interchanged; that is $A_{IN} \rightarrow B_{OUT}$.

(b)   Write out the truth table for a Fredkin gate.

(c)   Figure out Boolean expressions for C_{OUT}, A_{OUT}, and B_{OUT}.

(d)   Can you design an inverter with a Fredkin gate? Choose one input to be inverted and one output to be the inverted input.

(e)   Can you design a two-input AND gate with a Fredkin gate? One output will be the correct response to the two inputs, and the other two outputs to reconstruct the inputs.

Other schemes for reconstructing inputs will be seen in Chapter 9 when error-correcting codes are considered.

‡86. Think about a circuit for sorting the letters of the alphabet. The 26 letters of the alphabet need five bits minimum for coding. Let the two letters to be compared be positionally coded as numbers from 1 to 26, with A $= 1$ and Z $= 26$. Call the five individual bits $\beta_4\beta_3\beta_2\beta_1\beta_0$ and $\alpha_4\alpha_3\alpha_2\alpha_1\alpha_0$. The following circuit reports when bit β is "greater than" bit α.

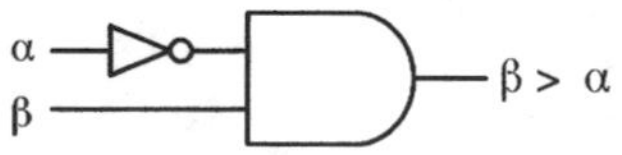

α ─▷○─┐
      ├─D── β > α
β ────┘

Figure P2.26

Let us follow the design for a two-bit cascade comparator. $\beta_1\beta_0$ and $\alpha_1\alpha_0$ are to be compared. Specifically,

$$\beta_1\beta_0 > \alpha_1\alpha_0 \text{ if } \beta_1 > \alpha_1 \text{ or if } \{\beta_1 = \alpha_1 \text{ and } \beta_0 > \alpha_0\}$$

Equality of β_1 and α_1 can be signaled by an XNOR gate,

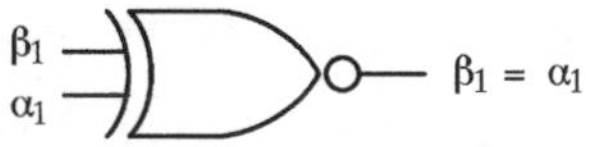

β_1 ─┐
)D○── $\beta_1 = \alpha_1$
α_1 ─┘

Figure P2.27

because $\text{XNOR}(\beta, \alpha) = \text{HI}$ only when $\beta = \alpha$. Therefore a two-bit greater-than circuit looks like the one in Fig. P2.28.

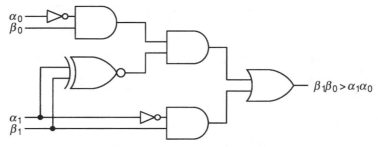

Figure P2.28 The statement $\beta_1 > \alpha_1$ or $\{\beta_1 = \alpha_1 \text{ and } \beta_0 > \alpha_0\}$ expressed in logic gates.

Now think about what would be needed to signal $\beta_2\beta_1\beta_0 > \alpha_2\alpha_1\alpha_0$. It is an extension of the circuit you see in Fig. P2.28. Express in logic gates

$$\beta_2 > \alpha_2 \text{ or } \{\beta_2 = \alpha_2 \text{ and } \{\beta_1 > \alpha_1 \text{ or } \{\beta_1 = \alpha_1 \text{ and } \beta_0 > \alpha_0\}\}\}$$

The part of the expression on the right has already been done. Keep going and design a modular serial network to find when $\beta_4\beta_3\beta_2\beta_1\beta_0 > \alpha_4\alpha_3\alpha_2\alpha_1\alpha_0$.

  (a) Think of five qualities not normally quantified, like *perseverance*, which would require fuzzy variables to represent their "magnitudes." Is color such a quality?

  (b) Consider the set of all of Picasso's paintings. Is the set of Picasso's paintings that contain some blue pigment a fuzzy subset?

  (c) Can you suggest a membership function for the fuzzy set of blue Picasso paintings?

  (d) Suppose $E(P)$ is the membership function for paintings in Picasso's early period. What is the membership function for paintings that are in the early period OR the blue period?

References

BOOLE, G. 1954. *An investigation of the rules of thought.* 1854. Reprint, New York: Dover.

COURANT, R., AND H. ROBBINS. 1947. *What is mathematics?* 4th ed. New York: Oxford University Press.

DERTOUZOS, M. 1965. *Threshold logic: A synthesis approach.* Cambridge, Mass.: MIT Press.

FLETCHER, W. I. 1980. *An engineering approach to digital design.* Englewood Cliffs, N.J.: Prentice Hall.

FREDKIN, E., AND T. TOFFIOLI. 1982. Conservative logic. *International Journal of Theoretical Physics* 21:219–253.

KANDEL, A., AND S. C. LEE. 1979. *Fuzzy switching and automata.* New York: Crane, Russak.

KOSKO, B. 1991. *Neural networks and fuzzy logic.* Englewood Cliffs, N.J.: Prentice Hall.

———. 1993. *Fuzzy thinking.* New York: Hyperion.

KOSKO, B., AND S. ISAKA. 1993. Fuzzy logic. *Scientific American,* July, 76–81.

TERANO, T., K. ASAI, AND M. SEGENO. 1992. *Fuzzy systems theory and its applications.* Boston: Academic.

ZADEH, L. A. 1965. Fuzzy sets. *Information and Control* 8: 338–353.

———. 1971. Toward a theory of fuzzy systems. In *Aspects of network and system theory,* edited by R. E. Kalman and N. DeClaris. New York: Holt, Rinehart & Winston.

ZIMMERMAN, H. J. 1985. *Fuzzy set theory and its applications.* Norwell, Mass.: Kluwer-Nijhoff.

Map and Table Methods for Minimizing Boolean Expressions

··

In Chapter 2 you learned how to design a sum-of-products (SOP) realization of any truth table, and you learned various Boolean algebra theorems that reduce the number of product terms in the realization. In Chapter 3 we press the issue of **minimizing** logic expressions from truth table output. We attack the problem first by graphic means. For $N \leq 6$, the 2^N lines of an N-input truth table can be rearranged as a graphic rectanguloid array of 2^N subsquares known as a **Karnaugh map (K-map).** With proper labeling of K-map subsquares, implicants (reduced products of inputs) will be easier to spot. Gathering the implicants as a sum will result (usually) in a smaller Boolean expression for output; in some cases it will be a **minimum cover,** or smallest set of **prime implicants** that can realize the given truth table with a sum of products.

The second approach, tabular reduction, will work for up to about $N = 16$ to 20 input truth tables (depending on the speed of the computer). The **Quine-McCluskey algorithm** starts with a column of all minterms associated with OUT = 1 from a truth table and combines in a second column various pairs of minterms that differ by only one bit. The **adjacency theorem** of Boolean algebra ($\mathcal{P} \cdot Q + \mathcal{P} \cdot \overline{Q} = \mathcal{P}$, where $\mathcal{P}$ is a product and Q is the differing bit) is used to combine minterms. Applying adjacency continues until a list of prime implicants is generated. The second part of the Q-M algorithm extracts from the set of prime implicants a minimum subset (cover), which contains the products to be summed for an SOP form. The first step in the minimum cover search is isolation of **essential prime implicants,** implicants that cannot be removed from any cover.

For large truth tables (inputs $N > 16$ or so), *heuristic* methods that require fewer comparison operations than the Quine-McCluskey algorithm are needed. Near the end of Chapter 3 we outline the **Espresso** method for finding minimum or near-minimum covers in much less computer time than the Q-M algorithm. Finally we compare the Espresso method to a bias-free **evolutionary algorithm,** Eve, as another method for minimizing the cover of a large truth table. Eve can be used to search for optimal forms other than sum of products.

When you finish Chapter 3, you will have a better appreciation of Boolean relationships hidden in truth tables, especially large truth tables. You will be able to exploit the adjacency relationship to find minimal and near-minimal hardware

program for finding near-optimal realizations of large truth tables, and you will understand a general-purpose evolutionary algorithm that competes well with Espresso in searching for optimal hardware solutions.

3.1 TRUTH TABLES COMPRESSED INTO TWO-DIMENSIONAL MAPS

3.1.1 Segue from Venn Diagrams to Maps

Venn diagrams are two-dimensional maps of overlapping sets that can demonstrate graphically the meanings of AND, OR, NOT, XOR, and so on. A Venn diagram has an outside border that defines the universe of possible inputs. The subset of the universe where a Boolean variable X is true is shown by a smaller boundary that encloses set X. Logic relationships can then be represented by overlapping boundaries of variables.[1]

EXAMPLE 1

Consider two sets A and B that overlap in their universe of possibilities as shown in Fig. 3.1. Inside area A variable A is true; inside area B variable B is true. Working with $\{A, B\}$ pairs, the diagram in the middle shows the universe divided into four regions marked by A, B minterms. For example, the minterm $\overline{A} \cdot \overline{B}$ marks the region in which NOT-A AND NOT-B is true. (How else could the $\overline{A} \cdot \overline{B}$ region be marked? Apply De Morgan's law to see $\overline{A} \cdot \overline{B} = \overline{A + B}$, the NOR operation.) On the far right in Fig. 3.1, the A and B shapes are changed to rectangles and the outside of the universe is labeled for two columns and rows.

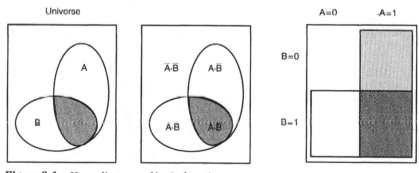

Figure 3.1   Venn diagram of logic functions.

---

[1]For example, a universe might be the containers found in a kitchen; variable A might be true for containers that hold solid foods, and variable B true for containers that hold liquid. Then a colander would be in set A, a juice box in set B, and a mixing bowl in set A *and* set B. Thus if a recipe calls for a container to hold something that changes from liquid to solid, such as beaten egg whites, an object in the *intersection* of sets A and B would produce a true output.

B	A	OUT
0	0	O_{00}
0	1	O_{01}
1	0	O_{10}
1	1	O_{11}

	0	1
B 0	O_{00}	O_{01}
1	O_{10}	O_{11}

Figure 3.2   Two-input K-map organization.

The Venn diagram for two variables suggests the following application to truth tables. Consider for now single-output truth tables, and start with a two-input truth table. In Fig. 3.2 the truth table outputs are labeled as O_{BA}, where B, A are minterm subscripts. In the box to the right, the truth table outputs are placed in squares where the values of the two inputs intersect. The truth table on the left and the two-dimensional map on the right contain the same information; nothing new is added by rearranging the way the inputs and outputs are listed.[2]

EXAMPLE 2

Let a two-input truth table have the outputs shown in Fig. 3.3. On the left, minterms associated with OUT = 1 are gathered in sums of products. The resulting expression is simplified by application of the Boolean adjacency theorem. In the map on the right, you can directly see the arrangement of outputs equal to 1 in a column with $A = 1$. The minimization can be solved by (visual) inspection.

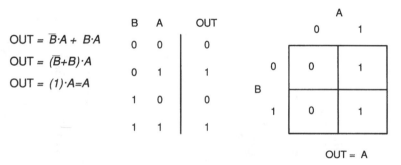

$$\text{OUT} = \overline{B}{\cdot}A + B{\cdot}A$$
$$\text{OUT} = (\overline{B}+B){\cdot}A$$
$$\text{OUT} = (1){\cdot}A = A$$

B	A	OUT
0	0	0
0	1	1
1	0	0
1	1	1

	A 0	1
B 0	0	1
1	0	1

OUT = A

Figure 3.3   Two-input function solved by algebra and a K-map.

The next example expands the map form to three variables. It is an orderly version of a Venn diagram with three overlapping sets.

---

[2]A trivial benefit of the map arrangement of a truth table is that fewer pen strokes are required to write it out. I have an Etch-A-Sketch with a four-by-four set of squares drawn in indelible ink to save writing down everything except the truth table output for a particular problem.

EXAMPLE 3

A car buzzer problem in Chapter 2 was worked into the form of a truth table, reproduced on the left in Fig. 3.4. The output is BUZZER. There are four 1s in the output, implying that a canonical SOP expression for BUZZER would have four minterms. On the right in the figure, the inputs label eight boxes in a large rectangle. The labeling is such that vertically or horizontally adjacent boxes differ by only one bit at a time. Inside each of the eight boxes is written the output corresponding to the input combination. An instance of BUZZER $= 1$ for input combination $KDB = 111$ is shown with an arrow connecting the truth table and the map.

KEY	DOOR	BRAKE	BUZZER
0	0	0	0
0	0	1	1
0	1	0	0
0	1	1	1
1	0	0	0
1	0	1	0
1	1	0	1
1	1	1	①

DOOR BRAKE

KEY	00	01	11	10
0	0	1	1	0
1	0	0	①	1

Figure 3.4 Three-input K-map for Example 3.

Our goal here is to find a simplified SOP expression for BUZZER from the 1s in the map. Look for connected groups of 1s that have inputs in common. We gather the output 1s that are horizontal or vertical neighbors until all the 1s have been covered. (*Covered* means that every 1 in the truth table output or map has been expressed as a sum of products.) In so doing, we will collect prime implicants (see Fig. 3.5). Circle P surrounds 1s that have prime implicant $\overline{K} \cdot B$ in common; that is, both of the squares inside circle P are associated with inputs $K = 0, B = 1$: $\overline{K} \cdot B \cdot (\overline{D} + D) = \overline{K} \cdot B$, an application of adjacency. Circle Q surrounds 1s that have prime implicant $K \cdot D$ in common; both input K and input D are 1 for the two squares inside Q. When we combine the two circles' input matches, we obtain

$$\text{BUZZER} = P + Q = \overline{K} \cdot B + K \cdot D$$

which is the same reduced formula we found after Boolean reduction (by law of consensus) of the original SOP problem.

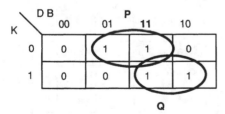

Figure 3.5 Gathering subcubes for three variables, $K, D,$ and B.

The previous examples illustrate Karnaugh maps, first worked out by Karnaugh (1953). A **Karnaugh map** (or K-map for short) is a rectanguloid set of connected squares; each square represents a minterm of an underlying truth table. Inside each square is written the output (either 0, 1, or X) of the truth table for the given minterm. A given square in the map differs by only one literal from each of its neighbors. For edge and corner squares, wrap-around is enforced to ensure that all squares on a two-dimensional map have four neighbors. (Only for four-input maps are all neighbors different.) To achieve the one-bit change per neighbor, the squares inside the map will be arranged as a larger rectangle of $2^P \times 2^Q$ sides, where P and Q are nonzero integers and $P + Q = N$, the number of inputs for the truth table. In Example 3 the K-map has $2^1 \times 2^2$ squares per side.

3.2.1 Labeling Inputs

Positional code won't work for labeling the minterm squares of a map. In the positional count 00, 01, 10, 11 there are two positional bits of change between 01 and 10. In Chapter 1 you were introduced to Gray code, which has the quality of changing one bit at a time that we want. A two-bit Gray code sequence is 00, 01, 11, 10, and we can apply that sequence to both sides of a four-input K-map, as shown in Fig. 3.6. The inputs are $DCBA$. Note that minterm $DCBA = 1111$ in Fig. 3.6 is not at the bottom right corner of the map. The neighbors of $DCBA = 0000$ are circled; two of the neighbors come from wrap-around. There is more than one way for labeling the inside squares to achieve a one-bit change per neighbor; the labeling method above—using Gray code—*defines* K-map labeling.

3.2.2 Veitch Diagram

Assign one variable to each side of the four-bit two-dimensional matrix, and alternate the labeling of the edges, as shown in Fig. 3.7. The result is a **Veitch diagram**. Since each square still differs from its horizontal or vertical neighbors by only one input

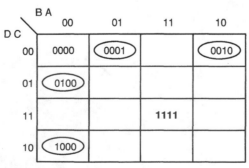

Figure 3.6   Labeling a four-variable K-map.

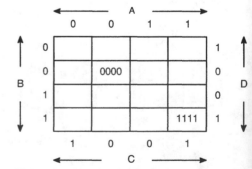

Figure 3.7   Veitch diagram labeling.

	Y	Y
$\overline{Z}$	$\overline{Y}\ \overline{Z}$	$Y\ \overline{Z}$
Z	$\overline{Y}\ Z$	$Y\ Z$

	$\overline{X}\ \overline{Y}$	$\overline{X}\ Y$	$X\ Y$	$X\ \overline{Y}$
$\overline{Z}$	$\overline{X}\ \overline{Y}\ \overline{Z}$	$\overline{X}\ Y\ \overline{Z}$	$X\ Y\ \overline{Z}$	$X\ \overline{Y}\ \overline{Z}$
Z	$\overline{X}\ \overline{Y}\ Z$	$\overline{X}\ Y\ Z$	$X\ Y\ Z$	$X\ \overline{Y}\ Z$

	$\overline{X}\ \overline{Y}$	$\overline{X}\ Y$	$X\ Y$	$X\ \overline{Y}$
$\overline{W}\ \overline{Z}$	$\overline{W}\ \overline{X}\ \overline{Y}\ Z$	$\overline{W}\ \overline{X}\ Y\ \overline{Z}$	$\overline{W}\ X\ Y\ \overline{Z}$	$\overline{W}\ X\ \overline{Y}\ \overline{Z}$
$\overline{W}\ Z$	$\overline{W}\ X\ \overline{Y}\ Z$	$\overline{W}\ \overline{X}\ Y\ Z$	$\overline{W}\ X\ Y\ Z$	$\overline{W}\ X\ Y\ Z$
$W\ Z$	$W\ \overline{X}\ \overline{Y}\ Z$	$W\ \overline{X}\ Y\ Z$	$W\ X\ Y\ Z$	$W\ X\ \overline{Y}\ Z$
$W\ \overline{Z}$	$W\ \overline{X}\ \overline{Y}\ \overline{Z}$	$W\ \overline{X}\ Y\ \overline{Z}$	$W\ X\ Y\ \overline{Z}$	$W\ X\ \overline{Y}\ \overline{Z}$

Figure 3.8 Labeling a K-map by minterms.

bit, the Veitch diagram works equally as well as the K-map. Notice on the map where the boxes for 0000 and 1111 appear, compared with their locations in a K-map. The K-map is more commonly used, since it can be scaled up to more than four inputs, so you should probably stick with it. A reference on Veitch diagrams is Blakeslee (1975, chap. 3).

3.2.3 Applying Adjacency

To underscore what the squares inside a K-map represent, the minterm literals are displayed in their associated boxes in Fig. 3.8. Shown are two-, three-, and four-bit K-maps, with the inputs as variables both outside and inside. The inputs are W, X, Y, and Z. The AND operation with the minterms is implicit. This rewrite enables us to connect K-maps with theorems of Boolean algebra for simplifying expressions.

EXAMPLE 4

Four minterms in the four-input map in Fig. 3.8 are circled. What simplified SOP would represent them if they were the 1s in the truth table output?

Answer The two minterms in the middle differ only by the W input. The two top corners differ only in the X input and illustrate the wrap-around feature of K-maps. Writing out the whole minterms for the two pairs of squares in the figure and applying the adjacency theorem:

$$\overline{W} \cdot Z \cdot X \cdot Y + W \cdot Z \cdot X \cdot Y = Z \cdot X \cdot Y \cdot (\overline{W} + W) = Z \cdot X \cdot Y \cdot 1 = Z \cdot X \cdot Y$$

for the two squares in the middle, and

$$\overline{W} \cdot \overline{Z} \cdot \overline{X} \cdot \overline{Y} + \overline{W} \cdot \overline{Z} \cdot X \cdot \overline{Y} = \overline{W} \cdot \overline{Z} \cdot \overline{Y}$$

for the two squares in the upper corners. Combine these two reduced expressions (prime implicants) together with an OR operation for the sum of products:

$$\text{OUT} = Z \cdot X \cdot Y + \overline{W} \cdot \overline{Z} \cdot \overline{Y}$$

EXAMPLE 5

Gather together four contiguous squares in a two-by-two shape, as shown in Fig. 3.9. The sum-of-products expression reduces to

$$\text{OUT} = W \cdot Z \cdot \overline{X} \cdot \overline{Y} + W \cdot \overline{Z} \cdot \overline{X} \cdot \overline{Y} + W \cdot Z \cdot \overline{X} \cdot Y + W \cdot \overline{Z} \cdot \overline{X} \cdot Y = W \cdot \overline{X}$$

by two applications of the adjacency theorem. Note that you can determine the simplified result by inspection: Look for what the four squares have in common as input (what cannot be eliminated by adjacency). Check along the edges and observe that W is common to all four of the circled boxes; $\overline{X}$ is common to all four also. Thus the product $W \cdot \overline{X}$ determines OUT.

	$\overline{X}\,\overline{Y}$	$\overline{X}\,Y$	$X\,Y$	$X\,\overline{Y}$
$\overline{W}\,\overline{Z}$	$\overline{W}\,\overline{X}\,\overline{Y}\,\overline{Z}$	$\overline{W}\,\overline{X}\,Y\,\overline{Z}$	$\overline{W}\,X\,Y\,\overline{Z}$	$\overline{W}\,X\,\overline{Y}\,\overline{Z}$
$\overline{W}\,Z$	$\overline{W}\,\overline{X}\,\overline{Y}\,Z$	$\overline{W}\,\overline{X}\,Y\,Z$	$\overline{W}\,X\,Y\,Z$	$\overline{W}\,X\,\overline{Y}\,Z$
$W\,Z$	$W\,\overline{X}\,\overline{Y}\,Z$	$W\,\overline{X}\,Y\,Z$	$W\,X\,Y\,Z$	$W\,X\,\overline{Y}\,Z$
$W\,\overline{Z}$	$W\,\overline{X}\,\overline{Y}\,\overline{Z}$	$W\,\overline{X}\,Y\,\overline{Z}$	$W\,X\,Y\,\overline{Z}$	$W\,X\,\overline{Y}\,\overline{Z}$

Figure 3.9 Gathering adjacent squares.

3.2.4 Subcubes and Prime Implicants

What shapes of 1s in K-maps can be gathered for compact expression? Squares and rectangles having $2, 4, \ldots, 2^N$ squares on a side work best for SOPs. Such groupings of 1s are called **subcubes.** In terms of subcubes, a **prime implicant (PI)** is a product term not contained in a larger subcube.

EXAMPLE 6

Find the PIs in the map of Fig. 3.10.

	$\overline{X}\,\overline{Y}$	$\overline{X}\,Y$	$X\,Y$	$X\,\overline{Y}$
$\overline{W}\,\overline{Z}$	1	1	1	1
$\overline{W}\,Z$	0	0	0	0
$W\,Z$	0	0	1	1
$W\,\overline{Z}$	0	0	1	1

Figure 3.10 Two subcubes of size 4 and their sum of products.

to $\overline{W} \cdot \overline{Z}$; the subcube of four 1s in the lower right can be reduced to $W \cdot X$. There is a third PI, $X \cdot \overline{Z}$, formed by wrap-around and not circled. As far as the circled PIs are concerned, the four squares in a row at the top of the map are all TRUE when and only when $\overline{W} \cdot \overline{Z}$ is TRUE, and the four squares at the bottom right corner are TRUE when and only when $W \cdot X$ is TRUE. If either condition is true, the output must be true, so the two AND expressions selected must be joined by an OR—as a sum of products—to cover all the 1s. So OUT $= \overline{W} \cdot \overline{Z} + W \cdot X$.

What about other edge-connected shapes of four 1s? Excluding two mirror images and various rotations, Fig. 3.11 shows all the connected shapes of four 1s in two dimensions. We know that the two subcubes on the left can be gathered into single ANDed PIs (see Fig. 3.12). The two shapes in the middle can be gathered in subcubes of two PIs, and the shape on the right requires three. All five shapes can be converted to smaller SOPs than a four-minterm canonical expression. Two terms can be eliminated from the canonical minterm expression of any rectangle or square shape of four boxes. For example, in a four-variable system a four-by-one shape can be reduced to a two-variable PI.

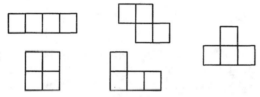

Figure 3.11 Groups of four connected minterms.

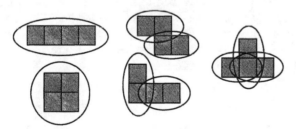

Figure 3.12 Gathering subcubes in groups of four adjacent minterms.

EXAMPLE 7

The shapes

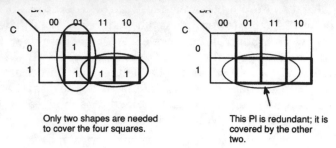

Only two shapes are needed
to cover the four squares.

This PI is redundant; it is
covered by the other
two.

Figure 3.13   Gathering subcubes from an L-shape.

can be used to prove the Boolean algebra law of consensus,

$$\overline{B} \cdot A + C \cdot A + C \cdot B = \overline{B} \cdot A + C \cdot B$$

Label a three-input K-map and place the corner L shape inside (Fig. 3.13). The expression $\overline{B} \cdot A + C \cdot B$ is covered. The L or S shapes could be placed at various other positions in a K-map matrix, to the same advantage, in proving the law of consensus and using the law to simplify SOPs.

3.2.5   Dealing with Wrap-Around

K-maps have the property that the edges wrap around: any subcube having sides on the edge of the map can be gathered with a matching subcube on the opposite side. A corner square can be gathered with two other sides. The extreme case of four corners is shown in Fig. 3.14 on a four-input map. The four corners are a subcube by wrap-around. In the four-corner map we assumed the particular case in which the empty boxes are all $0 = $ FALSE. If there were more 1s in the map, it might be possible to find larger subcubes and smaller resulting product terms. Note again the convention for writing out the unknowns: $DCBA$ means that D is the most significant input bit. OUT is the name of the entry in the K-map boxes. Other wrap-arounds are the left and right edges and the top and bottom edges.

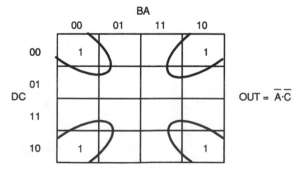

Figure 3.14   Wrap-around of four corners.

EXAMPLE 8

What SOP expression describes the four-input map in Fig. 3.15?

BA

DC \ BA	00	01	11	10
00	0	1	1	0
01	1	0	0	1
11	1	0	0	1
10	0	1	1	0

Figure 3.15 K-map to illustrate edge wrap-around.

Answer   The top and bottom edges wrap around, as do the two sides. So $\overline{C} \cdot A + C \cdot \overline{A}$ is a simplified SOP for the map. In fact we know $\overline{C} \cdot A + C \cdot \overline{A} = C \oplus A$, an even simpler expression.

3.2.6 Karnaugh Maps of XOR Functions

The preceding example motivates our interest in maps of XOR expressions. A thorough job of searching a K-map may produce a cover that minimizes an SOP expression, but there may be a simpler cover involving XOR operations. Figure 3.16 presents two patterns on three-input K-maps. The pattern on the right, resulting in $A \oplus B \oplus C$, is the SUM output of a one-bit full adder. An SOP expression would involve four four-input AND gates. K-maps are drawn to illuminate patterns among input and output, and if the pattern is zigzag, the relationship may be XOR or XNOR.

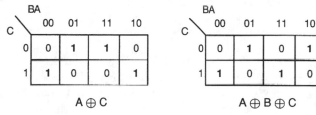

$$A \oplus C \qquad\qquad A \oplus B \oplus C$$

Figure 3.16 K-map of XORs.

EXAMPLE 9

Consider the map of 1s shown in Fig. 3.17, which would seem to require a cover of two three-input ANDs. Is there a simpler form?

Answer   Note that A and B have an XOR relationship on the line where $C = 1$, allowing the simplification shown on the right.

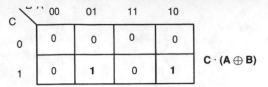

	00	01	11	10
0	0	0	0	0
1	0	1	0	1

$C \cdot (A \oplus B)$

Figure 3.17   K-map with buried XOR pattern.

EXAMPLE 10

Show the K-map for an even-parity check of four bits, and write out a Boolean expression for even parity.

Answer   Let the bits be W, X, Y, and Z. Even parity means that OUT is HI when there is an even number of 1s among W, X, Y, and Z. Zero (0000) counts as an even number. Figure 3.18 shows the K-map, and the expression $\text{OUT} = \text{XNOR}\{W, X, Y, Z\}$ is shown on the right.

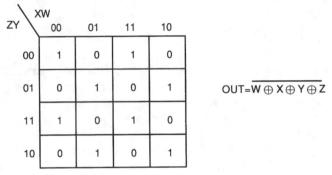

$$\text{OUT} = \overline{W \oplus X \oplus Y \oplus Z}$$

Figure 3.18   K-map for XNOR of four variables.

Unfortunately there are no simple ways to pick out XOR and XNOR patterns buried in K-maps, as there are for organizing square sum-of-product groups of prime implicants from K-maps. Nor can XOR functions easily be included in the systematic tabular reduction methods we will study later in Chapter 3. Nevertheless, for small-scale problems the zigzag patterns of XOR maps are worth keeping in mind as a possible means for expressing truth tables with a minimum of hardware.

3.3   GATHERING ZEROS

If a K-map presents only a few 0s in a field of 1s, you may gather 0s instead of 1s. There are two approaches to take: aim to cover the complement of OUT with an

SOP expression, or form reduced maxterms and generate a product-of-sums (POS) expression. Both approaches were developed for truth tables in Chapter 2, and you may want to review that material before studying the examples that follow.

EXAMPLE 11

Consider a square subcube of four 0s in a larger field of 1s, shown in Fig. 3.19. Form an SOP expression for $\overline{\text{OUT}}$.

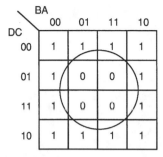

Figure 3.19 Gathering zeros.

Answer   The four input combinations associated with the 0 outputs have A and C in common. Since the output is zero for these four inputs, we can write

$$\overline{\text{OUT}} = A \cdot C$$

We can find what OUT is by complementing both sides of the expression and applying De Morgan's law.

$$\overline{\overline{\text{OUT}}} = \overline{(A \cdot C)} = \overline{A} + \overline{C} = \text{OUT}$$

Actually, gathering the 1s in this particular K-map isn't a difficult task if you notice that wrap-around results in a cover using only two groups of eight 1s. OUT $= \overline{A} + \overline{C}$, as computed above.

Now let us try a POS form by gathering the subcubes of zero. First we need to define the negative-logic version of a PI. Recall that one isolated 0 in a K-map is covered by a maxterm. As you learned in Chapter 2, to form a maxterm, you complement the literals of the corresponding minterm and replace AND with OR. In this case *cover* means that the output is reset to 0 when the input matches the literals in the maxterm. A minimum sum of literals that covers a subcube of zeros in a K-map is also called a **prime implicate**. Also recall from Chapter 2, in the same way a sum of products can be realized by a two-level NAND circuit, a product of sums can be realized by a two-level NOR circuit. The example that follows has two PIs.

EXAMPLE 12

Work the map of Fig. 3.20 into a simplified POS circuit.

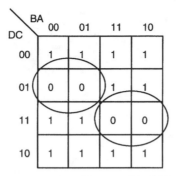

Figure 3.20 K-map with 4/16 zeros.

Answer The boxes circled on the left have the inputs $\overline{D}$, C, and $\overline{B}$ in common; their associated prime implicate is $D + \overline{C} + B$. In the circled boxes on the left, the literals that cannot be canceled by adjacency are D, C, and B; their associated prime implicate is $\overline{D} + \overline{C} + \overline{B}$. Therefore a POS that finds when OUT $= 0$ is

$$OUT = (D + \overline{C} + B) \cdot (\overline{D} + \overline{C} + \overline{B})$$

It is realized as an all-NOR circuit in Fig. 3.21.

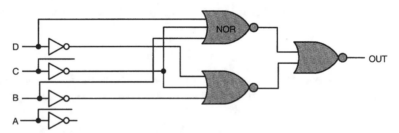

Figure 3.21 All-NOR realization.

The OUT expression does not depend on input A. By inspecting the map, can you see why? It turns out that an even simpler expression results if you notice the XNOR pattern buried in the map:

$$OUT = C \cdot (\overline{D \oplus B})$$

How can you tell whether a POS or an SOP realization will require less hardware? In many cases (Example 13 and Example 16) the number of literals is about the same. In general you may need to work out both versions for a problem to see any difference.

EXAMPLE 13

Consider the four-input, single-output truth table and the resulting K-map in Fig. 3.22. Which is a simpler realization, SOP or POS?

D	C	B	A	OUTPUT
0	0	0	0	0
0	0	0	1	0
0	0	1	0	0
0	0	1	1	0
0	1	0	0	0
0	1	0	1	1
0	1	1	0	1
0	1	1	1	1
1	0	0	0	0
1	0	0	1	1
1	0	1	0	1
1	0	1	1	1
1	1	0	0	0
1	1	0	1	1
1	1	1	0	1
1	1	1	1	1

DC \ BA	00	01	11	10
00	0	0	0	0
01	0	1	1	1
11	0	1	1	1
10	0	1	1	1

Figure 3.22 Four-input K-map with a three-by-three field of 1s.

DC \ BA	00	01	11	10
00	0	0	0	0
01	0	1	1	1
11	0	1	1	1
10	0	1	1	1

Figure 3.23 De Morgan's law applied to previous map.

Answer   First try gathering 0s, which can be formed into two subcubes of four 0s, as circled in Fig. 3.23. We form an SOP for $\overline{\text{OUT}}$:

$$\overline{\text{OUT}} = \overline{A} \cdot \overline{B} + \overline{C} \cdot \overline{D}$$

Taking its complement and applying De Morgan's law twice, we find the POS form:

$$\text{OUT} = (A + B) \cdot (C + D)$$

Using distributivity to expand this expression gives the SOP form:

$$\text{OUT} = A \cdot C + A \cdot D + B \cdot C + B \cdot D$$

The subcube for PI $A \cdot C$ is shown in bold in Fig. 3.23. For OUT, the POS form involves half as many literals. (Remember that a literal in a Boolean expression is any occurrence of a variable or its complement.) However, the (negative-logic) $\overline{\text{OUT}}$ version of the SOP is just as small as the POS.

EXAMPLE 14

Suppose the upper left-hand corner of a four-input K-map has the only 0 in a field of 1s. What is a simple Boolean expression for OUT? Assume that inputs are DCBA.

Answer   Gather the only 0 and write the complement of OUT as a minterm:

$$\overline{\text{OUT}} = \overline{D} \cdot \overline{C} \cdot \overline{B} \cdot \overline{A}$$

Complement both sides and apply De Morgan's law to obtain OUT:

$$\text{OUT} = D + C + B + A$$

The whole expression can be seen as one prime implicate or the sum of four PIs. In both cases the hardware to realize the truth table is the same (not counting inverters).

Some truth table lines have don't-care X's in their output columns. The set of min-terms associated with don't-care outputs is called the **dc set**.[3] The dc set can be used to advantage for minimizing the Boolean expression for OUT. First, transfer the don't-care X's directly to the K-map, and then, once you see where the X's land on the map, decide whether they can become 0s or 1s. The choice of what to declare the X's in order to minimize the Boolean expression for OUT may be easy or may involve more study. To begin with, decide whether you have a compelling reason to choose the product of sums or a form involving XOR; if not, use the sum of products. In any case a resulting expression will imply *some* choice for don't-cares: you cannot just ignore the don't-cares, because they'll end up being *something* in the final map.

One guideline: when you begin gathering subcubes for a Boolean expression, *make sure that no subcube is composed entirely of former don't-cares.* That doesn't mean all the don't-cares can't become the same value, but often don't-care choices should be tailored to complete subcubes started by members of the on-set or the off-set.

EXAMPLE 15

Suppose a truth table with four don't-cares is transformed into the K-map shown on the left in Fig. 3.24. Compare the resulting SOP expressions for OUT if all the X's become 0, 1, or the values shown on the right.

Answer   For all X's equal to 0, the simplest SOP is

$$OUT = D \cdot \overline{B} + D \cdot A + C \cdot \overline{B} + C \cdot A$$

For all X's equal to 1, the simplest SOP is

$$OUT = D + C + B \cdot \overline{A}$$

For the choice of X's shown on the right, the SOP simplifies to

$$OUT = D + C$$

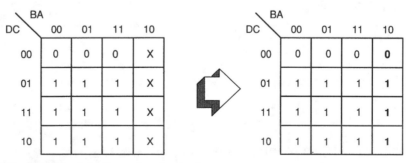

Figure 3.24   Selecting values for don't-cares.

[3]To express the other outputs in set terminology, call the set of minterms associated with OUT = 1 the *on-set* and the set of minterms associated with OUT = 0 the *off-set*.

The winner is the choice shown on the right. Neither of the subcubes for the SOP on the right is composed entirely of former X's.

Let us expand the guideline for choosing the status of don't-cares for a minimum SOP form: Declare an X to be a 1 if the X will complete or help complete a subcube of 1s *at least some of which are not other X's.* Conversely, declare an X to be a 0 if the X has no chance of completing a subcube of 1s *at least some of which are not other X's.* In the example above, the X in the top right corner of Fig. 3.24 cannot become part of an on-set subcube unless it's composed only of other X's, so the top right corner must be picked to be a 0. All the other X's can help form two-by-four on-set subcubes, so they are declared to be 1s. A couple of end-of-chapter exercises will help clarify these points. In a few cases you may see a chance to break the rules and draft don't-cares to bring forth valid XOR realizations for K-maps.

Whatever choices are made for output don't-cares, remember that after the choices are made, you must care what the values are! If something goes wrong with the resulting circuit, don't forget that a mistake may have been made either in thinking that a particular output could be a don't-care or in forcing a don't-care to become 0 or 1.

3.5 KARNAUGH MAPS FOR MORE THAN FOUR INPUTS

By using three-bit reflected Gray code along the top edge, we can generate a K-map for five bits as in Fig. 3.25. It's possible to gather across the reflection line; the subcube of 1s that crosses the line is product *VWY*. And wrap-around works to connect the far left and far right columns. But look at the column marked by the open stars on the left. Not only do the two columns on either side of it differ by one bit only, but so does the column marked by the solid stars on the right side! Now, with more than four bits, *flat* K-maps will have logically adjacent subcubes inside that do not border each other or wrap around. (See a six-variable K-map in Exercise 25.) If the five-bit map is cut along the reflection line and one half flipped under the other, logically adjacent columns can be brought in contact with each other.

	$\bar{X}\bar{Y}\bar{Z}$	$\bar{X}\bar{Y}Z$	$\bar{X}YZ$	$\bar{X}Y\bar{Z}$	$XY\bar{Z}$	XYZ	$X\bar{Y}Z$	$X\bar{Y}\bar{Z}$
$\bar{V}\bar{W}$		☆					★	
$\bar{V}W$		☆					★	
VW		☆	1	1	1	1	★	
$V\bar{W}$		☆					★	

Figure 3.25 Attempt at a five-input map.

EXAMPLE 16

How can the vertices of a wire frame be labeled for a 3D five-input K-map? Make sure each vertex is adjacent to all neighbors differing by only one bit.

Answer The vertices shown in Fig. 3.26 locate the 32 combinations. Now a vertex, not a square, must be labeled with truth table output. Not all the vertices are labeled—try to complete the job.

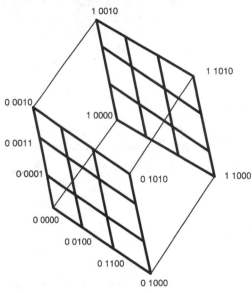

Figure 3.26 Three-dimensional map.

In a five-input 3D map every cube (vertex) has five adjacent neighbors (counting wrap-around); in a six-variable 3D map every cube (or vertex) has six adjacency neighbors. Exercises 25 and 26 help you visualize six-input K-maps.

Visualizing internal subcubes related by adjacency in maps for five or more inputs is challenging. In order to simplify truth tables with more than four inputs, we need a systematic method, one that can be applied directly to lists of minterms and PIs. Next we develop the Quine-McCluskey algorithms, a table reduction method that can be implemented as a computer program. As a practical matter, the Quine-McCluskey algorithms can find the minimum-size SOP realization for truth tables of up to 18 or so inputs on a Sparc 10 workstation within several hours.

3.6   THE QUINE-McCLUSKEY ALGORITHMS

3.6.1   Glossary of Terms Used in Describing Tabular Reduction

Most of the terms below have been defined before, but they are grouped together here so that we can review them and then illustrate them with an example before launching into a description of the Quine-McCluskey algorithms.

literal An explicit version of one variable, usually an input, in either its true or its false (complemented) form.

minterm An ANDed set of literals that include *all* input variables from a truth table. For N inputs there can be 2^N minterms. In what follows, *minterm* will be used to mean *minterm that results in TRUE output*.

on-set A shorthand term for the set of minterms associated with $OUT = 1$ (ON).

product The AND of a set of variables, whether a minterm or a subset of all input variables.

sum-of-products (SOP) The ORing of all products that lead to all the 1s in a truth table output column. If only minterms are summed, it is a **canonical SOP**.

cover Any expression, particularly an SOP, that accounts for the 1s in a truth table output. *Cover* usually suggests that *all* the 1s in a truth table are accounted for, but it can refer to a subset of the 1s (see *subcube*). In general there are many ways to cover a particular truth table.

minimum cover The cover of a particular truth table that uses the fewest literals in its Boolean expression.

adjacency theorem $X\mathcal{P} + \overline{X}\mathcal{P} = \mathcal{P}$, where $\mathcal{P}$ is any Boolean expression and X and $\overline{X}$ are the two literal forms of a Boolean variable. The expressions $X \cdot \mathcal{P}$ and $\overline{X} \cdot \mathcal{P}$ are *adjacent* in a K-map.

don't-care (dc) input A common input in a pair of implicants combined by adjacency.

imply If A implies B, then whenever A is true, B is true. It will not be the case that whenever B is true A is true, unless $A = B$.

implicant Any product, including minterms, that covers part or all of a truth table's true outputs. If an implicant is not a minterm, some 2^N minterms imply the implicant.

subcube The region of a map or the parts of a truth table covered by an implicant. A subcube can be as small as one minterm.

prime implicant (PI) An implicant that does not imply any other implicants in a cover of a truth table.

essential prime implicant (EPI) A PI that *must* be included in any cover of a given truth table.

cyclic cover A cover of a truth table or map that has no essential PIs; as a result, a cover will have overlapping PIs that form a closed loop (cycle) on the map.

necessary prime implicant Given a *particular* cover for a truth table or map, no necessary PI can be removed. All PIs in a noncyclic minimum cover are necessary.

EXAMPLE 17

Cyclic Covers A four-input, single-output truth table results in the K-map in Fig. 3.27. Each square in the map represents a minterm. There are several subcubes, including the four 1s circled in the upper left-hand corner. The subcube in the upper left-hand corner is described by the PI $\overline{D} \cdot \overline{B}$. Other implicants, such as $\overline{D} \cdot C \cdot \overline{B}$, and

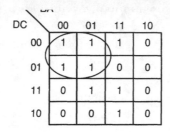 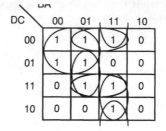

Figure 3.27 Cyclic cover of a K-map.

the minterm $\overline{D} \cdot \overline{C} \cdot \overline{B} \cdot \overline{A}$ imply $\overline{D} \cdot \overline{B}$. There are three literals in the product $\overline{D} \cdot C \cdot \overline{B}$. The adjacency theorem can generate the reduction of two implicants to a PI:

$$\overline{D} \cdot C \cdot \overline{B} + \overline{D} \cdot \overline{C} \cdot \overline{B} = \overline{D} \cdot \overline{B}$$

$\overline{D} \cdot \overline{B}$ could be described by $DCBA = 0X0X$, where the X's represent don't-cares for C and A.

The canonical SOP for the truth table is

$$\text{OUT} = \overline{D} \cdot \overline{C} \cdot \overline{B} \cdot \overline{A} + \overline{D} \cdot \overline{C} \cdot \overline{B} \cdot A + \overline{D} \cdot \overline{C} \cdot B \cdot A + \overline{D} \cdot C \cdot \overline{B} \cdot \overline{A}$$
$$+ \overline{D} \cdot C \cdot \overline{B} \cdot A + D \cdot C \cdot \overline{B} \cdot A + D \cdot C \cdot B \cdot A + D \cdot \overline{C} \cdot B \cdot A$$

One example of a cover is shown at the right in Fig. 3.27. It is a cyclic cover with six PIs. The only essential PI in the cover is $\overline{D} \cdot \overline{B}$; any one of the other PIs shown in the cover can be left out and all 1s will still be accounted for. Shown in Fig. 3.28 on the left is a cover with four PIs. All of the PIs in the cover on the left are necessary. The SOP for the cover on the left is

$$\text{OUT} = \overline{D} \cdot \overline{B} + C \cdot \overline{B} \cdot A + D \cdot B \cdot A + \overline{D} \cdot \overline{C} \cdot A$$

which has 21 fewer literals than the canonical SOP. A minimum cover of three PIs for the map on the left is $\text{OUT} = \overline{D} \cdot \overline{B} + \overline{C} \cdot B \cdot A + D \cdot C \cdot B$. On the right in Fig. 3.28 is a map with two fewer 1s in it, covered by a cycle with six PIs, none of which is essential; any one of the PIs on the right could be removed from the cover without exposing 1s. The cover is *not* minimum.

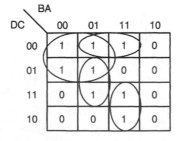 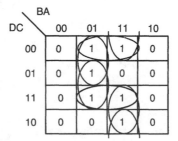

Figure 3.28 K-map covers for Example 17.

McCluskey (1956), find a minimum SOP cover as follows. First they apply adjacency over and over to pairs of minterms, producing a list of PIs. Next the PI list is searched for a minimum cover to the 1s of the underlying truth table. *For now, we restrict our examination of the Quine-McCluskey algorithms to SOP solutions of single-output truth tables with no don't-cares.*

3.6.2 Grouping Minterms and Applying the Adjacency Theorem

To apply the adjacency theorem, the first Quine-McCluskey algorithm needs to find minterms (associated with TRUE outputs) that differ by exactly one matching term. It does that by starting with a list of minterms and comparing pairs. Let's work through a five-variable example with six minterms associated with OUT=1. List the six minterms according to how many literals are TRUE in each. Then match each minterm with others that differ by exactly one TRUE bit, and use adjacency to combine possible matches into implicants. Adjacency will work on those minterm pairs for which the one TRUE difference *is in the same variable position*. Repeat the process until no more matching combinations are possible; you now have a second column of implicants to work with. If any minterms were left behind in the first pass, they are PIs.

EXAMPLE 18

Of the $2^5 = 32$ possible combinations of inputs for this five-input truth table, only the following six minterms cause OUT $= 1$:

E	D	C	B	A
0	0	1	0	0
0	1	1	0	0
0	0	1	0	1
0	1	1	0	1
1	1	1	0	1
1	0	1	0	1

Since the adjacency theorem works on input combinations that differ by one bit, regroup these minterms according to how many 1s there are in each expression:

E	D	C	B	A	Number of 1s
0	0	1	0	0	1
0	1	1	0	0	2
0	0	1	0	1	2
0	1	1	0	1	3
1	0	1	0	1	3
1	1	1	0	1	4

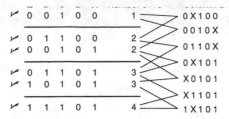

Figure 3.29 Q-M reduction table by application of adjacency.

Now compare each pair of minterms that differ by a 1 bit. If the differing bit is in the same variable position in both members of the pair, combine them by the adjacency theorem and enter the resulting implicant in a second column of the table. For example, the first two minterms differ in the D position only, so

$$\overline{E}\cdot\overline{D}\cdot C\cdot\overline{B}\cdot\overline{A} + \overline{E}\cdot D\cdot C\cdot\overline{B}\cdot\overline{A} = \overline{E}\cdot C\cdot\overline{B}\cdot\overline{A}$$

You can write 0X100 to denote that the D term is now a don't-care input. As soon as one of the original minterms finds a mate in an adjacency summation, put check marks by the two originals.

For the six minterms listed above, we can find the adjacency couples shown in Fig. 3.29. A total of seven matches were found. The first entry in the second column is the 0X100 term we found by adjacency above. One pair of minterms that differ by one 1 and do not match by adjacency is **01100** and **10101**, which has three mismatches. A check mark has been placed next to each minterm that has been combined by adjacency. In this case all of the minterms are checked off; if a minterm had not been combined by adjacency, it would have become a PI. Note that each of the minterms has participated in more than one adjacency reduction and that none of the implicants in the second column is a duplicate.

Next inspect the implicants in the second column, pair by pair, and try to apply the adjacency theorem again. In this second-column comparison, don't-care positions have to match, as well as all but one of the 0 and 1 terms. As shown in Fig. 3.30, four matches are found, resulting in two *different* third-column expressions. All of the seven second-column expressions are checked off, meaning that none of them survived to become PIs. The two remaining implicants in the third column cannot

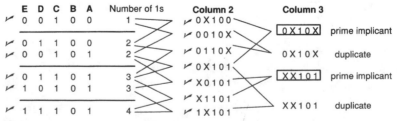

Figure 3.30 Third column of first Q-M algorithm.

be merged by adjacency because they mismatch in two positions. Therefore the two implicants in the third column are prime. No check marks are placed next to them.

In this example the remaining third-column PIs are essential PIs; they are necessary and sufficient to cover all the minterms of the original truth table. Normally more work (the second Quine-McCluskey algorithm) would be needed to verify a minimum cover. But here the minimum SOP cover for the original six minterms is $OUT = \overline{E} \cdot C \cdot \overline{B} + C \cdot \overline{B} \cdot A$, which has six literals.

It turns out that OUT can be realized by the expression $C \cdot \overline{B} \cdot (\overline{E} + A)$, which has only four literals. But $C \cdot \overline{B} \cdot (\overline{E} + A)$ requires three levels of logic, not the two levels of SOP. The basic Quine-McCluskey algorithm will find a minimum SOP cover, but not necessarily the minimum multilevel cover. Exercise 37 asks you to find the SOP result by writing out three-dimensional K-maps for the six minterms and gathering 1s.

At this point let's recall from Chapter 2 a compact notation for labeling minterms. Listed in Fig. 3.31 are the 32 combinations of five binary inputs that represent all

E D C B A	Decimal Equivalent
0 0 0 0 0	0
0 0 0 0 1	1
0 0 0 1 0	2
0 0 0 1 1	3
0 0 1 0 0	4
0 0 1 0 1	5
0 0 1 1 0	6
0 0 1 1 1	7
0 1 0 0 0	8
0 1 0 0 1	9
0 1 0 1 0	10
0 1 0 1 1	11
0 1 1 0 0	12
0 1 1 0 1	13
0 1 1 1 0	14
0 1 1 1 1	15
- - - - -	- -
1 0 0 0 0	16
1 0 0 0 1	17
1 0 0 1 0	18
1 0 0 1 1	19
1 0 1 0 0	20
1 0 1 0 1	21
1 0 1 1 0	22
1 0 1 1 1	23
1 1 0 0 0	24
1 1 0 0 1	25
1 1 0 1 0	26
1 1 0 1 1	27
1 1 1 0 0	28
1 1 1 0 1	29
1 1 1 1 0	30
1 1 1 1 1	31

BA

DC	00	01	11	10
00	0	1	3	2
01	4	5	7	6
11	12	13	15	14
10	8	9	11	10

E = 0

BA

DC	00	01	11	10
00	16	17	19	18
01	20	21	23	22
11	28	29	31	30
10	24	25	27	26

E = 1

Figure 3.31 Five-input truth table lines labeled by decimal numbers.

minterms, and next to them are decimal digits from binary positional code conversion (see Chapter 1). To the right are the four-variable K-maps for $E = 0$ and $E = 1$ with the decimal numbers of the minterms listed inside. Where convenient, minterms will be referred to by their decimal labels instead of their binary numbers. The minterms of Example 18 could be expressed in compact form by $\{m_4, m_5, m_{12}, m_{13}, m_{21}, m_{29}\}$ and the output could be

$$OUT = \sum \{m_4, m_5, m_{12}, m_{13}, m_{21}, m_{29}\}$$

With help from the decimal notation, here is another example of applying the adjacency theorem to minterm consolidation.

EXAMPLE 19

What is an SOP cover for OUT described by the following minterms?

$$OUT = \sum \{m_8, m_9, m_{12}, m_{13}, m_{18}, m_{21}, m_{23}\}$$

Answer Using the decimal-to-binary chart in Fig. 3.31, write out the binary versions of the seven minterms, grouped by how many 1s are in each minterm. Then use adjacency to combine as many of the minterms as possible. The implicants that cannot be combined are prime. The adjacency combinations in Fig. 3.32 result in three PIs, which are indicated by boxes. The two on the right are duplicates. Collecting PIs in an SOP form reveals that

$$OUT = E \cdot \overline{D} \cdot \overline{C} \cdot B \cdot \overline{A} + E \cdot \overline{D} \cdot C \cdot A + \overline{E} \cdot D \cdot \overline{B}$$

which we have not verified as a minimum cover. If you circle the decimal labels of the seven minterms for this problem on the K-maps in Fig. 3.30, you will see the PIs as subcubes on the maps.

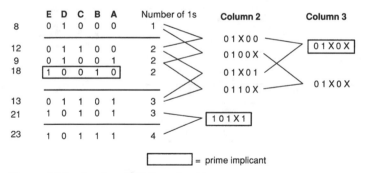

Figure 3.32 Another Q-M first algorithm.

We now collect our experience finding PIs and list the steps in the first Quine–McCluskey algorithm. We have listed the steps of the prime implicant search as if a human were writing down the solution; in fact the first Q-M algorithm is most sensibly expressed as computer code.

Quine-McCluskey Prime Implicant Search Algorithm

1. Expand decimal minterms to their binary form, and group them in a column on the left according to how many true literals (1s) each has.

2. Find all pairs of minterms in the right-most column that differ by one literal, and use adjacency to reduce those pairs that match the position of their differing literal.

3. Place all reduced implicants in a new column to the right. Eliminate duplicates.

4. If, after a search through all pairs that differ by one literal, any minterms have not participated in an adjacency combination, they become PIs.

5. For implicants in the second (right) column, search for pairs that differ by one literal *and* have don't-cares in the same position. Combine those implicants by adjacency, and put the new implicants in a new column to the right. Eliminate duplicates.

6. Label as prime any implicants that did not participate in adjacency in the current column being searched.

7. Continue looping between steps 5 and 6, creating new columns to the right, until no more reductions can be made. The implicants remaining in the final column and all others labeled prime are the set of PIs.

.6.3 A Computational Limit

The second Quine-McCluskey algorithm takes the PI list from the first algorithm as input and finds a minimum cover. Before going over the second algorithm, let us note a practical limitation on the first algorithm. A truth table with N inputs has 2^N minterms. For $N = 20$, $2^N \approx 10^6 = M$. The number of different pairs of M things is

$$\binom{M}{2} = \frac{M!}{(M-2)! \cdot 2} \approx M^2$$

If $M = 10^6$, the number of pairs is of the order of 10^{12}. Now a 22-input truth table will not have 2^{22} minterms associated with OUT = 1, but it might have 2^{21}. Not all of those minterms will differ from each other by one literal; maybe 10% (of 2^{20}) will. The first column of a Q-M search for the implicants of a 22-input truth table may then require on the order of 10^{21} pairwise comparisons, and even for a high-speed computer that is a lot of comparisons! Even if the computer could check one pair per microsecond, it might still take 10^6 seconds to do all the *first column* comparing; 10^6 seconds is a good fraction of a year ($\approx \pi \times 10^7 s$). The message here is that the number of comparisons required by the first Q-M algorithm goes up by something like 3^N for an N-input truth table, and at around $N = 20$ inputs the first Q-M algorithm becomes too much for a standard engineering workstation.

Examples 18 and 19 illustrated the first algorithm of the Q-M method. Repeated application of the adjacency theorem will result in a set of PIs. Simply ORing together the PIs will generate a valid cover to a truth table, and likely a much smaller solution than the canonical SOP. But it is unlikely to be a minimum cover. The second Q-M algorithm finds a subset of the PIs that completely covers the underlying truth table, and it does so at a guaranteed minimum cost. The following discussion will first describe loosely the second algorithm, then motivate its development with an example, and then spell out the algorithm step by step.

Start with a matrix whose columns are labeled by minterms and whose rows are labeled by PIs. Marks will be placed in the matrix where a PI includes a minterm. A search for a subset of covering PIs will require a row-by-row inspection of the matrix until all minterms have been accounted for. The order of the row search will take account of a PI's cost and thus will find an optimal SOP solution. Here is a five-input example that includes 10 minterms in order to generate a couple of unnecessary PIs.

EXAMPLE 20

Given a five-input truth table with OUT represented by the 10-minterm SOP

$$OUT = \sum \{m_4, m_5, m_6, m_7, m_{12}, m_{22}, m_{28}, m_{29}, m_{30}, m_{31}\}$$

what is a minimum sum-of-products expression that covers the minterms?

Use the first algorithm to find a set of PIs. Fig. 3.33 shows a chart of the first Q-M algorithm in action. A total of six PIs turn up. An SOP of the PIs is

$$OUT = \overline{E} \cdot C \cdot \overline{B} \cdot \overline{A} + \overline{D} \cdot C \cdot B \cdot \overline{A} + D \cdot C \cdot \overline{B} \cdot \overline{A} + E \cdot C \cdot B \cdot \overline{A} + E \cdot \overline{C} \cdot B + E \cdot C \cdot B$$

a total of 24 literals at the AND gate level.

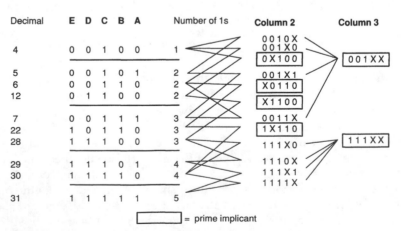

Figure 3.33   Reduction of minterms to PIs by first Q-M algorithm.

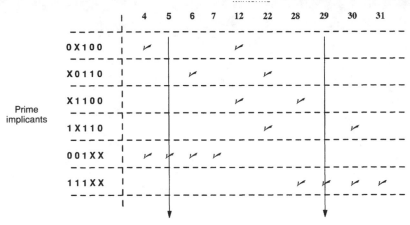

Figure 3.34 Finding a minimum cover among PIs: start of second Q-M algorithm.

Now we want a systematic method for finding a smaller (the smallest, in fact) cover. Let the PIs found from the first algorithm label the rows of a matrix, and the original minterms label the columns. Place check marks in the matrix where a minterm is involved with a PI. Such a matrix is called a **PI table.** The goal is to find a minimum set of PIs that covers the listed minterm columns. First look for obvious essential PIs—find any minterms covered by only one PI. In the matrix in Fig. 3.34, we see that minterms 5 and 29 are covered only by the last two PIs listed, and vertical arrows have been drawn through the minterms to highlight this fact.

Next (Fig. 3.35), horizontal arrows are drawn across the last two PI rows to indicate that they are essential and must be included in any covering. The minterms that are checked by the two essential PI rows are circled in the list at the top to remove them from further consideration about cover.

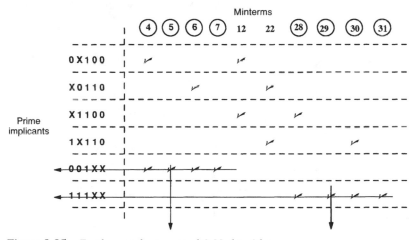

Figure 3.35 Further work on second Q-M algorithm.

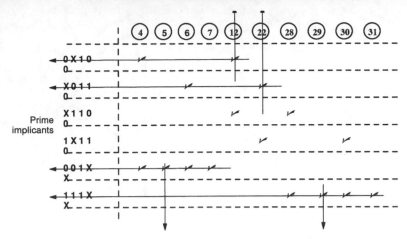

Figure 3.36 Selecting more PIs for a minimum cover.

At this point two minterms (12 and 22) are left uncovered. None of the remaining PIs is essential to cover m_{12} or m_{22}, so you have a choice as to which PIs to include in the cover. The four remaining PIs all have the same cost; four-input AND gates would be required to form the implied product terms. (The first two PIs included had lower costs: three-input AND gates.) Without further cost considerations the next choice of PI is arbitrary. Let us pick 0X100. That PI covers minterm 12, so two choices are left for a cover of minterm 22. Pick the next PI in the list, X0110. In the matrix of Fig. 3.36, our final two picks are shown with horizontal arrows knocking them out of the list of unused PIs. Selected vertical arrows are shown connecting minterm check marks with the horizontal arrows of the PIs included in the cover.

Our work with the PI table has produced a minimum cover that excludes two of the original PIs (those not lined out). A Boolean expression for this minimum cover is

$$\text{OUT} = \overline{E} \cdot C \cdot \overline{B} \cdot \overline{A} + \overline{D} \cdot C \cdot B \cdot \overline{A} + \overline{E} \cdot \overline{D} \cdot C + E \cdot D \cdot C$$

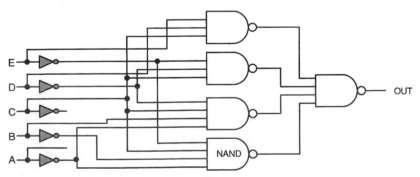

Figure 3.37 All-NAND realization of minimum-cover problem.

which has 14 literals and the all-NAND SOP realization shown in Fig. 3.37. Note that C is a literal in each product. A three-level expression using fewer literals is

$$\text{OUT} = C \cdot (E \cdot D + \bar{E} \cdot \bar{D} + \bar{D} \cdot B \cdot \bar{A} + \bar{E} \cdot \bar{B} \cdot \bar{A})$$

Given a set of minterms and a set of PIs for the minterms discovered through application of the first Q-M algorithm, we use the example above as an inspiration for listing the steps of a second algorithm to find a minimum cover of PIs for the minterms, as follows.

Second Quine-McCluskey Algorithm to Find Minimum Cover

1. Use the PIs discovered by the first Q-M algorithm to label the rows of a matrix. The columns of the matrix will be labeled by the minterms that were the inputs to the first algorithm.

2. Look for essential PIs. Some of them may be responsible for sole coverage of minterms labeling columns. Place all essential PIs in the minimum cover.

3. For each essential PI found, eliminate from consideration all minterms covered by it.

4. Select a minterm not covered by any essential PI. It will be covered by more than one of the remaining PIs.

5. Choose the lowest cost PI to include in the minimum cover.

6. Eliminate from consideration all other minterms covered by the chosen PI.

7. Continue looping around steps 4–6 until no more minterms are un-covered. The essential PIs and PIs placed in the cover are a minimum set.

This explanation of the second algorithm has not *proved* the resulting cover in minimum, nor have we discussed all the subtleties of finding essential PIs or picking nonessential PIs to complete the minimum cover. See Hill and Peterson (1993, chap. 6) for more detail.

In order to showcase the second algorithm apart from the effort to find PIs with the first algorithm, the following example is presented.

EXAMPLE 21

The goal is to select the minimum number of certain words that contain all the letters in a list. See Fig. 3.38. The letters are listed at the tops of the columns, and the words are listed to the left of the rows. Check marks show which letters are in which words. For example, q is covered only by the word *quakes*, so *quakes* is an essential word (EW). The other essential word is *pronto* for the letter p. Both EWs have boxes around them. Lines have been drawn through the rows containing *quakes* and *pronto*, and the columns having intersected check marks have their associated letters circled

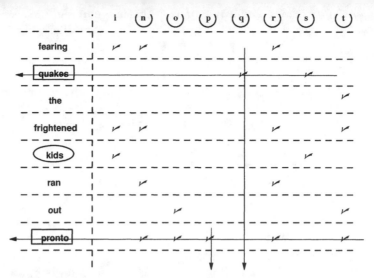

Figure 3.38 Application of second Q-M algorithm.

at the top. At this point all that remains is to cover the letter *i*. Three words contain letter *i*. The shortest of the three is *kids*, so including *kids* with *quakes* and *pronto* completes a minimum cover of the letters given.

The second Quine-McCluskey algorithm does not present as much computational burden as the first algorithm. If the PIs for a set of minterms are discovered, the second algorithm can usually find a minimum cover in reasonable time for truth tables of even 20 to 25 inputs. This fact gives the second algorithm more general use in other programs (such as *Espresso*, below) for circuit minimization.

Your use of the Q-M algorithms will almost certainly not involve the hand-checking of small examples used to explain the algorithms here. The Q-M algorithms for real problems are always implemented as computer code; the Q-M algorithms are used in the Macintosh program McBoole, for example.

Our review of Q-M tabular minimization has not considered optimization of multiple-output systems, nor have we dealt with tables containing don't-cares. A general-purpose Q-M program can handle both situations. The range of capability of the Q-M method matches up well with programmed logic devices to be discussed in Chapter 4. Programmed logic devices with more than 16 or so inputs are rare.

3.7 OVERVIEW OF THE ESPRESSO METHOD FOR HANDLING LARGE TRUTH TABLES

Techniques have been developed for finding nearly optimal realizations of large truth tables while avoiding the "combinatorial explosion" that the the Q-M method encounters in its pursuit of a true optimum. The best known of these approaches

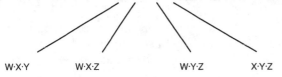

$W \cdot X \cdot Y$ $W \cdot X \cdot Z$ $W \cdot Y \cdot Z$ $X \cdot Y \cdot Z$

Figure 3.39 Expanding a minterm.

is *Espresso*, which we review below. Espresso was developed at the University of California at Berkeley and at IBM in the 1980s.

As you may appreciate from the discussion of the first Q-M algorithm, Espresso's main challenge is finessing the problem of finding a complete set of PIs. If Espresso is given a non-minimal Boolean expression F to start with, it will put the expression in SOP form and expand it out to other possible implicants. See the branching example in Fig. 3.39. Suppose $W \cdot X \cdot Y \cdot Z$ is in the Boolean expression given to Espresso. It will test each of the implicants for a match to function F. Basically, those that match will be expanded by implication again; those that do not match will be discarded. Duplicates will also be discarded. By expanding all products it is given, Espresso will come up with a set of PIs much faster than the pairwise testing of minterms that starts the first Q-M algorithm. Unfortunately there is no guarantee that the Espresso set of PIs will be *complete*.

With its incomplete set of PIs, Espresso next tries to find a cover for F. The cover so found will probably be nonminimal. Espresso can use something like the second Q-M algorithm for finding a cover. Espresso deviates from the Q-M method by application of various heuristics (reasonable rules) needed to deal with a possibly incomplete set of PIs.

Next Espresso tries pulling PIs out of the cover it has generated. This is the so-called reduction phase, and it reverses some of the generalizing expansion Espresso created in the beginning. Reduction goes from implicants back to cubes. Espresso evaluates the reduced cover, giving it a cost in terms of literals and other factors. For a large truth table the reduction is likely to result in a different set of products than Espresso started with.

With a revised set of products, Espresso then goes back to the expansion phase. See Fig. 3.40. The process cycles around the loop shown until the cost function stops

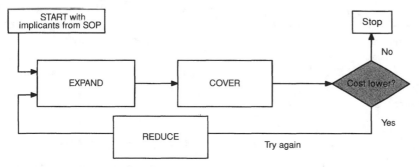

Figure 3.40 Espresso flowchart.

returning a lower value. At that point Espresso has found an optimal or nearly optimal SOP expression.

This overview of Espresso has failed to treat many subtleties, such as partitioning the PI set. Nor have various efficiencies been explained, such as the way input is represented as multi-valued variables. Typical results, shown in Rudell and Sangiovanni-Vincentelli (1987), are that Espresso can come within 1% of the cost of exact solutions to tough cyclic constraint problems, with only 6% of the execution time needed for an exact solution. See the following references as well: Biswas (1993, chap. 4), Brayton et al. (1984), De Micheli (1994, chap. 7), Hill and Peterson (1993, 144–152), and Katz (1994, 89–91).

Espresso finds practical usefulness minimizing SOP expressions of many-output truth tables (in which several outputs share the same inputs). Often the needed expressions must be reduced to fit in commercial programmable logic devices. Programmable logic devices and their role in realizing truth tables will be discussed in Chapter 4.

‡3.8 EVOLUTIONARY ALGORITHM FOR MINIMUM COVER SEARCH

Any algorithm, such as Espresso, that tries to hasten a search for a global optimal solution runs the risk that its efficiencies for speed-up will bias the search toward a local optimum.[4] There is, however, one optimizing method that deliberately introduces almost no bias, possibly at a cost in its speed of finding a solution. An **evolutionary algorithm** borrows ideas from the evolution of species in searching a space for an optimal answer. In contrast to the Q-M and Espresso methods, with their arcane features and their subtleties and nuances, an evolutionary algorithm is the essence of simplicity. Here's how it works: Have the computer make many random guesses as to what a minimum cover might be. Evaluate each guess using a cost function. Select only those guesses with low costs, and have the low-cost guesses become the parents of the next generation. "Mutate" each parent several times to fill out the next generation. Evaluate the parents and the children of the new generation and again select "survivors." Continue mutating survivors and creating new generations until the costs of the best survivors stop decreasing.

It may seem incredible that little more than random guessing about the best answer could result a good solution, yet that's what happens in evolutionary algorithms (and in real evolution!). The secret in both cases is a "survival of the fittest" mechanism that limits a broad search to variations of the best previous guesses. Evolutionary algorithms can be applied to virtually any optimization problem, from solving jigsaw puzzles to arranging baseball batting orders. See, for example, the special issue of *IEEE Transactions on Neural Networks* on evolutionary computation of January 1994. Or read Holland (1992). Genetic algorithms utilize a "sexual recombination" of two parents, instead of a mutation of one parent.

[4]Another example of a biased search technique intended to improve on the Q-M method is the "greedy" algorithm, illustrated in Hayes (1993, 343–346). The greedy algorithm starts with all essential PIs in partial cover and then adds other PIs on the basis of their cost until the cover is complete. It can find nonminimal covers when looking at cyclic maps.

Tyan and Daniels (1996) wrote an evolutionary algorithm called Eve in MATLAB to search for a minimum cover given a canonical set of minterms in decimal notation as input. The box below lists the steps (coded as subroutines or functions) in a relative of Eve.

Outline of Evolutionary Algorithm for Finding Minimum Cover

1. Convert minterms in decimal notation to binary.

2. Create a large number of mutations of the minterm list by introducing at most one don't-care per minterm in each mutated "individual."

3. Expand each mutated individual to see if it includes minterms not in the original list. Kill mutations that expand to too many minterms. Save the other mutations in the list for the first (or current) generation.

4. Once a list of valid mutants for the first (or current) generation is created, kill off clones (duplicates).

5. Evaluate each surviving member of the first (or current) generation by counting the number of don't-cares in all its minterms. Rank-order the first-generation members.

6. Select the highest-scoring members of the first (or current) generation to be parents of the next generation. Mutate each parent many times, again introducing at most one new don't-care per minterm (now an implicant).

7. Continue looping between steps 3 and 6 while the score of the best survivor continues to increase.

In a typical run of Eve, each generation consists of 1024 individuals, the top one-eighth of a generation is selected to survive, and each survivor has seven children. Scoring beyond the first generation will give extra weight to more than one don't-care per minterm. Putting more don't-cares in a minterm makes the subcube that the minterm (now an implicant) covers larger and larger. For example, implicant 001X001X covers four times as much space as a basic minterm. The more don't-cares in an implicant, the lower the hardware cost to realize the product.

Tyan and Daniels also wrote Espresso in MATLAB using the work of Brayton et al. (1984) as a guide. A comparison of the solution times of Eve and Espresso in MATLAB run on a SPARC 10 for 4–14 input truth tables is shown in Fig. 3.41. Note that the time to a stopping solution for Eve is about five times better than MATLAB Espresso for 12–14 inputs. MATLAB Espresso is about 100 times slower than Espresso in Octtools, written in C. For details see Tyan and Daniels (1996).

The user of the evolutionary algorithm needs to make some decisions about parameters, such as what percentage of one generation will become parents of the next, how many children there will be per parent, and what the probability of mutation per implicant in an individual will be, but otherwise neither the writer of the algorithm nor the user needs to know much about combinational design. No understanding of adjacency or essential PIs is needed, for example.

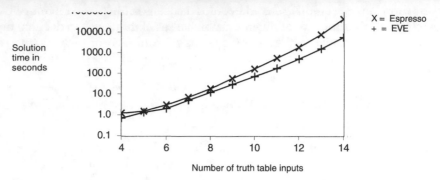

Figure 3.41 Espresso versus EVE: solution time.

By changing the way inputs are represented or by changing the scoring method in the program, the evolutionary algorithm can be made to consider multiple-output, multilevel solutions and even solutions involving XOR gates. This adaptability of the evolutionary algorithm to changing environments is more difficult to achieve with the Q-M and Espresso methods.

The evolutionary algorithm is always finding better solutions in each new generation, but for some problem requirements, a solution that merely beats a criterion—without being the best possible solution—is good. Espresso requires a significant amount of time to generate its first solution (on which it will iterate improvements), and during that initial delay an evolutionary algorithm can have made several generations of usable guesses. A rule of thumb for evolutionary algorithms is that a search over the cube root of (a large) number of possible combinations will yield a nearly optimal solution. In the case of a large truth table with, say, 40 PIs and minimum covers of about 20 PIs, the total search space is about

$$\binom{40}{20} = \frac{40!}{(40-20)! \cdot 20!} \approx 10^{11}$$

The cube root of 10^{11} is about 5000, so after approximately 5000 mutations over several generations an evolutionary algorithm might be "close" to an optimal answer.

If you are tempted to speed up an evolutionary algorithm by giving it "intelligence," beware. Just as the natural selection of biological evolution proceeds by random mutation and "survival of the fittest," so too should artificial evolution. Any attempt to help the algorithm may bias it toward a local optimum.

Something like an evolutionary algorithm (simulated annealing) is used to help optimize the placing of logic blocks and the routing of connections between them for field-programmable gate arrays. Field-programmable gate arrays will be discussed at the end of Chapter 4.

3.9 SUMMARY

Methods for reducing the complexity of truth table realization presented in this chapter fall in two categories: graphic map methods good for visualizing relationships on six or fewer inputs, and tabular methods good for computer coding to handle large truth tables. The emphasis in Chapter 3 has been on minimizing sum-of-product circuits; not much has been said about multilevel logic. Nor has much been said here about the efficiencies to be found in multiple-output synthesis.

- **Venn diagrams** of overlapping sets show logical relationships graphically and can lead to rectangular maps of input lists.

- To draw a **Karnaugh map** of a four-input truth table, create a two-dimensional matrix of squares. Each square represents a minterm from the truth table. The outside edges of the matrix are labeled with Gray code so that each inside square differs from its neighbors by only one literal of input. The output column entries of the underlying truth table are written into the squares of the matrix.

- **Subcubes** in a K-map are rectangular groupings of 1s; the number of subsquares on each side of the rectangle is a power of 2.

- Inspection of a K-map makes gathering subcubes of 1s an easier task. The edges of a K-map **wrap around.**

- Subcubes not fully contained in a larger subcube are **prime implicants (PIs).**

- PIs are products that can be summed for SOP realization usually smaller than the canonical SOP.

- XOR relationships form zigzag patterns on a K-map.

- Choose output don't-cares as 0 or 1 to simplify the expressions of PIs. Do not form subcubes composed exclusively of former don't-cares.

- Truth tables with five and six inputs can be represented in a three-dimensional cube or wire frame or on multiple two-dimensional maps.

- Truth tables with more than six inputs must be minimized by tabular methods expressed as computer algorithms

- The **Quine-McCluskey** method is a two-stage process amenable to computer automation. The first algorithm identifies all PIs. The second algorithm finds a minimum cover using PIs.

- Heuristic methods such as **Espresso** can be applied to truth tables with more than 20 inputs to find near-optimal covers. Espresso goes through a cycle of expanding implicants, finding a cover, reducing the cover, and then expanding the new set of implicants.

- An **evolutionary algorithm** applied to the search for minimum hardware configuration will go through cycles of randomly changing reasonable designs, looking for improvements in a cost function, and then using the best of a current generation to create a better set of reasonable designs.

Exercises

1. On the Venn diagram at the beginning of Chapter 3, show where regions for the maxterms $\overline{A} + \overline{B}$, $A + \overline{B}$, $\overline{A} + B$, and $A + B$ lie.

000 001 011 010 110 111 101 100

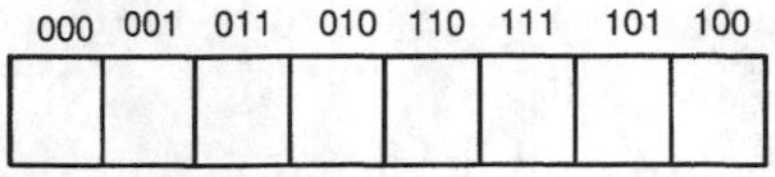

Figure P3.1

(a) Does this linear map wrap around properly?

(b) Write in the output for 1BFA carry-out. Can you gather 1s for a simplified expression?

(c) What disadvantage does a linear map have over the two-by-four K-map used for three-bit input?

3. Consider a K-map and a Veitch diagram for four bits of input. Number the squares inside the map from 1 to 16, starting in the upper left-hand corner. For how many of the 16 squares are the minterms for the K-map and the Veitch diagram the same?

4. Assume that three inputs should produce a HI output if only one or none of the inputs is HI. Write out a truth table and the K-map and find a hardware realization for this problem.

5. The following truth table has two outputs. Make a separate K-map for each output, and then use adjacency to simplify the sum-of-products expression for OUT_1 and OUT_2.

D	C	B	A	OUT_1	OUT_2
0	0	0	0	0	1
0	0	0	1	0	1
0	0	1	0	0	0
0	0	1	1	0	0
0	1	0	0	1	1
0	1	0	1	0	1
0	1	1	0	1	1
0	1	1	1	0	0
1	0	0	0	0	1
1	0	0	1	0	1
1	0	1	0	0	1
1	0	1	1	0	1
1	1	0	0	1	0
1	1	0	1	0	0
1	1	1	0	1	0
1	1	1	1	0	0

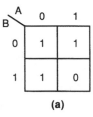

A B	0	1
0	1	1
1	1	0

(a)

DC \ BA	00	01	11	10
00	0	0	1	0
01	1	1	0	0
11	1	0	1	1
10	0	0	1	1

(c)

C \ BA	00	01	11	10
0	1	1	0	0
1	1	0	1	1

(b)

Figure P3.2 K-maps to reduce.

7. In a certain alarm system, both sensors A and B must be active for the alarm to sound, unless sensor C is active, in which case only one of A or B need be active for the alarm to sound. Assuming that inputs A, B, and C and output ALARM are digitized, write out a truth table for the three inputs and one output of this system. Turn the truth table into a K-map. Write out a Boolean expression f for ALARM $= f(A, B, C)$. Draw a sum-of-products realization of the Boolean expression.

8. The Tetris $\perp$ shape for a three-input K-map is the shape of CARRY$_{OUT}$ in the 1BFA. With the help of its K-map, fit the CARRY$_{OUT}$ SOP expression

$$\text{CARRY}_{OUT} = A \cdot \overline{B} \cdot C + A \cdot B \cdot \overline{C} + \overline{A} \cdot B \cdot C + A \cdot B \cdot C$$

in hardware that includes no three-input AND gate and no four-input OR gate.

9. Simplify the following expression by expressing it in a K-map and then gathering 1s:

$$C \cdot B \cdot A + C \cdot \overline{B} \cdot \overline{A} + C \cdot B \cdot \overline{A} + \overline{C} \cdot B \cdot A + C \cdot \overline{B} \cdot A$$

10. **Application of the law of consensus** At the end of Chapter 2 we looked at timing hazards in combinational circuits. In that regard consider the following SOP circuit. Suppose inputs A and C are both 1 and input B switches from 1 to 0. Imagine that gate AND$_2$ has a longer propagation delay than AND$_1$; let the OR gate have the same propagation delay as AND$_2$. By the looks of the logic, you would expect the output to remain 1, given the input change offered. The output does start at 1 and end at 1; however, as the timing diagram below the

logic circuit shows, there is a transient downward glitch on the output due to the unequal propagation delays of the two AND gates. The unwanted glitch is called a static hazard.

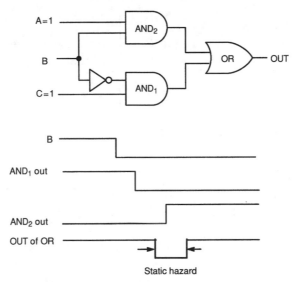

Figure P3.3   A static hazard.

Your problem is to add something to the circuit that will eliminate the static hazard.

11. **Wrap-around**   Write out one 1-variable expression for each of the following two K-maps. Use wrap-around to simplify your work.

BA

DC	00	01	11	10
00	1	1	1	1
01	0	0	0	0
11	0	0	0	0
10	1	1	1	1

BA

DC	00	01	11	10
00	1	0	0	1
01	1	0	0	1
11	1	0	0	1
10	1	0	0	1

12. Determine a Boolean expression for each of the following single-output, three-input K-maps (X stands for don't-care).

C\BA	00	01	11	10
0	0	1	1	0
1	0	1	1	0

(a)

R\QP	00	01	11	10
0	1	0	0	1
1	1	0	0	1

(b)

H\GF	00	01	11	10
0	1	1	0	X
1	0	1	1	0

(c)

Z\WY	00	01	11	10
0	0	1	1	0
1	X	0	1	0

(d)

13. What is the K-map for the following circuit, with inputs A and B? What changes are needed in the map and the circuit so that OUT $= A \oplus B$?

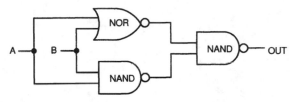

Figure P3.4

14. **(a)** Draw the three-input K-map for the expressions
    (i) $A \cdot (B \oplus C)$
    (ii) $X \oplus (Y \cdot Z)$

  (b) Draw the four-input K-maps for the expressions
    (iii) $A \oplus B \oplus C \oplus \overline{D}$
    (iv) $(W + X + Y) \oplus Z$

15. **Gathering zeros**   Determine SOP expressions for $\overline{\text{OUT}}$ by gathering 0s in the following two maps.

DC\BA	00	01	11	10
00	1	1	1	1
01	1	0	0	0
11	1	1	0	1
10	1	1	1	1

DC\BA	00	01	11	10
00	0	1	1	1
01	1	0	1	1
11	1	0	1	1
10	0	1	1	1

POS (NOR) expression of OUT.

XW
ZY \ XW	00	01	11	10
00	1	0	1	1
01	1	1	1	1
11	1	1	0	1
10	1	1	1	1

17. Find both SOP and POS expressions for the K-map below. Which expression has fewer literals?

B A
C \ B A	00	01	11	10
0	0	1	1	1
1	1	1	1	0

18. Here is the dual version of the first law of consensus:

$$(A + B) \cdot (\overline{A} + C) \cdot (B + C) = (A + B) \cdot (\overline{A} + C)$$

Prove the law by gathering 0s in a K-map and showing that the right-hand side covers the expression on the left-hand side.

19. (a) For the following K-map, will a POS or an SOP realization use less hardware?
    (b) Will any circuit involving XORs do a better job?

Q P
S R \ Q P	00	01	11	10
00	1	0	0	1
01	1	1	1	1
11	1	0	0	1
10	1	1	1	1

20. (a) List guidelines for choosing the status of don't-cares if a POS realization is desired.

    (b) Can you think of guidelines for choosing the status of don't-care X's if an XOR circuit seems possible?

21. **Don't-care choices** Determine POS expressions for $\overline{OUT}$ by gathering 0s in the following two maps.

DC \ BA	00	01	11	10
00	1	1	1	1
01	X	X	0	0
11	1	X	X	1
10	1	0	0	1

JH \ GF	00	01	11	10
00	0	1	X	X
01	1	0	X	X
11	1	0	1	1
10	0	1	1	X

22. What selections for the don't-cares below will generate minimum realizations?

F \ ED	00	01	11	10
0	0	X	X	0
1	1	0	0	1

F \ ED	00	01	11	10
0	0	X	0	X
1	1	0	1	0

23. Shown below is a five-variable K-map. Gather 1s and form a minimal SOP expression for OUT.

PQ \ RST	000	001	011	010	100	101	111	100
00	0	0	1	0	0	1	0	0
01	0	1	1	0	0	1	1	0
11	1	1	1	1	1	1	1	1
10	0	0	1	0	0	1	0	0

24. **Three-dimensional five-variable map** Draw two four-input K-maps side by side. Let both maps be labeled for D, C, B, and A, and let one map correspond

to $E = 0$ and the other to $E = 1$. The **Hamming distance** between two sets of N-bit binary combinations is the number of bits by which the sets differ.

(a) Which corresponding squares on the two maps are Hamming distance 1 away from each other?

(b) Use your five-variable maps to minimize an SOP Boolean expression for the following truth table (only OUT = 1 is listed):

A	*B*	*C*	*D*	*E*	OUT
0	0	1	0	1	1
0	0	1	1	1	1
0	1	1	0	1	1
0	1	1	1	1	1
1	0	1	1	1	1
1	0	1	1	0	1
1	1	1	0	1	1
1	1	1	1	0	1

Try to form subcubes across the two 4 × 4 maps.

25. **Six-input K-map** Below is a 64-square map for a six-input truth table. Note how the four quadrants are Gray code mirror images of each other. The 1s for a truth table are shown; assume that the other squares are filled with 0s.

FED \ CBA	000	001	011	010	110	111	101	100
000	1							1
001								
011			1			1		
010				1	1			
110				1	1			
111			1			1		
101								
100	1							1

Your problem is to write an expression for the on-set of 1s shown above using three PIs. Which set of 1s is most difficult to gather? Writing the map on tissue paper and cutting and folding carefully can help!

26. Time to get out the LEGO bricks or the Rubik's Cube.

(a) Label the *cubes* in Fig. P3.5 with 0s and 1s so that adjacent cubes differ from each other by only one bit.

(b) Stack bricks in a three-by-three-by-three cube and label the *vertices* (corners) of the bricks to accommodate a six-input K-map.

(c) If you have 63 bricks (3 × 3 × 7), stack them in a cube and see what a seven-input map would look like in three dimensions. Many of the vertices are buried inside and have logically adjacent vertices not within one brick distance!

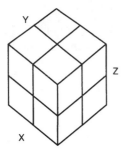

Figure P3.5 Three-dimensional cube for K-map.

27. List the minterms and all prime implicants (PIs) for the K-map below. What is a minimum cover of the map?

BA
C \ BA	00	01	11	10
0	0	0	0	1
1	1	1	1	0

28. Think of an example of a four-input truth table that has PIs of which at least one is not essential.

29. Circle the PIs in the three-input K-maps below. Which of the PIs are essential? Be sure to look for PIs formed by wrap-around.

BA
C \ BA	00	01	11	10
0	0	1	1	1
1	0	1	1	1

QP
R \ QP	00	01	11	10
0	1	1	1	0
1	1	0	1	1

GF
H \ GF	00	01	11	10
0	1	1	0	0
1	0	1	1	0

WY
Z \ WY	00	01	11	10
0	0	1	1	1
1	0	0	1	0

(a) When using adjacency to find PIs from a set of minterms in the Quine-McCluskey algorithm, what is wrong with comparing minterms that have the same number of 1s in them?

(b) Give an example of a five-bit input minterm that differs by exactly one 1 but that *cannot* be combined by adjacency.

31. What is the K-map for the products of Example 18 in the text?

32. The following input combinations are the only ones that generate 1s at OUT for a five-input truth table. Draw out two four-input K-maps, one for $E = 0$ and the other for $E = 1$, gather 1s, and show a minimal SOP expression for OUT.

E	D	C	B	A
0	0	1	0	0
0	1	1	0	0
0	0	1	0	1
0	1	1	0	1
1	1	1	0	1
1	0	1	0	1

33. Can you find a set of essential PIs for covering the following two sets of five-input minterms by the first Quine-McCluskey algorithm? Minterms are given as decimal numbers; that is, $11100 = 28$. Let the inputs be named $EDCBA$.

(a) 0, 3, 7, 13, 17, 24, 28

(b) 7, 25, 27, 29, 30, 31

‡34. **Numerology of notation**   Reproduced below are the decimal labels for a five-input truth table. The labels are placed inside four-by-four K-map grids. Inputs are $EDCBA$. The map on the left is for $E = 0$; the one on the right, for $E = 1$. Notice that each label has five neighbors; the five neighbors of 21 are underlined.

DC\BA	00	01	11	10
00	0	1	3	2
01	4	5	7	6
11	12	13	15	14
10	8	9	11	10

E = 0

DC\BA	00	01	11	10
00	16	17	19	18
01	20	21	23	22
11	28	29	31	30
10	24	25	27	26

E = 1

Your problem is to find a set of rules for combining decimal numbers by the adjacency theorem. To get you started, note that 21 can be combined by adjacency with all its nearest neighbors, and that the differences between 21 and its neighbors are 1, 2, 4, 8, and 16—all powers of 2. The exponent of the power-of-2 difference even marks which bit should be don't-care in the adjacency combination. *What's wrong with using the power-of-2 difference rule without qualification?*

35. Example 20 associates the following minterms with $OUT = 1$:

$$OUT = \sum\{m_4, m_5, m_6, m_7, m_{12}, m_{22}, m_{28}, m_{29}, m_{30}, m_{31}\}$$

Draw out two four-input K-maps, one for $E = 0$ and the other for $E = 1$, and find all the PIs. Can you find a cyclic cover for the problem?

36. Find a minimum SOP cover for the following two sets of five-input truth table minterms, expressed here in decimal notation:

(a)   1, 3, 5, 7, 19, 24, 27, 31

(b)   0, 4, 12, 13, 14, 15, 16, 17, 18, 19, 22, 30

‡37. Find a minimum SOP cover for the following set of six-input truth table minterms, expressed in decimal notation (0–63): 0, 1, 2, 3, 16, 17, 32, 33, 48, 49, 63.

38. Suppose a shorter word is less costly than a longer word. Find the least costly minimum cover of words for the set of letters shown below.

	m	n	o	p	q	r	s	t	u
quick									
brown									
fox									
jumped									
over									
the									
lazy									
dogs									

39. Without relying on K-maps, expand the following Boolean expression to find valid prime implicants.

$$OUT = \overline{A} \cdot \overline{B} \cdot \overline{C} \cdot \overline{D} + \overline{A} \cdot B \cdot \overline{C} + A \cdot B \cdot D + A \cdot C \cdot D$$

Start by expanding the first minterm to find four products.

‡40. If you have access to a computer and know a programming language, try following the steps given for the evolutionary algorithm and code your own version. It turns out mainly to be a problem of how to represent and manipulate sets of implicants. The evolutionary algorithm is perhaps the most accessible of the tabular methods discussed in Chapter 3. The basic evolutionary script we wrote in MATLAB calls functions for the following:

DEBIN   Converts decimal notation minterms to binary.

MUTATE   Selects whether and where to insert a don't-care in an implicant.

EXPAND Finds all minterms from expansion of a list of implicants.

MATCH Determines whether an expanded list contains minterms not in the original input list.

COMPRESS Compresses all valid guesses of a generation into a two-dimensional matrix.

NODUP Eliminates identical rows of a compressed matrix.

UNCOMP Uncompresses one row of a compression matrix.

SCORE Scores an uncompressed individual by counting the don't-cares in its implicant list and weights each extra don't-care per row by another power of 2.

SORT Rearranges a compressed list by row according to the score for each row.

For the rest, the main program contains various loops and tests to continue the evolutionary process.

References

BISWAS, N. N. 1993. *Logic design theory*. Englewood Cliffs, N.J.: Prentice Hall.

BLAKESLEE, T. R. 1975. *Digital design with standard MSI and LSI*. New York: John Wiley & Sons.

BRAYTON, R. K., C. MCMULLEN, G. D. HECHTEL, AND A. SANGIOVANNI-VINCENTELLI. 1984. *Logic minimization algorithms for VLSI synthesis*. Norwell, Mass.: Kluwer.

DE MICHELI, G. 1994. *Synthesis and optimization of digital circuits*. New York: McGraw-Hill.

HILL, F. J., AND PETERSON, G. R. 1993. *Computer aided logic design, with emphasis on VLSI*. 4th ed. New York: John Wiley & Sons.

HOLLAND, J. 1992. Genetic algorithms. *Scientific American*, July, pp. 66–72.

IEEE Transactions on Neural Networks. January 1994.

KARNAUGH, M. 1953. The map method for synthesis of combinational logic circuits. *Transactions of the AIEE on Communications and Electronics* 72:593–599.

KATZ, R. 1994. *Contemporary digital design*. Reading, Mass.: Addison-Wesley.

MCCLUSKEY, E. J., JR. 1956. Minimization of Boolean functions. *Bell System Technical Journal* 35:1417–1444.

QUINE, W. V. 1952. The problem of simplifying truth functions. *American Mathematical Monthly* 59:521–531.

RUDELL, R. L., AND A. SANGIOVANNI-VINCENTELLI. 1987. Multiple-valued minimization for PLA optimization. *IEEE Transactions on Computer-Aided Design* 6:727–750.

TYAN, H.-Y., AND J. D. DANIELS. 1996. Evolutionary algorithm compared to Espresso for minimizing 2-level truth table realizations. In preparation for *International Systems Circuits and Automation Conference*.

Programmable Circuits for Combinational Design

....

Up to now in dealing with truth tables we've treated each separate combinational logic problem as a new opportunity to exercise design skills with Boolean algebra, Karnaugh maps, or tabular minimization. In most cases a special-purpose sum-of-products design resulted. The AND gates of the SOP can have various numbers of inputs to accommodate exactly the literals of individual prime implicants. In Chapter 4 we relax our interest in strict minimization and explore the use of large-scale, standardized architectures on which to impress truth tables.[1]

Because of the importance of AND-to-OR circuits, logic chip manufacturers have labored to make larger and larger SOPs. These large circuits can have AND gates handling many inputs (as minterms); in most cases the inputs to the large circuit are each complemented inside the chip. **General-purpose combinational chips** come with **programmable connections**. By *programmable* we mean that some action of the designer or user of the circuit can reconfigure or limit the otherwise large number of potential connections inside the chip.

Multiplexers are the smallest of the circuits in Chapter 4; the user has continual access to 2^N data inputs of a multiplexer and can assert some of N select lines to choose which of the data inputs become output. In a **read-only memory (ROM)** the select inputs are relabeled "address," and more (up to 20 or so) can be accommodated; a special write operation determines (internally) which output is to be associated with each of the 2^N addresses. Both multiplexers and ROMs can realize *any* N-input truth table, at the expense that much more hardware than necessary may be placed in the circuit, but with the convenience that if a design change occurs, relatively simple reprogramming can adapt the device to a new specification.

The second half of Chapter 4 considers **programmable logic devices,** which are more efficient providers of SOP hardware. **Programmable array logic (PAL)** chips are tailored for many inputs with relatively few TRUE outputs. Exactly which minterms gain access to the output can be programmed at the AND gate level. The OR gates of a PAL don't share product terms. **Programmable logic arrays** combine features of both ROMs and PALs, allowing both AND-level and OR-level connections to be modified and accommodating shared product terms. At the end of Chapter 4,

---

[1]To optimize absolutely the hardware of large logic circuits that are to be produced in mass quantity, a designer may resort to *application-specific integrated circuits,* which make it possible to implement a minimum gate count necessary to realize a large truth table.

square arrays of multiplexer-like combinational blocks. The combinational blocks can be programmed internally as SOPs or as various multilevel configurations. The routing resources inside an FPGA are often exhausted before all the combinational blocks are used up. The chapter concludes with a review of CAD software for configuring and programming ROMs, PALs, and FPGAs to solve combinational logic problems.

4.1 MULTIPLEXERS

When you learned about toggle switches in Chapter 1, you were introduced to multiplexers (MUX). Here is a more general account of multiplexers. Consider for a moment *any* three-input, single-output truth table, one example of which is shown in Fig. 4.1. Every three-input, single-output truth table has eight separate OUT values, one for each row. How many different three-input, single-output truth tables are there? Not allowing don't-care outputs, there are $2^8 = 256$ different truth tables. A general-purpose method to solve any three-input, single-output truth table must be able to account for any of 256 different possible combinations of output.

In a general-purpose solution each input product must be capable of independently generating either a 0 or a 1 output. Let's attack one of the eight such outputs, say the one governed by input $CBA = 101$. An SOP realization of "$DATA_{101}$" will look like the subcircuit in Fig. 4.2, where $DATA_{101}$ is a value that equals the desired output *for truth table line CBA = 101*. Yes, we could have combined the two AND gates into one four-input AND gate, but for the time being we keep separate AND gates to distinguish the two kinds of input. The AND gate that selects data is colored.

To account for all truth table combinations, a total of eight of these subcircuits are required, and all eight must feed into an eight-input OR gate. The $DATA_{101}$ subcircuit is shown as one input to the eight-input OR gate in Fig. 4.3. The other seven inputs to the OR gate are similar subcircuits specialized to detect the other input combinations of the truth table. The complete circuit is a sum of products. For a particular CBA combination at least seven out of eight inputs to the OR gate will be 0; the eighth input may also be 0 if the selected $DATA_{CBA}$ is also 0.

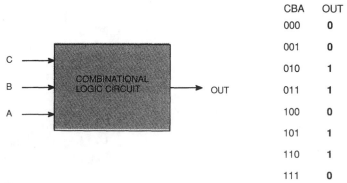

CBA	OUT
000	0
001	0
010	1
011	1
100	0
101	1
110	1
111	0

Figure 4.1 A black-box three-input combinational circuit and truth table.

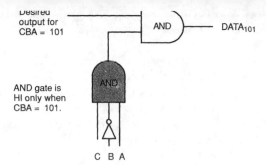

Figure 4.2 Selecting data with AND gates.

The truth table of the circuit described above has the general-purpose block diagram shown in Fig. 4.4. It can be used—as advertised—to realize any three-input truth table. (It can also be used for some four-input truth tables; see Exercise 6 and Example 1.) $DATA_{CBA}$ is the desired output for the input combination CBA; another term for $DATA_{CBA}$ is *data input*, to distinguish it from *select inputs*, which are the CBA lines. In this circuit the *possible* outputs are set by the user directly into the data inputs.

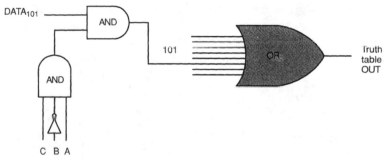

Figure 4.3 Data path through multiplexer.

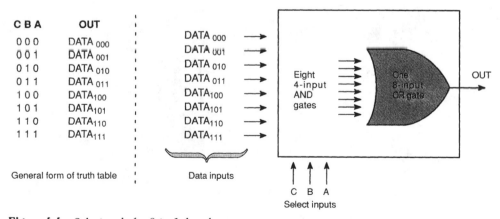

C B A	OUT
0 0 0	$DATA_{000}$
0 0 1	$DATA_{001}$
0 1 0	$DATA_{010}$
0 1 1	$DATA_{011}$
1 0 0	$DATA_{100}$
1 0 1	$DATA_{101}$
1 1 0	$DATA_{110}$
1 1 1	$DATA_{111}$

General form of truth table

Figure 4.4 Select code for 8-to-1 decoder.

combination of N select inputs. A circuit with these features is a $2^N \to 1$ **multiplexer,** or $2^N \to 1$ **encoder.**

In the case of eight data inputs above, an $8 \to 1$ MUX results. MUXs are so versatile for realizing small truth tables that they are standard chips in any integrated circuit family. In custom and semicustom logic chips multiplexers are ubiquitous. For example, the configurable logic block (CLB) of a Xilinx 3000 series gate array chip has 14 multiplexers for routing data in the block; a Xilinx 3090 gate array chip has 320 CLBs, which result in almost 5000 MUXs on one chip!

The hardware in an $8 \to 1$ MUX is more than enough for any *specific* three-input truth table. For example, a truth table with four TRUE outputs would really need only four AND gates and a four-input OR gate in a minimal SOP design, versus the eight AND gates and eight-input OR of the $8 \to 1$ MUX. If all of the AND gates of a MUX were given data 1s to send to output, the MUX output could be replaced by a single wire tied to HI!

Consider the following use of the smallest MUX. If the select input of a $2 \to 1$ MUX is hooked to a square-wave oscillator, the output of the MUX will switch periodically between its two data inputs, an action that can be useful for generating multiplexed 2-digit displays when the oscillation frequency is greater than the human flicker fusion rate.

In general, if several signals can share at different times a common path, the several signals are said to *multiplex* the path, or be multiplexed onto the path. Multiplexing— analog or digital—finds frequent use in networks such as the telephone system, where a connection from one point to another may be so costly that only one or two wires can be installed; those few wires must multiplex many messages.

EXAMPLE 1

Use a MUX to realize CARRY$_{OUT}$ for a one-bit full adder. The CARRY$_{OUT}$ truth table is reproduced on the left in Fig. 4.5.

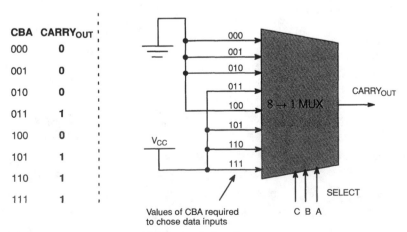

CBA	CARRY$_{OUT}$
000	0
001	0
010	0
011	1
100	0
101	1
110	1
111	1

Figure 4.5 Eight-to-one MUX example for carry-out.

is hard-wired to either LO (gnd) or HI (V_{CC}), depending on which output value from the truth table it should represent. As you will see in Chapter 11, it's possible to realize the carry-out truth table with an OR gate, an AND gate, and one $2 \rightarrow 1$ MUX, where C_{IN} is the select input.

4.1.1 Standard MUX Sizes

Here in Chapter 4 it will be worthwhile to name specific IC chips as realizations of various general-purpose circuits. For example, in the transistor-transistor logic (TTL) family an $8 \rightarrow 1$ MUX is a 74151 and has the pinout and truth table of Fig. 4.6, where STROBE is an input that can force OUT to LO no matter what the select inputs are. Notice that select inputs *CBA* are listed as XXX when STROBE = 1; this don't-care convention avoids the writing out of all *CBA* combinations associated with STROBE = 1. Another way to think about STROBE is that when STROBE is asserted LO, the chip is *enabled* (thus the strobe bubble on the diagram and its negative logic status). The 74151 provides both OUT and its complement, $\overline{\text{OUT}}$. *One 74151 chip can realize any three-input, single-output truth table.*

Besides the TTL 74151 chip, which has one $8 \rightarrow 1$ MUX, the following MUXs are available in the transistor-transistor-logic 7400 series (or the more up-to-date 74LS series):

74157	Four $2 \rightarrow 1$ MUXs per chip
74153	Two $4 \rightarrow 1$ MUXs per chip
74150	One $16 \rightarrow 1$ MUX in a 24-pin package

In some schematics a trapezoid is used for multiplexers (see Fig. 4.7).

The IEEE 1984–91 standard symbol for a 74150 is shown in Fig. 4.8. The "hat" on the top of the symbol is a common control block for the two rectangles underneath. The G in the control block refers to the gating of the strobe inputs, pins 1 and 15. The output of a MUX rectangle, on the right, comes from a numbered input pin (0–3) ANDed with the decoded 0-1 pair of pins in the control block. The EN input sent

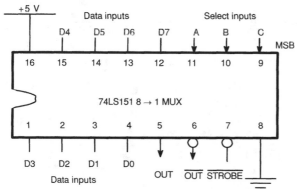

STROBE	C B A	OUT
0	0 0 0	D0
0	0 0 1	D1
0	0 1 0	D2
0	0 1 1	D3
0	1 0 0	D4
0	1 0 1	D5
0	1 1 0	D6
0	1 1 1	D7
1	X X X	0

Figure 4.6 74151 multiplexer pinout.

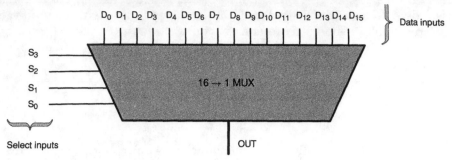

Figure 4.7 A multiplexer with four select inputs.

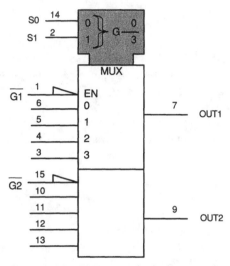

Figure 4.8 IEEE standard diagram for 74153 dual 4→1 multiplexer.

through a bubble is an active-low enable (strobe) without which the MUX output will remain LO. The second rectangle is assumed to be controlled like the first and with the same select pins, 2 and 14. Pin numbers for the 74153 chip are shown on the outside, near the I/O lines. Power and ground pins are assumed.

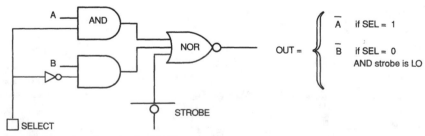

Figure 4.9 One-fourth of a 74158.

The '4157 and the '4158 are both quad 2 → 1 MUXs. Look at how the '158 inverting MUX can be realized with AND-OR-INVERT hardware primitives (see Fig. 4.9). Each MUX in a '158 is an AND-OR-INVERT with DATA, SELECT, and STROBE inputs.

To increase convergence, standard encoders can be connected end to end.

EXAMPLE 2

Show how to use two 2 → 1 MUXs to create a 3 → 1 MUX.

Answer Combine a '157 and a '158 as shown in Fig. 4.10 for a quad 3 → 1 MUX. The data paths, labeled A, B, and C, are four bits wide. Input word C is chosen by two combinations of select inputs ($S_1 S_0$). In color are the pins for one 2 → 1 MUX path. The quad 3 → 1 MUX shown is an inverting MUX.

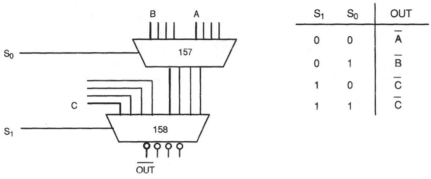

S_1	S_0	OUT
0	0	$\overline{A}$
0	1	$\overline{B}$
1	0	$\overline{C}$
1	1	$\overline{C}$

Figure 4.10 Two 2 → 1 MUXs used in design of a 3 → 1 MUX.

Continuing concatenations, appreciate that two '157s with their eight combined outputs feeding the eight data inputs of a '151 create a 16 → 1 MUX. Tie the two select inputs of the '157s together for the D input, and don't forget to enable the MUX's active-low strobe. (See Fig. 4.11.)

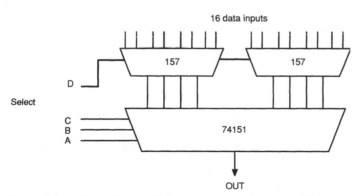

Figure 4.11 Cascading multiplexers create one larger multiplexer.

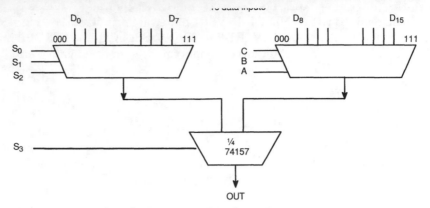

Figure 4.12 Small multiplexers cascade to form a larger one.

Two '151s and one-fourth of a '157 can realize the same $16 \to 1$ MUX capability. Both '151 selects receive the same $S_3 S_2 S_1 S_0$ input, while the '157 select is now D. (See Fig. 4.12.) But why bother? Two '151s and a '157 cost more than a $16 \to 1$ 74150 MUX, and the 74150 has half the propagation delay and (counting interconnects) takes up less space on a PC board. However, if you're stuck with all MUXs of the same size, say $N \to 1$ MUXs, then $N + 1$ of them can be arranged to make a $2N \to 1$ MUX.

4.1.2 Multiplexers and Karnaugh Maps

Each of the four columns of a 16-square K-map can be thought of as a select input for a $4 \to 1$ MUX. (The same could be done for the rows.)

EXAMPLE 3

Study the following Karnaugh map for OUT and find a way to realize it with one $4 \to 1$ MUX:

DC \ BA	00	01	11	10
00	0	0	1	0
01	1	0	1	0
11	1	1	1	0
10	0	1	1	0

Answer Notice that each of the four columns can be described by the following expressions:

When $BA = 00, \text{OUT} = C$.
When $BA = 01, \text{OUT} = D$.

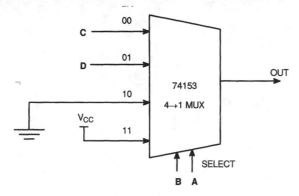

Figure 4.13 MUX with variable inputs.

When $BA = 11, \text{OUT} = 1$.
When $BA = 10, \text{OUT} = 0$.

Let the SELECT to a $4 \rightarrow 1$ MUX be governed by inputs BA (Fig. 4.13). Then the truth table for OUT can be realized by half of a 74153.

Sometimes variables present themselves as natural SELECTs for encoders. In the case of Fig. 4.13, inspection of the K-map columns reveals regularities favoring an encoder as a one-chip solution to the problem. If input pairs DC were used as the encoder selects, then more random logic[2] would have been required to process the data inputs to the MUX.

4.1.3 Multiplexers and Shannon's Expansion Theorem

There's nothing to stop you from putting expressions more complicated than 0 or 1 on the data inputs.

EXAMPLE 4

In Fig. 4.14 the K-map on the left is realized by the $2 \rightarrow 1$ MUX on the right. The Boolean expression for OUT restates the definition of $2 \rightarrow 1$ multiplexing in terms of the variables shown. Using the notation in the figure, the $2 \rightarrow 1$ MUX truth table could be listed as

C	OUT
0	A
1	B

[2]*Random logic* refers to irregular interconnecting gates necessary to make a system function properly. *Glue logic* is a small version of random logic.

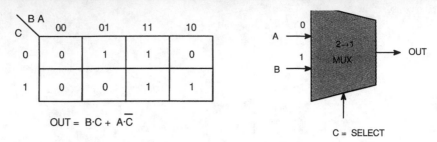

OUT = B·C + A·C̄

Figure 4.14 Two-to-one MUX realizing a three-input truth table.

where outputs now appear as data input variables. The pattern on the K-map covers the Boolean consensus law.

In general, a Boolean expression can be expanded according to Shannon's theorem to find a form that will fit in a multiplexer. Recall the SOP version of Shannon's theorem from Chapter 2: Let $F(X_1, X_2, X_3, \ldots, X_N)$ be any Boolean expression of N variables. Shannon's theorem says that

$$F(X_1, X_2, X_3, \ldots, X_N) = F(1, X_2, X_3, \ldots, X_N) \cdot X_1 + F(0, X_2, X_3, \ldots, X_N) \cdot \overline{X_1}$$

where F has been expanded in terms of X_1. Variable X_1 can be the input select to a $2 \rightarrow 1$ MUX that has $F(1, X_2, X_3, \ldots, X_N)$ and $F(0, X_2, X_3, \ldots, X_N)$ as its two data inputs.

Two passes of a function F through Shannon's theorem yield

$$\begin{aligned}
F(X_1, X_2, X_3, \ldots, X_N) &= F(1, X_2, X_3, \ldots, X_N) \cdot X_1 + F(0, X_2, X_3, \ldots, X_N) \cdot \overline{X_1} \\
&= F(1, 1, X_3, \ldots, X_N) \cdot X_1 \cdot X_2 + F(1, 0, X_3, \ldots, X_N) \cdot X_1 \cdot \overline{X_2} \\
&\quad + F(0, 1, X_3, \ldots, X_N) \cdot \overline{X_1} \cdot X_2 + F(0, 0, X_3, \ldots, X_N) \cdot \overline{X_1} \cdot \overline{X_2}
\end{aligned}$$

which results in the $4 \rightarrow 1$ MUX realization of Fig. 4.15.

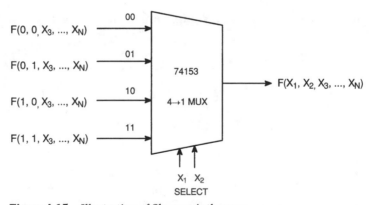

Figure 4.15 Illustration of Shannon's theorem.

EXAMPLE 5

Find a way to have a $4 \rightarrow 1$ MUX to help realize the Boolean expression $W \oplus X \oplus Y \oplus Z$ using only one XOR gate.

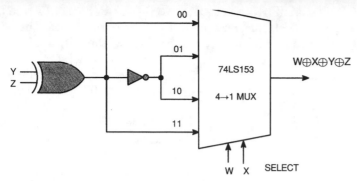

Figure 4.16 Circuit for Example 5.

Answer Try expanding $F = W \oplus X \oplus Y \oplus Z$ using Shannon's theorem twice.

$$F = W \oplus X \oplus Y \oplus Z$$
$$= W \cdot X \cdot [1 \oplus 1 \oplus Y \oplus Z] + \overline{W} \cdot X \cdot [0 \oplus 1 \oplus Y \oplus Z] + W \cdot \overline{X} \cdot [1 \oplus 0 \oplus Y \oplus Z]$$
$$+ \overline{W} \cdot \overline{X} \cdot [0 \oplus 0 \oplus Y \oplus Z]$$
$$= W \cdot X \cdot [Y \oplus Z] + \overline{W} \cdot X \cdot [\overline{Y \oplus Z}] + W \cdot \overline{X} \cdot [\overline{Y \oplus Z}] + \overline{W} \cdot \overline{X} \cdot [Y \oplus Z]$$

This expansion translates into the realization of Fig. 4.16.

4.2   DEMULTIPLEXER

From a multiplexer design, strip out the set of AND gates that detect different combinations of input. For an encoder with two select inputs, the set of input-detecting ANDs is as shown in Fig. 4.17. This subcircuit is important enough by itself

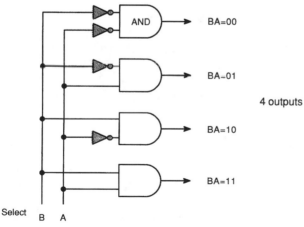

Figure 4.17   Two-to-four decoder.

to deserve its own name: **demultiplexer (deMUX) or decoder**—in this case a $2 \rightarrow 4$ decoder, to indicate two select lines fanning out to four output lines. The values of the select inputs that activate each output are shown near the output arrows in the figure. In general, a *demultiplexer*, or *decoder*, is a system in which one of 2^N output lines is selected to be active; the unselected output lines are all complementary to the selected output, which can be active HI or active LO. In the case of Fig. 4.17 the unselected outputs will be LO.

In a $2 \rightarrow 4$ decoder only one output out of four will be HI at any one time (positive logic convention). Compared with a MUX, a standard decoder has only select inputs, no data input.

EXAMPLE 6

It is possible to give a $2 \rightarrow 4$ decoder a *data input* by adding a common data line to each AND gate. In the circuit of Fig. 4.18 it's no longer true that the selected output will always be complementary to the $2^N - 1$ unselected outputs. Whenever data-in is LO, all the outputs will be LO.

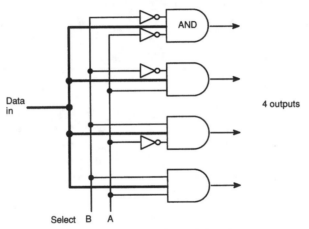

Figure 4.18   Two-to-four decoder with data input.

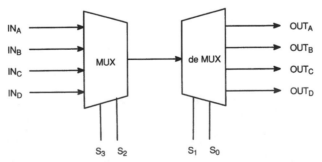

Figure 4.19   Multiplexed output into a demultiplexer creates a router circuit.

MUX is passed into a 2 → 4 decoder with data input, the four-in, four-out circuit of Fig. 4.19 results. Depending on the settings of the selects $\{S_3 S_2 S_1 S_0\}$, any one input can be routed to any one output. This router circuit is not a full crossbar switch because at any time only one output is active. As you will see in Chapter 9 on communication circuits, when $S_3 S_2$ and $S_1 S_0$ are synchronized, the circuit implements a form of time-division multiplexing.

In general, a decoder takes a few inputs and produces many outputs. In particular a circuit with N inputs that fans out to 2^N outputs is an N-to-2^N decoder. Sometimes, in the context of memory circuits, such a system is called an *address decoder* because it takes an N-bit address and asserts one of 2^N output lines headed for memory cells.

Decoder chips in IC families have no data input, and the convention for decoder outputs is normally active-low. The circuit of Fig. 4.18, showing AND gates fanning out from select inputs, can be converted to active-low form by replacing the ANDs with NANDs.

4.2.1 Standard Decoders

A 16-pin 74139 TTL chip has two 2 → 4 demultiplexers (see Fig. 4.20). The logic for each demultiplexer is described by the table on the right. The outputs are active-low. ENABLE is an active-low *control* input, and there is a separate ENABLE for each demultiplexer; ENABLE inputs allow separate demultiplexer chips to be cascaded together. When ENABLE is HI, a demultiplexer's outputs are all HI, regardless of the values of the select inputs, BA. Each demultiplexer has two select inputs, with input B the more significant bit.

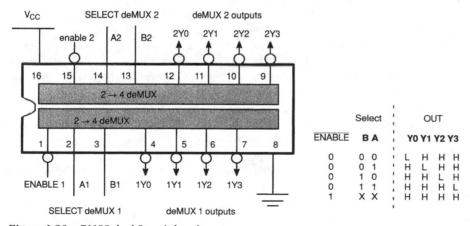

ENABLE	B A	Y0 Y1 Y2 Y3
0	0 0	L H H H
0	0 1	H L H H
0	1 0	H H L H
0	1 1	H H H L
1	X X	H H H H

Figure 4.20   74139 dual 2 → 4 decoder.

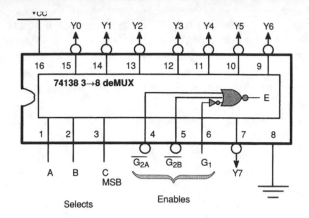

Select				Outputs							
E	C	B	A	Y0	Y1	Y2	Y3	Y4	Y5	Y6	Y7
L	L	L	L	L	H	H	H	H	H	H	H
L	L	L	H	H	L	H	H	H	H	H	H
L	L	H	L	H	H	L	H	H	H	H	H
L	L	H	H	H	H	H	L	H	H	H	H
L	H	L	L	H	H	H	H	L	H	H	H
L	H	L	H	H	H	H	H	H	L	H	H
L	H	H	L	H	H	H	H	H	H	L	H
L	H	H	H	H	H	H	H	H	H	H	L
H	X	X	X	H	H	H	H	H	H	H	H

Figure 4.21 74138 three-to-eight decoder and truth table.

Besides the 74139, the following TTL-family decoders (active low, inverters on inputs and outputs) are available:

74138   One 3 → 8 demultiplexer

7442   One 1 → 10 demultiplexer (binary-coded decimal)

74154   One 4 → 16 demultiplexer in a 24-pin package

A 74139 chip 3 → 8 decoder is shown in Fig. 4.21. The three enable pins converge on an internal NOR gate, giving the output E for the sake of the truth table to the right. The truth table is shown in terms of L and H, as is common in data books. As an example, check the truth table and see that if CBA = LHL, then the third output pin Y2 will be LO and the other seven will be HI.

Earlier, the example of the Xilinx 3000-series gate with 14 multiplexers per logic block was cited. That logic block has *no* demultiplexers, because a decoder is no more than a set of AND gates connected to a common set of inputs, a design that can be implemented by configuring several logic blocks. But we will find decoders plentiful in Chapter 8 (Memory), where they are used in addressing in memory chips.

A 1 → 2 decoder is a signal plus its complement, shown in Fig. 4.22. The outputs of the 1 → 2 decoder are literals because they represent a variable and its complement. When a pulse generator serves as the signal, the pair of outputs is a two-phase clock, and it will find use in timing circuits. In such a timing circuit, delay through the

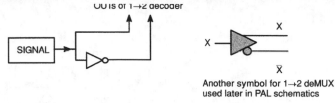

UU is of 1→2 decoder

Another symbol for 1→2 deMUX
used later in PAL schematics

Figure 4.22 Two-to-one decoder circuit and symbol.

two paths is equalized. A demultiplexer is the circuit of choice if only one of several targets can be on at a time, for example, only one of four positioning motors or one of eight arrows on a display.

4.2.2 Decoding Digits in a Display

In Chapter 2 the truth table of the conversion from BCD to a seven-segment display was worked out. You saw four bits of input decoded to become seven bits of output. Consider now the problem of displaying a three-digit decimal number if a multiplexed display, such as the HP 7433, is used. In a 7433 all three digits share common seven-segment control information; only when the correct BCD information for a particular three-digit number is available should the corresponding digit in the 7433 be enabled.

EXAMPLE 7

How can multiplexers and demultiplexers be used to coordinate segment and digit information in a three-digit HP7433 display?

Answer See the diagram in Fig. 4.23. The diagram shows the three digits of BCD segment information, available simultaneously on the left, heading into four MUXs, one for each bit in the numbers. The select inputs B and A determine which digit should be delivered to the BCD-to-seven-segment decoder. For example, the segments

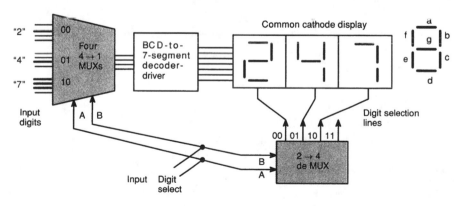

Figure 4.23 Three-digit multiplexed display.

a, b, d, e, and g must be active for pattern "2," and they are asserted when the BA inputs select MUX data inputs for 00.

On the digit selection side all of the segments for each digit funnel through a *common cathode* pin. It's the common cathode pin that must be "grounded" by an active-low decoder output, using a select code coordinated with the MUX. For example, when $BA = 00$ is presented to the decoder, the 00 output will be active-low and current from the left-most display digit will have a path to ground.[3] $BA = 00$ is at the same time selecting digit information for the "2" pattern, so "2" will be displayed on the left digit only. During that time the other two digits will be blank. If the digit-select BA is changed faster than approximately 30 times a second, a human will not perceive flicker in the display. As implied in the schematic of Fig. 4.23, 25% of the time (when $BA = 11$) all digits will be off. Again, this blinking will not be perceived if the BA select inputs alternate fast enough; however, the perceived brightness will be 25% less than in a $2 \rightarrow 3$ decoder design.

4.3 READ-ONLY MEMORY

Return to consideration of multiplexers. In terms of demultiplexing, an $8 \rightarrow 1$ multiplexer looks like Fig. 4.24, where the eight data inputs are tucked between a decoder and a final OR output gate. If a MUX is to handle larger truth tables, it must have more select pins. If we increase the number of select lines to 12, there must be an internal decoder with $2^{12} = 4{,}096$ outputs.[4] We still need only one output pin, however.[5]

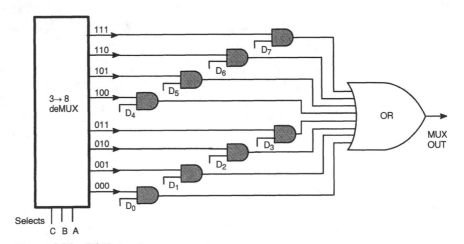

Figure 4.24 ROM structure.

[3] Assuming that the output of the decoder chip can sink the current from the display; if not, an extra transistor may be needed to handle current from the common cathode pin.

[4] It's not necessary to construct a demultiplexer of N selects using 2^N N-input AND gates. More efficient methods of decoding are addressed in Chapter 8, and a row-column method is brought forth in Exercise 2

[5] In Chapter 8, Memory, you will learn that the 2^N-input OR gate of a large encoder can be replaced by a 3-state bus.

Now, you can imagine 12 select pins on a chip and one output pin, but not 4,096 data input pins! How can we eliminate the need for external data input pins? Instead of external data inputs, arrange that each colored AND gate in the circuit above has an *internal* switch for data and that the internal switches can be flipped to either HI or LO by a special programming procedure that accesses only a couple of pins on the chip.

EXAMPLE 8

How can internal data for a large encoder be designed?

Answer   Figure 4.25 suggests how an internal data switch can become part of the path to output for a 12-bit-select MUX. Here the select combination 0011 0110 1011 enables an internal switch to the output OR gate.

The internal switch is set to HI here. Whenever SELECT = 0011 0110 1011, the output of the chip will be 1. At this point, let's not worry about how the internal switch was set to HI other than to say that it was programmed by a write process that accessed voltages or pins on the chip not normally used during the read mode illustrated in Fig. 4.25. Chapter 8 will provide more information about programming memory chips. Suffice it to say that the programming process is permanent enough that even when power to the chip is interrupted, the chip will still remember (for years) its correct output when power is reapplied and the proper select inputs are chosen.

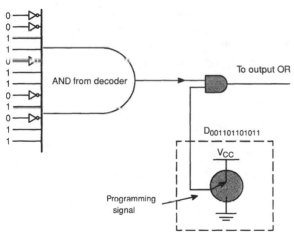

Figure 4.25   Internal structure of ROM.

Before going further, let's give these encoding devices another name to distinguish them from their evolutionary cousins, the multiplexers. A **read-only memory (ROM)** chip is an SOP integrated circuit that provides a preprogrammed output of one or several bits in response to combinations on **address** pins (corresponding to the multiplexer's select pins). The qualifier *read-only* isn't quite right; at some time in its past, a ROM had to be written to, by correlating **contents** with each different address. The connections between the AND gates and the final OR gates are programmable. The writing of contents into the ROM might have been a one-time-only process, done during semiconductor fabrication, in which case the chip is a plain ROM. Or the ultimate user may be able to program an individual ROM in a special machine, which typically raises the voltage on a pin above V_{CC} and sequences through all addresses while presenting the contents to be written. The unprogrammed ROM starts with all its contents set to either LO or HI. The programming machine changes only those values of contents that differ from the unprogrammed value. In such a case the chip is a **programmable read-only memory,** or **PROM.** If the contents of the PROM can be erased (brought back to the unprogrammed state) by ultraviolet light, the chip is an **erasable programmable read-only memory,** or **EPROM.** If the erasing process is electrical, the chip is an **electrical-erasable programmable read-only memory,** or **EEPROM.**

EXAMPLE 9

The 2764 chip is an eight-bit output EPROM chip capable of storing $2^{16} = 2^{13} \times 2^3 = 65{,}536 = 64$ Kbits (uppercase K is $1024 = 2^{10}$). The 2764 is a 28-pin IC, shown larger than life in Fig. 4.26. The 2764 has 13 address pins and 8 output pins. It contains $2^{13} = 8{,}192$ locations, or addresses. Each location has eight bits of contents. Pins A_0–A_{12} are the 13 address pins; pins C_0–C_7 are the data I/O pins. During normal operation (read mode), the C_i pins serve as eight bits of output for the contents of whatever address is currently selected. For the 2764 to be in the read mode, pins 20 and 22 (active-low chip-selects) must both be LO; furthermore, pin 27 (the active-low program pin) and pin 1 (V_{PP}) must both be at 5 V $= V_{CC}$ for reading. $\overline{OE}$ and $\overline{CE}$ are output-enable and chip-enable active-low pins, which must be grounded for the

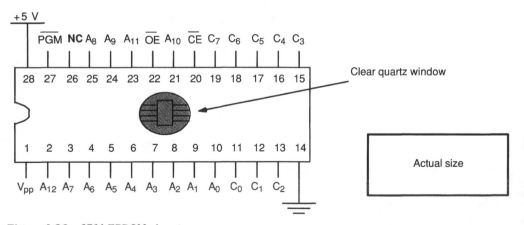

Figure 4.26 2764 EPROM pinout.

[6]A ROM has the kind of memory any combinational circuit has: the memory of the truth table it is programmed to remember. There is another kind of memory chip (RAM), which can have contents more easily written to its various addressed locations, but which loses the contents whenever power to the circuit is turned off. RAM will be derived from latches, which are to be introduced in Chapter 5.

chip to function as ROM. OE and CE will be discussed in Chapter 8 with regard to data and address buses in memory systems. Once all these settings are made, the 2764 looks up in a truth table whatever output corresponds to the input presented at the address pins.

Fantastic as it sounds, the entire contents of a 2764 can be erased by energetic ultraviolet photons beamed through the clear quartz window over the chip itself inside the plastic package. The erasing takes a few minutes of exposure, and it returns all contents to 1111 1111. If you find an EPROM and look through its quartz window with a magnifying glass, you can see the marvel of large-scale integration laid bare. Notice the fine gold wires leading away from the chip itself, to the pins on the periphery of the package.[7]

To place the 2764 in the programming (write) mode, switch V_{PP} to 25 V. Whenever pin $\overline{PGM}$ is pulsed low for about 50 ms, whatever values have been held on the C_i pins will be written to ("burned in") the contents of the location represented by the address pins A_j. Programming on a 2764 can only send bits LO that are initially HI. The programming process starts with a chip erased by ultraviolet light to all HI levels. *During the write mode, the C_i are input pins.* The programming process would normally be streamlined by using a PROM programmer connected to a computer. With an editor in the computer you can compose a file of eight-bit numbers, and after selecting the correct PROM chip from a software menu, you can activate the "program chip" feature. Your contents file would be burned into the PROM in a minute or less. The computer takes account of write timing, that is, how long a write pulse should be held for each address. The computer then exercises the ROM once to verify that all locations were properly programmed.

There's not much difficulty in realizing a truth table with ROM. Type (with the help of an editing program) each input combination of the truth table as an address for the ROM and type the corresponding truth table output as contents for that address. Insert an EPROM chip in the socket connected to the PROM programmer and execute the programming software using the keyboard or mouse. The ROM now realizes the given truth table. If you make a mistake or specifications change, erase the EPROM and try again. ROMs now (1995) come in sizes up to 16 megabytes per chip (about 2 million locations at eight bits contents per location). Two Mbytes ($= 2^{21}$) require 21 bits of address, so a 2-million-line, eight-output truth table could be accommodated.

ROMS are ubiquitous. They have a widespread practical role in modern digital hardware. As one example, every IBM PC has an assembly-language code called basic input-output system (BIOS). Nearly all PCs and their clones contain BIOS in ROM, usually in a 32K × 8-bit ROM. BIOS gets the computer started before the operating system is loaded from the hard drive. Besides storing computer program code, ROMs are used for other large-scale truth tables, such as table-lookup math (storing all the values of cosine, tangent, and so on), and for control of fonts in printers.

Why not use ROMs for realizing all truth tables? Skip the Boolean algebra, the Karnaugh maps, the minimizing algorithms. Just enter the truth table in a computer

[7] Years ago a student of mine walked her honors project across campus for a final demonstration. It was a sunny day, and the uncovered EPROM was erased by the ultraviolet rays in the sunlight by the time she got to her destination! Remember Einstein's result from 1905: $E = h\nu$, where ν is the frequency of the photon, E is its energy, and h is Planck's constant.

are some reasons why not: For one thing, minimizing (shrinking a canonical SOP design to a much smaller form) can pay big dividends. For another thing, a ROM is too much for small problems; it's like water-skiing behind an aircraft carrier. ROM chips may have a larger footprint on the circuit board than a smaller combinational chip, and a ROM costs more than a small TTL chip. In 1994, a 7400 quad NAND gate chip would cost 25¢ whereas a 2764 could be $8. Then, too, the cost of the PROM programmer must be considered. A Needham Electronics PROM programmer with ROM socket is about $125 (1992) and must be plugged into a slot in a personal computer. The hard-UV lamp for erasing the PROMs is another $50. Furthermore, the technology used to fabricate EPROMs results in propagation delays across the ROMs that are longer, by many nanoseconds, than the propagation delays across TTL chips. So speed can be a limitation for ROMs. In the next part of Chapter 4 we will see other programmable chips that are faster and more efficient at realizing large truth tables with limited numbers of TRUE outputs.

4.4 PROGRAMMABLE LOGIC DEVICES

A ROM is an example of a **programmable logic device (PLD).**[8] Here in Chapter 4 we consider PLDs only in the service of combinational logic. By *programmable* we mean that a designer, with a relatively low-cost machine such as the PROM programmer described previously, can configure a set of internal switches in the PLD that route signals to various logic gates in order to realize a particular circuit. Not only can the designer program the PLD, he or she *must*. A PLD arrives in a virgin state and must be configured at least once before being able to do something useful. With regard to combinational logic, nearly all PLDs give the user some version of a blank sum-of-products circuit, though some PLDs offer XOR gates at the output, for polarity control.

Let's start by reviewing where the programmable links are in a ROM. We know that N address inputs are turned into literals in the ROM and fan out to 2^N AND gates, with each AND gate representing a different possible minterm of an N-input truth table. In Fig. 4.27 the addresses come in at the bottom, where their complements are formed, and all $2N$ lines find their way to 2^N N-input AND gates. *The connections to the AND gates are not programmable.* For each bit of output, all the AND gates project to a common OR gate. *The links from the AND gates to the OR gates are programmable in a ROM.* If a link is removed during programming ("blown away" in the jargon), the associated AND gate has no influence on the output OR. The floating input of a blown link is LO for the OR gate.[9] The links that remain connect minterm AND gates with the output OR. Since the bank of AND gates acts as a decoder—with only one ac-

---

[8]Nonprogrammable logic devices, from the point of view of the logic system designer, are of two sorts: (1) off-the-shelf chips from standard logic families, which have commonly used functions (chips from the 7400 TTL series are in the off-the-shelf category), and (2) application-specific integrated circuits (ASICs), which are custom-designed chips for high-volume use in one particular application. ASICs are generally much larger-scale circuits—controllers for networks, high-speed calculators, etc.—than those found in standard logic families. In either case the user has no ability to alter the *internal* functions of nonprogrammable chips.

[9]Unlike standard TTL gates, where unconnected inputs typically float HI.

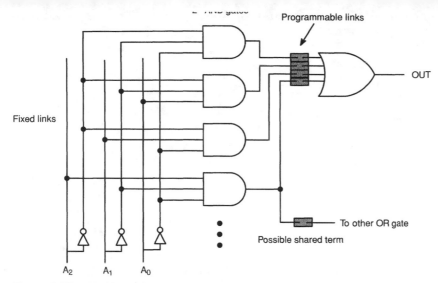

Figure 4.27 ROM logic diagram.

tive AND at a time—only when a TRUE line of the truth table is selected by the address will OUT be HI. In the ROM of Fig. 4.27 the demultiplexing process is started with $1 \rightarrow 2$ decoders on each address input A_i. A ROM doesn't need programmable links on the AND gate inputs because it accounts for all input combinations. The problem in configuring ROMs is choosing which AND gate outputs can be multiplexed to the final ROM output. The contents of the ROM locations can be more than one bit; if so, the output OR gates' inputs can share AND outputs, which fan out.

4.5   PROGRAMMED ARRAY LOGIC (PAL)

We now come to a programmable device more efficient than a ROM. If a logic function with many inputs generated relatively few TRUE conditions, most of a ROM would be wasted. Thus the motivation for the **programmable array logic,** or **PAL.** PALs have a limited number of N-input AND gates, but *the links from the PAL inputs to the AND gates are all programmable.* Again, there is (the equivalent of) an OR gate to supply the output of the PAL, but the links between the limited number of ANDs and the final OR are not programmable. In the PAL diagram shown in Fig. 4.28, each AND has $2N$ inputs, since complements of each input are generated internally. By the way, it wouldn't make sense to connect a PAL input *and* its complement to the same AND because the AND would always have 0 output; the software used to program the PAL can ensure that inputs to a PAL AND gate have such consistencies.

Compared with fixed-function logic chips, the use of a PAL entails two limitations: (1) The number of TRUEs in the truth table under consideration must be less than or equal to the number of AND gates per OR in the PAL. (2) A special programming system is needed to remove input-to-AND links in the PAL. (Once a link is blown, in most PALs, the process is irreversible. A different PAL chip must be programmed if a change is needed in the truth table.)

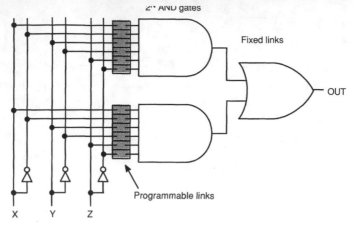

Figure 4.28   PAL connections.

On the other hand, a PAL has the following advantages: (1) Propagation delay is less than in a ROM. (2) Its footprint is smaller than that of a ROM or of random TTL gates (it takes up less room on a PC board). (3) A PAL generally costs less than a ROM. (4) Subsequent PAL chips can be reconfigured by programming to meet new specifications and then plugged into the sockets of the chips they're replacing. By these advantages PALs have come to occupy a large niche in the digital circuit design environment.

4.5.1   Schematic Conventions for PALs

PAL diagrams in data books have some special conventions. An input and its complement are represented by a dual-output triangle with one bubble to indicate inversion. It is a $1 \rightarrow 2$ decoder. See Fig. 4.29. The input decoder symbol on the right properly suggests that both the input and its complement have the same delay into the circuit.

Because ANDs are crowded together in PAL diagrams, a more compact notation is used. One line from the input side of a gate is crossed by all *possible* inputs. (See Fig. 4.30.) An X at an intersection represents a connection; the absence of an X means no connection. Thus a three-input AND gate for $F \cdot C \cdot A$ in this notation needs only a long input tail to which perpendicular inputs can attach or not. The AND gate shown has a limit of eight inputs, indicated by letters of the alphabet. The input lines

Figure 4.29   Generating both literals of a variable.

Figure 4.30   How AND gate inputs are represented in a PAL schematic.

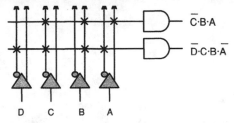

Figure 4.31 Two products in compact PAL form.

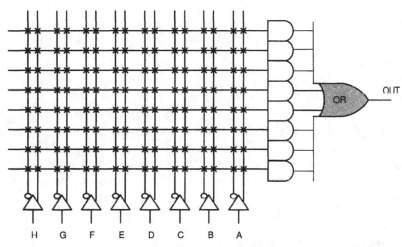

Figure 4.32 Uncommitted PAL cell.

are meant to cross all available AND gates and to do so through the $1 \rightarrow 2$ demultiplexers shown in Fig. 4.30. To extend the drawing of one AND gate to two, we have the diagram in Fig. 4.31. Now four inputs go to two AND gates, which realize the product terms $C \cdot \overline{B} \cdot \overline{A}$ and $D \cdot \overline{C} \cdot \overline{B} \cdot \overline{A}$.

In a PAL many AND gates must feed into one OR gate. To avoid drawing a huge gate, an OR gate with *input wings* is used to handle many inputs. An eight-input PAL OR gate is shown in Fig. 4.32. The PAL AND inputs are shown in their virgin state, fully connected with all intersections marked by X, before most connections are eliminated by programming. Commercial PALs normally have several (2, 4, 8, etc.) output OR gates, none of which share AND gate outputs.

4.5.2 Two Examples

EXAMPLE 10

Realize the Boolean expression

$$OUT = B \cdot \overline{C} \cdot E \cdot \overline{G} + A \cdot \overline{D} \cdot E \cdot \overline{H} + \overline{A} \cdot B \cdot C \cdot G \cdot \overline{H} + D \cdot E \cdot \overline{F} + G$$

with a PAL.

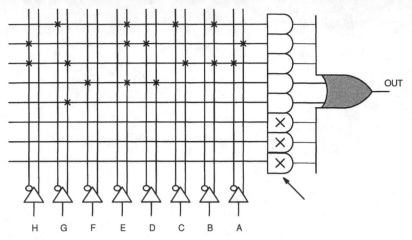

Figure 4.33 Committed PAL cell.

Answer Using the PAL grid of Fig. 4.32, we "program away" unwanted connections (Fig. 4.33). The top five AND gates realize the five product terms of OUT. Note that three of the AND gates are unused (completely unused AND gates are sometimes marked with a larger X). On a computer screen PAL programmer software would show each minterm as a string of 1s and 0s associated with input literals.

Commercial PALs generally have several (some power of 2) OR gate outputs per chip. As mentioned, the output ORs in a PAL don't share product terms. Let's look at such a prototype PAL in the next design example.

EXAMPLE 11

Two-Bit Comparators Suppose two two-bit numbers, B_1B_0 and A_1A_0, are to be compared. The comparator will have three outputs: "$B = A$," "$B > A$," and "$B < A$." Assume that B and A are unsigned positionally coded integers. Design a circuit to fit in a multiple-output PAL.

Answer Karnaugh maps for the three outputs are shown in Fig. 4.34. Notice how the columns of the map for $B > A$ are the rows of the map for $B < A$. By gathering the 1s of the largest subcubes (prime implicants), we find that the Boolean SOP functions for the three outputs are

$$\text{"}B = A\text{"} = \overline{B_1} \cdot \overline{B_0} \cdot \overline{A_1} \cdot \overline{A_0} + \overline{B_1} \cdot B_0 \cdot \overline{A_1} \cdot A_0 + B_1 \cdot \overline{B_0} \cdot A_1 \cdot \overline{A_0} + B_1 \cdot B_0 \cdot A_1 \cdot A_0$$

$$\text{"}B > A\text{"} = B_0 \cdot \overline{A_1} \cdot \overline{A_0} + B_1 \cdot \overline{A_1} + B_1 \cdot B_0 \cdot \overline{A_0}$$

$$\text{"}B < A\text{"} = \overline{B_0} \cdot \overline{A_1} \cdot \overline{A_0} + \overline{B_1} \cdot \overline{A_1} + \overline{B_1} \cdot \overline{B_0} \cdot \overline{A_0}$$

No product terms are shared. The diagram in Fig. 4.35 shows the format of a four-input, four-product-term, three-output PAL burned with the correct connections to realize the comparator function.

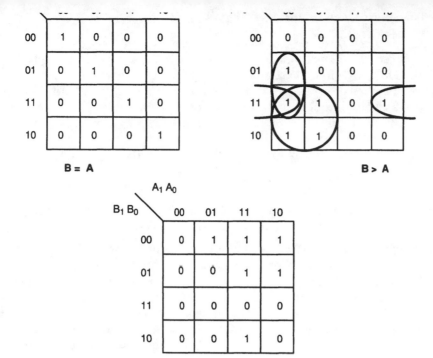

Figure 4.34   K-maps for two-bit comparator.

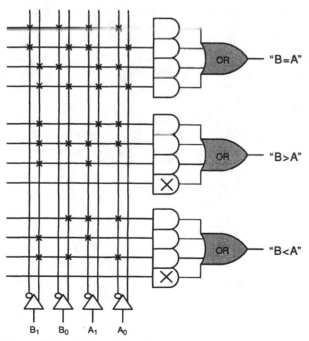

Figure 4.35   PAL configured as comparator.

223

Programmable array logic devices have been a commercial success since they were introduced in 1978 by Monolithic Memories; they are commonly used as replacement devices for fixed-function combinational TTL chips. Three parameters specify a PAL: (1) the number of input pins, (2) the number of output pins, and (3) the number of AND gates per output OR. The first two of these parameters are used in naming PAL parts; thus a 20-pin PAL 16L8 chip can have up to 16 inputs. The last number tells you that the 16L8 has eight outputs. Each output pin can be designated as an input. The middle letter in the chip name tells what form the output takes; for example:

L	Active-low
H	Active-high
C	Complementary outputs (both active-high and active-low)
X or P	Exclusive OR gate output (for external control of output polarity)

In general, the fewer the outputs of a PAL, the more AND gates it has per OR gate. The 16L2 PAL supports 16 product terms per OR gate.

The output portion of a 16P8 chip is shown in Fig. 4.36 programmed for noninversion (the XOR and the enabled inverter cancel each other). If the polarity control of the XOR is set to ground, the output is inverted. If the output of the final inverter gate is disabled, the square pin can function as input to other AND gates in the 16P8. The inverter with an enable input has a special **three-state output**, shown in detail in Fig. 4.37. Recall complementary switches from Chapter 1, a set of which is at the right in the circuit in Fig. 4.37. If output-enable (OE) is LO, both switches are open and PIN is disconnected from both data paths. In the truth table the disconnect condition is listed as "Hi-Z" (short for *high impedance*). In the Hi-Z state PIN can function as an input, and the route of the input is shown in the figure. If OE is asserted, the output of the OR gate can be fed back to the AND array. In Chapter 5 we will develop the possibilities of feedback circuits. For now we rule out feedback in combinational circuits, except to point out the potential for feedback in commercial PALs. In a 16L8 PAL, 10 of the inputs come from dedicated input pins and another six can come from I/O pins controlled by output-enable.

The schematic diagrams in data books for PALs follow a standard format. Figure 4.38 shows one OR gate's worth of a 16L8 schematic. None of the X's for connec-

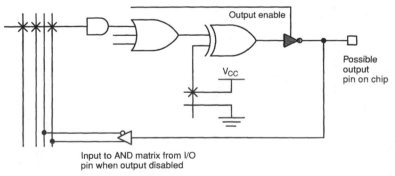

Figure 4.36 Output of a PAL chip.

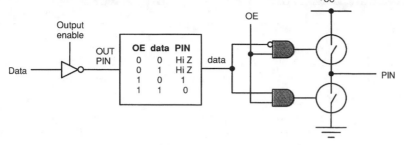

Figure 4.37 Detail of a Hi-Z control.

tions are indicated; the user is free to mark them in. Inputs on the left (only 2 of the 10 are shown) are demultiplexed 1 to 2. Then those pairs of lines make the connections indicated by dots with the vertical lines crossing the AND inputs. The eight AND gates are shown packed next to the OR gate, with the top AND heading directly for output enable control. If output is disabled, pin 18 can function as a possible input pin for the enabled outputs. Since there is an inverter on the output, the 16L8 PAL is active-low—the designer should pay attention to the LO outputs in the truth table he or she is trying to realize.

PALs have many more gates and internal connections than TTL gates with about the same number of pins. The 20-pin 16L8 has 72 eight-input AND and OR gates; a 16-pin 7485 comparator has 30 AND and OR gates, with about three inputs per gate. PAL propagation delay (in high-speed versions) is as low as in advanced TTL chips; a 74F85 (TTL comparator, four levels of delay) has about 10 ns t_{pd}, and an AMD 16L8 PAL can have as little as 5 ns of delay (three-level logic).[10]

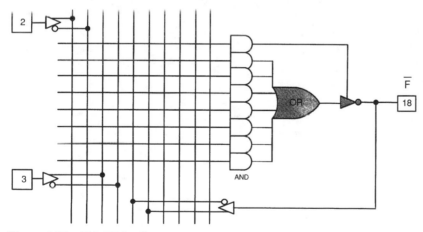

Figure 4.38 PAL 16L8 cell.

---

[10]The decreased propagation delay comes at a great expense in power consumption; a 5-ns 16L8 PAL will draw about 200 mA of current. On the other hand, there are slower, low-power 16L8s that consume less than a milliamp of current. In general there is a speed-power trade-off that a designer may need to consider. (See *Daniels' Digital Design Lab Manual* for more details.)

EXAMPLE 12

Design a four-bit equality detector using a PAL. That is, if B and A are two four-bit numbers $B_3B_2B_1B_0$ and $A_3A_2A_1A_0$, then the detector output is asserted only when $B_i = A_i$, for $i = 0$ to 3.

Answer   There are eight inputs to the truth table. But even though there are $2^8 = 256$ input combinations, only 16 of the combinations result in TRUE output. The 16 are shown in Table 4.1. A PAL with eight inputs and 16 product terms per output will be able to handle this problem. Each of the 16 combinations in Table 4.1 is a prime implicant minterm that requires an eight-input AND gate to form a product. Looking in a PAL data book, you will find that the 16L2, a PAL with 16 inputs, two active-low outputs, and 16 product terms per output OR, can do the job. What about the active LO output? Either the user can accept that LO output represents $B = A$, or an inverter is needed. Since only 8 of the 16 inputs on the 16L2 are used for inputs B and A, a ninth input to the second OR gate could receive the first OR gate output and be programmed for the inversion. The 16L2 has no internal feedback like the 16L8, so an external wire, as indicated in Fig. 4.39, would be needed.

In Chapter 2 we saw XORs in the service of comparators. Our problem here could have been solved with four TTL XORs feeding into a four-input AND. But the PAL approach is more versatile. If we wanted to change specifications and match, say, a four-bit number N with another number P greater by 1 (test for $P = N + 1$), it would be a straightforward matter to reprogram a PAL and plug it back in the same socket. It would be more problematic to redesign an XOR logic circuit and rewire such fixed-function logic chips.

Table 4.1   Input Combinations for OUTPUT = TRUE in Four-bit Comparator

$B_3 \ B_2 \ B_1 \ B_0$	$A_3 \ A_2 \ A_1 \ A_0$
0 0 0 0	0 0 0 0
0 0 0 1	0 0 0 1
0 0 1 0	0 0 1 0
0 0 1 1	0 0 1 1
0 1 0 0	0 1 0 0
0 1 0 1	0 1 0 1
0 1 1 0	0 1 1 0
0 1 1 1	0 1 1 1
1 0 0 0	1 0 0 0
1 0 0 1	1 0 0 1
1 0 1 0	1 0 1 0
1 0 1 1	1 0 1 1
1 1 0 0	1 1 0 0
1 1 0 1	1 1 0 1
1 1 1 0	1 1 1 0
1 1 1 1	1 1 1 1

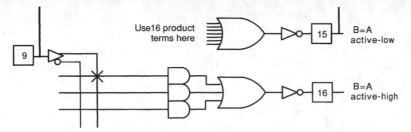

Figure 4.39 Feedback pin as input in PAL.

4.5.5 Folding, Factoring, and Partitioning

When a designer sends some PAL outputs back to become inputs, the operation is called **folding**. We saw that the 16L8 has internal folding that can be activated by choosing OR gate output feedback paths to the AND gate connection matrix. The 16L2 in Example 12 is folded *externally* to invert an output through an unused OR-INVERT gate. Folding does not necessarily violate our restriction against feedback in combinational circuits. It can sometimes be a way to cascade combinational circuits together for multi-level designs.

If a Boolean expression has too many inputs for one PAL, the expression must be **factored** so it can be **partitioned** into two or more PALs. Sometimes the distributive laws or Shannon's theorem, from Chapter 2, can be of help.

EXAMPLE 13

Consider a hypothetical small PAL chip with four inputs and two outputs. Use two such small PALs to realize the Boolean function

$$P = C \cdot \overline{E} \cdot F + C \cdot E \cdot \overline{F} + D \cdot A + D \cdot \overline{B}$$

There are six different inputs (*A–F*) so one PAL is not enough.

Answer   Factor P (by inspection, or by Shannon's theorem) into

$$P = C \cdot (\overline{E} \cdot F + E \cdot \overline{F}) + D \cdot (A + \overline{B})$$

So if $X = \overline{E} \cdot F + E \cdot \overline{F} = E \oplus F$ and $Y = A + \overline{B}$, we can say that $P = C \cdot X + D \cdot Y$, a sum of products with four terms. Form $(\overline{E} \cdot F + E \cdot \overline{F})$ and $(A + \overline{B})$ in one PAL, and fold X and Y to a second PAL to merge with C and D, as shown on the next page in Fig. 4.40, which uses a data book standard for PAL schematics. The second AND-OR circuit on the lower PAL is not shown. Notice how few of the PAL connections remain!

Folding effectively can increase the number of product terms one OR gate in a PAL can accept. For example, if all six of the output pins that can be folded are sent back to the same AND gate in a 16L8, the receiving OR gate can handle 15 inputs.

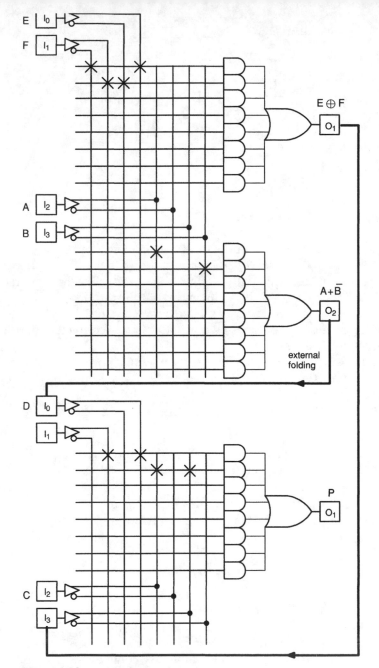

Figure 4.40 Folding a PAL design.

A sum-of-products array in which the connections from AND to OR are programmable is a ROM; a sum-of-products array in which the connections from input to AND are programmable is a PAL. If both the AND and the OR links of a chip are modifiable, the accepted terminology is **programmable logic array (PLA)**. PLAs have a limited number of AND gates, like PALs. But unlike PALs, PLA OR gates can share product terms. A small PLA is shown in Fig. 4.41, where the output OR gates share $\frac{2}{4}$ of the product terms. The AND gate outputs are demultiplexed like the external inputs; if OR gates are to share a product term and its complement, the complement must be formed on a separate AND gate. The greater fan-in of PLA OR gates creates more delay, so PLAs are a few nanoseconds slower than similar-sized PALs. And, too, the expense of programmable OR inputs on a PLA make a PLA chip more costly than a PAL with the same number of product terms.

Signetics Inc. has been well known for its PLAs. As an example, the Signetics PLS100 has 16 inputs that can contact 48 AND gates; the 48 AND gate outputs are shared by eight OR gates. The PLS100 is a 28-pin chip. PLA flexibility is often built into more general-purpose logic chips, containing flip-flops and other sequential hardware. The Signetics PLS105 sends 16 inputs to 48 AND gates, which are shared by 29 OR gates; the OR gate outputs control set and reset inputs on 14 flip-flops (in a way you'll learn in Chapter 5). Six of the flip-flops fold back as additional product term inputs, and the other eight provide the actual PLS105 output.

Programmable logic arrays with a full programmable interconnect of AND to OR gates actually preceded PALs into the marketplace in the mid-1970s, but they failed to catch on because their propagation delays were much greater than those of TTL chips. Only when the fan-in to the OR gates was restricted—resulting in the PAL format—did the resulting chips speed up enough to compete with TTL.

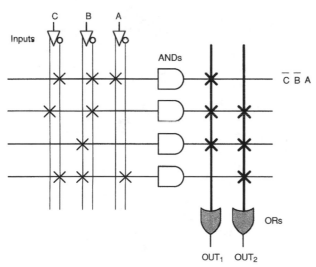

Figure 4.41 PLA sum of products.

Up to now we have fitted logic-problem realizations into two-level SOP formats. What has come to be known as a **field-programmable gate array (FPGA)** offers a more flexible approach to combinational design. Commercial FPGAs contain flip-flops and other circuitry we have not dealt with to this point; here we concentrate on the combinational features of FPGAs. Each FPGA manufacturer incorporates different features in the **logic blocks** and **I/O pads** of their devices, but all have in common a two-dimensional array ("sea of gates") of identical logic blocks surrounded by horizontal and vertical wiring resources. Figure 4.42 is a diagram of one corner of a typical FPGA. In the Xilinx 3090 FPGA there are 320 logic blocks, 72 input-output pads, and a total of 166 pins.

What you should appreciate at this point about FPGAs is their great difference from PALs. One FPGA logic block can be programmed to implement a two- to four-level combinational circuit, and the output(s) of that logic block can become the inputs to other logic blocks. (As more levels are involved, critical timing paths become important.)

A major challenge in the use of FPGAs is the routing of connections from one logic block to another and from the I/O pads to the logic blocks. Over half of the area of an FPGA is taken up with lines and switches that can be programmed for short and long connections between internal and external "pins" in the FPGA. Much of the routing is normally done by trial-and-error optimizing algorithms, similar in spirit to

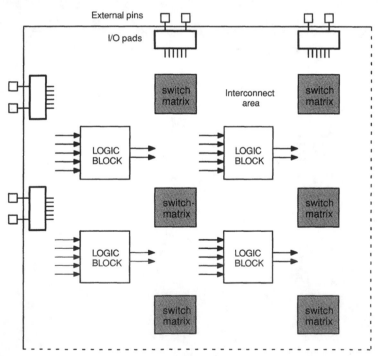

Figure 4.42   FPGA cells in corner of chip.

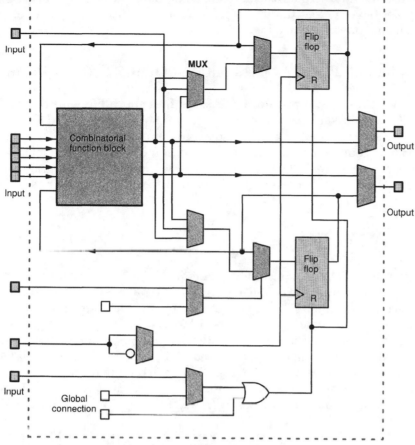

Figure 4.43 Cell in a Xilinx FPGA 3000-series chip.

the evolutionary algorithm presented at the end of Chapter 3. However, it is possible for a designer to learn about the wiring resources and "hand-connect," with software, circuits or parts of circuits.

Now we go down one level of detail and examine the diagram in Fig. 4.43 of the internals of one logic block from a Xilinx 3000-series FPGA. It has two flip-flops to the right, whose operation need not concern us at this point. Shown in the diagram are nine multiplexers, shaded in. The selects on all multiplexers must be specified and controlled. The seven-input **combinatorial function unit** on the left can be programmed to realize any two four-input logic functions, or any one five-input logic function. You can think of the combinatorial function unit as an embedded PLA; it contains another half-dozen multiplexers. The logic block accommodates up to eight inputs and two outputs. An FPGA containing over 100 logic blocks is capable of a stupendous variety of logic operations. A full understanding of FPGA capability awaits your learning about flip-flops, clocked sequencers, and state machines. For now it is enough to appreciate the combinational resources of the logic block of one

that do not have to pass through flip-flops and can therefore be part of a strictly combinational operation for a logic block.

4.8 SOFTWARE FOR PROGRAMMING PROGRAMMABLE LOGIC DEVICES

ROMs and PALs, and especially FPGAs, are brought to life with computer-aided design (CAD) software. As outlined near the end of Chapter 1, CAD is involved in both synthesis and simulation of designs. Programming a ROM is straightforward; you create a computer file of addresses and contents (the truth table itself). The software then downloads the file through a cable from a PROM programmer card in the computer. The cable contacts the ROM in a socket and transfers a voltage that programs the data file.

4.8.1 CAD Help for PALs

The design for a PAL may have to be optimized, because a PAL has far less than a complete set of minterms available for its N inputs. Software help for fitting a logic specification into a PAL starts with either truth tables or Boolean equations. Particular help can come from the proprietary software of manufacturers of PALs and PAL programmers. There are two widely used CAD packages, **ABEL** (Advanced Boolean Expression Language, developed by DATA I/O Corp.) and **PALASM**. ABEL[11] is a *language* because it comes with a compiler that translates a high-level (usually Boolean) description into a fuse pattern for a particular PAL chip. The expression-minimizing software in ABEL is adapted from the algorithms of Espresso, discussed at the end of Chapter 3.

PALASM (short for *PAL assembler*, and distributed free by AMD Inc.) was the first CAD software for PALs and is still widely used to convert Boolean expressions or truth tables into fuse maps for PALs. PALASM requires the user to put Boolean expressions in SOP form and to specify which pins on the target chip will handle the required input and output.

The end result of employing ABEL or PALASM to implement a Boolean equation in a PAL is the compilation of a fuse pattern for a specific PAL. The fuse pattern is downloaded as a JEDEC (Joint Electron Device Engineering Council) file to a PLD programmer. The PAL chip rests in a zero-insertion-force socket on the programmer hardware, connected by a ribbon cable to the computer. The programmer generates the correct timing and voltage waveforms to burn the fuse pattern into the PAL.

EXAMPLE 14

This example is adapted from Pellerin and Holley (1991).[12] Use ABEL to implement in a PAL a $3 \rightarrow 1$ MUX with a four-bit-wide data path. There will be 12 pins devoted

---

[11] As if you didn't have enough ways already to express Boolean operators, ABEL and some other keyboard-based Boolean expression software use the conventions AND=&, OR=#, INVERT=!, and XOR=$.

[12] See Chapter 2 of Pellerin and Holley for a good history of programmable logic devices.

to data input (3×4) and 4 pins for output. Two more pins will be needed for the select inputs on this MUX. The target PAL will be a P16H8. Active-high outputs are desired.

Answer Let the data inputs be a3, a2, a1, a0; b3, b2, b1, b0; c3, c2, c1, c0; let the select inputs be s1, s0; and let the outputs be y3, y2, y1, y0. The main features of the ABEL script for the $3 \rightarrow 1$ four-bit MUX are shown below:

```
                    device   'P16V8S'

a3, a2, a1, a0      pin      1, 2, 3, 4;
b3, b2, b1, b0      pin      5, 6, 7, 8;
c3, c2, c1, c0      pin      9, 11, 12, 13;
y3, y2, y1, y0      pin      14, 15, 16, 17;
s1, s0              pin      18, 19;

select  =      [s1..s0];
Y       =      [y3..y0];
A       =      [a3..a0];
B       =      [b3..b0];
C       =      [c3..c0];

equations
        Y =  (select == 1) & A
           # (select == 2) & B
           # (select == 3) & C;

end
```

The first line indicates the target device. The next section of the ABEL code declares which pins on the PAL the signals are assigned to. Variable names are then given to the signal sets. The key part of the ABEL code is the Boolean equation; it is shown in ABEL notation, using the variable names. The symbol $==$ stands for logical equality, & is AND, and # is OR. In the notation standard in this book, the Boolean equation would say

$$Y = \overline{S_1} \cdot S_0 \cdot A + S_1 \cdot \overline{S_0} \cdot B + S_1 \cdot S_0 \cdot C$$

If S_1 and S_0 are both 0, then the output Y will be all 0s.

When the ABEL script is compiled, the Boolean expression is expanded into four sums of products for each of the Y outputs. Further processing by ABEL results in a fuse map that can be downloaded to a programmer to convert a virgin 16H into a $3 \rightarrow 1$ four-bit MUX.

EXAMPLE 15

In the end-of-chapter problems of Chapter 1 is a greater-than design. Pellerin and Holley (1991, 209) revisit the problem and show that compiling the ABEL statement for greater-than,

```
A_GT_B = [a7...a0] > [b7...b0]
```

creates 255 product terms, which can't be realized in fewer than 10 PLDs! They go on to show that designing a one-bit greater-than circuit and then cascading eight of them together does result in a design that can fit in one PAL. It turns out that the partitioning of the eight-bit greater-than circuit into eight smaller problems is not a solution that ABEL can identify. An attentive designer can still prove his or her usefulness in spite of competition from computer algorithms!

4.8.2 CAD Help for FPGAs

The use of field-programmable gate arrays is much more tied to elaborate CAD software than other chips so far considered. Because the FPGAs of various manufacturers are so different from one another, proprietary software is the rule. The following will be an overview of the XACT software for Xilinx FPGAs.

The XACT steps from concept to verified design are shown in Fig. 4.44. The process starts with "schematic capture," the drawing and labeling of the circuit to be implemented. The designer may have used other CAD software to help with the design layout. While it is technically possible to hand-wire FPGA logic blocks from within the XACT design editor, the designer normally relies on an automated process after his or her schematic has been generated. In the steps in Fig 4.44 the place-and-route routine is by far the most computationally intensive. Using something like the evolutionary algorithm discussed at the end of Chapter 3, the place-and-route routine tries out various arrangements of logic blocks and connections, reducing delay in the process. An hour of computer time on a PC is not uncommon for the place-and-route phases. In designs that attempt to utilize over 70% of the logic blocks, placing and routing may run out of wiring resources before the design is finished.

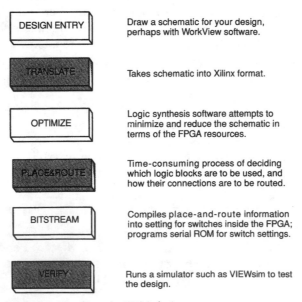

Figure 4.44   Steps in FPGA design.

In Chapter 4 you have learned about circuits with regular, repeating sum-of-products structures that can implement large truth tables. Multiplexers, ROM, and PALs can realize truth tables by versions of table look-up. These one-stop-shopping hardware solutions come at some cost in additional gates (and sometimes additional delay) compared with the minimization methods discussed in Chapter 3. For additional information see Pellerin and Holley (1991), *Xilinx Programmable Gate Array Data Book, 1995;* Haznedar (1991); and Geiger, Allen, and Strader (1990, chap. 8).

In Chapter 4 we've dealt with solutions to large-scale practical problems in truth table realization. We've made a closer approach to commercial practices than in the previous two chapters. As a result, we've named names. We've discussed real chips, from 7400-series MUXs to ROM to PALs to 160-pin FPGAs, and we have named companies: AMD, Data I-O, Signetics, Xilinx, and others. You should come away from Chapter 4 remembering more than names; you should appreciate that the SOP architecture has inspired MUX, ROM, and PAL chips. Even the combinational part of field-programmable gate arrays, when dissected down to its basics, is no more than a large collection of multiplexers, OR gates, sum-of-product circuits, and routing resources.

- **Multiplexers (or encoders)** use their N select inputs to choose from among 2^N data inputs; the selected data input becomes the output. The data inputs can be attached to ground or to $+5\,V$ to realize a truth table directly, or the data inputs can be connected to other logic gates for more complicated arrangements. A cascade of multiplexers sharing common selects can increase the size of the truth table served.

- **Demultiplexers (or decoders)** are the input-decoding AND gates that form a subset of a MUX. For N select inputs, a decoder has 2^N outputs. A convention in TTL chips has it that the *selected* output of a demultiplexer is LO, and the remaining $2^N - 1$ outputs are HI (active-low convention).

- By connecting truth table inputs to **read-only memory (ROM)** address pins and programming the memory to function as a lookup table for outputs, a one-chip solution can be created to realize a truth table in hardware. Unlike multiplexers, ROMs have no data-input pins; their representation of truth table output is internal to the chip.

- A **programmed array logic** chip **(PAL)** has a set of AND-to-OR gates that can handle a relatively small subset of the total number of minterms of many inputs. The links of input to the *first-level ANDs* in a PAL are user-programmable. To maximize speed, OR gates in PALs do not share product terms.

- ROMs and PALs are constrained examples of **programmable logic arrays (PLAs);** a general-purpose PLA has modifiable connections at both AND and OR inputs, and its OR gates can share product terms.

- **Field-programmable gate arrays (FPGAs)** offer a more flexible approach to programmable logic. The FPGA, sometimes referred to as a "sea of gates," is rich in multiplexers for combinatorial logic. Even the input-output pads of FPGAs have considerable logic devoted to data routing.

- Programming a PAL is done with the aid of software, such as **ABEL** (Advanced Boolean Expression Language) or **PALASM** (PAL assembler). Typically a user enters a Boolean expression by keyboard, and then the software creates a fuse pattern that specialized hardware burns into a particular PAL.

- CAD support for FPGAs is high-level and sophisticated. A package such as PowerView allows for *schematic capture* of a design. The designer then chooses a particular FPGA chip, and after internally configuring logic blocks, the software begins a laborious process of *place and route,* attempting to fit and optimize the design to the particular logic blocks and connections in the FPGA.

End of Combinational Logic   The end of Chapter 4 is the end of our look at circuits obeying the combinational logic restriction of no feedback. The concepts you have learned, however, are necessary building blocks for the sequential logic design to come next in the book. We leave combinational logic with a seven-fold mnemonic for remembering the tools we've developed for analyzing and synthesizing combinational circuits.

Minterms	The entry point for sum of products
Math	Boolean algebra and its theorems for reduction
Maps	Karnaugh maps as a way to find prime implicants
McCluskey	The Quine-McCluskey tabular reduction method
Multiplexers	A general-purpose method for realizing small truth tables
Memory	Read-only memory
Monolithic	Monolithic Memories, the company that launched PALs

Exercises

1. **(a)** Restrict your attention to outputs that can be only 0 or 1. How many different *truth tables* are there with
   (i) Two inputs and one output?
   (ii) Two inputs and two outputs?
   (iii) Four inputs and one output?
   (b) How would your answers change if don't-care outputs were allowed? For this problem consider a don't-care output to be different from a 0 or 1 output, even though after a circuit is realized an output will always be 0 or 1.

2. A Xilinx 3000-series field-programmable gate array has configurable logic blocks (CLBs) with combinatorial function generators a user can program. Shown in Fig. P4.1 is the combinatorial generator in its four-variable mode, with three MUXs helping route seven possible inputs. Select lines for the three MUXs are not shown, but they can be programmed by the user. The seven possible inputs are $A, B, C, D, E, X,$ and Y.

   How many different combinations of four out of the seven inputs are possible, given the arrangement of MUXs in Fig. P4.1? Let's say the four inputs of any combination must all be different; that is, A, X, X, D doesn't count.

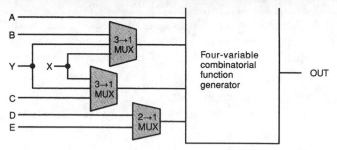

Figure P4.1   Xilinx 3000-series FPGA combinational logic block.

3. Consider a $4 \rightarrow 1$ multiplexer with select inputs X and Y and data inputs P, Q, R, and S. Write out the Boolean expression for the output of the multiplexer.

4. **(a)**   How many data inputs can a MUX with four select inputs accommodate?
    (b)   To realize a four-select MUX with a sum-of-product AND-to-OR form, how many AND gates are required? How many inputs will each AND gate need?

5. Realize the truth table for Example 1 in a $4 \rightarrow 1$ MUX. Look at the inputs CB in the rearrangement below. Do you see what to use as each of the four inputs?

ABC	$CARRY_{OUT}$	ABC	$CARRY_{OUT}$
000	0	001	0
010	0	011	1
100	0	101	1
110	1	111	1

6. Write a Boolean expression for the output of the MUX shown below. A, B, and C are inputs controlling the MUX select. D is a fourth input, connected to the line selected when $CBA = 000$.

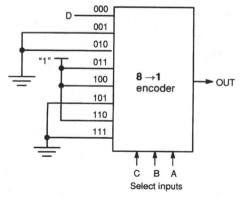

Figure P4.2

7. (a) Use a MUX with one select input to realize an inverter.
   (b) Use a MUX with two select inputs to realize a two-input NAND gate.
   (c) Use a MUX with three select inputs to realize a three-input NOR gate.
   (d) Use a MUX with three select inputs to realize an any-three-out-of-four circuit.

8. A $2 \rightarrow 1$ MUX has three inputs, including SELECT. Can a $2 \rightarrow 1$ MUX be used to mimic any of the following two-input gates, and if so, how?
   (a) XOR
   (b) AND
   (c) NAND
   (d) OR

9. What size of multiplexer could be used to realize the law of consensus for three inputs to eliminate static timing hazards? Draw out the circuit. Review the timing section at the end of Chapter 2 if necessary.

10. (a) Draw out the Karnaugh map of a 2/3 majority gate.
    (b) Use one multiplexer to design an any-two-out-of-three majority circuit.
    (c) With the two-out-of-three design as a building block, design an any-three-out-of-five majority circuit with multiplexers.

11. How many $2 \rightarrow 1$ MUXs would it take to make one $8 \rightarrow 1$ MUX? Draw out the circuit.

12. Show that five $4 \rightarrow 1$ MUXs can be arranged to design a $16 \rightarrow 1$ MUX.

13. Will the combination of three $2 \rightarrow 1$ MUXs shown below function as a $4 \rightarrow 1$ MUX? If not, how can it be fixed?

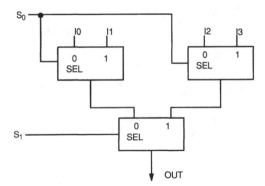

Figure P4.3

14. (a) Show that $N + 1$ of $N \rightarrow 1$ MUXs can be arranged to make one $4N \rightarrow 1$ MUX.
    (b) Show that $N - 1$ of $2 \rightarrow 1$ MUXs can be arranged to make one $N \rightarrow 1$ MUX.

15. What K-map describes the following $4 \to 1$ MUX set-up?

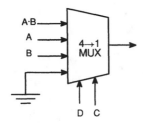

Figure P4.4

16. Draw out the four-input K-map for the following combination of $2 \to 1$ MUXs:

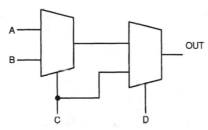

Figure P4.5

17. Realize the following K-map for OUT with the help of one $4 \to 1$ MUX. Use no more than two other gates and two other inverters besides the $4 \to 1$ MUX.

DC \ BA	00	01	11	10
00	0	1	1	0
01	1	0	1	0
11	0	1	0	1
10	0	0	0	0

WX \ YZ	00	01	11	10
00	0	1	1	0
01	0	0	1	1
11	0	0	0	0
10	1	1	0	0

(a) If W and X are used as the select inputs to a $4 \to 1$ MUX, what can generate the data inputs?

(b) If Y and Z are used as the select inputs to a $4 \to 1$ MUX, what circuit can form the data inputs?

19. Use Shannon's expansion theorem to realize the following expression with a $4 \to 1$ MUX:

$$OUT = (P \oplus Q) \cdot S + (R \oplus S) \cdot Q$$

20. How many different output combinations can a $3 \to 8$ demultiplexer produce?

21. Write out the truth table(s) for an active-low $3 \to 8$ demultiplexer.

‡22. **Four-by-four crossbar switch** You saw a two-by-two crossbar switch at the end of Chapter 1. Now design a circuit with four data inputs and four outputs so that the four inputs are routed to any of the four outputs. We want a permuting crossbar: at any one time one input can be routed to only one output. To select the permutation of inputs to outputs, other "nondata" inputs to the crossbar switch will be needed. The diagram below suggests that you might need four such selector inputs.

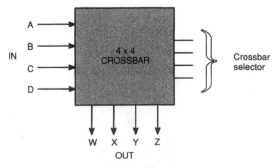

Figure P4.6 Crossbar switch.

Exactly how many different arrangements of inputs to outputs are there?

23. Unlike cascades of encoders, cascades of decoders aren't good for much. For the circuit below, however, what outputs will be LO for what combinations of inputs $S_1 S_0$?

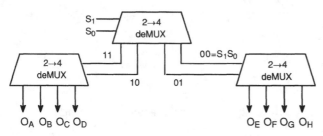

Figure P4.7

24. Show how to form a $4 \to 16$ decoder by using the enable inputs on smaller demultiplexers.

25. The need for a $2 \to 1$ MUX will arise when a two-digit display system has one data bus. Assume that you are given a display driver chip with four binary inputs $DCBA$ and seven-segment outputs in a circuit to display two digits.

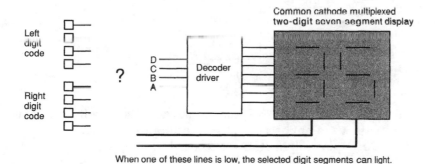

When one of these lines is low, the selected digit segments can light.

Figure P4.8

Show how a MUX and a decoder can be used to send left-digit and right-digit code information to the display unit. Where should the control signals for the active-low digit select lines shown in bold come from?

26. Design an active-low BCD decoder with four selects and 10 outputs. Call the select inputs $DCBA$. One of the 10 outputs will be active whenever the four selects code for the decimal digits 0–9. Let all outputs be HI if hex numbers A_{16}–F_{16} are presented at the select inputs.

27. Priority encoder Design a three-bit priority encoder. As shown below, input C has the highest priority.

IN			OUT	
C	B	A	X	Y
H	X	X	1	1
L	H	X	1	0
L	L	H	0	1
L	L	L	0	0

Whenever C is HI, the output is 11, no matter what B and A are. If C is LO, input B has priority over A. If all three inputs are LO, then OUT = XY = 00.

28. There are more efficient ways to decode the select inputs on larger decoders. Below is a diagram of a matrix decoder for a 4 → 16 decoder. Each of the 16 shaded boxes contains a two-input AND gate.

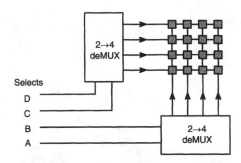

Figure P4.9 More efficient decoding.

(a) How many total AND gate inputs does the circuit above have, compared with a straight decoder of 16 four-input ANDs?

(b) Does the straight 16 × 4 decoder have more or less delay from input to output than the matrix decoder above?

(c) What would be the advantage of matrix decoding if eight selects were needed and the measure of cost were the total number of AND gate inputs (compared with a bank of eight-input AND gates)?

29. In a ROM is it possible for two different addresses to have the same contents? Is it possible for the same address to have two different contents? Define what is meant by *contents* before you answer the question.

30. A 7411 is a triple three-input AND chip. If all six AND gates on two 7411s are cascaded together, they can form a 13-input product. A 2764 ROM has 13 address pins. Say a 7411 costs 25¢ and a 2764, $10. How many TRUE lines must a 13-input truth table have before it becomes less costly to realize with a 2764 than

with a 7411? Assume that each minterm is a prime implicant for this problem.
(Notice we're not using the full output capability of the 2764, which can realize
eight different single-output, 13-input truth tables simultaneously.)

31. In Chapter 2 we considered a truth table for driving a seven-segment display,
shown below.

   (a) How can a read-only-memory be used as a decoder for a four-bit binary
        code for seven segments of output?
   (b) We can certainly make examples of the numbers 0–9 on such a display, but
        exactly how many *different* symbols can be made from a seven-segment
        display?

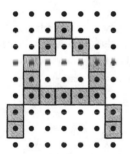
Labeling of the seven segments.

32. The font patterns for the 26 letters of the alphabet (uppercase and lowercase)
and 10 digits are to be specified in ROM chips. The patterns are to be displayed
in a seven-wide, nine-high array of LED lights. If 1M × 4 ROM chips are to be
used, how many will be needed for the whole font specification?

Figure P4.10   Dot-matrix
lettering.

33. Can you think of an exception to the following claim? "Every combinational
circuit is some form of read-only memory, in the sense that circuit input is the
address and circuit output is the contents."

34. Consider a 64K ROM in the form of 2^{16} words, each word with one bit of output.
While it is true that there are more efficient forms of addressing 64K words than
using 65,536 16-input AND gates, let's say that AND gates is the addressing
scheme for this particular ROM. Count as links in the chip all connects to the
AND gates and all connections to a final OR gate. What percentage of the links
in this ROM are programmable?

Shown below is a four-input PAL structure with some links blown and others intact. Intact links are colored. What Boolean expression results at OUT? Can the expression be simplified more?

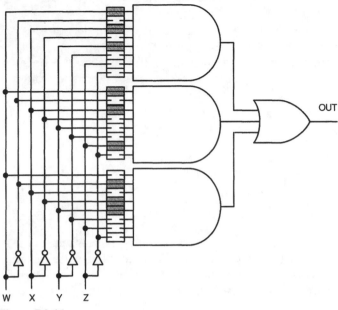

OUT

W X Y Z

Figure P4.11

36. In a PAL the inputs are sent through a 1 → 2 decoder, the outputs of which cross all possible AND gate input "tails." What happens if both outputs of the same input decoder are connected to the same AND gate?

37. Draw in conventional schematic form the three parts of programmed logic diagrams shown in Fig. P4.12.

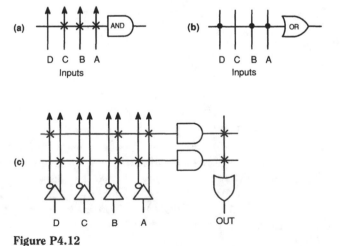

(a) AND
D C B A
Inputs

(b) OR
D C B A
Inputs

(c)
D C B A   OUT

Figure P4.12

38. Suppose a PAL is needed to indicate when three-bit numbers A, B add up to 8, that is, when $B_2 B_1 B_0 + A_2 A_1 A_0 = 1000$. How many product terms will be needed? Draw out a PAL design for the NOT EQUAL circuit.

39. The TTL 7485 comparator is a combinational chip that accepts two four-bit inputs, $B_3 B_2 B_1 B_0$ and $A_3 A_2 A_1 A_0$, and produces outputs for EQUAL, GREATER THAN, and LESS THAN. As you saw in an example in Chapter 4, 16 product terms would be required to realize the EQUAL function of a 7485 if an SOP form were used.

(a) How many product terms would be involved in determining greater-than?

(b) The 7485 has three other cascading inputs, also labeled $A = B$, $A > B$, and $A < B$. These inputs can come from the outputs of another 7485 to increase the size of the binary numbers being compared. If the cascaded form of the 7485 comparator chip were to be realized with PALs, how many product terms would be needed for the $A = B$ output (given now 11 inputs, that is, four As, four Bs, and three cascade inputs)?

(c) How many 16L8 PALs would be needed to implement the cascaded comparator?

If you look in a TTL data book, you can see that the 7485 is realized as a multi-level design to take advantage of XOR operations early in the processing of the inputs.

40. Fit the K-map and Boolean expression on the left into the PAL diagram on the right. The dots on the OR gates represent fixed connections. Only the AND gate inputs are programmable.

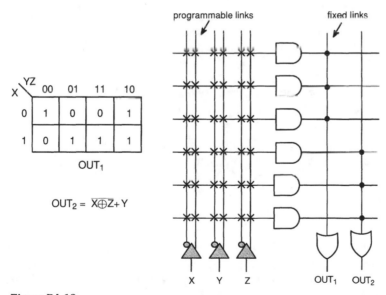

$OUT_2 = \overline{X \oplus Z} + Y$

Figure P4.13

41. See the 16L8 diagram in Fig. 4.38. How can pin 2 of a 16L8 PAL be used to disable the output of pin 18? Of what use is pin 18 if the OR gate output has been disabled?

43. **Folded NAND array** Consider the one-level array of NAND gates shown
below. The thick line on the input of each NAND gate represents a multiple-
input scheme to which can be connected the vertical lines of the inputs, C, B,
and A (and their complements), and the feedback inputs, O_1 and O_0. If an X
is placed at an intersection, a connection is made between the two lines. Four
connections are shown below. Only pins C, B, A, and O_i are accessible to the
user.

(a) What is a Boolean expression for O_2 given the connections shown?

(b) How should the connections be arranged to realize

$$OUT = A \cdot C + (B + \overline{C})$$

from one of the output pins?

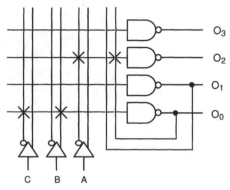

Figure P4.14 Feedback in NAND array.

44. **Folded NOR array** Imagine now that the NANDs in the previous problem
have been replaced with NORs. Answer the two questions of the previous
problem again.

45. **Factoring and folding** Consider a hypothetical PAL with five external inputs
and four outputs, two of which can be folded back as additional inputs. Realize
the following three Boolean equations with this PAL. Can you do it with two
PALs? A–F are external inputs, and P–R are required outputs.

(a) $P = \overline{E} \cdot F \cdot (\overline{D} + C) + B$

(b) $Q = \overline{D} + C + \overline{E} \cdot F \cdot B$

(c) $R = A \cdot B \cdot \overline{D} \cdot \overline{E} \cdot F$

46. Fan-in is the number of inputs to a gate. What is the fan-in of an OR gate in a
16L8 PAL? Suppose all the AND gates in a 16L8 architecture fanned in to each
OR gate. How many inputs would each OR gate have to handle?

47. **3000-series logic block** Study the diagram of the Xilinx 3000-series logic
block in Fig. 4.43. Assume that the combinatorial function unit carries out a
sum-of-products operation.

(a)   What is the shortest path from logic block input to output in terms of gate delays? Assume that each flip-flop contributes one gate's worth of delay.

(b)   What is the longest path from input to output (not allowing feedback)?

References

GEIGER, R. L., P. E. ALLEN, AND N. R. STRADER. 1990. *VLSI design techniques for analog and digital circuits.* New York: McGraw-Hill.

HAZNEDAR, H. 1991. *Digital microelectronics.* Palo Alto, Cal.: Benjamin-Cummings.

PAL device handbook, 1992. Sunnyvale, Cal.: Advanced Micro Devices.

PELLERIN, D., AND M. HOLLEY. 1991. *Practical design using programmable logic.* Englewood Cliffs, N.J.: Prentice Hall.

Programmable Gate Array Data Book, 1995. San Jose, Cal.: Xilinx Corp.

SEQUENTIAL DESIGN

Evolution of Flip-flops

OVERVIEW

Look at the signal flow in every one of the combinational logic circuits from the previous four chapters and you'll see all information moving from left to right, from input to output. No signal goes back—from right to left—to a preceding gate. Combinational logic has no **feedback.**[1] We now begin consideration of logic circuits with feedback. Properly arranged feedback in logic circuits can result in elements with **memory,** that is, elements whose present outputs depend on their history of inputs. We will build up feedback-containing elements using the hardware primitives introduced in Chapter 2. Most of the circuits we develop here in Chapter 5 will be **flip-flops,** whether clocked or unclocked, whether **edge-triggered** or **level-sensitive latches.** We start with the most basic feedback circuits and then "evolve" them by adding more features until you find out what an edge-triggered *JK* **flip-flop** with preset and clear inputs can do. The most useful flip-flop is the edge-triggered *D* **flip-flop,** because the *D* flip-flop input-output relationship is straightforward to work with and because in semiconductor fabrication a *D* flip-flop takes up a minimum of surface area on an integrated circuit.

A flip-flop is so called because, like a wall switch for a light, a flip-flop can be flipped into one of two **stable states,** where it will remain until prompted by other

[1]To qualify as feedback, signal flow from right to left must be part of a loop. If no loop is involved, the circuit can be straightened out to eliminate the right-to-left path. See below.

This circuit has no feedback. If the OR gate is pulled to the right, all signal flow will become left-to-right.

This circuit has feedback. The closed loop is shown in bold. No amount of rearranging of gates will eliminate all right-to-left signal flow.

251

input. important in describing flip-flops are timing parameters. In particular, if a flip-flop can change state only at the time of a clock edge (LO-HI or HI-LO transition), data must be constant during the **setup time** before the clock edge and during the **hold time** after the clock edge.

Motivation   Flip-flops constitute the basis of *sequential* design and are therefore one of the most important elements in digital hardware. By the end of Chapter 5 you will have grasped enough about the varieties of latches and flip-flops to move on, in Chapter 6, to the design of counters. Counters use more than one clocked flip-flop to step through the positional binary code. Then in Chapter 7 you will learn about *finite state machine* design, a general-purpose method of designing any controller.

5.1   CONSEQUENCES OF FEEDBACK

Feedback means sending a copy of an output signal back to an input part of the system, where it can influence the system components that helped form it in the first place. If this definition sounds circular, it is! An output signal fed back to become a system input can either subtract from (negative feedback) or add to (positive feedback) the other inputs. In the circuits we'll look at in this chapter, positive feedback is generally in effect. Positive feedback tends to drive a system to one of its extremes (or to cause oscillation). Even when external input goes to zero, the positive feedback can reinforce the output to stay locked at one limit or the other.

In Chapter 2 you found out that any real logic gate has a nonzero propagation delay. In a positive feedback circuit, propagation delay is an important factor in producing desired effects. Suppose the propagation delay of a gate or system $\mathcal{L}$ is Δ, and suppose the system sends its output back to be one of its inputs, as shown in the upper diagram in Fig. 5.1. The output of the system at time t is $y(t - \Delta)$. To highlight delay, consider the lower diagram, where delay is segregated in the box Δ. The user doesn't really have access to the undelayed result $y(t)$; it's there to emphasize that the input and output can be different values at the same time.

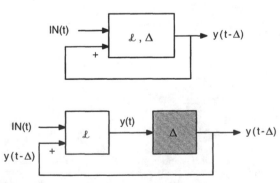

Figure 5.1   Feedback and delay.

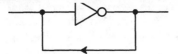

Figure 5.2 One inverter with feedback.

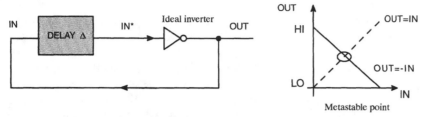

Figure 5.3 Inverter with delayed feedback.

Even negative feedback in a loop with significant delay can lead to oscillations, as Fig. 5.2 suggests. Consider a circuit in which the output of an inverter is fed back to its own input. How does the circuit respond? A HI output goes back to become the input, which causes (with some delay Δ) a LO output, which goes back to become input, which causes a HI output, and the cycle starts over again. The circuit oscillates with period Δ. In fact there's another possibility, namely, that the inverter gate output and input could settle at a value half-way between LO and HI, called a metastable state. See the right side of Fig. 5.3.

The timing diagram in Fig. 5.4 shows OUT becoming IN almost instantly, in rise time σ, but the feedback to IN must wait a longer *transport* time Δ before it starts to change to the new value of IN. Assume that $\Delta \gg \sigma$, and suppose the circuit has just been turned on, with IN at a LO level. As soon as power is applied, OUT goes

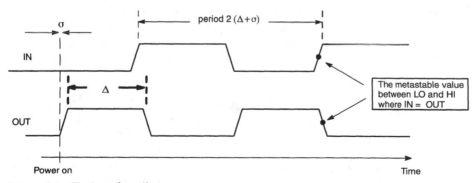

Figure 5.4 Timing of oscillation.

An oscillation (with period $2 \cdot (\Delta + \sigma)$) results, although theoretically it is possible for the inverter to hang up at the metastable point. The slope of the output-input line must be greater than 1 for the circuit to oscillate as shown. In practice, logic chips are designed to avoid metastable conditions as much as possible.

5.1.1 Sequential Circuits

The output of a circuit with feedback may no longer be predicted from its *present* input alone. The outputs of a logic circuit with feedback—now to be called a **sequential circuit**—depend on present input plus previous input. A sequential circuit therefore possesses the quality of **memory,** of output influenced by the past.[2] Other circuit elements, such as capacitors and inductors, can store charge or flux, and thus have memory, so feedback circuits aren't the only way to achieve memory electronically.

The two basic categories of digital logic circuits are combinational and sequential. The following example will illustrate their differences.

EXAMPLE 1

Suppose X and Y are binary vectors (sets of more than one binary number). Assume further that if arbitrary input X_1 causes a circuit $\mathcal{L}$ always to have output Y_1, and input X_2 causes the same circuit always to have output Y_2, then switching between X_1 and X_2 will cause the output to switch between Y_1 and Y_2. Circuit $\mathcal{L}$ is combinational, one whose present output depends only on its present input. But if the output of circuit $\mathcal{L}$ is Y_3 only if the sequence X_1 then X_2 occurs, and is output Y_4 only if the sequence X_2 then X_1 occurs, then the circuit has memory and is sequential. A sequential circuit can and does contain combinational elements, but as soon as it has memory due to feedback, it's more than combinational and cannot be described completely by a truth table.

A Stable Feedback Circuit We have looked at the delayed negative feedback of a one-inverter ring. Now what happens in Fig. 5.5 with the *positive* feedback of two inverters in a ring? (The feedback is positive because in going around the loop, the signal passes through an even number of inverters.) After binary signal A on the left passes with delay through the two inverters, it is A again. And since it is A that is fed back from right to left, the system is **stable**—it doesn't oscillate. There are two stable

---

[2] A *difference equation* can describe a discrete system whose output depends on past input; a differential equation can describe a continuous system with memory. See the beginning of Chapter 1 for a discussion of discrete versus continuous systems. In fact, the effect of previous input can be fully represented by the *state* of a system with memory; state (flip-flop outputs) for a sequential circuit will be defined more carefully later. Suffice it to say that if the present state, the internal mechanisms, and the future input are known, the future output of a system with memory can be predicted. In a differential equation (linear or nonlinear) the initial condition is the state needed to predict future output. More generally, the state can be defined as the minimum set of conditions that enables one to predict the future of a dynamical system, given future input.

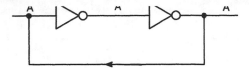

Figure 5.5 Bistable pair of inverters.

states: $A = 0$ or $A = 1$. As wired, the circuit is so stable that there's no way to get it to change from whichever initial condition it popped into. No finite delay can cause it to oscillate; it's a positive feedback system that is locked up at one of its two limits. A chief reason for the stability of this pair of inverters is that each inverter is limited to a range of 0 to 5 V. You'll see in Chapter 8 that a stable ring of two inverters forms the basis of static random-access read-write memory.

5.1.2 Mechanical Switch Debouncer for SPDT

Switch *bounce* occurs as a mechanical switch lever snaps to a new position: after reaching the new contact point, the pole bounces on a micrometer scale of millisecond duration. Bounce can cause problems in circuits that are expecting an input to stabilize without fluctuating, such as counters.

In the switch shown in Fig. 5.6, the ground input signal will be momentarily disconnected from both outputs during bounce. A circuit for *debouncing* a mechanical SPDT toggle switch uses the two inverters with feedback and rearranged (with respect to the circuit of Fig. 5.5) to emphasize symmetry. Each inverter in the circuit has two inputs (switch contact and feedback), both connected to the same wire. A grounded switch contact input will override any feedback signal and force the inverter input to LO. When the switch pole is in contact with, say, the lower output post, the bottom inverter input will be LO, the bottom inverter output will be HI, and the top inverter (the debouncer output) will be LO. What happens when the switch pole is flipped up? First, for a short time, both switch outputs will be disconnected from the debouncer. During the disconnection interval the inverter ring will remain in its stable state of OUT = HI. After the pole makes contact with the upper output post, the upper inverter input will become LO; after delay Δ the upper

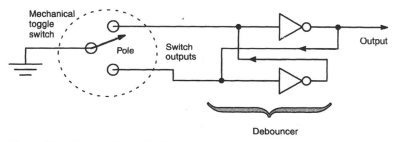

Figure 5.6 Debouncing with inverters.

inverter output will be forced HI (the other stable state of the inverter pair). When the pole arm bounces off the upper contact (neither input grounded), the inverter pair will remain in its new state. The debouncer will respond to the *first* contact of a switch flip by changing state; it will not change state again until the other post is grounded by a new flip of the switch. Secondary mechanical bounces will be ignored.

Note: This debouncer circuit causes a momentary connection of a HI chip output pin directly to ground, a circumstance that can create a current transient. The current transient will be of short duration and should not affect the inverter output. In general, connecting a HI output to ground can cause power drain and heat generation in digital ICs. See *Daniels' Digital Design Lab Manual*. A debouncer circuit that does not cause output grounding is described in Section 5.3.

We now continue development of feedback circuits whose output states can be controlled by external inputs.

5.2   A FLIP

Consider the positive feedback circuit of Fig. 5.7. A two-input NOR gate has replaced one of the inverters in the previous ring of two inverters. An external input F connected to a toggle switch has access to the second NOR input. Imagine that F is grounded and the circuit has just been turned on, with Q coming up LO. Both inputs to the NOR are LO, so its output N is HI. The NOR output of HI is the inverter's input, whose output $Q = $ LO feeds back to the NOR. The circuit is stable with $Q = 0$. Now flip the F switch to $V_{CC} = $ HI. The NOR output N heads to LO, and the inverter output Q heads to HI. The NOR's inputs of HI-HI agree with its output of LO, and the system is stable again. *But even if the switch is flipped back to $F = gnd$, Q remains at HI.* Once Q goes HI, it's stuck there. The circuit is a **flip.** Of what use is a flip? If the circuit initializes at power-on to $Q = 0$, the flip will wait for input F to go HI. Once F goes HI, Q will remain HI, even if F returns to ground. The circuit will remember the F-going-HI event as long as power is applied. See the timing diagram in Fig. 5.8.

Not to be flip, but flips have limited usefulness. Once flipped on, the flip's output cannot be reset to zero (except by turning the power off or by grounding the output). Flips will now evolve into set-reset latches.

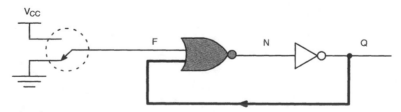

Figure 5.7   A flip.

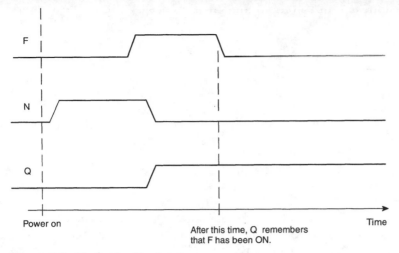

Figure 5.8 Timing for flip circuit.

5.3 SET-RESET LATCHES

Let the inverter in the flip be replaced by another two-input NOR gate. The circuit is redrawn symmetrically in Fig. 5.9 and labeled on the right. The output of each NOR projects back to one of the inputs of its partner. The circuit now has two inputs, SET and RESET, and is called an *SR flip-flop,* or more precisely, an *SR* **latch.**[3] The output of the NOR with the direct R input is labeled Q. The flip's problem of becoming stuck in the state $Q - 1$ now disappears for the *SR* flip-flop; it can be **reset** by the input combination $R = 1, S = 0$. (Remember that a NOR output is disabled to 0 whenever either input is 1.) Likewise, if $R = 0$ and $S = 1$, the flip-flop will be **set** to $Q = 1$.

If $S = R = 0$, the *SR* latch will remain in the state it was in before the change to $SR = 00$. In the condition $SR = 00$, Q can be either 0 or 1, depending on the past history of *SR* inputs. For example, if the latch had been set by the input $S = 1, R = 0$, then the $Q = 1$ generated by the set will remain in effect during $RS = 00$.

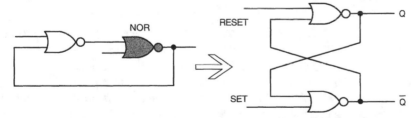

Figure 5.9 *SR* latch designed with NOR gates.

[3]A latch is a type of flip-flop without a clock, or it may have a level-sensitive clock. Clock inputs will be discussed later in this chapter.

Can we write a "truth table" for this circuit? Let's try.

R	*S*	*Q*
0	0	no change
0	1	1
1	0	0
1	1	0 ← a problem

$R = S = 0$ is called a no-change condition because the previous state (generated by either $RS = 10$ or $RS = 01$) persists. The *SR* latch remembers which set or reset action occurred just before $RS = 00$. A point of terminology: the expression *truth table* should be reserved for input-output relationships of combinational circuits, where outputs are either 0, 1, or X; the table above is more properly called an ***SR* excitation table** (or function table or state transition table).

When $RS = 01$, the latch output is set to 1; when $RS = 10$, the latch output is reset to 0. But the input combination $RS = 11$ presents a problem. Yes, in the NOR circuit underlying the excitation table, when $R = 1$ the top NOR gate is disabled (held at 0) and the output Q stays at 0. But what happens if we try to go to the no-change state of $RS = 00$ directly from $RS = 11$? Try as we might to avoid it, on a nanosecond time scale the inputs will pass through either $RS = 01$ or $RS = 10$ on their way to $RS = 00$. *The two SR inputs almost never change simultaneously.* Depending on which of the two intermediate states is reached first, no matter how briefly, two different outcomes may occur in going from $RS = 11$ to $RS = 00$. The two cases are shown below. Each line represents a different timing.

	Case 1			Case 2		
	R	*S*	*Q*	*R*	*S*	*Q*
t_0	1	1	0	1	1	0
t_1	0	1	1	1	0	0
t_2	0	0	1	0	0	0

The problem case is case 1. If $RS = 00$ is truly to be a no-change state, then case 1 is a disaster: $RS = 11$ and $Q = 0$ ends up after transition to $RS = 00$ with $Q = 1$. How can we deal with this problem? There is no way to ensure absolute simultaneity of changes in R and S, so we must declare that *only one input at a time can change* or that *input combination RS = 11 is not allowed.* The second limitation, not allowing $RS = 11$, is the more conservative, and it is the one usually enforced with *SR* latches. Not allowing *RS* to equal 11 has a couple of other benefits. For one thing, if S and R equal 1 at the same time, the notion that $S = 1$ will set Q to 1 is violated. Also, if $RS = 11$ is not allowed, the output of the other NOR is always the complement of Q, and a $\overline{Q}$ signal can be made use of. Later, when *JK* flip-flops evolve, the $SR = 11$

limitation on the two inputs will be lifted. Now our SR excitation table looks as follows:

R	S	Q
0	0	no change
0	1	1
1	0	0
1	1	not allowed

EXAMPLE 2

SR Latch Design with a Truth Table   Considering the *SR* latch defined by its excitation table, we can work backward to a gate design, adapting the truth table realization techniques of Chapters 2–4. First we need a labeling trick—one that will separate the output from the fed-back signal. Because there is some delay in the fed-back signal's influence on the output, let's call the fed-back signal Q_N and the output Q_{N+1}.[4] See Fig. 5.10. Let's use these labels in a truth table setting. For each *SR* input condition there will be two Q_N "input" values to consider. The truth table below lists the four *SR* combinations with the two Q_N and the Q_{N+1} output that should result.

	R	S	Q_N	Q_{N+1}
No change	0	0	0	0
	0	0	1	1
SET	0	1	0	1
	0	1	1	1
RESET	1	0	0	0
	1	0	1	0
Not allowed	1	1	0	NA
	1	1	1	NA

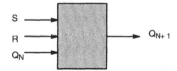

Figure 5.10   Labeling for an *SR* latch delay.

[4]Index N indicates time. If $N = 0$ is the present, then $N > 0$ is future and $N < 0$ is past. Later we will have index N incremented by a system clock.

Q_N \ R S	00	01	11	10
0	0	1	NA = X	0
1	1	1	NA = X	0

Figure 5.11 K-map for *SR* latch; the boxes contain the
values of Q_{N+1}.

For example, if $RS = 00$ (the no-change state), and $Q_N = 0$, then Q_{N+1} should also be 0; if $Q_N = 1$ and $RS = 00$, then Q_{N+1} should be 1, as shown in the table. For $RS = 11$ (the not-allowed input combination), we can write in two don't-care X's, because we expect never to encounter those input combinations. Transfer the truth table into the K-map of Fig. 5.11, in which *the values inside the map are the Q_{N+1} from the truth table.*

If we want to end up with a NOR circuit, we should gather 0s and organize a product of sums from the resulting maxterms. The product of sums can then be realized by a two-level NOR structure, as we saw at the end of Chapter 2.

Let both of the X's become 0s. Gather two subcubes, one by wrap-around. See Fig. 5.12. Express each subcube as an implicate for a POS form: $Q_{N+1} = \overline{R} \cdot (S + Q_N)$ (an implicate, or *maxterm*, contains the summed complements of the variables defining the subcube; see Chapter 2). The resulting equation can be realized as a two-level OR-to-AND circuit which, as we know from Chapter 2, can be replaced by the NOR-to-NOR circuit, drawn in Fig. 5.13. If you consolidate the input $\overline{R}$ to R by removing the top NOR gate (which is acting as an inverter), nothing will change. If

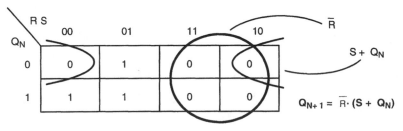

Figure 5.12 Maxterms for subcubes.

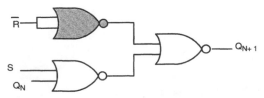

Figure 5.13 NOR realization for *SR* truth table.

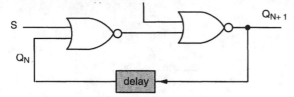

Figure 5.14 Replacing NOR with delay and feedback.

the delay path is shown, the circuit looks like Fig. 5.14. Figure 5.14 is the same as the NOR latch seen earlier!

5.3.1 An *SR* Latch Made with NANDs

What kind of latch circuit results if we gather 1s from the K-map of Fig. 5.11 and form a sum of products? Choose both don't-care X's to be 1s, and gather 1s, as shown in Fig. 5.15. Write the sum-of-products expression as $Q_{N+1} = S + \overline{R} \cdot Q_N$, which contains two implicants, and realize the expression as the two-level NAND circuit of Fig. 5.16. Again, by the protocol set forth earlier, Q_N represents the fed-back output signal. (The delay between Q_N and Q_{N+1} is the delay of two NAND gates.) Draw in the feedback and eliminate the NAND gate used as an inverter on S. The circuit can be redrawn as in Fig. 5.17.

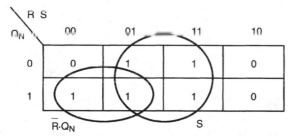

Figure 5.15 Don't-cares selected for NAND implementation.

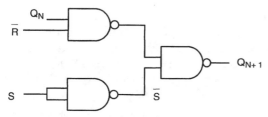

Figure 5.16 *S*-bar *R*-bar latch from K-map.

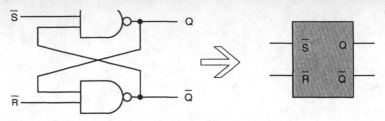

Figure 5.17 Cross-coupled NANDs.

This circuit is called an **S-bar R-bar latch.** A block diagram symbol is shown at the right. The $\overline{SR}$ latch has the following function table:

$\overline{R}$	$\overline{S}$	Q
0	0	not allowed
0	1	0
1	0	1
1	1	no change

It is the negative-logic version of the NOR-based SR latch. In this circuit, if both $\overline{S}$ and $\overline{R}$ are 0, the two NAND gates will be simultaneously disabled and you have the same problem of predicting output after releasing from the 00 state here as you do from the not-allowed NOR latch state $RS = 11$.

5.3.2 Switch Debouncing

EXAMPLE 3

You were introduced to switch debouncing in Section 5.1.2. Here we demonstrate an improved debouncer with an $\overline{SR}$ latch. Flip a mechanical SPDT toggle switch. As the central pin makes contact with a new pole, it will bounce a few times before settling. In Fig. 5.18 you can see that the voltage on the upper pole will change from ground to about +5 V each time the central pin bounces off. We don't want a counting circuit (to be considered later) to count the many brief spurious post-contact bounces before the switch settles on a new pole.

The SR debouncer circuit is drawn in Fig. 5.19. The switch's common terminal is connected to ground, and its other two contacts are pulled up to +5 V.[5] An $\overline{SR}$ latch has $\overline{S}$ and $\overline{R}$ inputs connected to the pulled-up contacts. Here's how the latch debouncing works: When the center pin is not in contact with either outside pin, the debouncer is in the no-change $\overline{RS} = 11$ state. As a consequence, the first contact with

---

[5]Lab note: If you make this debouncer with a 7400 NAND chip, you may not always need the resistors pulling up the NAND gate inputs since unconnected TTL gates float high. As a conservative design practice, however, connect the resistors as shown; use a resistor of about 1 kΩ.

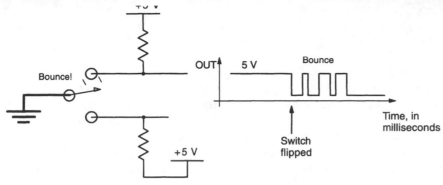

Figure 5.18 Bouncing switch.

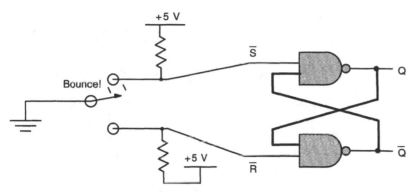

Figure 5.19 Debouncing with S-bar R-bar latch.

a pin that changes output Q will be the only contact registering a change for one flip of the switch; the latch won't transmit the subsequent switch chatter to Q.

Another way to think about a latch debouncing a toggle switch is as follows. The switch really has three states: output connected to one pole, output connected to the other pole, and output between the two poles, not connected to either of them. The latch debounce circuit ensures that the in-between state is associated with the no-change condition of the latch. The phrase *break before make* is sometimes used with this kind of switching.

Switch Condition	$\overline{R}$	$\overline{S}$	
Impossible	0	0	
Upper pin contacted	1	0	
Lower pin contacted	0	1	
Neither pin contacted	1	1	No change

5.4.1 Definition

By the **state** of one flip-flop or latch we mean one of two stable conditions for the outputs, either $Q\overline{Q} = 01$ (the reset state) or $Q\overline{Q} = 10$ (the set state). Notice that of four conceivable output combinations for the SR or $\overline{SR}$ latch, only two are allowed: $Q = 1$, $\overline{Q} = 0$, and $Q = 0$, $\overline{Q} = 1$. It is possible for latch outputs to be forced to $Q\overline{Q} = 00$ or 11, but those conditions are considered unstable because they can't persist in the no-change conditions of $SR = 00$ or $\overline{SR} = 11$. There will be more detail on state definition in the next chapter, which is concerned with sequencer design using multiple flip-flops.

5.4.2 N-flops

EXAMPLE 4

The first form of an SR flip-flop (latch) was a pair of NOR gates tied together with reciprocal feedback. Let that scheme be extended to three NOR gates reciprocally connected; we'll call the circuit a **3-flop.** Each NOR feeds back to the other two NORs, and each NOR receives one external drive. See Fig. 5.20. If they weren't in a circuit interconnected by feedback, outputs Q_1, Q_2, and Q_3 could be in any of 2^3 states. But with the feedback system as shown, Q_1, Q_2, and Q_3 are limited to three stable states:

Q_1	Q_2	Q_3
1	0	0
0	1	0
0	0	1

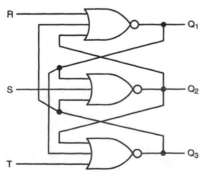

Figure 5.20   A 3-flop.

The R, S, and T conditions are entered when R, S, or T is LO and the other two inputs are HI as the table below shows. In the active-LO R, S, and T conditions the appropriate output (Q_1 for R, etc.) is HI and the other two outputs are forced LO. If the inputs are all 1 then the outputs are all RESET to LO. From the RESET condition the R, S, or T conditions can be entered by a 1-bit change. From an allowed condition, if all inputs are reset to LO, then the outputs remain unchanged.

It is possible for the 3-flop to oscillate. From the no-change condition set HI the input previously associated with the HI output. The other two outputs can start oscillating in lockstep. If you go back to the no-change state, all three outputs will oscillate because there are three inverters in series.

R	S	T	Q_1	Q_2	Q_3
0	1	1	1	0	0
1	0	1	0	1	0
1	1	0	0	0	1
0	0	0		no change	
1	1	1		RESET	

A 3-flop can be made with NAND gates, as Exercise 11 illustrates.

The oscillation possibility makes the 3-flop questionable as a practical circuit. The 3-flop can be generalized to a 4-flop and on to n-flops. They should remind you of decoders, with their several outputs, but like their SR cousins, n-flops have memory. A stabilized n-flop can be used as a building block in an associative memory, as you'll see in Chapter 8.

5.5   CLOCKED SR LATCHES

5.5.1   Glitches on SR Inputs

SR latches are sensitive to the timing of changes on their two inputs. To illustrate that sensitivity, recall Section 2.11, on timing in combinational circuits. There you saw that unequal delays through combinational circuits result in hazards that can produce glitches.

Suppose we place a glitch generator on the S input of an SR latch. See Fig. 5.21. Because of delay on the inverter, a change from LO to HI on A will generate a brief (and perhaps unwanted) glitch on input S. The HI S input on the latch will set output Q to 1, even if it was 0 before the change in A.

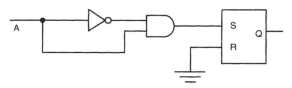

Figure 5.21   Glitch generator with SR latch.

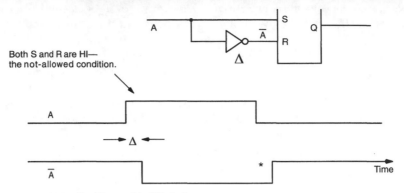

Figure 5.22 Problem with *SR* timing.

Here's another example, in Fig. 5.22, with just an inverter. Ironically, we might hope that an inverter from *S* to *R* would protect the *SR* latch from ever seeing the not-allowed *SR* = 11 state. Alas, just after the rising edge of *A*—for a duration Δ—the latch will see both inputs HI. Another property of the circuit of Fig. 5.22 is that except for brief glitch times (* in the figure), it can never be in the *SR* = 00 no-change state, and it's therefore a feedback circuit without memory!

5.5.2 Level-Sensitive Clock

How can the *SR* latch be made insensitive to glitches? Let it evolve to a **clocked *SR* latch**, as shown in Fig. 5.23. Two AND gates have been added to the *S* and *R* inputs in a demultiplexer-like arrangement. Now, only when the clock signal is HI will the latch accept input from *S* and *R*. When CLK is LO, the two AND gates on the left are disabled and the latch itself is in the no-change state. S_{int} and R_{int} are the *internal* set and reset controls. This arrangement is clock **level-sensitive,** not edge-sensitive. When CLK is HI on such a latch, the latch is said to be **transparent.** When CLK is low, *Q* retains its last value. (Why?)

The block on the right in Fig. 5.23 shows a symbol for a level-sensitive clocked *SR* latch, with the level-sensitive clock input shown as a box. Later, when we come to edge-sensitive clock inputs, the clock's box symbol will change to a triangle and the devices will be called flip-flops.

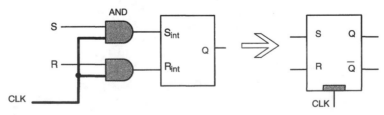

Figure 5.23 Level-sensitive latch.

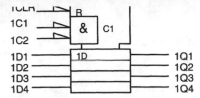

Figure 5.24 Half of a 74116 in IEEE schematic form.

The IEEE Standard 91-1994 graphic for one-half of the 24-pin 74116 dual four-bit latch with $\overline{\text{CLEAR}}$ is shown in Fig. 5.24. The ampersand (&) represents the AND of two clock signals; the R near the $1\overline{\text{CLR}}$ means reset. The inputs are 1D1, etc., and the corresponding latched outputs are 1Q1, etc.

To make the clocked *SR* latch useful, all that need be done is delay the HI portion of the clock until data on *S* and *R* have settled. See the waveforms in Fig. 5.25. By *settled* we mean that glitches due to different delays in input have time to disappear. In Fig. 5.25 the HI CLK region is confined to a time when we know that input *A* is not in transition. How to know when incoming data have settled must be left to an understanding of asynchronous sequential design, which you can read about in the *Supplemental Chapters* mentioned in the Preface. For now let's simply note that clocking the latch many propagation delays after input has changed will ensure stable data.

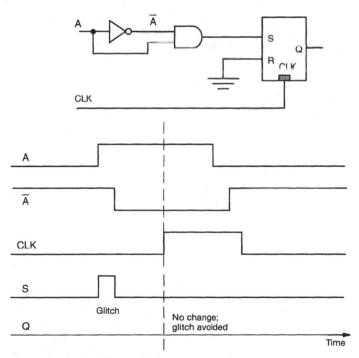

Figure 5.25 Avoiding a glitch.

A real integrated circuit latch requires a minimum pulse width in order for a SET or RESET command to be effective. For example, the data sheet for the old 7476 JK flip-flop lists a minimum active-low pulse width (t_w) of 25 ns for asynchronous SET or RESET. Clock pulses (or glitches) with pulse widths less than 25 ns *may* not be able to change the state of a 7476, or they may send the output into a metastable state for an indefinite time. In addition, there are propagation delays in latches. For example, asynchronous SET and RESET on the 74F112 flip-flop have 4.5-ns typical propagation delay t_{pd}. And there are clock propagation delays, which we will discuss after introducing edge triggering.

5.6   DATA LATCH

EXAMPLE 5

Let's improve on the *SR* latch by combining two circuit ideas, a clock and an inverter between *S* and *R*. See Fig. 5.26. If CLK goes HI after *D* settles, the delay through the inverter will not cause glitches on the flip-flop output. This is a **D latch**; when CLK is HI it's transparent for data to move from *D* to *Q* (with delay t_{pd}). When CLK is LO, both S_{int} and R_{int} are LO and *Q* holds the last value of *D* it saw; any changes in *D* during LO CLK will have no effect on *Q*. Thus CLK = LO is the memory, or no-change, state.

The basic design shown in Fig. 5.26 may have limitations because it has an asymmetric delay in the *R* path. An equal-delay $1 \rightarrow 2$ decoder may be more practical.

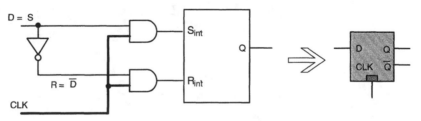

Figure 5.26   Level-sensitive *D* latch.

5.6.1   Use of a Data Latch

Data latches can be useful in situations where digital output from a circuit is valid only some of the time; during the times when the data is not valid, the latch will not be transparent. For example, analog-to-digital converters (ADCs) generally require considerable time (from nanoseconds to milliseconds, sometimes measured in the number of clock pulses) to convert an analog voltage to digital format. During

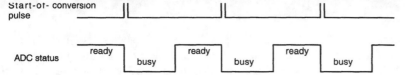

Figure 5.27 Timing in an analog-to-digital converter.

conversion time the ADC may send out a busy signal, which can be used to force a set of D latches (a **register**) to hold the previous conversion until a new answer is ready. The simplified timing for such a system might look like Fig. 5.27, and the circuit for a four-bit ADC with external latch could look as shown in Fig. 5.28. The user needs to supply start-of-conversion requests and clock pulses to the ADC. The D latches hold the last valid conversion, available after each busy signal is over. (Read more about analog-to-digital conversion in the *Supplemental Chapters* mentioned in the Preface.)

5.6.2   Attempted Shift Register Design

Sometimes binary data need to be moved down a pipeline of registers in time with a clock signal. The case of the ADC above may require the most recent answers generated by the conversion process to be in a pipeline while they are processed by a filter. What we're interested in here is the pipeline, called in the single-bit case a **shift register**. With every tick of the clock we want data to move to the next flip-flop in the chain.

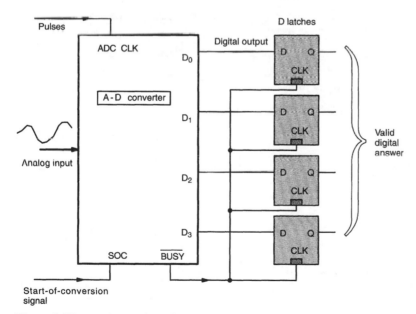

Figure 5.28 Latching a digital conversion.

EXAMPLE 6

In a shift register, such as the serial-in, parallel-out 74164 chip, several D flip-flops are chained together Q-to-D and connected by a common clock, and on each clock pulse DATA shifts to the right by one flip-flop. (In Chapter 8 we'll find out how to make a bidirectional shift register.) In Fig. 5.29 is an *attempt* at a three-stage right-shifting register using level-sensitive D-latches. In Fig. 5.30 is a timing diagram of what we

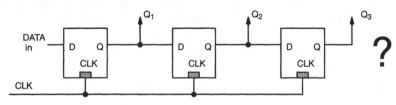

Figure 5.29   Clocked latch circuit that races.

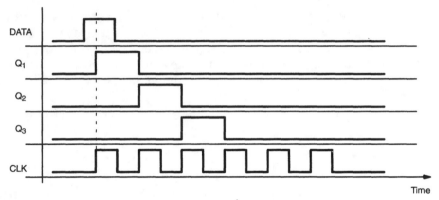

Figure 5.30   Expected output from shift register.

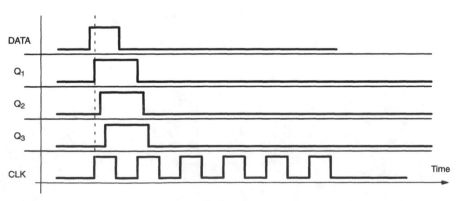

Figure 5.31   Actual output from racing latches.

flip-flop. Is this what will happen? No! As soon as the clock goes HI, *all* the latches will be enabled (made transparent) and the data will **race** through the system, as in Fig. 5.31.

We've drawn each Q_i turning on with a delay with respect to Q_{i-1}, but that slight delay (typically in nanoseconds, for TTL gates, but exaggerated here) is not enough to qualify our circuit as a shift register. Haste makes waste. What can be done to fix this condition in which data race through the circuit?

5.7 MASTER-SLAVE FLIP-FLOP

The inspiration for the master-slave idea comes from this observation: we could stop Q_i from gobbling up Q_{i-1} in a shift register by inverting the clock to the Q_i latch—that way, latch Q_i would have to wait until CLK goes LO before it takes in latched data from Q_{i-1}. If two latches with an inverted clock between them are combined in one package, a **master-slave flip-flop** results. See Fig. 5.32. The latch on the left is the master, dictating to the slave latch on the right what its input will be. The symbol on the right represents the master-slave D flip-flop; note the triangle with bubble where clock arrives. The triangle stands for an **edge-triggered clock.** Its meaning will become clear in the following discussion of the master-slave timing diagram, shown in Fig. 5.33.

Follow the timing diagram in Fig. 5.33 to see how the master-slave flip-flop works. At time (a) DATA goes HI. Since the master clock CLK_M is HI at that time, the master latch is transparent and its output Q_M goes HI at (b). At (c) CLK_M goes LO and the HI value of DATA is held at Q_M. Even though DATA goes low during the next clock phase, Q_M stays HI. For a time Δ both CLK_M and CLK_S are LO and no data can race through. At (d) the inverted CLK_S goes HI and the output of Q_M is passed through the slave to Q_S. At (e) the master latch opens again to take in DATA = LO, but not until (f) will the slave output Q_S drop to LO.

Because data can change in the master-slave flip-flop shown above only after the input clock (called CLK_M) shifts from HI to LO, the particular version of master-slave flip-flop is called a **negative-edge-triggered** flip-flop. In fact the term *flip-flop*

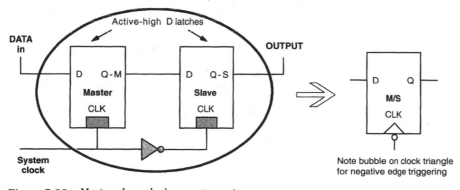

Figure 5.32 Master-slave clock arrangement.

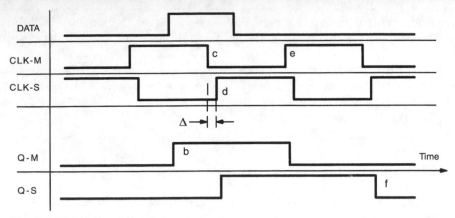

Figure 5.33 Master-slave timing.

is reserved for edge-triggered bistable memory storage elements; unclocked or level-sensitive elements are called *latches*.

The master-slave flip-flop (now containing two latches) will function correctly as an element in a shift register. Data won't race through. Correctly shifted waveforms may appear as in the timing diagram of Fig. 5.34, which is for a four-bit shift register. DATA enters the shift register asynchronously but is then transferred in lockstep

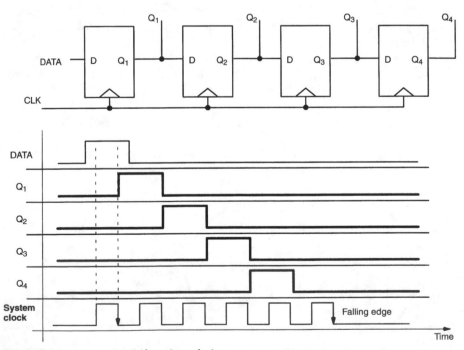

Figure 5.34 Successful shift register design.

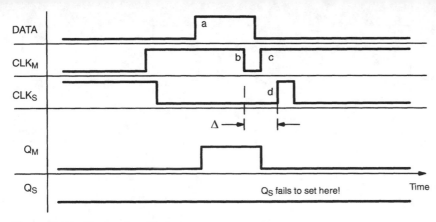

Figure 5.35 Master-slave timing.

on the *falling edges* of the system clock. Success with the shift register design using master-slave flip-flops has come at the expense of twice as much hardware compared to the failed design where data raced through level-sensitive latches.

5.7.1 Maximum Clock Rate in Master-Slave Flip-flops

In a negative-edge-triggered master-slave flip-flop, if the clock goes LO and then HI again in less time than the propagation delay of the inverter between the two latches, the flip-flop won't work properly. See Fig. 5.35, where $t_{pd} = \Delta$ is exaggerated for clarity and only the LO phase of the clock is shortened. As before, DATA going HI at (a) is held by the master latch at (b). If the master latch goes transparent (c) before the slave latch does (d), a LO instead of a HI will be passed to the slave. Therefore the duration of the LO-going part of master clock must be at least equal to the propagation delay. If we want the clock to have a 50% duty cycle (Fig. 5.36), the minimum *period* of the clock pulse is $2 \cdot \Delta$. The maximum frequency would then be

$$f_{max} = \frac{1}{2\Delta}$$

Look at the data sheet of the old TTL part 7476—a master-slave flip-flop—and see that t_{PLH} (propagation delay for a LO-to-HI transition on CLK) is 25 ns and the maximum clock frequency is 25 MHz. A frequency of 25 MHz implies a period of 40 ns, and $40 \div 2 = 20$ ns, close to t_{PLH}. A complete analysis of the maximum clock frequency would take into account second-order factors such as propagation delay through the latches themselves and the minimum duration of the clock pulse.

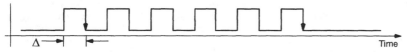

Figure 5.36 Fifty percent duty cycle clock.

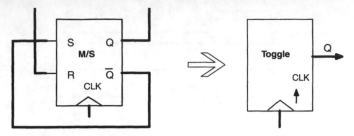

Figure 5.37   Toggle flip-flop.

5.7.2   Toggle Flip-flop

Recall that a D latch was created by sending S through an inverter to R, ensuring that the forbidden state $SR = 11$ would never be reached. Another way to ensure that the S and R inputs of a master-slave flip-flop are always complemented is to cross the Q and $\overline{Q}$ outputs with R and S as shown in Fig. 5.37. On every falling edge of the clock, output Q jumps to the opposite state it had before; if Q were LO before the falling edge, it would be HI after, and vice versa. Thanks to the protection of the master-slave clock timing, R and S are held until the next falling edge—the circuit is not an unstable oscillator. It is said that the clock **toggles,** and the circuit is a **toggle flip-flop.**[6] *This toggle flip-flop has only one input,* CLK. Look at the timing diagram in Fig. 5.38, where 0s and 1s chart the changes in CLK and Q.

With our toggle flip-flop we've created a **two-bit up-counter**—00, 01, 10, 11—where Q is the most significant bit (MSB) and CLK is the least significant bit (LSB). By cascading Q into the CLK of a second toggle flip-flop, we obtain a three-bit ripple counter (more often classed as a true two-bit counter, because the clock "doesn't

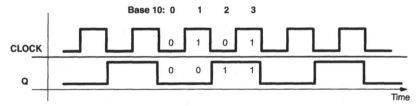

Figure 5.38   Toggle CLK-to-Q timing.

[6]You saw toggle switches in Chapter 1. The word *toggle* isn't in my 55,000-entry *American Heritage Dictionary;* by that standard, *toggle* is engineering jargon. As an adjective, *toggle* refers to a system in which the output moves from one output state to its opposite every time the input is activated. As a verb, *toggle* means to activate an input that will cause an output to go to its opposite state. For example, control panels often have toggle switches that, when toggled, cause a process to turn from ON to OFF or from OFF to ON.

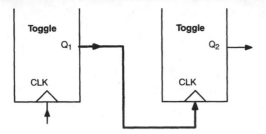

Figure 5.39 Two-bit ripple counter.

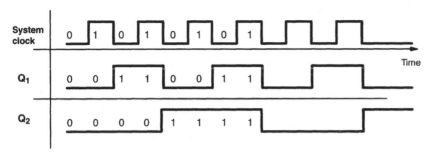

Figure 5.40 Two-bit ripple counter timing.

count"). See Fig. 5.39. Its timing diagram (sans delay) is shown in Fig. 5.40. Another way to think of a toggle flip-flop is as a divider of the clock frequency: the clock frequency is cut in two after it passes through a toggle flip-flop. Passing through a ripple cascade of N toggles divides the clock frequency by 2^N.

A toggle flip-flop is more useful if it has an *enable* input (see Fig. 5.41). Only when the enable is asserted will the clock toggle the output; otherwise the disabled toggle flip-flop stays in a no-change state. See the table to the left in Fig. 5.41. You'll see in Chapter 6 that toggle flip-flops can be connected to the same clock, like a shift register, and then have higher-order enables driven by lower-level Q outputs to create positional counters.

EN	CLK	Q_{N+1}
0	X	Q_N
1	active	$\overline{Q_N}$

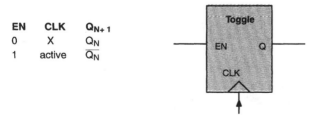

Figure 5.41 Toggle flip-flop with enable.

EXAMPLE 7

When the master latch in a master-slave D flip-flop is transparent, it is always passing DATA through to output Q. During D-latch transparency there is no memory condition in which DATA can be held. But a set-reset master-slave flip-flop will have an $SR = 00$ hold state that can occur during master transparency. (See Fig. 5.42.) Refer to the master-slave set-reset flip-flop labels in Fig. 5.42 for the timing diagram in Fig. 5.43. During the time CLK_M is HI, a pulse occurs on SET, at (a). Q_M goes HI as a consequence. Even after the SET pulse goes LO, at (b), Q_M continues to stay HI. When the clocks change at (c), Q_S "catches" the 1 on Q_M and goes HI itself at (d). *So even though the data are both LO at the time of the falling clock edge, the output can go to HI because of a prior SET on the master latch.* This behavior is known as

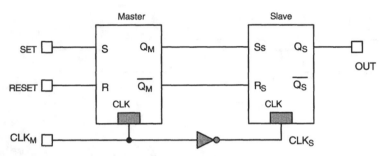

Figure 5.42   Master-slave clock circuit.

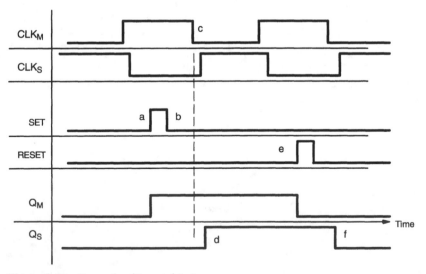

Figure 5.43   Example of 1s-catching.

0s-catching, where RESET pulses during master transparency (e) and then transfers the LO to output Q_S at (f), even though Q_S had been HI at the start of the clock cycle in question.

5.8   THE *JK* FLIP-FLOP

Unless the circuit in question is intended to capture glitches on the SET line, 1s- and 0s-catching is a problem for a master-slave *SR* flip-flop. A trouble-free SET-RESET capability can, however, be put into an edge-triggered flip-flop, by combining the toggle and *D* flip-flop ideas. Feed Q and $\overline{Q}$ back from the slave latch output to an AND-to-OR circuit that provides data to a *D*-latch master. The other two inputs to the AND-OR circuit are called *J* and *K*, and they are analogous to *S* and *R*, but without the restriction against both being asserted simultaneously. See Fig. 5.44, and note the inverter bubble on the *K* input. If $JK = 11$, only the *J* AND gate is enabled; since the AND gate's other input is $\overline{Q}$, the *JK* flip-flop output will toggle on each clock pulse. When $JK = 00$, the output Q will remain unchanged, because the *K* AND gate is the only one enabled. Think about holding $Q = 1$ during $JK = 00$: if $Q = 1$, both inputs to the *K* AND gate (Q and $\overline{K}$) are HI and the AND gate passes a HI to *D* and on to Q. For the third case, when $J = 1$ and $K = 0$, both AND gates are enabled. And when a falling clock edge occurs, Q will always become 1, because either

$\overline{Q}$ was 1 and the *J* AND gate would pass a SET through to Q, or

Q was 1 and the *K* AND gate would pass a SET through.

When $JK = 01$, both AND gates are disabled and Q will always be reset to 0 after a falling clock edge. Put all four cases together, and we have the **JK state transition table,** or excitation table, given in Table 5.1, where Q_{N+1} is the state of the *JK* flip-flop after a valid clock edge. Sometimes data sheets show the clock input explicitly as $\downarrow$ or $\uparrow$ symbols.

The improvement of the *JK* flip-flop over the master-slave *SR* flip-flop: *state 11 is no longer not allowed.* In state $JK = 11$, the flip-flop toggles: whatever state its output

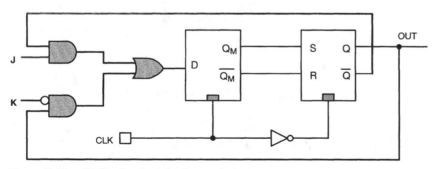

Figure 5.44   *JK* flip-flop from latches and gates.

Table 5.1 *JK* State Transition Table

J	K	Q_{N+1}
0	0	no change
0	1	0
1	0	1
1	1	toggle

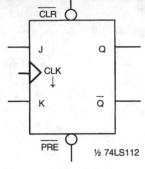

Figure 5.45 *JK* flip-flop with preset and clear.

was in, that state is complemented after a clock edge. Memorize the *JK* transition table; you'll need to recall it when designing *JK*-based sequencers in the next chapter!

Commercial *JK* flip-flops always include SET and RESET inputs that can override the clock. The block diagram in Fig. 5.45 shows a TTL 74LS112 negative-edge-triggered *JK* flip-flop. PRESET and CLEAR are *active LO* inputs that act independently of CLK. $\overline{PRE}$ and $\overline{CLR}$ are $\overline{SET}$ and $\overline{RESET}$ inputs having the limitation that they should not be asserted simultaneously. Both $\overline{PRE}$ and $\overline{CLR}$ need to be tied high for clocked *JK* operation. On the other hand, if the 74LS112 is to be used as a SET-RESET latch, the clock should be tied LO to prevent noise on the clock pin from interfering with operation when PRE = 1, CLR = 1, the no-change state.

$\overline{PRE}$	$\overline{CLR}$	Q
0	0	HI, but unstable
0	1	1
1	0	0
1	1	clocked operation (see *JK* transition table, Table 5.1)

There are no commercial TTL or CMOS packages that are only SET-RESET latches; the clock-independent SET-RESET feature is built into many IC edge-triggered *D* and *JK* flip-flops.

5.9   DESIGN FOR AN EDGE-TRIGGERED *D* FLIP-FLOP

A master-slave pair of latches is not the only way to create an edge-triggered flip-flop. Here is a design for a negative-edge-triggered *D* flip-flop that takes advantage of gate delay between three *SR* latches, an OR gate, and two extra feedback connections. The Q_1 *SR* latch in Fig. 5.46 has two resets, like a NOR gate in a 3-flop. Imagine that the

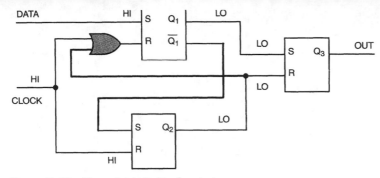

Figure 5.46 Three-latch D flip-flop design.

SR latches are made with NOR gates. *How* the circuit was designed won't concern us here, just *why* it works. When CLK is HI, both Q_1 and Q_2 are forced to reset, no matter what DATA is. As a result, both S and R for Q_3 are LO and OUT is not changed. See the labeling in Fig. 5.46.

Once you feel comfortable with the fact that CLK = HI is a no-change condition, assume that OUT has been LO, DATA is now HI, and a HI-to-LO clock transition is occurring. (See Fig. 5.47.) The two LOs on the Q_1 resets allow Q_1 to be set by HI DATA, in turn setting Q_3 to HI, as desired. The Q_2 latch goes into a no-change $SR = 00$ condition, and the circuit is stable. If now, while CLK is LO, DATA changes from HI to LO, all that will happen is that the Q_1 latch will go to a no-change condition, preserving the SET on Q_3. The only other case to analyze—that of a clock transition occurring when DATA is LO and the previous output was HI—is left as Exercise 31.

5.9.1 The Importance of D Flip-flops

Figure 5.48 shows the schematic convention for an edge-triggered D flip-flop. A triangle greets the clock as it comes into the flip-flop body. Depending on the direction of the arrow near the triangle, a rising- or falling-edge-triggered D flip-flop

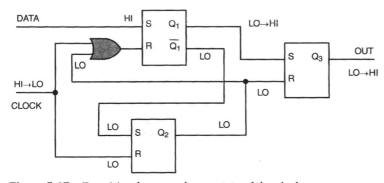

Figure 5.47 Transition from no-change state of the clock.

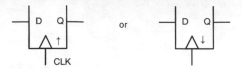

Figure 5.48 *D* flip-flop symbols.

is represented. An IC chip will be specified with a **minimum clock width,** t_W; for example, the 74F112 falling-edge-triggered *D* flip-flop has a 4.5-ns minimum clock width. And once the 74F112 is clocked, there is a maximum of 6.5 ns propagation delay, t_{PD}, before correct data appears at the output Q.

Of all the varieties of flip-flops you've seen in Chapter 5, edge-triggered *D* flip-flops are the most important in modern digital design. For example, only edge-triggered *D* flip-flops are found in the logic cell blocks of a field-programmable gate array IC. Edge-triggered *D* flip-flops predominate because they take up less area on a silicon die than their nearest competitors, edge-triggered *JK* flip-flops, and because their single input is easier to program. Compared with *D* flip-flops, *JK* flip-flops often have more capability than is needed in some designs. Why drive a station wagon to school when a bicycle will do? In fact, both *JK* and *D* flip-flops find extensive use in modern digital design. In the next two chapters *JK* and *D* flip-flops will become the building blocks of more complex synchronous sequential circuits. (*SR* latches have their niche in practical design, too, in *asynchronous* sequential design.)

5.9.2 *D* Flip-flops in Parallel Form a Register

As a preview of the work flip-flops can do together, consider the register, a set of *D* flip-flops all connected to the same clock. See Fig. 5.49. Shown is a parallel-in, parallel-out (PIPO) register. A PIPO register can store a binary word presented at the input pins during the time of a clock edge. The word will then be available at the output pins of the register until the next clock edge occurs. Chapter 11, on register-transfer logic, will discuss other register types and their use in computer systems.

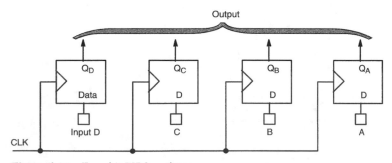

Figure 5.49 Four-bit PIPO register.

Edge triggering solves the problem of how a D flip-flop acknowledges and responds to data for only a limited time, but edge triggering brings up a new question: What if the input data changes at the same time the clock edge occurs? Which version of the data will be clocked in by the flip-flop, the data before the clock, or after? In a real flip-flop, new data must be continuously present slightly before and slightly after the clock edge in order for correct new data to reach the Q output.

The duration of time DATA needs to be present before the clock arrives is called the **setup time,** shown in the timing diagram in Fig. 5.50. Unless setup time is zero, if the data change appears simultaneously with the clock, it will not be logged in. Setup time accounts for the approach of data; what about its exit? How long does the data have to *stay* after the clock in order for it to be accepted? That interval is called the **hold time,** again indicated in Fig. 5.50. In a data sheet for an IC chip, setup and hold times are expressed as minimums.

EXAMPLE 8

Find a TTL data book and look at the data sheet for a 74LS112 negative-edge-triggered flip-flop. At the bottom of the list of switching characteristics, find t_{setup} and t_{hold}. For the 'LS112 the minimum (worst case) setup time for "data input" is 20 ns; data hold time is 0 ns. Therefore the data must change to its new value at least 20 ns before the clock edge in order for the new data to be accepted by the next clock to the 74LS112.

Zero hold time is not uncommon for real D flip-flops; once the clock edge arrives, all that matters is that the data was present for t_{setup} *before* the clock edge. By going back to the design of the negative-edge-triggered D flip-flop (Fig. 5.46), you can appreciate the need for setup time. If DATA is to go HI but the HI signal arrives late, $\overline{Q}_1$ will have time to reset the first flip-flop by circulating a HI through Q_2.

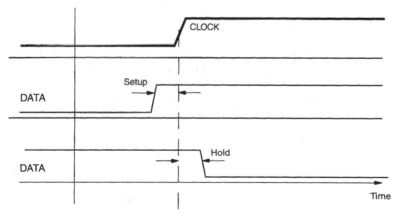

Figure 5.50 Setup time and hold time.

Another flip-flop timing parameter is the minimum duration of the clock pulse usually listed as t_W. In the case of the 74LS112, the width t_W is 20 ns minimum HI before another falling edge can arrive. Furthermore, edge-triggered clocks or flip-flops and counters expect that the edge will occur at a minimum **slew rate** or volts/second change. Inputs that make the transition too slowly may not be acceptable clocks.

5.10.1 Maximum Clock Rate for a Flip-flop

There is yet another timing constraint on flip-flops that is worth noting. After an asynchronous data pulse, a minimum **recovery time**, t_{rec}, must elapse before the clock can make an active transition. (See Fig. 5.51.) Given the timing constants of a D flip flop—propagation delay, setup and hold times, recovery time, minimum clock pulse width—it may be difficult to find the worst case for calculating the maximum clock rate of the flip-flop. Manufacturers therefore provide this specification in addition to the other switching characteristics of a clocked flip-flop. The maximum clock rate f_{max}, is given in hertz, usually megahertz (MHz, 10^6 cycles/second). As an example the 74F74 switching values are

$$t_{setup} = 2.0 \text{ ns (HI to LO)}$$
$$t_{hold} = 1.0 \text{ ns}$$
$$t_W = 4.0 \text{ ns (HI to LO)}$$
$$t_P = 4.6\text{–}7.0 \text{ ns } (t_{PHL} \text{ for } \overline{S} \text{ to } Q)$$
$$t_{rec} = 2 \text{ ns}$$
$$f_{max} = 125 \text{ MHz}$$

An f_{max} of 125 MHz implies an 8-ns delay; since

$$125 \text{ MHz} \approx \frac{1}{t_{setup} + t_{hold} + t_P}$$

8 ns is about equal to $t_{set} + t_{hold} + t_P$.

‡5.10.2 Metastability

(*This section is optional.*) Suppose the data for an edge-triggered D flip-flop arrives a little late for the next clock. Say it arrives 10 ns before and should have been there at least 20 ns before the clock edge. It was suggested in our discussion of setup time that such a late arrival would mean that the flip-flop output fails to change state. Unfortunately things can be even worse than that; the data may have just enough

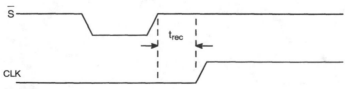

Figure 5.51 Recovery time.

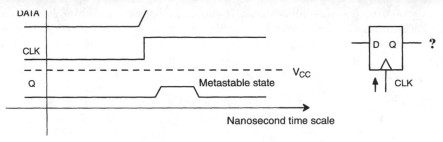

Figure 5.52 Metastable response to simultaneous DATA and CLK change.

influence to kick the output to a level between valid LO and HI levels, that is, to a **metastable state.** In the case shown in Fig. 5.52, a late-arriving D input manages to push Q halfway to V_{CC}, where Q stays for a few nanoseconds until falling back down toward ground and a valid LO level. While it's in the metastable state, the Q output will confuse the inputs it projects to. Is Q a LO or a HI? Errors may result. With probability that decreases with time, the output can remain indefinitely in the metastable state. And when it leaves the metastable state, the output can go either HI or LO with no predictable preference.

Why the term *metastable?* It's a state like a flipped coin landing on its edge. In short order the coin will fall to either heads or tails, but in rare cases the coin may hang up on its edge for quite a while before falling. Being on its edge is not a stable state for the coin, nor is being at a voltage half-way between the maximum of LO and the minimum of HI a stable state for a flip-flop output. If a coin balanced on its edge is pushed slightly one way or the other, even by a breath of air, it will fall to either heads or tails. A coin on its edge has fuzzy membership in the sets of heads and tails.

For a flip-flop it probably wouldn't matter that the output were caught between logic levels if it snapped to a valid logic level within a nanosecond, but as was said earlier, in real ICs it's possible for Q to pause for many nanoseconds in the "forbidden zone." If a metastable state lasts longer than the clock period, an error is likely to result.

EXAMPLE 9

Imagine a D flip flop shift register system with a clock rate of 50 MHz (period 20 ns). There is a low probability that setup-time-violating inputs will cause metastable outputs to endure longer than 20 ns. In fact, to the first order, the probability distribution of metastable durations under certain conditions is approximated as a Poisson-like exponential:

$$P(t) \approx \frac{1}{\tau} e^{-t/\tau}$$

P is the probability that a metastable state will last *at least* t ns, and τ depends on the particular semiconductor process used to make the flip-flop. For example, a 74AC74 D flip-flop from National Semiconductor is rated at $\tau = 0.39$ ns. If a data change occurs about t_{setup} from the clock edge, there's an 8% chance of 1-ns metastability.

in practice, the in effects of metastability become vanishingly small for clock rates less than 10 MHz. Above 10 MHz the problem can be further minimized by synchronizer circuits on input. Again, you need to remember that if data is not given enough setup or hold time, the metastable failure is *not* an unpredictable shift to 0 or 1, but rather a hang-up at an intermediate voltage and *then* a snap to 0 or 1.

Synchronizer   As the example about the late-arriving D input suggests, a flip-flop is most at risk for metastable output when its input violates setup or hold times. In a well-designed synchronous system, inputs are scheduled to meet setup times and metastability is minimized. It's when inputs arrive *asynchronously* (without regard to a clock) that a circuit is most at risk for metastable failure. To reduce the risk of metastability in a synchronous system, a **synchronizer** circuit can be placed between any asynchronous input and the at-risk synchronous system. You can think of the synchronizer as a "pulse stretcher" for brief asynchronous inputs. See Fig. 5.53, where synchronizer details are shown at the bottom. Both the synchronizer and the synchronous system are driven by the same clock CLK. The synchronizer delays the input through a two-stage *pipeline*, but that is the price to pay here for reducing the likelihood of error-causing metastable states. The asynchronous input arrives first at a fast D flip-flop that features short setup and hold times. If an unfortunately timed asynchronous input manages to cause a metastable output on Q_1, the metastable output may die between Q_1 and Q_2. Otherwise it is not possible to completely banish metastable conditions that last longer than the system clock pulse.

In engineering practice an empirical formula that takes into account the clock rate of the flip-flop and the effective "clock rate" of the data is used to calculate the *mean time between failure* (MTBF) of a synchronizing circuit.

$$\text{MTBF} = \frac{e^{+t/\tau}}{T_0 f d_r}$$

where T_0 and τ are empirical constants with units of seconds and nanoseconds, respectively, f and d_r are the clock rate and average data rate in hertz, and t is the duration from one clock edge to the next. Note the plus sign in the exponent of e.

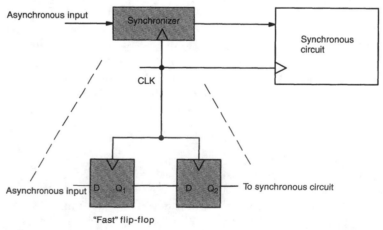

Figure 5.53   Synchronizer details.

EXAMPLE 10

A 74LS74 D flip-flop is rated at $T_0 = 7$ s and $\tau = 1.3$ ns, and a 74AC74 D flip-flop is rated at $T_0 = 0.3$ s and $\tau = 0.5$ ns. Compare the mean times between failure of the two flip-flops when used in a circuit with a clock frequency of 40 MHz and an average data rate of 15 MHz.

Answer A 40-MHz clock rate implies 25 ns between clock changes, so use $t = 25$ ns, ignoring nonzero setup time. Insert t, τ, T_0, f, and d_r in the formula for MTBF. For the 74LS74,

$$\text{MTBF} = \frac{e^{+t/\tau}}{T_0 f d_r} = \frac{e^{25/1.3}}{7(40 \times 10^6)(15 \times 10^6)} \approx \frac{2 \times 10^8}{4000 \times 10^{12}} \approx 50 \text{ ns}$$

For the 74AC74,

$$\text{MTBF} = \frac{e^{25/0.5}}{0.3(40 \times 10^6)(15 \times 10^6)} \approx \frac{5 \times 10^{21}}{200 \times 10^{12}} \approx 2.5 \times 10^7 \text{ s} \approx 1 \text{ year}$$

What a difference! And we haven't even taken into account the nonzero setup times of the flip-flops!

It is fortunate that metastability occurs only when stray input changes land in a small time zone, between the setup and hold limits of the clock edge. Even then the metastable state probably won't last long enough to cause an error. Rapidly changing inputs in a system where the clock ticks at a high rate can breed metastable errors. When data rates are kept low and flip-flops are connected to a common clock, metastability is a rare event indeed. But with the effort of system designers to force higher data rates through computer systems, error-causing metastability may become more common. It is a problem that can only be minimized, never avoided absolutely. See Mentzer (1990).

5.11 SUMMARY

Chapter 5 discusses two kinds of sequential circuits: latches and flip-flops.

- Properly arranged, **feedback** in a logic circuit can create outputs that depend not only on the circuit's present input but on the sequence of inputs that led up to the present. Such circuits with feedback are called **sequential** and have the quality of *memory*: their present output has been affected by prior input.

- A **set-reset latch** has two inputs, only one of which should be asserted at a given time. The SET input sends the output HI; the RESET input sends output LO. If neither input is active, the latch output stays in the last state it was sent to by a previously active input; in the no-change condition the flip-flop therefore "remembers" its previous state. Set-reset flip-flops can be made from cross-coupled NOR or NAND gates.

- *SR* latches can be used to **debounce** SPDT mechanical switches.

An SR latch is a digital feedback circuit with two stable states. An n-flop is a generalization of an SR latch. It is made by feedback connection of n n-input NAND or NOR gates and has n stable states, not 2^n.

- A **glitch** is a brief pulse that can be a by-product of asymmetric (skewed) signal delay through a combinational circuit. An SR latch is sensitive to glitches on its inputs.
- Gating SR inputs with another input called **clock** can decrease sensitivity to input glitches; the device is called a **level-sensitive latch.**
- If you put an inverter between S and R on a level-sensitive latch, you create a **data latch.** When the clock is asserted, the latch is said to be *transparent;* when the clock is not asserted, the data latch remembers its last value.
- If the output of one clocked latch is sent to another and the clock signal between the two is inverted, a **master-slave flip-flop** results. Only when the clock is changing from the master-enabled to the slave-enabled state can data be transferred from master to slave. The flip-flop is said to be edge-triggered.
- A **D flip-flop** is an edge-triggered sequential circuit that has one data input; data is transferred to the flip-flop's output on an active clock edge. D flip-flops are the most commonly used flip-flops in modern digital designs; they're found in registered PALs, gate arrays, and other large-scale ICs.
- A **register** is a bank of D flip-flops clocked simultaneously.
- A **shift register** is a cascade of D flip-flops with a common clock; the output of one flip-flop becomes the input of the next flip-flop. Only the initial flip-flop input is available for external data.
- A **toggle** flip-flop can be created by sending Q and $\overline{Q}$ of a master-slave SR flip-flop back to R and S, respectively. A toggle flip-flop output changes state on every active clock edge, as long as the flip-flop is enabled.
- An edge-triggered **JK flip-flop** has the following state transition table:

J	K	Q_{N+1}
0	0	no change
0	1	0
1	0	1
1	1	toggle

Q_{N+1} is the output of the flip-flop *after* the next clock edge. When $J = K = 1$, the JK flip-flop changes state on each clock pulse. The edge-triggered JK flip-flop with asynchronous PRESET and CLEAR is a common IC.

- **Setup** and **hold times** define a small region of time before and after the clock edge during which flip-flop data should not change if a valid data transfer to output is to occur.
- A **metastable** output, between valid LO and HI logic levels, can occur for a brief time in an edge-triggered flip-flop in which the timing of a data change violates the setup and hold limits around an active clock edge. A **synchronizer** circuit, featuring a D flip-flop with low setup and hold times, can minimize the occurrence of error-causing metastable outputs.

1. Which of the two circuits in Fig. P5.1 is sequential, and which is combinational? Inputs are *A*, *B*, and *C*. For the combinational circuit, write out its Boolean expression. For the sequential circuit, show how present output does not depend *only* on present input; i.e., find a set of inputs *CBA* for which there can be different outputs, depending on the circuit's history of inputs.

(a)   **(b)**

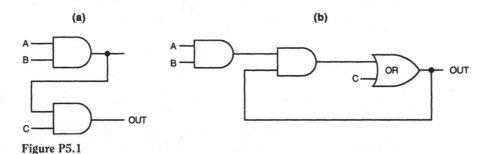

Figure P5.1

2. In Fig. P5.2 are three inverters in a ring. The result will be oscillation, because the delay back to the start is long enough to generate instability. With ICs it's straightforward to build a three-inverter oscillator like this in the lab and watch the oscillation on an oscilloscope. A ring of three 74C04 inverters oscillates at about 3×10^6 Hz.

   If the oscillation frequency is 2.5 MHz, what do you estimate to be the propagation delay t_{pd} of the inverter?

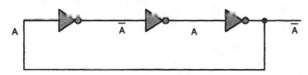

Figure P5.2

3. **Flips** Consider an OR gate in a feedback arrangement (Fig. P5.3). It's another flip circuit:

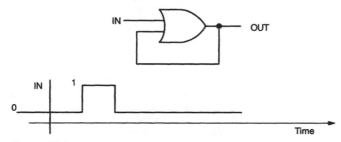

Figure P5.3

(a) Suppose, when we turn on the circuit at $t = 0$, both OUT $= 0$ and IN $= 0$.
What will OUT be in response to the IN waveform shown below the circuit?

(b) Now consider the circuit in Fig. P5.4, where the bubble on the input represents an inverter:

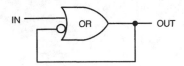

Figure P5.4

If the same initial conditions and waveform as in (a) occur, what will happen to this circuit?

(c) What will happen if the OR gate in (a) is replaced with an AND gate? (Again, at $t = 0$, both OUT $= 0$ and IN $= 0$.)

(d) What will happen if the OR gate in (a) is replaced with a NAND? Is this circuit the *dual* or the negative-logic version of the circuit in (a)? (Dual expressions were discussed in Chapter 2.)

4. Speaking of duals, a dual-control electric blanket has a warmth control for each of the two people sleeping (or in the case we're dealing with here, trying to sleep) in the bed. In normal operation the control for person A affects the heat only on the part of the blanket covering A, and vice versa for B. Imagine now a practical joke in which the controls have been reversed. Person A actually controls person B's blanket heat, and vice versa for B. Is this feedback system stable? How is it like a latch? Consider the outputs to be the temperatures of the two sides of the blanket. Draw an input-output processing diagram.

5. Can either or both of the two feedback circuits in Fig. P5.5 function as an SR latch? If so, which input would be S, and which R?

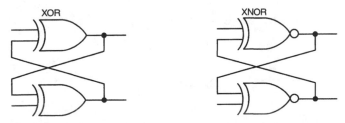

Figure P5.5

6. For an SR latch state $SR = 11$ is not allowed, but when $SR = 11$ the latch output stays at a definite logic level until released from input.

(a) For an SR latch made of NORs, what is the output for input SR = 11?

(b) Suppose one of the NOR gates has a much longer propagation delay than the other. Can you always predict the result of a transition from $SR = 11$ to $SR = 00$?

7. What is the function table for the feedback circuit in Fig. P5.6? X and Y are inputs, Q and P are outputs.

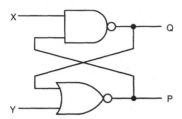

Figure P5.6

8. **Latches and K-maps**

   (a) What is the truth table in the form of a K-map for the circuit in Fig. P5.7?

Figure P5.7

   (b) Find a realization for OUT from the following K-map, *using only NOR gates.* Show the steps of your solution. Your answer will be a *start* to a JK flip-flop design.

K J	00	01	11	10	
Q					
0	0	1	1	0	
1	1	1	0	0	OUT

   ‡(c) What other input is needed for a *JK* design? Can you expand the K-map and complete a new *JK* circuit?

9. **Switch debouncer** Will the circuit in Fig. P5.8 work as a switch debouncer? If not, why not?

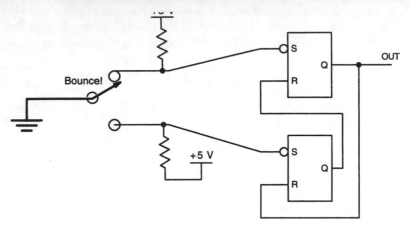

Figure P5.8

‡10. How can a single-throw switch be debounced by hardware? In Fig. P5.9 is an attempt, using an *RC* circuit and an inverter with input threshold θ. It takes time for the capacitor to charge up through the resistor from V_{CC}. Without the capacitor in place, when the button is pushed down it bounces momentarily, producing the unwanted pulses shown in the first time line.

(a) What will be the response OUT for the circuit with and without the capacitor? Assume, if you need to, the values of $R = 100 \text{ k}\Omega$ and $C = 1 \text{ }\mu\text{F}$.

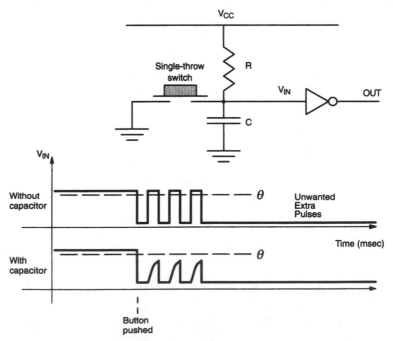

Figure P5.9 Debouncing a pushbutton switch.

(b) If the inverter is replaced with an S-R latch, where S receives V_{IN} and R receives OUT, will the design be improved?

11. **Three-flop NAND**   We can cross-couple three three-input NAND gates by feedback to achieve another 3-flop (Fig. P5.10).

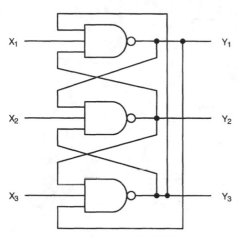

Figure P5.10   A 3-flop with NANDs.

(a)   If only one input can be HI at a time, what are the three output conditions?
(b)   For the input combination $X_1 X_2 X_3 = 101$, what are the possible outputs?
(c)   Find a sequence of inputs that can lead to oscillations in the circuit.
(d)   How would your answers for (a)–(c) change if the NANDs were replaced by NORs in Fig. P5.10, and the 1s and 0s swapped in (a)–(c)?

12.   A feedback circuit made with NAND gates is shown in Fig. P5.11, on the next page. Suppose all R_n are zero and then R_1 goes HI. What will happen to the R_n^*'s? Now, while R_1 is HI, R_2 and R_3 go HI. What happens? Now, with R_1–R_3 HI, R_1 goes LO, leaving R_2 and R_3 on. What happens now to the outputs?

13.   An active-HI input, active-LO output 2/3 majority gate has the following truth table:

C	B	A	OUT
0	0	0	1
0	0	1	1
0	1	0	1
0	1	1	0
1	0	0	1
1	0	1	0
1	1	0	0
1	1	1	0

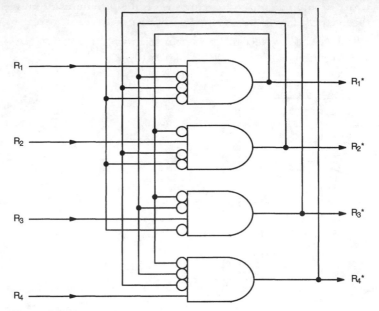

Figure P5.11 A 4-flop.

(a) Design a set-reset latch using only two 2/3 majority active-low gates.

(b) Can you design a 4-flop using only 2/3 active-low gates?

14. In the text we saw Fig. P5.12 and found that because of delay in the inverter, the condition $SR = 11$ could appear transiently. What input change on A will produce $SR = 11$? Assuming that the SR latch is made with NOR gates, what will be the state of the latch (value of output) *after* the transient $SR = 11$ event?

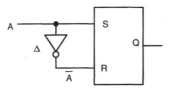

Figure P5.12 A transparent latch.

‡15. Assume that a microwave oven has an electronic thermometer attached to circuitry with two outputs: one is asserted when the temperature is above θ_H and the other is asserted when the temperature is below θ_L (one-bit analog-to-digital converters). Using RS latch(es), design a circuit that will turn the oven on when the temperature falls below θ_L; turn the oven off when the temperature is above θ_H; and when the temperature is between θ_L and θ_H, leave the oven in the condition it was in before θ_L or θ_H was last reached.

Start by drawing out oven response versus temperature on a graph. Such curves demonstrate **hysteresis**; at θ_L and θ_H the system changes the curve it operates on in order to minimize switching back and forth ("chatter") when the temperature is near the desired level.

16. In the circuit shown in Fig. P5.13, the output of an *SR* latch enables an AND gate through which an input called INT tries to pass. When the output of the AND gate goes from LO to HI, a subcircuit, called DELAY, goes HI for 1 s. While the 1-s delay is in effect, INT is disabled. Normally ENABLE is a pulse that occurs long before the INT pulse. After a DELAY has been executed, ENABLE is pulsed again. What if ENABLE = 1 and OUT = 1 occur at the same time? What should be the rule for the *SR* latch for input *SR* = 11 in order for the circuit to work as expected? Assume that the aberrant timing looks as shown in Fig. P5.14.

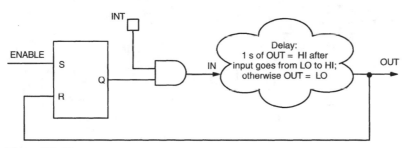

Figure P5.13

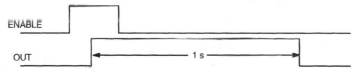

Figure P5.14

17. What will be the output of the circuit of Fig. P5.15 for a LO-HI transition on input *X* if the propagation delay is 20 ns per gate? Draw a nanosecond-scale timing diagram for *X*, *S*, *R*, and *Q*. Assume that NOR gates make up the *SR* latch.

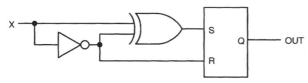

Figure P5.15

18. Suppose you are called upon to design an arbiter for a two-person game show. Both contestants have a button on their modified lecterns. A light comes on for whoever presses her button first, and in that case the opponent's light stays off, even though the opponent may have pressed his button only nanoseconds after the winner. There must be a master RESET that will turn off both lights to start another round. Assume that the button does a good job of providing a clean and fast LO-to-HI transition when pressed and that the light is driven adequately by the logic output of your circuit. You implement the design in Fig. P5.16. After the first contest the game show host runs back stage screaming that your design didn't work all the time—a couple of times, both lights came on.

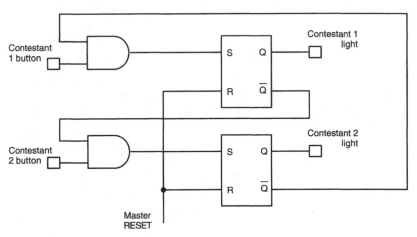

Figure P5.16   Start of arbiter circuit.

(a) What's wrong with the above design as an arbiter circuit?
(b) Using only one more logic gate and a little rewiring, how can you fix the arbiter?
(c) Design an arbiter circuit for three contestants.

19. Given the motivation in Section 5.5 for the evolution of clocked flip-flops, will the circuit in Fig. P5.17 work as a clocked flip-flop? If not, why not?

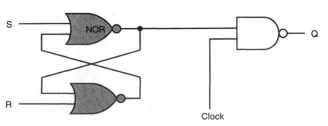

Figure P5.17

20. See the circuit in Fig. P5.18. Assume that each gate has a 10-ns propagation delay. Draw OUT as a function of time in response to a 30-ns pulse on IN.

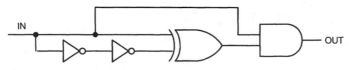

Figure P5.18

21. Shown in Fig. P5.19 are SET and RESET waveforms and four clock waveforms for a positive *level-sensitive* (not edge-triggered) clocked *SR* latch made from NORs. What will be Q, the latch output, for each of the clock waveforms at the time indicated by the vertical dashed line? Assume that Q is 0 before any clock pulses arrive. Assume also that all pairs of waveform edges are more than t_{pd} apart in time.

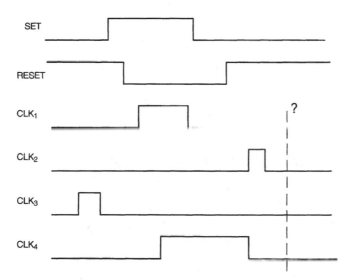

Figure P5.19

22. **One-shot** Normally, when SET pulses HI, the output Q is set to HI until a RESET pulse comes along. It's possible to modify an *SR* latch to deliver a HI pulse on output Q instead of Q staying HI until reset comes along. Such a circuit is called a *one-shot* and is useful in asynchronous design. See the timing waveforms in Fig. P5.20, which assume that external RESET is LO. It doesn't matter how long SET is asserted; Q_{1-s} will be asserted for a fixed duration.

Figure P5.20   One-shot timing.

Imagine you have available a circuit that delays output from input by Δ ms. Design the delay circuit into a sequential circuit that responds as required: when SET is asserted, the output Q_{1-S} pulses HI for Δ ms.

23. Can a level-sensitive master-slave flip-flop act as a transparent latch?

24. Look at the cascade of three toggle flip-flops shown in Fig. P5.21.

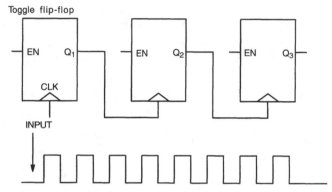

Figure P5.21   Ripple counter.

(a) Can this circuit function properly as a shift register?

(b) If the input is as shown, what will waveform Q_3 look like? Assume that propagation delay is negligible compared with input pulse width.

25. Assume that the clock input of a D-type master-slave flip-flop has a 2-ms clock period and a 50% duty cycle of ON and OFF. Assume that input D can change at any time. What is the longest time you might have to wait to see a change in input reflected at the output of the master-slave flip-flop?

26. A JK master-slave level-sensitive clock design is shown in Fig. P5.22. Given the clock and J and K waveforms shown below the schematic, draw what you expect the OUT waveform to look like.

   The second J pulse is an example of *1s-catching*. Why do you think it has that name? What J or K pulses would produce 0s-catching?

27. What would happen if Q and $\overline{Q}$ of an SR latch were connected directly back to R and S, respectively? No master-slave arrangement is involved.

28. Study Fig. 5.44, which shows a JK flip-flop made from a master-slave arrangement and an AND-OR input circuit. Show how to add $\overline{PRE}$ and $\overline{CLR}$ active-low inputs that will override the clocked inputs if either is LO.

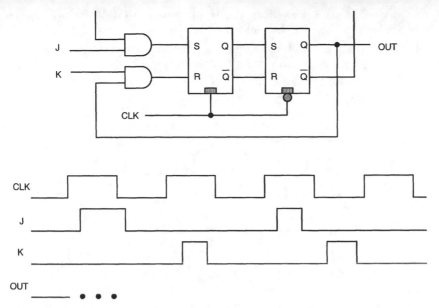

Figure P5.22

29. Using *one* toggle flip-flop with ENABLE and any AND, OR, and INVERT gates you wish, design a *JK* flip-flop.

30. Study the combinational logic plus edge-triggered *D* flip-flop shown in Fig. P5.23.

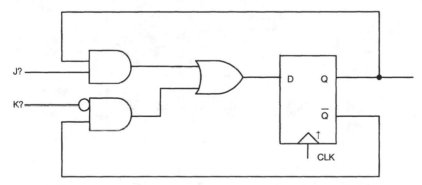

Figure P5.23

(a) Will the above circuit function as a *JK* flip-flop? If not, convert the design, with as few changes as possible, to one that will function as a *JK* flip-flop.

(b) What happens to the characteristics of the Fig. 5.23 flip-flop design if the OR gate is changed to a NOR?

31. The edge-triggered D flip-flop is reproduced in Fig. P5.24 at a time when CLOCK is falling, DATA is LO, and the previous output was HI.

(a) Trace through the sequence of changes that result in a LO at the output.
(b) Show that when CLOCK is LO, the output will be immune to DATA moving back up to HI.

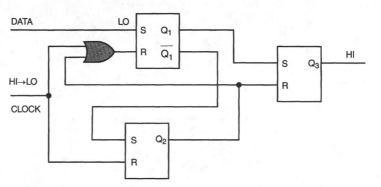

Figure P5.24 DATA LO for a clock transition on a D flip-flop.

32. The term *unclocked D latch* can refer to an unclocked SR latch with an inverter between the S and R inputs. A level-sensitive clocked D flip-flop does not have to be designed by tacking an inverter between the S and R inputs of a clocked SR flip-flop. It can be designed from scratch, as the SR latch was, using the Q_N, Q_{N+1} convention and a K-map. The map below defines a clocked D flip-flop.

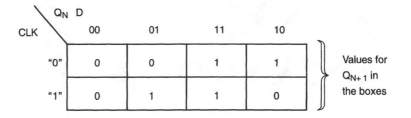

The terms for CLK are in quotation marks because the 1 may represent an active clock edge instead of a level-sensitive HI value. Notice there are no don't-cares in the D flip-flop map. Finish designing the circuit started with the map.

33. In an SR latch, when the input is 00, the latch remembers its previous state (00 is a no-change, or memory, input). What is the equivalent of the memory state for a D flip-flop? That is, in what condition does the D flip-flop remember previous data?

34. A rising-edge-triggered D flip-flop and a falling-edge-triggered D flip-flop are arranged as shown in Fig. P5.25. If the input wave and clock are as shown in Fig. P5.26, what will the output waveform look like? Does the rising- and falling-edge-triggered D flip-flop combination act like a master-slave flip-flop? Assume D_B starts at 0.

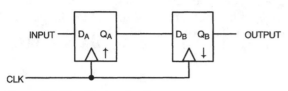

INPUT — D_A Q_A — D_B Q_B — OUTPUT

CLK

Figure P5.25 Master-slave?

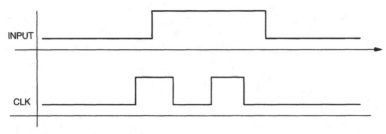

INPUT

CLK

Figure P5.26

35. A manufacturer of gate arrays includes in its library a "MUX flip-flop" (see Fig. P5.27). Using only a MUX flip-flop and no logic gates other than inverters, figure out how to arrange inputs such that the circuit in Fig. P5.28 is replaced by a MUX flip flop alone.

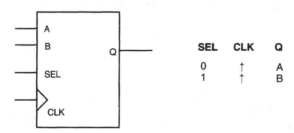

SEL	CLK	Q
0	↑	A
1	↑	B

Figure P5.27 A MUX flip-flop.

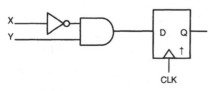

Figure P5.28

36. **(a)** Can you think of a situation where a latch can do something an edge-triggered flip-flop fails to do?

(b) Can you think of any way to add logic around a self-contained edge-triggered flip-flop to turn it back into a latch?

37. **Setup and hold times** Shown in Fig P5.29 is the rising clock edge of a rising-edge-triggered D flip-flop and four DATA waveforms. Setup and hold times for the flip-flop are indicated by the horizontal bars shown. For which of the four waveforms will the output Q definitely be HI one hold time + t_{pd} after the clock edge? Assume that Q (the flip-flop output) is 0 before the clock rises.

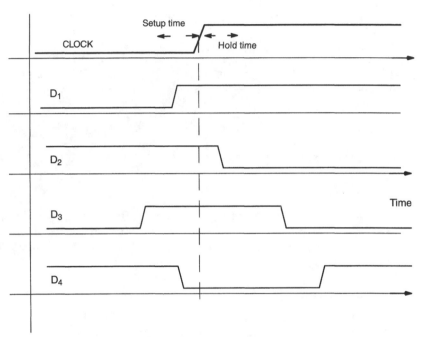

Figure P5.29 Timing problem.

38. **(a)** What would it mean for a flip-flop to have a *negative setup time?*

(b) Suppose a D flip-flop has a setup time of 3 ns, a hold time of 4 ns, a minimum clock width of 5 ns, and a propagation delay of 2 ns. What is the maximum frequency at which the flip-flop clock can operate before the flip-flop may make mistakes capturing data?

(c) What if the the flip-flop in (b) had a minimum clock width of 10 ns? How would the answer to (b) change?

(d) Suppose the output of the flip-flop specified in part (b) is connected to the D input of an identical flip-flop and both of the flip-flops are driven by the same clock. What will be the maximum frequency this two-stage shift register can be clocked at?

39. Suppose a rising-edge-triggered D flip-flop has

    A setup time of 4 ns
    A hold time of 5 ns
    A recovery time of 2 ns
    A propagation delay t_{PLH} from D to Q of 6 ns
    A propagation delay from clock to Q of 7 ns

What is the shortest time from a LO-to-HI data transition to a LO-to-HI Q output transition that can occur for valid data transfer? (*Hint:* Not all of the above parameters are needed for the calculation.)

40. (a) Assume, in the circuit of Fig. P5.30, that all Q_A–Q_D are initially 0 and that one CLK pulse occurs within a duration much greater than the setup and hold times of the flip-flops. Under what conditions of inputs A, B, C, and D does Q_D go HI? Draw out a timing diagram. The flip-flops are rising-edge-triggered D flip-flops.

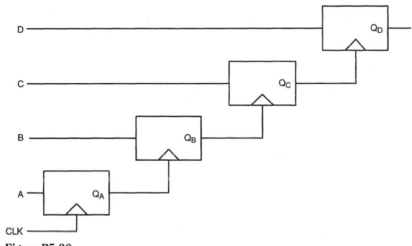

Figure P5.30

(b) Now assume that CLK is a steady 1-kHz stream of pulses. Show the timing for A–D so that Q_D could go through the sequence HI-LO-HI.

(c) Now assume that $\overline{\text{CLK}}$ is connected to A–D. What will be the output at Q_D?

41. Toggle flip-flops in series Suppose the propagation delay through a toggle flip-flop is 20 ns from the time of a rising clock edge to the change of the output. Assume that six toggle flip-flops are connected from the output of one to the clock of the next (with the first toggle flip-flop connected to a 1-MHz pulse generator). What is the period of the final flip-flop output? How long will it take for the last toggle flip-flop to change from LO to HI after the first rising edge is seen? Assume that all the flip-flop outputs are LO when the 1-MHz generator is enabled.

42. The formula for the mean time between failures of a metastable synchronizer is

$$\text{MTBF} = \frac{e^{+t/\tau}}{T_0 f d_r}$$

where τ and T_0 have units of seconds and nanoseconds, respectively, and f and d_r have units of hertz. Show that MTBF has the units of seconds.

‡**43.** Say that whenever an external, nonclock input fails to meet setup and hold times for a D input, the flip-flop goes metastable for a time. Divide time into nanosecond intervals, and let the probability $P(n)$ that the flip-flop stays for n nanoseconds in a metastable state be

$$P(n) = \lambda e^{-\lambda n} \qquad \lambda = \tfrac{1}{4}\,\text{ns}^{-1}$$

a Poisson distribution. What minimum clock period will ensure that 99% of metastable events will not cause errors in the system? Use the falling- and rising-edge-triggered circuit in the synchronization discussion in Section 5.10.2 as the basis for your design. Note: 99% reliability would be unacceptable in most critical applications.

44. Given the data in Section 5.10.1 on T_0 and τ for the 74AC74 CMOS D flip-flop, calculate the mean time between failures for a synchronizer built with a 74AC74 operating with a 50-MHz clock and a data rate of about 20 MHz. Assume a nonzero setup time of 4 ns.

45. Remember how a JK flip-flop was created from a clocked SR flip-flop, as shown in Fig. P5.31.

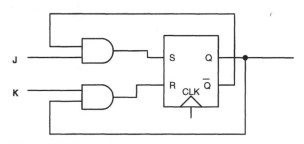

Figure P5.31

(a) What would happen if the AND gates were replaced by OR gates and the inputs to the gates were complemented? Would it still work as a clocked flip-flop?

(b) Recall the concept of duality from Chapter 2. Do you think the concept of duality makes sense for a flip-flop?

Reference

MENTZER, R. 1990. Designing to deter metastable conditions. *National Anthem* (published by National Semiconductor, Santa Clara, Cal.), May, 12.

Synchronous Counters

OVERVIEW

A **sequencer** is a circuit or system that cycles through a definite series of **states;** the cycling can be governed by a master clock (synchronous sequencer) or can occur in response to arbitrarily timed external stimuli (asynchronous sequencer). As an example, nearly all computer programs are executed in hardware as synchronous sequencers. The hardware of a sequencer can be partitioned into memory storage elements (such as you saw in Chapter 5) plus combinational logic. Sequencers have significance in biology as well as in digital electronics.

> The computer program that we call differentiation instructs some genes to turn on and others to turn off in a particular sequence. The turned-on genes make proteins and these then help to produce other molecules of the body. (Klein 1990, 13)

> A wealth of clinical evidence shows that lesions of the cerebellum characteristically entail a chronic disruption of the sequential order in bodily movement. ... When a patient with such an impairment is asked to extend his ipsilateral arm and then bring the index finger to the tip of his nose, he proves capable of obeying only with marked instability: his hand lurches from side to side, and the lurch grows worse as the finger nears the target. (Nauta and Feirtag 1986, 102)

Here in Chapter 6 we will be concerned with synchronous sequencers made of electronic flip-flops only—flip-flops all connected to a common clock. In fact, for most of Chapter 6, the clock will be the *only* external input to our sequencers; as such, the sequencers will be called **counters** (or *automatons*). After establishing a basic design method for counters, we will consider some global inputs, such as RESET, LOAD, and HALT. But not until Chapter 7 will we allow logic-steering nonclock inputs to complicate our sequencer designs. At that time we will refer to the resulting circuits as **finite state machines,** of which counters are an important subset.

One of the major concepts for understanding sequencers and their design is **state.** At any instant of time, the outputs of all the flip-flops in a circuit constitute its state. At the start of counter design your goal will be to associate a binary state with each step in the count sequence. A **present-state–next-state table** (PS-NS table) will set you up to finish the design of a counter. Examples in Chapter 6 will show you how the PS-NS table of the counter is expanded in terms of flip-flop excitation tables, which lead to combinational circuits for flip-flop drives. The outputs of the flip-flops

or toggle flip-flops can be used for counter designs. **Shift** registers will be shown as a particularly useful form of sequencer design. If the sequence you need to realize has repeating numbers, "hidden" flip-flops, which don't participate directly in system output, will be needed to complete your design. By the time you finish Chapter 6 you will be able to design any synchronous automaton.

In Section 6.1 the terms *sequential circuit, clock, state, synchronous circuit, counter,* and *finite state machine* are more carefully explained.

6.1 SEQUENTIAL CIRCUIT, STATE, AND CLOCK

In Chapter 5 latches evolved to flip-flops. As noted at the beginning of Chapter 5, any digital circuit with memory due to feedback—particularly a circuit with latches and flip-flops—is a **sequential circuit**. In a **synchronous circuit** all memory elements are flip-flops and all the flip-flops are connected to the same clock. In the first example we analyze a small synchronous circuit, a cyclic shift register with three D flip-flops.

EXAMPLE 1

Recall that a rising-edge-triggered D flip-flop (shown in Fig. 6.1) transfers the value of input D to output Q when CLK input changes from LO to HI. Now consider three such D flip-flops connected to a common clock, also as shown in Fig. 6.1. CLK is the only external input. In between the flip-flops are inverters, which transfer the complement of one flip-flop output to the D input of the next flip-flop; flip-flop A sends its uncomplemented output back to the input of the flip-flop C. Let's assume that when this circuit is first turned on, all the flip-flop outputs Q_C, Q_B, and Q_A are 0 (or that a reset mechanism ensures a 000 start). Thereafter none of the outputs will change until the clock makes a transition from LO to HI. In the first transition, flip-flops B and A will change to 1 because their D inputs had been 1 (for the duration of many setup times) before the rising-edge clock. The output of flip-flop C will remain 0 because its D input was 0 before the clock edge.

As the clock goes through several transitions, output changes will occur, which you can express in a timing diagram (sans delays) as shown in Fig. 6.2. Listing the

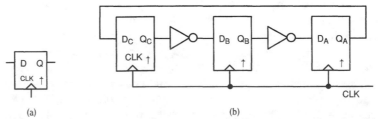

(a)   (b)

Figure 6.1   (a) Rising-edge-triggered D flip-flop; (b) cyclic shift register.

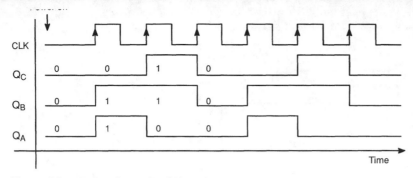

CLK

Q_C 0   0   1   0

Q_B 0   1   1   0

Q_A 0   1   0   0

Time

Figure 6.2 Timing for cyclic shift register.

outputs as $Q_C Q_B Q_A$, the system goes through the "states"

Q_C	Q_B	Q_A
0	0	0
0	1	1
1	1	0

and then it repeats 000 as the clock ticks. The flip-flop outputs cycle through three states before the sequence repeats. Think of it as a circuit that counts three clock pulses before starting over. If you know which of the three states the circuit is in, you can predict which state the circuit will go to after the next rising clock edge. The transition equations (excitation equations) for the circuit are the following:

$$D_C = Q_A$$
$$D_B = \overline{Q_C}$$
$$D_A = \overline{Q_B}$$

If the flip-flops had started in a state different from any of the three states in the sequence above, a different sequence would have resulted. Exercise 1 asks what sequence will result if the circuit starts in state $Q_C Q_B Q_A = 111$. The point is, in order to predict the future output (sequence of states) of a sequential circuit, you must know the complete current state and the transition equations; then you will be able to derive the resulting state after the next clock pulse.

It is instructive to redraw the circuit of Example 1 as shown in Fig. 6.3. In the dashed box at the top, the combinational circuitry from the flip-flop outputs to the flip-flop inputs is collected together. (One of the flip-flop inputs is a direct connection from a flip-flop output.) The clock is highlighted as the only external input. (The feedback from the flip-flop outputs to inputs through a combinational circuit can be considered "internal input.") The redrawing of Fig. 6.2 emphasizes that the flip-flops

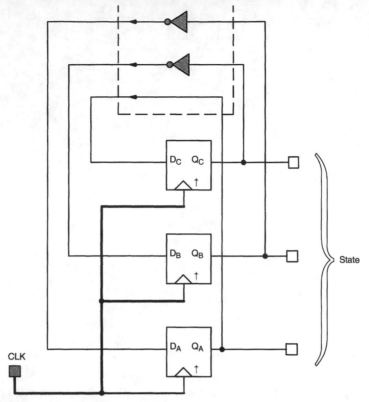

Figure 6.3 Finite-state machine.

in a synchronous counter circuit can be segregated together as a parallel-in–parallel-out register whose parallel inputs are formed by combinational logic of the parallel outputs.

6.1.1 State versus Output

To predict the future output of a combinational circuit, an engineer requires only the future *input* and a diagram of the gates representing the circuit. For predicting the future output of a sequential circuit containing latches and flip-flops, the circuit diagram, the previous history of the input, and the future input will be needed. It turns out that input history is summarized by the current outputs of all flip-flops in the circuit. The **state** of a circuit is all its flip-flop outputs at a given time. If a circuit has N flip-flops, it can have at most 2^N different states. In dynamical system analysis (sequential circuits are an example of a dynamical system) the *state* can be defined as the minimum system information needed to determine future output, given future

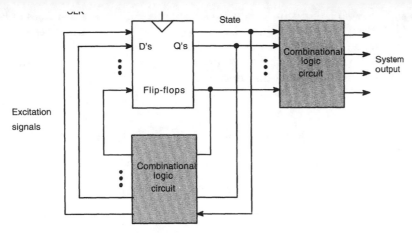

Figure 6.4 General form of Moore circuit.

input.[1] It is beyond the scope of this text to prove that the set of flip-flop outputs in a synchronous digital system constitutes a valid state in all circumstances; however, as you follow the examples in this chapter and the next, you will appreciate that flip-flop outputs do play a crucial role in determining the next state of a sequential circuit waiting for a clock edge.

Notice that *inputs*, including the clock, are not included in the definition of a state. Further, the state is not the same thing as the circuit's output. Some or all of the flip-flop outputs may be direct output, but in general, synchronous counter circuit output is a combination of flip-flop outputs, as shown in Fig. 6.4. Note that circuit output can change only after valid clock edges; a circuit in which output changes only in time with the clock is called a **Moore** circuit. Some flip-flop outputs may not participate in output at all. For example, only the last flip-flop in a serial-in–serial-out shift register provides circuit output. *All* of the flip-flop outputs, however, are necessary to describe the circuit state. Flip-flops that do not directly influence output may be described as "hidden." We will use hidden units for sequencer designs later in this chapter.

The flip-flop outputs of a sequential circuit are the minimum amount of information to qualify as a state. But any set of flip-flops helping to realize a circuit might not be the minimum-size set needed for an optimal design. In Example 1, three flip-flops starting at 000 sequenced through three states; it would be possible to realize the exact sequence in Example 1 with two flip-flops and combinational logic, which

---

[1]See, for example, Director and Rohrer (1972), who say, "A *state* of system at time t_0 is any amount of information, which together with any possible input function specified for $t_0 \leq t \leq t_f$ is adequate to determine uniquely the output function for $t_0 \leq t \leq t_f$ for any $t_f \geq t_0$. Often we are interested in a *canonic* representation and in such cases specify that an acceptable state be a *minimal* amount of such necessary information."

Here's a nondigital example: in a dynamical system described by differential equations and modeled with analog integrators, the state variables are the outputs of all integrators at a given time t_0. (The values of the state variables at the start t_0 of a process are the initial conditions at t_0.)

would take the two flip-flop outputs and generate three outputs. If a system must cycle through M states, then at least N flip-flops, where N is the smallest integer such that $2^N \geq M$, would be required. As we will see, it may be convenient to use more than the minimum number of flip-flops in some designs, and it may be inconvenient to eliminate extra flip-flops from other designs.

EXAMPLE 2

The circuit in Fig. 6.5 has three bits for its state ($Q_C Q_B Q_A$), but only one bit of output.

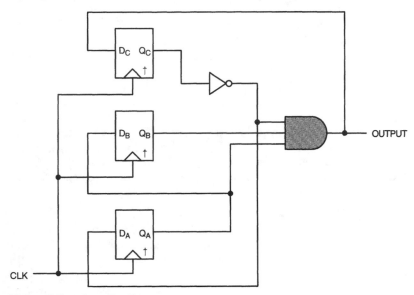

Figure 6.5   Three flip-flops, one output.

We have correctly defined the state of a sequential circuit as the values of all its flip-flop outputs at a given time. But in digital design *state* may also refer to the name of a condition, such as IDLE, WAIT, ACCEPT, or START MOTOR in a specification for a sequential design (state machine). As the design process goes ahead, the named state will be given a multiple-bit binary label comprising the values of the flip-flop outputs representing it. The secondary problem of figuring out flip-flop data input drives can sometimes be simplified by a well-chosen state variable assignment. Again, whether the number of states in a system is minimal or optimal is a separate matter from how the states are named and labeled.

6.1.2   One Clock and Its Maximum Frequency

In a synchronous circuit all flip-flops must be clocked by the same signal. In fact, all the flip-flops in the circuit normally must be either rising- or falling-edge-triggered; the two types should not be mixed in the same circuit. Furthermore, as the clock signal

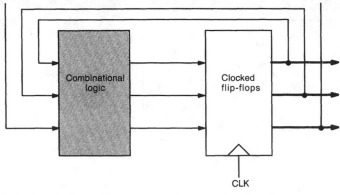

Figure 6.6 General form of synchronous circuit.

courses around the circuit, it should not be delayed or otherwise passed through logic gates. Such actions would **skew** the clock, that is, create different arrival times for the clock at different flip-flops in the circuit.

It's perfectly possible to create useful multi-flip-flop sequential circuits with more than one clock, or no clock at all, but because of the timing advantages of synchronous design, over 99% of practical sequential designs are synchronous. In Chapter 5 you saw the benefits of edge-triggering individual flip-flops. Only at the active clock edge will the flip-flop accept new data and change its output. Races and catching are avoided. These benefits hold for a multi-flip-flop synchronous circuit, too. Since all the flip-flops in a synchronous circuit act in parallel, the problem of stabilizing the flip-flop inputs is reduced to a single time frame.

Each new active clock edge will present an opportunity for the state of the circuit to change. Imagine a synchronous system in state P; after the next clock pulse the system must be in state Q. If the only external input to the system is CLK, only the current state P of the system need be used to determine the next state Q. The current state is represented by the flip-flop outputs, which are the inputs to a combinational circuit, which forms the actual flip-flop inputs (D, J, K, etc.). We have another layer of feedback around the flip-flops themselves, which already are designed with positive feedback! See Fig. 6.6. The circuit in Fig. 6.6 is a prototype for the counters we will design in Chapter 6. Its only external input is the clock, and the flip-flop outputs are the circuit's outputs.

How Fast Can the Clock Go?   In many cases the user of a clocked digital system wants to run the clock at its maximum rate. Consider the case of the counter shown in Fig. 6.7, with CLK input and with flip-flop outputs and combinational logic outputs in a loop. There is propagation delay Δ_F through the flip-flops and Δ_C through the combinational logic. Once those delays elapse, the combinational output, which forms the input to the flip-flops, must be stable for at least the setup and hold times before and after the clock edge. These timing limitations are shown in Fig. 6.8, where

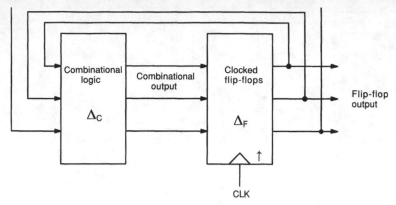

Figure 6.7 Moore circuit for clock speed.

signifies data not yet available. If we assume that t_{hold} is zero (as it is in many commercial flip-flops), the minimum period for the clock t_{min} is

$$t_{min} = \Delta_C + \Delta_F + t_{setup}$$

The frequency in hertz is $1/t_{min}$. Any delay in combinational logic between flip-flop outputs and circuit output does not affect the maximum clock rate because the output logic is not involved in the feedback path from flip-flop state back to excitation.

In addition to a high frequency, a clock signal may need a *precise* frequency. In some applications a maximum clock rate may be less important than an exact and repeatable clock rate. A clock frequency of 1.048576 MHz can be divided down 20 times to exactly 1 Hz, for example. In such cases, a **crystal oscillator** connected to a timing circuit will be needed to achieve the exact frequency.

Fan-out Since the clock signal may need to contact many flip-flops in a large synchronous circuit (such as a microprocessor), fan-out problems may arise. One IC output can project to only a limited number of gate inputs before logic levels and noise margins are compromised too much. There are two solutions: (1) design a

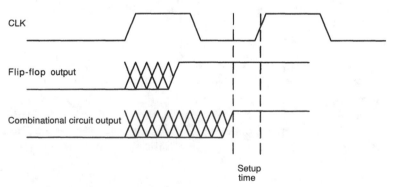

Figure 6.8 Timing diagram for speed analysis.

special output circuit for CLK that can supply hundreds of milliamps of current or
(2) send the clock generator output to buffer gates, which then supply the actual
clock signal to the flip-flops.

EXAMPLE 3

Here we'll improve clock fan-out by sending the clock generator signal to the six
inverters of one IC package (74LS14) of Schmitt trigger inverters. Since the inverters
are all in the same IC, they will have similar propagation delays and any change in
t_{pd} due to temperature fluctuations in the chip will affect all the inverters equally.
See Fig. 6.9. To the right are six clock lines with minimized skew that can project
to various flip-flop clock inputs. Use of the 7414 Schmitt trigger inverter to improve
fan-out will help maintain a fast rise time. The fact that the clock generator signal
is being inverted will not affect synchronous performance as long as only inverted
signals are sent to flip-flop clocks.

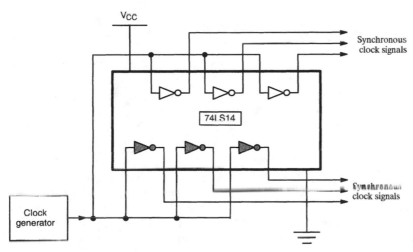

Figure 6.9   Schmitt trigger inverter for clock fan-out.

So far we have been insisting that CLK be the only external input to our synchronous circuits, and therefore we are considering simple *counters* or *automatons*.
Later we will allow other inputs unsynchronized with the clock to enter our designs;
at that point we will discuss *synchronizer circuits* for minimizing setup and hold times
and metastability problems. Furthermore, some synchronous circuits may need to
communicate with other independent synchronous circuits operating with different
clocks. In Chapter 9, on digital communication, you will learn about *handshake circuits*
for connecting together two circuits running on different clocks.

---

[2]In 1990 the Digital Equipment Corporation's Alpha chip microprocessor was described as "an arc welder
surrounded by a million transistors."

Table 6.1   State Changes for Three Flip-flops

$Q_N \rightarrow Q_{N+1}$	D Flip-flop D	Toggle Flip-flop ENABLE	JK Flip-flop			
			J	K	J	K
$0 \rightarrow 0$	0	0	0 0	1 0	0	X
$0 \rightarrow 1$	1	1	1 1	0 1	1	X
$1 \rightarrow 0$	0	1	0 1	1 1	X	1
$1 \rightarrow 1$	1	0	0 1	0 0	X	0

6.2   STEPS IN ANALYZING A SYNCHRONOUS COUNTER

Now that we've established what a synchronous circuit and its state are, let's look at two examples of already-built synchronous counters and figure out what sequences they step through. First we consider the steps you will go through to solve for a given circuit's sequence. (1) Separate the components into the flip-flops and the **excitation logic**—the combinational logic for each flip-flop input. In the cases below, and for most of the rest of this chapter, circuit output will be the flip-flop outputs, and no external input except clock and reset will be allowed. (2) Study the excitation logic, and extract a Boolean expression for each of the flip-flop inputs. (3) Assume to begin with that the circuit has been reset to an all-zero state, and put all zeros in the excitation equations. (4) Take the new state outputs and put them in the excitation equations, finding the next state. (5) Continue with step 4 until a previous state is encountered again. If possible, mark the binary-labeled states in a Karnaugh map.

The **state change table,** Table 6.1, will help you determine the next state given the excitation logic for the three types of edge-triggered flip-flops from Chapter 5. On the left are the states before (Q_N) and after (Q_{N+1}) the clock edge; on the right are three groupings of flip-flop input values. For D flip-flops the "drive" is just Q_{N+1}; for toggle flip-flops their enable is 1 only when Q_N and Q_{N+1} are different. The JK table, as you learned in Chapter 5, ends up with four don't-cares out of eight J and K possibilities. For analysis the table is used from right to left; for design you work from left to right, starting with flip-flop transitions and determining the required excitation logic.

EXAMPLE 4

Starting at $Q_C Q_B Q_A = 000$, what sequence does the synchronous circuit of three D flip-flops in Fig. 6.10 step through? State 000 can be reached by asserting the asynchronous $\overline{\text{RESET}}$ switch to LO and then sending $\overline{\text{RESET}}$ back to HI.

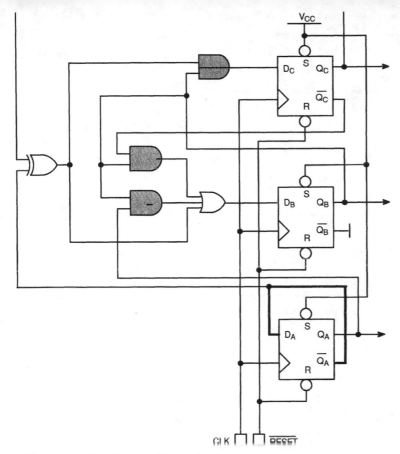

Figure 6.10 Synchronous Moore circuit.

Solution

Step 1 The excitation circuitry is fairly well separated from the flip-flops, except for the short connection, highlighted, from $\overline{Q_A}$ to D_A.

Step 2 Now we obtain the excitation expressions for the D inputs. Tracing through the connections in the circuit, we find

$$D_A = \overline{Q_A}$$
$$D_B = Q_C \oplus \overline{Q_A} + \overline{Q_C}Q_B + Q_BQ_A = \overline{Q_C}Q_A + Q_C\overline{Q_A} + \overline{Q_C}Q_B + Q_B\overline{Q_A}$$
$$D_C = Q_B \cdot (Q_C \oplus \overline{Q_A}) = \overline{Q_C}Q_BQ_A + Q_CQ_B\overline{Q_A}$$

Step 3 If $Q_CQ_BQ_A = 000$, then $D_CD_BD_A = 001$, so the first two states are

$$000$$
$$001$$

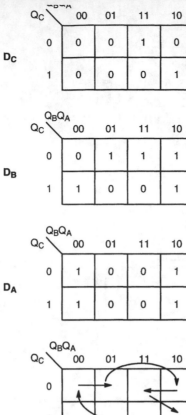

Figure 6.11 K-maps for Example 4.

Steps 4 and 5 Using the SOP excitation equations to fill in subcubes on K-maps for the D's, we find the K-maps of Fig. 6.11, where the last "map" shows the steps the sequence takes. These result in the following sequence:

Q_C	Q_B	Q_A	Decimal Value
0	0	0	0
0	0	1	1
0	1	0	2
0	1	1	3
1	1	0	6
1	1	1	7

and then back to 000.

Another way to find the sequence: lay out and simulate the circuit on a CAD system such as LogicWorks or Beige Bag. Simulating the circuit may be a good check that your pencil-and-paper prediction is correct.

EXAMPLE 5

Study the *JK* flip-flop circuit in Fig. 6.12, and find what sequence comes out of Q_D, synchronized with the clock.

Solution   The state of the circuit is $Q_D Q_C Q_B Q_A$, but only Q_D is output. The asynchronous $\overline{\text{SET}}$ input is permanently disabled, but $\overline{\text{RESET}}$ can be asserted by the user. Notice that flip-flops B, C, and D receive as inputs $J_M = Q_{M-1}$ and $K_M = \overline{Q_{M-1}}$, $M = B, C, D$; thus the last three flip-flops in the chain act as *D* flip-flops, passing input from the previous flip-flop through on each clock cycle (shift register). For the first flip-flop,

$$J_A = K_A = Q_A \oplus (\overline{Q_B + Q_C})$$

so flip-flop A will either toggle or hold, depending on the values of the three hidden units A, B, and C in the Boolean expression.

Go through the steps listed above.

Step 1   The excitation logic for J_A and K_A is segregated, and the drives for B, C, and D are in the form of a shift register.

Step 2 $J_A = K_A = Q_A \oplus (\overline{Q_B + Q_C})$

Step 3   For $Q_D Q_C Q_B Q_A = 0000$, $J_A = K_A = 1$, so the next state is

$$Q_D Q_C Q_B Q_A = \mathbf{0001}$$

Steps 4 and 5   Continued application of the excitation expression for $J_A = K_A$ yields

```
0 0 1 1
0 1 1 0
1 1 0 0
1 0 0 0
0 0 0 1
```

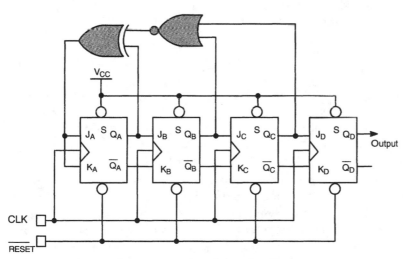

Figure 6.12   *JK* synchronous circuit with four flip-flops.

The last, 0001, is a repeat, so the sequence is complete. Notice that the repeating cycle of this counter does *not* include the reset state 0000. The output from the state cycling is

$$Q_D = 0000110001100011\ldots$$

with *four* 0s at the RESET start.

Both of the examples analyzed above are synchronous counters because all their flip-flops are driven by one clock signal, which is the only external input (save an asynchronous reset). In our analysis we didn't investigate systematically what happens if a circuit pops into a state not in the intended sequence, although in the second example we did see that state 0000 led into the main sequence. *Lockout* refers to an unwanted sequence generated by the same hardware, and a *trap* is a state that cycles on itself; *lockout* and *traps* will be considered in Chapter 6.

6.3 DESIGN OF SYNCHRONOUS COUNTERS

Part of the design method for synchronous counters follows backwards the steps in analysis. Remember that in the analysis of a counter circuit, the goal was to figure out the sequence a particular circuit would generate. In design you're *given* the sequence and need to work back to the hardware. Once you choose a sequence of binary-labeled states for the counting pattern, a present-state–next-state (PS-NS) table is used to develop excitation equations for the flip-flop drives. The equations then lead to the realization in hardware.

Other issues in the design process, however, will be new to you: minimizing or optimizing the number of states, assigning *state variables* (flip-flop outputs) to state names in the sequence, choosing an appropriate flip-flop (usually a *D* flip-flop), and avoiding lockout states. Before outlining all the steps of the basic counter design method, let's look at the state assignment problem.

6.3.1 Assigning Flip-flop Outputs to States

Sometimes the specifications for a synchronous counter start with a definite sequence of binary numbers that a design must step through. In that case the assignment of flip-flop outputs is established and you get no chance to be inventive matching state variables with state names. Other times you have carte blanche to encode state names with state variables. In that case, here are some guidelines:

1. If there are M states in the sequence, you will need at least N flip-flops, where N is the smallest number such that $2^N \geq M$.
2. You might find it convenient to use more than the minimum number of flip-flops for state assignments; doing so can help partition your problem.
3. The extreme of using more than the minimum number of flip-flops is assignment of one flip-flop output per state; this kind of assignment is called *one-hot* and will be seen in an example.

4. One state, which we will call the *ground state* (also called RESET, CLEAR, idle, start state, and others) should be designated as a return point for all unused flip-flop output combinations (unused states). Normally the ground state is all zeros and can be reached by an asynchronous clear command to all the flip-flops. (A ground state of all zeros assumes that 0000 ... is one of the states in the sequence!) Unused states will become don't-cares in excitation logic maps, so *if you want to minimize excitation logic* you can fill in 1s (instead of 0s) where convenient at don't-care map locations. *Minimizing excitation logic will mean that if an error pops the circuit into an unused state, a return to the main sequence is not guaranteed.* You'll see an example of nonzero ground state later.

6.3.2 Ten Steps to Design a Synchronous Counter

After state assignment you need to proceed with the generation of the present-state–next-state table, the development of the excitation equations, and the choosing of a flip-flop type. For the algorithm below we assume that all the numbers in the sequence are unique; the case of a number being repeated in the sequence can be solved with hidden units, as will be explained later.

Steps in Synchronous Counter Design Given a Labeled Sequence

1. Express each number in the sequence in binary code. Each number will be a state of the system.

2. Choose and implement a method of assigning flip-flop outputs (N) to states (M): either use one flip-flop output (state variable) per bit of the number code, or minimize the number N of flip-flops according to $2^N \geq M$, or use one-hot coding

3. Make a present-state–next-state table whose left-side rows have a state (number) and whose right side has the *next state* in the sequence. The next state for the last state in the sequence is the first state.

4. Choose *one* flip-flop type (D, JK, or toggle) to realize the circuit. D flip-flops are a default choice.

5. Find state transition relationships for each pair of present-state–next-state columns, using the state change table for the chosen flip-flop.

6. Use the complete *present state* as input to truth tables whose outputs are state transition values corresponding to each flip-flop input.

7. Send unused states to a ground state (usually all zeros).

8. With map or Boolean algebra methods find expressions (excitation equations) for each flip-flop input from the truth tables of step 6.

9. Form system outputs from combinations of the flip-flop outputs.

10. Realize the excitation expressions as combinational logic drives for the flip-flop inputs. Build in RESET to the ground state.

---

of the 10 steps. The rest of the steps can be and have been automated; in Chapter 7 we'll look at the use of a *Finite-State Machine Compiler* and the Moore machine option in PALASM CAD software.

EXAMPLE 6

Design a synchronous counter for the repeating sequence 0 3 6 9 12 0, etc. Use positional binary code for each of the numbers. Employ rising-edge-triggered D flip-flops, and have the flip-flop outputs code for the numbers in the sequence.

Solution

Steps 1 and 2   Flip-flop outputs Q_3–Q_0 are determined by the specifications:

Number	Q_3	Q_2	Q_1	Q_0
0	0	0	0	0
3	0	0	1	1
6	0	1	1	0
9	1	0	0	1
12	1	1	0	0

Step 3

Present State				Next State			
0	0	0	0	0	0	1	1
0	0	1	1	0	1	1	0
0	1	1	0	1	0	0	1
1	0	0	1	1	1	0	0
1	1	0	0	0	0	0	0

Step 4 D flip-flops will be used. Modern designs rely on D flip-flops because a D flip-flop occupies less area on an IC than a JK flip-flop does. Furthermore, you can read the state transitions for a D flip-flop directly from the "next state" column; it's more difficult to make a quick transfer from state transition table to excitation map with JK or toggle flip-flops.

Step 5   Table 6.1 shows the D inputs for state transitions. For example, when $Q_3Q_2Q_1Q_0 = 0000$, $D_3D_2D_1D_0$ must be 0011 in order for the next state to be $Q_3Q_2Q_1Q_0 = 0011$.

Step 6   The four maps in Fig. 6.13 show the state transition drives for the four flip-flops. Only 5 out of the 16 possible states need to be filled in at this point. The map for D_0 is labeled with arrows showing the sequence cycle of $Q_3Q_2Q_1Q_0$; further, each stop in the cycle is marked with the decimal number of the sequence.

You should make sure you understand how these maps are generated. The inputs to each map are the *outputs* of the four flip-flops; the output bit represented in the Nth K-map is the *input* to the Nth flip-flop. Remember that in a synchronous counter the flip-flop outputs are fed back through a combinational circuit to become flip-flop inputs. The inputs wait until the next valid clock edge before they direct the next state transition of all the flip-flops.

Step 7   All of the unmarked squares (unused states) from the maps in step 6 are don't-cares at this point. The safest strategy is to "care" that the unused states go

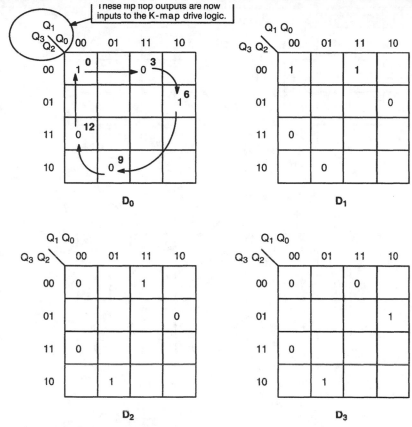

Figure 6.19 K-maps for Example 6.

to the ground state (which we normally designate as $Q_3Q_2Q_1Q_0 = 0000$). If you are sure that your system will never pop into an unused state or if you truly don't care if it does, or if you must minimize the cost of the combinational excitation logic, then you may fill in the don't-cares in such a way as to create large subcubes for prime implicants with few literals.

In the maps above, all the minterms are isolated from each other, so breaking the rule about sending unused states to 0000 would result in fewer gates needed for excitation logic. In the maps of Fig. 6.14, the drive inputs for the desired sequence are in bold and all the rest of the K-map squares are filled with zeros.

Step 8   Looking at the four maps in Fig. 6.14, the excitation equations for the D's are

$$D_0 = \overline{Q_3} \cdot \overline{Q_2} \cdot \overline{Q_1} \cdot \overline{Q_0} + \overline{Q_3} \cdot Q_2 \cdot Q_1 \cdot \overline{Q_0} \quad [m_0, m_6]$$
$$D_1 = \overline{Q_3} \cdot \overline{Q_2} \cdot \overline{Q_1} \cdot \overline{Q_0} + \overline{Q_3} \cdot \overline{Q_2} \cdot Q_1 \cdot Q_0 \quad [m_0, m_3]$$
$$D_2 = \overline{Q_3} \cdot \overline{Q_2} \cdot Q_1 \cdot Q_0 + Q_3 \cdot \overline{Q_2} \cdot \overline{Q_1} \cdot Q_0 \quad [m_3, m_9]$$
$$D_3 = \overline{Q_3} \cdot Q_2 \cdot Q_1 \cdot \overline{Q_0} + Q_3 \cdot \overline{Q_2} \cdot \overline{Q_1} \cdot Q_0 \quad [m_6, m_9]$$

which can't be minimized any more. Minterm numbers are in brackets to the right.

Step 9   The output comes directly from the flip-flops.

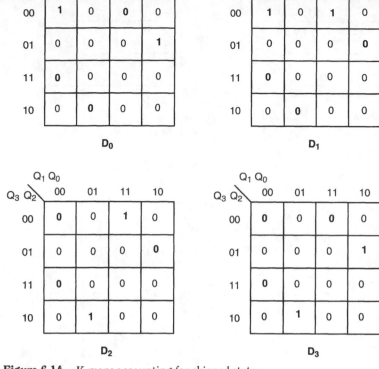

Figure 6.14   K-maps accounting for skipped states.

Step 10   The circuit in Fig. 6.15 (on the next page) is drawn in PAL format, where connections with AND gate inputs are shown with X's. The circuit realizes the excitation logic and shows a $\overline{\text{RESET}}$ input for the four D flip-flops. There is no straightforward way in the PAL for different OR gates to share the same product term, so states 9, 3, and 0 are each implemented twice. Not shown are where the clock comes from or how the outputs are displayed. On the far left are the numbers of the minterms that the ANDs realize. The circuit can be drawn on LogicWorks with "binary switches" for CLK and RST and "hex display" for output and then simulated to verify the correct sequence.

The next example allows the designer a chance to assign flip-flop outputs to states and to deal with outputs that are combinations of flip-flop outputs.

EXAMPLE 7

Say an engine needs to go through four strokes, all of equal duration. (See Fig. 6.16.) On the first stroke the inlet valve is open and the outlet is closed; on the next stroke the inlet is closed; on the third stroke a spark is delivered; and during the fourth

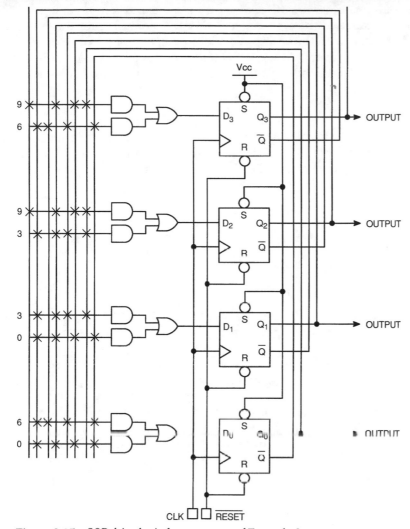

Figure 6.15 SOP drive logic for sequencer of Example 6.

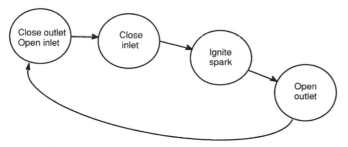

Figure 6.16 State sequence of engine cycle for Example 7.

stroke the outlet is open for the exhaust from the explosion to vent. Then the first stroke comes again and the cycle repeats. Design a controller for the system, with a clock for input and with three outputs: one to open the inlet, one to open the outlet, and one to ignite the spark. Assume that if the control to open a valve isn't asserted, the valve closes (spring-loaded valve). The frequency of the clock will determine the speed of the engine.

Solution

Step 1 Each of the four strokes is a different state. Since two flip-flop outputs can represent four states ($2^2 = 4$), let's try to design a controller with two flip-flops.

Step 2 How shall we assign flip-flop outputs (state variables) to the states? The most natural way would be to use positional binary code:

	$Q_B Q_A$
S_1	0 0
S_2	0 1
S_3	1 0
S_4	1 1

Such coding could work. But we observe that the system has three outputs, and the proper functioning of the engine requires that outputs be asserted only during their intended states. We see that in the sequence 00 **01 10** 11, two flip-flop outputs try to change at once between the second and third states and between the last and first states. Because of unequal propagation delays in the flip-flops, it's possible that the two flip-flops won't change simultaneously and that a glitch will occur that will throw the system into an unwanted state transiently before it gets to the expected next state. Since there's nothing special about a numerical code for this problem, try two-bit Gray code. In Gray code, numbers change only one bit at a time. Included in our state table now are what we think the values of the outputs should be at each phase of the engine.

	$Q_B Q_A$	INLET	OUTLET	SPARK
S_1	0 0	1	0	0
S_2	0 1	0	0	0
S_3	1 1	0	0	1
S_4	1 0	0	1	0

Step 3

Present State $Q_B Q_A$	Next State
0 0	0 1
0 1	1 1
1 1	1 0
1 0	**0 0**

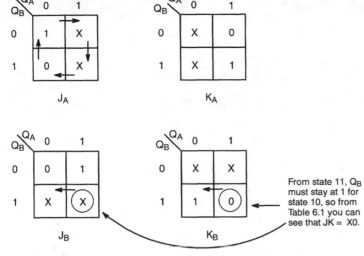

Figure 6.17 State transitions on a K-map.

Step 4 Let's use JK flip-flops for this example. Half of the JK state transition drives are don't-cares.

Step 5 Table 6.1 shows J and K inputs for state transitions. For example, when $Q_BQ_A = 00$, J_BJ_A must be 01 and K_BK_A must be XX in order for the next state to be $Q_BQ_A = 01$. See these pairs as entries in the map in Fig. 6.17.

Step 6 The four maps in Fig. 6.17 show the state transition drives for the four flip-flop inputs, J_B, J_A, K_B, K_A. Appreciate again that the inputs to the maps are the outputs of the flip-flops. The $11 \rightarrow 10$ transition for Q_B is explained in detail in Fig. 6.17.

Step 7 All states are used. The X's in the maps above are legitimate don't-cares from JK excitation tables; the X's can stay in the maps without affecting lockout. State 00 can still be a ground state, to which the system goes after RESET.

Step 8 We fill in the don't-cares to minimize excitation logic (see Fig. 6.18). Thanks to JK don't-cares, no gates are required to hook up the J and K inputs to the Q and $\overline{Q}$ outputs.

Step 9 The output combinational logic comes from the following table:

	Q_BQ_A	INLET	OUTLET	SPARK
S_1	0 0	1	0	0
S_2	0 1	0	0	0
S_3	1 1	0	0	1
S_4	1 0	0	1	0

We can see that

$$\text{INLET} = \overline{Q_B + Q_A} \qquad \text{OUTLET} = Q_B \cdot \overline{Q_A} \qquad \text{SPARK} = Q_B \cdot Q_A$$

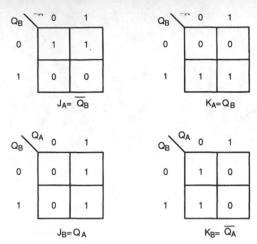

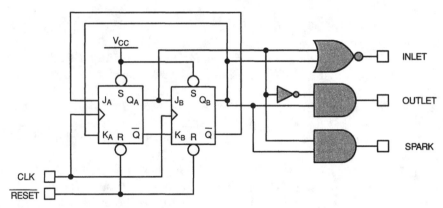

Figure 6.18   K-maps.

Figure 6.19   *JK* flip-flop solution to engine controller.

Step 10   Figure 6.19 can be laid out in LogicWorks with "binary switches" for CLK and RST and "probes" for output. Simulation of the circuit will verify that the correct sequence results.

6.4   POSITIONALLY CODED COUNTERS

The most important category of counter designs—and the one most associated with the term *counter*—concerns sequential circuits whose outputs increment or decrement one positionally coded number per clock edge. Positional counters invariably have

6.4.1 Up-Counter with Toggle Flip-Flops

EXAMPLE 8

Design a synchronous up-counter that cycles through the first 16 unsigned base-2 integers: on each valid clock edge the output will increment by one integer. When state 1111 is reached, the circuit will assert an active-low *ripple-carry-out*, $\overline{RCO}$. After 1111 and a valid clock edge the circuit will wrap around to state 0000.

Solution In Fig. 6.20 (on the next page), the first 16 positionally coded binary numbers are shown at the left, and at the right is a 16-state transition diagram of up-counting with the same numbers (in base 10) superimposed on a Karnaugh map.

Steps 1 and 2 The states and their assignments to flip-flop outputs are taken care of in the counter specifications. There will be four flip flops, and all $2^4 = 16$ possible combinations of their outputs will be used to code for the numbers in the sequence—no unused states. The state variables are $Q_3Q_2Q_1Q_0$.

Steps 3 and 4 Instead of writing out the complete PS-NS table, we'll use the K-map of Fig. 6.20 and select toggle flip-flops for the design. Remember that for a toggle flip-flop, no-change state transitions ($0 \rightarrow 0$ and $1 \rightarrow 1$) require the flip-flop to be disabled, and the state transitions for change ($0 \rightarrow 1$ and $1 \rightarrow 0$) need the flip-flop to be enabled.

Steps 5–8 Looking at the K-map and reading off the toggle flip-flop table (Table 6.1), we obtain the four maps for the toggle enables shown on the next page in Fig. 6.21. The least significant bit toggles on each clock, so its whole K-map is filled with 1s; the most significant bit toggles only twice, at 0111 → 1000 and at 1111 → 0000, so there are only two 1s in its map. There are no unused states to worry about. The circuit in Fig. 6.22 (see p. 327) realizes the four Boolean expressions for the enables gathered from the maps of Fig. 6.21.

Step 9 We need an active-low output when all Q's are HI. An AND will detect all Q's being HI; a NAND will send out a LO under the all-Q's-are-HI condition. Since EN_3 already has three of the Q's ANDed, let's try sending EN_3 to a NAND gate with Q_3.

Step 10 The complete circuit, shown in Fig. 6.22, was simulated on LogicWorks. The flip-flop outputs work as expected, cycling through the 16 positionally coded binary numbers, and $\overline{RCO}$ does produce a LO output when all four outputs are HI. However, the LogicWorks simulation also revealed that $\overline{RCO}$ generates an unwanted glitch at the transition 0111 → 1000. Why? Q_3 changes to 1 *before* the three-input AND gate changes from 1 to 0; for a brief time the $\overline{RCO}$ NAND gate sees two 1s on its input. How can this static-0 hazard be fixed? Replace the two-input NAND with a four-input NAND that receives the four flip-flop outputs directly. You'll see in data sheets for counter chips that $\overline{RCO}$ NAND gates always take direct flip-flop outputs—attempts to minimize logic by chaining together intermediate ENABLE controls are not used in practical circuits.

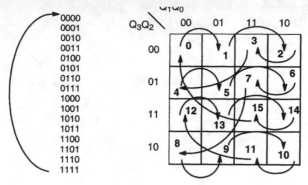

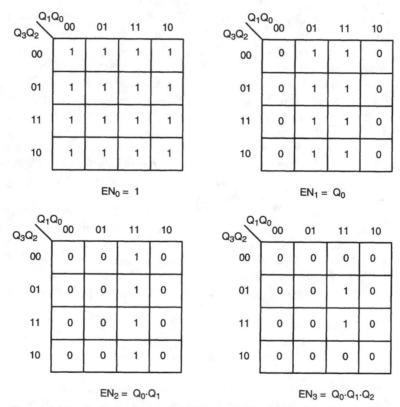

Figure 6.20 K-map state transitions for a four-bit counter.

$EN_0 = 1$

$EN_1 = Q_0$

$EN_2 = Q_0 \cdot Q_1$

$EN_3 = Q_0 \cdot Q_1 \cdot Q_2$

Figure 6.21 Excitation expressions for toggle flip-flop enables.

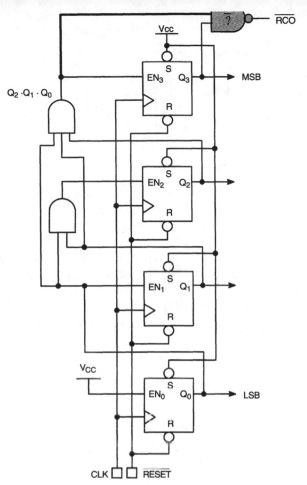

$Q_2 \cdot Q_1 \cdot Q_0$

Figure 6.22 Four-bit toggle counter.

6.4.2 Ripple Counter

EXAMPLE 9

Design a four-bit positional binary up-counter with no combinational logic needed on the flip-flop inputs.

Solution   Actually, it can't be done as a synchronous circuit. But if we break our rule about all flip-flops being driven by a common clock, it's possible. Use the output of one toggle flip-flop as the clock input to the next one in a chain. See Fig. 6.23, where JK flip-flops are always in the toggle mode because $JK = 11$. The output is $Q_3Q_2Q_1Q_0$. Falling-edge-triggered flip-flops have been used; if rising-edge-triggered flip-flops had been used, we would have ended up with a down-counter.

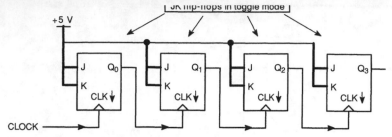

Figure 6.23   Ripple counter.

An asynchronous counter where outputs chain to clocks is a **ripple counter.** *It's not called a ripple counter for nothin'.* Because of propagation delay, the flip-flops in a ripple counter don't change state simultaneously. For example, in the transition from $Q_3Q_2Q_1Q_0 = 0111$ to 1000, Q_0 will change first and Q_3 last. The clock and Q waveforms for the ripple circuit of Fig. 6.23 are reproduced in Fig. 6.24 with exaggeration of the t_{pd} delay Δ between stages to show the rippling of outputs. The incrementing process of the up-counting is labeled with 0s and 1s. At the right side Δ_r is the accumulated delay between the falling clock and the response of Q_3. During the time Δ_r the ripple counter goes through the following sequence on its way from $Q_3Q_2Q_1Q_0\text{CLK} = 0111\ 0$ to $1000\ 0$:

Q_3	Q_2	Q_1	Q_0	CLK
0	1	1	1	0
0	1	1	0	0
0	1	0	0	0
0	0	0	0	0
1	0	0	0	0

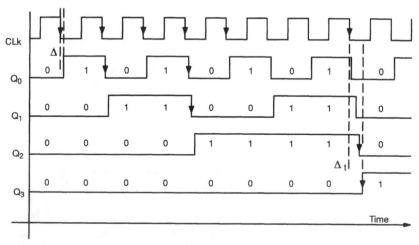

Figure 6.24   Ripple counter timing.

in a synchronous counter, on the other hand, all flip-flops would change simultane-ously.

You can use a ripple counter in an application where you're not worried about synchronicity or where the glitches at clock edges won't cause big problems. In fact, if asynchronous behavior is really not an issue, then the clock waveform can be included as the LSB with the four Q's to make a five-bit counter!

6.4.3 A Decrementing Decade Counter with D Flip-Flops

EXAMPLE 10

Let's work through the design of another positionally coded counter, this time one that counts down from 9 to 0, rolls over to 9, and does so using D flip-flops. A sequential circuit that cycles through 10 states is called a **decade counter**.

Solution

Steps 1 and 2 The sequence and its linkage on a K-map are shown in Fig. 6.25. Because $10 > 2^3$, a decade counter will require four bits for representation. As with other positionally coded counters, state variable assignment is fixed; 6 out of the 16 states are unused.

Steps 3 and 4 Instead of writing out the complete PS-NS table, we'll use the K-map in Fig. 6.25 and work through the state transitions for individual D flip-flops. Remember that for a D flip-flop the next state is the D input for the present state; after the clock edge the D input will become the flip-flop output.

Steps 5–8 Looking at the arrows in the state transition K-map in Fig. 6.25, we ob-tain the four maps of Fig. 6.26 for the D_0–D_3 inputs. Unused states are sent to $1001 = 9$. Each D_i is expressed as a minimum sum of products considering only its map. No attempt is made to gather 0s, share terms, or use multi-level logic since PAL OR gates can't share products and are set up for straight SOP expressions only. Besides, two-level SOP logic will have the least delay possible in case clock speed is an issue.

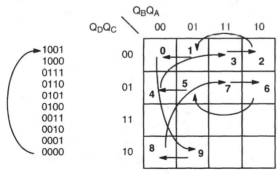

Figure 6.25 Decimal counter state table in K-map.

This is state 7, the next state is 6. The map is for D_1, so look at what you want Q_1 to become in state 6. 6 = 0110. Q_1 is a 1, so a 1 goes in this box.

Q_1Q_0

Q_3Q_2	00	01	11	10
00	1	0	0	1
01	1	0	0	1
11	1	1	1	1
10	1	0	1	1

$$D_0 = \overline{Q_0} + Q_3 \cdot Q_2 + Q_3 \cdot Q_1$$

Q_1Q_0

Q_3Q_2	00	01	11	10
00	0	0	1	0
01	1	0	1	0
11	0	0	0	0
10	1	0	0	0

$$D_1 = \overline{Q_3} \cdot Q_1 \cdot Q_0 + \overline{Q_3} \cdot \overline{Q_2} \cdot \overline{Q_1} \cdot \overline{Q_0} + Q_3 \cdot \overline{Q_2} \cdot Q_1 \cdot \overline{Q_0}$$

Q_1Q_0

Q_3Q_2	00	01	11	10
00	0	0	0	0
01	0	1	1	1
11	0	0	0	0
10	1	0	0	0

$$D_2 = \overline{Q_3} \cdot Q_2 \cdot \overline{Q_0} + \overline{Q_3} \cdot Q_2 \cdot Q_1 + Q_3 \cdot \overline{Q_2} \cdot \overline{Q_1} \cdot \overline{Q_0}$$

Q_1Q_0

Q_3Q_2	00	01	11	10
00	1	0	0	0
01	0	0	0	0
11	1	1	1	1
10	0	1	1	1

$$D_3 = \overline{Q_3} \cdot \overline{Q_2} \cdot \overline{Q_1} \cdot \overline{Q_0} + Q_3 \cdot Q_2 + Q_3 \cdot \overline{Q_2} \cdot Q_0 + Q_3 \cdot \overline{Q_2} \cdot Q_1$$

Figure 6.26   K-maps filled in for decimal counter.

Step 9   The specifications don't call for a ripple-carry-out, but if an $\overline{RCO}$ were needed, it would be $\overline{Q_3} \cdot \overline{Q_2} \cdot \overline{Q_1} \cdot \overline{Q_0}$; since one of the AND gates for D_3 already uses $\overline{Q_3} \cdot \overline{Q_2} \cdot \overline{Q_1} \cdot \overline{Q_0}$, $\overline{RCO}$ is there if we want it.

Step 10   The decrementing decade counter with D flip-flops is shown on the next page in Fig. 6.27 in a registered PAL schematic. The $\overline{RESET}$ line has been rerouted internally so that $Q_3Q_2Q_1Q_0 = 1001$ after an asynchronous reset. This tailored reset cannot normally be done with a PAL, but it can be done with discrete D flip-flops, such as 7474s.

By now you may have the impression that once state variables have been assigned to state names and a flip-flop type has been selected, the process is straightforward enough to be automated. You're right. After entering a sequence of state variables into a CAD system and writing code that tells the machine which transition you want from which state, the generation of excitation equations (and even the programming of a registered PAL) can be taken care of by the computer. In Chapter 7 we look at design automation for counters and other finite-state machines.

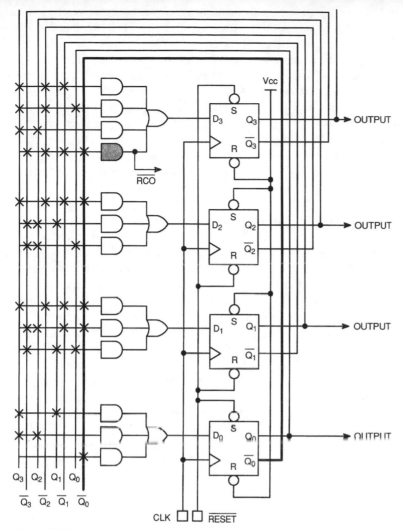

Figure 6.27 Synchronous decade down-counter.

6.4.4 Counting to Higher Numbers with Ripple-Carry-Out

In principle an 8-, 12-, or 16-bit counter can be designed by the methods described above. And in fact there are commercial single-chip eight-bit synchronous counters, such as the 74ALS869. But their cost—in combinational excitation hardware—increases at a rate proportional to the number of bits of counting. You saw in the toggle flip-flop design for up-counting that an $(M - 1)$-input AND gate was needed on the Mth toggle enable input and that the ripple-carry-out required an N-input AND gate, where N was the total number of bits in the numbers being incremented.

A common MSI chip in logic families is the four-bit rising-edge-triggered counter. In the next chapter we will analyze in particular the 74LS169, a four-bit up/down counter with $\overline{\text{RCO}}$, external load, and two external count-enable pins. A number N of 74169s can be tied together for synchronous $4N$-bit counting, but let's defer discussion of that to Chapter 7, where nonclock inputs (such as count-enable) to synchronous circuits are handled.

For now, consider the uses of ripple-carry-out (RCO) coming from a four-bit counter. First of all, RCO is a one-bit status pin that informs a user or another circuit when the counter has reached **terminal count**—its maximum (or minimum, if it's a down-counter) positional value. Next, the count range of a synchronous counter with RCO can be extended by one synchronous bit by sending RCO to a toggle enable (or both J and K inputs) on an external flip-flop. (See Fig. 6.28.)

To continue increasing the count size beyond one extra bit is more of an effort. The new MSB and the four counter-chip outputs must be sent to a five-input AND, and that signal must be sent to the ENABLE of another toggle linked to the common clock. As you may remember from the four-bit toggle flip-flop example, chaining the AND gates together to reduce pin count will result in static hazards on RCO.

How can RCO be used to increase the counting range of four-bit-packaged IC counters, such as the 74169? A low-range counter must influence a higher-range counter. To apply the *synchronous* method shown above, direct access to the control inputs of the first flip-flop of the next counter chip is needed, and that access is not available on an IC counter chip. If only CLK is externally available on the next counter chip, you must project RCO to the next counter's clock input.

In the circuit at the top of Fig. 6.29, RCO from up-counter 1 is sent to the CLK input of counter 2. Counter 1 changes state on the rising CLK_1 edge. Samples of the four outputs of counter 1 (Q_{1A} to Q_{1D}) are shown, leading up to the time between the dashed lines, when counter 1 reaches terminal count of 1111. Shown next are waveforms for RCO and the active-low $\overline{\text{RCO}}$. Which is correct to send to counter 2's clock? The expected waveform of the LSB for counter 2 (Q_{2A}) is shown, and its transition lines up with the rising edge of $\overline{\text{RCO}}$. Therefore all rising-edge-triggered IC counters have an active-low ripple-carry-out, in order to keep higher-order counters in phase with the base counter driven by the system clock.

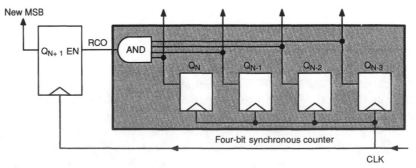

Figure 6.28   Extending the count by one bit using RCO.

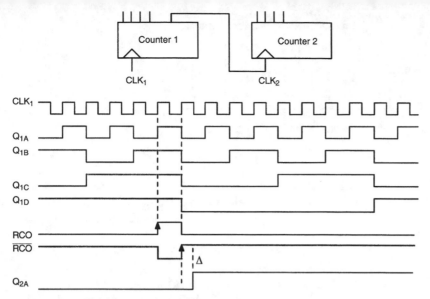

Figure 6.29 Ripple-count timing between ICs.

Projecting $\overline{\text{RCO}}_N$ to CLK_{N+1} can correctly expand the range of an IC counter system, albeit with the loss of synchronicity and the cost of extra delay. For eight bits of counting with one $\overline{\text{RCO}}_N \rightarrow \text{CLK}_{N+1}$ connection, the increased delay caused by waiting for the system to stabilize amounts to only one AND gate's worth of t_{pd}, compared with eight t_{pd}'s for a full ripple counter.

6.5   SHIFT REGISTERS IN SYNCHRONOUS COUNTER DESIGN

In Section 6.5 we step away from positional binary counter design to see what sequences can be generated by shift registers. Shift registers are one of the most important MSI (medium-scale integration) circuits in logic families. Recall from Chapter 5 that a shift register is a set of edge-triggered D flip-flops connected output to input and driven by a common clock. A four-flip-flop shift register is shown in Fig. 6.30. The only D input left unaccounted for is the first one, D_{in}. For a counter design with only the clock for external input, D_{in} must be a subset of $\{Q_i, i = 0, \ldots, N - 1\}$, where N is the number of flip-flops in the shift register. On the other hand, for all input $D_M, M \neq 0, D_M = Q_{M-1}$, so there are limitations on what sequences are

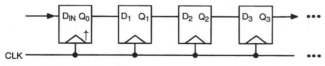

Figure 6.30   Shift register.

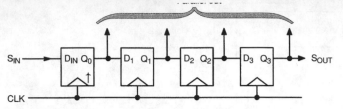

Figure 6.31   Serial-in–parallel-out shift register.

possible with a shift register. (When multiple-bit registers are chained together like a shift register, the arrangement is called a **pipeline.** You will see pipelines used in Chapter 11.) The shift register shown in Fig. 6.30 could be considered a one-bit-wide pipeline.

6.5.1   Serial-In–Parallel-Out and Cyclic Shift Registers

For counter design we need a serial-in–parallel-out (SIPO) shift register, as in Fig. 6.31, in which each flip-flop output can be accessed. S_{IN} now labels the serial input, and S_{OUT} labels the output of the last flip-flop in the chain. A TTL example of a SIPO shift register is the 74164 chip eight-bit shift register.

A **cyclic shift register** is a SIPO shift register in which the serial input is a combination of the subsequent flip-flop outputs only—no external inputs are allowed. The general form for a four-deep cyclic shift register is in Fig. 6.32.

6.5.2   Analysis of Cyclic Shift Registers

The flip-flop outputs of an N-bit cyclic shift register will shift $Q_i \rightarrow Q_{i+1}$, $i = 0$, $\dots, N-1$, and D_0 will be $f(Q_i, i = 0, \dots, N)$, where f is a Boolean function. After some number of clock edges (less than or equal to 2^N), the sequence pattern will begin to repeat. To find out what pattern results from a given CSR, you must either simulate the circuit or work through each step in the sequence by hand.

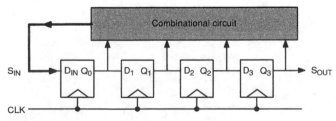

Figure 6.32   General form of a cyclic shift register.

EXAMPLE 11

One of the simplest combinational circuits for S_{IN} is an inversion of Q_N. What sequence does the circuit in Fig. 6.33 step through when $N = 4$ and the starting state is 0000?

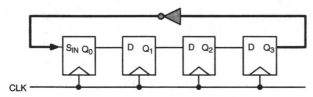

Figure 6.33   One inverter from last flip-flop to serial input.

Solution   Work your way through the sequence, starting at 0000. First the register fills up with all 1s, and then it empties and returns to the 0000 state. It goes through eight states in its cycle. Each pattern in the sequence differs from its neighbors by one bit. See the left side of Fig. 6.34. The pattern resembles a digital Moebius strip; it's called a **switch-tailed ring counter**. If the circuit starts outside the Moebius sequence, it locks into the eight-state series to the right in Fig. 6.34. The anti-Moebius sequence of the switch-tailed ring counter leaves only one flip-flop output unchanged after each clock pulse.

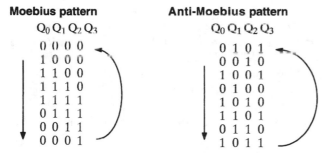

Figure 6.34   State sequences of switch-tailed ring counter.

If a sequence can be implemented in a cyclic shift register, the design problem boils down to finding the excitation equation for S_{IN}; all other D_M inputs are just Q_{M-1} outputs!

6.5.3   Design with Cyclic Shift Registers

What sequences are candidates for design with cyclic shift registers? Any sequence that unfolds with a horizontal shifting pattern can be implemented with a cyclic shift register. When assigning state variables to state names (Step 2 in the design method), see whether you can create a block of flip-flop outputs that show a shift-left or shift-right pattern. Sometimes just permuting the state variables will result in a valid shift register sequence.

EXAMPLE 12

Suppose five joints of a robot arm must be flexed in sequence. System outputs are assigned to specific joints. Use a cyclic shift register to implement a design. The robot user decides whether the exercise cycle is repeated.

Solution

Steps 1 and 2   To assign states to the sequence, write out the pattern of movement as a left-shifting sequence of joints to be flexed one at a time, as shown in the following table.

Shoulder	Elbow	Wrist	Finger	Knuckle
1	0	0	0	0
0	1	0	0	0
0	0	1	0	0
0	0	0	1	0
0	0	0	0	1

Use a CSR with five flip-flops; each flip-flop's output will directly control one joint. With five states in the sequence, we could have gotten away with three flip-flops, since $2^3 > 5$. The CSR will use two more flip-flops than the minimum.

We can skip Steps 3–7 in the design algorithm and go straight to the problem of the drive for S_{IN}, Step 8. What combinational feedback circuit will circulate a 1 around the shift register? Should the output of the last flip-flop be sent back to the input of the first flip-flop? It could be, but two problems arise: what if the circuit is reset to 00000, and what if the shifting 1 drops out or an extra 1 appears as an error, popping the system out of the sequence? It turns out that a better solution doesn't involve the output of the final flip-flop at all! Consider the $2^5 = 32$ possible inputs to the combinational circuit. The 2 cases out of 32 in which a 1 must be returned to S_{IN} are

Q_0	Q_1	Q_2	Q_3	Q_4	S_{IN}
0	0	0	0	1	1
0	0	0	0	0	1

All the other 30 combinations of $\{Q_0, \ldots, Q_4\}$ give $S_{IN} = 0$. The first line is the expected situation, when a 1 has reached the last flip-flop and must rotate around to the first flip-flop Q_0. *The second line covers RESET or bit-dropping conditions—if for some reason 0s appear on all flip-flop outputs, the system will self-correct and inject a 1 back to* S_{IN}. Q_4 is a don't-care! Apply the adjacency theorem to the two lines to see that

$$S_{IN} = \overline{Q_0} \cdot \overline{Q_1} \cdot \overline{Q_2} \cdot \overline{Q_3}$$

Apply De Morgan's law:

$$S_{IN} = \overline{Q_0 + Q_1 + Q_2 + Q_3}$$

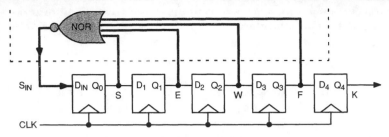

Figure 6.35 One-hot (active-high-output) CSR.

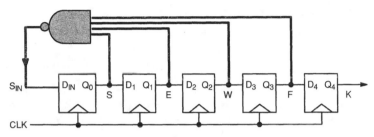

Figure 6.36 One-at-a-time active-low-output CSR.

The logic primitive that produces a 1 only when all inputs are 0 is therefore a NOR gate. (See Fig. 6.35.)

Make sure you understand why $S_{IN} = 0$ for the other 30 combinations of Q's. With this design, no matter what state the flip-flops initialize to at the time power is turned on, within five clock pulses one 1 will be circulating around the register. To eliminate the five-clock-pulse stabilization, reset all flip-flops to 00000; the next state will be 10000. Q_4 is a status output that informs the user that the cycle is complete. It can be utilized if additional control logic is needed to stop the system after one cycle.

The circuit we have just designed is called a **one-hot sequencer**, and it is probably the best known and most useful of all cyclic shift register designs. A one-hot sequencer assigns one flip-flop output per state and in that regard is not an efficient use of flip-flops.

What if the requirement is to circulate one 0 in a field of 1s? (A one-cold sequencer?) You could just put inverters on the one-hot sequencer outputs. A more efficient method would be to replace the NOR gate in the design of Fig. 6.35 with a four-input NAND gate. A NAND returns a 0 only when all its inputs are 1. Shown in Fig. 6.36 is a shift register for circulating one 0 in a five-bit shift register.

Not just sequences of circulating 1s or circulating 0s, but any fixed word advancing one step at a time to the right in a sequence can be realized with a CSR and appropriate combinational feedback logic. To show how, we need to generalize the method from the design of a one-hot sequencer. First, assume that your sequence shifts to the right and that you want to form a positive-logic sum of products for S_{IN}.

Understand that to *barrel-shift right* means to move the right-most bit (S_{OUT}) to the left-most position and shift all other bits right by one flip-flop on each clock edge. Here are the steps to find the combinational logic for S_{IN}:

1. Barrel-shift right until a 1 appears at S_{OUT}.

2. The pattern in the flip-flop outputs is responsible for *two* minterms in a list: one with a 1 in the right-most position (true literal for Q_N) and another with a 0 in the right-most position (error correction).

3. Barrel-shift right again until a different 1 is encountered at S_{OUT}. Two more minterms are revealed, one for $Q_N = 1$ and another for $Q_N = 0$.

4. Continue barrel-shifting right until all 1s in the pattern have been placed in Q_N and all pairs of minterms added to the list.

5. If there are N consecutive 1s in the pattern, then add $000\ldots0011$ through $000\ldots(N-1)$ 1s to the list of minterms.

6. Include $m_0 = [0, 0, \ldots, 0]$ in the list of minterms, to initialize (the brackets denote a state).

7. Use adjacency or any other technique, including the Quine-McCluskey method, to find a minimum expression for S_{IN} given the minterms in the list.

The resulting expression for S_{IN} will generate the required sequence and correct (within N clock pulses) for any state, including that of all zeros, not in the sequence.

EXAMPLE 13

Design a cyclic shift register to circulate the pattern 101 around eight flip-flops in the manner shown here:

	H	G	F	E	D	C	B	A
S_1	0	1	0	1	0	0	0	0
S_2	0	0	1	0	1	0	0	0
S_3	0	0	0	1	0	1	0	0
S_4	0	0	0	0	1	0	1	0
S_5	0	0	0	0	0	1	0	1
S_6	1	0	0	0	0	0	1	0
S_7	0	1	0	0	0	0	0	1
S_8	1	0	1	0	0	0	0	0

Solution We follow the steps of the method outlined above. In state S_5 two minterms are generated for the list:

	H	G	F	E	D	C	B	A	S_{IN}
M_5	0	0	0	0	0	1	0	1	1
M_4	0	0	0	0	0	1	0	0	1

In state S_7 two more minterms are generated:

M_{65} 0 1 0 0 0 0 0 1   1
M_{64} 0 1 0 0 0 0 0 0   1

Combine them with

M_0 0 0 0 0 0 0 0 0   1

These are the only five truth table rows out of $2^8 = 256$ that have 1 output.

To realize the S_{IN} circuit you could stop here and use five eight-input AND gates feeding one five-input OR gate. You could also do some simplifying. Following the lead of the first Q-M algorithm, adjacency can be applied to pairs of these minterms to find the following prime implicants:

$H\ G\ F\ E\ D\ C\ B\ A$

0 0 0 0 0 1 0 X   1 (m_5, m_4)
0 1 0 0 0 0 0 X   1 (m_{65}, m_{64})
0 0 0 0 0 0 0 0   1 m_0

Only three of these minterms are required for a realization: (m_5, m_4) and (m_{65}, m_{64}) are essential, and one of the remaining two are needed. If multilevel logic is permitted, the product $\overline{H} \cdot \overline{F} \cdot \overline{E} \cdot \overline{D} \cdot \overline{B}$ can be factored out of the SOP expression for the result

$$S_{IN} = \overline{H} \cdot \overline{F} \cdot \overline{E} \cdot \overline{D} \cdot \overline{B} \cdot (\overline{G} \cdot C + G \cdot \overline{C} + \overline{G} \cdot \overline{C} \cdot \overline{A})$$

If XOR gates can be used,

$$S_{IN} = \overline{H} \cdot \overline{F} \cdot \overline{E} \cdot \overline{D} \cdot \overline{B} \cdot (G \oplus C + \overline{G} \cdot \overline{C} \cdot \overline{A})$$

S_{IN} is the only flip-flop input requiring any work in a CSR! The other seven D inputs are just the outputs of the flip-flops to the left of the D's in question.

If the CSR powers up to an initial condition of 0000 0000, within three clock cycles the proper pattern of 101 will be circulating; if the initial condition is 1111 1111, the system will take nine clock cycles to settle down to the pattern 101.

Even if a design for a circulating shift register seems feasible, CSR counters have the limitation that more than one start-up clock cycle may be required to stabilize the proper sequencing pattern.

6.5.4 Pseudorandom Sequence Generator

A **pseudorandom sequence generator** (PRSG) is a cyclic shift register with a large N. It is designed to step through many of its 2^N states. PRSGs find use in encrypting serial transmissions (see Chapter 9) and in generating repetitive "noise" for test circuits.

EXAMPLE 14

Figure 6.37 shows a PRSG circuit for four bits that uses just one XNOR gate. It passes through 15 out of 16 states. The only state it skips is 1111. The circuit must be initialized to any state except 1111, which is a trap.

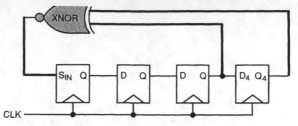

Figure 6.37   CSR with XNOR feedback to S_{IN}.

Randomness is in the eye of the beholder: the term *pseudorandom* is a catchall for ring counters built to step through as many states as possible without following a regular pattern. If there are N flip-flops in a CSR, it *is* possible to come up with a design that steps through the maximum 2^N states before repeating! Try Exercise 36. The output of a PRSG can be any of the flip-flop outputs, since presumably only the length and randomness of the sequence, not its pattern, are important. See Michelson and Levesque (1985) on linear function shift register counters, and see Berlekamp (1968).

6.6   HIDDEN UNITS

We continue Chapter 6 with a counter problem that at first blush appears to have changes we're not prepared to handle. But, taking a clue from cyclic shift register sequencers, we find that inserting flip-flops that have no direct influence on circuit output (hidden units) can solve the problem. To illustrate the sequencing problem, we start with an example.

EXAMPLE 15

Design a synchronous counter for the sequence

$$2\ 0\ 1\ 2\ 0\ 1\ 2\ 3\ 0\ 1\ 1$$

which repeats back to 2, 0, and so on.

Where did that 3 come from in the middle? How can 2 sequence to 0 *and* to 3? How can we stop at 1 twice near the end before repeating? How can the inner sequence 2-0-1 repeat twice before changing? Up to now a present state S_N in a sequence has always changed to a unique next state S_{N+1}; now we have two different destinations for one state, "2." And if a state cycled back to itself, we assumed it was a trap; now state "1" waits one clock cycle before ending the series and looping back to the start.

Solution   The output of the sequencer presents only four different numbers, so it might seem that a design with two flip-flops ($2^2 = 4$) could work. But because of the position-dependent state change and the waiting in the sequence, more states than four are actually required. Recall that the numbers in the sequence will be the outputs of the counter circuit. You can use *non-output* flip-flops *(hidden units)* to mark the events that appeared to cause problems. Call the hidden unit flip-flops D and C. The following table uniquely labels all the states necessary to generate the desired outputs.

Decimal	Binary BA	Hidden Units DC
2	10	00
0	00	00
1	01	00
2	10	11
0	00	11
1	01	11
2	10	10
3	11	00
0	00	10
1	01	01
1	01	10

There are now 11 states, the same as the length of the sequence. The hidden units D and C code for the transitions away from the basic 2-0-1 sequence. When $DC = 11$, the second 2-0-1 sequence is executed; when $DC\,BA = 10\,10$, the next state is $00\,11$; when $DC\,BA = 10\,00$, the next state is $01\,01$. There are four different "1" states, depending on where the "1" is encountered in the sequence! Flip-flops D and C are **hidden units** because they don't participate in the production of the binary output. Exactly which patterns of D and C are used to mark the different parts of the sequence is unimportant because D and C do not participate in output. With four flip-flops there are 16 possible states, so 5 states are unused.

At this point we have just completed the creative part of the counter design, steps 1 and 2 (state assignment) of the method outlined earlier. We continue with the steps of counter design.

Step 3 Here's the PS-NS table:

Present DC	BA	Next DC	BA
00	10	00	00
00	00	00	01
00	01	11	10
11	10	11	00
11	00	11	01
11	01	10	10
10	10	00	11
00	11	10	00
10	00	01	01
01	01	10	01
10	01	00	10

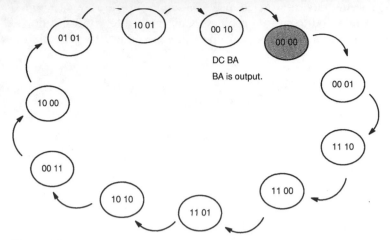

Figure 6.38 State diagram for hidden unit problem.

As a prelude to the next chapter, the 11 states are rearranged in Fig. 6.38 into a *state diagram*, which shows graphically the same thing the PS-NS table does.

Step 4 Which flip-flop do we use? Since we've used *D* flip-flops for most of the designs in Chapter 6 and will be using them again in the next chapter, let's give *JK*s a chance at this design. That means we will have eight four-input Karnaugh maps, two for each *JK* flip-flop.

Steps 5 and 6 Individual *JK* values for state transitions were determined with Table 6.1 at hand. The maps are shown in Fig. 6.39. The 5 unused states are marked with bold X's.

Step 7 Instead of sending all the unused states to 0000, we're leaving the maps with the don't-cares in place for a *minimum-cost solution*.

Step 8 Gathering subcubes of 1s from the maps, I come up with these SOP excitation equations. See if you agree with them.

$$J_A = \overline{Q_B} \cdot \overline{Q_A} + Q_D \cdot \overline{Q_C}$$
$$K_A = Q_D \cdot Q_A + \overline{Q_D} \cdot \overline{Q_C}$$
$$J_B = \overline{Q_C} \cdot Q_A + Q_D \cdot Q_A$$
$$K_B = \overline{Q_D} \cdot \overline{Q_C} + Q_C \cdot Q_B \cdot \overline{Q_A}$$
$$J_C = \overline{Q_D} \cdot \overline{Q_B} \cdot Q_A + Q_D \cdot \overline{Q_B} \cdot \overline{Q_A}$$
$$K_C = Q_B \cdot \overline{Q_A}$$
$$J_D = Q_A$$
$$K_D = Q_D \cdot \overline{Q_C}$$

Step 9 The outputs are $Q_B Q_A$.

Step 10 The above equations can be laid out as two-level SOP combinational gates. The eight *JK* flip-flop inputs will hook up to two AND and six OR outputs.

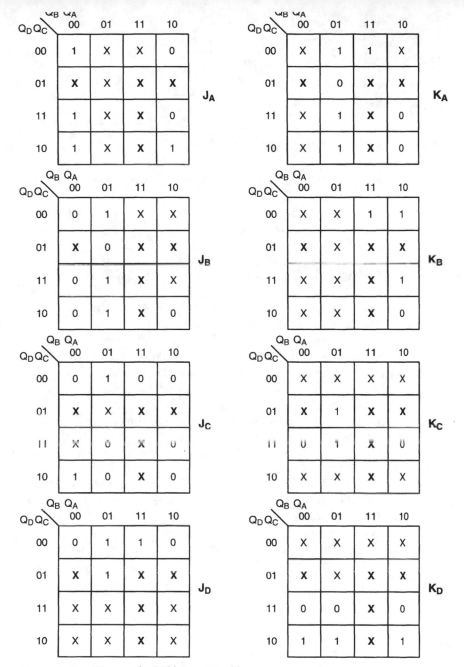

Figure 6.39 *JK* maps for hidden unit problem.

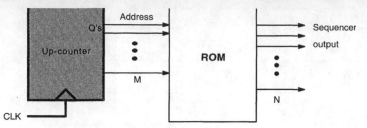

Figure 6.40 Counter plus ROM for sequencing.

The take-home lesson from Example 15: When necessary, create new states to work around repeats in a sequence. The same output can be part of as many different states as needed to find the end of the sequence. In fact, you are likely to need as many different states as there are steps in the sequence.

6.6.1 Counter plus ROM Can Generate an Arbitrary Sequence

Counter sequences in which the same output can go to different next outputs, depending on the position in the sequence, are examples of *arbitrary* sequences. At the end of Chapter 7 two systematic ways to generate arbitrary N-length sequences are outlined. In the first, you have a count-to-N sequential circuit address a read-only-memory combinational circuit (see Chapter 4 on ROMs). Program the contents of the ROM to be the sequence in question, and program the count to be the position in the sequence. (See Fig. 6.40.) Make sure the number of bits M of the counter is such that $2^M \geq N$, where N is the length of the sequence to be generated. If N is not a power of 2, either the counter must be specially designed to roll over after N clock ticks or a standard counter with synchronous CLEAR must be used. One of the ROM outputs can control the synchronous CLEAR. Only when the last number in the sequence is reached will the CLEAR line be asserted. (See Fig. 6.41.) Because synchronous CLEAR is a non-clock input, let's defer discussion of counter plus ROM until Chapter 7.

The second way to generate arbitrary N-length sequences: use a general-purpose sequencer such as found in microprogrammed controllers. The general-purpose

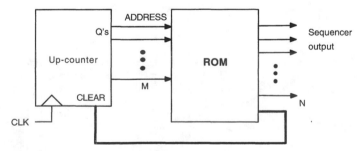

Figure 6.41 Counter plus ROM with feedback for restart.

sequencer will be able to handle conditional branching, looping, and subroutining. Microprogrammed control is a generalization of the counter-plus-ROM circuit and features a register with input from a MUX; MUX-select chooses from *increment, load,* and *return from subroutine.* The sequencing problem of Example 15 can be treated in a systematic way by such a general-purpose sequencer. We'll develop the use of the general-purpose sequencer in Chapter 7.

6.7 SUMMARY

By now you should be confident about designing a synchronous sequencer that has the clock as its only external input (also known as a counter or automaton circuit). You have learned a 10-step procedure that starts with the problem of state assignment and continues with the present-state–next-state table. Once a D, JK, or toggle flip-flop is chosen, the state transitions for the particular flip-flop are used to fill in maps or truth tables for flip-flop excitation. Unused states of the flip-flops can be sent to a ground state, usually all zeros. In some cases the output of the system can be logical combinations of flip-flop outputs. Realization of the maps results in excitation circuits to drive the flip-flop inputs and complete the circuit.

- **Sequential circuits** contain latches or flip-flops as memory elements. The output of a sequential circuit depends on previous input, as distinct from a combinational circuit, whose output is a function only of current input.

- The **state** of a sequential circuit is the set of latch or flip-flop output values at a given time. State is generally not the same thing as the circuit's *output.*

- A **synchronous sequential circuit** is composed of edge-triggered flip-flops all connected to the same clock signal. The flip-flops must all change state on the same edge, either the rising or the falling edge of the clock.

- A basic **up-** or **down-counter** is a synchronous circuit with only the clock as an external input. A counter has the general form shown in Fig. 6.42, in which the circuit can be partitioned into a flip-flop register and a combinational logic circuit that transforms the current state into flip-flop **excitation.**

- The **maximum clock rate** in hertz of a counter circuit must be less than

$$\frac{1}{t_{pd} + t_{comb} + t_{setup}}$$

where t_{pd} is the propagation delay through the flip-flop register, t_{comb} is the maximum delay through combinational logic feeding back to flip-flop inputs, and t_{setup} is the flip-flop setup time for data. The **skew** is the difference in arrival time of the clock edge at two flip-flops. It can be minimized by placing the clock generator physically in the center of the circuit.

- The sequence of a counter circuit can be **analyzed** by deriving the excitation equations and working through the various state transitions they generate.

- A 10-step method enables you to design counter circuits. Part of the 10-step synthesis involves the reverse of analysis: going from a list of states to flip-flop excitation equations.

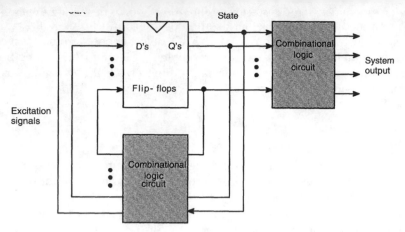

Figure 6.42 General form of synchronous automaton.

- The part of the design process that is most in need of judgment is **state assignment,** where the **state variables** (flip-flop outputs) are assigned to various named states.
- Once state variables are assigned, a **present-state–next-state** table is formed. The present state is the input and the next state is the output of the excitation logic. The PS-NS table can be turned into a set of Karnaugh maps or into a state diagram.
- D flip-flops are the standard choice for counter designs because their *one* input can be read directly off the PS-NS table or map and because their internal design can be built efficiently in integrated circuits.
- The **state transition table** of a flip-flop shows what values of its inputs are required to move the flip-flop from one state to another after a valid clock edge.
- To complete the design of a counter, form and solve the truth table for each flip-flop input. The truth table will depend on the type of flip-flop chosen. The resulting I/O tables are called **excitation tables.**
- **Unused states** should be directed to a ground state, usually $000\ldots0$; otherwise, if unused states accidentally pop up, for instance during start-up or because of noise, they may be **traps,** which **lock out** the system, preventing it from returning to its correct sequence.
- Additional combinational logic may need to be designed to transform flip-flop outputs to **system output.**
- **Positionally coded counters** increment or decrement through positional binary code. Positionally coded counters are the most widely used form of counter and are available as IC chips in logic families. **Decade counters** increment or decrement for 10 numbers of positional code and then wrap around to the ground state and start over.
- **Ripple-carry-out** from a positionally coded counter chip can be used for counting to higher numbers by projecting to another counter's clock input. Such an arrangement saves on hardware but makes the overall circuit asynchronous.

- **Shift registers** are synchronous chains of D flip-flops. The input D_N is the output Q_{N-1} of the flip-flop to the left. The input to the left-most flip-flop can be external or wrapped around.

- Sequences in the form of shifted patterns can be realized by **cyclic shift registers.** In the case of CSRs only the left-most flip-flop's D input needs to be figured out. CSRs with many flip-flops in their shift registers can be used as **pseudorandom sequence generators.**

- Sequences with looping and position-dependent state changes can be realized with **hidden units:** flip-flops that increase the number of internal states but do not participate in the formation of circuit output.

- An N-bit counter addressing an N-bit by M-bit read-only memory can implement any sequence of length less than or equal to 2^N and output per character less than or equal to M, with the ROM output expressing the desired sequence.

Exercises

1. **(a)** For the circuit below write down the sequence of states that will result from an initial condition of $Q_C Q_B Q_A = 111$ as a series of clock pulses are fed in.

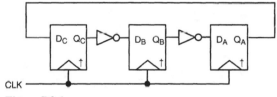

Figure P6.1

   (b) The circuit of Example 1 has three flip-flops and moves among three states. Redesign the circuit so that it uses only two flip-flops to sequence through the three states.

2. Find the best match for the following analogy: State is to flip-flop as
   (a) Bit is to gate
   (b) Input is to output
   (c) Automobile speed is to engine RPMs
   (d) Dress size is to body shape
   (e) Temperature is to color

3. Do you think, given the discussion of state in Chapter 6, that a purely combinational circuit can have a state? Give an example or a counterexample.

4. Which of the following problems will not *require* a sequential circuit for its solution?
   (a) OUT goes HI if input B is LO after input A has gone through a LO-to-HI transition.
   (b) An alarm goes off if the oven door is opened before the heat is turned off.

(c) OUT goes LO when exactly two keys in a row on a keyboard are pressed simultaneously.

(d) The movement of a spot from left to right over a series of photodetectors triggers an output pulse. No signal is output for right-to-left movement.

(e) The output of a circuit is the result of the multiplication of two two-bit binary numbers.

(f) Every second a different one of eight outputs is randomly chosen to be HI while the other seven remain LO.

5. In the Moore circuit below, the current state is $Q_C Q_B Q_A = 101$. All three clock inputs are connected to the same clock signal.

   (a) What will be the next state after a clock pulse occurs?
   (b) What is the current output, and what will be the next output?
   (c) Starting from 101, will the circuit OUTPUT ever be 0?

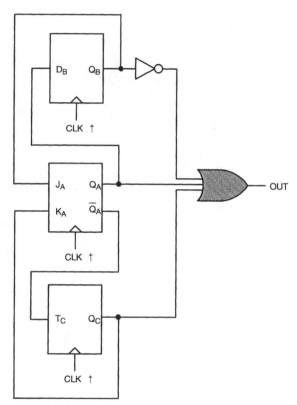

Figure P6.2

6. What is the maximum number of states for a cyclic shift register of eight flip-flops? Assume you have freedom to design the serial input as any function of flip-flop outputs.

7. What should the equation for the minimum time period of a clock look like if nonzero hold time is taken into account?

8. For the four-bit synchronous ripple counter shown in Fig. P6.3, assume that a flip-flop has a 16-ns propagation delay (CLK to Q) and an 8-ns setup time and that an AND gate has a 12-ns propagation delay.

   (a) If all the Q's are HI, how long will be the delay from the next rising clock edge to a change of Q_3 to LO?

   (b) If the same two-input AND structure is used for an eight-bit counter and the Q's of the counter are all HI, how long will the delay from the next rising clock edge to a change of Q_H to LO be?

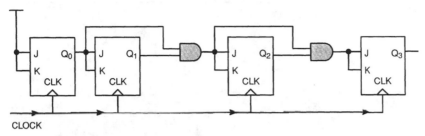

CLOCK

Figure P6.3   Synchronous ripple counter.

9. In the toggle mode a 74LS112 has a t_{pd} from clock to output of 13 ns, a setup time of 20 ns for enable, and zero hold time. The 74LS21 four-input AND gate has a t_{pd} of 11 ns.

   (a) At what maximum clock frequency could a fully synchronous four-bit counter run if it were made from 'LS112s and 'LS21s?

   (b) What is the maximum clock frequency if it's a 16-bit ripple counter made with 'LS112 toggle JK flip-flops?

10. (a) What J_N and K_N values are required for a flip-flop system to make a transition from $Q_3Q_2Q_1Q_0 = 1001$ to 0011, where N labels the flip-flops and runs from 0 to 3?

    (b) What would be the inputs to D flip-flops before a clock pulse in order to make the transition from 0000 to 1111?

11. What happens in the circuit used as the solution for Example 4 if it starts up at state 4 or 5? What sequence does it step through?

12. What sequences will the circuits in Fig. P6.4 count through, as the clock ticks, after power is applied? When the systems are turned on, $Q_BQ_A = 00$. Consider output as Q_BQ_A.

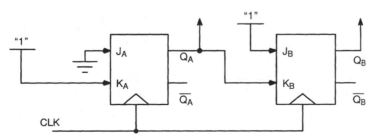

Figure P6.4

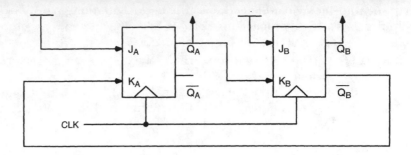

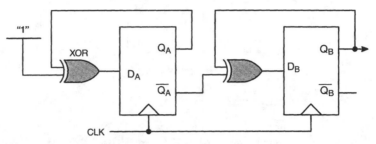

Figure P6.4 (Continued)

13. **(a)** How many different sequences can be made from the five symbols 4, 8, Δ, A, and C if each symbol can be used only once in the sequence?
    (b) How many can be made if each symbol *must* be used once and only once in the sequence?

14. For Example 6, what is an implementation of the combinational drive logic for the D inputs that uses fewer gates than the solution shown?

15. Design a synchronous counter that cycles through the hexadecimal sequence 2 4 8 A C and then repeats 2....

16. Redesign the engine sequencer of Example 7 using D flip-flops.

17. **(a)** In Fig. P6.5 are shown the K-maps for the J and K inputs to two clocked flip-flops whose outputs are Q_1 and Q_0. If the system starts up in state

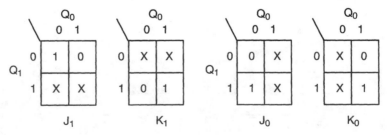

Figure P6.5

$Q_1Q_0 = 00$, what sequence will it cycle through? What happens if the system starts in state $Q_1Q_0 = 01$?

(b) In Fig. P6.6 are shown the K-maps for the D inputs to three clocked flip-flops whose outputs are Q_2, Q_1, and Q_0. If the system starts up in state $Q_2Q_1Q_0 = 000$, what sequence will it cycle through? Rewrite the K-maps so that the states not on the 000 cycle return to 000 after one clock pulse.

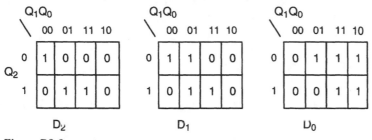

Figure P6.6

18. For a synchronous counter made of toggle flip-flops (Fig. 6.22), (a) what is the total delay from the clock input to the Nth flip-flop output in the counter? (b) total delay from clock to RCO output? Assume $t_{pd} = \Delta$ for the AND gate.

19. **(a)** What sequence results from a three-bit asynchronous ripple counter constructed with rising-edge-triggered flip-flops?
    (b) Assume that each flip-flop has a "write access time" of Δ nanoseconds, and draw a timing diagram like the one in Fig. 6.24, showing the build-up of delay from the clock to the output change of the third flip-flop.
    (c) What is the maximum clock rate the counter can be run at?

20. Refer to Fig. 6.26, which has the excitation equations for the four D_i inputs of Example 10, the decade down-counter.
    (a) In the K-map for D_0, what expression do you obtain if you gather zeros? Is it simpler than the SOP shown?
    (b) Can any of the circuits for the D excitation share terms? Which terms?
    (c) Can you see a way to use fewer gates in the expression for D_3 if you allow yourself to use multilevel logic?

21. **(a)** Design a synchronous decade up-counter using JK flip-flops that counts from 0 to 11.
    (b) Design one that counts from 00 to 59, possibly using a decade counter plus a count-to-six counter.
    (c) Design a four-bit decade down-counter using JK flip-flops. Say what happens if your circuit starts up in one of the states $A_{16}-F_{16}$.

22. Following the lead of Fig. 6.28, use extra flip-flops to extend the counting range of a four-bit up-counter IC by three bits.

23. **(a)** In a packaged four-bit up-counter such as the 74LS107, what internal logic will generate a correct ripple-carry-out? Look in a TTL data book.

(b) Coming out of a second four-bit IC counter in an eight-bit ripple counter is another ripple-carry-output. What skew (time difference) is there between this second RCO and the original clock pulse into the lower-order counter? Assume $t_{CLK \to RCO} = 20$ ns.

(c) What would go wrong with two 169s counting synchronously to FF if RCO were active HI instead of active LO?

24. Example 11 illustrates a switch-tailed ring counter. If a four-bit switch-tailed ring counter starts in state 0000, it goes through an eight-step sequence that reminds one of a Moebius strip. Design a cyclic shift register that gets back in the Moebius pattern if it pops into one of the eight states shown at the right in Fig. 6.34. Your combinational feedback circuit will have to be more complicated than one inverter!

25. Can Gray code be generated by a cyclic shift register? If so, show how for four bits.

26. See the cyclic shift registers in Fig. P6.7. If the flip-flop outputs start out as all zeros, what sequences of states will the CSRs step through as the clock ticks?

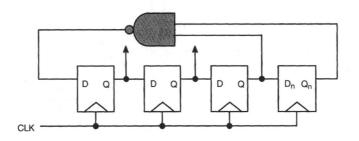

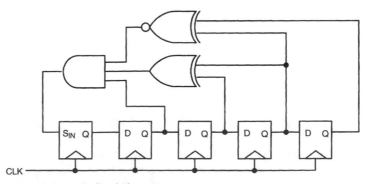

Figure P6.7 Cyclic shift registers.

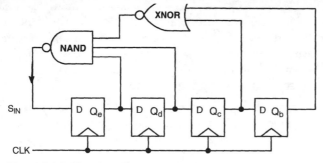

Figure P6.7 (Continued)   Cyclic shift registers.

27. What sequence does the synchronous JK circuit below step through if it starts at the 0000 state? Are any states locked out of the sequence starting at 0000?

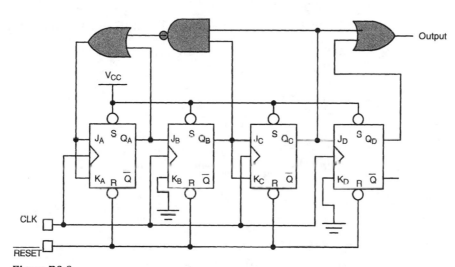

Figure P6.8

28. (a)   Serial-in for the five-bit 1-circulator shown in Fig. 6.35 is $S_{IN} = \overline{Q_3 + Q_2 + Q_1 + Q_0}$. What would the output pattern of the 1-circulator be if $S_{IN} = \overline{Q_4 + Q_3 + Q_2 + Q_1 + Q_0}$?

     (b)   Serial-in for the five-bit 1-circulator shown in Fig. 6.36 is $S_{IN} = \overline{Q_3 \cdot Q_2 \cdot Q_1 \cdot Q_0}$. What would the output of the 0-circulator be if $S_{IN} = \overline{Q_4 \cdot Q_3 \cdot Q_2 \cdot Q_1 \cdot Q_0}$?

29. A *two-hot sequencer* is a shift register around which two neighboring 1s circulate, so that at any time exactly two in a row of the shift register outputs are HI and

all the others are LO. (The pattern 1000 0001 is also included.) Design an eight-bit two-hot sequencer. The only input allowed is clock. You'll need an eight-bit serial-in–parallel-out shift register plus combinational logic to determine what goes to S_{IN}. Simply sending Q_8 back to S_{IN} is not good enough. Your design must be able to start up automatically and settle down within eight clock pulses and be able to recover from dropped or extra bits.

30. **Shift register sequencers** What combinational circuit, with inputs from a four-bit shift register set of outputs, can generate the following Moore output patterns? The output will come from the shift register flip-flops.

(a)	(b)	(c)	(d)
1010	0001	1110	1100
0101	1000	0111	0110
1010	0100	1011	0011
0101	0010	1101	1001
1010	0001	1110	1100
⋮	⋮	⋮	⋮

31. Use a shift register system to sequence through the following states:

(a)   00000
        10000
        11000
        01100
        00110
        00011
        00001
        00000
          ⋮

(b) 01010101
     10101010

(c) Begin at 0 1 0 1 0 1 0. Shift to the right, and let the right-most bit wrap around to the left side: 0 0 1 0 1 0 1 is the next state.

32. If a four-bit pseudorandom sequence generator starts in state 0000, what should the response of its feedback circuit to 0000 be? (The feedback circuit is a combinational circuit whose output goes back to serial-in and whose inputs are the flip-flop outputs.) What should be the response of the feedback circuit if the flip-flops start in state 1111?

33. Name *two* drawbacks of the circulating shift register approach to design of clocked sequencers.

34. Suppose a 10-bit cyclic shift register must circulate right the pattern 11 0100 0000. How many clock cycles will it take for the correct pattern to appear if the system is started up in state 11 1111 1111? Assume that a feedback circuit correctly decides whether to send a 0 or 1 back to the S_{IN} input.

‡36. **Maximum-length random sequence** For N flip-flops in a serial-in–parallel-out shift register, it's possible to find a PRSG that goes through 2^N states. A computer-assisted tree search is one way to find a complete cyclic path. For $N = 4$, find a feedback circuit for a PRSG that results in a 16-state cycle. It can be done with fewer than four gates in feedback!

37. In Example 15 there are five unused states. Does the minimum-cost design in the text prevent lockout (step 7)? If not, send all the unused states to 0000.

38. **(a)** Use hidden unit(s) to design a D flip-flop synchronous circuit to realize the following sequence:

	Binary
Decimal	BA
2	10
0	00
1	01
2	10
1	01
1	01
2	10
3	11
0	00
1	01
1	01

(b) Design, with three *rising*-edge-triggered JK flip-flops and a minimum of combinational logic, a synchronous sequencer that repeats the following series of six numbers in time with a clock:

3 2 1 3 2 0 and repeat

(c) Design, with *falling*-edge-triggered JK flip-flops, a clocked sequencer to cycle repeatedly through the following states:

000	0
110	6
110	6
010	2
000	0
111	7

Repeat:

000	0
110	6
$\vdots$	$\vdots$

Note that the sequencer stays at "6" for two clock pulses.

39. It is possible for a sequential circuit to support two or more independent sequences, depending on initial conditions. Recall the Moebius and anti-Moebius patterns of Example 11. Can *one state* of a circuit be part of two different sequences? If so, give an example; if not, say why not.

40. Using a four-bit up-counter, plus any additional combinational logic you may need, realize the two sequences expressed in decimal numbers as (a) 0, 4, 8, 12, 1, 5, 9, 13, etc. and (b) 5, 7, 1, 3, 1, 3, 5, 7, 4, 6, 4, 6, etc.

41. Two-phase clock To bring order to sequencer design, edge-triggered flip-flops all connected to a single clock are required. And this is as it should be, to reap the benefits of synchronous circuits. It has not been emphasized, but it is true that all the flip-flop clock inputs in a given synchronous circuit should respond to the same edge, either rising or falling. What happens when rising and falling edges are mixed in the same circuit?

What output (OUT_3, OUT_2, OUT_1) sequence will the following circuit go through? A state change can occur at either clock edge. Assume that the system initializes at state 0000. Flip-flops A and C are rising-edge-triggered, and B and D are falling-edge-triggered. The clock inputs are shown as short lines to avoid diagram clutter.

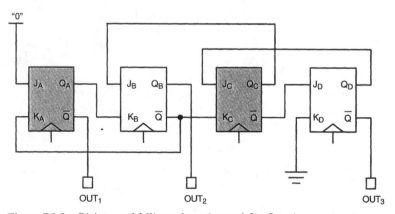

Figure P6.9 Rising- and falling-edge-triggered flip-flops in one circuit.

References

BERLEKAMP, E. 1968. *Algebraic coding theory.* New York: McGraw-Hill.

DIRECTOR, S., AND R. ROHRER. 1972. *Introduction to system theory.* New York: McGraw-Hill.

KLEIN, J. 1990. *Immunology.* London: Blackwell Scientific.

MICHELSON, A. M., AND A. H. LEVESQUE. 1985. *Error control techniques for digital communication.* New York: John Wiley & Sons.

NAUTA, W., AND M. FEIRTAG. 1986. *Fundamental neuroanatomy.* New York: W. H. Freeman.

Synchronous Finite State Machines

OVERVIEW

In Chapter 6 synchronous circuits were restricted to *automatons:* circuits with the clock as the only external input. Now we're ready to remove that restriction and allow *asynchronous inputs* to influence the sequence of states a synchronous circuit is stepping through. Examples of asynchronous inputs are up and down button signals for an elevator controller; LOAD, ENABLE, CLEAR, and DIRECTION inputs to multifunction counters; start-of-conversion input to a successive-approximation analog-to-digital converter; transmit and receive signals on RS232 serial interfaces; direct memory access interrupts; and computer keyboard strokes. We'll still maintain the restriction that all flip-flops be driven by the same clock, but otherwise we'll enter the world of **finite state machines (FSMs)**, sequential circuits that can be described by a finite number of states.[1] Examples of nonfinite state machines are Turing machines and counters that have no limit on the size of the number they count up to. Rest assured that nearly all the academic and real-world problems you will encounter in sequential circuit design can be solved by some sort of finite state machine. By the time you finish Chapter 7 you will know how to **synchronize** nonclock inputs and how to include such inputs in the tables and maps used to derive the excitation logic for the flip-flops in the circuit. In principle you will be able to tackle any specification or word problem that requires a sequential circuit for a solution, and you will have learned about computer-aided design help for such problems.

We'll first see how asynchronous inputs can directly influence circuit output and therefore allow the output to change at times other than clock edges. Then we'll study ways to synchronize input with the clock in order to minimize metastable responses in the flip-flops. Next an already-built FSM—a flip-flop lock—will be **analyzed** to find what sequence of external inputs will "unlock" the circuit. After that analysis a more general version of the method from Chapter 6 for synthesizing synchronous FSMs will be presented. As with the 10-step method for the design of counters, the FSM design procedure will feature state assignments leading to excitation tables for flip-flop inputs. Algorithmic state machine notation will be introduced. An example

---

[1] Finite state machines do not *require* a clock; they can consist of latches joined together with combinational logic, changing state whenever input changes, or they can have multiple clocks and subcircuits communicating with one another. In any case we will still call the outputs of all flip-flops and latches at any one time the state of the FSM.

357

we'll take another look at counters, this time adding external inputs for ENABLE, count DIRECTION, synchronous CLEAR, and LOAD of other external data. A **finite state machine compiler (FSMC)** and its syntax will be described and illustrated. The *FSMC* will take a state transition description and turn it into equations that can be downloaded to a device for programming a registered PAL. The FSMC will be illustrated with an elevator controller. Finally you will be introduced to a general-purpose sequencer architecture commonly found in microprogrammed computers. The microprogram sequencer will be a generalization of a counter-plus-ROM and will be able to handle looping, subroutines, and conditional branching in a sequence.

7.1 MOORE CIRCUITS EVOLVE TO MEALY CIRCUITS

In Chapter 6 you studied the general form of a synchronous counter. Now we add other external inputs, in addition to the clock. If the *outputs* of the circuit as a whole still come off the flip-flop outputs (state variables) it remains a **Moore circuit** (output changes only on valid clock edge). In some cases, though, an asynchronous external input modifies the system output directly without waiting for the next clock edge. A circuit whose output depends on the *internal state plus external influences* is a **Mealy circuit.** See the part of Fig. 7.1 highlighted by colored lines. In a Mealy circuit flip-flop outputs still represent the state; the input is not involved in the state, but it does influence circuit output. For a Mealy circuit, external inputs can head straight for the output combinational logic. Output in a Mealy circuit can change at *any* time.

7.2 SYNCHRONIZER CIRCUITS

Flip-flop input arriving randomly with respect to the clock may, unluckily, fail to meet setup or hold times. Flip-flop output may or may not switch as desired, or it may go to a metastable state, as discussed at the end of Chapter 5. To minimize

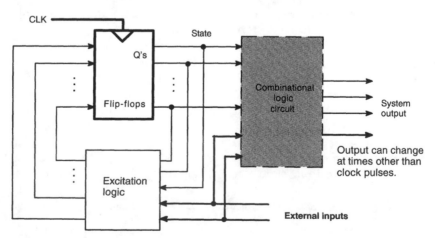

Figure 7.1 Mealy sequential circuit.

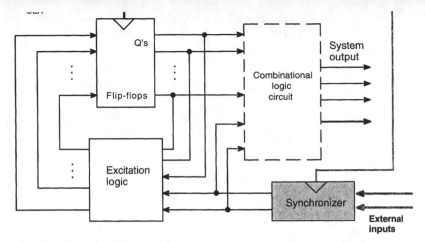

Figure 7.2 Placement of synchronizer.

the possibility of metastable outputs on flip-flops, the external inputs can be forced through a **synchronizer circuit,** which is basically a register of special flip-flops on the system clock. See Fig. 7.2. A metastable response will likely be trapped and die in the synchronizer flip-flops. Any change in a nonclock external input must first wait for a high-speed D flip-flop to capture it. The high-speed D flip-flop will be inside the synchronizer and will have short setup time and zero hold time. The synchronizer circuit lives up to its name, resynchronizing the system at the expense of some small delay from the actual occurrence of the external input changes. The first-order synchronizer for one asynchronous input is one fast D flip-flop. Possible timing for the synchronizer is shown in Fig. 7.3 for a rising edge triggered flip-flop. Notice that the synchronized input starts and ends later than the actual input. Normally these small delays will not matter to the synchronous system (it wasn't expecting the external input at any particular time anyway). In Fig. 7.3, even if the external

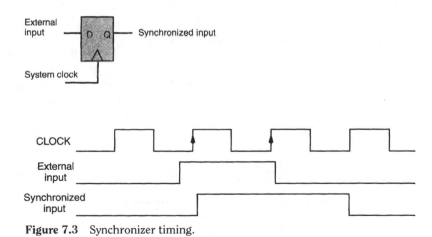

Figure 7.3 Synchronizer timing.

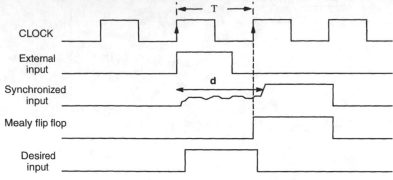

Figure 7.4 Metastable failure.

input violates the setup and hold times of the D flip-flop, things will be okay if the flip-flop output snaps to HI by the next clock edge. However, the synchronizer flip-flop will fail if its output goes metastable and stays metastable for more than one clock period. See the waveforms in Fig. 7.4, where the external input rises exactly with the clock and doesn't provide enough setup time. The metastable state lasts for duration d, which is seen to be greater than clock period T. It produces a much different result than desired! The synchronized input may be seen as a LO or a HI or may cause further metastability in the synchronous circuit itself.

The goal of synchronizer design is to minimize the probability of metastable failure. As you saw in Chapter 5, the probability of a metastable state of duration d falls off exponentially as a function of d/τ where τ is a characteristic of the particular IC chip.

$$P(d) \approx \tau e^{-d/\tau}$$

A synchronizer should be designed so that $P(T)$ is as close to zero as possible. The first and easiest—but most impractical—way to lower the probability of metastable failure is to increase system clock period (decrease the frequency and therefore increase d in the equation). But faster clock rates are generally so important to system performance that lowering clock frequency would be done only as a last resort. The other term in the exponential, τ, has to do with the particular flip-flop used in the synchronizer. Basically, the smaller the setup time, the smaller τ is. So you should use high-speed D flip-flops, such as 74AS74, for the synchronizer, in spite of their cost and power consumption. Special high-speed discrete D flip-flops will be better synchronizers than the D flip-flops that come packaged on registered PALs. For a general reference on synchronizers, see Fletcher (1980, 465–485).

It's possible to tamper with the synchronizer clock without slowing down the system clock. Divide the system clock with toggle flip-flops and have it drive a second synchronizer in series with the first. See the circuit of Fig. 7.5. Thanks to the longer clock cycle, the metastable timing problem of Fig. 7.4 is now solved. See Fig. 7.6. A short and a long external input are included in Fig. 7.6. Only the long input is captured by the synchronizer. The long input to the synchronous circuit no longer gives an erroneous HI output caused by the metastable mistake. True, it missed the

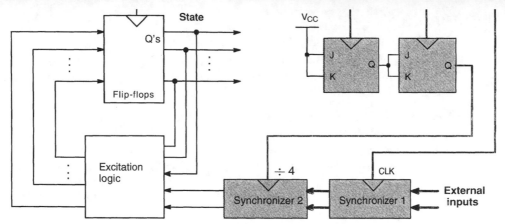

Figure 7.5 Divide-by-4 clock on synchronizer flip-flops.

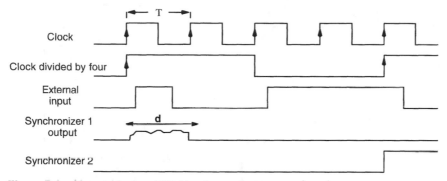

Figure 7.6 Metastable state killed by slower clock on synchronizer.

first brief external input, but as an end-of-chapter problem and Example 4 show, that miss can be cured by placing an *SR* latch on the input to the synchronizer.

For the rest of Chapter 7 a synchronizer will not explicitly appear on every external input, but you should keep in mind that for critical applications a synchronizer is required for every nonclock input to a synchronous circuit. We'll return to the issue of synchronizing circuits in Chapter 9 when we consider the issue of connecting two synchronous circuits running on different clocks (handshake circuit).

7.3 ANALYSIS OF A FLIP-FLOP LOCK

Analysis of synchronous FSMs with external input is similar to analysis of counters. Excitation equations for the flip-flop inputs must be expressed, and the state changes are then followed. The analysis is usually more complex because the external inputs can lead the FSM on different paths of sequences. In some cases, as in Example 1, attention can be directed to FSM *output* in a way similar to solving a maze: keep an eye on the goal while testing various passages through the routes.

EXAMPLE 1

What does the circuit shown in Fig. 7.7 do? In particular, what makes output Z (flip-flop output Q_2) go HI after a reset of all flip-flops to 000? There is one external input, IN. Assume that if IN is changed, the change occurs *between* rising edges of the clock.

Answer It is much more difficult to "step through" this circuit (as you could step through a counter's sequence) because you're not sure when to assert the input. While it may be possible to work backward from $Z = 1$, it may be better to write out the Karnaugh map for each of D_0, D_1, and D_2 using Q_2, Q_1, Q_0, and IN as inputs to the maps. Then find a path from $Q_2Q_1Q_0 = 000$ to $Z = 1$. Note now the difference between FSMs and counters: *external inputs enter the excitation K-maps of FSMs*.

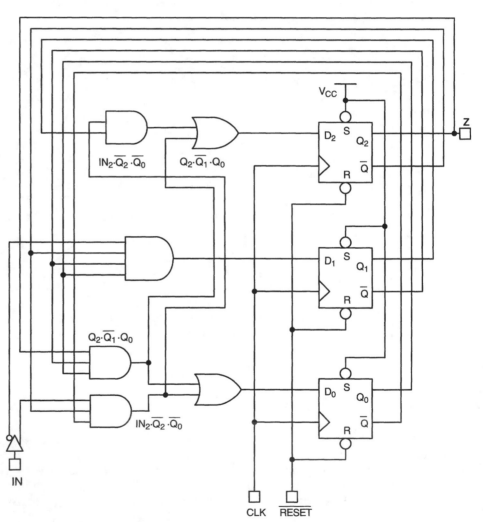

Figure 7.7 FSM circuit to analyze for Example 1.

	Q₁ Q₀						Q₁ Q₀						Q₁ Q₀			

(K-maps reproduced below)

Q_2 \\ Q_1Q_0

Q_2＼	00	01	11	10
00	0	0	0	0
01	0	1	0	0
11	0	1	0	0
10	1	0	0	1

$$D_0 = Q_2\cdot\overline{Q_1}\cdot Q_0 + \mathbf{IN}\cdot\overline{Q_2}\cdot Q_0$$

Q_2＼	00	01	11	10
00	0	1	0	0
01	0	0	0	0
11	0	0	0	0
10	0	0	0	0

$$D_1 = \overline{\mathbf{IN}}\cdot\overline{Q_2}\cdot\overline{Q_1}\cdot Q_0$$

Q_2＼	00	01	11	10
00	0	0	0	0
01	0	1	0	0
11	0	1	0	0
10	0	0	0	1

$$D_2 = Q_2\cdot\overline{Q_1}\cdot Q_0 + \mathbf{IN}\cdot\overline{Q_2}\cdot Q_1\cdot\overline{Q_0}$$

Figure 7.8 Excitation maps for D inputs of Example 1.

You can generate the Karnaugh maps of Fig. 7.8, where each D drive is worked out in SOP form. IN is shown in bold. There aren't many 1s in the maps, so a path to Q_2 isn't hard to find. Start at IN $Q_2Q_1Q_0$ = 0000. If IN stays at 0, then 0000 is a trap, but if IN = 1, you'll move on the map to 1000. *On the next clock pulse* the state will change to $Q_2Q_1Q_0$ = 001, but if IN doesn't change back to 0, the state will return to 000. Consider what will happen on a subsequent clock pulse with IN = 0 and IN = 1. On the K-map of Fig. 7.9 arrows have been drawn on the path from state 000 to Z = 1 (the squares where Z = Q_2 = 1 are circled). The following sequence leads to Z = 1:

IN	Q_2	Q_1	Q_0	
0	0	0	0	
1	0	0	0	CLK
1	0	0	1	
0	0	0	1	CLK
0	0	1	0	
1	0	1	0	CLK
1	1	0	1	trap
0	1	0	1	trap

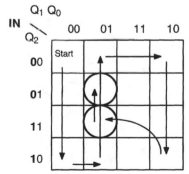

Figure 7.9 State transitions on a K-map.

we can say what the circuit does: it detects the sequence 0-1-0-1 on IN, at which time it keeps Q_2 set until a deliberate reset. It's a circuit that recognizes a certain sequence on IN in time with the clock. In that sense the circuit is an *electronic lock*, or a "flip-flop lock," which can be unlocked only if 0 then 1 then 0 then 1 appear on IN during consecutive clock pulses.

7.3.1 An Asynchronous Latch Lock

The flip-flop lock of Example 1 is annoying in that the user must coordinate the unlocking sequence with the clock. It's possible to avoid this problem by making an electronic lock out of set-reset latches—no clock involved. Although Chapters 6 and 7 focus on synchronous sequential circuits, in Chapter 6 you did see asynchronous ripple counters, and here in Chapter 7 an asynchronous electronic lock is presented.

EXAMPLE 2

Assume that there are five buttons for input labeled A, B, C, D, and R (RESET) and that only one button at a time can be asserted (mechanical lockout—like the function-select buttons on some stereos). Design a circuit that will assert the UNLOCK output after the sequence B-D-C-A is pressed.

Answer In Fig. 7.10 is a circuit that meets the specifications by using SR latches. The correct sequence is arranged as a series of SET inputs in a cascade of SR latches; each latch after the first one can be set only if the previous latch is set AND the next button in the unlocking sequence is pressed.

The design unlocks properly, but it doesn't conform to the spirit of a combination lock. For example, once B and D are pressed, they can be pressed again or A can be pressed without a reset penalty. What's needed is stricter reset policy. We must think

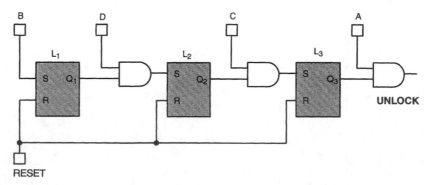

Figure 7.10 First try at an asynchronous sequential electronic lock.

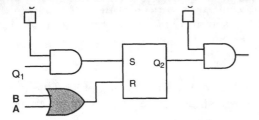

Figure 7.11 Reset for second latch.

about each latch in the pathway and decide when it should be reset. Let's start with the second latch (L_2), which has output Q_2. Imagine that L_2 has been set by pressing B and then D.

- If D is pressed again, we can leave L_2 alone in order to debounce the input.
- If C is pressed, we can leave L_2 alone, since C is the correct next input.
- However, if A or B is pressed, then L_2 should be reset; neither A nor B was responsible for setting L_2, and neither will be the next correct unlocking entry. See Fig. 7.11.

Since only one input at a time can be asserted, there is no danger that $SR = 11$. What about resetting L_1? By the same reasoning we used on L_2, we can see that inputs B and D should not reset, since they are part of the correct sequence around L_1; otherwise, inputs A or C should reset L_1. Continuing this line of thought, L_3 should be reset by B or D. The result is shown in Fig. 7.12, now with the reset shown going into each OR gate.

This reset logic is a better design. Even so, once the correct sequence is entered and Q_3 is HI, UNLOCK will flicker in time with repeated presses of A; this may be okay, or we may need a fourth latch. For the design above a way to reset (relock) to the all-zero state is to press B and *then* C or A. Another way: hook up a master RESET input to each OR gate. Actually, the specification for the electronic lock didn't say what should be done for relocking, so perhaps the design in Fig. 7.12 is acceptable. (Our circuit is almost as hard to relock as it is to unlock!)

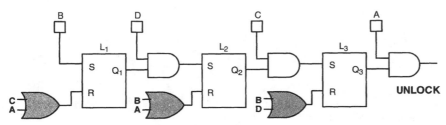

Figure 7.12 Better reset on an asynchronous lock.

Notice that our asynchronous lock has no feedback from a latch output back to any gate that forms its input. Feedback from Q output to gate input will turn out later to be an important feature of *synchronous* state machine design.

Example 2 is a nonsynchronous FSM. For the rest of Chapter 7 we will no longer use unclocked latches or multiply-clocked flip-flops for finite state machines.

7.4   REPRESENTING STATES AND INPUTS

When we studied counters in Chapter 6, we ended up with one fixed sequence that each counter stepped through. Here in Chapter 7, what an FSM does will depend on the status of its nonclock inputs. Before learning a design procedure for synchronous FSMs you need to develop ways to represent states and their input-dependent transitions.

We'll discuss three representations:

1. State-I/O table
2. Algorithmic state machine (ASM) flowchart
3. Software aids for FSM descriptions, such as *Finite State Machine Compiler* and *ABEL*.

For each of the representations we'll use the following scanner example.

EXAMPLE 3

A tuner moves among three stations. If the input select is off, the tuner changes stations once a second. If the input select is N ($N = 1, 2, 3$), the tuner stops at station N when it gets to it in the scan. When the scanner reaches a selected station, a lock light comes on; if the input select changes, the lock light goes off immediately and the tuner moves away from the current selection within one second and starts scanning again. If no station is selected, the scanning continues without stopping.

Given these specifications, we can begin the representation process by assigning state variables. There will be three states, one for each station, and we can give the states alphanumeric names and assign them flip-flop outputs:

Name	Q_1	Q_0
S_1	0	1
S_2	1	0
S_3	1	1

The design will be a Mealy machine because output must respond immediately to changes in nonclock input.

This tabular representation is an extension of the present-state–next-state table used in the automaton design of Chapter 6. Now there are separate columns for each possible nonclock input combination (in the scanner case, I_1I_0). $I_1I_0 = 00$ is the select-off condition. In the table we use state *names*, since state variable assignment can be arbitrary, but we list the inputs as *binary values* because nonclock input is normally fixed before the FSM design begins. When the output L is to be asserted, it is shown next to the state input combination (S_1/L, etc.). Here's the state-I/O table for the scanner control:

	I_1I_0			
Present State	00	01	10	11
S_1	S_2	S_1/L	S_2	S_2
S_2	S_3	S_3	S_2/L	S_3
S_3	S_1	S_1	S_1	S_3/L

The state-I/O table is an exhaustive list of all possible state transitions as a function of the input combinations. We have a column for $I_1I_0 = 00$, which represents a no-station-selected condition. It's not immediately clear from the state-I/O table that output L is a Mealy output and can change at times other than valid clock edges.

7.4.2   Algorithmic State Machine Flowchart

The flowchart of a finite state machine will give you a graphic feel for the relationships between states, inputs, and outputs. In Fig. 7.13 are the three shapes to be used in an algorithmic state machine flowchart. These blocks can be used for synchronous or asynchronous FSMs. For a synchronous FSM only the STATE blocks are associated with the timing clock. The conditional test is normally checked continuously whenever the attached state is in effect. The output condition block is needed for Mealy-type outputs, and it is a way to signify that an output changes before the next clock edge.

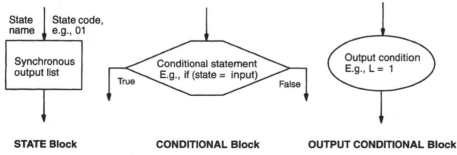

STATE Block   **CONDITIONAL Block**   **OUTPUT CONDITIONAL Block**

Figure 7.13   ASM blocks.

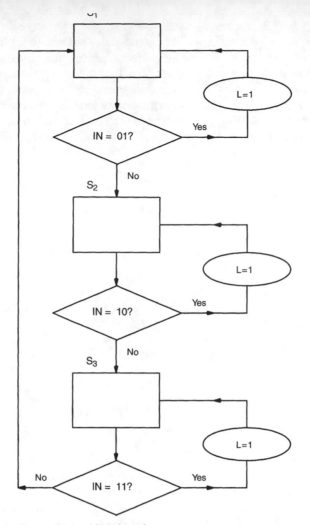

Figure 7.14 ASM chart for scanner.

The ASM chart for the scanner is shown in Fig. 7.14. Here the conditional test is put in the form of a question, and YES and NO are the outputs (instead of TRUE and FALSE). It's not clear from the flowchart where valid clock edges occur; the test on IN is happening continuously, and if it is TRUE, then L is asserted. *Output L is asserted in oval blocks because it is a Mealy output and can occur independently of clock edges.* If L were a synchronous output, it would be listed inside its state rectangle.

7.4.3 Finite State Machine Compiler

In a *state machine software description* each state is contained in a separate section of code that describes the input and state conditions under which the given state makes

ftp from Don Troxel at MIT; see Preface) takes a state-by-state description of an FSM and compiles it into D flip-flops and their Boolean excitation equations as a foo.jed file suitable for downloading to a PAL programmer. The user of FSMC at its highest level names states and describes how transitions are made from each state to other states. You can see FSMC syntax in the code below: A colon is placed after each state name, and each transition statement within a state block of code ends with a semicolon. If there is a Mealy output (such as L, below) a line in a state description says under what conditions the Mealy output is asserted. In the code below the first `stay` could be replaced by `goto S1`. The notation for Boolean expressions in FSMC and PALASM has / = complement and * = AND, so /I1*I0 means $\bar{I_1} \cdot I_0$ in the notation of this text. A complete input file for FSMC has some header information not shown below. (See *Daniels' Digital Design Lab Manual*; FSMC expects the name of a particular PAL, such as 22V10, so it can decide if the FSM represented by the state equations can fit in one registered PAL or if the representation needs to be partitioned.)

```
S0:     goto S1;
S1:     if /I1*I0 stay;
        L = /I1*I0;
        goto S2;
S2:     if I1*/I0 stay;
        L = I1*/I0;
        goto S3;
S3:     if I1*I0 stay;
        L = I1*I0;
        goto S0;
```

Coded state descriptions (such as foo.fsm files for FSMC or foo.pds files for PALASM) show off the correspondence between state machine hardware and state transition code. A foo.fsm file is filled with declarations, conditional branches, and Boolean equations in correspondence to the states, the input-dependent transitions, and the output expressions for the FSM.

At this point we will not finish the design of the scanner. We next use the representation of input-dependent state transitions to understand the general design method for synchronous FSMs.

7.5 DESIGN METHOD FOR SYNCHRONOUS FSMs

Like design of counters, design of synchronous FSMs will reverse the steps going from flip-flop drive logic back to state diagram. But unlike counter design, FSM design puts more emphasis on the overall state representation than on any one sequence through flip-flop states.

The seven steps outlined below generalize on the design method for counters from Chapter 6. We assume the design process starts with a word description of some problem, including conditional words such as *if, then, only, except when,* and *unless.*

Design Method for Synchronous FSMs

1. *Transform the problem specification into a state-I/O table, an ASM flowchart, or FSM software code.* This process will involve decisions about what are states and how nonclock inputs influence transitions from one state to another. All input combinations should be accounted for at each state. Outputs will be associated either with state transitions (Moore outputs) or with input combinations and states (Mealy outputs).

2. *Assign flip-flop outputs (state variables) to states.* This step can involve clever state-to-variable choices by the designer, or the assignments can be made by algorithm.

3. *Choose a flip-flop type.* Normally D flip-flops are used, but there may be special reasons for picking JK or toggle flip-flops. Each type of flip-flop has its own state-versus-input transition relationship.

4. *Derive the excitation equations for the flip-flop inputs.* The flip-flop drives will be functions of the state and of nonclock input. In cases where the number of flip-flop outputs plus nonclock inputs is less than five, you may want to write out K-maps for the inputs. In cases of more state variables and inputs you may be able to work individually on each state and its rules for transitions to other states.

5. *Either figure out the combinational logic for the outputs or take the outputs directly off the flip-flops* (see step 2).

6. *Send unused states to ground*, and account for all nonclock input combinations at each state transition.

7. *Realize circuit in hardware, and test.* Especially check responses to all combinations of nonclock inputs.

Before we illustrate the steps with an example, we make some remarks about step 1: Step 1 is the inventive design part of the method. For a vague or complicated specification, step 1 may take as much effort as the other six steps combined. In fact if the result of step 1 is the generation of state transition code, a software compiler may be able to handle the remaining steps, especially if the hardware end result will be a registered PAL. In this text, for the most part, we won't worry about minimizing the number of states used to represent the FSM. And in reading over a particular specification, try first to see how much of the problem can be solved by combinational logic alone.

EXAMPLE 4

A light pole on each side of a crosswalk on a one-way street has a WALK button for a pedestrian to push when he or she wants a WALK sign to light and traffic to stop. In the road to one side of the crosswalk is a digitized inductive sensor to detect the presence of automobiles; the sensor emits a HI pulse whenever a car passes over it.

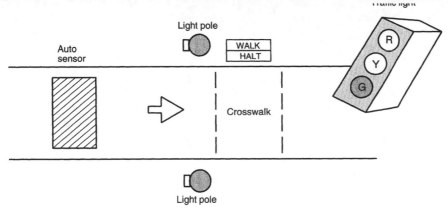

Figure 7.15 Pedestrian crosswalk layout.

If an automobile has tripped the inductive sensor, the pedestrian may have to wait 8–16 s before the traffic light turns yellow, then red. A yellow light will stay on for 2 s. The WALK light will stay on for 2 s. There will be a period of 2 s when the traffic light is red *and* the HALT light for the pedestrian is on. If the WALK button has not been pressed, the traffic light will remain green. See Fig. 7.15. Design a controller for the crosswalk.

Answer   Let's solve the state assignment problem in three stages, first by working out the traffic light and walk sign sequence without the external WALK and sensor inputs, then by considering the WALK button input, and then by considering both the WALK and the auto sensor inputs.

We begin with step 1. What are the states of the system? It makes sense that in the ground state the traffic light is GREEN and walk light on HALT. Including the ground state, the sequence of states to allow a pedestrian across the road must be:

GREEN	HALT
YELLOW	HALT
RED	WALK
RED	HALT

If we want to cycle through these states, a clock with a 2-s period should do the job; YELLOW will last 2 s, WALK will last 2 s and the RED-HALT state will last 2 s. This first stage is a synchronous counter problem; we can use as few as two flip-flops (perhaps from a standard up-counter) for four states, or we can assign state variables (step 2) as follows:

		$Q_2 Q_1$	Q_0
GREEN	HALT	0 0	0
YELLOW	HALT	0 1	0
RED	WALK	1 1	1
RED	HALT	1 1	0

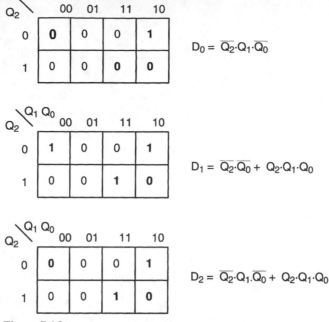

$$D_0 = \overline{Q_2} \cdot Q_1 \cdot \overline{Q_0}$$

$$D_1 = \overline{Q_2} \cdot \overline{Q_0} + Q_2 \cdot Q_1 \cdot Q_0$$

$$D_2 = \overline{Q_2} \cdot Q_1 . \overline{Q_0} + Q_2 \cdot Q_1 \cdot Q_0$$

Figure 7.16 Pedestrian crosswalk K-maps for D inputs.

Now Q_0 controls the WALK-HALT sign and Q_2 controls the RED light. Some decoding of Q_2 and Q_1 is needed for GREEN and YELLOW control. If we select D flip-flops (step 3) and form present-state-to-next-state K-maps for excitation of $D_2 D_1 D_0$ (step 4), we obtain the maps in Fig. 7.16. All unused states are sent to ground. The output decoding needed is

$$\text{YELLOW} = \overline{Q_2} \cdot Q_1 \quad \text{and} \quad \text{GREEN} = \overline{Q_2} \cdot \overline{Q_1}$$

Once the flip-flops, their combinatorial drive, and a 2-s-period clock are in place, the counter will cycle through the four states, albeit with a ridiculously short 2-s GREEN phase.

Now to stage 2 (and step 5 of the seven-step algorithm), incorporating external input from a WALK button. Assume both WALK buttons are OR'd together. First, with a 2-s-period clock, it's likely that the WALK button may be momentarily pressed and released before a clock edge occurs. We need to capture the button press with an SR latch; in the circuit of Fig. 7.17, pressing the WALK button sets an active-low $\overline{SR}$ latch and in the process debounces the switch; once the latch is set, it must wait for the FSM to send a reset signal $\overline{RST}$ before it returns to a $Q = \text{LO}$ output. The reset signal has priority; it inhibits the WALK pathway while it's active-low.

Figure 7.18 is an ASM flowchart for the system with external input W. In the state boxes the asserted outputs are listed. There is now a Mealy output reset for the latch used to capture the WALK signal. A ground state has been declared (step 6).

At this point we could reformulate the $D_2 D_1 D_0$ maps in terms of state $Q_2 Q_1 Q_0$ *and* external input W, and then figure out the D's again. But since we don't reset until the

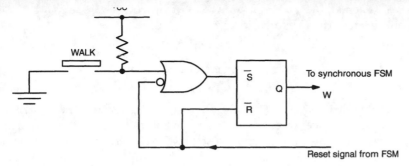

Figure 7.17 Capturing the WALK pulse.

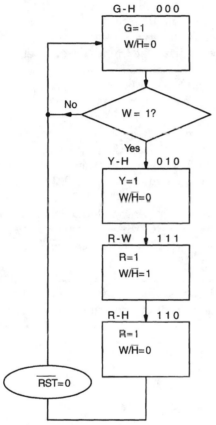

Figure 7.18 ASM chart for pedestrian crosswalk FSM.

W can enable each of the D expressions:

$$D_0 = W \cdot (\overline{Q_2} \cdot Q_1 \cdot \overline{Q_0})$$
$$D_1 = W \cdot (\overline{Q_2} \cdot \overline{Q_0} + Q_2 \cdot Q_1 \cdot Q_0)$$
$$D_2 = W \cdot (\overline{Q_2} \cdot Q_1 \cdot \overline{Q_0} + Q_2 \cdot Q_1 \cdot Q_0)$$

The reset signal is $\overline{RST} = \overline{Q_2 \cdot Q_1 \cdot \overline{Q_0}} = \overline{Q_2} + \overline{Q_1} + Q_0$, which is the detection of the last state of the sequence; once the last state (11 0) is entered, the WALK latch is immediately reset but the system stays in state RED-HALT until the next clock edge.

This design allows GREEN to stay on for the traffic as long as no pedestrian pushes the WALK button, but if the WALK button is repeatedly pressed, only 2 s will be allowed for the traffic light to remain green. We now need stage three of the design, in which we take account of the traffic sensor and use it to keep GREEN on a minimum of 8 s. There are two approaches. The first would be to use hidden units and introduce "wait" states associated with the outputs GREEN and HALT; these wait states would be entered when the traffic sensor is activated. The second approach notes that all the hidden units would do is count four or so clock pulses while GREEN and HALT are on: so why not have the traffic sensor reset an external counter whose output would delay the WALK signal from moving the FSM out of the ground GREEN-HALT state? (The counter could be built into a PAL such as the 22V10 shown in Fig. 7.23.) The counter approach is developed here.

Let the traffic sensor pulse reset a three-bit counter with no wrap-around, as seen in Fig. 7.19. This circuit is a kind of synchronizer–pulse stretcher for the traffic sensor pulse; it converts the sensor pulse into a delayed ripple-carry-output (RCO) response that is synchronous with the clock. After a reset, this up-counter's rising-edge synchronous waveforms look like the waveforms in Fig. 7.20. The counter stops at $QC_2 \, QC_1 \, QC_0 = 111$ and waits for another reset to 000. RCO in this counter is active-high. Such a counter is a type of design problem treated in Chapter 6.

Now all that's needed is for a LO value on the RCO line to inhibit the WALK signal *after* the latch. RCO does not need actively to reset the latch; reset will happen at the end of every WALK cycle anyway. See Fig. 7.21.

For step 7, the whole traffic control FSM circuit can be laid out and simulated with software such as LogicWorks. Three D flip-flops will be used; as you can see from the equations for the D's, two of the excitation product terms are shared by two of the

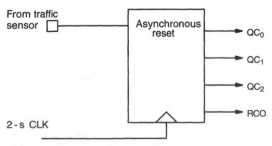

Figure 7.19 Counter to capture and extend traffic sensor pulse.

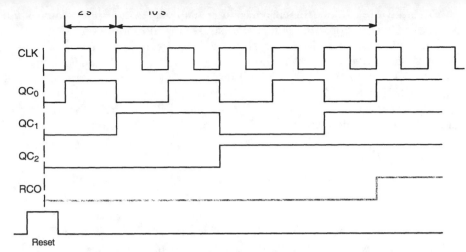

Figure 7.20 Timing diagram for capture and extension of traffic pulse.

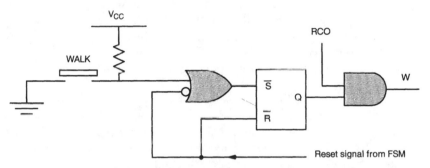

Figure 7.21 Latch for capturing WALK pulse.

D drives. The circuit must be tested correctly for all combinations of WALK and traffic nonclock inputs (step 7). By the approach here we have avoided introducing two more nonclock inputs by having one of them activate a counter that basically functions as a timer for delaying the pedestrian WALK light if cars are coming.

7.6   FINITE STATE MACHINE COMPILER

Look again at step 1—forming the state transition diagram—in the finite state machine design algorithm. In this subsection you'll learn a way to proceed from such an FSM description to hardware by using a software compiler that eventually generates a foo.jed file for the programming of a registered PAL or GAL (generic array logic) chip. Here we will concentrate on a particular compiler—FSMC—available by internet ftp from MIT, and on a particular registered PAL, the 22V10.

The software compiler itself will take a state description (foo.fsm file) and return a set of SOP equations (foo.eqn file) for the D flip-flop inputs needed in the system. The compiler will decide how many flip-flops are required and how the flip-flops will be assigned to the states given by the designer. The software FSMC has a number of features and capabilities, but here we want to focus on the capabilities necessary to describe FSMs. In an .fsm file the important entries are blocks of statements that define the conditions under which a given state will switch to other states on the next clock pulse. We illustrate a basic FSMC input file with an example.

EXAMPLE 5

A freight elevator can move between the first floor, the ground floor, and the basement. Suppose a system is required to control the movement of the elevator to the ground floor. The elevator can be either above or below the ground floor, and there is an active-high detector for each direction. If both ABOVE and BELOW detectors are LO, the elevator is at the ground floor. At the ground floor is a CALL button. Design a synchronous controller to move the elevator to the ground floor while the call button is pressed. Don't worry about opening the door at this point.

Answer   Your first problem is to think of what the states of the system might be. One answer is that the system will have three states: one for the elevator moving down, one for the elevator moving up, and one for the elevator stopped. Besides the clock, there will be three inputs: CALL, ABOVE, and BELOW. Although it didn't say so explicitly in the problem statement, we need two outputs: motor on/off and direction up/down.

In the spirit of using the finite state machine compiler, we will skip writing out a state transition table or drawing out an ASM chart. We plunge right into the C-like syntax of FSMC and code each state.[2] Call the moving-up state SMU, the moving-down state SMD, and the stopped state SS. The convention in an FSMC file is that a state is identified by a colon, a statement for defining a state transition condition ends with a semicolon, / is complement, * is AND, + is OR, and :+: is XOR.

```
SS:     if CALL*BELOW goto SMU;
        if CALL*ABOVE goto SMD;
        stay;
SMU:    MOTOR = 1;
        DIREC = 1;
        if /CALL+/(ABOVE+BELOW) goto SS;
        stay;
SMD:    MOTOR = 1;
        DIREC = 0;
        if /CALL+/(ABOVE+BELOW) goto SS;
        stay;
```

The blocks of statements above say the following: (1) if the elevator is in the stopped state SS, it will go to the moving-down state if CALL is pressed and the ABOVE

---

[2]See *Daniels' Digital Design Lab Manual* for more details about the use of FSMC, which does require the use of a computer workstation environment; I transferred FSMC by ftp to a Sun on a network at Brown University.

detector is HI, and from the stopped state a change to the moving-up state will occur on the next clock edge if CALL and BELOW are HI. (2) If the elevator is in the moving-up state, it will go to the stopped state if CALL is LO or if both ABOVE and BELOW are not HI. (3) Similarly, if the elevator is in the moving-down state, it will go to the stopped state if CALL is LO or if both ABOVE and BELOW are not HI.

The above code was written into file elevat.fsm. On the command line I typed `fsmc elevat` to invoke the compiler. The file elevat.eqn was returned as output of FSMC. The file elevat.eqn contained the following:

```
D0  =    CALL*BELOW*/Q1 +
         CALL*ABOVE*Q0*/Q1
D1  =    CALL*BELOW*/Q0 +
         CALL*ABOVE*/Q0*Q1
MOTOR = Q0 + Q1
DIREC = Q0
```

These equations for D inputs and system outputs are the result of the turn-the-crank work done by FSMC. Remember, in FSMC notation /Q0 is the complement of Q0. The state transition expressions do not need to be in reduced form; FSMC can call a program named "reduce" to minimize expressions. For the problem at hand, FSMC has created two flip-flops, Q_0 and Q_1, whose outputs represent the three states. The state names, SS, SMU, and SMD, do not appear explicitly in the excitation equations; if the `fsmc -s` option is put in the command line, the file elevat.sta will be created. In the problem here, opening file elevat.sta reveals that $Q_1 Q_0 = 00$ is state SS, $Q_1 Q_0 - 01$ is state SMU, and $Q_1 Q_0 = 10$ is state SMD.

In this example the freight elevator CALL button must be held down continuously for the elevator to come. And our fragment of a complete elevator controller hasn't taken into account the floor buttons inside the elevator car. The next example elaborates the three-floor elevator, taking into account the floor the rider wants to go to.

After FSMC has produced a valid elevat.eqn file, another program in the suite, PALASGN (also available by internet ftp), takes the .eqn file and compiles it to elevat.pal and elevat.pin; elevat.pal can be downloaded to a PAL programming device (I use DATA I/O and BP Microsystems boxes). Program PALASGN translates its input file into a PALASM file, elevat.jed. PALASM (*PAL Assembly* language) is Advanced Micro Devices Inc.'s standard PAL programming software. File elevat.jed is used directly by the PAL programmer to configure the PAL.

7.6.1   The 22V10 Registered PAL

As an example of a single IC that can accommodate the FSM designs we're working on for the elevator controller, here's the 22V10 registered PAL, or GAL (generic array logic). The *V* stands for *versatile*. A 22V10 has 24 pins in a dual in-line package (DIP): 12 pins are dedicated inputs, 10 pins are programmable input-outputs, and 2 pins are for power and ground. Each of the 10 I/O pins is part of a **macrocell**. The layout of one macrocell is shown in Fig 7.22. All of the 10 macrocells in a 22V10 are identical except for the number of product terms (AND gates) per OR gate. There is a variable product term distribution, from 8 to 16 per OR gate (8 10 12 14 16 and then 16 14 12 10 8 are the product terms for 10 macrocells).

Follow the output of the OR gate in Fig. 7.22. It's the D input to a rising-edge-triggered flip-flop, and it also bypasses the flip-flop to enter a $4 \rightarrow 1$ MUX along with its inverted form and Q and $\overline{Q}$ from the flip-flop. The S_1 and S_0 selects for the output MUX are user-programmable. The flip-flop's CLK, asynchronous reset (AR), and synchronous set (SP) inputs are all bussed together with the same pins on the other nine macrocell flip-flops; CLK is a dedicated input pin; AR and SR are driven by other AND gates (not shown above) whose inputs are also user-programmable. The output of the $4 \rightarrow 1$ MUX passes through a three-state inverter whose enable is controlled by another AND gate via pin 13. If the three-state inverter is disabled by the user, the I/O pin becomes an input. Either way, the pin input or the MUX output is fed back to a $2 \rightarrow 1$ MUX along with $\overline{Q}$ from the flip-flop. The same signal that controls S_1 on the $4 \rightarrow 1$ MUX is the select input for the $2 \rightarrow 1$ MUX. If S_1 is HI, the macrocell is "combinatorial" (output bypasses the flip-flop) and the $2 \rightarrow 1$ MUX selects the I/O pin. If S_1 is LO, the macrocell has a "registered" output and the flip-flop's $\overline{Q}$ is fed back to the connection matrix of AND inputs.

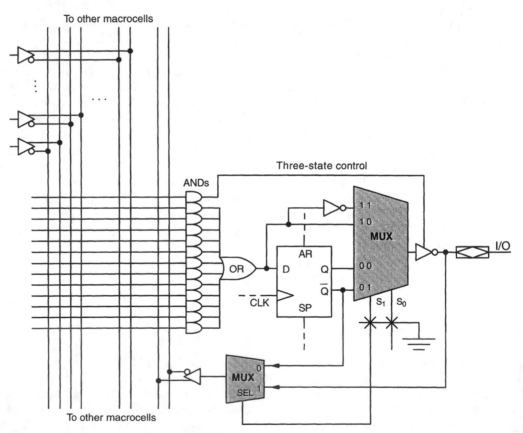

Figure 7.22   One macrocell of a 22V10 PAL.

(*PALCE* is the Advanced Micro Devices, Incorporated designation for electrically reprogrammable PALs. PALs without the PALCE marking are of lower cost but can be programmed only once.) The number of AND gates projecting to an OR is given by the number at the slash going through the OR input. The pinout is for the skinny DIP package. If the 22V10 is to be used purely for combinational logic, CLK is just another input.

The 22V10 has much more internal logic than a typical TTL chip; in its standard form it consumes about 180 mA of current and has propagation delays of 10–35 ns. Versions of the 22V10 for design and testing (the PALCE types) can be electrically erased and then re-programmed.

The pin assignments of the 22V10 are shown in parentheses in Fig. 7.23, but for the pinout of a 22V10 to have real meaning, the 22V10 must be programmed for a particular application (see Example 6, below). The user can assign inputs and outputs to specific pins, or CAD software can do the assigning. After FSMC has produced a foo.eqn file, the foo.eqn file is presented to another program, PALASGN (PAL assign), which prepares a PALASM file suitable for use in a PAL programmer device. PALASGN creates foo.pal and foo.pin; foo.pal is the PALASM-type file for use in a PAL programmer, and foo.pin is an ASCII graphic of the 22V10 pinout for a particular foo.eqn.

EXAMPLE 6

If the elevator controller file elevat.eqn of the previous example is given a "22V10" header and used as input for PALASGN,

```
% palasgn -p elevat
```

then the file elevat.pin shows (in ASCII graphics) how the excitation and flip-flop logic fit in one 22V10. See Fig. 7.24 on p. 381 for the elevator ground floor controller.

So many NCs ("no connections") suggest that a 22V10 is overkill for the ground-floor elevator control problem of Example 5; a smaller PAL would have done the job. If we stick with the 22V10, however, on subsequent design iterations it's possible to fix the pin positions of CALL, BELOW, DIREC, and so on in a header in the eqn file and to expand on the design. Notice that Q_0 and Q_1 are pins available from the chip for troubleshooting or for other post-programming custom wiring. FSMC is not the only route to a PALASM file; excitation equations can be entered manually or with some other software compiler, such as PALASM itself. All roads, however, lead to a PAL realizing a finite state machine, in this case a 22V10 for an elevator controller. In the next example we work through the state transitions of a finite state machine (step 1 in the algorithm) and then let FSMC and PALASGN turn the crank to implement the design in a 22V10.

EXAMPLE 7

Here we extend the freight elevator controller of the previous example. As before, the freight elevator goes between the basement, the ground level, and the first floor. At each floor is one call button on the wall near the elevator shaft. In the elevator

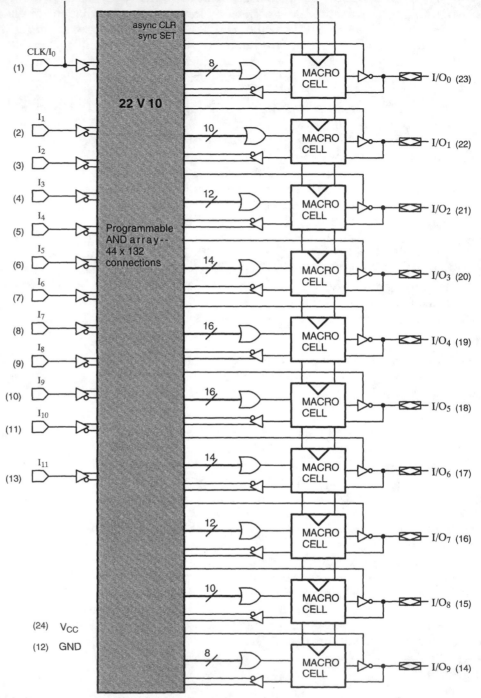

Figure 7.23 Overview of 22V10 PAL, with skinny DIP pinout.

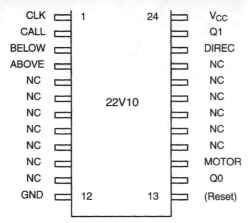

```
       CLK   1        24      Vcc
      CALL                    Q1
     BELOW                    DIREC
     ABOVE                    NC
        NC                    NC
        NC          22V10     NC
        NC                    NC
        NC                    NC
        NC                    NC
        NC                    MOTOR
        NC                    Q0
       GND   12       13      (Reset)
```

Figure 7.24 Pinout of 22V10 skinny DIP for elevator controller.

itself are three buttons, 1, G, and B, and at each floor is a sensor that detects when the elevator has arrived at that floor. The door of the elevator can be either open or closed; a motor controls the door. The motor controlling the elevator movement can be either on or off, and its direction of pull can be either up or down. See Fig. 7.25.

Design a controller that moves the elevator efficiently from one floor to the next, depending on which call buttons or which floor destination buttons have been pressed, and in what sequence.

Answer We have some latitude in the design. The specification calls for efficiency but doesn't say what the priorities should be if competing floor destination and call buttons are active simultaneously. Before starting to code state transitions for a 22V10, let's work on the input and output list. We now have four *motor control outputs.* Here they are listed with their code mnemonics:

Elevator motor on/off	MOTEL
Elevator motor direction	UPDOWN
Door motor on/off	MOTDR
Door motor direction	OPCLSE

We might also want to have, as "user-friendly" output, lights on the floor destination buttons that tell that a floor has been selected; such displays won't be necessary for the correct movement of the elevator, however.

Input In the previous elevator controller we had a crude call button: it had to be pressed continuously by someone until the freight elevator arrived at the ground floor. What we want to do here is *preprocess* the various inputs so that the user doesn't have to lean on buttons and the FSM code doesn't have to keep track of more inputs than necessary. Let's have set-reset latches capture the presses of call buttons for each of the floors, and let the elevator car destination buttons be OR'd with the

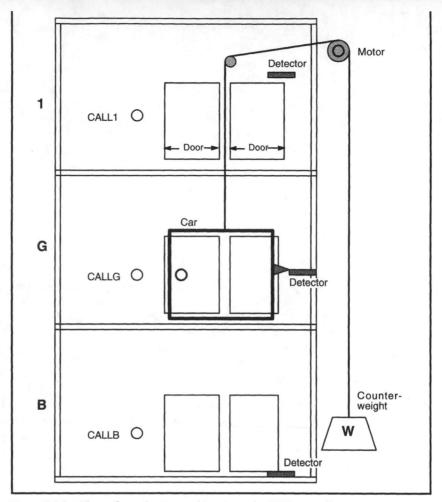

Figure 7.25   Three-floor elevator and inputs to the FSM controller.

appropriate floor calls, as in Fig. 7.26, where GO1, GOG, and GOB are the elevator car "go to" buttons. What should reset the latches? The detectors that signal arrival at the floors should reset them. As implied in the elevator diagram of Fig. 7.26, each detector is asserted when the elevator arrives at the floor in question. Let DET1, DETG, and DETB be the detectors; when one of them is asserted (and in normal operation only one at a time can be asserted), the latch for that floor is reset. DET has priority over CALL and GO, as shown by the inhibited ANDs in Fig. 7.27.

The preprocessing of inputs has reduced part of the FSM burden from nine inputs to three. Since the outputs of the three latches are inputs to the FSM, we call them IN1, ING, and INB. Yes, we could code the elevator FSM with the nine raw inputs, but something like the circuitry in Fig. 7.27 would be implemented anyway. If we include latches in the overall controller, the system has not been made asynchronous (that would happen if some flip-flops had one clock and others had other clock,

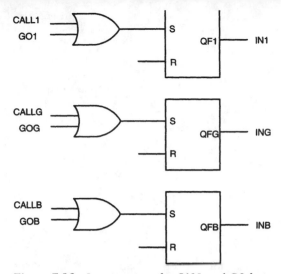

Figure 7.26 Input capture for CALL and GO buttons of elevator.

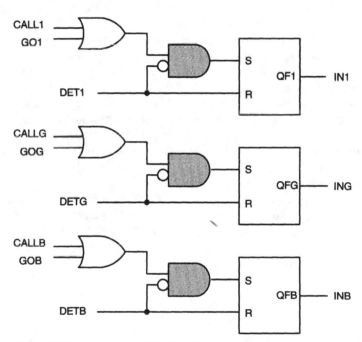

Figure 7.27 Reset control for input capture circuit.

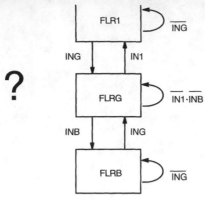

Figure 7.28 Start of ASM chart for three-floor elevator.

or gated clock, inputs). Think of the latch preprocessing as an elaborate switch debouncing circuit if you like.

States of the Elevator Controller Let's start with a state for each floor and see if that's enough; we draw them in an informal state diagram and call the states FL1, FLG, and FLB. The diagram in Fig. 7.28 says that a transition from a state occurs if the input latch from a neighboring state is asserted. At least two problems occur with this "machine": (1) Unless we have an extremely slow clock or an extremely powerful elevator motor, the system cannot move from one floor (state) to another in one clock pulse. (2) No account is taken of a request to move directly from the first floor to the basement, bypassing the ground floor. What we need are additional states to represent the elevator car moving. We need at least two states, one for moving up, the other for moving down. In fact, let's solve the problem of going directly from the first floor to the basement right now by creating two UP and two DOWN states, one of each in each direction, to bypass the ground floor. The system can remain in one of these states until the IN signals are not asserted. These thoughts lead to the more elaborate (and still informal) state diagram in Fig. 7.29.

At this point we can try coding the states for FSMC in a file elevat3.fsm, shown below. The first part of the code specifies the 22V10 as the target device. Where we place the name of an output (e.g., "down") in a state, FSMC sets that output to HI *while in that state*. The variables floor1, floorG, and floorB are outputs that control floor lights, and up and down are outputs that indicate the direction of the car's movement.

```
begin_p
device 22v10;
end_p

FL1:    floor1;
        if /ING*INB goto DWNB;
        if ING goto DWNG;
        stay;
```

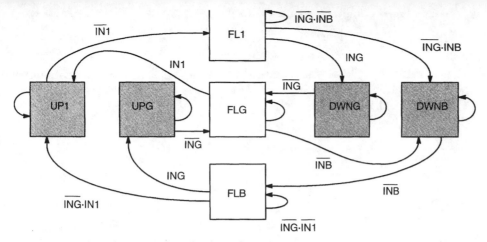

Figure 7.29 Complete ASM chart for three-floor elevator.

```
DWNG:    down;
         MOTEL;
         if /ING goto FLG;
         stay;

DWNB:    down;
         MOTEL;
         if /INB goto FLB;
         stay;

FLG:     floorG;
         if IN1 goto UP1;
         if INB goto DWNB;
         stay;

UP1:     up;
         MOTEL;
         UPDWN;
         if /IN1 goto FL1;
         stay;

UPG:     up;
         MOTEL;
         UPDWN;
         if /ING goto FLG;
         stay;

FLB:     floorB;
         if ING goto UPG;
         if /ING*IN1 goto UP1;
         stay;
```

```
>> fsmc -s elevat3.fsm
```

which returns a file elevat3.eqn and a file elevat3.sta. If we open file elevat3.sta, we find that FSMC has used three D flip-flops to represent the seven states. State $Q_2 Q_1 Q_0 = 111$ is not used.

	Q_2	Q_1	Q_0
FL1	0	0	0
DWNG	0	0	1
DWNB	0	1	0
FLG	0	1	1
UP1	1	0	0
UPG	1	0	1
FLB	1	1	0

When we open file elevat3.eqn, we see that the following Boolean equations have been figured out by FSMC, where Q_0, Q_1, and Q_2 are the internal flip-flops defined above.

```
D0 = Q0*Q̄1 + ING*Q1*Q2 + ING*Q̄1*Q̄2 + ĪNB*ĪN1*Q0
D1 = ĪNG*ĪN1*Q1 + ĪN1*Q1*Q̄2 + Q̄0*Q1*Q̄2 + ĪNG*INB*Q̄1*Q̄2 + ĪNG*Q0*Q̄1
D2 = IN1*Q0*Q1 + Q1*Q2 + ING*Q0*Q2 + IN1*Q̄0*Q2 + ĪNB*Q̄0*Q1
```

```
floor1 = Q̄0*Q̄1*Q̄2
floorG = Q0*Q1
floorB = Q1*Q2
down = Q0*Q̄1*Q̄2 + Q̄0*Q1*Q̄2
up = Q̄1*Q2
UPDWN = Q̄1*Q2
MOTEL = Q̄1*Q2 + Q̄0*Q1*Q̄2 + Q0*Q̄1
```

Note that some of the product terms (Q0*Q1, Q1*Q2, and so on) are made assuming that Q2 Q1 Q0 = 111 is not possible.
    If we run

```
>> palasgn -p elevat3.eqn
```

and then open file elevat.pin, we see Fig. 7.30, which is the pinout of *one* 22V10 programmed to implement the elevator control. Pin 13 is a dedicated output enable control that for one PAL should normally be grounded. Notice that by introducing outputs for the floor lights and the outputs up and down we used all 10 of one 22V10's outputs (pins 14–23). The other output of *palasgn*—elevat3.pal—can be converted to elevat3.jed and downloaded to a PAL programmer to configure a 22V10

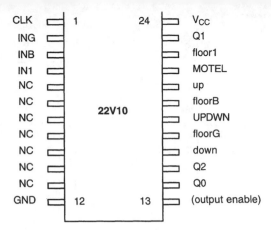

Figure 7.30 Pinout of skinny DIP 22V10 for elevator controller.

with the pinout of Fig. 7.30. When the sensors are hooked up to the preprocessing *SR* latch circuit worked out earlier and the outputs hooked up to appropriate lights, motor, and switches, the elevator works. The one issue we haven't considered is the clock speed. For a demonstration, the clock can be set to 1 Hz or less; with a slow clock the elevator will spend at least one second at each floor if it has to start up again.

Our first design cycle has produced a working elevator controller, but it still has some major and minor annoyances. For one thing, the elevator door must be operated manually. In order to incorporate control of the door, more states and more outputs need to be added. Since more than 10 outputs will be required, a second PAL will have to be recruited. The program *palasgn* has the capability of partitioning a large problem between several PALs, but let's leave such a project to *Daniels' Digital Design Lab Manual* for now. A minor annoyance is that once the elevator has started descending from the first floor to the basement, it can't be interrupted by a new call from the ground floor; that's not so bad for a three-floor elevator, but for more floors, more intelligence (more states) should be added.

Summary The Finite State Machine Compiler (FSMC) is an example of software that can take over after the designer has done the creative work of defining states and their transitions for a synchronous FSM. FSMC reads your state transitions and turns them into flip-flop assignments and *D* input combinational logic. Further processing of the equations generated by FSMC can result in a programmed PAL, such as the 22V10 highlighted here. (If you're working in PALASM, the "Moore Machine" option can be used in a way similar to FSMC. After you define state transitions in a file, PALASM can compile the file in a way that solves the excitation equations for the PAL specified.)

We shift now from finite state machine compiler software for general-purpose design of synchronous FSMs with PALs to specific consideration of positional counters and their control by nonclock inputs.

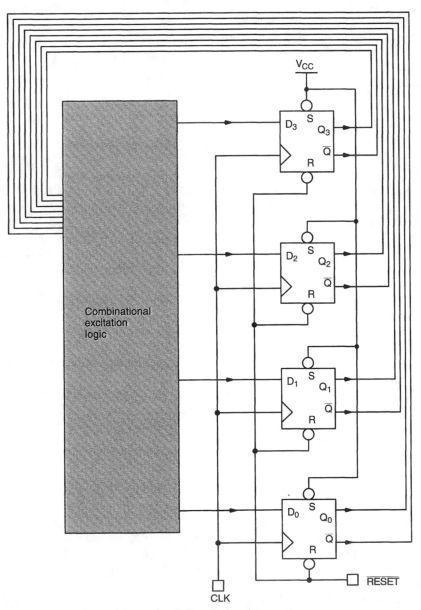

Figure 7.31   General form of a clock-only four-bit counter.

In Chapter 6 the word *counter* referred to a synchronous Moore automaton circuit that cycles through one fixed sequence. An asynchronous reset was used in some of the counters in Chapter 6, but otherwise only the clock was allowed as input to a counter. Now we will add nonclock inputs to positional binary counters. The nonclock inputs will be LOAD, which will load data directly into the counter flip-flops; CLEAR, which sends all flip-flop outputs to zero; HALT, which will stop the counter from incrementing or decrementing; and DIRECTION, for counting up or down. All these control input features will be *synchronous*. Each control signal must remain asserted until the next valid clock edge, at which time its effect will take place. A counter with these nonclock inputs becomes a Moore machine (except for Mealy output $\overline{RCO}$). With their versatility these multifunctional counters will be able to help program various sequences. We will use as our prototypes of IC counters the 74LS169 and 74LS569 TTL chips.

7.7.1 LOAD for Positional Counters

Recall a general form of the four-bit positional counter, where the outputs are the Q's of D flip-flops. The Q's and their complements form the inputs to a combinational logic circuit (drive logic). See Fig. 7.31. What's presented to the D's before a clock edge will become the Q's after the edge. In order to break into the counter control loop and insert external data onto the D inputs, a **load** operation is needed. One way to achieve a load operation is by adding a multiplexer: see Fig. 7.32. Now the combinational logic from the original counter is one set of inputs, and pins I_0–I_3 are the other set of inputs, to a quad $2 \rightarrow 1$ MUX whose select is the LOAD input. If LOAD picks the external inputs I_0–I_3, then after the next clock pulse, $Q_i = I_i$. LOAD must be asserted long enough to see a valid clock edge, but once it has the clock edge, the Q's will be the external data for as many clock pulses as LOAD is asserted.

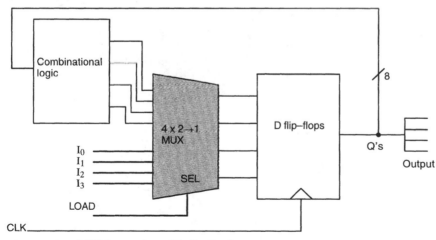

Figure 7.32 MUX for routing of D flip-flop inputs.

III IIIUSL COMMERCIAI IC COUNTERS LOAD is active-low for selecting external data. If you look at the logic diagram in the data sheet for a 74LS169 counter chip, you can find the four MUX's driving the four D inputs. LOAD in some cases is called **parallel enable** (active-low $\overline{PE}$ in the '169).

In fact, inserting a MUX as shown in Fig. 7.32 would add another two gates' worth of delay to the path from the Q's back to the D's. To keep the delay at the minimum of two gates' worth for an SOP, the decoder, with its external data and LOAD input, would have to be incorporated into the combinational logic design, for a larger SOP realization.

EXAMPLE 8

Starting with a four-bit up-counter that has active-low LOAD, design a counter that sequences through 11 states instead of 16.

Answer   If we connect the counter's active-low ripple-carry-output $\overline{RCO}$ to $\overline{LOAD}$, as in Fig. 7.33, the chip can start counting 11 numbers below the value $15 = F_{16} = 1111$, then wrap around at 0101 and do another 11, and so on. The sequence will be:

0101
0110
0111
1000
1001
1010
1011
1100
1101
1110
1111

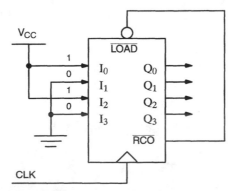

Figure 7.33   Using RCO to LOAD at a set number.

State 1111 will be held for the same duration as the other states because LOAD is a *synchronous* operation and waits for the next clock edge, even though $\overline{RCO}$ is asserted as soon as 1111 is detected.

7.7.2 Synchronous CLEAR

Clearing a counter to 0000 output can be a special case of loading 0000, and that's true for the 74LS169; there's no separate CLEAR pin. However, clearing a counter is so frequent an operation that some counter chips have separate CLEAR inputs in addition to LOAD. The 74LS569 counter chip has separate pins for synchronous CLEAR, asynchronous reset, and $\overline{LOAD}$, for example. Active-low synchronous reset ($\overline{SR}$) in the '569 works by ANDing $\overline{SR}$ with all the DATA inputs and ORing $\overline{SR}$ with the LOAD input. See Fig. 7.34.

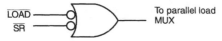

Figure 7.34 Synchronous reset and load control in '569 counter.

EXAMPLE 9

Since synchronous clearing means making all D's zero before the next clock pulse, another way to build in an active-low synchronous clear input is to send $\overline{SR}$ directly to all AND gates in the SOPs of the excitation logic. See Fig. 7.35 on the next page. $\overline{SR}$ is synchronous reset, and $\overline{MR}$ is asynchronous reset (master reset). When $\overline{SR}$ is LO, all AND gates are disabled. This method has the virtue that excitation logic propagation delay does not increase.

EXAMPLE 10

Starting with a four-bit hex counter, make a decade counter.

Solution   Detect when 9 = 1001 is reached, and use an active-low version (NAND) of that detection to synchronously reset the counter (see Fig. 7.36 on p. 393). (If it were a '169 counter, you could send the 1001 detection to $\overline{LOAD}$.) Actually, for up-counting, a two-input NAND gate would work as well, detecting $Q_3 \cdot Q_0$. The first time in the decade up-counting sequence that the pattern $Q_3 \cdot Q_0$ is reached is at 9. As soon as the next clock edge arrives, the counter will jump to 0000 and the detector will go off, allowing more up-counting. If you sent the 1001 detection to *asynchronous* reset, the 10th state, 1001, would last only a brief time, until the counter cleared to 0000. (Designing a decade counter from scratch or from a hex counter is a somewhat academic exercise, because each commercial hex counter has a decade counterpart. The 74LS168 is a decade counter with the same pinout as the 74LS169.)

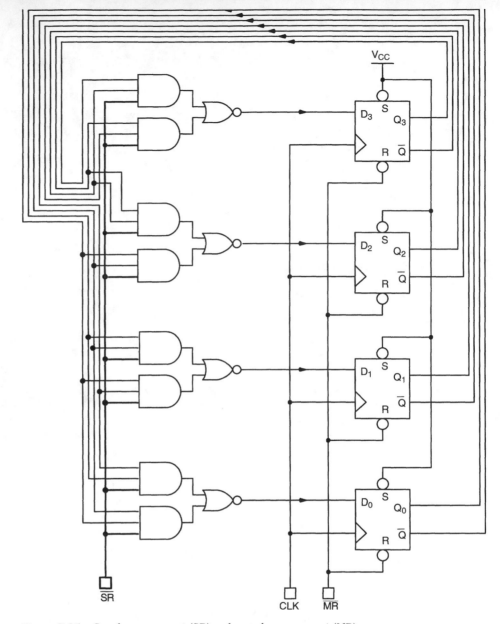

Figure 7.35 Synchronous reset (SR) and asynchronous reset (MR).

7.7.3 Enabling a Counter

Suppose you want your counter to stop incrementing when its output matches the value in some other register. The counter output and the register contents both go to a combinational four-bit comparator. You could be tempted to intercept the clock

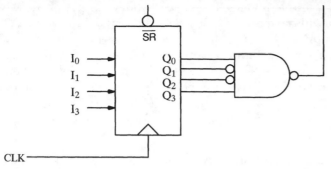

Figure 7.36 Counter clearing itself.

with an AND gate, but we saw earlier that gating the clock is a bad idea for a synchronous circuit. It is better to build an **enable** function into the counter. When enable is asserted, the chip counts normally. When enable is not asserted, the current value of the counter output is held (no resetting involved).

Here's one way to hold the current output: make sure that $D_i = Q_i$. We can expand on the MUX idea for LOAD. In the diagram of Fig. 7.37, Q_D, Q_C, Q_B, and Q_A are the counter outputs and the multiplexing arrangement is shown for one drive, that of D_A. The external input for LOAD is I_A. Enable is active-low. If enable is LO, the combinational logic for incrementing is passed to the next MUX; if enable is HI, then Q_0 (the current state) is passed back to the next MUX.

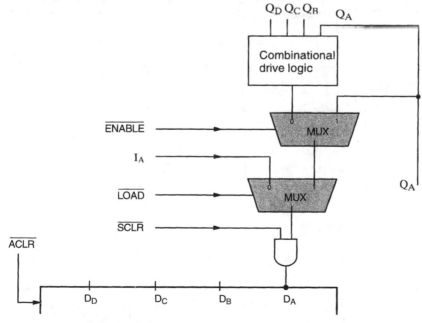

Figure 7.37 MUX cascade for counter options.

les, there are seven levels of gates in Fig. 7.37, from Q to D, but the actual realization in an IC chip will have fewer logic levels and less delay. Figure 7.37 shows in a modular way the **priority** of the various operations: asynchronous clear ($\overline{\text{ACLR}}$) has the top priority, then synchronous clear; if $\overline{\text{SCLR}}$ is asserted, the outputs will go to zero after the next clock edge. If $\overline{\text{SCLR}}$ is HI, then $\overline{\text{LOAD}}$ has the next highest priority; otherwise it matters only whether enable is asserted or not (*hold* or *continue* operations).

EXAMPLE 11

We illustrate one use of counter-enable by considering how four-bit counters can be used to count synchronously to higher numbers. For multi-chip counting we will use the 74LS169. Before we go further, let's look at the pinout of the 74LS169, a four-bit synchronous up-down counter TTL IC that changes state on rising clock edges. See Fig. 7.38. $\overline{\text{RCO}}$ is active-low ripple-carry-out, $\overline{\text{CET}}$ and $\overline{\text{CEP}}$ are active-low enable pins, and DATA are clocked in when $\overline{\text{LOAD}}$ is LO. There are two enable pins, 7 and 10, called $\overline{\text{CEP}}$ and $\overline{\text{CET}}$[3] (count-enable trickle and count-enable parallel). *Both* $\overline{\text{CET}}$ *and* $\overline{\text{CEP}}$ must be LO for the '169 to count. You've seen all the other pins[4] on the '169 except pin 1, which determines count direction and which we will discuss in Section 7.7.4. $\overline{\text{CET}}$ and $\overline{\text{CEP}}$ project to a common NOR gate, as shown in the circuit fragment of Fig. 7.39.

Let's start with eight-bit synchronous counting. Hook up CLK to both chips and send the $\overline{\text{RCO}}$ of one chip to the other chip's $\overline{\text{CEP}}$ pin; the other enable pins are grounded. See Fig. 7.40. Since $\overline{\text{RCO}}$ and $\overline{\text{CEP}}$ are active-low pins, the connection works as long as the design of RCO ensures that it is LO until the next clock edge. The counter on the left will increment only once every 16 clock pulses, when $\overline{\text{RCO}}$ goes LO at 1111. The counter on the left handles the four most significant bits of the

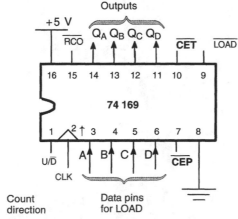

Figure 7.38   Pinout of 74169.

---

[3]Some manufacturers' data sheets label the $\overline{\text{CET}}$ and $\overline{\text{CEP}}$ pins as $\overline{\text{ENT}}$ and $\overline{\text{ENP}}$, respectively. The *T* stands for *trickle* and the *P* for *parallel*. Disabling is sometimes called a HOLD operation.

[4]Some manufacturers' data sheets refer to $\overline{\text{RCO}}$ as $\overline{\text{TC}}$, active-low terminal count.

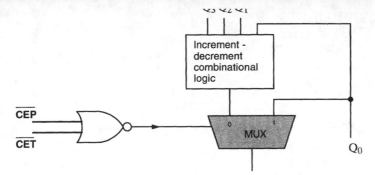

Figure 7.39 Parallel and trickle enable used together.

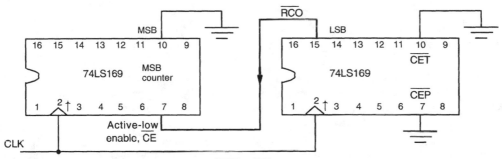

Figure 7.40 Synchronous counting with $\overline{RCO}$ to $\overline{CE}$.

count. The projection from $\overline{RCO}$ of the lower counter to $\overline{CEP}$ of the upper counter adds another stage of delay to the whole counting process; the delay is generated by the NAND gate on the lower chip, which forms the $\overline{RCO}$ output.

Let's add a third synchronous '169 and be able to count up to 2^{12}. Two enables per counter now come in handy. The $\overline{RCO}$s of the two lower-order counters (A and B, Fig. 7.41) can project in parallel to the higher-order counter, C (and eliminate one ripple's worth of delay).

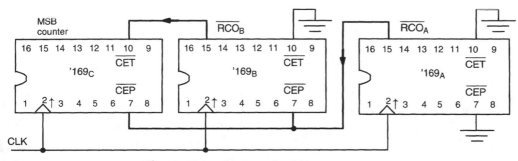

Figure 7.41 Counting to 2^{12} with CET and CEP on the '169.

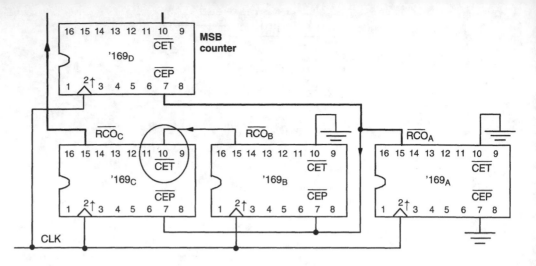

Figure 7.42 Counting to 2^{16}.

When the up-count reaches XXXX 1111 1111, both lower-order counters send $\overline{RCO}$ signals to the most significant counter and enable it to increment on the next clock edge—no delay waiting for a ripple through the second counter.

How can we add a fourth counter to perform 16-bit counting? Will the extension in Fig. 7.42 work? Yes, it works, but we must consider an interaction between $\overline{CET}$ and $\overline{RCO}$ in order to justify it. As you can see, the first and third lower-order counter $\overline{RCO}$s project up to the fourth counter. Because the influence of the second counter on the fourth is missing, an error could occur when an up-count reaches XXXX 1111 XXXX 1111. Instead of waiting for XXXX 1111 1111 1111 before advancing the four most significant bits, the MSB counter could tick ahead prematurely. This potential fault is corrected in the '169 by directing $\overline{CET}$ to gate $\overline{RCO}$, as shown in Fig. 7.43. For up-counting, $\overline{RCO}$ will go LO if all Q's are 1 *and* CET is 1. Because of CET's presence, the third counter in Fig. 7.42 won't activate its $\overline{RCO}$ until the second counter signals its advance to state 1111, through the $\overline{RCO}_B \rightarrow \overline{CET}_C$ connection circled in the figure. $\overline{CET}$ acts as a conduit for chaining the $\overline{RCO}$s together ("trickle" operation). Therefore it's important that $\overline{CET}$ be used as the destination for the second $\overline{RCO}$.

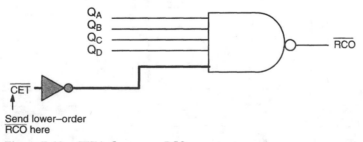

Figure 7.43 CET influence on RCO.

fourth counter must wait for the third counter to roll over), but counter D does use $\overline{RCO}_A$, the ripple-carry-out from the most rapidly changing lowest-order counter. As a result, the 16-bit design with two enables is still faster than a 16-bit ripple design. To extend the count to more than 16 bits, the idea for 16-bits is repeated over and over: send $\overline{RCO}_A$ to $\overline{CEP}_N$ and $\overline{RCO}_{N-1}$ to $\overline{CET}_N$, where N is the number of a higher-order counting chip.

It's taken four four-bit counters to demonstrate the need for the two different counter enables $\overline{CEP}$ and $\overline{CET}$ on a 74169! The result is a counter with a higher maximum clock rate. It is an exotic example of *carry look-ahead* (CLA). You'll see a more basic version of CLA in Chapter 10, on hardware for parallel adders.

7.7.4 Count Direction

By addition of a nonclock input, a positional counter can be made to switch between up-counting and down-counting. Here's a design example to illustrate control of count direction.

EXAMPLE 12

Design an external input that tells a three-bit positional binary counter whether to increment or decrement on the next clock pulse. Let the circuit have a ripple-carry-out when it reaches 111 *and* is counting up *or* when it reaches 000 *and* is counting down. Follow the seven steps of FSM design.

Answer

Steps 1 and 2 The problem is well defined. Let's establish that direction = 1 asserts up-counting—so direction input can be called $U/\overline{D}$. Choose D flip-flops for implementation. We need three four-input K-maps, one for each D flip-flop. The four inputs are the three flip-flop outputs plus the $U/\overline{D}$ control. See Fig. 7.44.

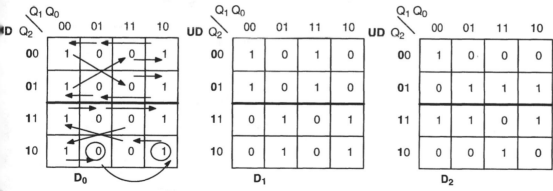

Figure 7.44 K-maps for count direction in three-bit counter.

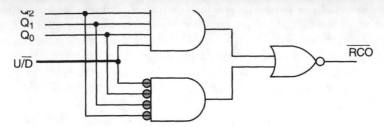

Figure 7.45 Influence of up/down control on RCO.

Steps 3 and 4 Follow the arrows on the D_0 map and verify that 1s and 0s are placed to set up for a transition to the box the arrowhead rests in. For example, the curved arrow in the map indicates a transition from $U/\overline{D}\, Q_2 Q_1 Q_0 = 1\,0\,0\,1\ \text{to}\ 1\,0\,1\,0$; to move Q_0 from 1 to 0 requires a 0 on the D input, where the arrow's tail is. In Fig. 7.44, $U/\overline{D}$ is shown as the variable UD.

$$D_0 = \overline{Q_0}$$
$$D_1 = UD \cdot (Q_1 \oplus Q_0) + \overline{UD} \cdot (\overline{Q_1 \oplus Q_0})$$
$$D_2 = \overline{UD} \cdot \overline{Q_2} \cdot \overline{Q_1} \cdot \overline{Q_0} + UD \cdot \overline{Q_2} \cdot Q_1 \cdot Q_0 + UD \cdot Q_2 \cdot \overline{Q_1}$$
$$+ \overline{UD} \cdot Q_2 \cdot Q_0 + Q_2 \cdot Q_1 \cdot \overline{Q_0}$$

The map for D_1 shows the XOR and XNOR patterns, so an exception to two-level logic was made for the D_1 drive.

Step 5: Count direction and RCO Ripple-carry-out depends on count direction $(U/\overline{D})$. $\overline{\text{RCO}}$ for a three-bit up-down counter must look like Fig. 7.45. Only if all

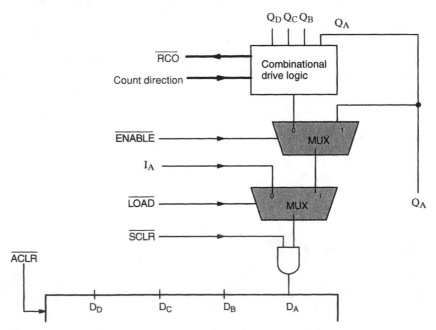

Figure 7.46 Priority for counter controls including count direction.

flip-flop outputs are HI *and* the count direction is UP or all the outputs are LO *and*
count direction is down should $\overline{RCO}$ be asserted. $\overline{RCO}$ is a Mealy output; if the 111
or 000 condition is satisfied, $\overline{RCO}$ can change back and forth with changes in $U/\overline{D}$
without waiting for a clock edge. (That means that our multi-chip counting circuits
from Section 7.7.3 would be subject to error if count direction changes back and forth
while a lower-level counter is at 1111. This up-down chatter can be cured by using
the 74LS569 hex counter, which has an active-low clocked carry-out. $\overline{CCO}$ waits for
the next clock pulse before asserting itself.)

Step 6   As derived from Fig. 7.44, there are no unused states, so we don't have to
worry about traps and lockout.

Step 7   The equations can be expressed as logic gates in a CAD simulation, and
the circuit can be tested.

We can add direction and RCO to our general counter hierarchy. See Fig. 7.46.
Direction changes will be noticed in the counter output only if the counter is enabled
and the LOAD and CLEAR controls are turned off.

7.7.5   Priority in FSMC Code for the 74163 Counter

Earlier, three ways of representing FSMs were described: state transition tables, ASM
flow charts, and computer code. We said that coding an FSM was the most flexible
and high-level approach for reasonably complex systems. Here we'll code a counter
using the FSMC language introduced previously. The order in which statements are
listed in the *while* loop below gives the priority of the various nonclock inputs to the
counter. Thus CLEAR has higher priority than LOAD, and LOAD has higher priority
than count ENABLE. Carry_out is a Mealy output and is defined before any state
transitions are described.

EXAMPLE 13

Describe the 74163 counter in FSMC code.

Answer   The 74163 is a four-bit up-counter chip with LOAD, synchronous CLEAR,
and two enable pins, P and T. It has a ripple-carry output. It can be described in
FSMC by the following, which was adapted from Troxel (1994).

```
while #statenum < 16            ' The states will be 0-15.
{                               ' Curly bracket is start of while loop.
#statenum:            ' A colon is the beginning of a state definition.
        Carry_out = T*Q0*Q1*Q2*Q3; ' Defines RCO active HI
        if Clear goto #0;
        if Load
               then     Q0=a,    ' a,b,c,d are the inputs to be loaded.
                        Q1=b,    ' FSMC picks up the Q's to be outputs.
                        Q2=c,
                        Q3=d;
```

```
if /P + /I                                   if either P or I enable is not true,
        goto #statenum;                      ' stay at current state
#statenum += 1;                      ' += means increment by the next number (1)
                                             ' #statenums become the 16 states
}                                            ' End of while loop
goto #0;                             ' Rolls over back to state 0000 after 1111.
```

The C-like iterative loop above shows off the descriptive power of FSMC. If the file above is named c163.fsm and

```
>> fsmc -s c163.fsm
```

is executed, the file c163.sta is created, which lists the 16 states, their outputs, and their transitions. (More details can be found in *Daniels' Digital Design Lab Manual*.)

7.8   MICROPROGRAMMED SEQUENCING

We now shift from the specific designs for external controls on positional counters back to general discussion of sequencing. In Chapter 6 we saw how a counter can be used to address a ROM whose contents form a sequence. We can say more about such synchronous circuits (FSMs) now that we have positional binary counters with LOAD, CLEAR, ENABLE, and DIRECTION control. The general form is shown in Fig. 7.47. The counter addresses a memory whose contents form the desired sequence. Thanks to the LOAD and CLEAR inputs, the sequence can be of any length less than or equal to 2^N, where N is the number of flip-flops in the counter. A subsequence (*subroutine*) within a sequence can be entered by use of the LOAD input and the subroutine address of $I_3I_2I_1I_0$. Before going further with sequence examples, let's reconfigure a positional counter for better use in these applications.

7.8.1   Counter as Register plus Incrementer

A positional up-counter can be separated into D flip-flops and a combinational *incrementer* circuit. The incrementer is an adder circuit with one input from the Q's

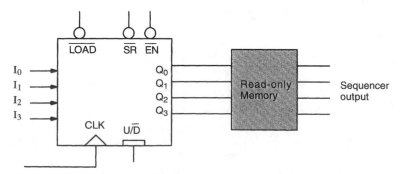

Figure 7.47   Counter plus ROM.

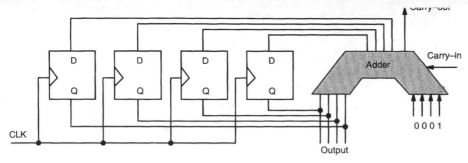

Figure 7.48 Up-counter realized as incrementer plus register.

and the other input equal to 1. The input of 1 could be carry-in. In the circuit of Fig. 7.48, carry-in is set to zero. (Does carry-out play the same role as ripple carry-out in a standard counter?) The circuit has some flexibility compared with a hard-wired up-counter; by making the increment input on the right 2 or 3, we can change the count sequence; by setting the increment input to zero, the counter can hold. It can even count down! See Exercise 29.

We can compress the drawing above into the icons in Fig. 7.49. Carry-out is not needed as part of the sequencer, and carry-in can be used to increment. We'll ignore the second input to the adder for now. A numbered slash through a connection ───/4─── means a bus of that many wires in parallel; it is a convention to reduce drawing clutter.

The diagram in Fig. 7.49 is a basic up-counter; carry-in can function as an enable; if carry-in is not asserted, the register holds its current value on each clock tick. We can add a synchronous LOAD feature by placing a MUX on the input to the register, as in Fig. 7.50. The four bits of DATA are external input and become the output if MUX select (an external control input) routes DATA through to the register. If DATA = 0000, the sequencer is synchronously cleared. By properly setting the inputs to the adder and the MUX, we have constructed a counter with LOAD, CLEAR, ENABLE, and DIRECTION control.

Now we're ready to connect read-only memory to the output of what can be called our **address generator**. See Fig. 7.51. In general, for a microprogrammed sequencer,

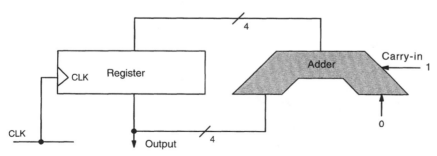

Figure 7.49 Four-bit up-counter as FSM.

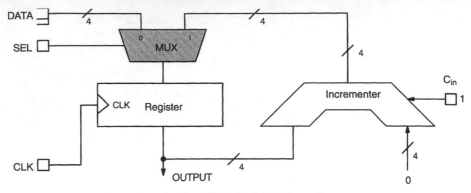

Figure 7.50 Input to register is from MUX with DATA channel.

the ROM output may have many more bits than the *data paths* internal to the address generator. Six outputs from the ROM are shown in the circuit of Fig. 7.51. *To make the sequencer self-contained, the ROM can store the control signal for the next MUX select and the value of the next DATA inputs.* See Fig. 7.52, where a way to CLEAR the register has also been added. The data path around the address generator is shown as having N bits. To design the circuit of Fig. 7.52 for a particular sequence, the engineer must program the ROM to be aware of when the sequence must *jump* to a new location and set that information in the ROM. The jump address goes to the MUX on the DATA path. The *next* address to jump to will be in the *current* instruction from ROM. Because select and DATA have been buried in the sequencer itself, the circuit is back to looking like a clock-only counter (except for the C_{in} input, which we

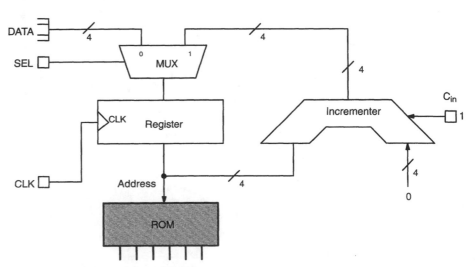

Figure 7.51 ROM on output of register-counter.

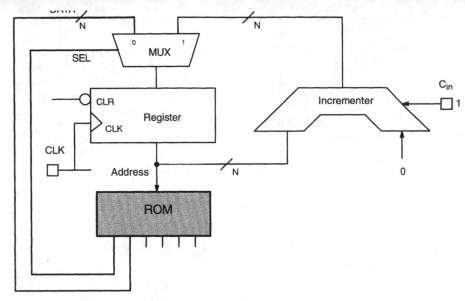

Figure 7.52 ROM field for JUMP address fed back to DATA input of MUX.

leave asserted as an enable for now). ROM outputs that select MUX input and jump address on DATA are **microinstructions** for the sequencer; they are hidden outputs that do not project out of the circuit.

7.8.2 Jump to and Return from Subroutine

It is common in programs and other sequences influenced by external events that the response to an external event (**interrupt**) is a subsequence (subroutine), entered from the main sequence and returned to after the subroutine has finished. Figure 7.53 shows that during address M in the main program, EVENT becomes true, requiring a conditional jump to address S. After completion of instruction $S + 3$, a return to

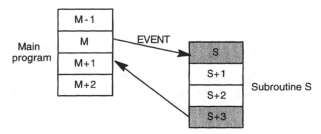

Figure 7.53 Example of jump to and return from subroutine.

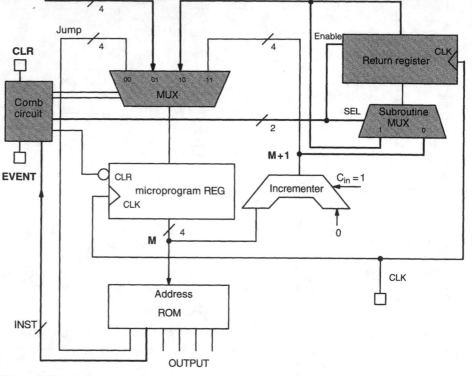

Figure 7.54 Register included to store return address for subroutine.

the next address in the main program, $M + 1$, is needed. A sequencer that can handle subroutines must be able to remember the return point(s) in the main program. The return address is in fact waiting in our microprogrammed sequencer: it is the $M + 1$ value on the output of the incrementer! In Fig. 7.54 our microprogrammed sequencer has been redrawn with various additions (in color) necessary to handle subroutining. Say that address M is at the output of the microprogram register; then $M + 1$ is at the output of the adder. If EVENT occurs, a combinational circuit output selects the adder input to the subroutine MUX and on the next clock pulse $M + 1$ will be stored in RET REG (return register). (Assume for now that EVENT lasts only long enough to meet the next clock pulse.) RET REG will hold $M + 1$ because the subroutine MUX will revert to selecting RET REG output for its RET REG input. EVENT must also help select the address for jumping to the start of the subroutine. Thus the event signal is shown going into a combinational circuit that drives the main MUX for the microprogram register. As a fourth input to the main MUX there is DATA, which contains the subroutine's starting address. Part of the control must enable the return register only when a jump-to-subroutine instruction is in progress. You will see more about registers with external control in Chapters 10 and 11. Exercise 31 asks about register holding.

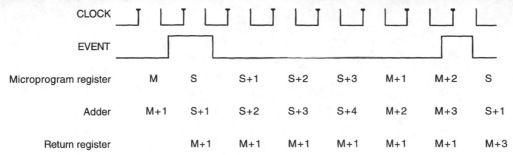

CLOCK										
EVENT										
Microprogram register	M	S	S+1	S+2	S+3	M+1	M+2	S		
Adder	M+1	S+1	S+2	S+3	S+4	M+2	M+3	S+1		
Return register		M+1	M+1	M+1	M+1	M+1	M+1	M+3		

Figure 7.55 Timing diagram for subroutine return.

What causes the return from the subroutine to address $M + 1$? When subroutine address $S + 3$ reaches the ROM, the contents of the ROM will have an INST signal that tells the main MUX to select RET REG as input. Then on the next clock edge $M + 1$ is delivered as the address to the ROM and the main program picks up where it left off. The subroutine is finished.

The diagram in Fig. 7.54 is rather formidable! Two multiplexers, two registers, an adder, a ROM, and an extra combinational circuit! In fact, most of the "brains" of the sequencer have been pushed into the combinational circuit. The good news about the microprogrammed sequencer is that any changes to the sequence can be handled by reprogramming the ROM; there is no need to redesign or add any hardware to the microprogrammer.

To gain more confidence about our general-purpose sequencer, let's make a timing and address diagram with an asynchronous event input, as in Fig. 7.55. In the timing diagram the EVENT signal lasts exactly one clock pulse and does not occur again until the subroutine finishes. What if an event interruption occurs during execution of the subroutine, S through $S + 3$? We would like the combinational circuit to prevent the return register from being loaded with the adder output. (No nesting of subroutines in this version—see Exercise 32 for nesting subroutine returns with PUSH and POP instructions on a stack.)

7.8.3   Microprogramming Example

EXAMPLE 14

Here's a sequencing puzzle: Suppose you're given the following ROM code for a four-bit address microcode. The *content* of each ROM address is 10 bits wide, and divided into the three fields SEL, JUMP, and CONTROL, as shown in the table below. Your problem is to figure out what sequence of *control* outputs is stepped through. Assume that you are working with the circuit of Fig. 7.54, and that the first action is a CLEAR to ROM address 0000, at which CONTROL = 1010. The subroutine address is set at 1011. Finally, assume that an *event* pulse occurs after the third clock edge and during the fourth clock edge.

ROM Address	SEL I_2 I_1	JUMP J_3 J_2 J_1 J_0	CONTROL $C_3C_2C_1C_0$
	ROM Contents		
0 0 0 0	0 0	X X X X	1 0 1 0
0 0 0 1	0 0	X X X X	1 0 0 0
0 0 1 0	0 0	X X X X	0 1 0 0
0 0 1 1	1 0	0 1 1 1	0 1 0 1
0 1 0 0	1 0	0 0 0 0	X X X X
0 1 0 1	1 0	0 0 0 0	X X X X
0 1 1 0	1 0	0 0 0 0	X X X X
0 1 1 1	0 0	X X X X	1 0 0 0
1 0 0 0	0 0	X X X X	1 0 0 1
1 0 0 1	1 0	0 0 0 0	X X X X
1 0 1 0	1 0	0 0 0 0	X X X X
1 0 1 1	0 1	X X X X	1 1 0 1
1 1 0 0	1 0	1 1 1 0	0 0 0 1
1 1 0 1	0 0	0 0 0 0	0 0 0 0
1 1 1 0	1 1	X X X X	1 1 1 1
1 1 1 1	1 0	0 0 0 0	X X X X

Don't care X's in the control field are at addresses (unused states) not in the sequence; they are associated with jump-to-0000 instructions. To solve the problem, you need to know what's inside the instruction circuit (called the combinational circuit in Fig. 7.54) and how the selects of the MUXs work. When the return MUX-select is HI, the adder output is selected for loading in the return register. The main MUX-select enforces the instruction set below, with instruction names at the right:

$S_{\mu 2}$	$S_{\mu 1}$	Main MUX = Select	Instruction Name
0	0	Adder	Continue
0	1	External address	Jump to subroutine
1	0	DATA (to $J_3J_2J_1J_0$)	Jump
1	1	Return register	Return from subroutine

A combinational instruction circuit to realize the MUX-selects is shown in Fig. 7.56. The circuit has some restrictions with regard to subroutining and EVENT. When EVENT is asserted HI, we want two things to happen: the main MUX should select the subroutine start address and RET MUX should select the adder input. At the next clock edge the subroutine start address and the adder input will be stored in the microprogram REG and RET REG, respectively. As wired up with the XNOR gate, the instruction circuit of Fig. 7.56 will carry out the go-to-subroutine task only if $I_2 = I_1$.

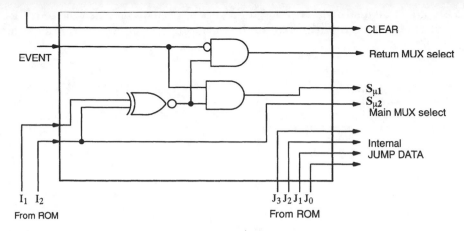

Figure 7.56 Instruction circuit for microprogrammer.

The hardware for $S_{\mu 1}$ realizes the K-map

$I_2 I_1$

E $\backslash$	00	01	11	10
0	0	0	0	0
1	1	0	1	0

$S_{\mu 1} = E \cdot (\overline{I_2 \oplus I_1})$

which means that a jump-to-subroutine event will be suppressed if it occurs during a regular jump instruction ($I_2 I_1 = 01$). Furthermore, if the $I_2 I_1$ code in the subroutine itself is 01 or 10, the subroutine won't be able to interrupt itself. With all these details noted, we can now figure out the answer!

Answer The answer will be the sequence of control field outputs, $C_3 C_2 C_1 C_0$. It starts with 1010, because $C_3 C_2 C_1 C_0$ is that value at ROM address 0000. $I_2 I_1$ at ROM address 0000 is 00, which calls for the adder output to be the next ROM address (continue instruction). The control field for the next address of 0001 is 1000. The third clock pulse also brings in a continue operation, so the third control field in the sequence is 0100. We're saying that after the third clock pulse the event line goes HI through the fourth clock pulse, so the select for the main MUX becomes 01, letting the SUB ADDR of 1011 go to the ROM. The contents of the ROM address 1011 are 1101. Now you're in the subroutine, which comprises one continue instruction, one jump instruction, and a return-from-subroutine instruction. Since you left for the subroutine at ROM address 0011, you will return to 0100. At ROM address 0100 a jump to 0111 is called for. Two

over. There are no more events, so the main program cycles. The entire sequence is as follows:

	ROM Address	$C_3C_2C_1C_0$	Hex
	0 0 0 0	1 0 1 0	A
	0 0 0 1	1 0 0 0	8
	0 0 1 0	0 1 0 0	4
(Subroutine)	1 0 1 1	1 1 0 1	D
	1 1 0 0	0 0 0 1	1
(Jump)	1 1 1 0	1 1 1 1	F
(Return)	0 0 1 1	0 1 0 1	5
(Jump)	0 1 1 1	1 0 0 0	8
	1 0 0 0	1 0 0 1	9
(Jump)	0 0 0 0	1 0 1 0	A

The hex sequence continues (if no event interrupts) 8, 4, 5, 8, 9, A, and so on.

Whew! Yes, it's fairly tedious to figure out what the sequence is, but that would be doubly true if you were reverse-engineering a real microcontroller! By the way, not all the ROM addresses are used in the program, and those addresses that aren't in the program are filled with jumps to 0000, the ground state. If noise knocks the sequencer into an unused state, it will start over at 0000.

Let's point out again the advantage of a microprogram controller: a new sequence can be set up by reprogramming the microprogrammed controller's ROM (and perhaps by resetting the external subroutine address); there is no need to add chips or rewire anything. In this sense, microprogram controllers are like FSMs designed with PALs: once the initial circuit is built, only reprogramming is required to change the sequence.

EXAMPLE 15

Given the microprogram controller of the previous example, write microcode for ROM that will step through the address sequence 5, 7, B, D, 3, 3, 7, (repeat) 5, 7, B, D, and so on unless an interrupt occurs, in which case the sequence 8, 10, 12 is stepped through and the sequence returns to where it was interrupted.

Answer Assume that when the microprogrammed controller is cleared to ROM address 0000, the contents are 0101 = 5. Assume also that 1011 is still the address set in the SUB ADDR input to the main MUX. From there we can fill in the ROM contents as in the table on the next page.

ROM Address	ROM Contents SEL $I_2\,I_1$	JUMP $J_3\,J_2\,J_1\,J_0$	CONTROL $C_3C_2C_1C_0$	
0 0 0 0	0 0	X X X X	0 1 0 1	5
0 0 0 1	0 0	X X X X	0 1 1 1	7
0 0 1 0	0 0	X X X X	1 0 1 1	B
0 0 1 1	0 0	0 1 1 1	1 1 0 1	D
0 1 0 0	0 0	X X X X	0 0 1 1	3
0 1 0 1	0 0	X X X X	0 0 1 1	3
0 1 1 0	1 0	0 0 0 0	0 1 1 1	7 (and jump to 0000)
0 1 1 1	1 0	0 0 0 0	X X X X	
1 0 0 0	1 0	0 0 0 0	X X X X	
1 0 0 1	1 0	0 0 0 0	X X X X	
1 0 1 0	1 0	0 0 0 0	X X X X	
1 0 1 1	0 1	X X X X	1 0 0 0	8 (start of subroutine)
1 1 0 0	0 1	1 1 1 0	1 0 1 0	A
1 1 0 1	1 1	0 0 0 0	1 1 0 0	C (and return)
1 1 1 0	1 1	X X X X	0 0 0 0	
1 1 1 1	1 0	0 0 0 0	X X X X	

7.8.4 Architecture of a Computer

Microprogrammed controllers are often used in computer central processing units. We will explore computer organization more in Chapter 11 (Register Transfer Logic). Here we can note that the ROM output is to be held in a pipeline register and used as a one-cycle machine instruction, choosing *source, function,* and *destination* operations in an arithmetic logic unit (combinational circuit) and in the computer's memory. A highly simplified (believe it or not!) diagram of a microprogrammed controller's (μPc) place in a computer is shown in Fig. 7.57. The microprogrammed controller now receives *external* and *internal* interrupt signals; the internal signals come from status on the ALU (carry-out, overflow, and so on). The memory receives address and read/write signals from the microcode appropriate for the machine instruction (add, compare, load, store, and so on) being carried out. The memory system receives the same clock as the microprogrammed controller, so the computer stays synchronous.

The term **architecture** refers to the arrangement of components in a system. Figure 7.57 is an architecture of a microprogrammed computer. It is beyond the scope of this text to explore architectural optimizations (such as pipelining) for the microprogram controller or computer. Exercise 36 looks at what happens to the microprogram controller if output to ROM is taken from the main MUX instead of a register. Such a component arrangement is seen in the old AMD 2911 and 2910 microprogram controllers, which also feature a five-deep stack for nesting of subroutines and a loop counter for repeating sections of microcode. (*Daniels' Digital Design Lab Manual* has exercises with more details about microprogram sequencers.)

References: Chapter 11 of Mick and Brick (1980), on microprogrammed design, goes over features of the 2910 sequencer. Chapter 4 of Myers (1980) discusses the

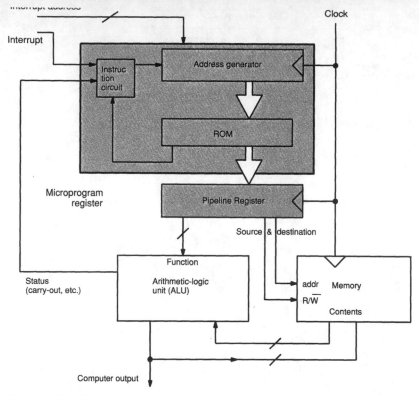

Figure 7.57 Microprogram sequencer in a computer.

2910 and similar chips from other manufacturers. See also the memoirs of Maurice Wilkes (1985), who originated the idea of microprogramming.

7.9 SUMMARY

- A **Mealy** sequential circuit's output may depend on clocked flip-flop outputs and on instantaneous combinations of external nonclock inputs; therefore a Mealy circuit's output can change at times other than clock transitions.

- The metastable errors from external nonclock inputs can be minimized by passing the inputs through **synchronizing circuits**. A synchronizer is a flip-flop circuit driven by the same clock as the FSM.

- Analysis of an FSM with nonclock input can be challenging. For a small synchronous FSM, generate the K-map for each flip-flop drive and try to work backward from the output state to the start state.

- Three ways to represent the **input-dependent transitions of states** were given: the state transition table, the algorithmic state machine diagram, and finite state machine compiler code.

- The rows of a state transition table are states, and the columns are possible nonclock input combinations. The entries in the table say what the next state after a clock pulse is. State transition tables enable a designer to account for every possible transition.

- An **algorithmic state machine (ASM) diagram** forces the designer to account for all state transitions in a specification. It contains symbols for state, conditional test, and asynchronous output that are joined by arrows representing clock transitions.

- **Finite state machine compiler (FSMC)** codes each state as a block of declarations about output and about state transitions. The compiler turns your state descriptions into a PALASM-compatible file, which can be downloaded to a PAL programmer. Because FSMC does all the work except making state definitions, a designer can build up an FSM step by step, adding features on successive programming cycles.

- The 22V10 registered PAL is a one-chip solution to many small and moderate FSM designs. The 22V10 has 10 D flip-flops, each one driven by 8–16 product terms in a sum-of-products format.

- The nonclock inputs for a positional counter, LOAD, CLEAR, ENABLE, and DIRECTION, can all be synchronous operations. Asserting **LOAD** causes the outputs of the counter to be loaded with special DATA inputs on the next clock edge; unless **ENABLE** is asserted on a counter, the counter will stay at its current state (different from clearing to 0000). **DIRECTION** determines whether the counter increments or decrements.

- Positional counters were illustrated with the 74169, the 74LS569, and the 74163. In the 74163 case, FSMC code was shown that would implement the '163 as a registered PAL. The code had the following operation **priority:** CLEAR, LOAD, ENABLE, with CLEAR having the highest priority.

- The use of counters in FSM design can be extended by **microprogramming.** A counter can be separated into a parallel-in–parallel-out register and a combinational adder circuit. The adder takes its input from the register and sends its summation back to a multiplexer providing register input. See Fig. 7.58.

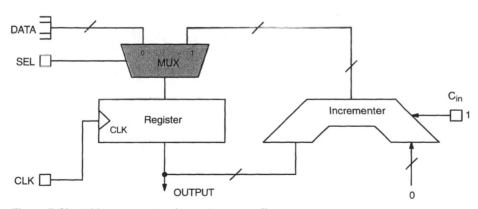

Figure 7.58 Address generator for a microcontroller.

develops more capability. If the adder output goes to another register, the return from subroutine address can be one of the MUX inputs.

- One application of a microprogrammer is inside a computer, where it can control the source, function, and destination of instruction data moved in and out of an arithmetic logic unit and memory system.

Exercises

1. **(a)** Is the circuit in Fig. P7.1 a Moore or a Mealy circuit? Explain. Inputs are INT and CLK on the left, and there are three outputs on the right.

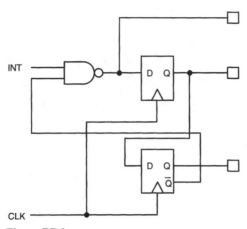

Figure P7.1

(b) True or false: A Mealy circuit must have more than two inputs.

2. Consider the Mealy circuit of Fig. 7.1. Redraw the circuit so that the combinational logic is consolidated into one block.

3. **(a)** Which of the following restrictions help define Moore circuits?
   (i) Only flip-flops can be in the circuit.
   (ii) All flip-flops in the circuit must trigger on the same edge.
   (iii) The output of the circuit comes from flip-flop outputs.
   (iv) The only external input allowed is the clock.
   (v) The combinational part of the circuit can receive flip-flop outputs as inputs.

   (b) **Mealy versus Moore circuits** Which of the following statements are not true?
   (i) The outputs of Mealy and Moore circuits can depend on other input than present input.
   (ii) Moore circuit outputs change only on the active edge of the system clock.

- **(iii)** Flip-flops in a Mealy circuit can be driven by different clock signals.
- **(iv)** The output of a Mealy circuit can change at any time.
- **(v)** A Moore circuit can be made entirely of NAND gates.
- **(vi)** The outputs of some flip-flops can be connected directly to the inputs of other flip-flops in both Moore and Mealy circuits.
- **(vii)** Clock inputs must be edge-triggered in Moore and Mealy circuits.
- **(viii)** Synchronizers are needed in Mealy circuits.

4. Suppose the assertion of a nonclock input to a synchronous FSM is so brief that it falls between two consecutive clock edges. Assuming that the user of the system wants a response to such a brief event, what can be done to capture the pulse and minimize metastability?

5. A certain Moore circuit has a clock input and one other external input, EXT, feeding its combinational subcircuit. Suppose EXT can change at any time with respect to clock. Will the out-of-phase synchronizing circuit of Fig. P7.2 solve potential input timing problems? If not, why not?

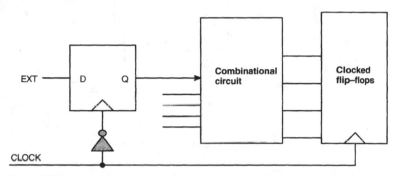

Figure P7.2   Inverted clock on external input flip-flop.

6. In Fig. P7.3 is a circuit similar to the circuit in Example 1.

   (a) What pattern on IN, in synchrony with the clock, will make output Z go HI?

   (b) What kind of circuit is created if output Z in Fig. P7.3 is ANDed with input IN? Is it possible for Z to change at times other than valid clock edges?

7. The solution to Example 2 shown in Fig. 7.12 uses three SR latches and can chatter after unlocking if input A is toggled. Show how to eliminate the chatter by adding a fourth SR latch to the chain.

8. Design a circuit with SR latches to unlock after the input sequence B, D, C, B, D, C, A is pressed. Make sure that the RESET inputs reduce the possibility that random hacking will find the combination.

9. **(a)** You have learned that the state at time t_0 of a synchronous circuit is all the outputs of the flip-flops in the circuit at that time. Do you think the same definition of state can hold for the state of an *asynchronous* sequential circuit such as we developed for the electronic lock?

   (b) The combination lock worked out in Chapter 7 is a *sequential* lock: the numbers in combination must be entered one after another. What would an

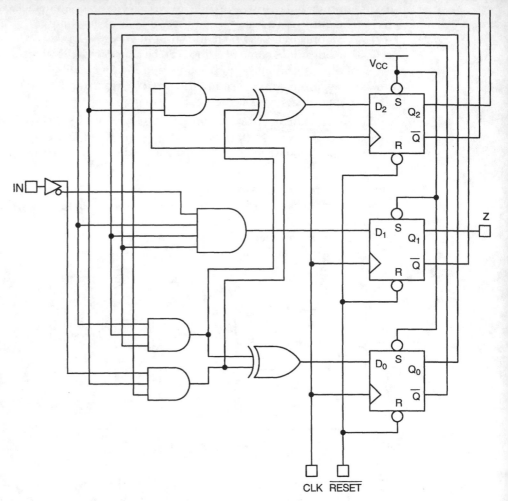

Figure P7.3 Synchronous lock.

electronic lock look like (block diagram) if the correct numbers have to be entered on separate tumblers and all the correct numbers have to appear simultaneously? (Some bicycle locks are of this design.)

10. **(a)** In the scanner of Example 3, what convention tells the lock light to go out once it has been turned on? Answer for each of the three kinds of state descriptions: table, ASM chart, and FSMC code.

(b) Show a new ASM chart description for a scanner in which a fourth station is added and the order of scanning is reversed, from 4 to 1 and back again. Let the system have an output that goes HI whenever the system is scanning the new station 4.

11. **(a)** Consider the state diagram in Fig. P7.4. The sequence skips state 101 when EXT = 1. Design a Moore sequencer that steps through the states and avoids lockout if the system is initialized to one of the unused states. Let state 111 be the ground state to which unused states are directed.

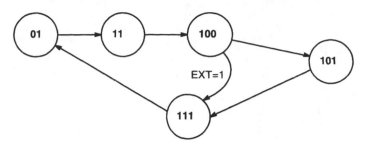

Figure P7.4

(b) A system with one external input, S, has the state diagram in Fig. P7.5. The three bits in each circle are the outputs of three flip-flops. On paths where S is not marked, S is a don't-care (for example, only a clock pulse is needed to take the system from 010 to 111). Design the combinational driving logic for the flip-flop inputs to realize the state diagram. If states not shown are entered, arrange that they change to the 000 ground state after the next clock pulse.

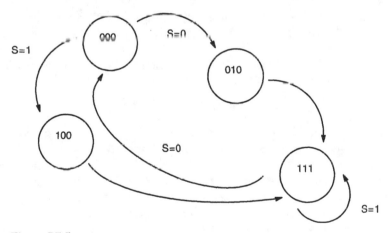

Figure P7.5

12. Compare the 7-step algorithm of Section 7.5 with the 10-step algorithm of Chapter 6, Section 6.3. Which steps from the first algorithm were consolidated? Which step(s) in the FSM algorithm is (are) new?

Imagine four photodetectors arranged in a vertical column, detector spacing is 1 cm. Each detector sends out a HI signal when light falls on it and a LO signal when it is in the dark. Also providing input is a one-per-second clock. See Fig. P7.6. A client wants a system that will give a 1-s output pulse if a spot of light travels from D_1 to D_4 at a speed of 1 cm/s. The spot can illuminate only one detector at a time.

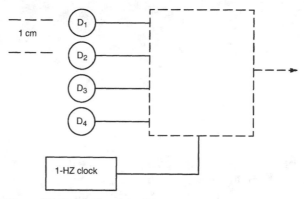

Figure P7.6   Motion detector.

Can the problem be solved by combinational logic alone? If not, design the states and their transitions for a system that meets the client's needs. There's no need to finish the design at this point. Show your answer three ways: as a state table, as an ASM chart, and as FSMC code. As you figure out the states and their transitions, you will clarify the specifications. For instance, because the system wants only one small spot at a time shining on the detectors, back-and-forth motion occurring within 1s will not result in a response. You still need to decide what will RESET the system, that is, cause it to begin waiting again for a valid movement to detect.

14. Suppose there are two motors for control of a robot forearm: one that flexes or extends the arm and another that rotates the forearm clockwise or counterclockwise. Both motors are stepping motors having direction and speed inputs. Motor speed is controlled by rates of pulses into the speed input. Each pulse rotates the motor shaft 1 degree. The arm has a sensor that detects whether the arm bumps into something. A client wants you to design a controller that will make the arm flex at five pulses per second until it reaches 90 degrees and then stop in the 90-degree position. If the arm bumps into something on its way to 90 degrees, it extends for five pulses, rotates counterclockwise, and then starts flexing again. If it bumps into a second object, it stops altogether and displays a flashing light. The client can arrange that the arm begins straight.

Define the states and their transitions for a system that meets the client's needs. There's no need to finish the design at this point. Show your answer three ways: as a state table, as an ASM chart, and as FSMC code. Have an accompanying block diagram that shows the inputs and outputs of the system.

(a) Why doesn't the auto-sensor input need a latch to capture it?

(b) Come up with a design for a three-bit up-counter that stops at 111 and doesn't roll over until a CLEAR occurs. Recall the Chapter 6 algorithm.

(c) Consider Fig. 7.21, the circuit for capturing a walk request pulse. What would go wrong if RCO inhibited the AND gate before the latch instead of after it?

(d) Propose a modification of the state diagram to allow the WALK signal to stay on 4 s instead of 2 s.

16. For the elevator controller of Example 5 draw out an ASM chart to show the connections between the states and the nonclock inputs.

17. Study the organization and pinout of the 22V10 PAL given in Section 7.6.1. Suppose you have a problem that needs only one output. What is the maximum number of inputs a 22V10 can offer for such a problem?

18. **Elevator controller**   Recall Example 7.

(a) Suggest in an ASM chart what would be needed to control the elevator doors—on the wall and on the car.

(b) Suggest in an ASM chart what additional states would be needed for the elevator to stop at the ground floor if G is pressed on the way from the basement to the second floor.

(c) What about elevator safety? Suggest a way to send the elevator to the basement if the wall sensors give inconsistent readings. Have a FAIL light come on in the elevator car, and have the door open when the elevator reaches the basement.

19. What sequence does the counter circuit in Fig. P7.7 step through?

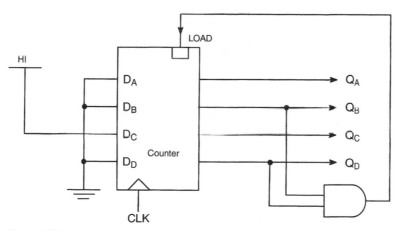

Figure P7.7   Feedback to synchronous LOAD.

20. Show how to configure a four-bit counter with a synchronous LOAD feature as a shift register (right shift).

21. Assume that just before clock edge (a) a '74169 is counting up and that after edge (a) ripple-carry-out goes LO. What were the four outputs $Q_D Q_C Q_B Q_A$ just before edge (a)? What will the four outputs be after edge (b)? When will RCO go HI again? (c) When will RCO go LO again after the HI of (b)?

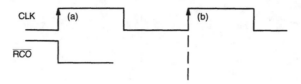

22. What is the first mistake the 16-bit counter in Fig. P7.8 will make in counting up from 0000 0000 0000 0000?

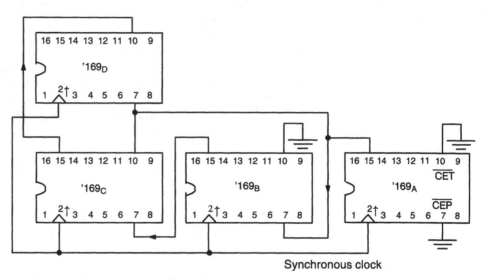

Figure P7.8 A 16-bit counter from 4-bit-counter ICs.

23. A data book lists the following propagation delay times t_{pd} for a 74169 four-bit counter IC: from CLK to Q_N, 20 ns; from CLK to $\overline{RCO}$, 17 ns; and from $\overline{CET}$ to $\overline{RCO}$, 9 ns.

(a) Suppose four 74169s are *rippled* together to form a 16-bit counter. In the worst case, how long must the MSB RCO wait for the circuit to increment by 1?

(b) What would be the maximum delay for an increment if four '169s ganged together, as shown in Fig. 7.42, using both $\overline{CET}$ and $\overline{CEP}$ enables?

(c) The 20-bit counter circuit sketched in Fig. P7.9 is built with '169s chained together from $\overline{CET}$ to $\overline{RCO}$. The most significant bit, Q_{5D}, is on the left.

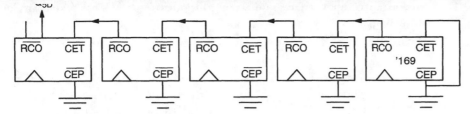

Figure P7.9   A 20-bit counter.

Given the timing data for '169s in part (a), what is the delay from CLK to Q_{D5} when the counter changes from $7FFFF_{16}$ to 80000_{16}?

(d)   Using the inspiration of Fig. 7.42, design a better 20-bit counter.

24. Design a **clocked carry-out** for an up-down counter with CET input. A clocked carry-out will not toggle like a Mealy output when count direction changes. A clocked carry-out will wait for a clock edge.

25. Study the clock gate circuit in Fig. P7.10. The inverter is in the CLOCK path to produce an edge. Clock enable is now situated to control an AND gate through which the clock signal must pass before it reaches the flip-flops inside the counter. What's wrong with this circuit as a way to implement LOAD and COUNT ENABLE?

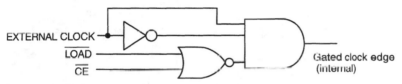

Figure P7.10   Wrong way to implement LOAD and ENABLE.

26. The 74160 pinout is shown in Fig. P7.11. Assume that the control pins $\overline{CLEAR}, \overline{LOAD}, \overline{CET}$, and $\overline{CEP}$ are connected as shown to enable counting

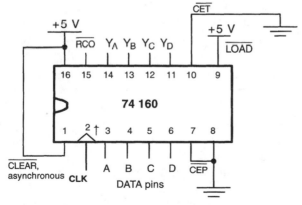

Figure P7.11   74160 up-counter.

up. What other logic can be placed around the 160 so it takes part in down-counting?

27. Assume that a 74169 chip is counting up and is at state 1100. Its data pins are set to 0101.

    (a) Between clock edges the LOAD and count direction pins are grounded. What will be the chip's output after the next clock pulse?

    (b) What if the ENABLE pin is set HI during the same interval as in (a), when DIRECTION and LOAD are sent LO? What will be the output of the counter after the next clock edge?

28. Study the FSMC code for the 74163 in Example 13.

    (a) Modify the code so that the counter can count up or down.

    (b) Add code so there is *asynchronous* clear on the FSM counter.

    (c) An optional question for those with access to FSMC: Will four-bit 74163 code fit in one 22V10 PAL?

29. The register plus adder of Fig. P7.12 has 1111 on its second adder input and carry-in of zero. How does the circuit output change after every clock pulse? What is the next output if the present output is 0000?

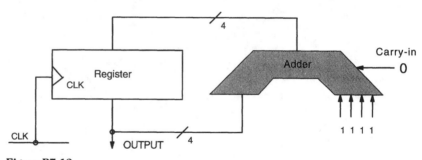

Figure P7.12

30. Study the microprogram counter of Fig. 7.50. Can a ripple-carry output be the carry-out of the adder? What prevents the incremented value of the output from racing around through the multiplexer and increasing without control?

31. Study the return register of Fig. 7.54. Only when a jump-to-subroutine instruction is called for should the return register load the value of the incrementer. Design a register with an enable such that the register holds its current contents unless the enable is asserted for data. The register enable will be like LOAD on a multifunctional counter.

32. **Nested subroutines** The microprogram sequencer of Fig. 7.54 allows for only one subroutine at a time to be entered. Suppose you need the capability of jumping to another subroutine on interrupt. The sequencer will need to go from the second subroutine to the first and then to the main program. Suggest, in block diagram form, a way to handle two-deep nesting of subroutines. You will need a second register to hold the return address from the first subroutine jump. A systematic solution to the problem of nesting must wait for Chapter 8, on

memory, where a static RAM will be developed, which can be written to with various subroutine return addresses.

33. Study Example 14, the coded microprogram sequence. Say what the answer to the sequence would be if the event occurred on the fifth clock pulse instead of the fourth.

34. Using clocked flip-flops and a minimum number of AND, OR, and INVERT gates, design a circuit that meets the following specifications:

   (a) In the normal mode the system output will step by clock pulses through the sequence 0, 1, 2, 4, 7, 6, 0, 1, 2, 4, 7, 6, 0, etc. Let the decimal numbers be represented by positional binary coding. You will need to figure out six J and K inputs, profitably using Karnaugh maps. Show these maps as part of your solution.

   (b) If the system output is 4 and a switch asserts the abbreviated mode, then stepping of the clock will show 3, 5, 3, 5, 3, 5, etc. Otherwise, if the ABBR switch is on and 4 is not the output, the long 0, 1, 2, 4, ... sequence will display until 4 appears as output, and then the abbreviated 3, 5, 3, 5 sequence will start. The abbreviated mode can be exited only when the ABBR switch is turned off *and* the output is 5, at which point the next output will be 0. Consider ABBR as external input and add its influence to the K-maps you generated for (a). Assume that ABBR switching always occurs at least several setup and hold times away from active clock edges. Show the K-maps for the abbreviated mode as part of your solution. See the figure below.

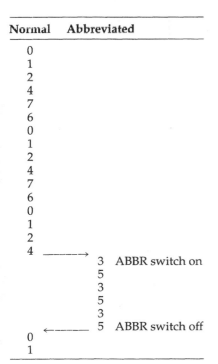

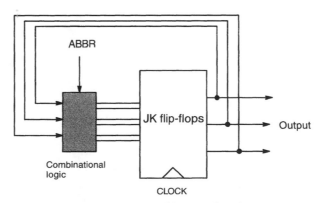

Figure P7.13   Counter with abbreviated mode.

machine of Fig. 7.54 to step through the sequence 0, 5, 7, 9, C, D (repeat) unless EVENT is asserted, in which case the routine 2, 3, 4 is executed and the main program is returned to.

36. It's possible for the multiplexer to be the output of the microprogram sequencer, as seen in Fig. P7.14. The AMD 2911 looks something like the diagram in the figure. Now there is a clocked register on the output of the incrementer and a return register for subroutining. The output of the MUX must provide the address to a ROM, which in turn has the microprogram of next instructions, the jump address, and computer control outputs. Your question: How do you prevent a race condition in the external jump path? The ROM will provide a jump address, but it can't go directly to the MUX or it will race around a loop. Draw the sequencer in an architectural block diagram that handles the ROM output in a satisfactory way. Study Fig. 7.57 for guidance. *JSR* stands for *jump to subroutine*, and *RR* stands for *return register*.

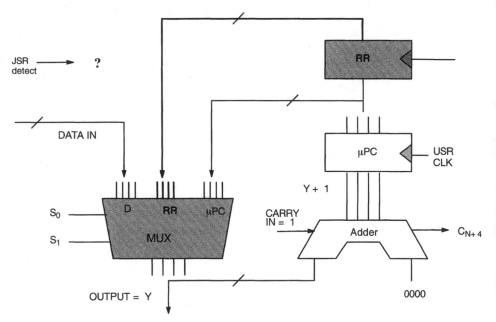

Figure P7.14 Another microprogram architecture.

37. Design extra hardware around a 74169 counter so that if it is counting up and the count reaches 1111, the counter stops and does not roll over; if the count is at 1111 and count direction changes to DOWN, then the '169 counts down. Likewise, if the '169 is counting down and reaches 0000, it stops there until the count direction is reversed to UP.

Bonus: Design an eight-bit synchronous counter that stops at 1111 1111 when counting up and stops at 0000 0000 when counting down. Build the terminal-

inputs of the '169!

38. What sequence $Q_D Q_C Q_B Q_A$ will the counter circuit in Fig. P7.15 step through?

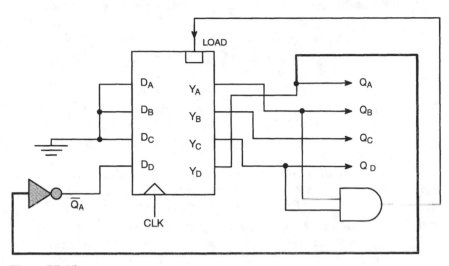

Figure P7.15

39. **Counters used in keyboard decoding** Consider a four-by-four matrix keyboard, diagrammed in Fig. P7.16. When a button (shown as a circle in the figure)

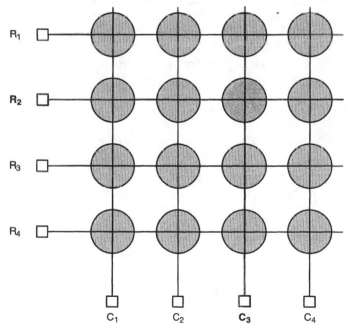

Figure P7.16 Matrix keyboard.

is pushed, a row wire and column wire are connected together; otherwise no wires are touching. Your problem is to decode the keyboard, that is, have a four-bit word representing a particular button be presented by the system as long as that button is pushed. At your disposal are the following:

A 4 → 1 MUX
A 2 → 4 deMUX
A four-bit synchronous binary counter, like the 74169
A 1000-pulses/s generator for CLOCK input
A hexadecimal display with blanking input

Connect the pulse generator to the counter and let the counter output represent the button pushed. How should the MUX and deMUX be connected to the counter and the keyboard to finish the job? Should the R's and C's be input or output?

In your design, what happens if more than one button is pushed at the same time? What is the worst-case reaction time (delay between contact and appearance of valid output) to a button push in your system?

‡40. In the computer game Tetris, pressing keyboard letter N allows the player to toggle between viewing the next shape and not viewing it. (Viewing the next shape costs points in scoring.) Sketch what additional sequential circuitry would be needed in a Tetris hardware system in order to implement the "next" feature. Assume you have available blocks for random generation of the next shape (one of six) and for sending a "next" shape to the screen. Show your answer as additional blocks in a diagram.

‡41. **Finite versus infinite state machines**   Virtually any practical sequencer problem can be solved with a *finite* state machine—one that contains a finite number of flip-flops. Can you think of a problem, any problem, that would require an infinite number of states for its solution? (Think of a computational problem, but note that computational problems are not the only infinite state problems.)

References

FLETCHER, W. I. 1980. *An engineering approach to digital design.* Englewood Cliffs, N.J.: Prentice Hall.

MEYERS, G. J. 1980. *Digital system design with LSI bit-slice logic.* New York: John Wiley & Sons.

MICK, J., AND J. BRICK. 1980. *Bit slice microprocessor design.* New York: McGraw-Hill.

TROXEL, D. 1994. *Notes for a short course in PAL design.* Cambridge, Mass.: MIT.

MASTERING DESIGN

Memory

I suspect we never really remember very much about a particular experience. Instead, our various agencies selectively decide, unconsciously, to transfer only certain states into their long-term memories—perhaps because they have been classified as useful, dangerous, unusual, or significant in other respects. It would be of little use for us simply to maintain vast stores of un-classified memories if, every time we needed one we had to search through all of them. (Minsky 1986, 153)

OVERVIEW

How does a student remember the truth table for an XOR gate? Maybe she remembers what page it's on in a book; maybe she writes it down on page six of her own notebook; maybe she writes it down over and over on scrap paper until it becomes imprinted in her brain; or maybe she is able to derive it from the words *OR* and *exclusive*. Each strategy is possible, and each has its counterpart in digital memory. Each of the first three ways of remembering involves knowing *where* the information is and being able to interpret *what* the information is. In terms of computer memory, these are issues of **address** and **contents,** and they will be fundamental to what you learn in Chapter 8. What about the student's fourth approach to recalling the XOR truth table? It's related to **content-addressable memory,** which is one of the final topics in this chapter.

In Chapter 8 you will study the organization of *digital random-access read and write semiconductor* memory. Let's deconstruct: to say "semiconductor" memory contrasts it with magnetic and optical memory, such as tapes, floppy disks, hard drives, and CD-ROMs.[1] While issues of address and contents apply also to magnetic and optical memory, their detailed consideration is beyond the scope of this introductory material. **Semiconductor memory** comes in the form of silicon IC chips, which can hold millions of bits of information each. A memory **cell** (or word) is one memory location (identified by a unique address) and its contents. Chapter 8 starts by showing you

---

[1] Hodges (1977, 130) divides digital memories into categories of moving-surface and entirely electronic. Tapes, disks, and CD-ROMs all involve moving surfaces and mechanical drives. Typical access time for moving-surface memories is about 20 ms to reach a sector of the disk; then data can be read at about 10^7 bits per second. Moving-surface storage media retain their data when power is off; they are often used for archival storage of information (e.g., databases), which may change little compared with semiconductor RAM in a computer.

427

how one memory cell can be constructed from latches. After making a small memory system with addressed cells, you will see how to link together multiple memory chips into large memory systems; the three-state outputs you were introduced to in Chapter 1 will play a role. **Random-access** memory contrasts with the shift registers you were introduced to in Chapter 6: any memory location in a random-access memory has the same access time as any other location, whereas information stored in different locations in a shift register will become available at the output after different numbers of clock pulses.

We've already looked at **read-only memory;** in Chapter 4 you saw that ROM is a type of combinational circuit wired, or programmed, to contain information that cannot easily be changed on the fly. The contents of **random-access read/write memory (RAM)** can be changed (be written to) at the same clock speed it can be read at. We will consider two types of RAM: **static RAM** and **dynamic RAM.** Both static RAM and dynamic RAM require power to be applied continuously (unlike ROM), or their contents will disappear. Dynamic RAM costs much less per bit than static RAM but requires periodic *refreshing,* or its contents may fade away. Methods for **addressing** memory will be considered later in Chapter 8. You will see that having separate row and column decoders for a square matrix of memory cells provides an efficient method of finding the one location in 2^N sought by N bits of address input to a memory system.

8.1 THE IMPORTANCE OF MEMORY

8.1.1 The Economics of Memory

If this text were written with regard to the *economic* value of various digital ICs, this chapter on memory would take up 40% of the book. And a particular type of semiconductor memory—dynamic RAM—would account for 60% of the memory pages. (Later in Chapter 8 the difference between dynamic and static RAM chips will be spelled out.) For now consider the following table from the January 1990 issue of *Electronics* on United States sales of *digital*[2] integrated circuits:

Category	Dollars (in Billions)	
Memories:		
Dynamic RAM	$2.84	(60%)
Static RAM	0.75	(16%)
ROM	1.19	(24%)
Memories, total	**$4.78**	**(40%)**
Custom ICs (PALs, etc.)	2.93	(25%)
Microprocessors (486, etc.)	2.56	(22%)
Standard logic families (TTL, etc.)	1.07	(9%)
Special-purpose processors (DSP, etc.)	0.51	(4%)
Total	**$11.85**	

[2]The same table shows that linear ICs accounted for $2.5 billion in sales—21% of the digital IC total. Discrete semiconductors (such as transistors and diodes) amounted to $2.2 billion, and optoelectronic devices (such as LEDs) were $0.72 billion in sales.

The great majority of memory chips end up in computers. As an example of the tremendous increase in memory use in computers, consider that in the mid-1980s a PC-AT computer had a random-access memory capacity of 640,000 words × 16 bits/word ≈ 10^7 bits; in the mid-1990s a 486-type personal computer typically has an order of magnitude more RAM. The fastest-growing segment for memory chips in the 1990s, however, is in telecommunications circuitry. You'll learn more about digital communication circuits in Chapter 9.

8.1.2 Moore's Law Applied to Memory Chips

It's worth noting a few facts about the evolution of memory chips over the past couple of decades. Each new memory chip on the market has more bits of storage, less power consumption per bit, and faster access time than its predecessors. Gordon E. Moore (not related to Moore of the Moore-machine!) observed in 1964 that the number of components per integrated circuit (pick the most densely populated circuit at the time, usually a memory chip) doubled every year, starting with a one-component planar IC transistor in 1959. Moore's "law" has held up fairly well. In 1995, 64-Mbyte dynamic RAM chips contained something like 10^8 components; $10^8 \approx 2^{27}$, so over 35 years there have been 27 doublings in chip density, or about one doubling every $1\frac{1}{4}$ years. Correspondingly, the price per bit of memory drops about 25% a year. Users of memory find delight in these numbers, and manufacturers of IC chips feel economic pressure to make more memory just to stay even. See Prince (1991); Noyce (1977); and the special issue of *IEEE Transactions on Solid State Circuits* (November 1991) devoted to memory.

8.1.3 RAM versus ROM

Recall that read-only memory chips are combinational SOP circuits able to remember the output (contents) of a truth table when prompted by a line of the truth table's input (address). Once programmed with the contents of a particular truth table, a ROM chip has a brief propagation delay,[3] in the tens of nanoseconds range. But the programming of a UV-erasable EPROM requires many seconds to erase the old contents, requires the application of special voltages for writing in new contents, and requires further hundreds of milliseconds to step through all the addresses in synchrony with the writing pulses for a new contents file. In most applications that's

---

[3]Propagation delay (or access time) t_{pd} is the interval between appearance of a new address and appearance of correct contents at the output pins. In the figure below, the address changes to HI and then, a time t_{pd} later, the contents change to HI.

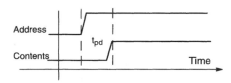

at the end of Chapter 5 when the register (a set of D flip-flops all connected to the same clock) was introduced. However, a register represents only one memory cell, whereas we need to design fast memory systems that rival ROM in the number of words per chip. For a dense memory system we don't need to use clocked flip-flops.

8.2   MEMORY CELLS FROM LATCHES

We start with what will be called **static RAM**: memory cells made from set-reset latches. Recall that once a set ($SR = 10$) or reset ($SR = 01$) signal is applied (even briefly) to the latch, the output Q changes within nanoseconds to a set ($Q = 1$) or reset ($Q = 0$) value. The output remains in its "programmed" state (is remembered) after latch inputs return to a no-change condition ($SR = 00$).

Each latch in a memory system can store one bit of data. To begin, we will deal with one-bit words, where a word is one location in memory, accessed by a unique address code. A one-bit word has one bit of contents, so each word will be handled by one latch.

EXAMPLE 1

We start small, with two unclocked latches—the smallest memory system possible bigger than one latch! Our first memory will therefore have two words: one latch with address 0, the other with address 1. Shown in Fig. 8.1 is a circuit for reading outputs Q_0, Q_1. The top latch has address 1; when ADDRESS = 1, whatever is on Q_1 will be DATA$_{OUT}$. The AND-OR circuit on the right is a $2 \rightarrow 1$ MUX. So far, this circuit is a read-only memory.

Can we can make our system a read *and write* memory by sending the address signal to the left in order to control routing on a decoder, as shown in Fig. 8.2? Yes, data will reach its designated latch; the S and R inputs are connected by inverters,

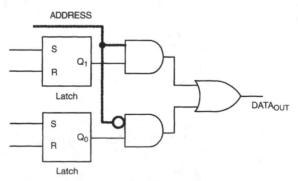

Figure 8.1   Latches with output address.

---

[4]Electrically erasable, programmable ROMs (EEPROMs) are blurring the RAM-ROM distinction. Especially significant is the *flash* EEPROM chip, in which all cells can be quickly erased at once (Haznedar 1991, 490).

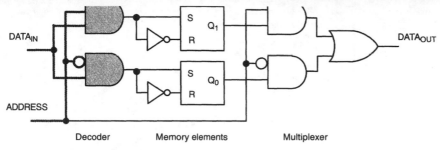

Figure 8.2 Latches with data and output address.

making the input similar to the data input of a D flip-flop. But the circuit has two limitations. First, it doesn't take advantage of a latch's no-change state—here S or R is always 1; second, there is no signal to tell the circuit when the user wants to write to a particular latch. These limitations can be fixed with three-input AND gates that accommodate a read/write line. The circuit in Fig. 8.3 adds the read/write feature, highlighted. The addresses of the two memory locations are shown on the latches. Data (either 0 or 1) can be written to a memory location only when two conditions are met: WRITE mode enabled, $W/\overline{R} = 1$, and address location selected.

The write signal acts like a level-sensitive clock (see Chapter 5). As long as WRITE is HI, data can be written to the latch in question; in fact, the value of $DATA_{IN}$ at the time $W/\overline{R}$ makes a transition back to read is the *only* data that will stay in the memory location contents! The $W/\overline{R}$ control, the data input, and the address will normally come from a controller with a synchronous FSM, but the RAM cell itself is constructed with unclocked latches.

The design of Fig. 8.3 sends the $W/\overline{R}$ line to the output multiplexer as an enable control; therefore during a WRITE operation, $DATA_{OUT}$ will be LO. Normally the user doesn't care what the RAM output is during a WRITE operation. Later we will combine the IN and OUT pins with a bidirectional three-state arrangement, so new contents will take over the data line during a WRITE.

We can symbolize our 2×1 RAM unit and package the design as shown in Fig. 8.4. We call the memory a 2×1 RAM cell because it has two addressable locations with

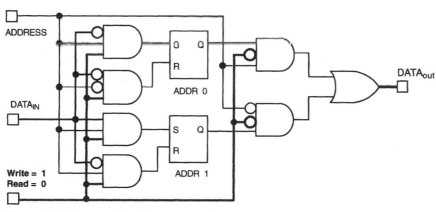

Figure 8.3 Improved two-bit memory element.

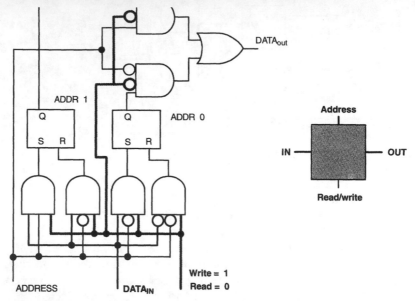

Figure 8.4 2×1 memory redraw, with icon.

one bit output per location. *Notice that the data input (for writing) and data output are on separate "pins."*

The design of memory cells when the same cell is to be repeated thousands of times on an integrated circuit is a challenging task. There must be a minimum of transistors, silicon area, power consumption, and access time if the chip is to be practical and competitive. The design above would require many more than four transistors, which is the minimum needed for a static RAM IC cell. See Haznedar (1991, 468–469) for transistor-by-transistor schematics of minimal static RAM cells. See also Geiger et al. (1990, chap. 8) and Sedia and Smith (1991, 961).

8.2.1 An Efficient Static RAM Layout

EXAMPLE 2

A static RAM (SRAM) cell in a commercial IC memory chip is a model of simplicity. Figure 8.5 shows how a bistable pair of inverters (like what you saw in the beginning of Chapter 5) can form the heart of a static RAM. Either inverter 1 is HI and inverter 2 is LO or vice versa. If the memory cell is selected by the address line, the two switches in the diagram will be closed (see Fig. 8.6; the switches are actually MOS transistors). The lines DATA and $\overline{\text{DATA}}$ project down a column (in which they contact other cell switches) to sense amplifiers that detect whether the voltage on DATA is greater or less than the voltage on $\overline{\text{DATA}}$. The other cells in the column share the same sense

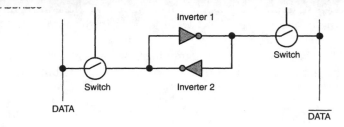

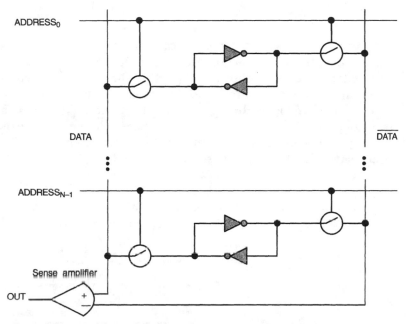

Figure 8.5 Bistable memory element implemented with two inverters.

Figure 8.6 A row of the efficient memory elements of Fig. 8.5.

amplifier. Since only one address line at a time can be active, only one of the memory cells in a column has access to the sense amplifier inputs. If the output of the sense amplifier is positive, the content of the addressed static RAM cell is reported as a 1.

8.2.2 Three-State Outputs and Memory I/O

In the commercial static RAM cell above, where does data enter for writing? It seems that data to be written must share the same line used for reading. To share the same wire, signals must either be multiplexed or have **three-state control**. In practice, the data-in and contents-out of RAM often share a common pin through utilization of three-state outputs. Three-state outputs were discussed in Chapter 1. Remember that the third state of a three-state output is disconnection (sometimes the disconnection state is called the THI-Z state, short for *high impedance*). Read/write control determines the three-state status of the I/O pin and whether it is in the input or the output mode.

A three-state buffer is a noninverting gate whose output can be put in a state of disconnection. A three-state buffer is shown by the following symbol:

The arrow input is the three-state control. Typically an active-low signal asserted on the three-state control enables connection between input and output of the buffer.

A **bidirectional transceiver** is shown in Fig. 8.7. It has two noninverting three-state buffers. From outside, the bidirectional transceiver looks like a $1 \rightarrow 2$ decoder. Inside, data to be written passes through a three-state buffer and then joins up to the data wires connected between a column of memory cells and a sense amplifier. The multiplexing scheme of Fig. 8.7 and the single memory element of Fig. 8.5 are combined in the small RAM cell symbol shown in Fig. 8.8.

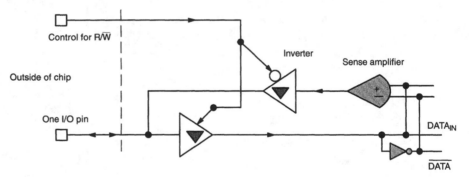

Figure 8.7   I/O Multiplexing for $1 \times N$ memory element.

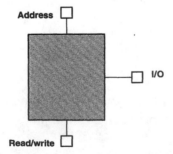

Figure 8.8   Single I/O pin version of SRAM cell.

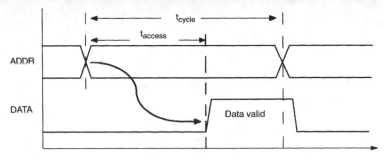

Figure 8.9 Read cycle timing diagram.

8.2.3 Access and Other Timing Parameters

Having set up the static design of a RAM, we are now ready to look at timing performance. RAM cells are governed by some of the same timing parameters as flip-flops. Notice that WRITE and ADDRESS inputs act like level-sensitive clocks. When a level-sensitive clock leaves its enable state, setup and hold times govern when DATA should be valid.

Let's start with READ timing, so the only enabling input will be a properly decoded address. In the READ mode, the parameter of interest is **access time** from the application of a new address to the appearance of correct data. Address access time is often listed as t_{AA} in data sheets. In the 1990s a static RAM chip may have an access time in the 10–40 ns range. For some chips a longer **cycle time** (total delay from one memory access to the next) governs the rate at which data can be read from consecutive locations. But for many chips memory cycle time equals access time. If data must be available for another minimum amount of time (hold time) before the next read can occur, then $t_{cycle} > t_{access}$, as shown in Fig. 8.9. Data are not valid after address changes until the next access time elapses.

The timing diagram of Fig. 8.9 introduces two conventions. The first is that crossed ADDR lines represent transitions. The second convention is that a curved arrow indicates cause and effect. The address change is the cause of the subsequent data change.

Write Cycle Timing   Our RAM cell is sensitive to the level of write signal; therefore, *when* the edge of an (active-low) $\overline{\text{WRITE}}$ pulse rises determines *what* data will be written to a location. However, if the address changes while $\overline{\text{WRITE}}$ is LO, false data may be written into the previous address. Address and data must be stable for reliable writing.

The following timing parameters are illustrated in the write cycle of Fig. 8.10.

t_{ASW} Write address setup time

t_{AHW} Write address hold time

t_{WP} Minimum write pulse width

t_{DS} Data setup time

t_{DH} Data hold time

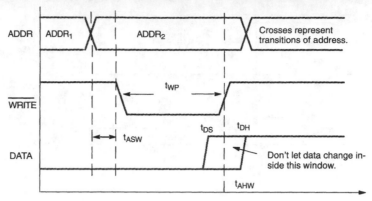

Figure 8.10 Write cycle for SRAM.

In the timing diagram in Fig. 8.10, $\overline{\text{WRITE}}$ is an active-low signal that must go low after address changes and before data changes in order for a proper write operation to take place. The falling of the WRITE line makes the I/O pin a receiver of data. In the waveforms of Fig. 8.10, ADDR_2 is first stabilized and then, after address setup time t_{ASW}, the WRITE line goes active-low. What happens if WRITE goes low before t_{ASW} elapses? Data stored in location ADDR_1 may be affected. The WRITE signal must be asserted for at least t_{WP}, or a valid write operation may not occur. Data must be valid for the setup time t_{DS} before and the hold time t_{DH} after the rising edge of the WRITE signal.

8.3   MEMORY CHIPS WORKING TOGETHER

A **memory system** is a set of memory cells organized to be read from and written to by another system (often the central processor of a computer) that supplies addresses and control signals and handles incoming and outgoing data. A memory system generally needs more cells, with wider contents, than a single RAM chip can provide. Many memory chips must be wired together—for address, data, and read/write control—to make a memory system work. A new control signal is needed for a multi-chip memory system: **chip-enable.** Chip-enable selects which chip or chips are to be read from or written to.

8.3.1   Chip-Enable Control

Consider first combining the I/O pins of two chips. Because input and output paths now share the same wire on the RAM chip, using a multiplexer for two chips is not straightforward; DATA_{OUT} needs to be multiplexed, but DATA_{IN} needs to be decoded. Extending three-state output is a better idea. We start by separating read/write control from the control that selects one chip out of many. In Fig. 8.11 we

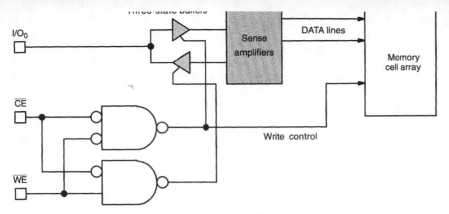

Figure 8.11 Interface between memory cells and external controls.

have two RAM chip control signals, write enable ($\overline{\text{WE}}$) and chip-enable ($\overline{\text{CE}}$), both active low. Notice that if $\overline{\text{CE}}$ is HI, both NANDs are disabled and both three-state buffers are disabled. If $\overline{\text{WE}}$ is HI and $\overline{\text{CE}}$ is LO, the chip is selected for reading; if both $\overline{\text{WE}}$ and $\overline{\text{CE}}$ are LO, the chip can be written to. Some RAM chips have separate chip-enable and output-enable pins for more control of output. Our 2×1 RAM chip black box[5] now looks like Fig. 8.12.

8.3.2 A Multichip Memory

A multichip memory system may need more address pins than one chip can handle. The higher-order address pins of the system must be decoded as chip-enable controls, shown in the next example.

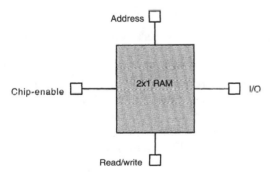

Figure 8.12 Black box symbol for a two-bit SRAM with chip-enable.

[5]In the notation $N \times M$ *RAM, N* is the total number of memory locations and *M* is the number of output bits. A static RAM may be $16K \times 1$ or $4K \times 4$ and use the same number of bits for storage.

EXAMPLE 3

Use two 2 × 1 RAM chips to create a 4 × 1 memory system.

Answer A 4 × 1 memory needs two address pins, but it needs only one data wire. Figure 8.13 shows the two RAM chips with their I/O pins tied together for the one-bit system data path width. The least significant address line goes to the address pin of each chip. Note that the most significant address bit is decoded, so that chip 1 responds to addresses 00 and 01 while chip 2 responds to 10 and 11. Active-low $\overline{CE}$ is acting like a second address pin, and during a READ operation $\overline{CE}$ selects which chip gains control of the DATA wire. What does $\overline{CE}$ do during a WRITE operation?

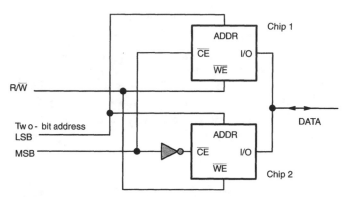

Figure 8.13 Decoding higher-order address bit (the MSB).

EXAMPLE 4

Use 2 × 1 RAM chips to create a 4 × 2 memory system.

Answer Now the content of each location is two bits wide. The diagram in Fig. 8.14 on the next page shows four 2 × 1 RAM chips organized for a 4 × 2 system. Again, the LSB address line goes to the ADDR input of each chip, and the MSB address is decoded at the inverter in order to chip-enable the bottom or top row of chips. Chips 3 and 4 provide the more significant data bit, while chips 1 and 2 are joined for the LSB data. Together the output wires form a **bus.**[6] In fact, the address, data, and $W/\overline{R}$ bits can be considered the memory system bus. The presence of a chip-enable control on a RAM chip greatly facilitates designing RAM into multichip memory.

---

[6] A bus is a parallel set of wires in which each wire has a defined function. The definition of bus functions is called the **bus protocol.** A bus connects one system with another, and each system must use the protocol for successful operation. A bus, for example, may connect a memory system to a computer, and wires in the bus may be defined for address, contents, read/write, clock, and so on. Some well-known buses are the S100 bus, VME bus, STD bus, microchannel, RS-232, and Macintosh's nuBUS. The complete specification of a bus may include the physical arrangement of the wires and the connectors and may define timing, parameters, and maximum and minimum voltages allowed.

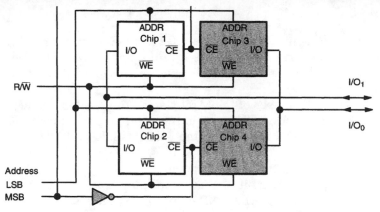

Figure 8.14 Two-address memory, with two bits at each address.

8.4   TWO COMMERCIAL STATIC RAM CHIPS

Next we consider the pinouts of two static RAM chips, one that saw its sales peak around 1980, the other a more recent chip. Commercial memory chips have on-board decoders for addressing.

EXAMPLE 5

An older MOS static RAM chip that multiplexes incoming and outgoing data is the Intel 2114, a 1024-words $\times$ 4-bits-per-word chip. Its pinout is shown in Fig. 8.15. The 2114 has 10 address pins ($1024 = 2^{10}$), four data pins, $\overline{\text{CHIP-SELECT}}$, $\overline{\text{WRITE-ENABLE}}$, power, and ground—a total of 18 pins. It does not have a separate output-enable. Compare its pinout with the pinout of the 2764 EPROM memory chip from Section 4.3 of Chapter 4. The access time of the 2114 is about 200 ns, quite slow by 1990 standards.

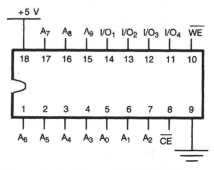

Figure 8.15   Pinout of 2114 SRAM.

EXAMPLE 6

A newer, 22-pin CMOS static RAM with both $\overline{CE}$ and $\overline{OE}$ is the Micron MT5C1605. The '1605 is a 4K × 4 chip, meaning that its 16K bits are arranged as 4K words of 4 bits each. Since 2^{12} = 4K, 12 address pins are needed if the whole address is to be presented in one cycle.

The '1605 is a smaller member of the MT5C family of SRAM chips, which range up to a size 1M × 4 (MT5C1M4B2). The 5 in the family name means the chips are powered by 5 V, not 3.3 V. Each chip in the MT5C family is designed with four transistors per cell.

A logic block diagram for the '1605 is shown in Fig. 8.16. Input and output are combined on a single pin for each bit, as shown. The three-state buffers in the chip are disabled for a LO control signal. The AND gates to the right result in the following operation table for the '1605:

	$\overline{OE}$	$\overline{CE}$	$\overline{WE}$	I/O
READ	L	L	H	Contents
WRITE	X	L	L	Data in
Disabled	H	L	H	HI-Z

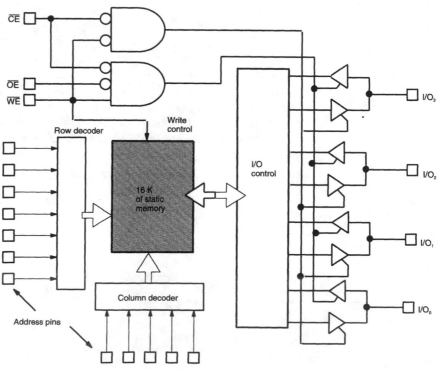

Figure 8.16   Internal organization of MT5C1605 SRAM.

For the chip to be read from, CE must be LO and WE HI. In that case the I/O pins are enabled as output. If a '1605 is ganged with other '1605s for a larger memory system, the $\overline{CE}$s must be tied to decoder outputs that are selected by higher-order address pins. Only when $\overline{CE}$ and $\overline{WE}$ are both LO will the chip write to the location specified by the address pins. If $\overline{CE}$ is HI, I/O is also disabled and the chip goes into a low-power standby state.

The fastest version of the MT5C1605 has an access time of 9 ns. Address setup and hold times are zero! Data setup and hold times for the fastest version are 5 ns and 1 ns minimum, respectively.

8.4.1 Sizing Memory System for Memory Chips

Memory chips and memory systems are sized by the number of words (locations, addresses) and by the number of bits per word. To generate a formula for calculating the number Q of memory chips required, consider a memory space of 2^N words, M bits/word, to be served by RAM chips of word size 2^J, K bits per word. The values J and N are normally powers of 2. Assume that $N > J$ and $M \geq K$; if *both* these assumptions are not true, then the memory system can be built with one chip! The system will need at least $2^{N-J} = Q$ chips. If $M = K$, exactly 2^{N-J} chips will be needed. A total of N address lines will be needed, which the memory system must decode for 2^N locations. If the word size M of the system is greater than the word size K of the memory chip to be used, either M/K is a number with no remainder, in which case

$$2^{N-J} \cdot \frac{M}{K} = Q$$

memory chips will be needed, or M/K has a remainder, in which case we compute $row = (M \bmod K) + 1$ and find that

$$2^{N-J} \cdot ((M \bmod K) + 1) = 2^{N-J} \cdot row = Q$$

memory chips will be needed.

EXAMPLE 7

My 1988 IBM-RT workstation had 8 Mbyte of RAM comprising 4M ($4M = 2^{22} = 4,194,304$) words of memory, each word 16 bits in size. My 1994 Sun Sparc 5 has 32 million words of RAM, each word 32 bits wide. If the two computers were to be given SRAM chips for their computer RAM, how many chips would have been needed in (a) 1987 (b) 1991 (c) 1995?

Answer In terms of the equation above, for the RT computer the exponent is $N = 22$ and the word size is $M = 16$. For the newer Sun, $N = 26$ and $M = 32$. Typical commercially available SRAMs in 1987, 1991, and 1995 were 16K × 4, 64K × 4, and 256K × 4 bits, respectively, which result in J's of 12, 16, and 20. Applying the

$$2^{N-J} \cdot \frac{M}{K} = 2^{22-12} \cdot \frac{16}{4} = 4096 \text{ chips in 1987}$$

$$2^{22-16} \cdot \frac{16}{4} = 256 \text{ chips in 1991}$$

$$2^{22-20} \cdot \frac{16}{4} = 16 \text{ chips in 1995}$$

The 1995 number seems reasonable, but not the 1987 and 1991 chip requirements. Applying the sizing formula to the Sparc 5 RAM requirements, we get

$$2^{N-J} \cdot \frac{M}{K} = 2^{26-12} \cdot \frac{16}{4} = 64K \text{ chips in 1987}$$

$$2^{26-16} \cdot \frac{16}{4} = 4096 \text{ chips in 1991}$$

$$2^{26-20} \cdot \frac{16}{4} = 256 \text{ chips in 1995}$$

which are all large numbers of chips! Later in Chapter 8 you'll see that *dynamic RAM* chips have even greater storage density than SRAM chips; DRAM is the memory technology that makes large computer RAM practical.

8.5 GENERAL FORM OF A MEMORY SYSTEM

Memory systems are part of many digital circuits, from calculators to data acquisition units. Sometimes, as in data acquisition, memory systems are used mainly to write newly acquired data; sometimes, as in table lookup calculations, memory is used mainly to read out stored values of math functions.

A semiconductor RAM system in a computer has the general appearance shown in Fig. 8.17, where input and output share the same bus; which way signals go on the data bus is determined by the read/write control line. The three divisions of the memory signals—address, data, and control—will find use later in the text (Chapter 11).

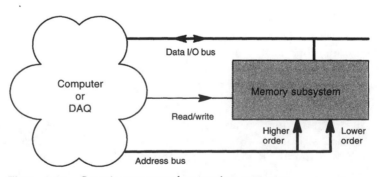

Figure 8.17 Generic memory subsystem in a computer.

features of a memory controller:

1. In the memory system there must be a decoder for higher-order address bits so that chip-enable inputs can select which memory chip is to be read from or written to.

2. There must be a three-state enable on the $DATA_{OUT}$ register of the controller; during read operations the $DATA_{OUT}$ buffer will be disabled.

3. **DATA storage register** holds output of RAM.

4. A finite state machine can be used to load a **memory address register** *before* a write pulse is sent to the memory. In Fig. 8.18, four memory chips on the right plus a higher-order address decoder form the memory system. The controlling is done by a synchronous FSM that uses the same clock as do three allied registers. The enable of a three-state buffer is controlled by the FSM, too. Where the next address comes from and where the data go to are suggested by the data oval. Even though the memory chips are not clocked, they are part of a synchronous system.

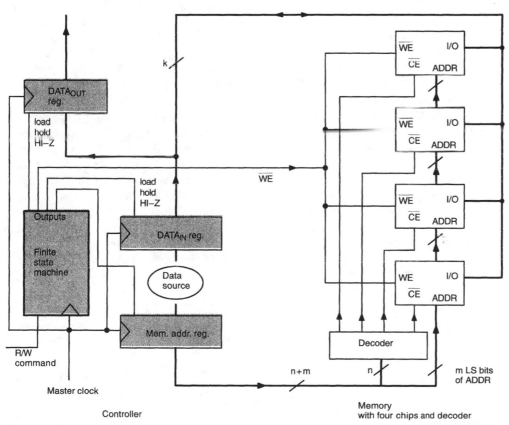

Figure 8.18 FSM memory controller.

The FSM has two main functions: controlling READ and WRITE operations. If you look back at the timing waveforms for WRITE, you see that the address must be stable before $\overline{WE}$ is sent LO. The controller can create this delay with a multiphase clock or a one-hot sequencer like you saw in Chapter 7, or the WRITE cycle can be segmented into several states that the FSM sequences through. Either way, the FSM clock ticks faster than the cycle time for a WRITE or READ operation. See chap. 4, "Function RAM Chip Testing," in Van de Goor (1991).

8.6 DYNAMIC RANDOM ACCESS MEMORY

A 1-million-bit memory chip (like the MT5C1005 static RAM) with multiplexed I/O pins and chip-select input streamlines memory chip design to a great extent. But more can be done to make a denser memory chip. We now consider another design efficiency: **dynamic RAM (DRAM).** DRAM is important from technical, space-saving, and economic perspectives.

Up to this point, we have dealt with memory contents stored in ROM (Chapter 4) and in bistable latches (this chapter). An electronic circuit can also "remember" by storing charge on a capacitor.[7] Charge storage on a tiny capacitor is the idea behind dynamic RAM. It's called dynamic because the charge on the capacitor can leak off through a large resistance unless the DRAM cell is refreshed by special circuitry.

Static RAM, based on latches, needs no refreshing. Why go to the trouble to build leaky memory and the refresh circuitry required to keep it from forgetting? Because DRAM can be the *lowest-cost* and *most densely packed* of semiconductor memory. State-of-the-art DRAMs can have four times as many bits per chip as state-of-the-art static RAMs. A static RAM bistable latch cell can be as small as four transistors, but a DRAM cell can be as small as one transistor! See Fig. 8.19. (See Sedra and Smith 1991, 964. In some designs the capacitor can be connected to V_{DD} instead of ground—see Haznedar 1991.) Millions of memory cells can be placed on one IC; the advantage of a one-transistor DRAM cell over a four-transistor SRAM cell can be measured in terms of the millions of transistors (three per cell) *not* needed. A small part of a million saved transistors can be used for the extra refresh circuitry.

When the address line in Fig. 8.19 is active, the MOS transistor acts as a closed switch. If the memory is to be read, the voltage on the capacitor is detected on the data (out) line by a sense amplifier, similar to the sense amplifier mentioned in

---

[7] A capacitor remembers charge the same way a bucket remembers water. In both, the amount of the thing stored can be read out through the effect of a "force," either voltage or water pressure. The water pressure at the bottom of the bucket is proportional to the height of water in the bucket, so measuring the water pressure in the bucket reads out how much water has been stored. Dynamic RAM stores charge as water is stored in a leaky bucket. The amount of charge stored is proportional to the voltage across the capacitor: $V = Q/C$ where V is voltage, Q is charge, and C is capacitance. Since current $I = dQ/dt$, then

$$I = C\frac{dV}{dt} \quad \text{or} \quad V_C(t) = \frac{1}{C}\int_{t_0}^{t} I(t)\,dt + v_C(t_0)$$

The capacitor voltage is proportional to the time integral of current. Therefore, the capacitor voltage cannot change instantaneously: it "remembers" the history of its current input. If there is a "leak in the bucket," it can be modeled by a first-order circuit having resistor in parallel with the capacitor. See, for example, Cunningham and Stuller (1994).

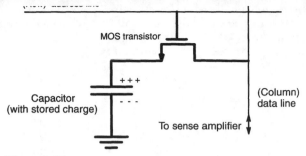

Figure 8.19 Schematic of one DRAM memory cell.

the discussion of SRAM design. In a practical DRAM, many (thousands of) memory locations may be connected to the same data I/O line; except for the particular address line activated, all the MOS transistors involved will be OFF, with high-impedance three-state outputs.[8]

If a write or refresh operation is called for, the data line becomes an input line. When the proper address turns on the MOS transistor in the DRAM cell, the capacitor can be charged or recharged from data-in.

In Fig. 8.20 a DRAM is shown with two cells, both in the same column; a three-state driver for writing; and a sense amplifier for reading. The address lines are now labeled as *row lines* for a reason to be explained in Section 8.6.1. The capacitor in a DRAM cell is tiny, on the order of femtofarads (10^{-15} farad); it's a stray capacitance associated

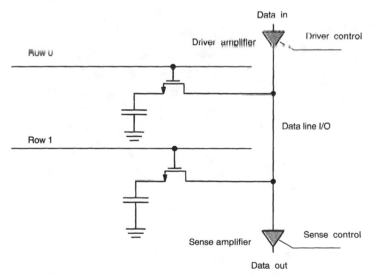

Figure 8.20 Organization of single two-cell DRAM column.

---

[8]In the 4116 dynamic RAM chip, 16,384 locations are all connected to one output line. This connection strategy saves pins on the chip—only an I/O pin is required. Even with this pin-saving, the entire address of 14 bits is read in two seven-bit phases on a 4116 ($2^{14} = 16K$).

MOS transistor can provide enough of a path to ground to discharge the capacitor to below noise level in less than 10 ms.[9] Now, before attacking the problem of dynamic RAM refresh, we discuss how a DRAM chip is addressed.

8.6.1 Row-Column Addressing of DRAM

Like a static RAM chip, a typical DRAM chip is physically organized as a square matrix of cells. DRAM chips contain 2^M cells, where M is an even integer. If access time is important, then a user will look to static RAM chips, whose access times can be a factor of 5 shorter than those of comparable DRAMs. If a user is looking for many memory cells per chip at lower cost, DRAMs are the choice. DRAM users often want to pack as many chips as possible onto computer circuit boards that have restricted surface areas. DRAM manufacturers accommodate the desire for small footprint by cutting in half the number of address pins and introducing row and column pins.

Figure 8.21 shows the basic organization of the row-column system for a chip with 2^M cells. The row and column latches (registers) and the address decoders are inside the DRAM chip. A row address will activate one row line, which will select all the cells in the activated row. When the column address arrives and activates one column line, the column line selects, by three-state-enable, one sense amplifier to take over the external output line. The selected sense amplifier is shaded in the figure. Exercise 32 asks you to place data-in and write-enable in the diagram. By virtue of the row signal

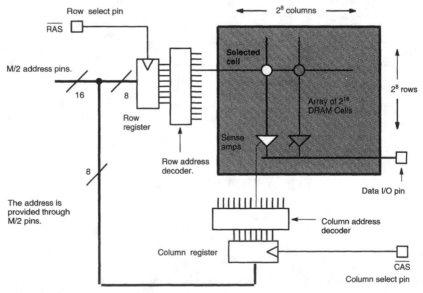

Figure 8.21   Internal organization of $M = 16$ (64 Kb) DRAM.

[9]If you've had a course in circuits, you may recall that the time constant associated with the decay of a capacitor is $C \cdot R$, where R is the parallel resistance across the capacitor.

selecting all cells in a row and the column signal then selecting only one of the row
cells for final output, the DRAM allows only one cell access to the external I/O pin.

In most popular DRAM chips, the row and column select inputs are active-low and referred to as $\overline{\text{RAS}}$ and $\overline{\text{CAS}}$ ("rass" and "cass"—row-address strobe and column-address strobe). Since the row and column registers share the same set of address pins, it normally takes two steps to bring a complete address to a DRAM chip. The row address always comes first. You can appreciate that the need to address a DRAM in two steps will make the DRAM twice as slow as it would be if it had all the address pins on the chip. However, DRAM chips are often used in large-scale memory systems where data or instructions are read out from one consecutive cell after another. When the memory cells to be accessed are consecutive, efficiency can be gained through **page-mode addressing** (it could be named "same-row addressing"). To perform page-mode addressing, maintain the row address constant while stepping through a sequence of column addresses. Page-mode addressing speeds up the reading of many same-row locations because $\overline{\text{RAS}}$ need only be asserted once per row, or "page." If a DRAM chip is to be read out in its entirety (for example, in the transfer of DRAM contents to a hard disk), then page-mode addressing makes the process faster. The timing of page-mode addressing for a sequence of read cycles will look like Fig. 8.22, where a long $\overline{\text{RAS}}$ provides an envelope for many $\overline{\text{CAS}}$s. The *falling* edge of $\overline{\text{RAS}}$ is coincident with the row address, and the *falling* edges of $\overline{\text{CAS}}$s are coincident with column addresses *on the common address lines*. $\overline{\text{RAS}}$ need be incremented only after a whole row, or page, is read out (or written to). In Fig. 8.22 setup and hold times are approximated.

DRAM Output   A DRAM chip can have many cells and few outputs. In 1994 chips with 16M ($= 2^{24}$) cells and 1, 4, 8, or 16 bits of output were commercially available. The mechanism of the column signal selecting one of many sense amplifiers explains how one output pin can be fed by many inputs. Figure 8.23 isolates the column decoder and sense amplifiers to illustrate the idea. In the case of 4M × 1-bit DRAM, the square root of 4M ($2048 = 10^{11}$) is the number of column address outputs. The one-bit output is formed by 2048 sense amplifier three-state outputs, all of which are

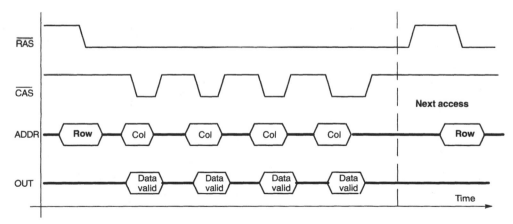

Figure 8.22 Timing of fast page-mode addressing of DRAM.

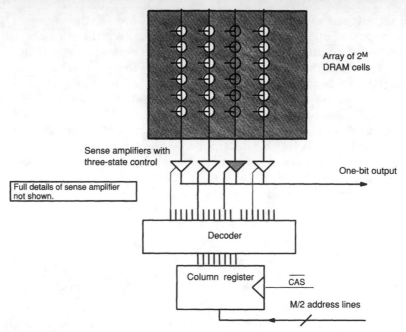

Array of 2^M DRAM cells

Sense amplifiers with three-state control

One-bit output

Full details of sense amplifier not shown.

Decoder

Column register

$\overline{\text{CAS}}$

M/2 address lines

Figure 8.23 Multiplexing of sense-amplifier outputs.

connected together. The active column signal selects which one of the sense amplifier outputs will be the chip output.

Difference between SRAM and DRAM   DRAM chips with one-bit output maintain separate input and output pins; for four or more bits per word, DRAM chips have input and output share I/O pins, as you saw for SRAMs. DRAMs substitute $\overline{\text{RAS}}$ and $\overline{\text{CAS}}$ signals for the chip-select on a SRAM.

8.6.2   Two Examples of Commercial DRAM Chips

EXAMPLE 8

Look at the pinout of the Micron Technology MT4264, a 64K × 1 DRAM chip, in Fig. 8.24.

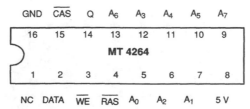

GND $\overline{\text{CAS}}$ Q A_6 A_3 A_4 A_5 A_7

| 16 | 15 | 14 | 13 | 12 | 11 | 10 | 9 |

MT 4264

| 1 | 2 | 3 | 4 | 5 | 6 | 7 | 8 |

NC   DATA $\overline{\text{WE}}$ $\overline{\text{RAS}}$ A_0 A_2 A_1 5 V

Figure 8.24   Pinout of MT4264 DRAM chip.

Q is output.

DATA is input (separate from output).

$\overline{RAS}$ is row-address strobe, active-low.

$\overline{CAS}$ is column-address strobe, active-low.

$\overline{WE}$ is active-low write enable.

A_0–A_7 are address pins. When $\overline{RAS}$ edge falls, A_0–A_7 are loaded in a row register; when $\overline{CAS}$ falls, A_0–A_7 are loaded in a column register.

Only 16 pins needed, and one of them is NC = no connection! Keeping pin count to a minimum in DRAM is important for maintaining a small footprint, which helps in placing as many chips as possible on a circuit board of limited size. See the data sheets in *Texas Inst. MOS Memory Data Book* (1986) for details. The data sheets also list a worst-case refresh time of 4 ms.

In order to read or write with the 4264, two sets of eight-bit addresses must be sent to the chip, one after the other, synchronous with $\overline{RAS}$ or $\overline{CAS}$ signals. Such two-stage addressing is one reason DRAM access time is about four times longer than static RAM access time. For a write operation, the value on the DATA pin is transferred to the loaded address on the rising edge of $\overline{WE}$. See the timing diagram in Section 8.8.2. When write-enable is asserted, a three-state buffer on the input pin is enabled and the input pin then has access to the data column line. More details about writing will be given when refreshing is discussed.

Now consider Micron Technology's 256K × 16-bit CMOS dynamic RAM, the MT4LC16256. It's a 40-pin chip, with pinout as shown in Fig. 8.25. The MT4LC16256 comes only in **surface-mount** style, with curved pins that must be soldered to the

V_{CC}	1		44	V_{SS}
DQ1	2		43	DQ16
DQ2	3		42	DQ15
DQ3	4		41	DQ14
DQ4	5		40	DQ13
V_{CC}	6		39	V_{SS}
DQ5	7		38	DQ12
DQ6	8		37	DQ11
DQ7	9		36	DQ10
DQ8	10		35	DQ9
		MT4LC16256		
NC	13		32	NC
$\overline{WEL}$	14		31	NC
$\overline{WEH}$	15		30	$\overline{CAS}$
$\overline{RAS}$	16		29	$\overline{OE}$
NC	17		28	A_8
A_0	18		27	A_7
A_1	19		26	A_6
A_2	20		25	A_5
A_3	21		24	A_4
V_{CC}	22		23	V_{SS}

Figure 8.25 Pinout of MT4LC16256 DRAM chip.

surface the chip rests on. Notice the gap in the middle and the numbers skipped in the numbering of the 40 pins. The MT4LC16256 chip is different in another way from all other chips considered up to this point in the text: the chip uses 3.3 V instead of 5.0 V. V_{CC} is connected to 3.3 V, and V_{SS} is grounded. A lower supply voltage means less heat dissipated in the chip. $\overline{WEL}$ and $\overline{WEH}$ stand for write-enable-low and write-enable-high and are separate write-enable controls for the upper and lower bytes of data. In the pin numbering in the figure, addresses start at A_0 and data pins start at DQ1. There are nine address pins because 256K requires 18 address bits (nine are for row, and nine are for column address). The 512 rows must be refreshed either every 8 or 64 ms, depending on the version of the chip used. Access time from $\overline{RAS}$ is 60–80 ns; the chip consumes 175 mW.

8.7 REFRESHING DYNAMIC RAM

Like a juggler keeping balls in the air by feats of timing and coordination, a dynamic RAM system must generate refresh signals that keep the charges on its cell capacitors. Leakage of charge off each DRAM cell capacitor must be corrected by refresh. During refresh, the sense amplifier is electronically connected back to the internal data I/O line for a time long enough for charge to be restored to the cell capacitor. Because a DRAM chip can contain up to 64 million storage capacitors, a way must be found to refresh more than one capacitor at a time, or the DRAM would spend nearly all its time refreshing and hardly ever be available for external reading or writing![11] Here's where the row-column organization of a DRAM chip comes in again: *all the cells in one row are refreshed at the same time.* Refresh generally occurs on the rising edge of $\overline{RAS}$.

EXAMPLE 9

The 4264 chip requires 16 address bits ($2^{16} = 65,536$). The square root of 2^{16} is $2^8 = 256$, so the chip is configured with 256 rows and 256 columns. As noted above, all the cells of one column are connected to one of 256 sense amplifiers. A refresh command is started by a row selection, after which all the cells of the selected row are refreshed simultaneously. For the 64K × 4 DRAM chip 4264, a complete refresh cycle for all 256 rows must finish every 4 ms to avoid loss of data.

To begin with, we'll consider only refresh initiated by $\overline{RAS}$ (imagine $\overline{CAS}$ and $\overline{WE}$ held high). The refresh timing then looks like Fig. 8.26. A_0–A_7 are latched by the

---

[10]Dual-in-line package (DIP) chips have pins that pass through holes in the printed circuit board and are soldered to the side opposite where the chip is. Surface-mount technology (SMT) chips have smaller spacing between pins and are normally soldered onto the PC board, in a special oven. Surface-mount pins are harder to get at for testing purposes, but SMT boards are less subject to noise, are smaller, and are on the whole more reliable in construction.

[11]Actually refreshing 64 million bits sequentially would not be possible with typical minimum per-bit time of 200 ns and a total time of 4 ms available for a refresh cycle: $200 \times 10^{-9} \times 65 \times 10^6 = 13,000$ ms—way too long! Even if the DRAM were only 64K in size, a sequential refresh would take 13 ms, still greater than a 4 ms refresh time.

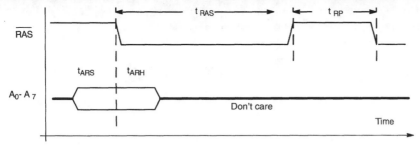

Figure 8.26 DRAM refresh timing.

falling edge of $\overline{\text{RAS}}$ into the row register. The total refresh cycle time per row is $t_{RAS} + t_{RP}$, where t_{RP} is *recharge time*. For the fastest version of the MT4264, the data sheet gives a cycle refresh time of

$$t_{RAS} + t_{RP} = 100 + 100 = 200 \text{ ns}$$

Not until 200 ns has elapsed after the falling edge of $\overline{\text{RAS}}$ can you be certain all the cells in a row have been properly refreshed. As shown, the row address must be valid around the falling edge of $\overline{\text{RAS}}$, with setup and hold times of t_{ARS} and t_{ARH}, which stand for time of address row setup and time of address row hold, respectively.

8.7.1 DRAM Sense Amplifier

A sense amplifier for a static RAM column can in principal be as simple as a noninverting buffer. But something special must go on in the DRAM sense amplifier; it must be able to capture the decaying charge of a DRAM cell capacitor and "remember" what to refresh the cell with. To accomplish the remembering, a sense amplifier contains an analog *SR* latch (more properly, a differential amplifier; see Haznedar 1991, 450–52, for details). A simplified diagram of a two-cell DRAM column is shown in Fig. 8.27. In the figure, which provides a simplified explanation of refresh, the *S* input is connected to a cell's data line and the *R* input is connected to a "$\frac{1}{2}$." The $\frac{1}{2}$ is not a legitimate logic level, but it serves the purpose of being larger than 0 and smaller than 1; it is called a **dummy cell**, or **reference cell**. The set input will be either 0 or 1, and the modified *SR* flip-flop will then snap into either a 0 or 1 state accordingly. The *Q* output is fed back on an antiparallel line to the cell's data input, resulting in a refresh of the capacitor.

Two DRAM cells are included in the figure to remind you that many cells from one column are connected to the same sense amplifier. Since only one column cell at a time is selected, refresh will only affect that selected cell. The next falling edge of $\overline{\text{RAS}}$ will introduce a new active row line, which finds another cell ready for refresh. What happens to the previous value of *Q*? Think about the upper cell in the figure becoming active, after the lower cell has been refreshed. Simply put, $\overline{\text{RAS}}$ generates a brief pulse from an internal timer, which clears the feedback path and allows the

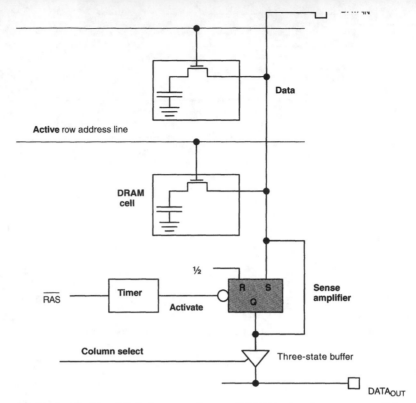

Figure 8.27 Simplified diagram of two-cell DRAM, showing sense amplifier structure.

next cell to begin refresh. See the exercises for more details about the timing of the DRAM sense amplifier, the reference cell, and refresh.

What the User Must Do for Refresh   Although some DRAMs have built-in refresh, with built-in timers,[12] refresh for DRAM is usually the responsibility of the memory system designer. For the 4264 chip, every 4 ms all of the rows must be refreshed; therefore the user must supply a sequence of row addresses and $\overline{RAS}$ pulses. Since $\overline{RAS}$ is the first action of any DRAM cycle, it doesn't matter whether a READ or WRITE operation accompanies the refresh. In a few happy circumstances, such as memory for graphics screen display, all the memory cells are read from and written to frequently enough that no additional circuitry is needed for refresh. Otherwise the user must supply a counter and logic to determine when the user's address takes over the address bus. See Fig. 8.28.

---

[12] Values of refresh time in data books are conservative. Actually, for some chips, you can *turn off the power* to a DRAM chip for a few seconds, turn it back on, and find it still has the same contents!

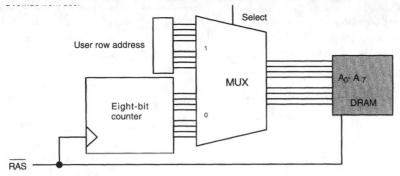

Figure 8.28 Refresh circuitry required for data retention.

8.8 DYNAMIC RAM TIMING

8.8.1 DRAM READ Timing

Assume that a row address has been been captured by the row address register in a DRAM. What happens when an active $\overline{CAS}$ arrives at the DRAM chip? By the time $\overline{CAS}$ goes low, the user should have changed the address pins to be a column address, and the falling edge of $\overline{CAS}$ will latch the new address pin values into a column address register. $\overline{CAS}$ will also select one of the sense amplifiers to control the external data line(s). As long as $\overline{WE}$ stays HI, the chip can assume that a read operation will take place, and in the case of a read, the feedback of sense amplifier to data line won't interfere with the reading process. The column signal should enable only one sense amplifier for the data output pin. Read cycle timing (for 256 rows) generally looks like Fig. 8.29, where the output pin data becomes valid a time t_{CAC}

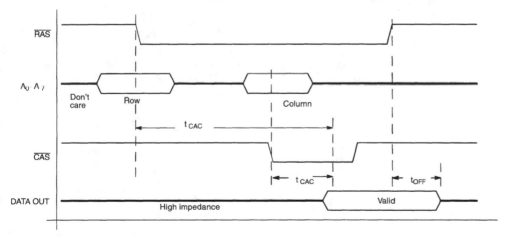

Figure 8.29 DRAM read cycle that accommodates refresh.

$\overline{CAS}$ returns to HI. The parameter t_{CAC} is the access time from $\overline{CAS}$, and t_{OFF} is the output buffer turn-off delay after the end of $\overline{RAS}$ or $\overline{CAS}$. Data are valid until t_{OFF} expires. When $\overline{RAS}$ returns to HI, refresh for the entire row occurs.

8.8.2 DRAM WRITE Logic and Timing

Suppose now that a write operation is required. A $\overline{WE}$ pulse is asserted after $\overline{RAS}$ but before $\overline{CAS}$. Why should the $\overline{WE}$ pulse occur then? For one thing, if $\overline{RAS}$ and $\overline{CAS}$ are asserted one after another before a write signal, it will look like a read operation. And because page-mode writing requires $\overline{RAS}$ to go LO and stay LO for a whole column's worth of writing, it makes sense that $\overline{WE}$ should occur after $\overline{RAS}$ but before $\overline{CAS}$. Such timing allows a $\overline{RAS}$ refresh and then makes sure the external data line is connected to the cell's internal data line. And there's no worry about output enable ($\overline{OE}$, active-low) if $\overline{WE}$ comes before $\overline{CAS}$.

Let's look at the logic required for routing external data to be written to *one* cell's capacitor. See Fig. 8.30. In this simplified picture of DRAM data routing for a common I/O pin, $\overline{WE}$ inactive (HI) keeps a three-state buffer on the output of the sense amplifier enabled, allowing refresh and reading. Two three-state buffers are shown on the output of the sense amplifier; one three-state buffer determines connection with the DATA$_{OUT}$ line, and the other three-state buffer is used to allow DATA$_{IN}$ access to the cell's capacitor. A successful write will occur only when the appropriate column line is active. The Boolean expression for describing data on a

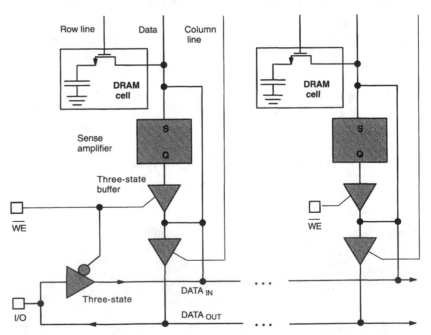

Figure 8.30 Strategic placement of buffers allows common write-enable.

$$\text{DATA}_{\text{COL}} = \text{WE} \cdot \text{COL}$$

There are various setup and hold times for data, $\overline{\text{WE}}$, and $\overline{\text{CAS}}$. They result in a minimum time between writing to one cell and writing to the next, expressed as $t_{WC}(t_{RC})$, the write cycle time. (See Fig. 8.31.) Notice again the $\overline{\text{RAS}}$-before-$\overline{\text{CAS}}$ timing, and note that the edge of $\overline{\text{WE}}$ falls between the $\overline{\text{RAS}}$ and $\overline{\text{CAS}}$ edges.

Practical DRAM The logic schematics and timing diagrams for DRAM read, refresh, write, and page-mode addressing shown here should provide you with an understanding of DRAM function, but they don't do justice to the sophistication of design in a practical DRAM chip. The internal workings of DRAMs span the range from simple to sublime—from one-transistor storage cells to refresh timing and sense amplifiers. Look at data sheets for a recent DRAM, and you will see a dozen or so timing diagrams for different read, write and refresh cycles. There may be 50 or more timing parameters listed under "AC characteristics." All the sense amplifiers, address registers, internal timers, and three-state buffers needed for smooth operation can be fabricated on the chip and still produce a DRAM physically smaller and less costly than an equivalent static RAM chip.

DRAM versus SRAM Here's a justification for using large DRAM chips: A 1-megabit DRAM uses 1 million transistors for memory cells, whereas a static SRAM uses 4 to

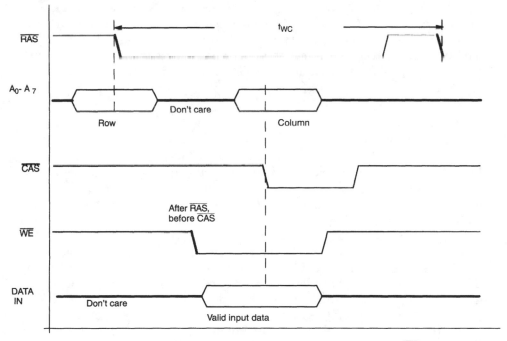

Figure 8.31 Early write cycle timing. If the DRAM chip has an output-enable, $\overline{\text{OE}}$, it should be held high during the early write cycle diagrammed here.

sense amplifiers can be fabricated for a fraction of a million transistors. The result is a slower, but smaller and less costly memory chip.

EXAMPLE 10

A 256K × 4 DRAM chip costs about as much as a 16K × 4 SRAM chip; the access time of the DRAM is about 100 ns; for the SRAM, it can be as low as 15 ns. (The DRAM price does not include extra circuitry for refresh.) A rule of thumb is that when a memory system requires eight or more chips, it is cost-effective to choose DRAM over SRAM.

EXAMPLE 11

In 1975, 4 MB of dynamic RAM chips cost about $8000; in 1985, 4MB of dynamic RAM chips cost about $500; and in 1995 *one* 4-MB dynamic RAM chip cost about $8. (What do you extrapolate for the cost of the same memory in 2005?)

8.9   ADDRESSING MEMORY

Now that we've established dynamic RAM as a compact means of laying out memory cells, we return to the problem of decoding addresses. With two strokes, three-state output and chip-select greatly streamlined memory bus output. But earlier another awkward aspect of our memory cell design was mentioned—the extra decoding circuitry needed to address each word in memory. We saw one method of efficient addressing with the row-column system of dynamic RAMs; now we look more carefully at address decoding.

8.9.1   Demultiplexer Addressing

In a random-access memory system, each equally accessible memory location must have a different address; in other words, each of 2^N addresses is a unique combination of the N address bits. The most straightforward way to generate one address is with an N-input AND gate. Figure 8.32 presents an example of an AND gate in the service of an $N = 6$–bit address. If nothing more clever is done, it will take 64 six-bit AND gates to address the whole of the memory system (shown in the figure is one such AND gate). In effect, we would be making a 64-output *demultiplexer* (Chapter 4). Note that in the six-bit decoder design we need to count (for every AND gate) six pins for the inputs (called **counting literals**) plus an output pin, for a total of $64 \times 7 = 448$ pins. (To achieve this efficiency, we assume that complements to all addresses are generated elsewhere or that inverter bubbles cost us nothing.) Let's examine a couple of addressing schemes that are more gate-efficient than a full-scale demultiplexer.

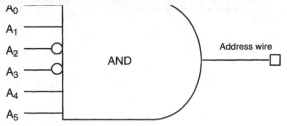

Figure 8.32 One AND gate decoding the address 110011 in binary.

8.9.2 Tree Decoding

EXAMPLE 12

Here's a method that uses more AND gates but fewer total pins. See Fig. 8.33. Consider the six-bit address 100011, shown decoded in the circuit with six two-input AND gates. Look first at the output of the AND on the right, which receives $A_5 = 1$ and $A_4A_3A_2A_1A_0 = 00011$. Address A_5 will project to 64 two-input AND gates; half the projections will be as literal $\overline{A_5}$.

If we look at the circuit starting from the left, we see that the tree decoding method builds up addresses systematically, as more address pins are added. The two bits A_1A_0 form part of a four-output decoder; the three pins $A_2A_1A_0$ form an eight-output decoder, and so on. The problem with tree decoding is that delay increases as more address bits are added. In Fig. 8.33, at least five gates of delay impose themselves from A_0 to the final outputs on the right.

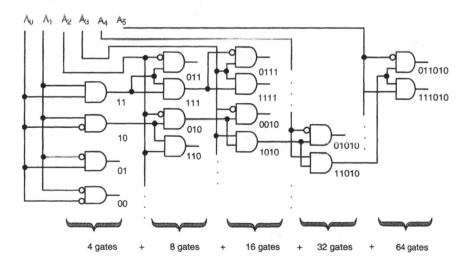

Figure 8.33 Address decoding with an AND-gate tree.

We've already worked with row and column decoding in DRAMs, albeit with a system ample enough to have a separate sense amplifier controlled by each column line. If each cell needs to be addressed by row *and* column lines, more AND gates are needed, as we'll see now. Start with an even number of address bits. Divide the address into two balanced ranges. To illustrate, let's attack the $N = 6$ example again. See Fig. 8.34. As we saw in the discussion of the *tree decoder* circuit, each $3 \rightarrow 8$ decoder can be built with twelve two-input ANDs. Each decoder output for a row is paired with every one of the eight decoder outputs for the columns, requiring 64 more two-input ANDs, for a total of 264—40% fewer than the tree decoder needed! As you can now appreciate, row and column decoding is the method of choice for RAM chips.

The final AND gate in row-column decoding adds one more gate's worth of delay, compared with a demultiplexing addresser. It is normally replaced by a column address multiplexer that selects which column buffer gains access to the output data line.

8.9.4   Higher-Order Address Bits

Let's continue to worry about our small six-bit address space. Suppose we are limited to chips that have only $16 = 2^4$ locations per chip. How can four-bit chips be used in a six-bit memory system? We've already done the groundwork for the solution: giving our chips a chip-select feature (see SRAM design). In Fig. 8.35 the worry is about addressing, not about the input/output bus. A decoder is placed between the higher-order address bits and the chip-select pins of the memory chips; for example, when $A_5A_4 = 11$, chip 3 is selected (active HI) to have its three-state outputs enabled. Exercise 38 asks you to figure out how chip-select works on a DRAM.

Addressing takes up a significant part of the real estate of a large memory chip. All large commercial memory chips are square arrays of cells addressed by row

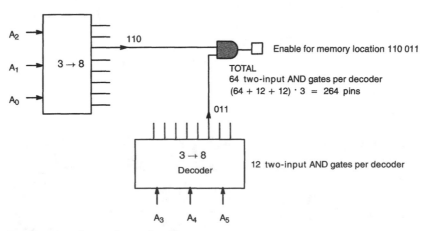

Figure 8.34   Row-column decoding.

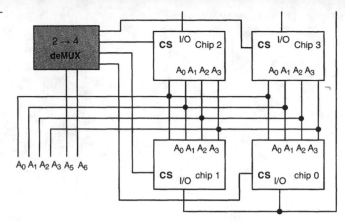

Figure 8.35 Memory subsystem using chip-select to expand address space.

demultiplexers and column multiplexers. A 1-Mb static RAM chip is organized as 1024 rows by 1024 columns; 30% of the area of the chip is devoted to addressing.

8.10 CONTENT-ADDRESSABLE MEMORY (CAM)

That's right, *content*-addressable memory. It sounds oxymoronic, but you can appreciate CAM's usefulness by considering the problem of *searching* for a particular pattern of bits through the contents of a large number of memory locations. Ordinarily hardware or an algorithm has to look for the pattern one word at a time, like the Prince searching for Cinderella by going from house to house with one glass slipper. After addressing a new location, the FSM (or the program) reads the location's contents into a register and compares it with the desired pattern in another register. If the match is not found, the next word in memory is tested, and so on, until the desired pattern and the one fetched from memory are equal.

Recall the quote from Marvin Minsky at the beginning of this chapter: of what use are "vast stores of unclassified memory" without an efficient means to search through them? By adding more hardware, it's possible to turn the pattern search problem into a content-addressable *parallel search*, which finds the answer(s) in one cycle. The CAM system takes content as input and returns address as output.

Figure 8.36 develops the hardware needed for an individual CAM cell. Assume that contents have already been stored in the CAM cell and that the problem now is to compare the cell contents with a test pattern. The memory contents and test pattern are compared in a bank of XOR gates. If the test pattern is identical to the contents of the memory cell, all of the XOR outputs will be 0. (If all of the inputs to a NOR gate are 0, its output is 1.) The figure emphasizes the digital comparator associated with each memory location, and it leaves the RAM read/write mechanism as a bidirectional arrow in the block on the right.

Now in Fig. 8.37 2^N CAM cells are combined in an array. Each of the CAM cell outputs projects to a priority encoder. We saw priority encoders in Chapter 4; the

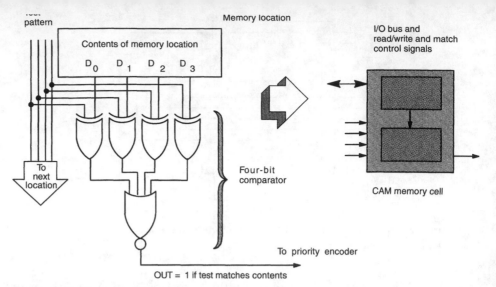

Figure 8.36   Content-addressable memory for one cell.

2^N inputs to a priority encoder determine which N-bit combination becomes output. If more than one input to a priority encoder is 1, the highest-priority input dictates which N-bit address is expressed. If all inputs are inactive, the priority encoder signals "no match" on a separate status line.

An example of a priority encoder chip is the 74148. It has eight active-low inputs, three "address" outputs, and two status pins that signal whether or not at least one of the inputs is LO.

8.10.1   A CAM Chip: The 99C10

To get a better feel for content-addressable memory, consider a commercial CAM chip, the 99C10 from Advanced Micro Devices. The 99C10 is a 28-pin chip containing 256 words. Its block diagram appears in Fig. 8.38. All data, including addresses and instructions, are sent to and from the chip by 16 I/O pins (D_{15}–D_0). If the contents of a word match the test pattern, the address of the matched word is sent to the status register, from which it can be sent onto the I/O bus. With the parallel search of the 99C10 a match can be found in less than 100 ns.

An instruction register and four active-low control pins determine what the 99C10 does; three of the pins are featured in Table 8.1. Whether the I/O bus is acting as input or output is determined by pin $\overline{G}$: if $\overline{G}$ is HI, the I/O pins act as input. For example, if you want to write data to a CAM cell, $\overline{G}$ is HI while valid contents are on the I/O bus. If you want to read data from the 99C10, $\overline{G}$ must be LO; the contents to be read are first sent to the CAM register. $\overline{W}$ and G shouldn't both be LO at the same time. If $\overline{W}$ and $\overline{G}$ are both HI at the same time, the I/O bus goes into a high-impedance state.

If a write operation is to be performed, then $\overline{W}$ must be LO. Writing to the command register is signaled by a LO on the $\overline{C}$ control pin. The command register

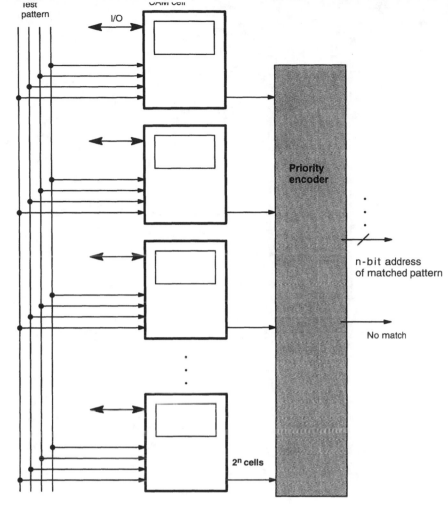

Figure 8.37 Organization of content-addressable memory.

contains six bits of instruction and eight bits of address. The address sent to the command register is the address to which data will be written. As with DRAMs, writing to the 99C10 is a two-phase operation: first the eight-bit address to be written to is stored in the command register, and then the actual write operation sends data to the word specified by the address.

There are two status pins, $\overline{\text{MTCH}}$ and $\overline{\text{FULL}}$, on the 99C10. If a match is found, $\overline{\text{MTCH}}$ goes LO; if all 256 of the cells in the CAM are in use, $\overline{\text{FULL}}$ is LO. Internally the 99C10 CAM cells have a couple of other nondata bits associated with match and full bits. If the skip bit is set, then even if a match is found, the next lowest priority match is sent out. If the empty bit is set, the CAM cell is available for data writing and does not participate in matches. By using the command register, it's possible to empty the whole chip (clear its registers) with one instruction.

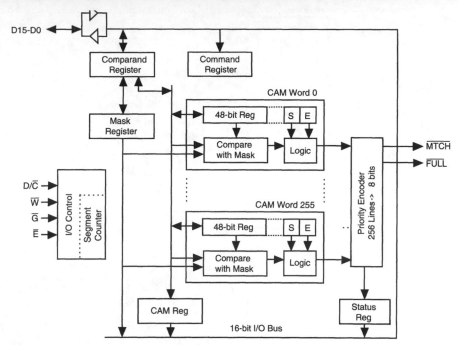

Figure 8.38   CAM 99C10A block diagram from AMD data sheets.

Table 8.1   Command, Write, and Output Pins of 99C10A CAM Chip

Command $\overline{C}$	Write $\overline{W}$	Output $\overline{G}$	Action
H	H	L	Read data
H	L	H	Write data
L	H	L	Read address (status)
L	L	H	Write to command register

Command Register and 99C10 Instructions   When 16 bits are written to the command register, the first four bits are instruction, and the last eight bits are address. The sixteen different instructions enable you to do such things as initialize and look for more than one match. The details of the instructions are left to the data sheets in *Daniels' Digital Design Lab Manual*.

Uses for CAM   If a string of bits represents a pattern detected by a sensor, such as in a machine vision system, a CAM can be used to match the pattern with other patterns stored in the CAM. The address found by the match would then represent the name of the pattern found. Another use of CAM is in local area networks. Messages traveling between computers can be intercepted by CAMs, and then a header in the message can be matched quickly with names of machines on the network. When a match is found, the complete message is routed to the correct machine. Since the local area network may be a high-speed system, a CAM is essential for fast determination of machine-to-message matches. In a similar way, a computer with an extensive directory system on its hard drive can handle a request to change file directory through a CAM.

For more information on content-addressable memory see Shiva (1988, 482 and 494); Mano (1988, 415); and Cole (1988).

8.10.2 Associative Memory

(This section is optional.) Suppose you are willing to accept memory contents that *nearly* match the test pattern—say, if only 1 bit out of 16 is different—and you want the address of a memory word with the closest match to your test pattern. An **associative memory**—a variation of content-addressable memory—will do the job. In principle there are three approaches to associative memory design: combinational logic (such as the CAM XOR), a finite state machine, or a computer algorithm to search for a near match, such as the evolutionary algorithm of Chapter 3 that searched for smaller Boolean expressions of truth tables. Exercises 44 and 45 explore some issues with associative memory.

In each case it would be useful to find the Hamming distance between the test pattern and the various memory contents you are trying to match. The Hamming distance is the number of bits different between two words of equal length. If two words are identical, their Hamming distance is 0. In the example offered above, a method would be to look for a Hamming distance of 0 or 1 between the test pattern and any of the memory contents to be matched. A finite state machine that takes input one bit at a time from the two patterns and has a counter driven by an XOR gate can compute Hamming distance.

There are parallel search methods for finding a closest match, and these methods can be implemented in hardware by digital or analog techniques. The parallel methods basically involve multiplying the test pattern with a correlation matrix derived from the contents patterns. The result of the multiplication indicates which contents pattern provides the closest match to the test pattern.

Human memory appears to be associative; it excels at matching imperfect patterns, say, views of faces, where computer vision algorithms presently fail. Human memory is also said to be **distributed:** a particular "content" may be distributed over many cells, and loss of a few memory cells does not seem to wipe out particular contents, but degrades all memories slightly. And, in human memory, contents are seldom lost forever; memory failure is usually a failure of **recall,** and often a temporary failure at that. Can't remember the name of those small blue and purple flowers on a shrub you're looking at? Half an hour later the word *hydrangea* may spontaneously occur to you. Kohonen (1980) and Hinton and Anderson (1981) are two classic references on associative memory.

Up to now we have concentrated on *random access* memory, in which all memory cells are only one address call away from revealing their contents. If access is not random, it must be *serial:* the memory must be searched sequentially for the desired location. Serial memory in semiconductor form is generally a shift register, and it can have specialized functions, such as **last-in–first-out (LIFO) stacks** and **first-in–first-out (FIFO) buffers**.[13] You saw shift registers in Chapter 5, on flip-flops; a shift register is a set of clocked D flip-flops with the output of one flip-flop being the input of the next, and so on down the line.

EXAMPLE 13

Design a combinational circuit for controlling shift direction in a shift register.

Answer   What's needed is a multiplexer on the input to each flip-flop in the register. In Fig. 8.39, a direction control circuit, shown in bold, is placed between each D flip-flop in the shift register.

One instance is shown of a $2 \to 1$ MUX, with left/right control as the select line. The input to the (one-bit wide) shift register above is the data input on the left; the output can be the delayed taps of the various D flip-flop outputs, but at this point we don't have a good way of keeping track of the location of data in the serial shift register. As shown, the left-right shifter will shift direction on each clock pulse; it doesn't have a no-shift mode.

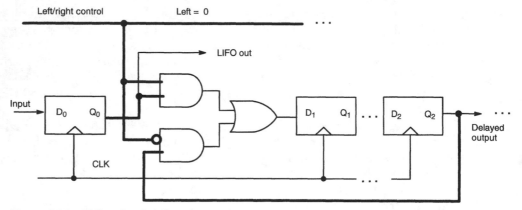

Figure 8.39   Bidirectional shift register.

Various other shift registers (circular, arithmetic, etc.) will be designed in Chapter 11, "Register Transfer Logic."

---

[13]Most serial memory is not semiconductor-based. For example, magnetic tape is a common form of serial memory: the information at the wound-up end of the tape will be read only after all the intervening tape has streamed by the head. Magnetic disks have much faster access times than tape, but they are not truly random access because a head must wait for a few milliseconds for the spinning disk to bring the correct part of the disk underneath. Optical memory (CD-ROM) has access characteristics similar to those of magnetic disks.

You saw in Chapter 7, when microprogrammed controllers were being designed, that it would be useful to remember the return addresses for nested subroutines. The *last* exited subroutine would be the *first* to be returned to. A last-in–first-out stack (LIFO) can be used to store a series of addresses. The bidirectional shift register of the previous example can be used to build a LIFO. First the shift register must be widened, so that there are as many D flip-flops at each level as there are bits in the words to be stored on the stack. *The output of the LIFO is at the first register in the chain, where data enters.* Now when data is written onto the stack, it is a shift-right operation and is called a **push** operation. When data is read from the stack, a shift-left operation takes place and is called a **pop** operation. At all other times the shift register should *hold* the data and not shift either direction when the clock signal arrives. Notice that a LIFO is a *synchronous* FSM. Exercise 44 has you design LIFO features.

8.11.2 First-In–First-Out Buffer

A first-in–first-out (FIFO) buffer can be thought of as a queue, or waiting line. The *first* person *in* line is the first person to buy a ticket when the booth opens and is the *first* person *out* of the line to enter the theater. FIFO memories can act as buffers between fast and slow memory systems, for example, when data is sent from fast static RAM in a computer to the slower magnetic medium of a disk drive. The FIFO will respond to two commands, WRITE and READ (push, pop).

EXAMPLE 14

In a shift-register version of FIFO, WRITE activates a right-shift and READ activates a left-shift. Every FIFO needs a **pointer** to indicate where the bottom of the stack is. The data at the top of the stack is the next to be sent out after a READ operation.

Figure 8.40 shows one way to implement a one-bit wide FIFO, if we're willing to let the clock be driven by the WRITE signal. Every time the circuit sees a WRITE pulse, it shifts data to the right in the D flip-flops and increments a counter in the

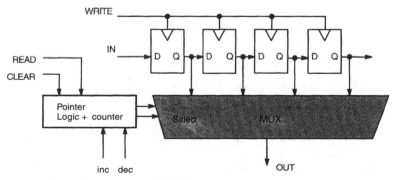

Figure 8.40   FIFO memory of depth 4.

are asserted simultaneously, the designer must build in *priority* to determine which operation to perform. See Exercise 45. The counter points to a multiplexer select. OUT from the MUX therefore always shows the first-in data *not yet read*. For the four-deep register in the figure, if the counter reads 11, a FULL status bit can be set. The FULL status bit can disable writing until at least one READ operation (or a CLEAR operation) has been performed.

The *depth of a FIFO* is the number of words it can store before filling up; in the case above, the depth is 4. The *width* is the number of bits per word the FIFO stores. In the case of Fig. 8.40, it is a 4×1 FIFO. As a FIFO increases in depth, the shift register plus MUX used above becomes awkward; yes, the MUX could be replaced by three-state output buffers, but considerable decoding would still be needed.

8.11.3 Static RAM FIFO

Another approach to FIFO replaces the shift registers with a static RAM array and an address generator. The address generator contains two counters, one for WRITE and one for READ. The static RAM array has separate input and output buses, *and separate WRITE and READ address lines*. The general form of the static-RAM-based FIFO is shown in Fig. 8.41, where N and M are normally powers of 2.

A WRITE pulse can push DATA to be stored in the word specified by the write address, and then increment the counter on the left side. $DATA_{OUT}$ is always showing the contents of the word specified by the read address; a READ pulse pops by *decrementing* the counter on the right side. When either of the counters reaches the value 2^{N-1}, the next pulse sends it to zero—hence the label "rollover counter" in the

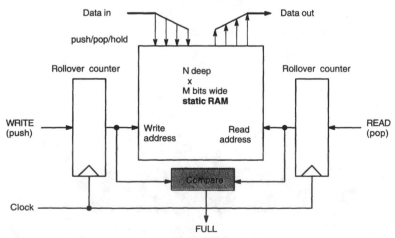

Figure 8.41 SRAM implementation of FIFO.

diagram. How can the system tell when the FIFO is full? It's not a matter of waiting for the write counter to reach $2^N - 1$, since READ operations may have freed up words at the bottom of the RAM for more writing. The WRITE and READ counters must be compared, as indicated in the schematic.

What condition must be satisfied for the FIFO to be full? Keep in mind that the write address (WA) rolls over when it reaches the end, and it can legitimately begin writing over the start of the RAM if the read address (RA) has moved ahead. Therefore, when

$$WA + 1 \text{ (with no carry-out)} = RA$$

the memory is full.

EXAMPLE 15

Consider two full examples from a 16-deep FIFO:

1. $WA = 1111$ and $RA = 0000$; $WA + 0001 = 10000 = 0000$ with no carry out $\Rightarrow$ FULL
2. $WA = 0000$ and $RA = 0001$; $WA + 0001 = 0001 = RA \Rightarrow$ FULL

We started the discussion of serial memory by contrasting it to random-access memory; now we find that an important example of serial memory, the first-in–first-out stack, is most effectively made from random-access memory! Is turning static RAM into a FIFO like grinding filet mignon into hot dogs? Not in one sense. Static RAM has much shorter access time than dynamic RAM, and as an interface between SRAM and DRAM, the FIFO must be able to keep up with rapidly changing input while it loads up its buffer waiting for read operations.

Can a cell in the FIFO static RAM handle both write and read addresses? Yes. We borrow a transparent latch RAM figure from the first part of this chapter and split the address line, as shown in Fig. 8.42. The value of the read address will determine the output of the RAM, independent of the write address.

A Static RAM FIFO Chip   In the late 1980s SGS-Thomson made a series of static RAM FIFO chips, one of which was the MK4503, a 2048-deep by 9-bits-wide FIFO (in 1995 IDT Inc. was making a more modern line of FIFOs). The MK4503 has 28 pins, 18 of which are for input and output (nine bits each). The other 10 pins

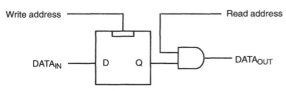

Figure 8.42   Addressing for FIFO RAM cell.

are WRITE, READ, RESET, FULL, HALF FULL, EMPTY, power and ground, and expansion in and out. None of the pins are for address; address information is kept internally in two counters. The MK4503 employs a static RAM with separate write and read addresses. Logic on the chip can account for expansion in depth by revising the computation for FULL. The MK4503 can complete a write cycle in 65 ns. Another benefit of the 4503: by cascading chips and using the expansion pins, you can increase the FIFO depth.

8.12   SUMMARY

The topic of memory pervades digital circuit design. Memory will be "addressed" again in the text, especially in Chapter 11, on register transfer logic. Like the food pyramid, there is a memory pyramid for computer systems, shown in Fig. 8.43. At the top of the pyramid is the central processing unit, with its registers and cache memory; the memory chips in the CPU (SRAM) are selected for speed. Main memory is large-capacity addressable RAM and is often constructed of lower-cost, denser DRAM chips. Archival memory provides an enormous capacity of storage (albeit with slower access time due to mechanical and serial limitations) in the form of magnetic disks and optical CD-ROM.

- In terms of sales, memory **chips,** especially dynamic RAM chips, are the single most important type of digital logic chip.
- Static random access memory (**SRAM**) is created from latches by adding address and read/write logic. Pin count on individual chips is often reduced by requiring input and output to share the same bus. Output pins can be put in a high-impedance state by a **chip-select pin;** control of chip-select enables many chips to share one data bus.
- Data input and output for a memory chip can share the same pin by means of three-state switching in a **bidirectional transceiver.**
- Both write-enable and chip-enable control access of a chip I/O pin to a data **bus.**
- The speed of memory reading is measured in **access time,** the time from presentation of address to appearance of data at output.

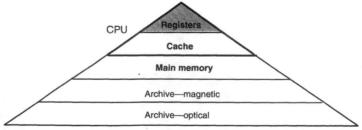

Figure 8.43   Memory hierarchy, with fastest type at apex of pyramid.

- Memory size in bits is the number of words times the number of bits per word. A memory system uses many memory chips to increase the address space and word size. A memory system is usually controlled by a synchronous finite state machine that oversees a memory address register, output bus controller, and read/write control.

- **Dynamic RAM** requires only one transistor per cell and therefore has a lower cost per bit and can be more densely packed on a chip than **static RAM (SRAM),** which requires four to six transistors per cell; however, DRAM must be refreshed every few milliseconds, or the memory stored as charge on a capacitor will leak off.

- DRAM is addressed in two phases: by row and then by column. The column address selects one of N sense amplifiers to be on the I/O bus. Because of two-phase addressing and the time required to sense charge on the DRAM capacitors, DRAM has longer access time than static RAM, made from latches. **Row address strobe** can be used like chip-enable as an address path for higher-order bits.

- **Refresh** of all the cells in a row of dynamic RAM occurs every time the row is accessed; the sense amplifier, which has the qualities of an analog latch, feeds its output back to the data line of the cell, recharging, if necessary, the DRAM capacitor.

- 2^N memory locations require N address bits.

- **Addressing** is a matter of decoding. N bits can address 2^N locations. One-layer AND gate decoding is the fastest addressing scheme. Considerable savings (at a slight expense in delay) in pin count occur when **tree** or **row-column** methods are used to decode address pins. (Row-column decoding is internal to large RAM chips)

- **Content-addressable memory** searches for particular contents to match a test pattern and returns the address of the location with a match. If each CAM cell has a built-in comparator, a CAM search can be done in parallel, in one clock cycle.

- **Serial memory** does not have the same access time per location; some cells may be further away from the reading mechanism than others. Serial memory can come in the form of magnetic tape or magnetic or optical disk. When made of D flip-flops in series, serial memory is called a shift register. A last-in–first-out stack **(LIFO)** made of a bidirectional shift register can be used to store return addresses for subroutines.

- An important use of flip-flop-based serial memory is in first-in–first-out **(FIFO)** buffers, which temporarily store data from a fast processor to be sent at a slower rate to a receiving device. A deep FIFO buffer can be made from a static RAM with two address ports, one for writing, and the other for reading.

Exercises 8

1. The first page of this chapter describes four ways a human may memorize the XOR truth table. Discuss briefly what might be considered the "address" and "contents" in each of the four memory schemes.

2. List three reasons why memory chips account for such a large percentage of the sales of digital integrated circuits.

3. A commercial RAM chip has a product lifetime for its sales. The curves below (adapted from Prince, 1991, fig. 2.8) show seven generations of dynamic RAM sales. Note that the vertical scale is $\log_{10}$(number of chips per year) $\times 10^6$. How well does Moore's law hold up for DRAM chips? What is the doubling time, in years, for chip density? Not shown is the start of sampling for 64-MB DRAM chips in 1994. Static RAM chips require more transistors per cell and therefore are about a generation behind dynamic RAM in cell density.

    (a) Why are 1K, 4K, 16K, ..., 4M the sizes of the DRAM families? Why not 2K, 8K, or other values of address size?

    (b) What will be the next chip size after 4M, and how many address pins will it need?

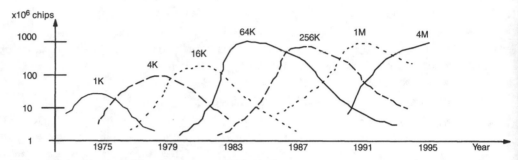

Figure P8.1   Memory chip sales per year, 1975–1995.

4. Explain the difference(s) between RAM and ROM. What speed advantages does RAM have over ROM in semiconductor memory?

5. Complete the following analogy as best you can, given the five choices below: RAM is to ROM as telephone is to

    (a) Telegraph
    (b) Newspaper
    (c) Answering machine
    (d) E-mail
    (e) Television

6. Consider the read/write memory cell made from two *SR* latches (see Fig. 8.4); input signals are presented at the following times:

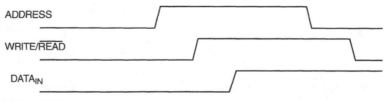

Figure P8.2

What will the DATAOUT waveform look like, considering circuit delay? Can any of the input signals look like CLOCK input?

7. Consider again the read/write memory cell made from two *SR* latches, shown below. What changes in the answer to Exercise 6 if the $W/\overline{R}$ line to the output ANDs (shown in bold below) is cut? Is each memory cell a *transparent latch*?

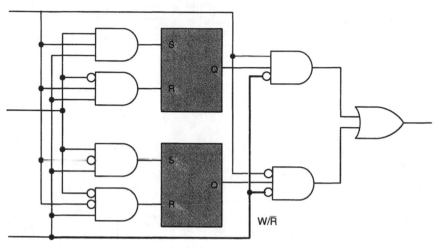

Figure P8.3

8. Using *SR* latches, design a *4 locations × 1 bit of output* read/write memory system.
9. A possible memory cell made with a *D* flip-flop is shown below. The clock is level-sensitive. What will be the responses of DATAOUT to the input waveforms of Exercise 6? Can you design a 4 × 1 memory system with this memory cell?

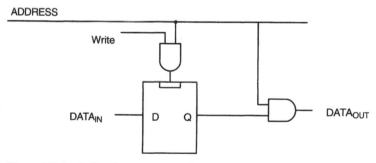

Figure P8.4 *D* flip-flop memory cell.

10. Consider the SRAM design made with two inverters shown in Fig. 8.5. What contributes to the delay from address presentation to output change in the design?

12. What are two advantages and two disadvantages of combining memory input
and output on one set of bidirectional wires?

13. Several write-timing parameters for static RAM were discussed: t_{ASW}, t_{AHW},
t_{WP}, t_{DS}, and t_{DH}. Which combination of these parameters will add up to the
minimum access time for writing to static RAM? (That is, what will be the
minimum time between successful write commands to two different memory
locations?)

14. Assuming the 2×1 memory cells are okay, what, if anything, is wrong with the
4×2 memory system in Fig. P8.5?

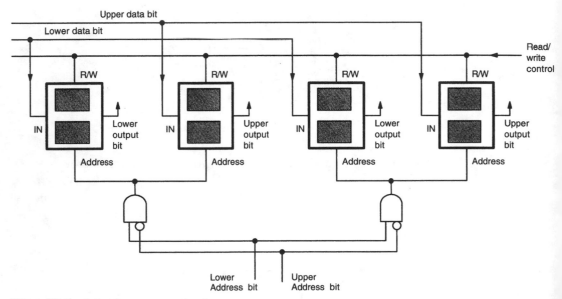

Figure P8.5 A 4×2 memory system?

It is supposed to be a 4 words $\times$ 2 bits/word memory system, where each box
is a 2×1 package (no three-state output).

15. **(a)** For the memory chip shown in Fig. P8.6, write out the truth table for the
inputs of address, write-enable, chip-enable, and IN; and for the outputs
of WRITE and OUT.
   (b) What happens at the I/O pin of the RAM chip when $\overline{CE}$ is not LO?
   (c) Draw out what the user of the memory chip must do with the multiplexed I/O line in order to read and write properly from the memory cell.

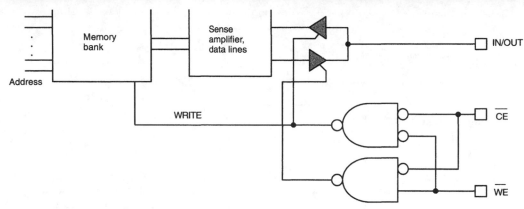

Figure P8.6

16. Design a 16 × 2 read/write random-access memory system with 4 × 1 chips. Show what will be necessary for address decoding, assuming that each of the chips has an active-low chip-enable.

17. Show how four 4K × 4 memory chips (MT5C1605) with $\overline{OE}$ control can be arranged for an 8K × 8 memory system.

18. Say a personal computer system needs RAM main memory with 32 bits per word and 8,388,608 locations.

    (a) How many 256K × 1 memory chips will be needed to build the memory system?
    (b) How many MT5C1M4B2 chips would be needed?

19. What advantages can you think of for having memory systems with exactly 2^N cells, where N is a positive integer? For example, why would a system with 64 locations be preferred to one with, say, 60 or 70 locations?

20. A read/write memory system has 4,194,304 locations, each with 16 bits of contents. How many wires would be needed on a bus to connect the memory to a computer, assuming the whole memory must be addressed and read from or written to on one clock cycle?

‡21. In a computer, memory is one of several components normally governed by a microprogrammed controller such as you saw at the end of Chapter 7. Let's concentrate on memory control. Consider the memory system diagram in Section 8.5. Design an FSM that controls read and write operations. The read/write command is an external input to the FSM. The controller has five outputs as shown in Fig. P8.7. Assume that the data for the DATA$_{IN}$ register and the memory address register have already been loaded.

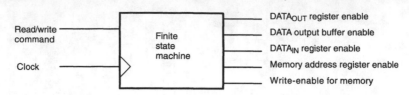

Read/write command

Clock

Finite state machine

DATA$_{OUT}$ register enable
DATA output buffer enable
DATA$_{IN}$ register enable
Memory address register enable
Write-enable for memory

Figure P8.7

‡22. Study the one-transistor DRAM cell of Fig. 8.19. Where is the resistance that causes the charge on the capacitor to leak off? If the capacitance C is 10^{-14} F, approximately what resistance would be needed to discharge C from 5 V to 0.5 V in 10 ms?

23. As the text says, most dynamic RAM chips with the need for N address bits have $N/2$ address wires, and the whole address must be read in two cycles, one for the row and one for the column. What advantage and what disadvantage accompany the use of row-column addressing as described for DRAM?

24. For a DRAM chip, does it matter whether the higher-order or lower-order bits of address are clocked by $\overline{RAS}$?

25. Show in a diagram how $\overline{CAS}$ and the output sense amplifiers are organized for a four-bit-wide output. Is the symmetry of row-column addressing disturbed by a 16M DRAM with two or eight output bits per location?

26. Consider the MT4LC16256 chip described in the text.
    (a) How many cells total does the chip have?
    (b) Why do you think the MT4LC16256 has two write-enable pins?

27. If both $\overline{RAS}$ and $\overline{CAS}$ were connected to the same line and the row and column addresses were the same value, how many locations of the total could be read from and written to?

‡28. The diagram in the following figure shows details of a practical DRAM sense amplifier connected to one storage cell (adapted from Prince 1991; she notes that this circuit was first used by Intel for its 16K DRAM chip in 1976). The circuit in the middle is a differential amplifier; notice how its crossed connections give it the appearance of a latch. There are three internal timing signals, ϕ_0, ϕ_1, and ϕ_2.

   Consider each MOS transistor as a switch; in simplified terms, when the gate voltage on the transistor is positive, the switch closes. See the timing in Fig. P8.9. Initially $\overline{RAS}$ and ϕ_2 are HI, causing the bit-line side of the reference capacitor to be at ground voltage and the bit lines (B_S, B_R) to be charged to V_{DD}. When $\overline{RAS}$ is asserted LO, it isolates the charge on the reference cell and disconnects

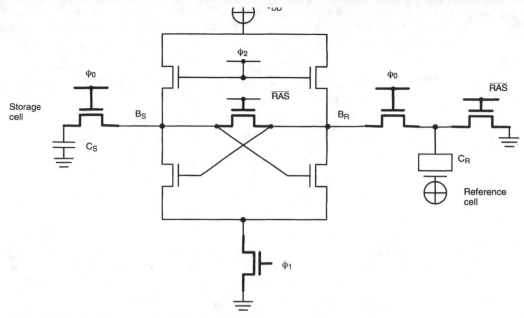

Figure P8.8   Transistor-level schematic of DRAM sense amplifier.

the two bit lines. The rising of control ϕ_2 disconnects the bit lines from V_{DD}. The rising of ϕ_0 brings the bit lines to the storage and reference levels. Next, the rising of ϕ_1 engages the differential amplifier. The secondary pulse on ϕ_2 balances the amplified difference between B_S and B_R. Your question: Draw the waveform for B_S in the case (a) where the data stored is a "0" and (b) where the data stored is a "1."

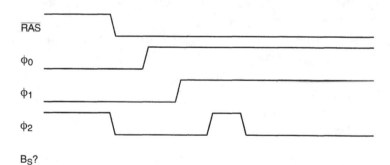

Figure P8.9   Internal DRAM timing signals.

29. What percentage of time is taken up with refresh if a complete refresh cycle must be completed in 5 ms, 256 Kb need to be refreshed row by row, and each refresh operation takes 150 ns?

30. Data sheets for DRAM chips show a late-write cycle, in which WE is asserted *after* $\overline{\text{CAS}}$. Draw out a late-write cycle timing diagram and indicate when data can be read from the I/O pins.

31. Draw out a DRAM write timing diagram for page-mode writing, that is, writing sequentially to all the cells in one column of a DRAM. Show what happens when the page changes.

32. Study Fig. 8.21, which describes DRAM logic.

(a) Show where data-in should be and how write-enable may control data-in.
(b) Can a dynamic RAM cell be written to if $\overline{\text{CAS}}$ is always HI? Can it be read from?

33. Draw out the timing waveforms needed to perform a write operation on the MT4264 of Fig. 8.24.

34. Suppose a computer memory of 1 million (actually 2^{20}) words with 16 bits per word is to be designed. You, the designer, have a choice of using 1-Mb DRAM chips of configuration 1M × 1 or 64K × 16. Each type of DRAM chip uses a row-column addressing scheme.

(a) Where should the upper four bits of address go for the 64K × 16 chip design?
(b) To minimize pin count *on the controller*, which chip should you choose? Consider that each chip may have V_{CC}, ground, $\overline{\text{CS}}$, $\overline{\text{RAS}}$, $\overline{\text{CAS}}$, $\overline{\text{OE}}$, and $\overline{\text{WE}}$ pins as well as address pins and data I/O pin(s).

35. Tree decoding Suppose you have a six-input tree decoder, such as the one in Example 12. Show how to increase the decoding for eight inputs, with the restriction that only two-input AND gates are available. Assume that complements of all inputs are available.

36. Row-column decoding Show a row-column addressing design for a seven-bit address. Include three-state buffers for the cells on each column.

37. Addressing Say that pin count includes input and output pins on a chip. Compare the pin count needed to address *eight-bit* memory for

(a) A standard one-layer demultiplexer
(b) Tree decoding
(c) Balanced row-column decoding

Which method has the shortest delay from address to decoded output?

38. A DRAM chip does not normally have a chip-enable input. Show how to use RAS and CAS inputs on DRAM chips to handle higher-order addresses. Assume that the number of address bits in the *system* is greater than the number of address bits per chip.

39. How could the Prince's search for Cinderella, which required him to go in serial fashion from house to house comparing maidens' feet with a glass slipper, be turned into a parallel, content-addressable search?

40. The IEEE-1984-91 schematic of the TTL priority encoder 74LS148 from the Texas Instruments *TTL Logic Data Book* is shown below.

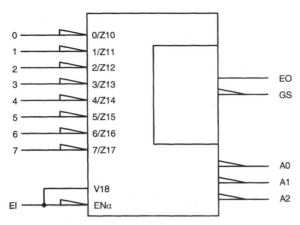

Figure P8.10   74LS148 schematic.

Notice that almost all inputs and outputs are negative logic, or active-low. Find a data book and look at the truth table for the 'LS148. Explain how two '148s can be cascaded through enable-in (EI) and enable-out (EO) pins to give 16 → 4 priority.

41. The 99C10 content-addressable memory chip has a mask register. When a bit in the mask register is HI, the comparator doesn't test for that bit in looking for a match.

(a)   Study the 99C10 block diagram and say how information gets from the data bus to the mask register.

(b)   How could masking be used to help a 99C10 perform an *associative* memory match?

42. Small associative memory problem   Design a circuit that will respond with a HI when any three out of four bits of a test pattern match with the four bits of the contents of a memory.

‡43. General-purpose associative memory   Consider an N-bit pattern represented as a vector $\mathbf{x}$, and a matrix $\mathbf{W}$ that maps $\mathbf{x}$ to an output vector $\mathbf{y}$. Find the matrix $\mathbf{W}$ such that $\text{sign}(\mathbf{Wx}) = \mathbf{y}$, where the sign function is 1 for argument > 0 and -1 when argument < 0. (Hint: Use a transpose of $\mathbf{x}$ to help find an answer with pseudo-inverse.) If several such $\mathbf{x}$-$\mathbf{y}$ pairs are "learned" by a series of matrices $\mathbf{W}_1, \mathbf{W}_2, \mathbf{W}_3$, then a matrix $\mathbf{W}_T = \sum_i \mathbf{W}_i$, the sum of the $\mathbf{W}_i$'s, will be a good associative memory.

If $\mathbf{W}$ is a symmetric matrix ($w_{ij} = w_{ji}$) with $w_{ii} = 0$, then $\mathbf{W}$ will relax to a stable state without oscillating and it will be a good model of animal memory. See Haykin (1994, chap. 8) for discussion of Hopfield memory.

44. A LIFO stack needs a hold condition and a full indicator.

    (a)   Draw out an eight-deep LIFO stack for four-bit words, showing connections between the four-bit registers.

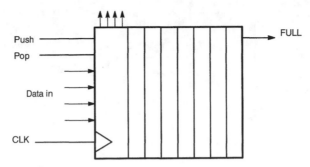

Figure P8.11

    (b)   Show a design in which the clock may be gated by push and pop instructions. If push and pop are asserted simultaneously, give pop priority.

    (c)   Show a circuit that will generate a HI output when the stack is full (all eight registers loaded).

45.   (a)   In the 4×4 FIFO of Fig. 8.40, complete the design of the pointer unit. Let WRITE have precedence over READ if both are asserted simultaneously.

    (b)   The following DATA-IN, WRITE, and READ operations are performed in a 4×1 FIFO. What will OUT be after each operation?

DATA	WRITE	READ	OUT	
02	✓		?	
03	✓			
X		✓		
04	✓			
05	✓			
X		✓		
X		✓		
X		✓		
CLEAR			?	clock ticks

46. What condition will signal FIFO *empty* for a static RAM FIFO? The empty condition will prevent reading from an empty buffer.

47. In the static RAM FIFO described in the text (Fig. 8.41), can a push and a pop happen simultaneously?

48. Design the compare unit (with empty and full output and WA and RA input) for the RAM FIFO shown in Fig. 8.41. See the following figure.

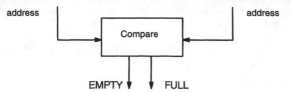

address   address

EMPTY ▼ ▼ FULL

Figure P8.12

49. Consider a 256-deep FIFO stack made with static RAM, as described in the text (Fig. 8.41). Every time data is added to the stack, a write counter is incremented. Every time data is read from the stack, a read counter is incremented. Both counters roll over to zero after they reach 255. Pairs of write and read addresses are given below in hex. Which pairs represent the stack's being full? Which represent its being empty?

Write Address	Read Address
0A	FA
00	02
FF	01
FE	FF
01	01
AB	AC

50. A 1024-deep FIFO buffer is fed data at a rate of 10 MHz; at the same time the FIFO is read at a rate of 5 MHz. How long will it take before the FIFO is full? How many words of data will have been read in that time?

51. In 1885 Hermann Ebbinghaus published *Uber das Gedächtnis* (On Memory), about his years of research investigating the powers and limitations of his own memory. Ebbinghaus would try to memorize three-letter nonsense syllables composed of two consonants surrounding a vowel: TAJ, ZIN, VEC, YOK, DAK, and so on. One result he called the "serial-position effect." On one day he would attempt to memorize a list of nonsense syllables, then test for recall the next day. Ebbinghaus found that syllables near the beginning of the list were easiest to remember, followed by items near the end; items in the middle of the list were most difficult to recall.

Inspired by Ebbinghaus's finding, design a digital logic memory system that recalls only the first and last items of a list. To be specific, suppose that on each clock pulse a random four-bit number is presented to your system. Let there be a CLEAR pulse that can erase all the contents of the memory and restart the list. After CLEAR, the clock starts ticking and new random numbers appear. When a RECALL input is activated, the system will respond by displaying (presenting as output) the number most recently acquired and the first number acquired after CLEAR. Try to minimize the number of flip-flops you need for your "Ebbinghaus memory."

52. Compare (qualitatively!) human memory and semiconductor SRAM memory on these counts:

Speed
Capacity
Addressing method
Ease of erasing
Writing method
Memory retention during power failure
Error rate
Associative capability

‡53. **Dual-port RAM** Memory can be a bottleneck in a digital system; only one read or write operation at a time is allowed, even though the memory may contain millions of useful data. A parallel processor may be able to use several words from memory simultaneously but be frustrated by one-at-a-time access to the information. Let's consider a way to widen the memory bottleneck.

What if two addresses could be presented simultaneously, and two words read at once? Even better, what if the memory could be read from and written to at the same time? Design, in block-diagram form, a memory with two *ports*.[14] A common block of memory cells, say 4×4, must be able to be read from or written to by two different addresses specified by two independent address ports. The actions must occur during one clock cycle.

References

COLE, B. 1988. Content-addressable memories catch on. *Electronics*, February, 65.

CUNNINGHAM, D. R., AND J. A. STULLER. 1994. *Basic circuit analysis.* New York: John Wiley & Sons.

GEIGER, R. L., P. E. ALLEN, AND N. R. STRADER. 1990. *VLSI design techniques.* New York: McGraw-Hill.

HAZNEDAR, H. 1991. *Digital microelectronics.* Reading, Mass.: Addison-Wesley.

HINTON, G., AND J. ANDERSON, eds. 1981. *Parallel models of associative memory.* Hillsdale, N.J.: Lawrence Erlbaum Assoc.

HODGES, D. 1977. Microelectronic memories. *Scientific American*, July, 130–138.

IEEE Transactions on Solid State Circuits, November 1991.

KOHONEN, T. 1980. *Content-addressable memories.* Berlin: Springer-Verlag.

MANO, M. 1988. *Computer hardware engineering.* Englewood Cliffs, N.J.: Prentice Hall.

Micron DRAM Data Book. 1994. Boise, Idaho: Micron Technology Inc.

[14] A *port* is a set of pins on a chip ready to be connected to a bus. A memory chip has address and data ports. If the memory chip has one bit of output, the one bit is not usually referred to as a port. Often *port* particularly refers to a set of input/output pins, as in an I/O port.

MINSKY, M. 1986. *The society of mind.* New York: Simon & Schuster.

NOYCE, R. 1977. Microelectronics. *Scientific American,* September, 67–76.

PRINCE, B. 1991. *Semiconductor memories: A handbook of design, manufacture, and application.* New York: John Wiley & Sons.

SEDRA, A. S., AND K. C. SMITH. 1991. *Microelectronic circuits.* 3d ed. Philadelphia: Saunders.

SHIVA, S. G. 1988. *Introduction to logic design.* Boston: Scott-Foresman/Little, Brown.

VAN DE GOOR, A. J. 1991. *Testing semiconductor memories.* New York: John Wiley & Sons.

Digital Communication and Serial Transmission

OVERVIEW

Communication is one of the major themes of twentieth-century electronic technology. In Chapter 9 we'll explore the world of **digital communication,** paying particular attention to the serial transmission of data. Design of systems that transmit or receive digitized information will allow you to exercise your skills with combinational and finite state machine circuits. You will learn that the sender and receiver circuits are likely to run on different, independent clocks; therefore **synchronization** of received data is an important issue in digital communication.

It is appropriate to consider digital communication at this point in the text because you now have a full set of basic tools with which to engineer designs for practical problems. You could just as well proceed to Chapter 10 (on arithmetic hardware) after Chapter 8, but the growing importance of digital communication is motivation enough for Chapter 9.

Here we focus on the digital logic (combinational and sequential) needed for sending and receiving multiple-bit messages one bit or one character at a time. We'll limit ourselves to one sender and one receiver—no network involved. If a multiple-bit word is ready to be transmitted one bit at a time in the sender circuit, a **parallel-to-serial shift register** is needed for transmission. On the receiving side a **serial-to-parallel shift register** can reverse the transmission process and make the serial message available as a whole word. Often one end or the other of a serial transmission system is in charge of the transmission and is called the **server,** whereas the **client** (which requested it) awaits data. (There's not a good match between client/server and master/slave terminology, but in one sense many clients may use one server as a slave for them.) After establishing general methods of sending and receiving data, we'll consider issues in **error correction** and the **encrypting** of messages. The extra bits needed for error correction in a message will be contrasted with the need for **data compression.** Finally, more detailed design of a back-and-forth communication link between client and server, governed by a sequential **handshake** circuit, will be sketched.

9.1   INTRODUCTION TO SERIAL TRANSMISSION

We saw in Chapter 1 that transmission of digital data is less prone to error than transmission of analog data. Digital data, however, may require many wires for

482

handling the many bits in a message. Over long distances it may become too expensive to lay out and maintain many parallel wires from one system to another. The solution is **serial transmission,** communicating information on *one* wire. Serially transmitted digital information invariably travels in the form of pulses, so one bit can be distinguished from another. It can be important how narrow the pulses are and at what rate they're sent. A pulse train either needs to be as fast (high-frequency) as possible or it needs to be timed precisely at a certain rate to match an oscillator in a receiving circuit.

Serial communication can in fact be digital or analog. Here in Chapter 9 we will stick to transmission of *digital* information. Some forms of communication—notably speech and music—are naturally sent in serial form (time series) anyway and are ideal for transmission on single wires. Other forms of information, such as two-dimensional images and maps, are naturally suited to parallel transmission but can be formatted for serial communication.

For successful transmission, the sending and receiving units must use the same transmission **protocol,** or method of encoding and transmitting data. We can classify serial transmission systems in a few ways. If data *and a clock signal* are sent, the system can be synchronous. If transmission is one-way, from a sender to receiver, it's called (in the modem[1] business) **simplex.** If transmission can be two-way but only one side can be the sender at any one time, the system is **half-duplex. Full duplex** describes a system in which both sides can simultaneously transmit and receive. See Bingham (1988).

Once sent from a transmitter, a message may enter a **network.** A network is a means of connecting more than two machines together for communication. A transmission from one machine has associated with it the names or addresses of the machines for which the message is intended. The network delivers the message only to those machines specified in the *receiver field* of the transmission. A contemporary example of a network for delivering digital messages is the **Internet,** the worldwide distributed network for electronic mail and the World Wide Web.

General reference: The September 1991 issue of *Scientific American* is devoted to the theme of "Communications, Computers and Networks," with special emphasis on networks.

EXAMPLE 1

Chapter 1 noted that telegraphy (invented 1835) was the first digital electronic communication system. Operator key pulse widths helped determine the information content of the telegraph message, which was sent out serially. Telegraph transmission was from point to point; no network other than first-come–first-served was involved.

The telephone system (started in 1876) replaced telegraphy with analog transmission that can send voice. Bandwidth is normally limited to about 3 kHz. There are

---

[1]*Modem* stands for *modulate-dem*odulate and normally refers to the processes of modulating digital data onto acoustic phone lines and demodulating the received acoustic signal back to digital pulse form. A self-contained modem also has an encoder, a decoder, and filters and has the capability of automatically dialing the phone number of another modem for the exchange of data. If the all-digital phone network (ISDN) becomes a reality, the widespread need for modems may be obviated. Also, two-dimensional images can be transmitted via modem by use of a facsimile (fax) machine.

during most power failures!) and one each for transmit and receive. The keyboard of a Touch-tone phone uses a frequency code to transmit different numbers as network addresses; the network address is transmitted on the same lines that the message will be carried on after point-to-point connection is established. The telephone companies of the world are in the process of shifting service to ISDN (Integrated Services Digital Network), which will transform the telephone system to an all-digital network.

Serial transmission is suitable for information generated at a low rate. An example is a computer keyboard. As Chapter 1 showed, the ASCII code for letters, numbers, and other text formatting symbols uses seven bits per character. Each time a key is pressed, the seven bits of the character plus a parity bit are transmitted on one wire to the computer, where a serial-to-parallel operation brings the character into a computer register and displays it on the monitor (unless it's a password character or a control character such as ENTER).

Television images are transmitted serially. In the case of broadcast television (and radio) the transmission doesn't use wires. Television and FM radio signals are broadcast on frequencies of about 100 MHz that carry by modulating the much lower frequency audio and video information. Serial transmission for television starts with the camera. A video camera scans a scene one pixel at a time, where the pixel locations are arranged in hundreds of row-column combinations. The analog intensity at each pixel is transmitted along with signals about the end of each row and the end of each picture. Present-day TV is a combination of digital position and analog intensity. New American standards are currently being considered by the Federal Communications Commission for high-definition TV, which will convert television transmission to an all-digital format.

9.2 BITS OF INFORMATION

Imagine you've just found out something new, like the next letter in a *Wheel of Fortune* round. How much **information** does the new event Q provide? We can give a quantitative answer by the following argument. Suppose the **probability** of the event Q was p; intuitively, discovery of a low-probability event should provide more information than discovery of a high-probability event. In the high-probability extreme, if $p = 1$, the event provides no new information—you knew in advance that the particular event would happen. Can we therefore make the following the information content of event Q?

$$\text{information} = \frac{1}{\text{probability}} = \frac{1}{p}$$

It's a good start, but consider what happens when data starts coming in a stream (time sequence) as it will during serial transmission. Suppose two events are received, each of probability $\frac{1}{8}$. The probability of two such (independent) events is $\frac{1}{8} \times \frac{1}{8} = \frac{1}{64}$, suggesting 64 units of information, or eight times as much as one event. The calculation is correct as far as probability theory is concerned, but wouldn't it make more sense that two events should provide *twice* as much information as one, instead of eight times as much? Is there a function that will turn the product into a sum? Yes:

$$\log(a \cdot b) = \log a + \log b$$

What base should we choose for the logarithm? For binary systems, 2 is a convenient choice. Now let the information content of an event be

$$\text{information} = \log_2\left(\frac{1}{\text{probability}}\right)$$

By this formula an event of probability $= 1$ will have information $= 0$. An event of probability $\frac{1}{2}$ will have 1 unit of information. The more improbable an event, the more information its arrival provides. The name of a unit of information is the **bit** (*binary unit* of information). Yes, since Chapter 1 we have used the term *bit* to describe one *binary digit* in a binary number: 1011 is a four-bit number, and we have been referring to four-bit counters and 256 Kb memories, and so on. In fact the term *bit* has more specialized meaning to a communications engineer. Strictly speaking, only when the probability of receiving a 1 or a 0 is $\frac{1}{2}$ will a communications engineer say a wire in a digital system is a one-bit wire, and even then the engineer may be more interested in the bits/s data transmission rate of the wire, rather than the message being transmitted.

Resuming the mathematics of information, reception of the above event of probability $\frac{1}{8}$ bears $\log_2(8) = 3$ bits of information. Two events of probability $\frac{1}{8}$ have

$$\log_2\left[\frac{1}{\frac{1}{8} \times \frac{1}{8}}\right] = \log_2(64) = 6 \text{ bits}$$

of information, just the additivity we want.

Channel capacity (of a serial line) can be expressed in bits per second. The term **baud** refers to symbols per second; if the symbols in a certain alphabet can be represented by a five-bit code, then for this certain alphabet, 100 bits/s $= 20$ baud.

For more "information" see Ash (1965) and Gray (1990).[2]

9.3 ONE-WAY TRANSMISSION

Suppose a multiple-bit message is ready to be sent from one system to another over a serial line. The sender and receiver must be on the same page—the receiver must

---

[2]The basis of information theory was first developed by Claude Shannon working at Bell Labs in the late 1940s. Richard Feynman considered Shannon's work, along with the work of Sadi Carnot (who formulated the second law of thermodynamics), the two most important contributions of *engineers* to fundamental understanding of nature. Carnot's and Shannon's work are not unrelated: information is essentially the opposite of the thermodynamic concept *entropy*, a measure of system disorder.

received message. What general characteristics should the sender have in order to transmit one bit at a time, and what design should the receiver have to accept the multiple-bit message? Let's assume one-way transmission. One-way transmission prevents the receiver from acknowledging or initiating the transmission, so the receiver must be vigilant for the next message. In fact, the sender can transmit anytime (asynchronously with respect to the receiver). We know from the design of synchronous sequential circuits that a single clock must be distributed to all flip-flops involved. Should the clock be transmitted along with the data? In many protocols that's not possible; the transmitted message contains start information that synchronizes a clock on the receiving side. We continue with an example.

9.3.1 Sending Four Bits

EXAMPLE 2

Assume that four bits, D_3–D_0, are ready to be transmitted one-way (simplex mode). Because the sender cannot receive feedback from the receiver in one-way transmission, the sender will need its own clock to define the time intervals over which the bits are to be sent. To send bits out one at a time, use a shift register. Load the flip-flops in the shift register all at once with a **parallel-in–serial-out (PISO)** chip. (The 74195 TTL IC chip is a four-bit PISO register; it also has a parallel-out port.) See Fig. 9.1 for the sender using a PISO register. There are four data inputs (D_3–D_0), a clock, and a shift-load control. Each D input on the four D flip-flops has a MUX whose SELECT input is controlled by $S/\overline{L}$ (shift-load control). When $S/\overline{L}$ is LO, the MUXs select the data input for a parallel load; when $S/\overline{L}$ is HI, the MUXs select the Q output from the flip-flop on the left and, at the CLOCK edge, data are shifted to the right.

If $S/\overline{L}$ changes out of phase with the active CLOCK edge, timing skew problems will be minimized. If rising-edge-triggered D flip-flops are used, transmission of one four-bit message could have the timing diagram shown in Fig. 9.2. The controller stops the message by returning $S/\overline{L}$ to LO. The LSB will be transmitted first.

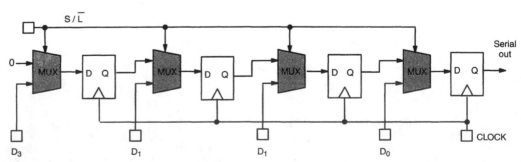

Figure 9.1 Parallel-in–serial-out shift register.

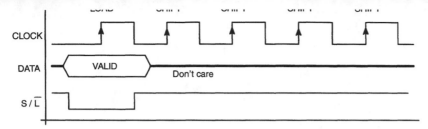

Figure 9.2 Timing of four-bit PISO sender for parallel-to-serial conversion.

Does the process need four shifts or three? The receiver needs four shifts to bring in all the data, but the sender may need only three pulses to move all the data to the serial-out port. Does it matter if 0 is shifted in at the left MUX? No. We'll worry about how the receiver deals with starting and stopping the message shortly.

Another way to deliver one bit at a time from a multiple-bit word is to use a multiplexer. Let a counter connected to the MUX SELECT sequence through the bits to be sent. Figure 9.3 shows eight bits on the data-in pins of an $8 \to 1$ MUX. Whether D_0 or D_7 is sent first depends on the protocol of the transmission. The MUX approach is a "memoryless" method in which the data need to be available from a source for the whole duration of the transmission, unlike the shift register approach, in which data path contents can be loaded into a memory register and then the data path used for other purposes. You do need three flip-flops in the counter to remember what state the transmission is in.

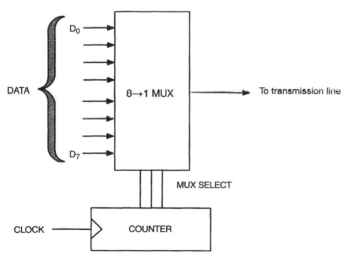

Figure 9.3 Multiplexer-based PISO transmission.

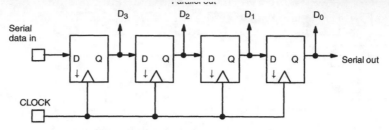

Figure 9.4 Parallel-in–serial-out SIPO shift register.

9.3.2 Receiving

Consider two kinds of message transmission: first, information accompanied by a clock signal on another wire, and then asynchronous messages on which the receiver must perform an **asynchronous-to-synchronous conversion (ASC)** to recover the message.

When transmission includes a clock we can directly use a **serial-in–parallel-out (SIPO)** shift register to capture the message (see Fig. 9.4). If the data have been transmitted on the rising edge of CLOCK, they should be captured on the falling edge. Look at the clock and data edges in Fig. 9.5 to see why.

The sender and receiver circuits must agree on which bit is to be the most significant. If the PISO from earlier in the chapter is used to transmit the data, the MSB will end up in the left flip-flop. A timing diagram for sending and receiving one four-bit word might look like the waveforms in Fig. 9.5, with receiving highlighted.

Is this timing all right for receiving a four-bit word? The receiver must ignore the first clock pulse (or the sender must not transmit it) for this circuit correctly to shift in one four-bit word. But how does the receiver know where one word ends and the

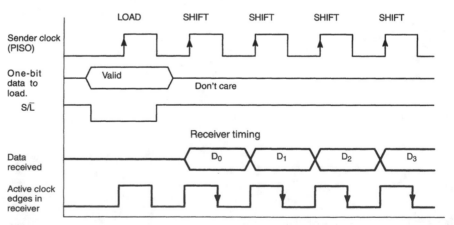

Figure 9.5 Sender and receiver timing for a four-bit PISO-SIPO.

next one begins? A new word could come immediately after one transmitted, or a variable amount of time could elapse before the next message. There are a number of different methods by which a protocol can mark the boundaries of a transmitted word, or block of words.

1. The receiver can count the number of pulses, but that still leaves the question of when to *start* counting. Since the clock is being sent to the receiver, we can expect that all the receiver counter needs to know is when a many-word message block starts and that it can capture the words faithfully until the end of the block. (We assume that the words are of constant bit length and that there is an end-of-block signal.)

2. The *amplitude* of the data or clock line can be sent to an unusual voltage (mark), such as +7 V or −7 V, at the start of a new word or block. An analog comparator can be used to detect the unusual event. The logic output of the comparator could then clear a counter or something else to begin the receiving process. If DATA and CLOCK go first to a *line receiver* chip, then the line receiver will not be harmed by +7-V or −7-V input.

3. The *quality* (width or frequency) of a pulse, on either the clock or the data line, can vary at the start or end of a word. For example, a clock pulse that is missing or is narrower or wider than a normal clock pulse could signal the start of a new word. A burst of narrow pulses is another possibility for a word-starting marker. Television uses variation in pulse width to mark end-of-line and end-of-frame locations in the time signal that carries pixel information. (If you tune a cable TV box to an unsubscribed premium channel, you'll see a wavy, desynchronized picture; the box strips off end-of-line pulses before the signal gets to the television set itself.)

4. The *pattern* of pulses could signal termination. If DATA input goes HI after the word has been transmitted, it always goes LO for one clock cycle at the start of the next word. The always-LO start and always-HI stop bits would not be part of the variable-content message transmitted in between start and stop. We'll see pulse coding in use for asynchronous transmission.

It might be helpful for the receiver to tell the sender when a word has been completely received, but such feedback is not allowed in one-way transmission; its use will come later, and it will be included in a handshake design.

9.3.3 Asynchronous Receiving

An asynchronous receiver can use the same SIPO shift register to log in data, but it must use its own clock. The receiver's clock rate must be fairly close to the sender's, or asynchronous transmission won't work. Furthermore, the beginning of every word must be signaled by a start bit so that the receiver can resynchronize and minimize the skew (timing offset) between the two clocks. By limiting clock rates to baud rate standards, an RS-232 system avoids the need for special synchronizer circuits to minimize metastable responses in the receiver.

EXAMPLE 3

RS-232 Protocol   Let's consider an example of how asynchronous serial transmission **RS-232 protocol** sends information back and forth between (some) computers and peripherals such as keyboards, floppy disks, and video terminals. RS-232 is an 11-bit code of which 8 bits are an ASCII-coded message. (The eighth message bit can be used for parity check, or it can be always 0.) Each eight-bit message is responsible for one character (letter, number, and so on). See Chapter 1 for more details on the ASCII code.

RS-232 uses negative logic—low voltages are logical HI, and high voltages are logical LO. In its idle state the RS-232 output is at a *mark value*, a voltage less than −5 V. The start of a character transmission is signaled by the rising edge of a *start bit*, from mark up to logical LO. The start bit is always at LO for one clock pulse (see Fig. 9.6). Then the eight information bits are sent, followed by two *stop bits*, which are always at logical HI. After the two stop bits another character can follow immediately or an indefinite interval of mark value can be sustained.

Computer Terminal Interface   If I hook an oscilloscope channel to (and trigger on) pin 2 ("transmit") of the RS-232 connector on the back of my computer terminal and hold down the S key, I see the pattern in Fig. 9.7 repeated. Notice the negative logic on the RS-232 bus; the signal will be translated immediately to TTL levels by a 1489 line receiver chip in the computer interface. The seven-bit ASCII code for uppercase S (101 0011) is transmitted last-bit-first with a 0 filling in the eighth bit place for even parity.

There is 0.1 ms per bit, implying about 900 characters/s maximum rate. If I put another oscilloscope probe on pin 3 ("receive") of the RS-232 connector, I see

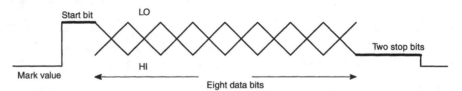

Figure 9.6   Representation of a generic 11-bit RS-232 transmission.

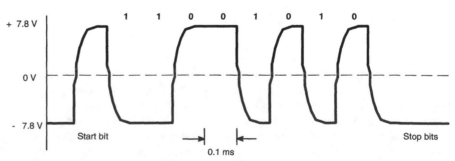

Figure 9.7   RS-232 transmission of seven-bit ASCII code for uppercase S: 101 0011. Start and stop bits are not shown.

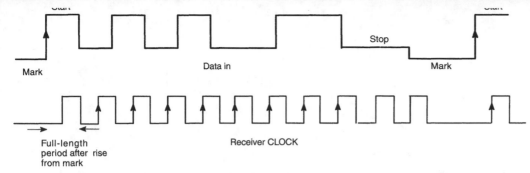

Mark

Data in

Stop

Mark

Full-length
period after rise
from mark

Receiver CLOCK

Figure 9.8 Eight-bit data word 0011 0101 (ASCII 5) surrounded by a start bit and two stop bits.

the same waveform for S returned (echoed) about 50 ms after the keyboard waveform was transmitted, implying a sustained typing rate of 20 characters/s. Most of the 50-ms delay is taken up with the echo process in the computer.

Timing To make RS-232 asynchronous transmission succeed, the clock in the receiver must be set to about the same rate (±5%) as the clock in the sender. For example, at 110 b/s (11 characters per second) the clock period should be about 9 ms. In addition, the receiver clock has to be reset at the start of the character message. See the waveforms in Fig. 9.8. The clock in the receiver is inhibited until the start bit occurs, and then it begins with a *full period*. It then clocks in, with a rising edge, the first message bit near the middle of the first bit's tenure on the DATA-IN line. The receiver then captures data for a shift register on the rising edges of its clock pulses. If the receiver clock active edge starts in the middle of the sender clock period, after 10 cycles it can't move more than half a waveform, or errors may result:

$$\frac{(1/2)}{10} = \frac{1}{20} = 5\%$$

Thus the 5% rule.

The two stop bits at the end of the RS-232 transmission also give the receiver time to move the data out of the eight-bit SIPO register to another register for processing or storage. The SIPO register is then available for the next word. Again, with no feedback to the sender, the receiver must assume that another data cycle can start any time after the present stop bits have passed.

EXAMPLE 4

What kind of oscillator-sequencer will start with a full-length period, and then stop after 11 pulses, as shown above? Its only valid starting stimulus is a rising edge from mark of the signal, and it has to ignore other rising edges of the signal until the sequence is over. (Actually, inside the receiver, a 1489 line driver will invert the DATA line, but let's ignore that sign change for now.)

Answer A design with two 1-shots and an **analog-to-digital comparator** is shown in Fig. 9.9. A 1-shot produces one pulse whose width is proportional to *RC* in response to a rising or falling edge. The analog comparator output is logical HI if its "+" input

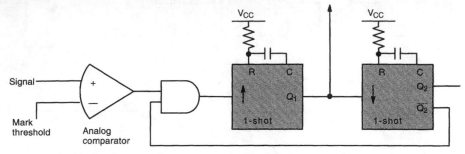

Figure 9.9 Mark voltage used to generate clock pulses to capture data.

is greater than its "−" input; otherwise the output is LO. Notice that the analog comparator *inputs* don't have to be logical values! The analog comparator acts as a one-bit A-to-D converter.

Assume to begin with that the 1-shots are off, in other words, that the $\overline{Q_2}$ output of the second 1-shot is HI, enabling the AND gate. When the signal rises above the mark threshold (a level slightly above the mark voltage), the comparator output goes HI. The AND gate *output* goes from LO to HI, triggering a calibrated pulse on the first 1-shot. When the first pulse falls from HI to LO, the second 1-shot is triggered and its $\overline{Q_2}$ output goes from HI to LO, and then back from LO to HI. On the $\overline{Q_2}$ transition from LO to HI, a new rising edge will be presented to the first 1-shot, and the cycle repeats. The AND gate stays enabled the whole time that the signal is less than the mark. When the signal falls below the mark at the end of a transmission, the first 1-shot input is held LO and the second 1-shot doesn't trigger.

Figure 9.10 shows what timing for the circuit looks like. The widths t_1 and t_2 of the two 1-shot pulses must be adjusted so that their sum equals the period of the

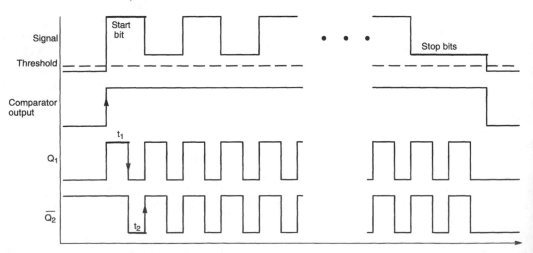

Figure 9.10 Timing for circuit in Fig. 9.9.

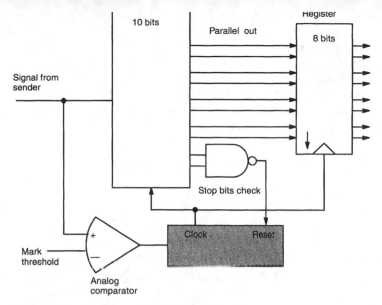

Figure 9.11 RS-232 receiver with two stop bits.

oscillator required to time the signal bits: $t_1 + t_2 = T_{CLOCK}$. Thus the 1-shot approach does need fine tuning of its timing circuits to function properly.

A complete receiver circuit, with a 10-bit up-shifting SIPO register, is shown in Fig. 9.11. The analog comparator together with the pulse generator with reset is basically the *phase-locked oscillator* of Fig. 9.9. The main problem is picking off the eight message bits from between the start and stop bits. In this design is a 10-bit PISO, which shifts in all 11 bits but saves only the last 10, which are the eight message bits and two stop bits. The shifting occurs during the time when the analog comparator output is HI (the signal is greater than the mark). When the signal input drops below the mark, the comparator output goes from HI to LO and latches the eight-bit message into another shift register. The two stop bits are passed through a NAND gate; if at the end of the word's transmission the NAND gate isn't HI, something went wrong. Error detection and correction will be discussed further in Section 9.4.

Summary for Receiving Circuits A common transmission protocol must be incorporated in both sending and receiving circuits. If the receiving circuit has access to the sender's clock, then a serial-in–parallel-out (SIPO) shift register will solve most problems of the receiver. If the receiver must be asynchronous (no sender clock), the receiver must maintain its own clock near the frequency of the sender. In the asynchronous mode the receiver can take in only one word at a time before resetting its clock phase in response to the next start bit.

What should happen to a received character? Storage or processing in the receiver is eventually necessary, but perhaps the first step is a check of the received word for errors, as described next.

The transmission line of a serial communications system can be susceptible to noise pulses that flip bits to incorrect values. In fact, even inside a computer, alpha radiation from packaging and cosmic radiation from outer space can alter the contents of memory chips. As in the case of a musician hearing a wrong note during a recording and needing to correct it on a second try, there is a need for altered digital transmission data to be identified and perhaps corrected.

9.4.1 Parity Check

If the total number of 1s in a word is *even*, the word has *even parity*. Odd parity is the other possibility. A binary number with even parity is not the same as an even number: an even number always ends in 0. Especially if the error rate is low, giving all message words the same parity can help the receiver determine whether an error in transmission has occurred. Restricting messages to only even or odd parity words eliminates half the possible code words for a message of a fixed bit length. Instead a code such as ASCII normally allows different characters to be represented by odd- or even-parity words, and an extra bit is appended to the transmission to make the parity constant. Once it has taken in a complete word, the receiver circuit can check parity. Similarly, some manufacturers of memory chips sell memories utilizing nine-bit words, where the ninth bit is used for parity check.

The parity of a word can be checked efficiently with XOR gates.

EXAMPLE 5

In the following figure, seven XOR gates are used to detect the parity of an eight-bit word.

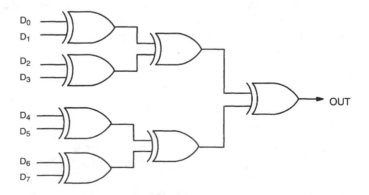

Discovery of a parity error means only that an error occurred; it doesn't tell us which bit the error occurred in. Further, exactly two flipped bits (or four or any other even number) in a word will pass through parity check disguised as a correct transmission. How likely are two errors per word? Let's say that the probability of one bit being reversed (causing an error) in the transmission process is a relatively high $0.1 = 10\%$ (probability of correct transmission is 90%). The probability that *no* error occurs in an eight-bit transmission is $0.9^8 = 0.43$. The probability of exactly one error out of eight bits can be calculated from the binomial formula

$$p^{n-r}q^r\binom{n}{r} = p^7 q^1 \frac{n!}{r!(n-r)!} = 0.9^7 \cdot 0.1 \cdot \frac{8!}{1\cdot 7!} = 0.38$$

where p is the probability of correct transmission and $q = 1 - p$ is the probability of error. Using the same combinatorial formula, the probability of exactly two errors in an eight-bit transmission is 0.15. Thus a parity checker would have a two-out-of-eight-bit error rate of 15% if a single bit is wrong 10% of the time! Therefore 10% is an unacceptably high rate of single-bit error even when eight-bit words are concerned; error rates that are much lower (by orders of magnitude) are needed in practical transmission systems. When low (but nonzero) rates are achieved, parity checking for one error per word becomes worthwhile.

9.4.2 Error Correction

Can the receiver *correct* messages with errors? Remember, we're still not allowing the receiver to send back a message reporting a parity check error. One way to make sure the right message gets through is to repeat the message every time. Suppose we want to send a four-bit message and make sure that the correct message is received in spite of errors. We could send a repeat of the message, but what if one bit is different between the original and the repeat? We'd have no way of knowing which of the two different bits was the correct one. So we'd have to send three copies of the message, 12 bits in all. Now if one bit is different in one of the three versions, majority rule could decide the correct 0 or 1. Of course, two bits in the same position can be incorrect, so the triple repeat would still make an occasional error.

Is there a way that uses fewer bits? Consider a transmission in which N bits represent one symbol. For N bits in a code word, 2^N different words are possible. If $N = 8$, the number of combinations is 256. But there's no law that says we can't use our N bits to account for fewer message states. If only a subset of the 2^N possible words are selected as valid code words, then all other combinations of the N bits will be errors. For example, if only $\{0000, 0011, 0110, 1001\}$ are valid code words, then receiving 0001, 0111, and so on means an error has occurred in transmission. (False negative errors can occur, too. If 0000 were sent and 0011 were received, the two-bit error will go undetected.) With this thought in mind, we next consider a specific means of coding in which certain errors can not only be detected, but corrected. We can achieve the same result using the **seven-bit Hamming code** as we could using the 12-bit triple repeat of four bits: we can *correct* any one-bit error. Further, the **eight-bit Hamming code** can *detect* any two-bit error in the four-bit message.

associative memory in Chapter 8. Consider two strings A and B of equal length, described by

$$A_N A_{N-1} A_{N-2} \ldots A_2 A_1 A_0 \quad \text{and} \quad B_N B_{N-1} B_{N-2} \ldots B_2 B_1 B_0$$

where each A_i and B_i is a bit in position i.

The **Hamming distance** between these two binary strings of equal length is the number of pairs $\{A_i, B_i\}$, $i = 0$ to N, in which $A_i \neq B_i$. If two strings are identical, the Hamming distance is zero; for every bit-pair that is different, the Hamming distance increases by one. For N-bit strings, the maximum Hamming distance possible is N: all bits are different. The Hamming distance between 0010 and 1101 is 4. You will see in the following coding scheme that a minimum Hamming distance between code words is a necessary condition for a successful error-detecting and -correcting code.

The 7,4 Hamming Code   A message of four bits is embedded in a transmission of seven bits. The three *check bits* provide enough information that a one-bit error anywhere in the seven bits can be corrected. First we consider the encoding process. For four bits, you will see that three check bits will suffice for single error correction. Let's call the message bits $M_3 M_2 M_1 M_0$. It turns out that we need a minimum of three check bits $C_2 C_1 C_0$, giving a total transmission of $M_3 M_2 M_1 M_0 C_2 C_1 C_0$. The C's will depend on the M's. Let $C_2 = f_2(M_3, M_2, M_1)$, $C_1 = f_1(M_3, M_2, M_0)$, and $C_0 = f_0(M_3, M_1, M_0)$. M_3 is in all three functions; the other M's are in two out of three. What Boolean functions f did Hamming choose? Here's Hamming's recipe which leads to the ability for error *correction*. Have each C_i be the bit that makes the parity of the string $\{C_i, M_x, M_y, M_z\}$ always the same. Then C_i becomes 0 or 1, whichever is needed to make the number of 1s in the set $\{C_i, M_x, M_y, M_z\}$ *even*. Said another way, $C_i = (M_x + M_y + M_z) \bmod 2$, or $C_i = M_x \oplus M_y \oplus M_z$.

Figure 9.12 is a Venn diagram that shows the same set of relationships. Parity is even for the four elements inside each circle; for example, the upper left circle, P_2, contains C_2, M_3, M_2, and M_1; since there must be an even number of 1s (zero, two, or four), the *sender (encoder)* adjusts C_2 for correct parity. The four message bits are the independent variables here; their expression in a truth table results in $2^4 = 16$

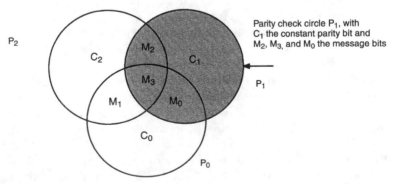

Figure 9.12   Venn diagram illustrating group parity checks for 7,4 Hamming code.

M_3	M_2	M_1	M_0	C_2	C_1	C_0
0	0	0	0	0	0	0
0	0	0	1	0	1	1
0	0	1	0	1	0	1
0	0	1	1	1	1	0
0	1	0	0	1	1	0
0	1	0	1	1	0	1
0	1	1	0	0	1	1
0	1	1	1	0	0	0
1	0	0	0	1	1	1
1	0	0	1	1	0	0
1	0	1	0	0	1	0
1	0	1	1	0	0	1
1	1	0	0	0	0	1
1	1	0	1	0	1	0
1	1	1	0	1	0	0
1	1	1	1	1	1	1

lines with three outputs C_1, C_2, C_3, as shown in Table 9.1. Look, for example, at every group of $\{M_3, M_2, M_1, C_2\}$: thanks to C_2, there's an even number of 1s in each group. The constant-parity bits C_i must be appended in the sender circuit (see Fig. 9.13).

9.4.3 Correcting One-bit Errors

Assume that an error is introduced during transmission *after* the check bits are appended. For a seven-bit transmission, the error may be in the message bits or in the check bits. First consider what things look like if no error occurs. Our decoder will find that all three of the check/parity relationships have even parity. The decoder works on each relationship by XORing the four bits concerned together (cascading three XOR gates) and finds 0s on each output (0 = OK, no error).

Let's say each parity check circuit OUT drives an LED in our hardware. Now suppose one check bit is missent. Our decoder will find a parity error in only one of the Venn diagram parity-check relationships; that relationship names the *location* of the check bit error. For example, suppose 0000 001 is received. If we assume that only one error was made, we humans can tell by inspection that the message must have been 0000 000. Our receiving decoder, however, has no such powers of inspection, so it must work through the C_0 decoder XOR circuit, and one LED C_0, will light up because $f_0 = P_0 = C_0 \oplus M_3 \oplus M_1 \oplus M_0 = 1$; *the other two decoder XOR circuits don't*

Figure 9.13 Block diagram of transmission and reception of parity-encoded message.

Table 9.2   Decoding Outputs for
One-Bit Message Errors

Erroneous Bit	P_2	P_1	P_0
M_3	1	1	1
M_2	1	1	0
M_1	1	0	1
M_0	0	1	1

depend on C_0, so they will stay 0. Because only the C_0-based circuit lights up, we and our circuit know that the one-bit error was in the C_0 position.

Now look what happens if a message bit is missent. Whichever message bit is incorrect will participate in two or more decoding XOR circuits, so two of the LEDs will light. For example, suppose 0100 000 is received. The message 0100 000 is not in our set of 16 allowed transmissions. By your human "maximum likelihood estimator" you can, with some effort, tell that 0000 must have been the intended message. The three decoding circuits will automatically have 110 as their output, which represents the *position* of the one message bit error. You can verify by a few more tests that the decoding outputs for the four possible one-bit *message* errors are as listed in Table 9.2. The three bits to the right are the decoder outputs of parity checks:

$$P_2 = C_2 \oplus M_3 \oplus M_2 \oplus M_1 \qquad P_1 = C_1 \oplus M_3 \oplus M_2 \oplus M_0 \qquad P_0 = C_0 \oplus M_3 \oplus M_1 \oplus M_0$$

These are the parity check expressions for the three circles in the Venn diagram of Fig. 9.12. Because M_3 participates in all three parity check relationships, all three P's light up for an error in M_3.

EXAMPLE 6

The following Hamming 7,4 message has been received:

$$M_3M_2M_1M_0 \, C_2C_1C_0 = 0111\,101$$

Is it a valid character, and if not, what was the intended character?

Answer   No, it's not valid. The combination is not one of the 16 in the *M-C* table (Table 9.1).

Is the error in the message or in the check bits? The three parity-check outputs are $P_2P_1P_0 = 101$. Since there are two parity-check errors, the mistake must be in the message part of the transmission. Looking at Table 9.1, we see that an error in M_1 gives 101, so the intended message must have been 0101 101, which is in the table of allowed transmissions.

What all this means is that if any one-bit error occurs in the seven-bit message, a circuit can decode where the error was. With more combinational logic it can correct the one-bit error. See Exercise 25 to continue with a design that does the actual error correction.

before transmission to the serial line, the message must be **encoded** (combined) with its error-correcting bits. The input to the encoding circuit is the message bits, and the output is the message bits plus the check and parity bits.

9.4.4 Detecting Two Errors

An occurrence of *exactly* two errors can be detected with an eighth bit, which creates the 8,4 Hamming code. By adding an overall parity bit in the eighth position, we can design a decoder that will *detect* (but not find the positions) when a two-bit error transmission has occurred. The eighth bit will depend on the other seven, so on the transmit side the check bits must be computed before the parity bit P is appended. The P bit ensures that there are an even number of 1s in the string of eight. A combinational circuit of XOR gates could do the encoding.

If one error occurs, the eighth parity bit will always be incorrect, and Table 9.2 will still be valid for correcting the error.

What if two errors are created during transmission? Suppose 1100 0000 is received. The eighth parity bit will be correct (as it will for every two-bit error), but the first seven bits will give an incorrect message, and not one that fits a one-bit error pattern. Since the eighth bit *isn't* in error, we can assume that a two-bit transmission error occurred, but we will not be able to tell where. What happens if the eighth bit is in error? See Exercise 26 for practice with two-error detection. If three or more errors occur during one transmission, our Hamming decoder will make mistakes. Presumably, three-bit errors will be rare events.

9.5 ENCRYPTING

Just as noise can *enter* a serial transmission line inadvertently, the signal can *leave* the transmission line inadvertently. In such a case the possibility of eavesdropping occurs. If the eavesdropper has a decoding circuit, he or she can decipher the message. But if the message is **encrypted** before it's sent, its transmission will be more secure. Only a receiver with the proper **key** can finish decoding its content.

EXAMPLE 7

Let's consider an encrypting scheme that uses the pseudorandom sequence generator (PRSG) of Chapter 6 plus an XOR gate to scramble the message (Fig. 9.14). If our message about to be sent is XORed with a synchronized set of bits from a PRSG, the signal on the transmission line will be scrambled and will not obey any obvious decoding scheme. In asynchronous transmission only the message, not the start and stop bits, should be encrypted, or the receiver won't know where one character ends and another begins.

At the receiving end we apply *the same pseudorandom sequence* of bits to the incoming signal, and the message will reappear on the other side. We depend on the relationship $M = M \oplus E \oplus E$, where M is the message and E is the encrypting

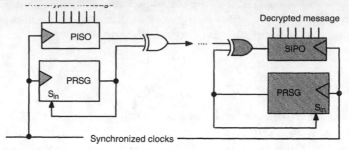

Figure 9.14 Crude encryption scheme using two identical, synchronized PRSGs.

sequence. The receiver must be able to tell when a received signal represents the start of an encrypted-message sequence so that the receiver can start its PRSG at the right time.

EXAMPLE 8

Circuit for the PRSG The circuit in Fig. 9.15 generates a pseudorandom sequence of length 2^8. (You've seen this circuit before, in Chapter 6.) The pseudorandom sequence generator provides the key for this encrypting system. By tapping different outputs of a serial-in–parallel-out shift register (such as the 74164 TTL chip), we can generate different pseudorandom sequences. The eight-bit shift register in this example will generate at most a 256-bit-long sequence, which is too short for a persistent spy not to be able to crack. In practice much longer (56-bit or longer shift registers) sequences are used, which effectively eliminate code cracking by algorithmic means.

The sender and receiver encrypting circuits need a way to reset all outputs to 0 in order to start the PRSG at a definite point; the 74164 has a CLEAR pin for resetting. On the receiving side, decrypting must be done *before* error detection and correction.

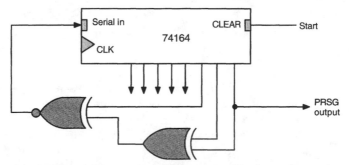

Figure 9.15 Pseudorandom sequence generator of length 256.

Encrypting can be done at the software level. For example, the UNIX operating system has a `crypt` command; if you crypt a file twice, it returns to its original form.

The crypt command prompts for a key to generate a 256-bit scrambler, and then it converts your file to an encrypted form. If the key is known by a distant receiver, electronic mail can be used to send coded messages. In an era of questionable security on the Internet, encrypting of e-mail is becoming common. A de facto standard for nongovernmental encrypting on personal computers is PGP (Pretty Good Protection; see Zimmerman 1995).

Encrypting is big business, and it is a national security issue for the United States. In 1994 the U.S. Senate considered a telecommunications bill that would require each telephone sold in the United States to have a "clipper chip" in it that would both provide for encrypting of voice data and enable the FBI, with a court order, to obtain a key and listen to encrypted messages during wiretaps. In 1995, a telecommunications reform bill passed, but without the clipper chip authorization.

Schiller (1994) discusses the Kerberos security and password system on the Athena network at MIT, a system that is being used to secure communications by other academic networks around the United States.

9.6   DATA COMPRESSION AND DECOMPRESSION: HUFFMAN VARIABLE-LENGTH CODE

Data compression is also big business. To the extent that the number of bits in a message can be reduced, the time and cost of the message's transmission can be reduced.

The first attack on compression starts at the code level. An optimal way to code a set of characters for *minimum transmission lengths* depends on knowing the probability of occurrence of each character. If these probabilities are known, the **Huffman algorithm** produces an optimal **variable-length code.** The Huffman algorithm has two phases: one phase that compresses the probability list down to two numbers, and another phase that expands the list back, assigning more bits to the parts of the expansion from the bottom of the list. The following example illustrates the Huffman algorithm.

EXAMPLE 9

Consider an alphabet of seven characters whose probabilities of occurrence in messages are as follows:

α	.26
β	.22
δ	.20
γ	.15
ε	.12
σ	.03
ξ	.02
	1.00

Find an optimal coding scheme for the small alphabet that will result, on average, in the fewest bits per message.

Answer Add together the smallest two probabilities and form a max-min column to the right, with one fewer entry than the parent column to the left, as shown below. Do the same for the new column, and continue doing the same for every new column. Continue until only two numbers remain in the last column.

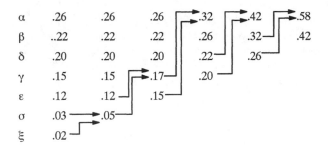

Now to generate the code: Label the two right-most numbers with bits 0 and 1. Follow the arrows back to the column to the left and add a bit to each of the two entries that were combined.

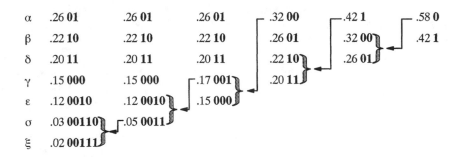

The binary patterns that reach the left-most column by this means are the optimal variable-length code for the probabilities given. Notice that shorter patterns match with more probable characters. (Huffman codes can also be visualized with a tree technique. For a quick tutorial on the World Wide Web go to http://www.crs4.it/~luigi/MPEG/huffman_tutorial.html.)

Because it's a compressing variable-length like Morse code, Huffman code doesn't look very easy to decode. But here's the beauty of the Huffman recipe: it's possible to string together letter codes in a word transmission and not have to use spacer bits. The decoder can unambiguously pick out the sequence of letters if it knows where the transmission starts. Try the message $\alpha\gamma\epsilon$ = 01 000 00111. The only code that starts with 01 is α, so the first letter must be 01 = α. If you strip off 01, you find that 000 is the only code letter that starts with 000, so 000 = γ is the second letter. The remaining code can fit only ϵ = 00111, and the message is complete.

One of the disadvantages of Huffman-type code is that if one bit of the message is lost in transmission, then the rest of the message cannot be decoded. For that reason, special symbol codes are introduced into long messages to act as restart markers. In the MPEG compression algorithm, start control codes begin with 23 0s followed by a 1. Since there is no other code word with 23 consecutive 0s, a restart is unambiguous.

Many compression algorithms do not work on the codes for individual characters or pixels; instead, they look for redundancies in the message and eliminate unnecessary letters, words, or frames. For example, skipping a few television frames because nothing is moving in the image can cut down considerably on the bandwidth required for transmission. In practice, a series of algorithms—JPEG, MPEG, and MPEG2—have been standardized over the last decade and applied to the problems of TV image compression.

It is the responsibility of the receiving circuit to decompress the message or image or file. In that regard, single-chip decoders for MPEG2 video compression are an area of great interest. We have developed only one compression method in this section; for other information see Bhaskaran and Konstantinides (1995) and Frank, Unangst, and Daniels (1981). See also Gonzalez and Woods (1992, chap. 6) on image compression.

9.7 TWO-WAY TRANSMISSION AND UARTs

Knowing now that noise can contaminate serial transmission, you can appreciate the benefits of two-way transmission, if for nothing more than to let the receiver request a retransmission when an error is detected. Transmission between a computer and its peripherals is sometimes two-way. Although some peripherals (such as keyboards and monitors) make sense only on the one-way sending or receiving end of a transmission, other systems need both to send and to receive information. For example, a floppy disk drive is read from and written to. In relation to the computer it's attached to, the floppy drive being read is a **server,** and the computer RAM is the client requesting information.

9.7.1 Transceivers

At long distances, where properties of the transmission line may limit the speed of data transfer, two-way systems fall into the categories half-duplex and duplex. In the half-duplex mode the same line or lines are used for transmitting in both directions. A two-way line needs to terminate in an interface element called a **transceiver,** which contains a three-state driver in parallel with a noninverting buffer. (See Fig. 9.16.)

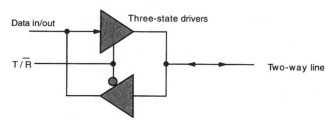

Figure 9.16 One-bit transceiver.

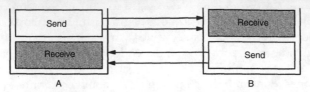

Figure 9.17 Simultaneous transmission and reception: full-duplex mode.

$T/\overline{R}$ is a transmit-receive control signal; when the three-state driver is disabled, the system is in receive mode. The three-state output driver of a transceiver can deliver considerably more power (current) than a standard logic chip; the increased power is necessary because a long transmission line accumulates capacitance that can load down and distort pulses.

9.7.2 Universal Asynchronous Receiver-Transmitter

IC manufacturers make support chips called **universal asynchronous receiver-transmitters (UARTs),** which, along with line driver/receivers, can interface between two digital systems that may have different clock rates and serial or parallel data to transmit or receive. A UART is normally a full-duplex chip with sending and receiving circuits on each side, and separate sending and receiving wires in the transmission line. Each side may have its own clock. (See Fig. 9.17.)

The UART typically converts a serial data stream from a peripheral or modem to parallel data for the computer, and it works in the other direction, too, converting bytes of data from the computer to a serial stream for the peripheral. In Fig. 9.18 one side of a UART has a parallel connection to a computer port and the other side has a serial connection to a peripheral through a pair of transceivers.

In fact UARTs are single-chip solutions to several digital communication interface problems. What makes a UART universal is its ability to be programmed for various word lengths (from five to eight bits), appended bits (parity bits and stopping and starting bits), and clock rates and the fact that its transmit and receive sides can have independent clock rates. Thanks to its independently clocked parts, a UART can

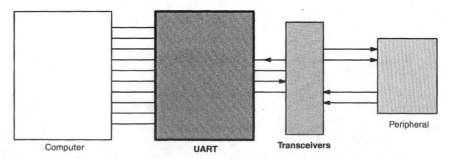

Figure 9.18 Diagram of UART in computer system.

compare two commercially available 40-pin UART chips that found wide use in the late 1980s.

EXAMPLE 10

The Intel 8250, a 40-pin chip, is a popular UART for X86-type personal computers. As an example, the 8250 can control a modem chip so that the computer can send and receive data on phone lines; the 8250 is also used in PC keyboard reading. The 8250 has nine eight-bit parallel-load registers and two shift registers on S_{IN} and S_{OUT}.

The National Semiconductor 16550, a version of the 8250 with FIFO registers, has the register organization shown in Fig. 9.19. Not all control pins are labeled. Having FIFO registers reduces the number of interrupts the UART must make on the computer side. The transmitter's external clock comes from a crystal oscillator attached between the X_{IN} and X_{OUT} pins. A number loaded into the *divisor latch* determines how the external clock is divided down to achieve the desired baud rate. Input RCLK allows for an independent receiver clock. The *line control register* has eight bits that can select for word length (5, 6, 7, or 8 bits), for the presence of a parity bit, and for whether the parity should be even or odd. See pp. 4-3 to 4-18 in National Semiconductor's *Data Communications, Local Area Networks and UARTs Handbook* (1990).

EXAMPLE 11

General Instruments makes a 40-pin UART, the **AY-3-1015D,** which has had good market success in digital communications. A block diagram for the AY-3-1015D is shown in Fig. 9.20. The AY-3-1015D has double-buffered, full-duplex operation. Compared to the 8250, the 1015D has parallel eight-bit ports on both transmit and receive sides, but it doesn't have specialized connections for modem operation. Two pins ("number of data bits") determine whether the words will be formatted with 5, 6, 7, or 8 bits. The 1015D has no internal divider for external clock oscillator.

There are separate TRANSMIT and RECEIVE parts of the chip, each with its own clock inputs. Each part of the chip has data and control lines. The TRANSMIT side has a "serial out" pin that is the output of the last flip-flop in a shift register. It is clocked by "16 X T CLK" that should be set by the user at 16 times the desired transmission rate.

To see the 1015D receive and transmit data, apply eight bits to the transmit data pins. Send different clocks to the transmit and receive sides. Connect the serial-out of the transmit side to the serial-in of the receive side. Set both number-of-data-bits pins HI to select for eight-bit word length. Set the control strobe, odd/even, number-of-stop-bits, and no parity pins HI also. Ground the external reset, $\overline{SWE}$, and $\overline{RCE}$ pins. Watch the data appear on the receive data bus each time the control strobe input is pulsed.

UARTs eliminate the need for special synchronization circuitry because their clock rates are arranged to approximately match the incoming data stream.

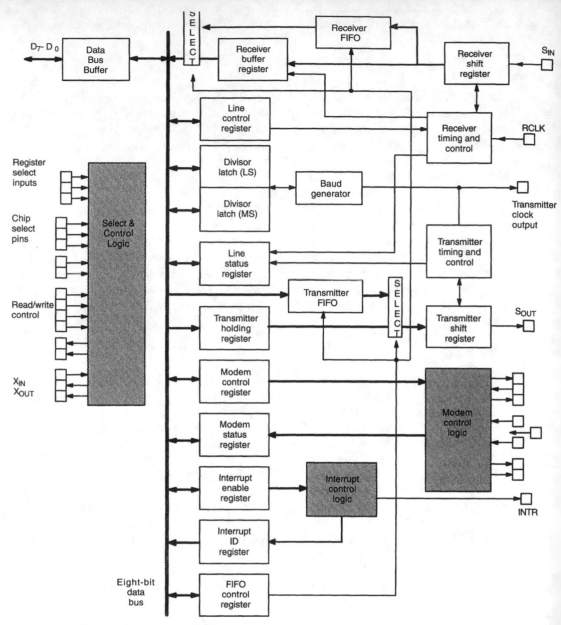

Figure 9.19 Organization of UART 8250 from Intel.

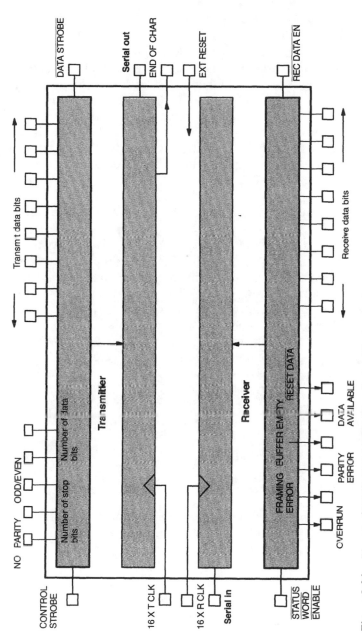

Figure 9.20 Pinout of UART AY-3-1015D from General Instruments.

507

A client is a digital system that requests information (data) from a digital server system. For example, computer clients on a network can request that licensed software be loaded from a server; the server may then request a license number from the client. There are a number of issues, large and small, associated with transmission between clients and servers, but here we'll focus on the control signals sent between the two systems. There are two cases: client and server can share the same clock, or, more often, the two systems will operate with independent clocks. In the second case the transfer of data from server to client is called a **handshake** operation. (See Fig. 9.21.) In the handshake case, the client **requests** data from the server and the server **acknowledges** the request while sending data.

9.8.1   Data Transfer between Client and Server Sharing the Same Clock

Suppose a synchronous digital system can be divided into two finite state machines (FSMs), each running independently of the other (no common control inputs). Now imagine that machine M_C (client) needs data from machine M_S (server). The data will be loaded in register R_{CD} in the client machine. A request line (REQ) is run from M_C to M_S, thus linking the two machine controllers (data lines have to be strung on a bus from the server to R_{CD}, too). The client machine M_C asserts the request line (REQ). However, there is no guarantee the data will be available immediately. The REQ input must prompt state machine M_S to enable or select the data needed, and that may take a few clock cycles. Nevertheless, when the data is on the output bus, M_S should issue an acknowledge (ACQ) signal to M_C. At that time REQ $\cdot$ ACK in M_C can load register R_{CD}. See the timing diagram in Fig. 9.22. The block diagram in Fig. 9.23 shows the client and the server with the control and data lines for a synchronous hookup.

9.8.2   Handshakes between Circuits with Different Clocks

As was said, if the client and server FSMs needing to communicate are driven by independent clocks, the control and timing between them is called a handshake. In

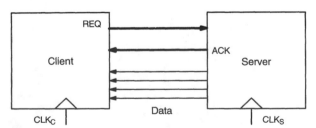

Figure 9.21   Common-clock client-server communication.

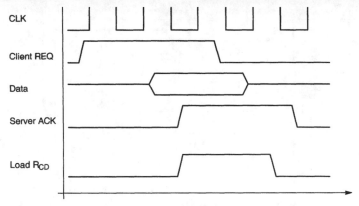

Figure 9.22 Client-server request timing.

contrast with the synchronous communication of the preceding section, there is now a need for synchronizer circuits to handle REQ and ACK in the server and client, respectively. You saw synchronizer circuits in Chapters 5 and 7; synchronizers reduce the chance of metastable behavior in a clocked circuit. The diagram in Fig. 9.23, used for synchronous communication, can be modified as shown in Fig. 9.24 to illustrate handshaking. The synchronizers and their clocks are in color.

The waveforms in Fig. 9.25 show the timing of a *return-to-zero handshake.* When the client wants data from the server, it asserts the REQ line. After the server sees the REQ (through its synchronizer and on its own clock edge), it incorporates the request into its FSM transitions and eventually enables or selects the needed data onto a bus between server and client. Once the data is available to the client, the server raises a signal on its ACK line back to the client. When it sees the REQ return to zero, the server knows that the client received the acknowledgment. Finally the ACK line is returned to zero and the data transfer cycle is finished. Notice that REQ and ACK go through four states: REQ, ACK = 00, 10, 11, and 01. Because it is a time when data

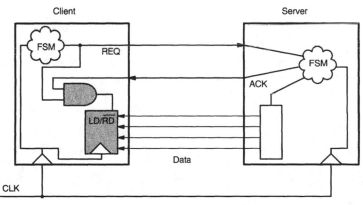

Figure 9.23 Diagram of a client and server with control and data lines.

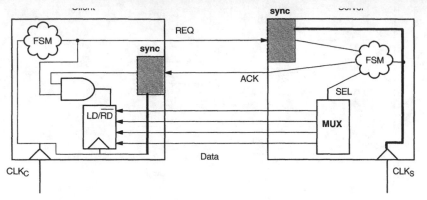

Figure 9.24 Asynchronous client-server communication.

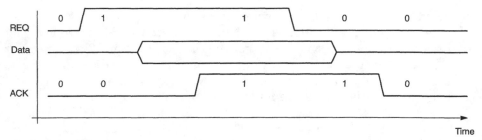

Figure 9.25 Data transfer using acknowledge signal.

are certain to be valid, it is appropriate for the client to latch the data during the REQ, ACK = 11 state.

Because acknowledge signals go in both directions, the chance for error in the transmission is reduced. If one or the other acknowledgment isn't received in a set time, the waiting circuit can either reset and try again or signal an error to the user.

9.8.3 Handshake Design Sketch

The following example will illustrate some of the issues associated with handshake design. It will specify the need for communication between various digital systems and will sketch some of the state machine design (from the server's point of view), but details of the design are left as a set of exercises.

EXAMPLE 12

Consider an electronic card dealer.[3] Suppose a server circuit called dealer needs to communicate with four client circuits called players. The player circuits are autonomous, and each operates with its own clock, as does the dealer circuit. On

[3]Speaking of circuits for gambling, see Bass (1990) for a description of a digital effort to beat roulette.

card from the dealer.

As soon as the first request for a card is received by the dealer, the dealer starts searching for a pseudorandom number from 0 to 51 that has not been picked since the previous SHUFFLE command. The number so chosen is enabled onto a data bus, and an ACK signal is sent to the player that requested the card. After the dealer sees the current HIT request signal return to LO, the dealer resets the player's ACK output (return-to-zero handshake). If another request is in the queue, the dealer immediately starts serving that; otherwise it waits in an idle state for a new request to be asserted.

The block diagram in Fig. 9.26 shows the overall design for the dealer. A count-to-52 (00 0000 to 11 0011) circuit is running continuously on the dealer's clock. After REQ has been received, the dealer's FSM latches the current value of CNTR in REG. Previous values (cards) that have been sent to players since the last shuffle are stored in a content-addressable memory (CAM; see Chapter 8). The CAM is tested for the contents of REG. If REG is not in CAM, the FSM enables the bus output to carry REG to the players. The player that sent the current REQ will have its acknowledge asserted, and that assertion can be used to capture the card number off the data bus in the player's circuit. After the player captures the card data, it will return its REQ to zero. After that REQ goes LO, another REQ can gain access to the dealer.

The flowchart in Fig. 9.27 shows part of the dealer's finite state machine flow-chart. The shuffle (reset CAM) input is not included. REQ comes from a queuing circuit, described below.

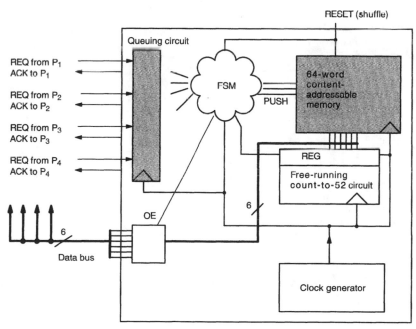

Figure 9.26 CAM and FSM used to implement electronic card dealer.

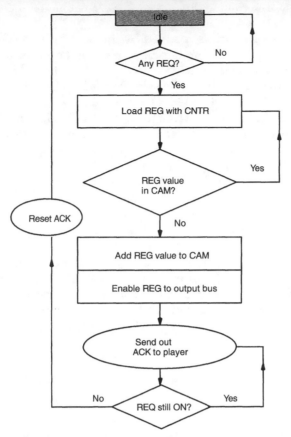

Figure 9.27 Flowchart depicting state changes (control flow) in FSM card dealer.

Handling Multiple Requests   Since the dealer can deal with only one player at a time, another FSM in the dealer system must be used to handle **queuing.** If, by some chance, several players press their HIT buttons at nearly the same time, the requests may be made faster than the dealer can handle them. The queuing circuit presents

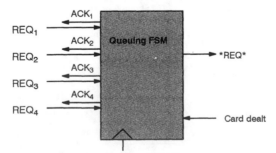

Figure 9.28   Queuing FSM used to handle multiple requests.

some subtleties in its design, which can be explored in Exercise 33. Figure 9.28 shows the queuer as a black box with player REQ_n inputs, one output $*REQ*$, a card-dealt input, and four ACK outputs. The main FSM of the dealer system only needs to know that a request has been received; the queuing FSM keeps track of *which* player sent the REQ. Any new requests received while the current request is being served are put in the queue and presented in order of their appearance. The queuing FSM handles the ACK signals too.

The dealer could be implemented as software, provided the software could control various input and output registers. Even if the design results in hardware, such as registered PALs, the design process may utilize a programming-language-like aid such as ABEL or *Finite State Machine Compiler*, as discussed in Chapter 7.

One master circuit, called the player, can send out next-card and shuffle signals to the slave system, called the dealer. When asked for a card by the player, the dealer will present code to the data bus for a card that has not yet been dealt since the last shuffle. As the dealer goes deeper into the deck, it takes longer (more dealer clock pulses) to find a valid card. During the time the dealer is looking for a new card, it turns off the READY flag, which the player circuit can use as asynchronous handshake information. Only after READY is on will card data be valid. When player asserts the shuffle signal, it is accompanied on the data bus by a code that helps randomize the new deck. Thus the data bus must be bidirectional. If the player asks for 53 cards in a row without a shuffle signal, the dealer will leave the READY light off until a shuffle signal is received. Every time player asks for a new card, it starts a count-down timer. In this design, if the timer reaches zero before the READY goes on, then the player asserts the shuffle line, requests another card, and starts the timer again.

*9.9   SUMMARY

Digital communication, including serial transmission, is an important application area for combinational and sequential circuit design. In Chapter 9 we have covered a number of related topics having as a common theme the transfer of information between independent circuits, each of which may have its own clock. We have concentrated on communication between two circuits; when more than two circuits or systems must communicate with each other, a network is required.

- **Serial transmission** is an economical method of moving data, and is called for in cases where transmission rates are naturally low (keyboard-to-computer, for example), or where the cost per wire of connection between two systems is high (undersea phone cable). Wireless electromagnetic radiation is a common means for serial transmission; interface circuits to transduce voltages into frequency or amplitude changes of electromagnetic radiation (and back again to voltages on the receiver side) are needed.

- **Information** is measured in bits and defined in terms of the probability of the signal received:

$$\text{information in bits} = \log_2\left(\frac{1}{\text{probability}}\right)$$

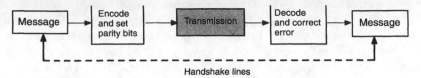

Figure 9.29

- Parallel-in–serial-out shift registers are useful for sending data; serial-in–parallel-out registers reverse the process on the receiving end.

- A signal on a transmission line may attenuate or be contaminated with noise. Errors, that is, bits flipping from 0 to 1 or from 1 to 0, can occur. As the wire length of a transmission line increases, so do series resistance and parallel capacitance, both of which increase the time-constant of the transmission line. Special line driver and receiver **(transceiver)** chips (1488, 1489) may be needed where sender and receiver contact the transmission line.

- The 8,4 Hamming code can *correct* any one-bit error and *detect* any two-bit error in an eight-bit transmission in which four bits are message.

- Transmitted data can be **encrypted** by XORing the message bits with bits from a **pseudorandom sequence generator.** If the encrypted transmission is XORed with the same pseudorandom sequence on the receiver side, the message is recovered.

- Channel size for transmission can be reduced if the messages can be **compressed.** The **Huffman coding** algorithm to minimize the length of messages depends on the probabilities of occurrence of various characters in the transmission alphabet.

- **Two-way** transmission between systems can be aided by commercially available **universal asynchronous transmitter-receiver (UART)** chips.

- A **handshake** scheme joins two systems with different clocks by having the systems exchange control signals. See Fig. 9.29 for the general form of a client/server system with handshake.

Exercises 9

1. Consider the electromagnetic radiation (broadcast) of radio and television signals. Currently most of such broadcasts are analog, but in the next few years digital television will be transmitted. Is the broadcasting of data a serial or parallel transmission? Defend your answer.

2. One-way transmission from keyboard to computer is serial, but there is more than one wire in the cable from the keyboard. What do you think the other wires are doing?

3. (a) A certain digital monochrome (black and white) television camera scans a scene in 640 columns and 480 rows; at each point in the scan matrix it re-

solves the intensity of light entering the camera to 32 levels. How many bits are needed to store one such TV image? If images are captured 30 times per second, how many bits are needed to store a minute's worth of TV images? (We're neglecting the audio signal here; it requires orders of magnitude less channel capacity than the video.)

(b) A certain high-resolution monitor used to display digitized x-rays has 2048 rows and 2048 columns, and intensity of each pixel is resolved to one of 256 gray levels. How many bits are needed to store one such x-ray?

(c) A certain phone line can transmit 56 Kb/s. How much compression (ratio of total bits to transmitted bits) is needed to transmit one TV image per second?

(d) Each human retina contains about 100 million photoreceptors (rods and cones). These photoreceptors converge on about 1 million optic nerve fibers, which project from the eye to the brain. If each optic nerve fiber is capable of sending about 100 pulses per second, what is the channel capacity of two optic nerves? Assume that each pulse represents one bit.

4. How many bits of *information* are received after the following events? Qualify your answer where needed.

   (a) The number 1 on a six-sided die
   (b) The birth of a baby boy
   (c) Reception of a 1 from the LSB of a four-bit counter
   (d) Reception of a 1 from the MSB of a four-bit decimal counter
   (e) Two losses in a row by the Patriots football team, who you know won 1 and lost 15 the year before

5. My word processor global search and replace feature says that in the introduction to Chapter 9, vowels are the following percentages of all 7653 characters:

a	6.69%
e	9.21%
i	6.96%
o	6.04%
u	1.54%
y	1.01%

   How much information, in bits, does reception of an *e* generate? Reception of a *y*? Reception of a vowel?

6. What is the baud rate of characters sent at 1000 bits/s in ASCII code with parity bit?

7. A clock gates a transparent latch; when the clock is HI, DATA passes through to OUT; when the clock is LO, the value of DATA just before the HI → LO transition is held at OUT. (See Fig. P9.1)

   OUT is sampled at the two arrows on the LO portion of the CLK waveform. What is the value of OUT at each sample, and how much *information* do you estimate is received from the two samples?

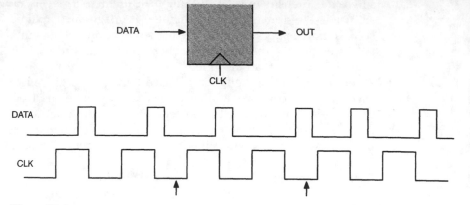

Figure P9.1

8. A clock is divided down by a toggle flip-flop. It also goes to a three-bit counter and a PISO chip.

   (a) Using additional combinational logic, design a controller for the PISO so that after loaded data is shifted out in four clock pulses, new data is loaded in and shifted. Make sure that the actual loading is done out of phase with the shift-load command.

   (b) Is the PISO like a FIFO or a LIFO shift register?

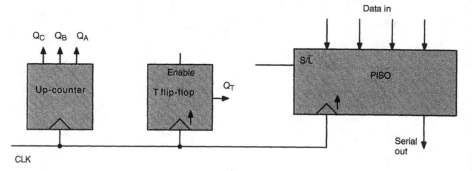

Figure P9.2

9. Compare the load-and-shift and the multiplexer methods of parallel-to-serial transmission of *one* message. If the clock speed is increased, which method do you think will make errors first? Compare the propagation delays in the two circuits. (The answer may change if you consider reloading data for repeated transmissions.)

10. A transmitted message is likely to be composed of many characters, one after the other. Which of the four methods mentioned in the text for identifying the end of a word of many characters do you think would use the fewest resources in the receiver?

11. At what bit in RS-232 transmission will a mistake first occur if the synchronized receiver clock is 10% *slower* than the transmission clock?

12. A timing problem What happens in the parallel-in–serial-out circuit in Fig. P9.3 if the same pulsing waveform goes to both CLOCK and $S/\overline{L}$? After four clock pulses, what will be at serial OUT? Assume that when $S/\overline{L}$ is HI, the MUX selects the Q inputs. Notice that the Q input to the MUX on the left is a 0. Assume that D_3–D_0 are all 1, the MUX has propagation delay time 10 ns, and the D flip-flop has setup and hold times of 2 ns and propagation delay of 5 ns. Answer for the D flip-flops being (a) rising-edge-triggered or (b) falling-edge-triggered.

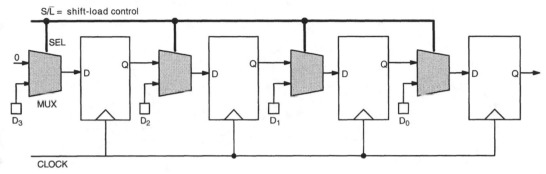

Figure P9.3

13. What will go wrong with the circuit in Fig. P9.4? It is intended to synchronize a signal pulse to the receiver clock. Assume that the 1-shot loop has been calibrated to match the correct frequency needed to clock in data. The arrows on the 1-shots indicate on which edges of input they trigger the start of their pulses. Assume that both 1-shots are off to begin with, that is, Q is LO for both.

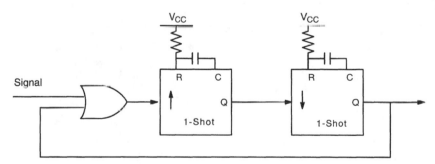

Figure P9.4 Two 1-shots in series.

14. Study the RS-232 timing for transmission of one character, given in Example 3 of the text. Assume that the design for Exercise 13 is done correctly; now design a circuit that ignores the start cycle and the two stop cycles and clocks a shift register eight times for the message bits. Assume that the receiver clock has correctly started with a full period and is within ±5% of the sender clock rate.

15. What's wrong with the circuit of Fig. P9.5 for controlling the receiver of a serial transmission system for eight-bit words? $\overline{RCO}$ stands for ripple carry-out, and $\overline{ENT}$ is the toggle enable of the counter; both are active-low.

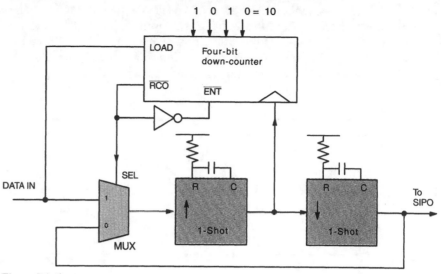

Figure P9.5

16. What, if anything, is wrong with the circuit of Fig. P9.6 as a receiver of a four-bit message? DATA IN and CLOCK come from the sender. DATA IN

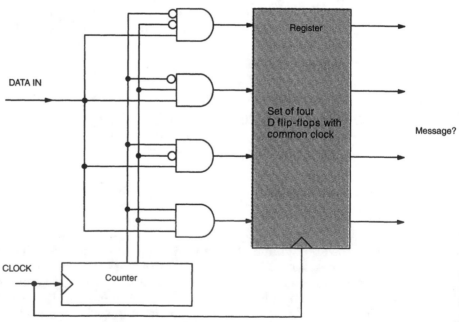

Figure P9.6 DeMUX input to register.

and correct data in phase with CLOCK. The four three-input AND gates attached to the counter form a *decoder*. Can you modify this circuit to function as a valid message receiver?

‡17. **Serial transmission formats**   If the signal on a serial transmission line varies from 0 to 1 and back again frequently enough, a special circuit on the receiving end, called a **phase-locked loop (PLL)**, can reconstruct the clock waveform that was used to generate the serial transmission. If a non-return-to-zero (NRZ) scheme is used to create the serial transmission, a long string of 1s or a long string of 0s will cause no variation in the transmission and will make it difficult for the PLL circuit to determine the sending frequency. However, if both 1s and 0s are sent as transitions (Manchester code), the PLL will have an easier time. Shown in Fig. P9.7 are transmissions of a sequence of eight bits with NRZ and Manchester codes. What is the rule for determining the Manchester transmission in the waveform?

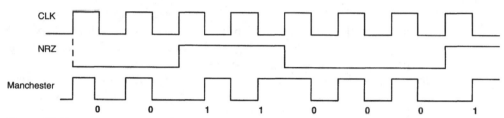

Figure P9.7

18. Suppose inputs are eight-bit words that can have from zero to four 1s in them. Design a circuit with a five-bit output such that the first four bits are the starting word and the fifth bit makes the five-bit word have *odd* parity.

19. Design a circuit to detect parity in a nine-bit word. Arrange that even parity results in a HI output from your circuit.

20. **(a)** For what range of single-bit error rate is the probability of exactly two errors out of eight greater than 25%?
    (b) At what single-bit error rate does the probability of eight consecutive correct transmissions rise above 90%?
    (c) If the error rate is 5%, what is the probability that a 16-bit word will have exactly three errors? Three errors (or any odd number) will also appear as a parity error.

21. Consider a four-input Karnaugh map. Describe how to measure, on the map, the Hamming distance between two minterms. Make sure your method reports that the Hamming distance from 0000 to 1111 is 4.

22. **Parity check for error correction**   Suppose the three check bits of a seven-bit message are formed by the following:

$$C_2 = M_3 \oplus M_2 \oplus M_1$$
$$C_1 = M_3 \oplus M_2 \oplus M_0$$
$$C_0 = M_3 \oplus M_1 \oplus M_0$$

groups? The parity test will take place in the receiver circuit.

23. One-bit errors in a four-bit message can be corrected by three check bits. How many check bits are needed to correct a five-bit message? Can you figure out the answer with a Venn diagram?

24. **One-bit error corrections** The following seven-bit codes are received, and each code has zero or one error. Which codes are correct, and which single bits are wrong in the message with the check codes with one-bit errors? The check bits C_2, C_1, and C_0 are defined by the Venn diagram of Fig. 9.12.

	C_2	C_1	C_0	M_3	M_2	M_1	M_0
(a)	0	0	0	0	0	0	1
(b)	0	1	1	1	0	1	0
(c)	1	0	1	0	0	1	0
(d)	1	0	1	1	1	1	0
(e)	1	1	1	1	1	1	1
(f)	1	1	1	0	1	1	1

25. Design a combinational circuit that will *correct* any one-bit mistake in a four-bit message with three bits of parity check. Your circuit will have seven inputs and seven outputs, one for each bit. When a correct message plus check is received, the message itself will be the output. For any single-bit error the mistake will be automatically corrected so that the output is the seven-bit code without the mistake. (Hint: XOR gates will be involved in an efficient realization.)

26. **Two-bit error detections** The following eight-bit codes are received, and each code has zero, one, or two errors.
    (a) Which codes are correct, which have one error, and which have two errors?
    (b) Correct the one-bit errors.

	P	C_2	C_1	C_0	M_3	M_2	M_1	M_0
(i)	1	0	0	0	0	0	0	1
(ii)	0	0	1	1	1	0	1	0
(iii)	0	1	0	1	0	0	1	0
(iv)	0	1	1	1	1	0	1	0
(v)	1	1	1	1	1	1	1	1
(vi)	1	1	1	1	0	1	1	1

27. Consider an eight-bit message in which the eighth bit is for setting overall parity to be even.
    (a) Find a 3-bit error identical to a 1-bit error pattern.
    (b) Can you think of a way to extend the code to catch (but not correct) exactly three-bit errors?

28. **Make up your own error-detecting code.** Consider the set of 16 four-bit binary numbers.
    (a) Demonstrate that in a successful one-bit error-detecting code the code words must have a minimum Hamming distance between them of 2.
    (b) Make up a four-word code using four-bit numbers such that a one-bit error can be *detected*.

(c) Is it possible to make up a code of four-bit numbers such that any error of one or two bits can be detected? If so, how many words can be in the code?

(d) Can a one-bit error always be detected with these valid four-bit code words?

0 0 0 0

0 1 1 0

0 1 1 1

1 1 1 0

29. **Encrypting** Consider the PRSG encrypting scheme described in Section 9.5.

(a) What would be unintelligent about sending the pseudorandom sequence on another wire so that the receiver would have the decrypting information immediately available for XORing with the scrambled message?

(b) Show that the formula $M = M \oplus E \oplus E$ for decoding an encrypted message is correct, where M is message and E is encrypting pattern of same size.

30. Here again are the percentages of vowels in the characters from the introduction to Chapter 9.

a	6.69%
e	9.21%
i	6.96%
o	6.04%
u	1.54%
y	1.01%

If we coded the vowels with a fixed-length code, three bits per vowel would be needed.

(a) What would Huffman say is an optimal variable-length code for vowels only?

(b) Can you compute the average code length of an all-vowel transmission?

‡31. Study the block diagram of the 8250 UART in Fig. 9.20 plus Data Sheets.

(a) What would need to be the setting on the control inputs for the UART to transmit parallel data as serial data?

(b) What would need to be the control settings for the UART to be a *receiver* of serial data? Where does the serial data go to be read out parallel?

32. Describe a reasonable protocol for a server to send data to a client. Show your answer in the form of a flowchart suitable for an FSM. Consider the possibility that the client receives data with errors or the server is busy with other clients.

33. Assume that a client and a server share the same clock and that four bits serial need to be transferred from client to server. Draw out a timing diagram, starting with CLOCK, that shows when various control signals need to be asserted.

34. **Handshake** Draw a timing diagram for a server/client handshake system in which four bits are to be sent from the server to the client on a serial line after the client requests the data. Show both client and server clocks on your diagram.

35. **(a)** Finish the design of the dealer's handshake control circuit for the card-dealing example started in the text, Fig. 9.27. Pay particular attention to the queueing circuit.
(b) Can you think of an efficient algorithm for dealing cards that takes account of cards already dealt?

36. Sketch a design for one player's internal circuit to handle interactions with the dealer.

‡**37.** Add a card-shuffle feature to the card-dealer system in Example 11.

38. Draw the OUT responses of the following "synchronizer" circuits given the input shown below. The clocked flip-flops are rising-edge-triggered.

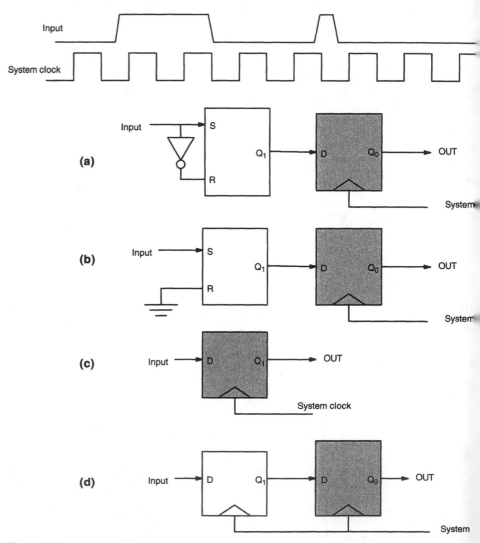

Figure P9.8

39. The text discusses how external input can interrupt a server. Does a handshake circuit interrupt the server when it's activated?

References

Ash, R. 1965. *Information theory.* New York: John Wiley & Sons.

Bass, T. A. 1990. *The Newtonian casino.* New York: Penguin.

Berlekamp, E. 1974. *Key papers in the development of coding theory.* New York: IEEE Press.

———. 1968. *Algebraic coding theory.* New York: McGraw-Hill.

Bhaskaran, V., and K. Konstantinides. 1995. *Image and video compression standards.* Boston: Kluwer Academic.

Bingham, J. A. C. 1988. *The theory and practice of modem design.* New York: John Wiley & Sons.

Data communications, local area networks and UARTs handbook. 1990. Santa Clara: National Semiconductor Corp.

Frank, A., D. R. Unangst, and J. D. Daniels. 1981. Progressive image transmission using a growth-geometry coding. *Proceedings of the IEEE* 68: 897–909.

Gonzalez, R., and R. Woods. 1992. *Digital image processing.* Reading, Mass.: Addison-Wesley.

Gray, R. M. 1990. *Entropy and information theory.* Berlin: Springer-Verlag.

Lathi, B. P. 1983. *Modern digital and analog communications systems.* New York: Holt, Rinehart, Winston.

Mano, M. 1988. *Computer engineering: Hardware design.* Englewood Cliffs, N.J.: Prentice Hall.

McEliece, R. J. 1985. The reliability of computer memory. *Scientific American,* January, 88–95.

Schiller, J. 1994. Secure distributed computing. *Scientific American,* November, 72–76.

Zimmerman, P. R. 1995. *The official PGP user's guide.* Cambridge, Mass.: MIT Press.

Arithmetic Hardware

This system of working out the same problem in two groups, which could then compare the results independently arrived at, was already traditional at Los Alamos. It was practiced there, candidly, as a kind of intellectual sport. Rolf Landshoff, an emigrant from Berlin to the United States, who had belonged to Teller's group during the war, remembers in connection with this "racing" that "there was a meeting in Teller's office with Fermi, von Neumann and Feynman in which I took part because I was to carry out the calculations planned at that meeting. Many ideas were thrown back and forth and every few minutes Fermi or Teller would devise a quick numerical check and then they would spring into action, Feynman on the desk calculator, Fermi with the little slide ruler he always had with him and von Neumann in his head. The head was usually first, and it is remarkable how close the three answers always checked."

(Jungk 1958, 292)[1]

OVERVIEW

Computers compute. The heart of digital computing is the hardware addition of two binary numbers. Chapter 10 concentrates on methods for adding two numbers together, and extends the notion to repeated adding and shifting, yielding the multiplication of two binary numbers. Who knows? With a Macintosh running MATLAB Feynman might have been able to beat Fermi and von Neumann every time.

In theory, all binary arithmetic problems could be solved by table lookup. The input (or address) would be the numbers to be added, multiplied, have their cosines taken, or whatever, and the output (contents) would be the answer. The answer would appear in tens of nanoseconds after presentation of input. But the cost of table lookup mounts as (roughly) the square of the number of bits in the input words. Consider the multiplication of two eight-bit words. There are $2^{(8+8)} = 64K$ (65,536) different combinations of input, and the output for each can be up to 16 bits: $16 \times 64K = 1$ megabit (1,048,576 bits), a fair piece of memory. However, to multiply two 16-bit words by table lookup would require $2^{32} \times 2^5 \approx 1.4 \times 10^{11}$ bits. Using 1-Mb

[1]Jungk's *Brighter Than a Thousand Suns* (1958) is about the Manhattan Project: the development of the atomic bomb in the early 1940s. John von Neumann went on to develop a number of key concepts for modern digital computers: see Aspray (1990).

ROMS, over 10 would be required. In practice, methods more clever (but perhaps slower) than table lookup are needed for large-scale computer arithmetic.

Chapter 1 introduced combinatorial methods for binary addition, including addition of signed numbers. We used the one-bit full adder (1BFA) module in multiple-bit designs. In the present chapter we'll expand on those designs to include hardware-efficient sequential methods. To increase the speed of combinational adders, we introduce **carry look-ahead** circuits, which bypass the ripple-carry bottleneck of standard adders.

In the second half of Chapter 10 we'll extend the domain of arithmetic hardware to include combinatorial and sequential multipliers for signed and unsigned numbers. Among the combinational designs will be an **array** multiplier—a matrix of full adders that efficiently realize the 2n-bit product of $n \times n$ multiplication. Two designs for an **add-and-shift** sequential multiplier will be worked out in detail. Booth's algorithm for fast signed multiplication will be explained. At the end of Chapter 10 you'll see how large and small real numbers represented in **floating point** can be added and multiplied together. We'll conclude with a demonstration of hardware division.

10.1 HALF ADDERS INTO FULL ADDERS

Recall from Chapter 1 the definition of a half adder:

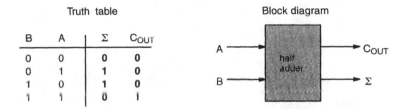

A one-bit full adder (1BFA) can be made from a modular combination of two half adders and an OR gate (Fig. 10.1). The 1BFA made from two half adders has three

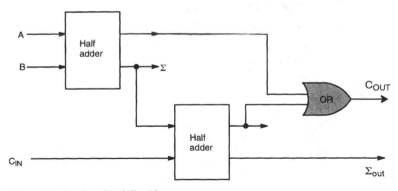

Figure 10.1 One-bit full adder.

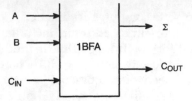

Figure 10.2 One-bit full adder icon.

gates' worth of delay to C_{OUT}, versus two gates' worth of delay for a 1BFA realized directly as a sum of products. We consolidate the 1BFA into a building block, as shown in Fig. 10.2.

10.2 RIPPLE ADDER

EXAMPLE 1

Hook up two 1BFAs to add together two two-bit numbers, $A_1 A_0 + B_1 B_0$. The answer is in Fig. 10.3. The *three bits* of output are Σ_0, Σ_1, and C_{OUT}. If half-adder-to-full-adder 1BFAs are used, then C_{OUT} for one 1BFA has three gates' worth of delay and the circuit of Fig. 10.3 must wait four gates' worth of delay for the final C_{OUT} to settle. (Think about the final OR gate in the lower 1BFA.)

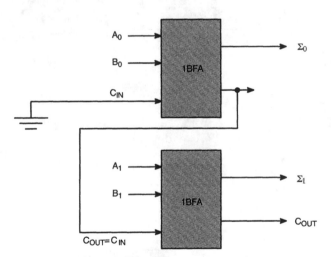

Figure 10.3 Two-bit full adder.

If we use 1BFAs made as sums of products, then delay to C_{OUT} for one adder is $2t_{pd}$. If we want an eight-bit full adder using the ripple scheme above, we would have to accept 16 gates' worth of delay before the final C_{OUT} settled. The ripple adder can be extended indefinitely for more bits by sending the carry-out of one 1BFA to the carry-in of the next most significant bit.

EXAMPLE 2

By inverting one set of inputs and letting the carry-in of the least-significant 1BFA see a 1, a subtracter is formed. If a subtraction signal SUB is used for the first carry-in and to gate XORs, a combined ripple adder–subtracter results.

Figure 10.4 shows what the first couple of stages look like for $B + A$ and $B - A$. For clarity, C_{IN} has been moved from the side to the top of the 1BFA icon. If the first C_{IN} is set to HI, it takes care of the 1 in the formula $\overline{A} + 1$, which generates the 2's complement of A. Extra circuitry is needed to detect 2's complement overflow or underflow; work it out in Exercise 6.

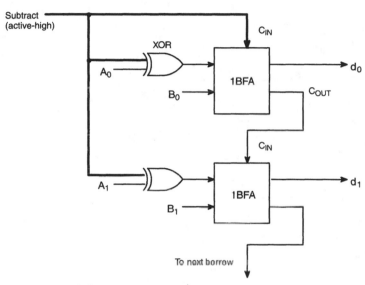

Figure 10.4   Subtracter.

10.3   CARRY LOOK-AHEAD

Let's shorten the worst-case delay of the ripple adder. We need to find one big expression for carry-out that can be computed as a two-level SOP (plus one level of input processing). What follows is a modular approach to minimizing C_{OUT} delay.

First recall the Boolean expression for the carry-out of a 1BFA,

$$C_{OUT} = A \cdot B + C_{IN} \cdot (A \oplus B)$$

where the "+" sign stands for OR.[2] Now change notation, assuming that the equation above applies to the least significant 1BFA of a chain. Let $C_1 = C_{OUT}$, $C_0 = C_{IN}$, $G_0 = A \cdot B$, and $P_0 = A \oplus B$, where G is the *generate signal* and P is the *propagate signal* of the zeroth-level 1BFA. With this notation the equation for the first carry-out is

---

[2]With regard to computer arithmetic, be careful when you see "+"; it may mean arithmetic addition or logical OR, depending on the context!

where again the "+" sign indicates OR.

Generalizing, let $G_i = A_i \cdot B_i$ and $P_i = A_i \oplus B_i$. The expression we've written for $C_{OUT} = C_1$ can be cast in a recursive form, $C_N = G_{N-1} + C_{N-1} \cdot P_{N-1}$; the present C is defined in terms of the previous C. With the recursive formula in hand, work backward from C_4, forming expressions for C_N down to $N = 1$:

$$
\begin{aligned}
C_4 &= G_3 + C_3 \cdot P_3 \\
&= G_3 + (G_2 + C_2 \cdot P_2) \cdot P_3 \\
&= G_3 + (G_2 + (G_1 + C_1 \cdot P_1) \cdot P_2) \cdot P_3 \\
&= G_3 + (G_2 + (G_1 + (G_0 + C_0 \cdot P_0) \cdot P_1) \cdot P_2) \cdot P_3
\end{aligned}
$$

C_0 is the first carry-in. We now have C_4 in a long form with C_0 and P's and G's only. If we expand the last version of C_4, we obtain the following sum of products:

$$C_4 = G_3 + G_2 \cdot P_3 + G_1 \cdot P_2 \cdot P_3 + G_0 \cdot P_1 \cdot P_2 \cdot P_3 + C_0 \cdot P_0 \cdot P_1 \cdot P_2 \cdot P_3$$

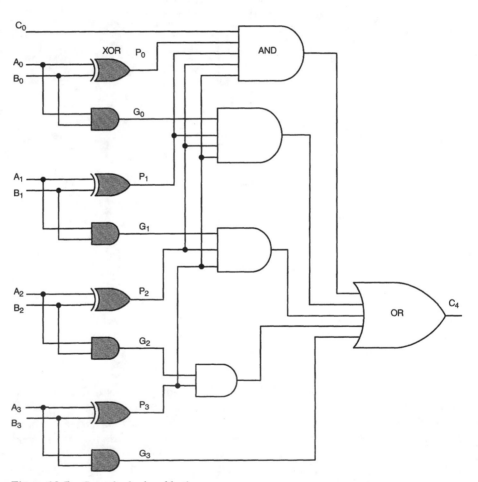

Figure 10.5 Carry look-ahead logic.

vve can ueciaie

$$\mathcal{G} = G_3 + G_2 \cdot P_3 + G_1 \cdot P_2 \cdot P_3 + G_0 \cdot P_1 \cdot P_2 \cdot P_3 \quad \text{and} \quad \mathcal{P} = P_0 \cdot P_1 \cdot P_2 \cdot P_3$$

as the generalized four-bit generate and propagate signals. Therefore

$$C_4 = \mathcal{G} + C_0 \cdot \mathcal{P}$$

and $\mathcal{G}$ and $\mathcal{P}$ can be made available as outputs of a multiple-bit adder.

The OR-of-ANDs (sum of products) expression for C_4 can be realized in hardware shown in Fig. 10.5. Carry-out C_4 is only three gates' worth of delay away from the adder input, instead of the eight gates' worth of delay in a plain vanilla ripple-carry four-bit adder. In fact, *any* bit-size combinational adder can add just three gates' worth of delay to the final C_{OUT} if it incorporates **carry look-ahead (CLA).** But a price is paid in more hardware to achieve this decreased delay. The more bits in the adder, the more CLA hardware is required. In fact if you draw out the logic circuits associated with each C_n and count gate input pins Q_n, you will find

$$Q_n = 4n + (n+1) + \sum_{j=1}^{n} (j+1)$$

It turns out that CLA complexity increases almost with the square of n.

Four-bit TTL arithmetic-logic chips—the 74181 and the 74LS381—have on-board CLA for C_4, and the '181 sends out $\mathcal{G}$ and $\mathcal{P}$ signals (as defined above). A CLA companion chip, the 74182, uses $\mathcal{G}$'s and $\mathcal{P}$'s from four '181s to form C_{16} in 16-bit arithmetic. With a two-layer CLA, C_{16} has 6 gates' worth of delay, versus 32 gates' worth of delay in a 16-bit ripple adder. Depending on the settings of its function-select pins, the '181 can do various other arithmetic and logic operations, which will be discussed in the next chapter.

EXAMPLE 3

See Fig. 10.6 for 16-bit addition with four 74181 chips and one 74182 chip. The C_{OUT}'s from the four 74181s are not needed when the 74182 is involved. If the first carry-in, C_n, is 0, the final carry-out from the '182 chip is $\mathcal{G}$.

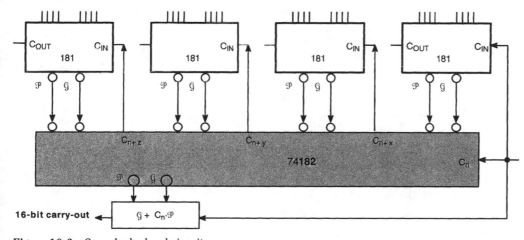

Figure 10.6 Carry look-ahead circuit.

10.4 SEQUENTIAL ADDER CIRCUITS

Next we develop two types of sequential adders: the one-bit serial adder and the faster accumulating adder. The accumulating adder will be used later as a template for the sequential add-and-shift multiplier.

10.4.1 One-Bit Serial Adder

It's possible to add together two N-bit numbers using only *one* 1BFA. The key idea is to store the previous C_{OUT} in a flip-flop and use it on the next cycle of adding. (See Fig. 10.7.) The numbers to be added can be stored in shift registers, and the answer can accumulate in another shift register.

With the appearance of flip-flops, we are now in the realm of *finite state machine* design. The shift registers and the flip-flop all need clock pulses. The guts of an eight-bit design are shown in Fig. 10.8. A few features needed for a self-contained design are missing from Fig. 10.8:

1. There's no way to load the starting numbers A and B or to clear the carry flip-flop at the start of an addition cycle. A parallel-in–serial-out (PISO) register could solve the loading problem.

2. A counter must stop the clock after eight ticks, or the answer register may fill up with zeros. The clock should project to a counter, as well as to the various registers.

3. Adding two eight-bit numbers can result in a nine-bit answer, and our answer register has only eight bits—the system needs to know that the ninth bit is in the carry flip-flop.

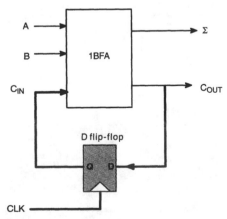

Figure 10.7   Sequential adder.

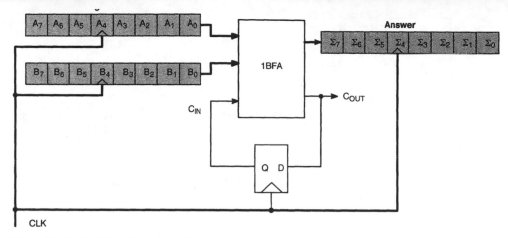

Figure 10.8 Multiple-bit serial adder.

Our serial adder design could benefit from start-of-add and end-of-add signals. "Add" them in Exercise 11.

The serial adder takes N clock pulses to finish an N-bit addition; it is likely to be much slower than the combinational ripple adders shown earlier. The combinational ripple adder, with carry look-ahead, is an example of parallel processing—several operations carried out simultaneously.

The sequential circuit presented here is an important stepping-stone for the synchronous multiplier circuits to come later in this chapter.

10.4.2 Accumulating Adder

EXAMPLE 4

The one-bit-at-a-time serial adder can be expanded to add one number at a time, as would be required if a column of numbers were being totaled. The result is a **multiple-bit path sequential adder.** See Fig. 10.9, which introduces a new symbol for the multiple-bit adder. The numbers to be added, four-bits in size, are fetched from memory by a counter providing addresses; the current number from memory is presented to the adder along with the previous sum, which is held in a register that accepts the adder's output. Here the adder output is seven bits plus carry-out, so it can add up more than a few four-bit numbers before the register overflows. Seventeen four-bit numbers can be totaled in an eight-bit register ($1111 \times 10001 = 1111\,1111$). This sequential multiple-bit path adder should be about seven times as fast as the one-bit serial adder because the multiple-bit path adder has seven 1BFAs working in parallel in the adder symbol.

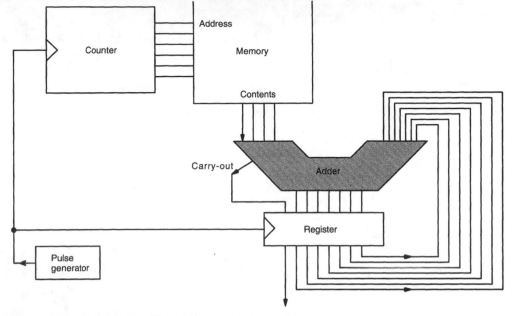

Figure 10.9 Multiple-bit adder with accumulating register.

10.5 HARDWARE FOR TWO'S COMPLEMENT AND OVERFLOW

All the adders we've designed will give correct answers to signed arithmetic problems provided that the inputs are in 2's complement form and that overflow is prevented or detected.

10.5.1 Two's Complement

As you learned in Chapter 1, the 2's complement of a four-bit number A is $10\,000 - A$. But $10\,000$ is five bits, too big for a four-bit system. Another way is to say $10\,000$ is $1111 + 1$ (like saying $9,999 + 1 = 10,000$ in 10's complement decimal). Now our 2's complement conversion can be stated as $2C(A) = 1111 + 1 - A$. And since (in four-bit words) $1111 + A = \overline{A}$, the formula boils down to $2C(A) = \overline{A} + 1$. In this notation, $2C(2C(A)) = A$.

Figure 10.10 shows a combinational circuit that will either pass A through unchanged or take the 2's complement of A. If the control line COMP-SIG (complement signal) is HI, the output of the circuit is the 2's complement of the number A on the data lines. In Fig. 10.10, the XOR gates invert the bits of A when COMP-SIG is HI. Further, the incrementer is a ripple adder for which COMP-SIG is carry-in. If COMP-SIG is HI, then 1 is added to the input (increment operation). Remember that $2C(A) = \overline{A} + 1$; therefore, when COMP-SIG is HI, the output is $2C(A)$. If

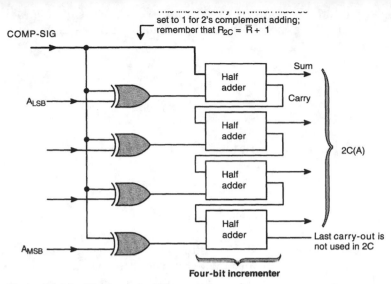

Figure 10.10 Hardware for 2C conversion.

COMP-SIG is LO, the data input is not inverted and 0 is added to the input (pass operation).

Ask yourself why full adders aren't needed for this incrementer. Is a combinational incrementer different from an up-counter?

10.5.2 Overflow Hardware

An expression for 2's complement overflow is

$$\text{overflow} = C_{N+1} \oplus C_N$$

For 2's complement addition our hardware must route the last two carries to an XOR gate for overflow status. If the addition is done by a ripple adder composed of 1BFAs, the appropriate carries are available internally, as shown in Fig. 10.11. In four-bit

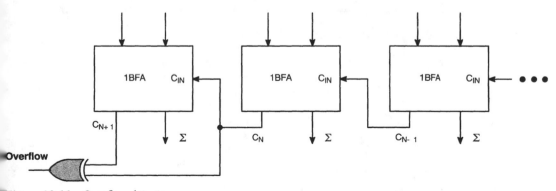

Figure 10.11 Overflow detector.

2's complement answer; it's the fifth bit and does not participate in the answer. For example:

$$\begin{array}{rcl}
 & & \textcircled{1}1\ 1 \\
-2 & & 1\ 1\ 1\ 0 \\
-2 & & 1\ 1\ 1\ 0 \\
\hline
-4 & & \textcircled{1}1\ 1\ 0\ 0
\end{array}$$

Here the fifth bit, circled, is not needed to define -4, which is not an overflow condition for four-bit 2C of $-2 - 2$.

10.6 MULTIPLIERS

Now we're ready to implement **multiplication** hardware, using some of the ideas gained from adder design. Both unsigned and signed multiplication will be considered. As with adder hardware, we'll start with combinational designs and then graduate to more general-purpose sequential designs. To understand the motivation for developing multiplier hardware, we point out that in *digital signal processing* circuits there is constantly a need for *sums of products* (the real algebraic SOPs, not the Boolean SOPs!); the weighted sum of a digital filter is an example. The general form of an algebraic SOP is shown in Fig. 10.12, where $m_0 \ldots m_{n-1}$ are n input signals and $w_0 \ldots w_{n-1}$ are the weights by which the filter controls the influence of the respective inputs in the final summation. Inputs $m_0 \ldots m_{n-1}$ may be from a tapped delay line of a single-input signal $IN(t)$ such that $m_i = IN(t - i\Delta t)$. In any case, in special-purpose digital signal process hardware *multiply-accumulate* units keep track of the running sum of a series of multiplications. Algebraic sum of products is also an important part of *neural network* hardware. In the case of neural networks the weights

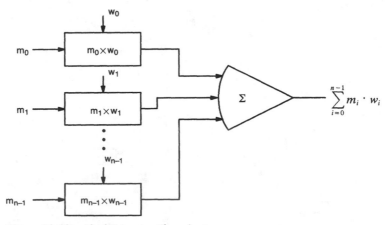

Figure 10.12 Algebraic sum of products.

may vary through supervised learning (adaptive filtering, see Widrow and Stearns 1985).

EXAMPLE 5

In the same way that multiplying by 10 is easy with decimal numbers, the simplest binary multiplication is multiplication by 2. If the number to be multiplied is stored in a shift register, multiplication by 2 is one shift to the left. Each square below represents a flip-flop. The clock is not shown; also not shown is how the multiplicand was loaded into the shift register in the first place. The number $1011\,1001 = B9_{16}$ multiplied by 2 is $1\,0111\,0010 = 172_{16}$.

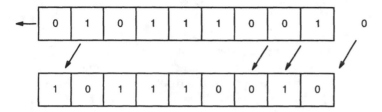

The shift register will have a serial input, which normally will be fed a 0, and its MSB should have another register or flip-flop for overflow.

10.7 COMBINATIONAL MULTIPLIERS

Earlier in Chapter 10 you saw how memory requirements can mount rapidly for table lookup arithmetic. For even modest numbers of bits per multiplier and multiplicand, the number of bits needed can be formidable; for example, the product of a 16×16 multiplication needs $2^{16+16} \times 2^5 = 2^{37} \approx 10^{11}$ bits for its table to be stored. For smaller products combinational designs are feasible and can be cascaded in modular fashion for much larger multipliers. We start with an example of how adders can be linked in a matrix array to generate combinational products, and then another example offers a two-by-two multiplier built into a larger multiplier.

10.7.1 Array Multiplier

EXAMPLE 6

Design a multiplier using only one-bit adder units.

Answer Hooking together adders to generate products makes an **array multiplier.** To follow the array construction process, study the four-by-four unsigned

				Q_3	Q_2	Q_1	Q_0
			$\times$	R_3	R_2	R_1	R_0
				Q_3R_0	Q_2R_0	Q_1R_0	Q_0R_0
		$+$	Q_3R_1	Q_2R_1	Q_1R_1	Q_0R_1	
	$+$	Q_3R_2	Q_2R_2	Q_1R_2	Q_0R_2		
$+$	Q_3R_3	Q_2R_3	Q_1R_3	Q_0R_3			
P_7	P_6	P_5	P_4	P_3	P_2	P_1	P_0

Each QR pair in the partial sums columns represents a two-input AND operation:

$$Q_0 \cdot R_0 = Q_0 \text{ AND } R_0$$

The P_i, $i = 0, \ldots, 7$, are the product answer, bit by bit. A nonzero P_7 would be due to a carry-out from the P_6 column addition. P_0 comes directly off the first AND gate; P_1 is the sum of two products. By referring to the multiplication chart above, you can verify that the array in Fig. 10.13 computes all the P_i sums. Each block is a one-bit full adder (1BFA), shown isolated at the top left of the figure.

Each column in the array multiplier corresponds to a column in the multiplication expansion shown in the figure. The column for P_1 is shown in color. Two products, Q_0R_1 and Q_1R_0, are added together, with no carry-in, to create P_1. What is the delay on the longest pathway, the one from presentation of input to appearance of valid output P_7? Start with P_3, which is three adders away from the AND gates at the top of the circuit. The adder at the top left of the circuit, in the same column as P_3, is three carries away from the highlighted adder on the top right. Finally, P_7 is four carries

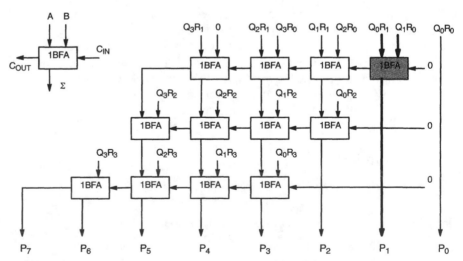

Figure 10.13 Array multiplier for four-by-four signed product.

$$t_{max} = t_{AND} + 3 \cdot t_{1BFA} + 7 \cdot t_{carry}$$

Exercise 20 asks you to analyze a modification of the array multiplier that has less total delay than the one in Fig. 10.13. Rabiner and Gold (1975, 514–524) have a good discussion of combinational array multipliers.

10.7.2 A Two-by-Two Combinational Multiplier Used in a Larger Design

In this section you will study a two-by-two multiplier and see the resulting design used in another array-type circuit for larger products.

EXAMPLE 7

Design a two-by-two binary multiplier.

Answer A multiplier for two two-bit unsigned numbers $A \times B = P$ realizes the four-output sparse truth table presented in Table 10.1. Seven of the lines of the truth table have all 0 outputs. The MSB output is HI for one minterm only: $P_3 = A_1 \cdot A_0 \cdot B_1 \cdot B_0$. The LSB output is HI only when $A_0 \cdot B_0$ is true. Figure 10.14 shows P_3 and P_0.

Table 10.1 Truth Table for a Two-by-Two Unsigned Multiplication, $A \times B = P$

A_1	A_0	B_1	B_0	P_3	P_2	P_1	P_0
0	0	0	0	0	0	0	0
0	0	0	1	0	0	0	0
0	0	1	0	0	0	0	0
0	0	1	1	0	0	0	0
0	1	0	0	0	0	0	0
0	1	0	1	0	0	0	1
0	1	1	0	0	0	1	0
0	1	1	1	0	0	1	1
1	0	0	0	0	0	0	0
1	0	0	1	0	0	1	0
1	0	1	0	0	1	0	0
1	0	1	1	0	1	1	0
1	1	0	0	0	0	0	0
1	1	0	1	0	0	1	1
1	1	1	0	0	1	1	0
1	1	1	1	1	0	0	1

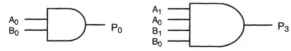

Figure 10.14 Combinatorial products for a two-by-two multiplier.

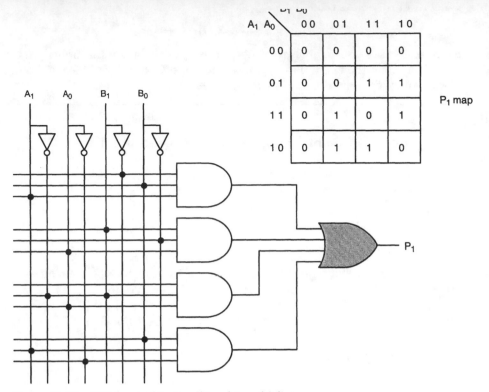

The P_1 map:

$A_1 A_0$ \ $B_1 B_0$	0 0	0 1	1 1	1 0
0 0	0	0	0	0
0 1	0	0	1	1
1 1	0	1	0	1
1 0	0	1	1	0

Figure 10.15   SOP for combinational two-bit multiplier.

If you draw out the symmetric K-map for the second LSB, you'll see that the four-input OR gate circuit of Fig. 10.15 realizes P_1.

In Exercise 21 you can finish the design for a two-by-two multiplier. The design can fit in one PAL, such as the 22V10 you saw in Chapter 7.

Now use the two-by-two multiplier as a building block in a hierarchical design for a larger multiplier. Follow the advice offered in Chapter 1 to design in modules. Use four copies of the two-by-two block and three five-bit adder blocks to build a four-by-four combinational multiplier.

EXAMPLE 8

Design a combinational circuit to multiply two input numbers $A_3A_2A_1A_0$ and $B_3B_2B_1B_0$. The answer can have as many as eight nonzero bits: $\Pi_7\Pi_6\Pi_5\Pi_4\Pi_3\Pi_2\Pi_1\Pi_0$. First write out the subproducts of the pairwise combinations, shown at the top of Fig. 10.16. Each pairwise product is handled by a separate two-by-two combinatorial multiplier, as shown in the figure. The four combinatorial multipliers are labeled W, X, Y, and Z, and the four outputs of each are labeled as to each output's position in the final eight-bit product. For example, multiplier Z's outputs are $Z_7Z_6Z_5Z_4$ since Z

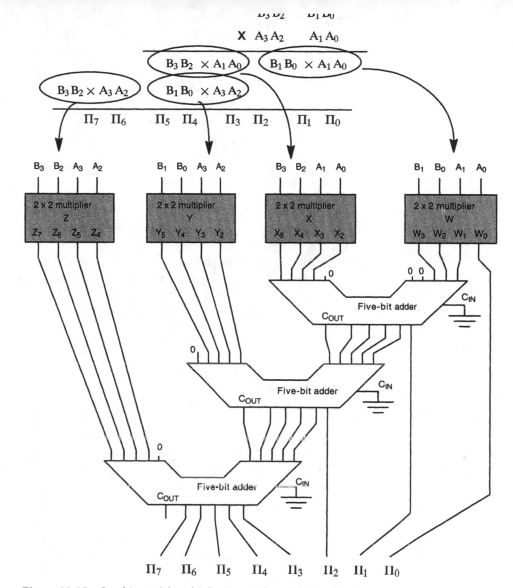

Figure 10.16 Combinatorial multiplication with multiplier subunits.

is four shifts away from W. Use four copies of the two-by-two block and three five-bit adder blocks to build a four-by-four combinational multiplier.

Answer Five-bit adders were chosen for the design to consolidate the adding hardware; all carry-ins have been set to 0. In the diagram, Π_i is the ith bit of the final product.

The largest eight-bit number to result from four-bit by four-bit unsigned multiplication is $F \times F = E1_{16}$. Here the output of each two-by-two multiplier block is

$$
\begin{array}{r}
1111 \\
1111 \\
\hline
\end{array}
$$

1001	W
100100	X
100100	Y
10010000	Z

$$11100001$$

2C answer

Notice that the lower four bits of 1111×1111 are 0001, which is the correct answer for $(-1) \times (-1)$, because $1111 = -1$ in 2C notation. Thus by limiting attention to the lower four bits, a 2C answer can be seen. You may need to test the answer for overflow using the fifth bit or checking $C_4 \oplus C_3$.

What's the maximum delay through the circuit of Fig. 10.16? Each of the adders will have three gates' worth of delay to C_{OUT}, and the combinational multipliers can be designed with two gates' worth of SOP delay. There are 11 gate delays of propagation through the circuit, less than in the array multiplier of the previous example.

10.7.3 Commercial Combinatorial Multipliers

EXAMPLE 9

A pair of TTL chips, the 74LS284 and the 74LS285, can finish a four-by-four combinational multiplication in 40 ns. The 74LS285 generates the first four bits and the 74LS284 generates the next four bits of the eight-bit answer. Two unsigned binary numbers, B and A, are multiplied together in Fig. 10.17; the chips do *not* test for 2C

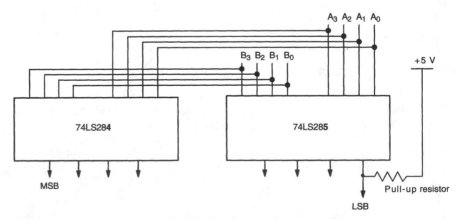

Figure 10.17 Two commercial multiplier chips working in tandem.

resistor of approximately 1 kΩ connected to +5 V, as shown in Fig. 10.17 for the LSB. Not shown are two active-low enable pins, $\overline{G_B}$ and $\overline{G_A}$, on each chip (for a total of 16 pins per chip). Notice that the two chips are independent of each other. There is no ripple-carry-out from the lower-order multiplier '285 to the higher-order '284.

10.8 ANALOG MULTIPLIERS

Electronic multiplication does not have to be done digitally. Here are two ways to multiply using continuously variable voltages to represent numbers.

Analog Multipliers In an *analog multiplier* both multiplicand and multiplier are in analog form. Analog multipliers, such as the AD534 chip from Analog Devices, take advantage of a temperature-compensated exponential voltage-current relationship across a semiconductor junction. The current I_D through a diode as a function of diode voltage V_D is

$$I_D = I_S\left(e^{V_D/V_T} - 1\right)$$

where V_T is about 25 mV at room temperature. I_S is the reverse saturation current and is the small leakage current of a reverse-biased diode. By this relation the chip generates voltages that are approximately proportional to the log of the applied currents. The circuit finds products by adding logarithms with a summation amplifier. Recall

$$\log(a \cdot b) = \log a + \log b$$

Analog multiplication needs no multiwire data buses and no clock, but it is somewhat costly and is limited in accuracy. The '534 analog chip is a four-quadrant multiplier with 2-μs settling time, but it costs approximately $40 and has a total error specification of 2%.

Multiplying Digital-to-Analog Converter An analog voltage and a digital number can be multiplied in a digital-to-analog converter (DAC). The *analog* result is proportional to the *analog* reference voltage supplied to the DAC. The analog reference can be a positive or a negative voltage, so in its basic form the multiplying DAC is two-quadrant.

EXAMPLE 10

In Fig. 10.18 you see a diagram from *Daniels' Digital Design Lab Manual* of a circuit that demonstrates exponential decay. VCO stands for *voltage-controlled oscillator*. The VCO supplies pulses to an eight-bit down-counter, which in turn provides the digital input to the DAC. The analog output voltage $y(t)$ is proportional to the reference

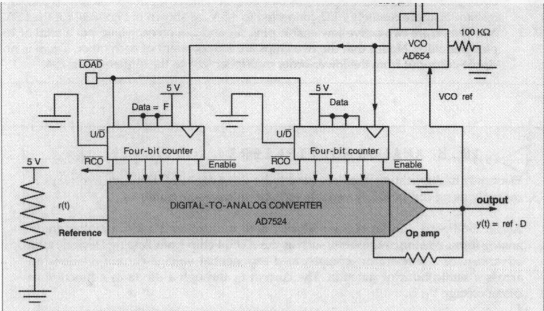

Figure 10.18 Multiplying DAC to demonstrate exponential decay.

voltage $r(t)$ and the eight-bit digital input from the counter. Reference $r(t)$ can be positive or negative voltage. The output of the AD7524 DAC is converted from current to voltage by an op amp and the result used to control the VCO rate at the VCO's reference. Since the count direction is down, the VCO slows down its rate and the output voltage declines to zero at an exponentially decreasing rate. The exponential decay starts when LOAD of FF_{16} is asserted LO, then released for counting down.

10.9 SEQUENTIAL ADD-AND-SHIFT MULTIPLIERS

To reduce the amount of hardware in a multi-bit multiplier, we can adapt the sequential adder approach developed earlier and design a finite state machine multiplier. We start with unsigned four-bit numbers and work through two designs, both add-and-shift multipliers. The first circuit is an FSM with a two-phase clock, and the second circuit is a fully synchronous design.

Add-and-shift multiplication means just what it did in elementary school: the multiplicand is multiplied by one digit or bit of the multiplier, and for each more significant bit of the multiplier the subproduct is shifted left. A column of N shifted subproducts (for an N-digit multiplier) is then added for the result. Before designing the hardware, let's work out what's expected to happen with a specific pair o

Multiplicand B:	1011
Multiplier D:	1101

Form a partial sum. $\left\{ \begin{array}{l} {}_1 1011 \quad \leftarrow \text{LSB of multiplier ANDed with multiplicand} \\ {}_1 0000 \quad \leftarrow 0 \text{ bit of multiplier ANDed with multiplicand} \\ {}_1 1011 \qquad\quad \text{and shifted to the left} \\ 1011 \end{array} \right.$

$$10001111$$
$$8 \qquad F_{16}$$

After each subproduct is formed, it can be added to the previous total. Observe that only four bits at a time need to be added together; previous bits can be shifted down into a register that holds the LSBs of the final answer. (Note: In 2C notation, $1101 = -3$ and $1011 = -5$; $(-3) \times (-5) = -15 > -8 = 1000$, so the 2C "answer" produces overflow: $C_3 \oplus C_4 = 0 \oplus 1 = 1$.)

10.9.1 A Two-Clock Design for Add-and-Shift Multiply

EXAMPLE 11

Design a sequential circuit to multiply together two four-bit positive numbers using an add-and-shift method. The design does not have to be fully synchronous (a gated clock or a two-phase clock is allowed).

Answer   Start with something that looks like the sequential adder, containing

- A parallel-in–serial-out register loaded with the multiplier
- A bank of AND gates receiving the multiplier-gated multiplicand
- A four-bit adder
- A parallel-serial register for *accumulating* the answer

Call the bits of the multiplier $M_3 M_2 M_1 M_0$ and the bits of the multiplicand $T_3 T_2 T_1 T_0$. The PISO register has a clock and a SHIFT/$\overline{\text{LOAD}}$ control. Notice that the multiplier is loaded so that the LSB is nearest to the serial-out pin. The first operation in the multiplication process is a *load* of the multiplier into the PISO register. (See Fig. 10.19.)

Not shown are the input to the other side of the adder, where carry-out goes, and where the other four-bits of the answer will accumulate. But this circuit fragment does get the process started. M_0 gates the bits of T and presents them to one side of the adder. If the other side of the adder is zero and carry-in has been reset to zero, then ACC can store the first add operation.

After the first partial sum has been stored in ACC, then the PISO can be clocked again, forcing M_1 to appear at the PISO serial-out pin and gating the multiplicand, T. On this second cycle of the multiplier, the multiplicand should be added to the three most significant bits of ACC and the former LSB of ACC should be sent down to a serial-in–parallel-out shift register. *The LSB of the first (addition) cycle is the correct answer for the LSB of the final answer.*

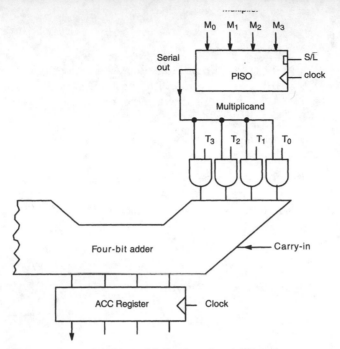

Figure 10.19 One-bit multiplication of multiplicand.

Figure 10.20 shows carry-out and the three most significant bits of ACC projecting back to become the inputs to the left side of the four-bit adder. *Notice that the MSB of ACC goes to the second-most-significant bit of the adder's left input.* In effect, this skewed projection of ACC to the adder provides a down-shift of the whole accumulator. To complete the combinational shift, the LSB of the adder's left input receives the second-least-significant bit of the previous partial sum. As a result of the combinational shift, the most significant bit of the final answer is held in the carry-out flip-flop, as shown at the bottom of the schematic. In Fig. 10.20 the following have been added to the design:

- A serial-in–parallel-out (SIPO) register for storing the LSBs of the answer
- A D flip-flop for holding the previous carry-out

We are left with a control problem for the four clocks, numbered in Fig. 10.20. What timing should govern the clock inputs?[3] Can they all be clocked by the same signal? No. There are two phases to the overall operation: add and shift. In the add phase the accumulator register and the carry-out flip-flop should be loaded to store the partial sum. In the shift phase the PISO and the SIPO should be clocked to shift down the LSB of the partial sum and to push out the next bit of the multiplier for

[3]If this were a fully synchronous design, all clocks would have to be the same signal, but for this first try at add-and-shift, we are allowing a *multiphase clock* design.

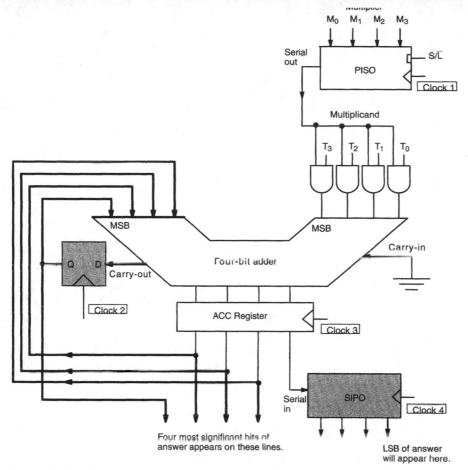

Figure 10.20 Final design for two-phase add-and-shift multiplier.

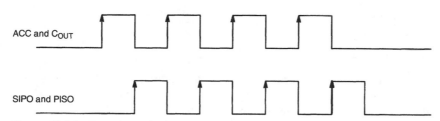

Figure 10.21 Two-phase clock.

ANDing with the multiplicand. See Fig. 10.21 for rising-edge-triggered timing. If the accumulator is rising-edge-triggered and the SIPO is falling-edge-triggered, only one clock is needed for loading and storing.

Notice how the accumulator and the carry-out flip-flop prevent a race condition from the adder output back to its own input. Even though the inputs to the adder

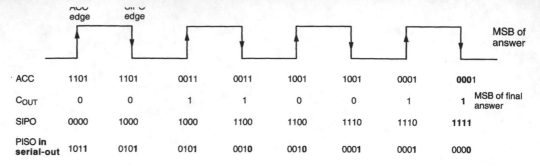

ACC	1101	1101	0011	0011	1001	1001	0001	**0001**
C_{OUT}	0	0	1	1	0	0	1	**1** MSB of final answer
SIPO	0000	1000	1000	1100	1100	1110	1110	**1111**
PISO in serial-out	1011	0101	0101	0010	0010	0001	0001	0000

Figure 10.22 Register values during multiplication sequence.

change and the adder output changes, the accumulator remains at the previous partial sum, waiting for its next valid clock edge.

Because the accumulator register output is shifted into the adder after the fourth SIPO clock edge (clock 4), *the correct answer is held in carry-out, the three most significant bits of ACC, and SIPO.* In the example of Fig. 10.22, the final answer is $1\,000\,1111 = 8F_{16}$.

As an example of the actions of the design, the intermediate register values of the hex multiplication $D \times B = 8F_{16}$ will be determined. Use one clock, with ACC and the D flip-flop rising-edge-triggered and SIPO and PISO falling-edge-triggered. The multiplicand is $D = 1101$, and the multiplier is $B = 1011$. See Fig. 10.22. On each SIPO edge the LSB of ACC is shifted down to SIPO and C_{OUT} is shifted into ACC.

In the example above, it was assumed that before the multiplication clocking started, the multiplier had been loaded into the PISO, ACC had been cleared to 0000, the carry-out flip-flop had been reset, and carry-in of the adder had been tied to LO. A self-contained design might accept a start-of-multiplication (SOM) command, which would in turn perform the following:

- Load the multiplier in the PISO register
- Clear the accumulator register
- Reset the carry-out flip-flop
- Clear a counter

The counter would take a system clock and form internal control signals. For a four-bit multiplier the counter would allow only four cycles before halting the process. The halt signal could serve as an end-of-multiplication (EOM) signal to a user or display latch.

Shown in Fig. 10.23 is a rough schematic for a counter to control the overall multiplication process. The LSB of the counter can provide edges for ACC and SIPO, using an inverter to create two phases. When the MSB goes HI after four LSB pulses, it can enable LOAD and CLEAR, and let the outside world know that an answer has been produced (EOM = MSB). Figure 10.23 also shows the timing of LSB and MSB, and the projections of LSB and MSB to the clocked elements of the add-and-shift multiplier. *Figure 10.23 shows only the clocked elements (the combinational adder is not*

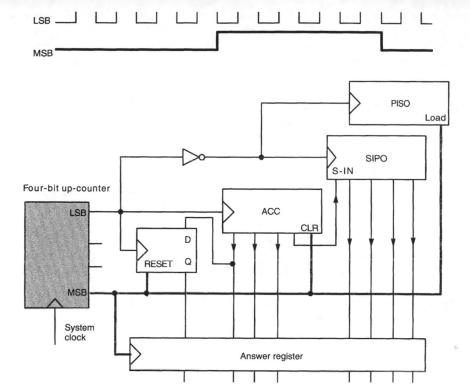

Figure 10.23   Using a counter to control a two-phase multiplier.

included). An answer register has been added, which is clocked by the rising edge of the counter MSB. The details are not shown, but while counter MSB stays HI, it can gate active clock edges into ACC and PISO to clear and load, respectively. During the time MSB is HI, another circuit can change the multiplier and the multiplicand. When MSB goes LO again, everything is ready to begin a new multiplication.

10.9.2   A Synchronous Design for Add-and-Shift

The design in Section 10.9.1 is an intuitive introduction to add-and-shift multiplication of four-bit numbers. However, not all the flip-flops in that circuit are driven by the same edge of the same clock, so the design is not truly synchronous. It is a finite state machine, but it uses more than one clock.

EXAMPLE 12

Design a single-clock four-bit by four-bit add-and-shift multiplier, following systematically the guidelines of synchronous FSM design developed in Chapter 7. If we were to build a synchronous multiplier from *D* flip-flops up, it would have an enormous number of states. In order to reduce the number of apparent states, our FSM design takes advantage of modern digital IC packages. We will allow building blocks consisting of a counter and three universal shift registers. A universal shift register such as the four-bit 74194 has a control port to decide whether shift left, shift right, load, hold, or clear occurs on the next active clock edge. The important operation for the problem at hand is *hold:* we need some way to have a register do nothing on some clock cycles.

You will see in the following design that the same basic scheme of add-and-shift from the previous two-clock design is used; however, more control logic will be generated to guide the machine synchronously from one state to the next. The synchronous design will be more self-contained than the two-phase clock design.

To begin, assume that the four-bit unsigned multiplier and multiplicand are available at data ports; the multiplier will be loaded into a register, and the multiplicand will face four AND gates. A start pulse will take the machine out of a WAIT state and into the INIT state, during which INIT will reset the accumulator, the carry flip-flop, and the counter and load the multiplier in a shift register. The FSM will then go to the LOAD state and then back and forth between the LOAD and SHIFT states until a count maximum is reached. The machine will return to the WAIT state, holding the correct answer until another start pulse is received. The ASM chart in Fig. 10.24 shows the states.

Since there are four states, at least two flip-flops are needed. Let's use two-state variables and assign the following codes to the four states:

	Q_1	Q_0
WAIT	0	0
INIT	1	1
LOAD	1	0
SHIFT	0	1

We can transform the flowchart into the following present-state–next-state chart, including the start (S) and finish (F) active-high inputs. The *start* input will come from an external source; the *finish* signal will be generated by a counter-comparator circuit shown later in Fig. 10.29.

Present State $Q_1 Q_0$	Next State $Q_1 Q_0$	S	F
0 0	0 0	0	X
0 0	1 1	1	X
1 1	1 0	X	X
1 0	0 1	X	X
0 1	1 0	X	0
0 1	0 0	X	1

Notice that if a start signal arrives during a WAIT state, then the finish signal is a don't-care. From the present-state–next-state chart we can write out the following excitation equations for the D_1 and D_0 flip-flop inputs. Look at the second and fourth lines of the present-state–next-state table: D_0 must be 1 when Q_0 is to become 1, that

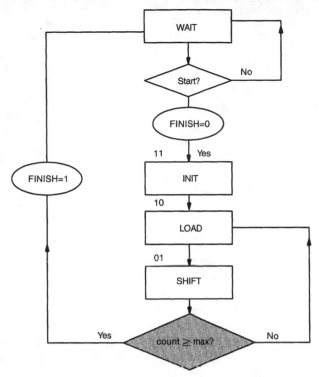

Figure 10.24 Algorithmic state machine flowchart for multiplication.

is, when $\overline{Q_1} \cdot \overline{Q_0} \cdot S$ is true or when $Q_1 \cdot \overline{Q_0}$ is true. Therefore

$$D_0 = \overline{Q_1} \cdot \overline{Q_0} \cdot S + Q_1 \cdot \overline{Q_0}$$

There are three lines in the table for which the D_1 drive for Q_1 must be 1. Forming a sum-of-products expression for those three conditions, we have

$$D_1 = \overline{Q_1} \cdot \overline{Q_0} \cdot S + Q_1 \cdot Q_0 + \overline{Q_1} \cdot Q_0 \cdot \overline{F}$$

where S and F are the active HI start and finish signals, respectively. After we turn the SOPs into hardware, the state machine part of the multiplier looks like Fig. 10.25. On the right, Q_1 and Q_0 are decoded through AND gates to become signals for each of the four states.

At this point we've completed the design of an FSM. By the steps of Chapter 7, we've specified the problem and assigned flip-flops to states (steps 1 and 2). We've chosen D flip-flops and determined the excitation equations (steps 3 and 4). Now we are left with a large output problem (step 5) that involves directing the state outputs to other registers.

If the machine is in the WAIT state, S (start) is asserted, and F (finish) has been true, then the machine will advance to the INIT state on the next clock edge. In the INIT state the accumulator and carry-out flip-flop will be reset, the multiplier will be loaded into a shift register, F will be reset, and the operation counter will be reset.

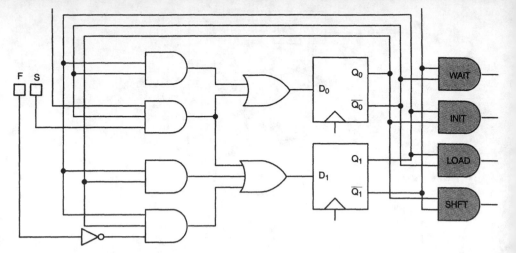

Figure 10.25 State machine for synchronous multiplier.

Figure 10.26 shows the INIT state signal carrying out these functions. Figure 10.29 also shows INIT clearing a counter, which resets the finish signal. Each of the sequential elements in Fig. 10.26 is driven by the same clock signal. $M_3 M_2 M_1 M_0$ is the multiplier to be loaded. Other connections in the multiplier circuit are not shown here; only the projections from INIT are necessary to initialize the circuit.

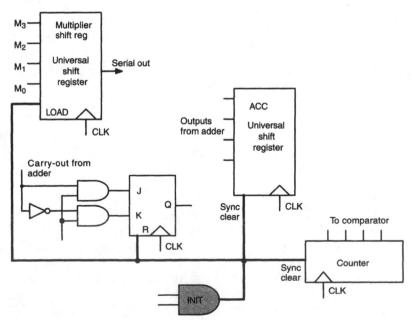

Figure 10.26 Start of synchronous multiplier design.

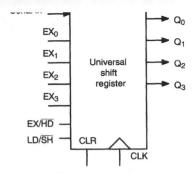

Figure 10.27 Universal shift register.

Before you see what happens to the circuit during the other states, we need a digression to learn about the four-bit universal shift register (USR, patterned after the 74194 IC). For our purposes the USR has the schematic symbol shown in Fig. 10.27. When LD/$\overline{\text{SH}}$ is HI, then on the next clock edge the USR is loaded with either *external data* (EX$_3$–EX$_0$) or with current outputs Q_3–Q_0, depending on the setting of EX/$\overline{\text{HD}}$. When Q_3–Q_0 are loaded, the operation is a HOLD. If LD/$\overline{\text{SH}}$ is LO, then on the next clock edge serial-in goes to Q_0 and Q_i goes to Q_{i+1} for $i = 0, 1, 2$. If CLR is HI, then on the next clock edge all Q's become 0, no matter what LD/$\overline{\text{SH}}$ or EX/$\overline{\text{HD}}$ is. Our USR has no shift-left operation, and it has a synchronous clear.

To continue with the design process, make a systematic list of the actions that occur at each of the four clocked elements in the multipliers. Refer to the USR in Fig. 10.27 to see how the control inputs are to be filled in below. ACC, MULT$_{\text{SH}}$, and LSB$_{\text{SH}}$ are USRs. For example, during INIT, ACC is cleared, the carry flip-flop is reset, and the LSB shift register is cleared.

	Q_1Q_0	ACC		Carry-Out Flip-Flop		MULT$_{\text{SH}}$		LSB$_{\text{SH}}$	
		LD/$\overline{\text{SH}}$	EX/$\overline{\text{HD}}$	J	K	LD/$\overline{\text{SH}}$	EX/$\overline{\text{HD}}$	LD/$\overline{\text{SH}}$	EX/$\overline{\text{HD}}$
WAIT	00	1	0	0	0	1	0	1	0
INIT	11	CLEAR		RESET		1	1	CLEAR	
LOAD	10	1	1	C_{OUT}	$\overline{C_{\text{OUT}}}$	1	0	1	0
SHIFT	01	0	X	0	0	0	X	0	X

Look at each of the three LD/$\overline{\text{SH}}$ columns. The only condition in which they are asserted LO is during the SHIFT state. Therefore $\overline{\text{SHIFT}}$ is a valid input to each of the LD/$\overline{\text{SH}}$ pins. Driving the LD pins with $\overline{\text{SHIFT}}$ is therefore an efficient way for shifting to be carried out. See Fig. 10.28. Continuing to examine the columns of the state table, we see that the INIT signal is the appropriate input to the MULT$_{\text{SH}}$ register EX/$\overline{\text{HD}}$ input and that the LSB$_{\text{SH}}$ register's EX/$\overline{\text{HD}}$ input can always be 0. Finally, the accumulator's EX/$\overline{\text{HD}}$ input is to be HI only during the LOAD state. The carry-out flip-flop is enabled during LOAD, and otherwise $JK = 00$ to HOLD the previous carry.

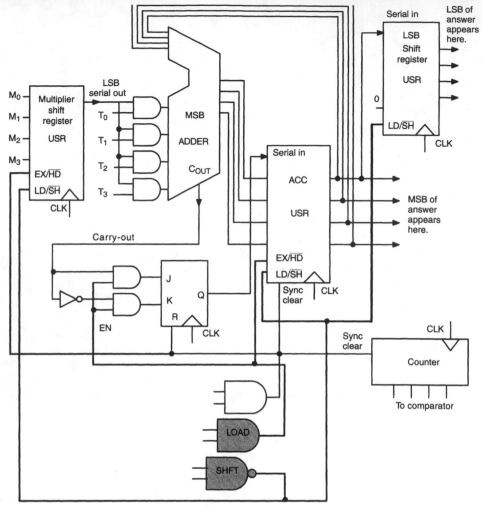

Figure 10.28 Synchronous four-by-four multiplier.

In the circuit shown in Fig. 10.28, the serial output of the MULT_{SH} shift register is ANDed with the multiplicand (T) bits. The result—either T or 0—is added to the previous value of ACC. The sum is stored in ACC on a LOAD cycle. During SHIFT the LSB of ACC is sent down to the LSB register and the carry-out is brought into ACC at the MSB side. After a clock edge initializes the circuit, a LOAD occurs. During a LOAD operation the adder output is sent to the accumulator and the carry-out flip-flop. The counter advances, and the shift registers hold their current values.

With the LOAD and SHIFT wiring done, the design is almost finished. The last question to answer is, How should the FINISH signal be generated? See the circuit in Fig. 10.29. When the operation counter is greater than $0110 = 6$, the FINISH signal goes HI. Greater-than is used so FINISH will stay HI until the counter is cleared

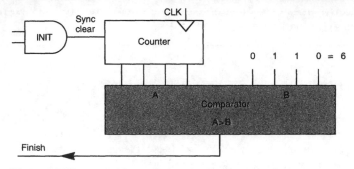

Figure 10.29 Detail for end-of-multiplication signal.

by INIT. You saw earlier that FINISH is used by the FSM flip-flops to gate moves from SHIFT to WAIT and from WAIT to INIT. Why count > 6? Basically, INIT clears the counter to 0000, so a LOAD occurs *after* 0000 and other LOADs occur after even numbers. Therefore FINISH will go HI on CNT = 7, during an odd-numbered shift operation. FINISH will signal the FSM to move from SHIFT to WAIT.

We account for step 6 and the Chapter 7 algorithm by noting there are no unused states. For step 7, testing the hex outputs of all the registers in step with the operation counter, register values are shown below for the hex product $F \times F = E1$:

Count	State	Carry	ACC	LSB$_{SH}$	MULT$_{SH}$	Comparator
0	LOAD	0	0	0	F	0
1	SHIFT	0	F	0	F	0
2	LOAD	1	7	8	7	0
3	SHIFT	1	6	8	7	0
4	LOAD	1	B	4	3	0
5	SHIFT	1	A	4	3	0
6	LOAD	1	D	2	1	0
7	SHIFT	1	C	2	1	1
8	WAIT	1	E	1	0	1

Remember: the operation shown for a particular count is executed on the *next* clock edge. Therefore the result of the LOAD at count 0 appears in registers on the line for count = 1. Once in the WAIT state, the FSM stays there until another START pulse comes along. The WAIT state AND gate in Fig. 10.25 doesn't have to control anything; it just waits.

It should be emphasized again that the main FSM design here was the four-state WAIT-INIT-LOAD-SHIFT sequence. Other parts of the design (counter, USR, and so on) are "slave" FSMs controlled by the main sequence.

The synchronous multiplier uses somewhat more combinational logic than the two-phase multiplier; it also has a separate pair of D flip-flops to generate states. The extra hardware is the price paid for fully synchronous operation. But the synchronous

10.10 BOOTH'S ALGORITHM FOR FAST SIGNED MULTIPLICATION

Any of the designs—combinational or sequential—seen so far in Chapter 10 can generate the correct answer for signed 2's complement of $N \times N$ products *if only the lower N bits of the 2N-bit product are allowed as the 2's complement answer*. For example, $-3 \times 2 = -6$ computed in four-bit 2's complement is

$$
\begin{array}{rrrrrrr}
(-3) & & & & 1 & 1 & 0 & 1 \\
\times(+2) & & & & 0 & 0 & 1 & 0 \\
\hline
& & & & 0 & 0 & 0 & 0 \\
& & & 1 & 1 & 0 & 1 & \\
& & 0 & 0 & 0 & 0 & & \\
& 0 & 0 & 0 & 0 & & & \\
\hline
& 0 & 0 & 1 & 1 & 0 & 1 & 0 \\
\end{array}
$$

If we look at the last four bits of the multiplication, we see the correct answer 1010 in four-bit 2's complement. Notice that in this example the algorithm went ahead and added 0000 to the accumulator three times when all that was needed was one left-shift of the multiplicand. A functional 2C multiplier will also need an overflow status output.

Booth's algorithm speeds up 2's complement multiplication by taking advantage of consecutive strings of 0s and 1s in the multiplier. Consider first a string of 0s. Reading the multiplier bit by bit, from LSB to MSB, you must eventually encounter a 1 (or the number would end with the string of 0s). An example is $1000\,0000 = 2^7$. As you saw with power-of-2 multiplication, a 1 followed by a string of 0s in the multiplier represents a sequence of pure left shifts.

EXAMPLE 13

The two eight-bit signed multiplications below confirm that when the multiplier is a series of 0s terminated by a single 1, left-shifting the multiplicand gives the correct answer. Two's complement code is used.

$$(+5) \times (+4) = 20_{10} = 14_{16} = 0001\,0100$$

0000 0101	Multiplicand
0000 0100	Multiplier
0001 0100	5 shifted twice

$$(-5) \times (+8) = -40_{10} = D8_{16} = 1101\,1000$$

1111 1011	-5 in 2's complement
0000 1000	
1101 1000	-5 left-shifted three times

Notice in the -5×8 example that the 5 multiplicand has been filled in with 1s to the left. The conclusion is that the presence of N consecutive 0s leading to a 1 on the left in the multiplier implies an N-bit left-shift of the multiplicand.

Next consider the case when the multiplier is a string of N 1s. Such a number can be expressed as $2^N - 1$. For example, for $N = 5, 1\,1111 = 10\,0000 - 1 = 2^5 - 1 = 31_{10}$. Multiplication of T by N 1s is $T \times (2^N - 1) = T \cdot 2^N - T$. We already know how to compute $T \cdot 2^N$: it's just an N-bit left-shift. So to compute $T \times (2^N - 1)$, left-shift T N times and add the 2's complement of T to the result.

EXAMPLE 14

Consider multiplication by 7:

$$111 = 1000 - 1$$

Let T be the multiplicand. For this example let $T = -2 = FF_{16}$ for eight-bit representation. So

$$111 \times (T) = (1000 - 1) \times (T) = 1000 \times (T) - T$$

by the distributive law. We've already worked out what to do with a number like 1000, which is to left-shift three times. In eight-bit format, -2×7 is

$$
\begin{array}{r}
-2 \\
\times\ +7 \\
\hline
F2_{16}
\end{array}
$$

$$
\begin{array}{ll}
1111\ 1110 & \\
0000\ 0111 & \\
\hline
1111\ 1111\ 0000 & \text{Three left-shifts} \\
0000\ 0010 & \text{Subtract } -(-2) \Rightarrow \text{Add } +2. \\
\hline
1111\ 0010 & = F2_{16} = -14 \text{ in eight-bit 2's complement}
\end{array}
$$

In general, N 1s in the multiplier followed on the right by M 0s results in the expression $2^{(N+M)} - 2^M$.

EXAMPLE 15

$$1111\ 0000 = 2^{4+4} - 2^4 = 256 - 16 = 240_{10}$$

Compound sequences can be done by parts:

$$
\begin{aligned}
1111\ 0000\ 1111\ 0000 &= 1111\ 0000\ 0000\ 0000 + 0000\ 0000\ 1111\ 0000 \\
&= (2^{4+12} - 2^{12}) + 256 = 65536 - 4096 + 256 = 61696_{10}
\end{aligned}
$$

Any consecutive set of 1s in the multiplier implies a subtraction when the first 1 is encountered and then an addition when the last 1 is encountered. For the 1s between the first and the last, only shifting is needed.

Only when the multiplier bits change from 0 to 1 or from 1 to 0 is anything other than a shift called for. Let the bits in the multiplier be $Y_7Y_6Y_5Y_4Y_3Y_2Y_1Y_0$. Further, define Y_{-1} to be 0 (we need a fictitious bit to the right of the LSB). Now move one bit at a time from Y_{-1} to the MSB. For every pair of Y's encountered, shift the partial sum (called ACC) and, depending on the pattern of the Y_N, Y_{N-1} pair, perform the action indicated in the following multiplier-pair action table:

Y_N	Y_{N-1}	Action
0	0	No operation
1	1	No operation
1	0	SUBTRACT multiplicand from ACC.
0	1	ADD multiplicand to ACC.

Each pair of multiplier bits defines an action that includes a shift. What do we mean by SUBTRACT? Add the 2's complement of the multiplicand! Booth's algorithm moves one bit at a time from the LSB of the multiplier on to the left until it encounters the final 1 in the multiplier.

Booth's algorithm is a sequential process that speeds up multiplication of signed numbers to the extent that there are repeated 1s or 0s in a multiplier. More information can be found in the following: Booth (1951); Kline (1977, 287); Rabiner and Gold (1975, 517–518).

EXAMPLE 16

Multiply 6×5 using Booth's algorithm for eight-bit registers.

Answer   The multiplier is 5 and goes by the notation $Y_7Y_6Y_5Y_4Y_3Y_2Y_1Y_0Y_{-1} = 0000\,0101\,0$, where Y_{-1} is needed to start the sequence of pairs of Y's. The numbers are listed out to eight places below; since they're both positive, 0s hold the most significant bits. Y_{-1} is in parentheses. To subtract 6, add the 2's complement of 6 ($-6 = 1111\,1010$). The accumulator starts out with zero.

$$
\begin{array}{rl}
6 = & 0000\,0110 \\
5 = & 0000\,0101(0) \\
\hline
& 1111\,1010 \qquad Y_0Y_{-1} = 10 \Rightarrow \text{Subtract 6.} \\
& 0\,0000\,110 \qquad Y_1Y_0 = 01 \Rightarrow \text{Add 6.} \\
& 11\,1110\,10 \qquad Y_2Y_1 = 10 \Rightarrow \text{Subtract 6.} \\
& 000\,0011\,00 \qquad Y_3Y_2 = 01 \Rightarrow \text{Add 6.} \\
& \qquad\qquad\quad\ \ \text{Rest of } Y\text{'s are all zero.} \Rightarrow \text{Do nothing but shift.} \\
\hline
& 101\,0001\,1110 \qquad \text{Add up the four numbers.}
\end{array}
$$

Examine the last eight bits, and see that $1E_{10} = 30_{10}$ is the correct answer.

EXAMPLE 17

Multiply 6×-5.

$$
\begin{array}{rl}
6 = & 0000\,0110 \\
-5 = & 1111\,1011(0)
\end{array}
$$

1111 1010	$Y_0 Y_{-1} = 10 \Rightarrow$ Subtract 6.
0 0000 000	$Y_1 Y_0 = 11 \Rightarrow$ Do nothing.
00 0001 10	$Y_2 Y_1 = 01 \Rightarrow$ Add 6.
111 11101 0	$Y_3 Y_2 = 10 \Rightarrow$ Subtract 6.
	Rest of Y's are all ones. $\Rightarrow$ Do nothing.
1000 **1110 0010**	Add up the four numbers.

Examine the last eight bits: the hex code for the answer is E2 $= -30_{10}$. To test that the overflow didn't occur, make sure that

$$
\text{(sign bit)}_{\text{ANS}} = \text{(sign bit)}_M \oplus \text{(sign bit)}_T
$$

where M is the multiplier and T is the multiplicand.

In these two examples we, as humans, are not bothering with partial sums; we find the $+6$ or -6 terms, shift them accordingly, and then add up the whole column at once.

A Booth's Algorithm Chip Booth's algorithm can compute 2's complement products within a single IC. In the late 1970s Advanced Micro Devices designed the 25LS14 chip for hardware execution of Booth's algorithm. Also called the 74LS384 TTL chip, it is an eight-bit by Y-bit multiplier, where the Y-bits enter on a serial line and the output is produced as another serial stream, S. The '384 uses a modified add and shift design.

The pattern of the multiplier bits Y_n, Y_{n-1} determines whether the next operation in Booth's algorithm is a PASS, ADD, or SUBTRACT of the multiplicand. The circuit in Fig. 10.30 compares the previous value of Y with the present value of Y and forms two control signals to enforce the Booth algorithm action table.

Y_n	Y_{n-1}	
0	0	PASS
0	1	ADD
1	0	SUBTRACT
1	1	PASS

Consider the XOR gate in Fig. 10.30.

If XOR $= 1$ and $Y_n = 1$, SUBTRACT.

If XOR $= 1$ and $Y_n = 0$, ADD.

If XOR $= 0$, PASS.

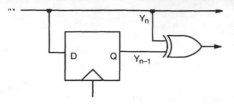

Figure 10.30 Booth's algorithm instruction circuit.

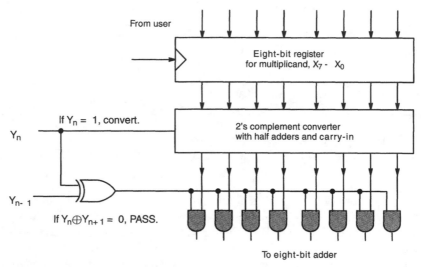

Figure 10.31 Booth's algorithm registers with AND gates for resetting outputs.

The eight-bit multiplicand, stored in an on-chip register for the duration of the computation, sees two stages of combinational circuitry, which use two control signals. First is an eight-bit 2's complement converter, controlled by the Y_n value. Next is a bank of eight two-input AND gates, whose outputs will be zero if $Y_n \oplus Y_{n+1}$ is zero. (See Fig. 10.31)

We now have one input to an eight-bit adder; the other comes from an accumulator (Fig. 10.32). The circuit of Fig. 10.31 is in the colored box of Fig. 10.32. In imitation of our previous add-and-shift circuit, the ACC LSB projects out as the latest bit of the answer. A separate flip-flop is shown on the C_{OUT} pathway.

An eight-by-eight multiplication will produce a 16-bit answer, so 16 clock pulses are necessary to shift out the entire answer. A serial-in–parallel-out register must be ready to receive the answer. The 74LS384 can handle a 25-MHz clock; therefore an eight-by-eight multiplication can be done in less than a microsecond. Figure 10.33 provides the 74LS384 pinout. The X_i's project to a register for the *multiplicand*; CLEAR loads a new multiplicand and clears ACC, the carry-out flip-flop, and the Y_{n-1} flip-flop. The *multiplier* bits are serially sent to the Y input, least significant bit first. The answer comes out of S, one bit at a time, on each clock pulse. K and M are

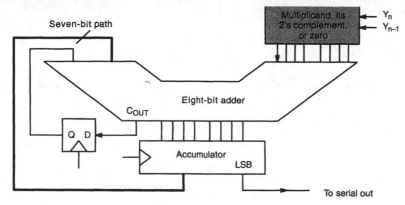

Figure 10.32 Accumulator on output of adder.

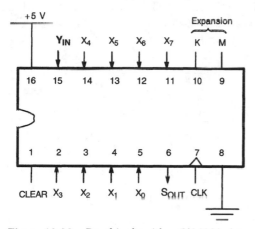

Figure 10.33 Booth's algorithm 74LS384 chip pinout.

pins for expansion to multiplicands having more bits. Find the data sheet for more details.

10.11 FLOATING-POINT ADDITION AND MULTIPLICATION

In Chapter 1 we covered a spectrum of binary numbers: unsigned integers, signed numbers, fractions, and numbers represented by scientific notation. For the last category—referred to as **floating-point numbers**—we now *outline* methods of addition and multiplication. In scientific notation, a real number X is expressed as

$$X = (-1)^S \cdot F \cdot R^E$$

where S is the sign, F is the fraction or mantissa, and E is the exponent. R, the radix (base), will always be 2 for computer arithmetic.

Consider base-2 real numbers. In the IEEE 754 (1985) floating-point standard for *single precision*,[4] one number takes up 32 bits, as shown below:

S	E	E	E	E	E	E	E	E	F	F	F	F	F	F	F	F	F	F	F	F	F	F	F	F	F	F	F	F	F	F	F

The number is

$$X = (-1)^S \cdot (1.F) \cdot 2^{(E-127)}$$

Thus the 23-bit fraction F is added to a hidden 1, and that number (the mantissa) is multiplied by 2 to the $E - 127$ power, where E is an eight-bit number. The form $E - 127$ is called "excess-127" notation. Use of excess-127 exponents allows for very large and very small numbers while E itself remains a positive integer. The exponent can range directly from -127 to $+128$. Note that $2^{128} \approx 3.4 \times 10^{38}$. Positive and negative numbers are expressed as **signed magnitudes**, not in 2's complement! A sign bit of 0 represents a positive number, and 1 represents a negative number. There are two zeros, $0+$ and $0-$, one for each sign bit.

EXAMPLE 18

Convert -4444.4414_{10} to binary and express it as a floating-point number.

Answer   Using one of the conversion methods of Chapter 1 (repeated division or repeated subtraction), you can find that

$$-4444.4414_{10} = -1\,0001\,0101\,1100.0111\,0001$$

Expressed as a number with magnitude between 1 and 2,

$$-4444.4414_{10} = -1.0001\,0101\,1100\,0111\,0001 \times 2^{12}$$

Because $12 = 139 - 127$ and $139 = 1000\,1011$, the IEEE 32-bit single-precision binary floating-point number would be

1	1	0	0	0	1	0	1	1	0	0	0	1	0	1	0	1	1	1	0	0	0	1	1	1	0	0	0	1	0	0	0

10.11.2   Floating-Point Addition

Two floating-point numbers must have equal exponents before they're added together. Assume that two floating-point numbers are in registers 1 and 2 in a memory system and that their sum is to be placed in register 3. To understand their addition, we use a pipelined flowchart, which suggests passage of data from one register

---

[4]There are four sizes of IEEE floating-point numbers: single precision has 32 bits, single extended format has 42 bits, double precision has 64 bits, and double extended format has 78 bits.

to another, as in a shift register: the data pipeline is the linkage of registers. As a pipe-lined flowchart, floating-point addition looks like the following, where we assume mantissas are between 1 and 2.

▷○ FLOATING–POINT ADDITION

↓ Place number with larger exponent in register 1.
↓ Let DIFF $= E_1 - E_2$.
↓ Right-shift mantissa M_2 by DIFF bits. Take account of hidden 1.
↓ Add mantissas M_1 and M_2; store in register 3 with exponent $E_3 = E_1$.
↓ If $M_1 + M_2 > 2$, renormalize by dividing by 2 and incrementing E_3.

The chart doesn't account for all contingencies (such as overflow), but it does have the key feature of mantissa shift by the difference in exponent size. For more discussion on floating-point arithmetic, see Stone (1990, chap. 3).

10.11.3 Floating-Point Multiplication

Recall that

$$M_1 \cdot 2^{E_1} \cdot M_2 \cdot 2^{E_2} = M_1 \cdot M_2 \cdot 2^{E_1 + E_2}$$

As you know from algebra, two numbers in scientific notation are multiplied by adding their exponents and multiplying their mantissas. The same holds for floating-point number multiplication. Since the product of two numbers between 1 and 2 may be greater than 2, a floating-point multiplication may need a renormalization (divide the product's mantissa by 2 and increment its exponent) as a final step. Here is a flowchart for a floating-point multiplication:

▷○ FLOATING–POINT MULTIPLICATION

↓ PROD $= M_1 \cdot M_2$
↓ If PROD > 1, normalize to PROD $\cdot 2^{E_3}$, where $E_3 = 1$ and PROD is a right shift of the original PROD.
↓ $E = E_1 + E_2 + E_3$
↓ ANS $=$ PROD $\cdot 2^E$

Not taken into account is the possibility of overflow or underflow. *Underflow* means the exponent is *less* than some negative limit. The next chapter, "Register Transfer Logic," will continue discussion of pipeline methods for floating-point arithmetic.

In microprocessors for personal computers, either there is built-in floating-point arithmetic hardware or the motherboard on the computer has a slot for a special floating-point unit (FPU) chip. The FPU is used as a peripheral to the central processing unit (CPU) microprocessor when the CPU carries out floating-point multiplication, addition, and so on.

10.12 SUBTRACT AND COUNT FOR DIVISION

As a final topic for Chapter 10, we introduce the problem of hardware division by looking briefly at a sequential method for finding the quotient and the remainder of an unsigned integer division.

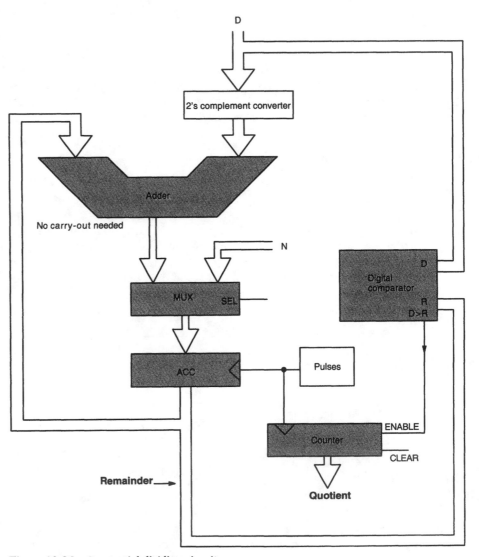

Figure 10.34 Sequential dividing circuit.

EXAMPLE 19

The sequential subtract-and-count design sketched in Fig. 10.34 (see p. 562) will find the positive-integer quotient and remainder for an M-bit number N (numerator) divided by another number D (denominator). To initialize the circuit, select the numerator path to ACC, load N into ACC, and clear the counter. Make sure that the denominator is presented to the 2's complement circuit at the top. As soon as the MUX-select is switched to the output of the adder, successive cycles will decrement ACC by the value of the denominator, D. Since a positive and a negative number are being added on each cycle, there is no need for a carry-out.

When the digital comparator detects that the remainder is greater than the denominator, the process is halted. The output of the comparator is therefore an end-of-division signal. The quotient appears at the output of the counter, and any remainder stays in ACC. The shifting operations of sequential multiplication have here been replaced by a counting process.

10.13 SUMMARY

- Two **half adder**s can be combined into a **one-bit full adder** (1BFA).
- Concatenating 1BFAs from carry-in to carry-out creates an N-bit **ripple adder.** The worst-case propagation delay for a ripple adder is from input to final carry-out.
- Combinational **carry look-ahead** circuitry can reduce the carry-out delay of ripple addition.
- Sequential **serial adding** can be done with one 1BFA, a flip-flop to hold the carry-out as an input for the next carry-in, and shift registers to hold the answer and the two numbers to be added. Adding together two N-bit numbers takes N clock pulses.
- An accumulating adder is a clocked circuit that uses a multiple-bit combinational adder with its output latched in an **accumulator.** One input to the accumulating adder is the next number to be added, and the other input is the partial sum stored in the accumulator.
- **Subtraction** hardware can be a combinational circuit that realizes a subtraction truth table; more useful, however, is conversion of the subtrahend to 2's complement form and then addition with an accumulating adder. A 2's complement adder requires a specified width in bits; the left-most bit is the sign bit.
- Two's complement conversion hardware is a bank of inverters whose outputs can project into an **incrementer** composed of rippling half adders with $C_{IN} = 1$.
- A 2's complement adder circuit needs an **overflow** status indicator.
- For modest-sized products (less than 30 bits or so), table lookup of answers is feasible; the two numbers to be multiplied form the address, and the product is the contents of a read-only memory.
- An **array multiplier** is a hierarchical matrix of AND gates and adders. An array multiplier can duplicate add and shift multiplication in a combinational design.

The heart of **add-and-shift** hardware for **sequential multiplication** is a multiple-bit adder projecting to an accumulator and a flip-flop to hold carry-out. A two-phase clock design for a sequential multiplier was compared to a fully synchronous design. The two-phase design used less hardware but the fully synchronous design conformed to the finite-state machine design standards proposed in Chapter 7.

- Booth's algorithm speeds up multiplication when the multiplier has sequences of consecutive 0s or 1s. It automatically takes care of signed products and can be implemented in a single chip.

- The **IEEE standard for floating-point numbers** takes account of $(-1)^S \cdot 1.F \cdot 2^E$ for representation in 32 to 78 bits, where S is the sign, F is the fraction of the mantissa, and E is the exponent. Algorithms exist for adding and multiplying floating-point numbers. Pipelined flowcharts show their general form.

- Hardware for **division** requires a counter to keep track of repeated subtractions. A digital comparator monitors the numerator and the remainder and halts the repeated subtraction when the numerator becomes greater than the remainder.

Exercises 10

1. **(a)** Suppose you want to create a truth table for looking up the square of any 16-bit 2's complement number. How many bits of memory will be needed?
   (b) What if you want to look up the result of dividing any 16-bit unsigned integer by any other nonzero 8-bit integer, with the result rounded off to the nearest integer? How many bits of memory will that require?

2. Computing a sum of products (inner product, dot product) of two sets of numbers is a common calculation in digital signal processing. Suppose you have two sets of four-bit vectors, w_0, w_1, w_2, w_3 and v_0, v_1, v_2, v_3, and you wish to compute $\sum_{i=0}^{3} w_i \cdot v_i$. Assuming that you have two-input adder and multiplier blocks, draw out in block diagram form an efficient way to find the required dot product. A dot product is a demonstration of the *distributive law* of algebra.

3. What does the cascade of half adders in Fig. P10.1 do to data $D_3 D_2 D_1 D_0$ in forming the five-bit output at the bottom of the circuit?

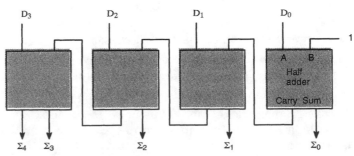

Figure P10.1

4. Design a combinational ripple adder for four-bit addition. Assume that your building blocks are 1BFAs made as two-level SOPs. What is the maximum delay through the adder circuit, assuming that each gate has an equal propagation delay Δ?

5. Shown in Fig. P10.2 is an arithmetic circuit composed of full adders. If

$$N_5 N_4 N_3 N_2 N_1 N_0 = 101111$$

what is the output $S_5 S_4 S_3$? What does the circuit do?

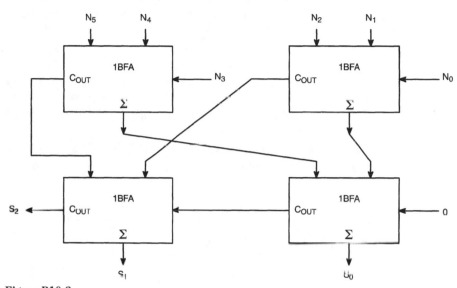

Figure P10.2

6. Draw out the four-bit version of the ripple adder/subtracter shown in Fig. 10.4. Add the extra circuitry needed to detect overflow in 2's complement. Show that the overflow indicator works for the case $0110 + 0110 = 1100$, where two positives result in a wrong negative answer.

7. (a) Does the plus sign in the formula $C_{k+1} = G_k + C_k \cdot P_k$ for carry look-ahead stand for addition or OR?

(b) Draw out the two-level logic circuits of *carry look-ahead* for C_1, C_2, C_3, and C_4 in terms of G_i, P_i. Count the number of input pins Q_i on the gates for each C_i. Can you find a function of i that computes any Q_i?

8. Show all the gates in a two-bit full adder design with carry look-ahead, and three gates' worth of delay.

9. The carry-look-ahead circuit developed in Chapter 10 has a total delay of 3. Estimate how much more hardware would be needed to get the delay down to 2. Draw out a complete answer for a two-bit adder.

PROPAGATE signals out of a four-bit CLA adder? G and P are needed as inputs to a chip such as the 74LS182. See Ercegovac & Lang, *Digital System and Hardware/Firmware Algorithms* (John Wiley & Sons, 1985), pp. 185–87.

11. The serial adder shown in Fig. 10.8 needs a START signal and an END signal to become a self-contained arithmetic peripheral. Look at the design in the text, and add the necessary components to make it self-contained. Assume that the two numbers to be added are already in parallel-output registers and that the answer register is a serial-in–parallel-out type. Consider a counter and USR.

12. Study the sequential adder in Example 4. Say what will be the contents of the register on each clock pulse if the register starts out at 0000 0000 and C_{16}, A_{16}, F_{16}, and E_{16} are brought in sequentially to be added together.

13. A cascade of half adders can make a combinational incrementer circuit, that is, a circuit that adds 1 to a number. Draw a design for a four-bit combinational *decrementer*. Assume that the number being decremented is unsigned—not 2's complement. Write out the truth table for a "half subtracter" to start your design. What happens when the number "underflows" at 0000? Is your decrementer different from a down-counter?

14. Use subtraction in the design of a combinational circuit that reports when two four-bit numbers are equal. Use the same idea to design greater-than and less-than outputs.

15. Suppose you don't have access to *all* the internal carries of a multibit adder. Think of another way to detect 2's complement overflow.

16. Consider a one-bit full **arithmetic** circuit, diagrammed in Fig. P10.3. The table listing the four operations of this circuit as functions of S_0, and S_1 is

S_1	S_0	Σ	
0	0	$A + C_{IN}$	If $C_{IN} = 0$, PASS; if $C_{IN} = 1$, INC.
0	1	$A + B + C_{IN}$	If $C_{IN} = 0$, ADD.
1	0	$A + \overline{B} + C_{IN}$	If $C_{IN} = 1$, SUBTRACT $A - B$.
1	1	$A - C_{IN}$	If $C_{IN} = 0$, PASS; if $C_{IN} = 1$, DEC.

(a) Show details of the data input for the MUX to satisfy the truth table above.
(b) Show how this circuit can be cascaded with others for multiple-bit arithmetic.

When drawn out as gates, this circuit starts to look like a 74181. It has more delay than a 1BFA.

17. In Fig. P10.4 is a four-bit adder chip configured to have five inputs and one output. What does it do? The inputs are I_1, I_2, I_3, I_4, I_5. The output comes from S_2, the second most significant bit of the adder output.

18. Look at the feedback circuit in Fig. P10.5, made with the carry-out of a 1BFA.

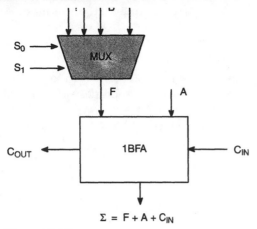

$$\Sigma = F + A + C_{IN}$$

Figure P10.3

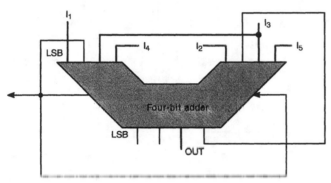

Figure P10.4

(a) What are the stable states of the circuit?
(b) If Σ is fed back to C_{IN} (instead of C_{OUT}), what are the stable states of the circuit?
(c) Can either version work as a set-reset flip-flop, where B and A would become S or R?

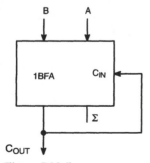

Figure P10.5

19. **(a)** Draw a combinational circuit that multiplies a four-bit number by 2.

(b) Draw a circuit that divides by 2.

(c) Repeat (a) and (b) for sequential circuit designs.

(d) Design a sequential multiply-by-8 circuit.

20. Here in Fig. P10.6 is a four-by-four multiplier array with four rows of three-per-row one-bit full adders. Because of the way the carries are propagated, it's faster than the array multiplier in Fig. 10.13. What is the total delay from presentation of multiplier and multiplicand (Q and R) until valid data appears on output P_7?

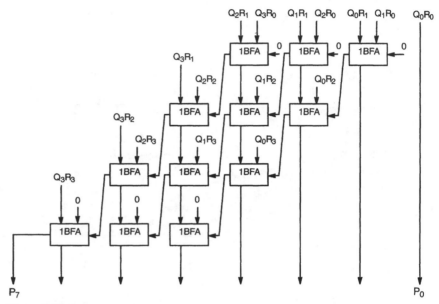

Figure P10.6 Faster array multiplier.

21. Consider Example 7, the two-by-two combinational unsigned multiplier.

(a) Realize P_2, the second MSB, as an SOP.

(b) Do any of the four outputs share the same implicants?

(c) What is the total gate and pin count for the whole design?

(d) Can use of XOR gates make the design any more efficient?

22. Study the combinatorial design of the four-bit by four-bit multiplier using five-bit adders.

(a) Redesign the multiplier with *four-bit* adders. How many do you need?

(b) What is the worst-case delay through the multiplier?

(c) What size of adder would be required to realize the four-by-four multiplier in one level?

23. **(a)** What's the truth table size for the 74285 multiplier chip described in the text? Look at its pinout in a TTL data book if you need help.

(b) Show how to use several of the 74181/85 chip pairs to multiply two six-bit numbers.

‡24. Section 10.8 shows you a multiplying digital-to-analog converter. In the test circuit of Fig. P10.7, what would happen on $y(t)$ if there were up-counters instead of down-counters, and 0F were loaded instead of FF?

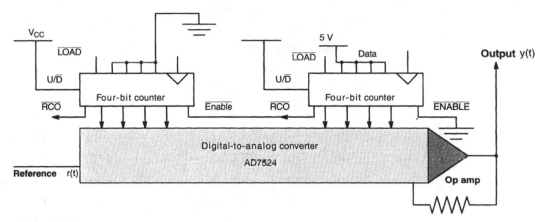

Figure P10.7

‡25. Write code in MATLAB, C, PASCAL, or BASIC to multiply two unsigned *binary* integers. Let the multiplier M and multiplicand T be eight bits each, and let the output be the 16-bit binary number that is the product $M \times T$. Don't multiply in decimal and then convert the decimal number to binary!

‡26. Use LogicWorks, Beige Bag 3.0, or other layout and simulation software to build the two phase four-bit add-and-shift multiplier shown in Section 10.9.1. Does the SIPO in the design need to be cleared before the multiplication starts?

27. Can add and shift operations of the two-phase multiplier design take advantage of chip delays and be executed on the same master clock edge, thereby speeding up the multiplication by a factor of two? Justify your answer.

‡28. In Fig. P10.8 is another way to do four-by-four add-and-shift multiplication using multiple clocks. Note that carry-out now goes down to the serial input of the serial-parallel shift register, which serves as ACC. Your problem: Design the control system for all the clock signals in this system and for S/L on the accumulator. One method of solution starts with the timing diagram shown in Fig. P10.9.

29. Follow the development of the *synchronous* add-and-shift multiplier (Example 12).

    (a) A universal shift register is used to capture the multiplier data $M_3, \ldots, M_0$. What should the control input external-hold, EX/$\overline{\text{HD}}$, be during the INIT state?

    (b) Look at the comparator in the counter circuit used to regulate the whole cycle of multiplication. What, if anything, will go wrong with the

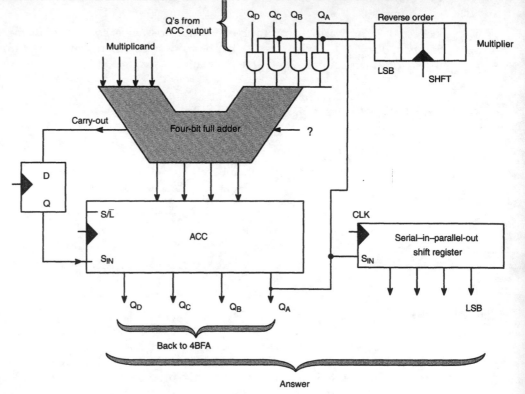

Figure P10.8   Another FSM multiplier.

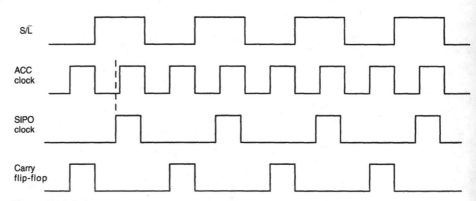

Figure P10.9   Timing for two-phase add-and-shift.

multiplier if the comparator output is asserted when its two inputs are *equal?*

30. For the fully synchronous four-bit multiplier, write out the register values for computation of $D \times B$ as a function of count number.

multiplication? How should the counter-comparator circuit be modified?

‡32. In Fig. P10.10 is another way to implement a four-bit sequential multiplier using a **systolic array**. X and Y are two unsigned four-bit numbers. We want to form the product $Z = XY$ using Fig. P10.10. See Lawson & Mirzai, *Wave Digital Filters* (Prentice-Hall, 1990), chapter 6.

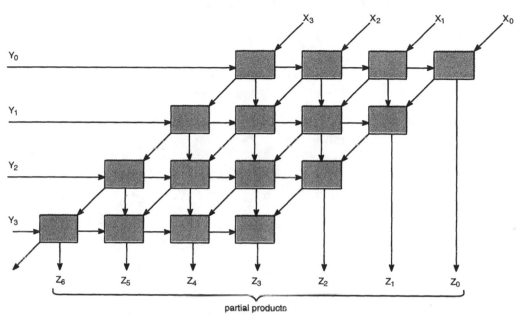

Figure P10.10 Systolic array.

There is a common clock, not shown, to all of the boxes.

(a) Each box takes three inputs and gives three outputs. What must the box do for Z to equal XY? Draw a circuit diagram of its internal workings.

(b) Assume that the clock for the boxes runs at 10 MHz. If the values of X and Y are not allowed to change when Z is being calculated, how many numbers can be multiplied in 1 second?

(c) How can the partial products be summed up for the final answer?

(d) Can the systolic array be a combinational circuit, with no clock?

33. What is a way to use a self-contained 4×4 multiplier to make a $K \times 4$ multiplier, where K is a multiple of 4?

‡34. **Deriving the Booth's algorithm rules**

(a) Verify that an $n + 1$-bit 2's complement number Q can be expressed in the form

$$Q = -2^n q_n + \sum_{j=0}^{n-1} 2^j q_j$$

where q_j is a bit in the n-bit number Q.

$$QR = 2^{2n}q_n r_n - 2^n q_n \sum_{j=0}^{n-1} 2^j r_j - 2^n r_n \sum_{k=0}^{n-1} 2^k q_k + \sum_{j=0}^{n-1}\sum_{k=0}^{n-1} 2^j 2^k q_j r_k$$

If the most significant bits q_n and r_n are 0, then the equation above reduces to the final summation, which is the unsigned product.

(c) Now show that you can write the multiplier Q as

$$Q = (q_{n-1} - q_n)2^n + \sum_{j=0}^{n-1} 2^j(q_{j-1} - q_j)$$

where $y_{-1} = 0$. When Q multiplies R bit by bit, it will operate on successive instances of r_j, accumulating shifted sums according to the following rules:

(i) If $q_{j-1} = q_j$, then a row of 0s is placed in the summation column.

(ii) If $q_{j-1} = 1$ and $q_j = 0$, then the multiplicand R is added to the accumulation.

(iii) If $q_{j-1} = 0$ and $q_j = 1$, then R is *subtracted* from the accumulation.

Thanks to Rabiner and Gold (1975, 517) for inspiration.

35. Consider each of the following pairs of hex numbers:

	M	T
(a)	-3	7
(b)	-7	8
(c)	$-E$	-4
(d)	$-A$	5

(i) Represent the numbers in eight-bit 2's complement notation.

(ii) Show the add-and-shift steps in multiplying $T \times M$ according to Booth's algorithm for an eight-bit signed product.

36. Study the Booth's algorithm chip, the 74LS384. What, if any, other hardware would be needed with the '384 in order to make a self-contained eight-by-eight signed-number multiplier?

37. (a) Design a circuit to find the *square* of a four-bit positive number.

(b) Think of a way to square a negative number already in 2C form.

38. List the last eight ROM entries in a table for looking up the answers to four-by-four signed multiplications. The inputs will be four bits of one number and four bits of the other.

39. (a) Suppose you have a ROM that looks up any four-bit by four-bit unsigned product. Think of a way to include more copies of such a ROM in a six-by-six multiplier design.

(b) What if the ROM is good for all four-by-four 2C products? Can you find a way to design copies of such a ROM into a six-by-six signed-product multiplier?

40. (a) Convert the following IEEE 754 single-precision floating-point numbers to decimal numbers expressed as scientific notation.

1	0	1	0	1	0	1	1	0	0	0	0	1	1	1	0	0	1	1	0	0	1	1	1	0	0	0	0	0	0	0	0

(ii)

0	0	1	1	1	1	1	1	1	1	1	1	1	0	0	0	0	0	0	0	0	0	0	0	0	0	0	0	0	0	0	0

(iii)

1	0	0	0	0	0	0	0	1	1	1	0	0	0	0	0	0	0	0	0	0	0	0	0	0	0	0	0	0	0	0	0

(b) Express the following numbers in IEEE 754 notation:
- **(i)** 22/7
- **(ii)** 10^{10}
- **(iii)** −4095

41. What are the decimal sum and the decimal product of the following two IEEE 754 floating-point numbers?

0	0	1	1	1	1	1	1	0	0	1	1	0	1	0	0	0	0	0	0	0	0	0	0	0	0	0	0	0	0	0	0

1	0	1	1	1	1	1	1	1	1	1	1	1	0	0	0	0	0	0	0	0	0	0	0	0	0	0	0	0	0	0	0

42. Write out a flowchart for *signed* floating-point multiplication.

43. Consider the subtract-and-count division design of Example 17. Design the synchronous FSM that will control SEL and CLEAR in the circuit.

References ··

ASPRAY, W. 1990. *John von Neumann and the origins of modern computing.* Cambridge, Mass.: MIT Press.

BOOTH, A. D. 1951. A signed binary multiplication technique. *Quarterly Journal of Mechanics and Applied Mathematics* 4: 236–240.

JUNGK, R. 1958. *Brighter than a thousand suns.* New York: Harcourt Brace.

KLINE, R. 1977. *Digital computer design.* Englewood Cliffs, NJ: Prentice Hall.

RABINER, L. R., AND B. GOLD. 1975. *Theory and application of digital signal processing.* Englewood Cliffs, N. J.: Prentice Hall.

STONE, H. S. 1990. *High performance computer architecture.* Reading, Mass.: Addison-Wesley.

WIDROW, B., AND S. D. STEARNS. 1985. *Adaptive signal processing.* Englewood Cliffs, N. J.: Prentice Hall.

Register Transfer Logic

OVERVIEW ....

The combinational and sequential arithmetic circuits from the previous chapter were hardwired to solve only addition problems or multiplication problems. The sequential arithmetic circuits—with accumulators—showed promise of evolving into general-purpose devices that could handle more than one kind of problem. In this chapter we pursue that evolution from single-register operations up to multiregister systems connected to data buses. We begin with a description of a clocked register, the main building block for this evolution, and finish with a multiregister *machine* that has the features of a computer with central processing unit and random access memory.

Chapter 11 ties together many of the topics introduced earlier in *Digital Design from Zero to One*. We begin with parallel-access registers, and then we add combinational circuits in a feedback loop around the registers, reprising a finite state machine approach we saw originally in Chapter 6. We first see what can be done with one register and a combinational circuit: logic, arithmetic, and shift operations are possible. Because of the need to load and store data, a second register becomes necessary. The design of a two-register circuit leads to a machine that can do sequential arithmetic. A **register transfer language** is introduced to describe the movement and transformation of data from one register to another. Finally, multiregister machines and parallel computing are brought forth and used in an example of multiplication.

For this final chapter of *Digital Design from Zero to One*, we want to develop a minimum-size, general-purpose, multiregister synchronous *architecture* that can add, multiply, or divide two numbers, depending on the sequence of instructions given the control inputs of the circuit. You will see that each instruction (which takes up one clock cycle) can be subdivided into *source, function,* and *destination* fields. By the end of Chapter 11 we will have moved from specific, hardware solutions of binary arithmetic problems to general, software solutions.

11.1 A PIPO REGISTER

By *register* we mean a set of D flip-flops connected to the same clock: normally their inputs and outputs are separately accessible (a parallel-in–parallel-out PIPO device). Figure 11.1 shows a four-bit register. In Fig. 11.2 are input and output labels for

575

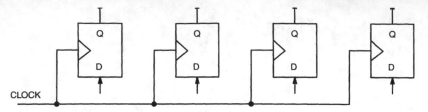

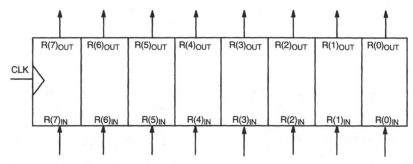

Figure 11.1 A four-bit PIPO register.

Figure 11.2 Eight-bit register R.

an eight-bit register, named R. The clock input on the left is common to all eight flip-flops. $R(i)_{IN}$ is data waiting to be loaded. $R(i)$ without an IN/OUT subscript refers to the *contents* of the ith flip-flop of register R and is the same as $R(i)_{OUT}$. For example, if register R holds a signed number, then $R(0)$, the right-most bit, is the LSB and $R(7)$ is the sign bit. The contents of R is also denoted [R], and since the contents are normally available at output, [R] is a name for all the outputs considered together. If register R is part of a multiregister system, R will have a three-state enable control; in some circumstances then a disabled register's pins may have a different value from [R].

The contents of register R can change only at an active clock *edge*, and then each $R(i)_{OUT}$ becomes the $R(i)_{IN}$ value. R_{IN} is likely to be the output of some other register. Here we generalize from concern about single flip-flops in synchronous machine design to concern about whole registers. We assume in this chapter that setup and hold times for the flip-flops are always met. A register can be shown by a more compact symbol: see Fig. 11.3. The slash through the data line and the letter N next to it indicate that N bits of data come and go in parallel.

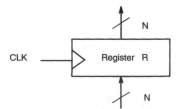

Figure 11.3 Compact icon for N-bit register named R.

Next we show you what operations can be done with one register and a combinational circuit in feedback. You saw an architecture like Fig. 11.4 at the end of Chapter 7, when a register with an incrementer was used to make a microprogrammed counter. Let one N-bit register R send its outputs back to its inputs through a combinational circuit. See Fig. 11.4. The slashed lines are the N-bit data path. This configuration should remind you of the Moore form of a clocked sequencer, from Chapter 6. The register must be edge triggered to prevent signals from racing around the feedback loop.

Single-register operations can be grouped into three categories, as listed below.

Logical operations:
   CLEAR/SET
   COMPLEMENT
   NO-OP

Arithmetic operations:
   INCREMENT/DECREMENT
   Two's COMPLEMENT

Shift operations:
   LEFT/RIGHT
   CIRCULAR/STRAIGHT
   BIT-BY-BIT/ARITHMETIC

Logical operations treat bits individually. The bits $R(i)$ are each set to 1, reset to 0, complemented, or not changed at all—the no-op operation.

Arithmetic operations for a single register treat the contents of register R as a number and either add 1 (increment), subtract 1 (decrement), or complement and add 1 (2's complement) to the current value of R. Because the register has a finite width, the possibility exists that an increment operation on an unsigned number will result in carry-out or that an increment operation on a signed number will result in overflow. The combinational circuit needs status pins for these possibilities. Likewise, repeated decrements will lead eventually to *borrow-in*.

Shift operations move bits either left or right, usually one bit at a time. There are a number of options concerning what to do with $R(N-1)$ and $R(0)$, the end bits of R: a special shifter circuit will be designed later in this chapter that will even include a no-shift option. A *signed arithmetic shift* takes account of the MSB as the sign bit and does not involve it in the shifting.

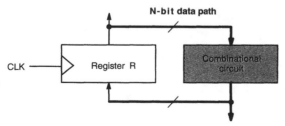

Figure 11.4 Single-register architecture.

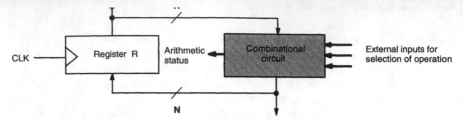

Figure 11.5 I/O pins added to combinational circuit.

We can add some I/O lines to the combinational circuit, including pins for selecting operations, and put the combinational circuit in the form of a cloud, indicating that more design work is needed. See Fig. 11.5.

11.2.1 Register Transfer Language

We can describe how the contents of a register change by using a notation called **register transfer language (RTL).** More detail will be given about RTL later, when we use it to describe multiregister machines and algorithms for multiplication. RTL was the forerunner of **VHDL** (Very High-level Description Language), a more modern and elaborate system for expressing algorithms in digital hardware. The following list presents basic RTL forms for single eight-bit register operations. Note: To the left of the arrow in an RTL statement a *location* is specified; to the right of the arrow a *value* to be loaded in the location is specified. As you can see, in some cases (shift instructions) an RTL statement can focus on single flip-flops in a register. The word *plus* is used for addition with the whole register, while the symbol + is used for incrementing an index.

Logic operations:
  CLEAR/SET $R \leftarrow 0 \quad R \leftarrow 1$
  COMPLEMENT $R \leftarrow \overline{R}$
  NO-OP $R \leftarrow R$

Arithmetic operations:
  INCREMENT/DECREMENT $R \leftarrow R \text{ plus } 1 \quad R \leftarrow R \text{ minus } 1$
  TWO'S COMPLEMENT $R \leftarrow \overline{R} \text{ plus } 1$

Shift operations:
  LEFT/RIGHT $R(i) \leftarrow R(i-1)/R(i) \leftarrow R(i+1) \quad i = 1 \ldots N-2$
  CIRCULAR/STRAIGHT $R(0) \leftarrow R(N-1)$ circular left shift
                            $R(0) \leftarrow S_{\text{IN}}$ straight left shift
  BIT-BY-BIT/ARITHMETIC $R(N-1) \leftarrow R(0)$ right shift
                            $R(N-1) \leftarrow R(N-1)$ arithmetic shift

The sign bit $R(N)$ is left alone during an arithmetic shift.

11.2.2 Logic and Arithmetic Subcircuits

The combinational design box from Fig. 11.5 must be capable of any of the one-register operations in the RTL list. If separate subcircuits take care of the three

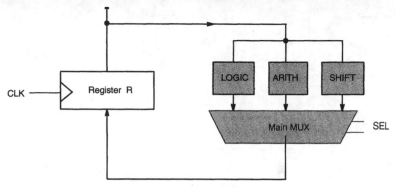

Figure 11.6 Multiplexer for combinational logic.

categories of operation, then a multiplexer can be used to *select* one of the operations. See Fig. 11.6. As we fill in the subcircuits, more multiplexers will be used, so we refer to the multiplexer in Fig. 11.6 as the main MUX. So far we assume that register R is already loaded with data of interest (we could add a fourth input to the MUX for external data).

EXAMPLE 1

We present here a combinational logic design for a single-register transfer system. Consider each of the three subcircuits in turn.

Logic   Since logic operations occur on each bit in isolation, we can draw out one bit's worth of the logic subcircuit and expect that N such subcircuits in parallel will complete the job. We assume that all the parallel one bit logic circuits will be connected to the same SELECT input; this assumption rules out the possibility of, say, setting one bit while clearing its neighbor; all bits will be similarly affected on any one clock cycle. (*Cycle* means one clock period, during which one machine operation takes place.) Figure 11.7 presents a multiplexer for one bit of the logic subcircuit. Two more control bits are now required to specify and select a logic operation.

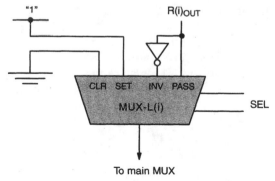

Figure 11.7   Multiplexer for logic subcircuit.

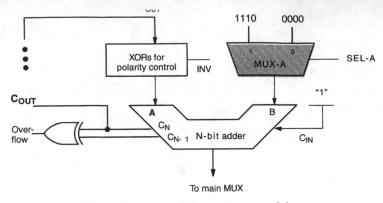

Figure 11.8 Arithmetic subcircuit for increment and decrement.

Arithmetic Increment and decrement require interaction between the bits of R_{OUT}. An N-bit ripple adder made with half-adder subunits and given a carry-in of 1 would be a basic nonsynchronous incrementer, but we need decrementing too. To proceed, assume that the number in register R is in 2C code, with sign bit in $R(N-1)$. (Decrementing in 2's complement means adding minus one: in four-bit 2's complement, -1 is $1110+1 = 1111$). The design of Fig. 11.8, with an N-bit full adder, will provide four arithmetic functions. The multiplexer needed in the arithmetic subcircuit is called MUX-A. Four-bit numbers are shown in Fig. 11.8. C_{IN} is always HI. When INV is HI, $\overline{R}$ is sent to the left side of the adder. When SEL-A is HI, 1110 is chosen as the B input. The arithmetic subcircuit generates status of carry-out and overflow.

In the list below are the functions from the arithmetic circuit for $C_{IN} = 1$. With $C_{IN} = 1$, the three required arithmetic functions result, plus a fourth oddball.

INV	SEL-A	Function
0	0	Increment
0	1	Decrement
1	0	Two's complement of R
1	1	Decrement complement of R(?)

If C_{IN} is set to zero, then when INV, SEL-A $= 0,0$, a pass operation results, and when INV, SEL-A $= 1,0$, an invert operation results. When SEL-A is 1 and C_{IN} is 0, the resulting operation is a dud.

That we've thrown an N-bit full adder into the one-register design is an extravagance. One input to the adder sees only 1110 or all 0s. Now two more control signals—INV and SEL-A—are required to specify register operations. Exercise 6 lets you explore the consequences of an N-bit *half adder* in the one-register system.

11.2.3 Shifter Design

Now we consider the various shift operations, bit by bit. To right-shift the bits in register R, the hardwired scheme in Fig. 11.9 can be used, which turns our PIPO into

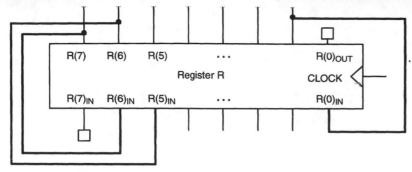

Figure 11.9 Hardware right-shift.

a SIPO. The figure shows an eight-bit register set up to right-shift. $R(7)_{OUT}$ projects to $R(6)_{IN}$, leaving $R(7)_{IN}$ unconnected. Notice also that output $R(0)_{OUT}$ is unconnected, since $R(1)_{OUT}$ projects to the right-most input $R(0)_{IN}$. If two registers were chained together, an unconnected $R_1(0)_{OUT}$ would project rightward to a waiting $R_2(7)_{IN}$.

On each clock pulse the bits move one more flip-flop to the right. If a left-shifter were desired, then $R(0)_{OUT}$ would project to $R(1)_{IN}$, $R(1)_{OUT}$ would project to $R(2)_{IN}$, and so on. A no-shift would look like the following:

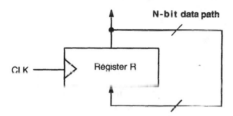

We can consolidate all three cases into one combinational shifter. Each input $R(i)_{IN}$ will be fronted by a $3 \rightarrow 1$ MUX that selects from $R(i+1)_{OUT}$, $R(i)_{OUT}$, and $R(i-1)_{OUT}$. In Fig. 11.10 is the fragment of the shifter for input $R(3)_{IN}$. The $R(3)$ region of R is shaded on the left of Fig. 11.10. For bits $R(0)$ and $R(7)$, the least and most significant

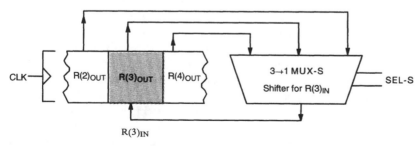

Figure 11.10 Combinatorial shifter for $R(3)$.

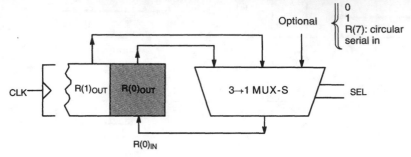

Figure 11.11 Terminal bit selection for shifter.

bits of R, the typical arrangement is not appropriate. For Shift left, $R(0)$ could take in 0, 1, or data from another register's $R(N)_{OUT}$ on the right, or it could become involved in a circular shift, in which $R(7)$ would be moved to $R(0)$. The modification in Fig. 11.11 shows what the MUX for $R(0)_{IN}$ should look like. Also included is a serial-in option so that registers can have their shifting cascaded together. For the other end bit, $R(7)$, we have in addition to the four $R(0)$-type options another possibility: leave $R(7)$ alone during the shift *when $R(7)$ is considered the sign bit* of a 2's complement number.

Shift operations can be considered multiplication by 2 (left) or division by 2 (right). For a signed arithmetic shift the sign bit $R(7)$ should not be changed.

11.2.4 IEEE Symbol for a 74LS323 Register

While we normally want the registers in our register-logic machines to be PIPO, it is possible to find IC shift registers with more functions built in. In Chapter 10 you saw such registers (74194) used in design of the synchronous add-and-shift multiplier. Here we describe another IC, called an *eight-bit universal shift register (USR)* in TTL data books.

EXAMPLE 2

The 74LS323 eight-bit storage and shift register is a 20-pin IC with IEEE-91-1984 symbol shown in Fig. 11.12. The '323 is an example of a stand-alone IC with the one-register *shift* functions we've been looking for. Pins 8 and 17 support inversions of the terminal bits; the other inputs and outputs share common pins, shown on the left of Fig. 11.12. The top part of the symbol is the control block. The triangles on the top three control inputs, $\overline{CLR}$, $\overline{G1}$, and $\overline{G2}$, are inverters (active-low inputs). The first four control signals (0–3) say what function is selected; you can infer this information from the S_0, S_1 part of the M_3^0 symbol. Control signal 4 is the clock, called C4 at the bottom of the control block. Control signal 5 is EN5, which is asserted when $\overline{G1}$ AND $\overline{G2}$ is asserted. At the top of the control block, 4R means that RESET depends on control signal 4, the clock, and is therefore a synchronous reset. The 5 near the

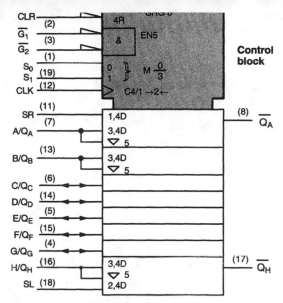

Figure 11.12   74LS323 universal shift register, eight-bit path.

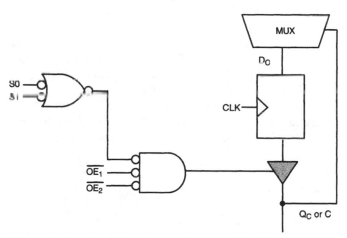

Figure 11.13   Detail of output enable control for '323 chip.

three-state ∇ indicators on the schematic mean that when control signal 5, ENABLE, is asserted, the outputs are enabled (not in Hi-Z mode). The chip pin numbers are shown in parentheses. The notation 3, 4D on each of the data pins indicates that data will be loaded when control condition 3 ($S_1S_0 = 11$) AND condition 4 (CLK) are asserted. The 1, 4D on Q_A and 2, 4D on Q_H say that when control is $S_1, S_0 = L, H$, data is shifted right into A, and when control is $S_1, S_0 = H, L$, data is shifted left into position H.

From this exercise in reverse engineering, it's possible to construct the following table of operations for the 74LS323, controlled by $\overline{\text{CLR}}$, S_1, and S_0 (output C is given as an example):

	$\overline{\text{CLR}}$	S_1	S_0	Output Q_C
RESET	X	X	LO	O
HOLD	HI	LO	LO	Q_C
Shift R	LO	HI	Q_B	Q_B
Shift L	HI	LO	Q_D	Q_D
LOAD	HI	HI	HI	c

For the LOAD operation, lowercase c indicates that output Q_C is disabled and the pin then functions as an input. The function table assumes that neither pin $\overline{\text{G1}}$ nor pin $\overline{\text{G2}}$ is HI: if either is HI, the eight I/O pins can become disabled (Hi-Z). The output control subcircuit for the C flip-flop in the '323 is shown in Fig. 11.13. The I/O pin can become an input when the three-state output is disabled.

11.2.5 The Complete One-Register Machine

We can now bring back our block diagram of the one-register system, with added details. The register R could be a universal shift register, but we've chosen to keep the shift functions in the combinational path. The control inputs in Fig. 11.14 are all devoted to selecting a **function** for the combinational circuit. A fourth input has been added to the main MUX: external data for a LOAD operation. Again, we assume that the inputs do not change at times that would trouble register R for setup or hold limits. As you know from Chapter 2, the combinational design in Fig. 11.14 could

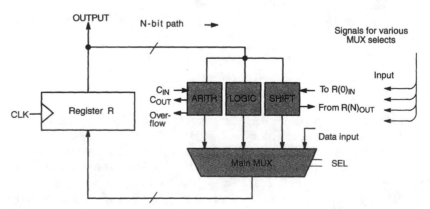

Figure 11.14 One-register machine.

be collapsed into a two-gate-delay SOP circuit. As shown, the circuit illustrates the subfunctions of the register-transfer operations at the cost of extra delay. Exercise 10 asks you to consider replacing the whole combinational circuit with a ROM.

11.3 TWO-REGISTER SYSTEM

A one-register machine is good for incrementing and decrementing, and it can be adapted for microprogram sequencing (see the end of Chapter 7), but it takes some imagination to think of other practical uses. A single register can't sort or add two numbers, for example. The one-register limitation is easy to fix: add a second register driven by the same clock. Try a multiplexer to combine the two register outputs. Then replace the multiplexer with a two-input arithmetic unit in the combinational path, and the two-register machine will be able to add numbers.

To begin with, call the two registers R1 and R2 and try an architecture in which $R1_{IN}$ is controlled by a $2 \rightarrow 1$ MUX having inputs R1 and R2, and $R2_{IN}$ receives R1, as shown in Fig. 11.15. We indicate the contents of a register, available at the output, as [R1] or [R2]. This minimal arrangement focuses on R1 and allows the contents of R1($= $ [R1]) to be loaded into either R1 or R2 on the next clock pulse and allows [R2] to be held if register R2 is disabled.

11.3.1 Arithmetic Logic Unit

We can give more capability to the minimal two-register system by replacing the MUX with a general-purpose **arithmetic-logic combinational circuit** (arithmetic-logic unit, or ALU). Selecting [R1] alone or [R2] alone as the input to register R1 can be a subset of the ALU instructions. See the architecture in Fig. 11.16. We ignore shifting operations for the moment.

Now that two inputs can be combined in various ways, we can have a richer *instruction set* than in the one-register system. Consider arithmetic first: we certainly want R1 *plus* R2. Adding two numbers together may generate a carry-out, so our ALU needs a C_{OUT} status pin. Further, it may be necessary to bring a carry-in, so the ALU needs a C_{IN} input pin, too. (C_{IN} and C_{OUT} are shown as arrows in Fig. 11.16.)

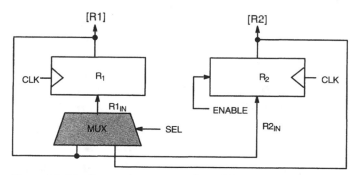

Figure 11.15 Two-register, two-path machine with MUX.

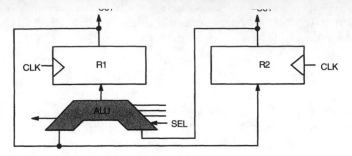

Figure 11.16 Two-register machine with ALU.

What about $R1 \times R2$? The problem with multiplication in two registers is that the product may be $2N$ bits wide. For now we want to maintain an N-bit data path around our registers, so direct combinational multiplication is ruled out. Is *addition* all we need for arithmetic? In principle, yes. If the ALU can complement and increment input, then the two-register system can subtract integers by 2's complement.

Before going further, let's examine two commercial ALU IC chips to see what's commonly available for basic arithmetic and logic functions on four-bit paths.

EXAMPLE 3

The 74LS382 arithmetic-logic unit is a 20-pin chip with two four-bit inputs (A and B), four-bit output (F), and status pins for carry-out and overflow ($2C$); see Fig. 11.17. The 74LS382 has three function-select pins that account for the following operation table:

Inputs			
S_2	S_1	S_0	Operation
0	0	0	CLEAR all four outputs to 0
0	0	1	B minus A
0	1	0	A minus B
0	1	1	A plus B
1	0	0	$A \oplus B$
1	0	1	$A + B$
1	1	0	$A \cdot B$
1	1	1	SET all four outputs to 1

Here $A + B$ means A OR B bit by bit ($A_i + B_i$, $i = 0, 1, 2, 3$), and the other two logic functions are also performed bit by bit. There is no direct complement operation in the '382 instruction set. The minus operations in the '382 are *1's complement*:

$$A \text{ minus } B = A \text{ plus } \bar{B} \text{ plus } C_{IN}$$

Thus 0000 minus 0000 = 1111 by 1's complement subtraction. To perform 2's complement subtraction with the '382, set $C_{IN} = 1$; then, for example, 0000 minus 0000

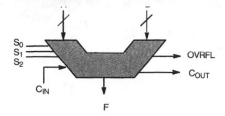

Figure 11.17 Block diagram of 74LS382.

plus $1 = 0000$. In the $A = 0$, $B = 0$ case $C_{OUT} = 1$, but presumably the user will ignore carry-out in 2C addition. The overflow output of the '382 is logically equal to $C_3 \oplus C_4$, where C_3 is an internal carry and $C_4 = C_{OUT}$. The operation 0000 minus 0000 plus $1 = 0000$ generates no overflow, but the operation $-8 - 8 = 1000$ minus 1000 plus $1 = 0000$ will have $C_{OUT} = 1$ and OVFL $= 1$ because -16 is too large for four-bit 2C notation.

The '382 uses internal carry look-ahead but does not "propagate" and "generate" CLA as separate outputs; the '382 can be used in N-bit by four-bit additions by ripple-carry from one chip's C_{OUT} to the next chip's C_{IN}. Only the first C_{IN} in the cascade need be controlled for 2C arithmetic.

An older chip, the 24-pin 74181 ALU, has four function-select pins and a mode-select (logic or arithmetic), so it's capable of 32 different operations. Most of the 32 operations are of dubious value, but to its credit the '181 (in its logic mode) can output A alone, B alone, $\overline{A}$, $\overline{B}$, and $\overline{A \oplus B}$; however, it has no 2C overflow output. To access the arithmetic mode of the '181, the MODE pin is asserted LO, enabling all of the internal carries; otherwise, when MODE is HI, only bit-for-bit logic is performed. A 74181 data sheet in a TTL Data Book will give logic and arithmetic results for active-low and active-high conventions; here we will stick with active-high. In active-high carry-in is $\overline{C_{IN}}$. With $\overline{C_{IN}}$ HI (no carry-in) the '181 performs 1's complement subtraction. Thus 0001 minus $0001 = 0001$ plus $1110 = 1111 = -1 = A$ minus B minus 1 in 2C notation. The '181 finds A minus B when carry-in is asserted.

When A minus B minus 1 is computed, an internal AND looking at all the F outputs will go HI; this AND is pinned out to an $A = B$ pin, which is therefore valid when the subtract-without-carry mode is selected. The $A = B$ pin is open-collector for wired-AND connection to other '181s, so N-bit by four-bit pattern equality can be tested.

The '181 has CLA outputs GENERATE and PROPAGATE (as $\overline{G}$ and $\overline{P}$); up to four '181s can be connected to the CLA chip 74182 to speed up 16-bit arithmetic.

An ALU can be constructed with the help of an N-input $2 \rightarrow 1$ multiplexer; see Fig. 11.18. Slashed lines represent the N-bit data pathway. In Chapter 10 you saw designs for a multiple-bit *combinational* adder that will do the job of the arithmetic block in Fig. 11.18. The logic unit can be broken down into another MUX, *one bit* of which is shown in Fig. 11.19. Four two-input logic gates are included in addition to the supply of functions from the one-register system. Figure 11.18 is a conceptual

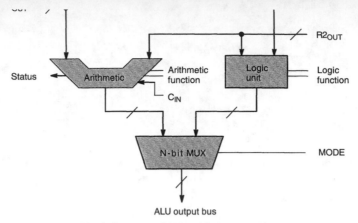

Figure 11.18   Block diagram of ALU with $2 \rightarrow 1$ MUXs.

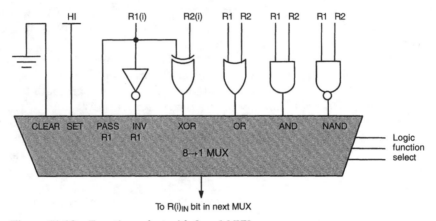

Figure 11.19   Function-select with $8 \rightarrow 1$ MUX.

design of an ALU. Look in a TTL data book at the logic diagrams for the 74181 and 74LS382 to see an efficient two-level SOP logic implemented; in commercial chips the truth tables for arithmetic and logic have been combined and the design minimized for gate count and propagation delay.

11.3.2   ALU Output Directed to a Combinational Shifter Circuit

Where should the shifter go? The one place in the two-register machine where a single data path emerges is the ALU output: that's the logical site for a shifter. The combinational shifter designed for the one-register machine will work here, too. See Fig. 11.20. In case no shifting is needed, remember that one of the "functions" of the shifter circuit is NO-OP (no-shift).

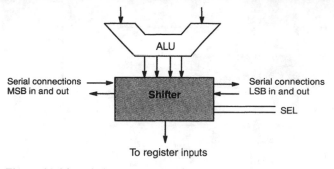

Figure 11.20 Shifter on output of ALU.

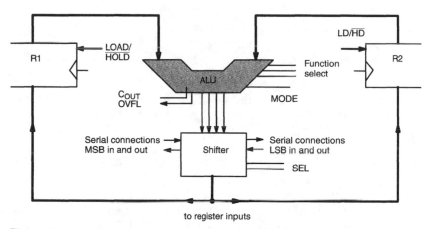

Figure 11.21 Symmetric architecture for two-register machine.

Figure 11.21 shows a more symmetric arrangement for a two-register machine; both R_1 and R_2 receive the shifter output. Now each register needs a control line, in addition to a clock input. The control input will determine whether the register loads new data or holds its current contents on each clock tick (you have seen load and hold as capabilities of a universal shift register). There's nothing to stop both registers from being loaded simultaneously with the shifter output, if desired.

Let's include a means to load either register with external data. In Fig. 11.22 a $3 \rightarrow 2$ MUX with external data now controls the two inputs to the ALU. By this architecture, external data must pass through (and be delayed by) the MUX, the ALU, and the shifter before landing in one or the other of the two registers.

In order to load the registers, operate on the ALU inputs, and shift the ALU output, the user must *program* the various control inputs. There are three categories of control:

1. *Source* of the ALU inputs (select on the $3 \rightarrow 2$ MUX)
2. *Function* of ALU and shifter
3. *Destination* (the LOAD/$\overline{\text{HOLD}}$ pins on R_1 and R_2)

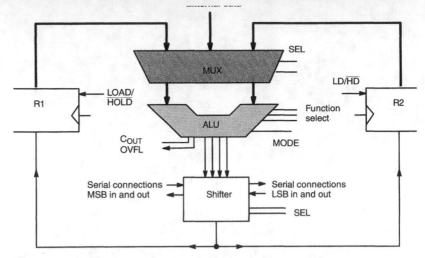

Figure 11.22 Source for external data in two-register machine.

Call the source, function, and destination *SFD*. To minimize metastability, changes on SFD inputs should not occur near the clock edges for the registers.

11.3.3 A Counter plus ROM to Control Source, Function, and Destination

At the end of Chapter 7 you learned two ways to generate arbitrary sequences: counter plus ROM and microprogramming. The most straightforward control for our two-register machine will be by counter plus ROM: Let the contents of ROM be the SFD signals. Then Fig. 11.23 shows how the counter and the registers can be timed by the same clock and the SFD controls can be supplied by ROM output. To gain

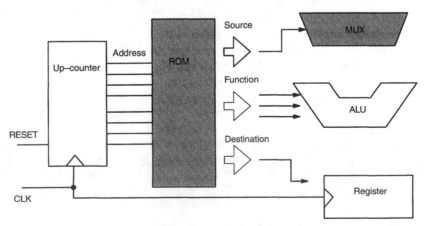

Figure 11.23 Source, function, and destination from ROM.

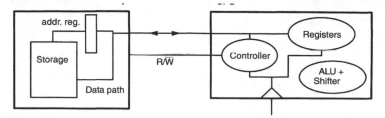

Figure 11.24 A computer is a CPU plus memory.

better separation between register input change and clock edge, the counter and the register could be on rising and falling edges of the clock, respectively.

So far we have not built in any means to change the counter output other than increment or reset. Control of program flow was discussed in terms of microprogramming at the end of Chapter 7, and in the next example we will use microprogramming to solve a division remainder problem.

Our two-register machine has enough functionality now to be called a **central processing unit (CPU)**. A CPU is a system of synchronously clocked registers and combinational logic with a synchronously clocked controller that delivers instructions for the source and destination of data, and for control of the function of the combinational logic that operates on the data. The SFD signals are called **microinstructions**, and a series of microinstructions given a binary number label for ROM address is called a **machine language instruction**. When the machine language instruction is coded for the programmer as an alphanumeric mnemonic, it's an **assembly language instruction**. All that a CPU lacks to be a full fledged computer is a memory system large enough to hold programs and store data. Therefore a **computer** is a CPU attached to a memory system, such as the kind of system we saw in Chapter 8. The memory must be supplied with address and read/write information from the CPU; in turn it gives data to the registers in the CPU ($DATA_{EXT}$ in our diagrams) and instructions (user program) to the controller. See Fig. 11.24.

Our two-register machine can certainly add two numbers together and combine two bit patterns logically (OR, AND, and so on). Let's see it try a more ambitious task.

11.3.4 A Two-Register System Used to Find U_1 mod U_2

EXAMPLE 4

Suppose two unsigned integers, U_1 and U_2, are available on $DATA_{EXT}$, on two successive clock pulses after a reset to the counter in our machine. We want to know what remains after division of U_1 by U_2 (modulo operation).

Answer To solve the modulo problem, use microprogramming: a ROM address control method that allows for conditional branching. A microprogram controller

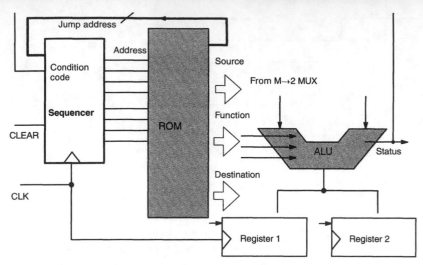

Figure 11.25 Sequencer to control microcode ROM.

suitable for a two-register CPU is shown in Fig. 11.25. The microcontroller is on the left in the figure. Status from the ALU can affect whether the sequencer jumps to an address contained in the ROM code. The status projects to condition code input on the sequencer. With this change from counter to sequencer for addressing ROM, we can have a streamlined set of microinstructions to solve the modulo problem.

Here is RTL code, which starts with a CLEAR to the sequencer, after which the machine loads unsigned integers U_1 and U_2 to registers R_1 and R_2. The second column is the address of the ROM. The "if" statement at A5 is not a standard RTL statement.

Operation	Address	RTL	Comment
CLEAR			
LOAD	A0:	R1 ← U1	;Load U1.
LOAD	A1:	R2 ← U2	;Load U2.
2C	A2:	R2 ← $\overline{R2}$ plus (C_{IN} = 1)	;Make R2 a 2C number.
ADD	A4:	R2 ← R2 plus R1	;Subtract U2 from U1.
Conditional jump	A5:	(if MSB = = 0) goto A4	;Jump back to subtract again.
2C	A6:	R2 ← $\overline{R2}$ plus (C_{IN} = 1)	;Change R2 back to an unsigned number.
ADD	A7:	R2 ← R2 plus R1	;Subtract U2 from U1.
HOLD			Stay at A7 with answer in R2 until another CLEAR signal.

The microinstructions repeatedly subtract U2 from U1, storing the result in R2, until the sign bit changes; if the sign bit has changed, then one subtraction too many has

11.4 MULTIREGISTER CPU

A two-register machine offers much more capability than a one-register machine, but it is still limited in what it can do. A two-register machine cannot, for example, multiply two numbers together. It can't even sort two numbers by size! Let's call a multiregister machine a CPU with more than two registers. A multiregister machine can in principle do anything we want if it has enough registers.[1]

We can expand the basic two-register machine architecture from above; our goal is to add more registers in a systematic way. Figure 11.26 shows a bank of synchronously clocked registers plus combinational MUX, ALU, and shifter. Assume that all load and select control points (bold lines) have a connection with a microcode ROM not shown. The MUX is called $N + 4 \rightarrow 2$ because of registers 0 to N, a $DATA_{EXT}$ input, and all-0 and all-1 inputs, adding up to 4 more than N. In a microprogrammed CPU, the ALU status would be a condition code input to a sequencer that would address the microcode ROM. One of the control fields from the ROM would go to SELECT

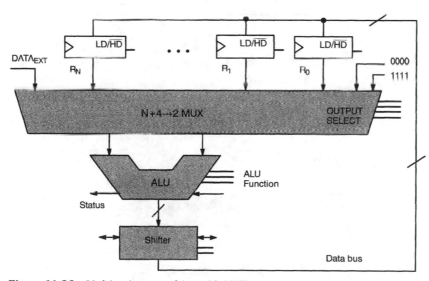

Figure 11.26 Multiregister machine with MUX.

[1] A register transfer machine with a finite number of registers is an example of a *Turing machine,* a device capable of carrying out any finite computation. If the computation mechanism is connected to an "infinite tape" of memory, a *universal Turing machine* is created, capable of *any* computation. There are no guarantees on how long the computation may take! For a discussion of Turing machines, see Penrose (1989, chap. 2).

control. Call the architecture in Fig. 11.26 a **horizontal register machine.**

11.4.1 Addressable Bank of Registers in a CPU

Accessing the LOAD pins on many registers can create a burden for the microcode in ROM if a separate line is needed for each register load. Another burden is created for the $K \to 2$ MUX if so many registers need separate access and so many combinations of K things taken two at a time need to be accounted for in the MUX. Here's a solution: if the registers are linked together with a common three-state output, they can be addressed by microcode using fewer bits. You've seen register outputs tied together in Chapter 8, in the form of static RAM cells. The common memory output can be one input to the ALU. See the new architecture in Fig. 11.27. Now all but one of the CPU registers are in the SRAM bank (when a static RAM is in the CPU of a computer, it is often called **cache memory**). The cache memory of 2^M words needs only M address lines from microcode. Only one cache register at a time can be written to, and only one at a time can become an ALU input, compared to the horizontal register system. In compensation, another register separate from the cache is created. This register is given the special designation of **accumulator (ACC)** and has private access to one of the ALU inputs through a small $3 \to 1$ MUX. The output of the (unclocked) cache

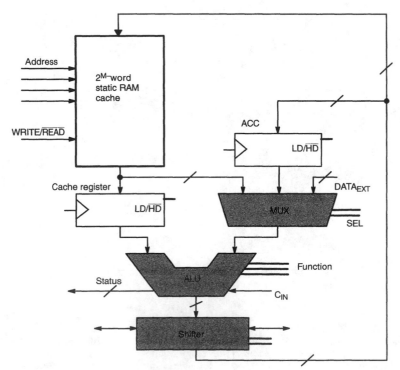

Figure 11.27 Memory bank supplying registers.

goes to its own ALU input register (cache register) and can be selected by the 3 → 1 MUX. The other input to the 3 → 1 MUX is external data, for loading registers. Notice that a clock cycle is needed to transfer a cache word to the cache *register*. [2]

The cache-based multiregister CPU doesn't have the regular structure of the horizontal register architecture, but it can accommodate more registers with less hardware overhead. The cache-based CPU, with its accumulator register, is close in spirit and form to the digital computer first proposed by John von Neumann and colleagues after the end of World War II. In fact each of the machines we are designing here in Chapter 11 comes under the category of von Neumann machine because each requires all operations to funnel through one ALU and shifter path. See Burks, Goldstein, and von Neumann (1963, 34–79).

11.4.2   Multiplication in a Multiregister Machine

Think back to the synchronous add-and-shift multiplier design in Chapter 10. We needed five clocked elements: one for counting, one for accumulating, and three for shifting (one of the "shift registers" was a flip-flop, which held carry-out from the adder). We now want a multiregister machine to be able to multiply. Since we don't need more than four or five registers, let's use the horizontal register architecture for our design and RTL code.

EXAMPLE 5

Show how a synchronous four-bit multiregister machine can be used for multiplication. The controller for the multiplier will be able to select the multiplier (M_1) and multiplicand (M_2) onto the $DATA_{EXT}$ bus; both M_1 and M_2 must be loaded into registers. For this problem consider four-bit by four-bit unsigned multiplication. Since the product may have up to eight bits of answer, and since we are restricting ourselves to four-bit data path and registers, let us find *the four most significant bits of the product* and place the answer on the output of the ALU. (Exercise 25 can lead you through refinements that capture the four LSBs in an ancillary register.)

We want our machine to have the minimum number of registers, and we want the ALU and the shifter to have the minimum number of operations required. The circuit in Fig. 11.28 shows five registers whose inputs are connected to a common SHIFTER-OUT bus. On a clock edge each register can be loaded or can have its contents held. The $N \to 2$ MUX, the ALU, and the shifter are all combinational circuits. Shown in color are the select and load pins that must be controlled on each clock edge. There are five register load pins, ALU function-select and C_{IN}, shifter function-select, and $N \to 2$ MUX-select.

Let's begin by identifying the logic and arithmetic functions we may need to effect unsigned multiplication. Suppose four-bit inputs to the ALU are A and B; A and B

---

[2]The cache memory architecture described here has much in common with the now-obsolete AMD 2901 bit slice microprocessor, first marketed in the late 1970s. The 2901 had a 16-word memory with a dual-port output and two sets of address lines, so two locations in the cache could be placed simultaneously in data registers. The 2901 was the predecessor of AMD's 29000 series of microprogrammed controllers.

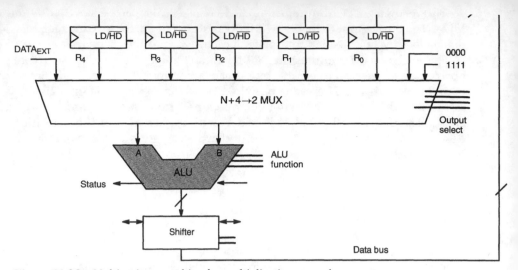

Figure 11.28 Multiregister machine for multiplication example.

will be the *outputs* of the $N \rightarrow 2$ MUX (four bits at each of the two outputs). We need only A plus B plus C_{IN} as an arithmetic function; it may generate a C_{OUT}. For logic functions we may want a reset of all bits to zero, we may want to pass one or the other of the inputs through unchanged, we may want to complement either input, we may want $A \cdot B$, and we *will* want a special logic function in which all bits of one input are ANDed one at a time with the LSB of the other input. Call such a function one-bit gating: $A \cdot B(0)$, where $B(0)$ is the LSB of input B.

The minimal list of ALU functions is as follows:

Logic:
  0
  Pass A
  Pass B
  $\overline{A}$
  $\overline{B}$
  $A \cdot B$
  $A \cdot B(0)$

Arithmetic:
  A plus B plus C_{IN}

Next decide what shifter functions may be needed for unsigned multiplication:

Shifter functions:
  No shift
  Shift right $SH(3) = C_{OUT}$
  Circular shift right $SH(3) = SH(0)$
  Shift left $SH(0) = SL_{IN}$
  Circular shift left $SH(0) = SH(3)$

where $SH(n)$ is the nth bit of the shifter output and SL_{IN} is a left-side input bit. (Shift left will come in handy for moving around the four least significant bits of the eight-bit answer.)

Now we're ready to write out a register transfer language version of an algorithm to compute the four most significant bits of four-by-four unsigned multiplication. Note that the second column labels the time (TN:) of the operation. Consider M1 the multiplier.

CLEAR	T0:	R3 ← 0000	;Clear the accumulator.
LOAD	T1:	R0 ← DATA	;LOAD M1, multiplier.
LOAD	T2:	R1 ← DATA	;LOAD M2 in R1.
AND	T3:	R2 ← R1 · R0[0]	;AND M2 bits with LSB of M1.
ADD	T4:	R4 ← R2 plus R4, {shift right}	;Add R2 to ACC and shift right.
SHFT	T5:	R0 ← R0, {shift right}	;Shift next LSB down to R0[0].

;Now repeat the T3–T5 operations three more times.

AND	T6:	R2 ← R1 · R0[0]	;AND M2 bits with LSB of M1.
ADD	T7:	R4 ← R2 plus R4, {shift right}	;Add R2 to ACC and shift right.
SHFT	T8:	R0 ← R0, {shift right}	;Shift next LSB down to R0[0].
AND	T9:	R2 ← R1 · R0[0]	;AND M2 bits with LSB of M1.
ADD	T10:	R4 ← R2 plus R4, {shift right}	;Add R2 to ACC and shift right.
SHFT	T11:	R0 ← R0, {shift right}	;Shift next LSB down to R0[0].
AND	T12:	R2 ← R1 · R0[0]	;AND M2 bits with LSB of M1.
ADD	T13:	R4 ← R2 plus R4, {shift right}	;Add R2 to ACC and shift right.

;Final multiplier shift isn't needed.

The four most significant bits of the answer are at the shifter output; note that the final carry-out has been shifted down. We needed only four registers; the fifth would come in handy for trying to save the full eight-bit answer. In RTL notation the colon indicates a conditional operation; the operation can be conditional on time (T1), address (A2), or logic (X · Y). So far, our RTL has no provision for IF statements, so we have had to write out all add-and-shifts.

How are the RTL statements for the four-by-four multiplier to be implemented? Because we created a machine with a regular structure whose only inputs are a clock and various select and load lines, we can assign each select and load bit to a different microcode ROM output. Because we can sequence straight through the algorithm without the *necessity* for conditional jumps or looping, a counter is sufficient to address the ROM; this scheme is microprogrammed control (introduced at the end of Chapter 7). See Fig. 11.29. Six pins are shown for 8 → 2 MUX SEL because $2^6 = 32 > 28$, the number of combinations of eight things taken two at a time ($8!/(2! \cdot 6!) = 28$).

After the counter is reset to 0000 0000, it begins to step through ROM addresses in time with the clock. The ROM is programmed at each location to execute one of the TN: lines of the multiplication program. The 18 control lines at each ROM location can be grouped in three categories: source, function, and destination. The MUX-select

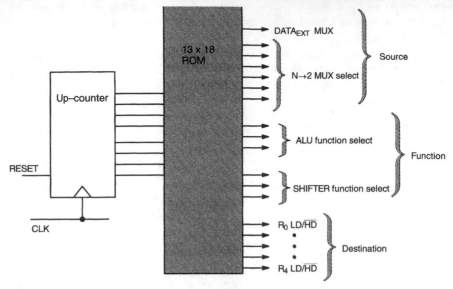

Figure 11.29 Source, function, and destination fields.

determines the sources for the ALU, and the RN LOAD signal or signals determine the destination(s) of the result. Exercise 24 shows a table of function fields for such a ROM.

Our five-register machine with counter-plus-ROM control can perform various logic and arithmetic functions on pairs of register contents and accumulate answers to problems that can be solved without conditional branching. For example, an algebraic sum of products $(A \cdot B + C \cdot D)$ can be computed if the machine is told when to fetch the values of A, B, C, and D. The important point developed here in Chapter 11 is that, in contrast to the hardware-specific circuits of the previous chapter, a general-purpose RTL von Neumann machine can be programmed to solve many problems simply by changing the instructions to the machine, with no modification required of the hardware.

Text References on RTL For more information on RTL, see Mano (1988, chap. 7), Myers (1980), Taub (1980, 161 and 326), and Bartee (1985, 443–446). RTL was devised by I. S. Reed and first described in Bartee, Lebow, and Reed (1962).

11.5 INCREASING COMPUTATION SPEED

Before concluding Chapter 11, we bring up one final hardware issue in register transfer logic: speed of computation. Speed can be increased in several ways, such as employing wider registers, using faster logic gates, and devising more clever algorithms. Here we look at a bottleneck in von Neumann architecture and offer a way to alleviate the bottleneck. Take as a benchmark the problem of adding up four numbers (called D1, ..., D4; assume that they're already in horizontal registers R1–R4 or cache locations W1–W4). Keep in mind that a sum of four numbers may need two registers to express the answer correctly.

EXAMPLE 6

Let's start by figuring out how many machine cycles it takes to add four numbers with cache memory architecture. We haven't yet written out RTL statements for the von Neumann machine with a cache memory (Fig. 11.27). Let's use the following notation: ACC is the accumulator register in the cache machine; [Wn] is *the contents of* location n in the cache memory itself, and RC is the cache register, which holds data in the cache architecture. Here are the cycles of RTL code to sum up four numbers:

T0: ACC ← W1
T1: RC ← W2
T2: ACC ← ACC plus RC;   RC ← W3
T3: ACC ← ACC plus RC;   RC ← W4
T4: ACC ← ACC plus RC;

A minimum of five clock cycles is needed for the answer to appear in ACC. To speed up the computation at times T2 and T3, the ACC is loaded with the sum of RC and ACC on the same clock edge as another number is loaded into RC.

Suppose a *horizontal register machine* (like Fig. 11.28) instead of a cache machine is used to compute a sum. Now how many machine cycles does it take to add four numbers?

ADD   T0:   R0 ← R1 plus R2
ADD   T1:   R0 ← R0 plus R3
ADD   T2:   R0 ← R0 plus R4

The answer appears in register R0 and on the shifter output after three clock pulses. No loading of the first two numbers from memory was necessary.

Is there a way to beat the speed of the horizontal register machine? Yes. Figure 11.30 introduces another ALU-shifter path. The arithmetic logic unit at the second level is called *ALU*. The two-level architecture here should remind you of an array multiplier from Chapter 10. Now four numbers can be added in two clock cycles if the four numbers are already loaded in registers R1–R4. The $(N + 2)$-bit answer appears at the output of the shifter and the status bits of *ALU*. If all registers R1–R4 are loaded with the same number M, we have a $4 \times M$ circuit—a 4-times multiplier.

Our radical new architecture deserves six comments.

1. At the cost of adding more hardware, we've created a rudimentary parallel processor.

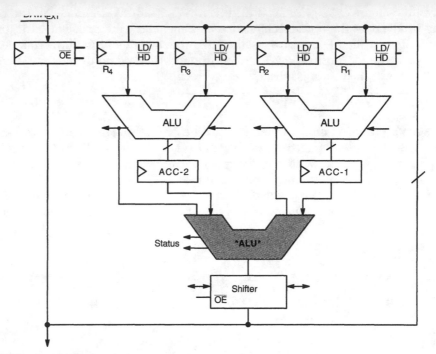

Figure 11.30 Parallel processing.

2. External data from system memory enters the CPU through a register tied by three-state outputs to the shifter outputs.

3. By adding a second ALU pathway, we no longer have a strict von Neumann machine; there are now ALUs that some data do not have to pass through.

4. Since the two first-level adders can each generate a carry-out, the second-level ALU (*ALU*) must be a special circuit with at least two bits beyond the nominal data path size. The extra two bits may be expressed as two-bit carry-out status.

5. The two clocked register accumulators ACC_1 and ACC_2 are placed between the first- and second-level adders to avoid timing skew. ACC_1 and ACC_2 can be considered *pipeline registers.*

    The maximum clock rate is determined by the longest combinatorial delay in the CPU. If the data must pass through a long sequence of gates, the long delay will limit clock rate. Worse, if there are different delays in different parts of a circuit, data may not arrive at registers at proper times. The pipeline registers break up a long combinational path and separate the two branches of it.

6. The general effort to program a parallel processor is much more involved than programming a von Neumann machine. Not only what instruction, but *where* it is to be executed, must be decided. Conditional branches pose more problems.

Our effort to increase the speed of the basic von Neumann CPU has succeeded, but it has opened up too many questions to pursue in an introductory text. We stop here, with a final comment. *Digital Design from Zero to One* began in Chapter 1 with a description of the fundamental feature of digital systems: binary codes and their expression in hardware switches. In this final chapter we see again the duality of software numbers and hardware gates: a general-purpose multiregister hardware system controlled by a microcode sequencer driven by a software program is capable of a great many different algorithmic computations without any change in its physical structure.

> We shall not cease from exploration
> And the end of all our exploring
> Will be to arrive where we started
> And know the place for the first time.
>
> *T. S. Eliot*

11.6 SUMMARY

- A **register** is a set of D flip-flops with a common clock. All bits of a register can be loaded (write operation) or read simultaneously (parallel-in–parallel-out). A register commonly has 2^N bits, where N is an integer.

- **Register transfer language** is a notation for describing register operations as functions of time or logic condition. A general form is $R_1 \leftarrow f(R_1, \ldots, R_N, C_1, \ldots, C_M)$ where the expression to the left of the arrow names a *location* and that to the right of the arrow computes a *value*, which may be an arithmetic or logic function of several registers R or several *control* variables $(C_1, \ldots, C_M)$.

- Logic, arithmetic, and shift account for **single register operations.**

- A **shifter** is a set of three-to-one MUXs; one choice represents no-shift, and the other two are for left and right shift. A shift can be circular or straight, arithmetic or logical. Special treatment is needed for the left- and right-most bits of the data being shifted.

- By means of an **arithmetic-logic unit (ALU)**, the contents of two registers can be combined. Examples of TTL-type ALUs are the 74181 and 74LS382. An ALU is a multiplexer plus extra combinational circuit that selects a FUNCTION to operate on incoming data.

- The control signals for a register-ALU-shifter machine can come from a wide-word ROM whose address is controlled by a counter or by a condition-dependent sequencer (microprogram).

- A multiregister machine can be efficiently organized around a static RAM **cache** with its own address and output bus. Combined with a special register, called an **accumulator**, the cache-based machine provides an example of **von Neumann architecture**, in which all operations must pass through one ALU-shifter path.

- A five-register CPU was used in the design of a multiplier for unsigned numbers. The multiplication steps were directed by unbranched register transfer language.

The same architecture could be used for other computational tasks simply by reprogramming, without the need for changes in hardware.

- *Parallel processing* can be combined with **pipelining.** Computation speed will increase because operations can be carried out simultaneously and synchronously.

Exercises 11

1. Consider two four-bit PIPO registers, R0 and R1, hooked up for shifting as seen in Fig. P11.1. If the contents of both registers start out all 0s, what will be the sequence of states (the cycle) that the registers will step through as the clock ticks?

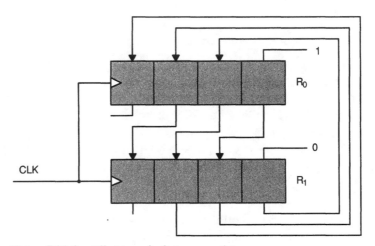

Figure P11.1 Offset transfer between registers.

2. Consider one register with a combinational circuit in feedback from register output back to its input. Show on a diagram a modification so that the one register can be loaded with external data.

3. (a) The serial input for a shift register needs to be specified in an RTL instruction; what is a notation for the S_{IN} specification, for shift-left?

   (b) A shift for a signed number should not change the sign bit. Draw the details of a register that may be involved in a left or right arithmetic shift. Consider an eight-bit register, and concentrate on what happens at the seventh and eighth bits of the register.

4. Figure 11.8 shows an arithmetic circuit for single-register operation. The register output projects back to the polarity control box.

   (a) Write out a program of INV, SEL-A, and C_{IN} instructions that will take a register from an initial setting of 0000, count up to 6, count back down to 4, invert all bits, and then hold at that final value 1011.

   (b) What happens to the circuit in Fig. 11.8 if C_{OUT} is connected to C_{IN}?

(c) Figure out the worst-case delay for a cycle around the register. Assume that each gate in Fig. 11.8 has a 25-ns delay. What is the maximum frequency the register can be clocked at?

(d) Design a two-level SOP with the same inputs and outputs as the block diagram design of Fig. 11.8.

5. Design a combinational box for an eight-bit one-register system that will make bits R_1–R_6 individually become 0 (reset) after the next clock pulse if their left *and* right neighbors are the same as R_i, $i = 1, \ldots, 6$. For example, if $R = $ [00011110], it will become [00010010] after the next clock.

6. The arithmetic subcircuit of a four-bit one-register system looks like Fig. P11.2. The only control over the circuit is the MODE input.

(a) What arithmetic functions can it perform?
(b) Is it possible to form ripple carry-out and borrow-in outputs and overflow?
(c) What is the maximum delay through the "incrementer" circuit?

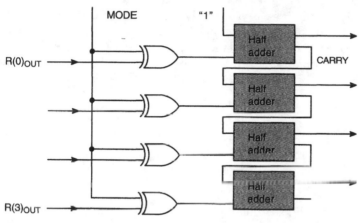

Figure P11.2

7. **Hardware shifter**
(a) Consider an eight-bit register and show connection details for a hardware circular shift left.
(b) Show the multiplexer connections for a full-function shifter's left-most bit (including signed arithmetic shift).
(c) Left-shifting is like multiplying by 2. What is a hardware status output for overflow in an arithmetic left-shifting register?

8. Design a seven-bit shifter that moves bits either two positions to the left or two positions to the right. The shift must be *circular*—bits going off one end should wrap around to the other.

9. **74LS323**
(a) Redraw the 74LS323 of Fig. 11.12 in the form of a 20-pin IC. Label the pins and show in a separate diagram as much as possible of the internal logic of the chip, using the standard logic notation of this text.

have separate complemented outputs on the chip?

(c) If either output enable pin is not asserted, can the '323 still be loaded with new data?

(d) The 74LS323 has a companion chip, the 74LS299, identical in all respects except that the clear on 74LS299 is asynchronous (independent of the clock). Can you think of a situation in which an asynchronous clear would be preferred to a synchronous clear?

10. Can the combinational part of a four-bit single-register design like the colored part of Fig. 11.14 have its circuit replaced by a ROM? If so, what would be the size of the ROM?

11. Design a four-bit ALU (no shifter) for a one-register system. The output can be no more than four-gates of delay from input, for logic and arithmetic, *including carry-out*. Implement the following four logic functions and 1 arithmetic function: CLEAR, SET, PASS, INVERT all bits, INCREMENT.

If you look at the section in Chapter 10 on CLA, you will see that the CLA expression simplifies if one of the inputs is zero. Use a simplified CLA to achieve the delay goal. Since there are five operations, you can select them with three inputs. Call the inputs Mode, Logic, and C0. When $M = 1$ and $C0 = 1$, Increment is enabled. Let the table below define the operations when $M = 0$.

Logic	C0	OP
0	0	CLR
0	1	SET
1	0	PASS
1	1	INV

12. Look at Fig. P11.3, a one-register system with no capability to be loaded externally.

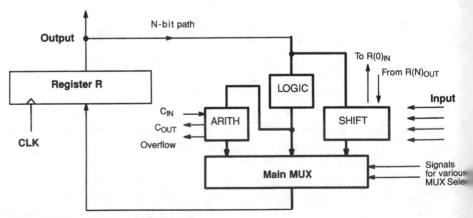

Figure P11.3   One-register machine.

(a) Write out a table, in terms of the MUX inputs, that lists all the instructions for this circuit.

(b) Assume that this is an eight-bit system and that at power-on, register R has all zeros. Without a second register for parallel loading of R, can you think of a way (a sequence of MUX selects) to get the pattern 0101 0101 into R?

13. Let a two-register machine have positive numbers in R1 and R2. Show how the 2C difference R1 − R2 can end up in register 1. That is, what settings on the machine for source, function, and destination can do the subtraction? Because both numbers are positive, no overflow can occur. See Fig. 11.22.

14. What are two ways to complement input A using the 74LS382 ALU chip of Example 3?

15. You know from Section 11.3.1 that the 74181 computes A minus B by 1's complement. Different results occur depending on whether C_{IN} is asserted or not. You also know that the adder circuit inside the '181 has a C_{OUT}. Your problem: Figure out a way for C_{OUT} to indicate $A > B$ when the subtraction mode is used. For help, find a TTL data book and study the 74181 data sheets.

16. **Minilogic unit** Suppose a device with two inputs A and B must provide at its output the logic function A AND B when MODE is LO or A OR B when MODE is HI. Here's a truth table description:

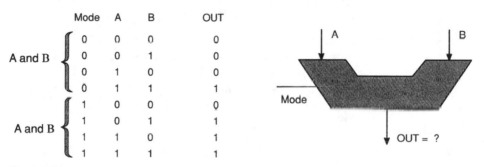

	Mode	A	B	OUT
A and B	0	0	0	0
	0	0	1	0
	0	1	0	0
	0	1	1	1
A and B	1	0	0	0
	1	0	1	1
	1	1	0	1
	1	1	1	1

Figure P11.4 Mini ALU.

(a) What *arithmetic* function is this truth table?

(b) Realize the truth table with one multiplexer.

(c) How can the design be expanded to select 1-bit full adding and XOR logic in addition to OR and AND?

17. External data for a two-register machine was loaded through a 3 → 2 MUX.

(a) Design a 4 → 2 MUX for a four-bit data path.

(b) What is the total access time (in gate delays) for writing an external value to a register in the machine of Fig. 11.22?

(c) Let the registers in Fig. 11.22 have three-state output, and let external data be stored in a three-state register. Redesign the two-register machine to eliminate the 3 → 2 MUX and handle data routing by control of three-state registers.

18. **Bit flicking** Suppose the user of a register transfer machine desires control over SET and CLEAR down at the level of single bits; that is, the user wants to

be able to SET or CLEAR certain $R(i)$ on a given machine cycle without affecting the other bits of R. Such an action is in the category of logic operations on one register. Call one such operation MASK, and let it be of the form MASK(1XX0) of R in a four-bit system, where the particular pattern [1XX0] means [SET, PASS, PASS, CLEAR] the individual bits of R.

(a) If $R = 0101$, what is the result of MASK(1XX0) of R?

(b) How can MASK be implemented at the hardware level (logic unit or shifter)?

19. In Example 4—computing the remainder (mod) after division with a two-register machine—how can the conditional branch be implemented? What must be in the microcode ROM? Assume that the ALU has status pins you can utilize.

20. Design a circuit for a two-register machine that detects for overflow in 2C addition. Consider what status pins you have from the ALU and what that status can do for the detector.

21. If a number in a register has even parity, it has an even number of 1s in it. Assume that in an eight-bit, three-register system a number has been loaded in register R_1. Write a program of function and destination instructions to determine whether the number in R_1 has even parity. Show where your answer comes out, and describe any hardware in addition to the basic two-register system you may need.

22. Consider the cache memory architecture of Fig. 11.27.

(a) Say what operations must occur and give the number of clock cycles required in order to transfer the contents of addresses 0010 to a cache register to the accumulator.

(b) If the ALU has two gates' worth of delay and the shifter one, what is the maximum clock rate the cache machine can be run at if one gate has 10 ns of delay?

‡23. The code in Example 5 for multiplying two unsigned numbers repeats itself four times to accomplish the four add-and-shifts. How could the code for add-and-shift be reduced to a *loop* that is executed four times? How does the hardware need to be augmented in order to support looping? Sketch your extra hardware or extra data paths, and show how to implement looping in the RTL code.

24. Control fields are shown in Fig. 11.29 for the microcode ROM outputs. Let's define the bits of the fields to accomplish the following functions:

DATA MUX (1 bit):	1	Latch external data onto off-board register.
$8 \rightarrow 2$ MUX SEL (3 bits):	000	Select 1 and R_1 for inputs A and B.
	001	Select 1 and R_2 for inputs A and B.
	010	Select $DATA_{EXT}$ and R_3.
	011	Select R_4 and R_1.
	100	Select R_5 and R_2.
	101	Select R_5 and R_3.
	110	Select R_5 and R_4.
	111	Select R_1 and R_2.

ALU function (3 bits):	000	$F = $ zero	
	001	$F = A$ plus B plus C_{IN}	
	010	$F = A$	
	011	$F = B$	
	100	$F = \overline{A}$	
	101	$F = A \cdot B$	
	110	$F = A \oplus B$	
	111	$F = A \cdot B(0)$	
Shifter function (3 bits):	000	No shift	
	001	Shift right; $SH(3) = C_{OUT}$	
	010	Circular shift right; $SH(3) = SH(0)$	
	011	Shift left; $SH(0) = SR_{IN}$	
	100	Circular shift left; $SH(0) = SH(3)$	
	101	Arithmetic shift left (MSB undisturbed)	
	110	Arithmetic shift right (MSB undisturbed)	
	111	No shift	
Destination (5 bits):	00001	Enable R_1.	
	00010	Enable R_2.	
	00100	Enable R_3.	
	01000	Enable R_4.	
	10000	Enable R_5.	

Write out in *machine code* an algorithm for multiplying two four-bit numbers together and finding the four most significant bits of the answer.

25. Devise a register transfer machine capable of forming all eight bits of a four-bit by four-bit unsigned product. Start with the instructions given in Example 5 to generate RTL code for the multiplication. Show where the answer is stored.

‡26. Assume that three different unsigned four-bit numbers are stored in registers R_1, R_2, and R_3. Propose a multiregister machine and an algorithm for sorting the three numbers such that the largest of the three numbers ends up in R_1 and the smallest in R_3. Develop and use a conditional code.

‡27. Recall from Chapter 9 that the Hamming distance between two equal-length binary strings is the number of *different* bit-pairs. Write a program (sequence of source, function, and destination instructions) for an eight-bit multiregister system to compute the Hamming distance between two eight-bit patterns already loaded in registers R_1 and R_2. Sketch any additional hardware, outside the register system, you may need to complete the job. If necessary, give your logic unit the capability of masking.

28. Imagine a six-register machine in which are stored two vectors, $\mathbf{V}_1 = (Ai + Bj)$ and $\mathbf{V}_2 = (Ci + Dj)$. The dot product of the two vectors is required: $\mathbf{V}_1 \cdot \mathbf{V}_2 = A \times C + B \times D$, where + and × are integer addition and multiplication. Write a program to compute the dot product and leave it on the output bus (with

perhaps the ninth MSB on the ALU carry-out). Assume that A, B, C, and D are positive *four-bit* integers and have already been loaded into four of the registers. Assume also that all registers, the ALU, and the shifter are capable of dealing with eight-bit numbers. Let the instruction set for the ALU be ADD, SUBTRACT, AND, and OR. The ALU has a carry-out that the user has access to.

(a) Sketch the machine architecture, showing the registers, the ALU, and the shifter.

(b) Decide on a function-select code for the ALU, a source-select code for the three-state enables of the registers, and a destination-select code for the register clock inputs (or use the tables from Exercise 24).

(c) Write a sequence of machine cycles showing source, function, and destination for each step, until the sum of products is finally available at ALU output.

‡29. Recall Booth's algorithm from Chapter 10. Use a multiregister machine to find the product of two eight-bit 2's-complement signed numbers with Booth's algorithm. Draw out the hardware architecture and write down the RTL code. See if you can do the job with five registers.

30. In Example 6 (the part about adding four numbers in a cache machine), why can't loading of ACC and R_C be done on one clock cycle?

31. Some computers have over 100 registers in the CPU. What do you think are two advantages and disadvantages of having so many registers?

32. Fig 11.30 has a parallel processor machine that can add four numbers in two cycles.

(a) Show what source, function, and destination fields may be needed to control the two-level, three-ALU machine. Pay attention to how the second-level registers (ACC-1, ACC-2) should be dealt with. Name the functions.

(b) What must *ALU* be like, with regard to status, in order to handle the four-number sum?

(c) With your new source, function, and destination codes, write out the two instructions needed to add together four numbers.

(d) Can you think of hardware for the four numbers to be summed up in one machine cycle?

33. Because of extra levels in the data path of the parallel processing, one of the machine cycles in Fig. 11.30 will take longer than in a von Neumann machine. If an ALU has a propagation delay of 2Δ and other blocks in Fig. 11.30 have delay Δ, what is the maximum clock rate at which the parallel processing machine can be run?

References

BARTEE, T. 1985. *Digital computer fundamentals.* 6th ed. New York: McGraw-Hill.

BARTEE, T. C., I. L. LEBOW, AND L. S. REED. 1962. *Theory and design of digital machines.* New York: McGraw-Hill.

BURKS, A. W., H. H. GOLDSTEIN, AND J. VON NEUMANN. 1965. Preliminary discussion of the logical design of an electronic computing instrument. U.S. Army ordnance report. 1946. Reprinted in *Collected works of John von Neumann*. Vol. 5. New York: Macmillan.

MANO, M. 1988. *Computer engineering: Hardware design*. Englewood Cliffs, NJ: Prentice Hall.

MYERS, G. J. 1980. *Digital system design with LSI bit-slice logic*. New York: John Wiley.

PENROSE, R. 1989. *The emperor's new mind*. New York: Oxford University Press.

TAUB, H. 1980. *Digital circuits and microprocessors*. New York: McGraw-Hill.